Cambridge Studies in Speech Science and Communication

Advisory Editorial Board J. Laver (Executive editor), A. J. Fourcin, J. Gilbert,
M. Haggard, P. Ladefoged, B. Lindblom, J. C. Marshall

Neurolinguistics and linguistic aphasiology
An introduction

Neurolinguistics and linguistic aphasiology

An introduction

David Caplan

Montreal Neurological Institute

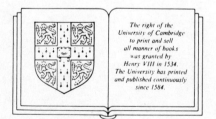

The right of the
University of Cambridge
to print and sell
all manner of books
was granted by
Henry VIII in 1534.
The University has printed
and published continuously
since 1584.

Cambridge University Press

Cambridge

New York   New Rochelle   Melbourne   Sydney

Published by the Press Syndicate of the University of Cambridge
The Pitt Building, Trumpington Street, Cambridge CB2 1RP
32 East 57th Street, New York, NY 10022, USA
10 Stamford Road, Oakleigh, Melbourne 3166, Australia

First published 1987

Printed in Great Britain by
The Bath Press, Avon

British Library cataloguing in publication data

Caplan, David, *1947–*
Neurolinguistics and linguistic aphasiology: an introduction. –
(Cambridge studies in speech science and communication)
1. Aphasia
I. Title
616.85'52   RC425

Library of Congress cataloguing in publication data

Caplan, David, 1947–
Neurolinguistics and linguistic aphasiology.
(Cambridge studies in speech science and communication)
Bibliography.
Includes index.
1. Asphasia.   2. Neurolinguistics.
1. Title.   II. Series.
RC425.C375 1987   616.85'52   86–31049

ISBN 0 521 32420 3 hard covers
ISBN 0 521 31195 0 paperback

To the memory of my father and teacher,
Dr. Hyman Caplan

Contents

Preface

The purpose of this book is to present an introduction to the emerging fields of neurolinguistics and linguistic aphasiology. It seems to me that many students, whose backgrounds are restricted to neurology, psychology, speech pathology, linguistics, or artificial intelligence, do not find the study of language disorders and the neural correlates of language accessible because basic aspects of the other fields are not familiar to them. Many neurology students, who must deal with the clinical phenomena of aphasia, shy away from linguistic descriptions of these conditions, and students in linguistics and psychology often consider neurolinguistics tangential to the central questions of their disciplines. My goal in writing this text is, therefore, to provide a basis from which to approach the more technical texts and articles which constitute the field. I hope readers come away from this volume able to locate articles they may later read within the general framework of theory and observation that constitutes neurolinguistics, and with enough detail to allow them at least to begin to evaluate an article in this area.

The first major problem facing students who might be interested in neurolinguistics – the number of different disciplines, each with its own vocabulary and technical aspects, that are relevant – can be approached in several ways. I have tried to introduce concepts from neurology (especially neuroanatomy, but also neurophysiology), linguistics, psychology, and aphasiology in ways which simplify but do not misrepresent essential features of these disciplines. Rather than devoting separate chapters or appendices to this, I have incorporated the material into the text at points where it seemed logical to do so. I hope that readers can bear with somewhat elementary expositions in their fields of expertise; hopefully they will find these sections helpful in those areas with which they are not as familiar.

Besides the interdisciplinary nature of the field, neurolinguistics and linguistic aphasiology can be hard to approach because of the large number of different types of models which have been advanced regarding language–brain relationships and language breakdown. Many articles dealing with aspects of neurolinguistics are only interpretable if one has an idea of the underlying theoretical framework and assumptions, and many writers do not make these explicit. Furthermore, there are tendencies in the literature towards simply reporting data without indicating the theories such data address, and towards presenting data as evidence for a particular theoretical approach without considering whether it could be accommodated in another framework. The fact that so many different basic approaches are present in the field might lead the student of neurolinguistics to ask whether it is possible to choose between them, and even to use data gathered within one conceptual paradigm to prove or disprove another approach. There is very little attempt to present and compare different frameworks in neurolinguistics, and existing introductions tend to present multiple analyses within a single framework (e.g. Benson 1979) or to review a large number of approaches without critically comparing them (e.g. Lecours *et al.* 1983). The result is a neglect, in introductory material at least, of how data bear on the choice of theories, and an inappropriate tolerance of any approach, as if neurolinguistics were a sort of "equal opportunity employer" of theories. This is less true of recent studies in linguistic aphasiology but remains a problem for much of the literature.

I do not think that we are yet in a position to choose definitely among the various theories in this field, and it is also likely that many approaches are complementary not contradictory. What seems to me to be possible and appropriate is to try to characterize the major theories, examine the data that have been used to support each and the logic used to give this support, identify strengths and weaknesses of each, and make some judgements as to which have been productive and which seem to be reasonably justified. This text does provide the student with this sort of preliminary assessment of theories, conditioned by my own views. The goal is to begin to equip readers to do this sort of analysis on their own.

As the title indicates, this book deals with two related areas: "neurolinguistics" and "linguistic aphasiology". The first of these, neurolinguistics, consists of the study of language–brain relationships. Its origins are in clinical neurology of the late nineteenth century, and it continues to be a clinically related field of observation and theory construction. Modern imaging techniques have greatly increased the ability of scientists to visualize lesions in the brain during life, and thus allow greater scope for lesion–symptom correlation and the construction of neurolinguistic theory. Modern techniques also allow for observation of normal brain metabolic and physiological functions during tasks which focus on the use of language. These techniques include the recording of event-related potentials, and PET and SPECT scanning. Several researchers have experimentally activated small areas of brain during neurosurgical procedures, to investigate the role of these areas in language functioning. These new techniques extend the traditional clinical–pathological correlation approach through the use of new technologies. In many cases, the use of these techniques is closely tied to questions about neurolinguistics which originated with the clinical tradition. I have tried to make explicit the areas of innovation and tradition found in this technologically newer work.

The second major area, linguistic aphasiology, is also in large measure derived from clinical studies and concepts, but adds a significant new perspective. Linguistic aphasiology is concerned with the psychology of language breakdown: it seeks to describe what aspects of the language code and its processing are disturbed after brain injury, and to account for the pattern of breakdown in terms of principles of language structure and processing. Linguistic and psycholinguistic analyses of aphasic symptoms are required for the clinical–pathological and clinical–radiological correlations that provide the basis for neurolinguistic theorizing and, in this sense, all neurolinguistics presupposes some level of linguistic aphasiological analysis. But modern work in linguistic aphasiology does not relate to neurolinguistic concerns and existing neurolinguistic theories in any simple way. In large part, modern linguistic aphasiology has been developed by psychologists and linguists whose interests are in how language breaks down, and in what the pattern of breakdown reveals about normal language and its processing. Much work has gone on in this area without concern for the details of the correlation between symptoms and neural lesions. Moreover, many of the analyses of aphasic symptoms which have been developed in linguistic aphasiology challenge classical analyses. Challenges at the functional, psychological level lead to challenges of the neurolinguistic theories which the traditional analyses propose. I have tried to chart the relationships among modern linguistic and psychological analyses of aphasic symptoms, traditional analyses, and neurolinguistic theory.

I wish to stress again that this book is an introduction and in no way a definitive text. I have tried to touch on the most important of the contributing fields, as I see them, but some (such as comparative neuroanatomy) have been omitted entirely and others treated lightly. In keeping with the objectives mentioned above, I have also tried to be selective in another sense: rather than present sketches of a large number of results in each area, I have usually opted to present related groups of studies in some depth, so that the reader can understand how evidence is gathered in the field and how theory has developed. Even so, there is much more to be said about every topic covered here. I hope that readers will be interested in reading the literature on the subject to achieve a broader and deeper understanding of the field, and that the book will prepare them to do so.

Preface

I have had a lot of help in developing the ideas presented here. I wish to acknowledge the contributions made by students in classes at the University of Massachusetts, the Summer Institute of the Linguistic Society of America (University of Maryland, 1982), and McGill University. I am profoundly indebted to many colleagues and friends, and to many teachers. Noam Chomsky, Merrill Garrett, Jerry Fodor, André Roch Lecours, John Marshall, Edward Walker, and Edgar Zurif are notable among the colleagues whose professional and personal support have in large measure contributed to the writing of this volume; many others have also been instrumental in helping me formulate ideas. Dan Bub, Harold Goodglass, Nancy Hildebrandt, John Marshall, Jack Ryalls, Mark Seidenberg, and Elizabeth Warrington were kind enough to comment on drafts of Chapters 11–14. Howard Chertkow made many useful editorial comments, and Nancy Hildebrandt verified many bibliographical references and provided the index. A special mention must be made of the late Dr. Norman Geschwind, my teacher, mentor, and colleague, whose untimely death has deprived me and the rest of the field of an invaluable mind. Jennifer Anderson's work in manuscript typing has been of the greatest help. Penny Carter and Sarah Barrett of Cambridge University Press have been particularly helpful.

I appreciate the institutional support afforded by the Sloan Foundation, the University of Massachusetts (Departments of Linguistics and Computer Science), the University of Maryland, the University of Ottawa, the Montreal Neurological Institute and McGill University, and the Centre Hospitalier Côte des Neiges (Montreal), at various stages of writing. This volume has been prepared while I held a Chercheur-boursier award from the Fonds de la Recherche en Santé du Québec, without which I would not have had the time to work on it. Finally, I wish to thank many friends and my family for their tolerance and support of my preoccupation with intellectual and professional activities, which has allowed me to prepare this book.

Part I

Introduction

1

Issues in neurolinguistics and linguistic aphasiology

The terms "neurolinguistics" and "linguistic aphasiology" are new ones, in use for a little over a decade. The areas of study to which they refer, the nature of language breakdown and the relationship between language and the brain, are much older than the term. Indeed, the study of language–brain relationships can be seen as one aspect of the more general study of the relationship between mind and brain (or mind and body) which has occupied Western philosophy since its beginning. The scientific study of language–brain relationships began in the last half of the nineteenth century, and detailed descriptions of language disturbances after brain injury began to be published before the turn of this century. However, despite their distant and recent histories, these fields have recently developed new directions and vigor, and the new terms are appropriate and increasingly popular. An increasing number of scientists from the fields of linguistics, psychology, speech pathology, and neuroscience are beginning to make their primary study the questions of how language is represented and processed in the brain, and how it breaks down after brain injury. Thus, the subject has a life of its own, independent of the disciplines which contribute to it. Techniques and concepts from linguistics, psycholinguistics, artificial intelligence, neuroanatomy, and other sciences are increasingly being applied to what was traditionally a medical preserve, yielding new discoveries about language disorders and their neural determinants which in turn have led to more detailed understanding of language and the brain. In short, while still very dependent upon contributing areas, neurolinguistics and linguistic aphasiology are becoming viable, autonomous areas of study. The new terms both reflect and announce the development of these new areas of study.

   This book is designed to provide an introduction to these new areas. We shall trace the history of scientific studies of language breakdown and language–brain relationships from the first scientific paper on the latter subject by Paul Broca in 1861 to contemporary work consisting of computer models, psycholinguistic experiments, and brain stimulation and recording. The central questions to which we shall return, again and again, are how

3

language breaks down, and how it is represented and processed in the brain. We shall come across fascinating case descriptions of patients, such as individuals who cannot read what they have written; we shall find that electrically stimulating certain brain structures can disturb some language functions while stimulating other structures improves them; we shall consider mathematical analyses of sets of neurons which model some features of human language. It is important, in all this fascinating material, not to lose sight of the central questions we want to try to answer. In this chapter, we shall consider some of these questions, trying to draw the boundaries of this field at least in general terms, and to relate this area of science to other areas, such as linguistics, psychology, and neuroscience.

What do we want to know about language breakdown and the relationship between language and the brain? It has been said that the most important thing a scientist must learn is which questions to ask, and it is certainly true that which questions we ask will determine the type of information we seek and, ultimately, the understanding that we attain. If we are concerned as, for instance, are medical practitioners, about whether various types of patients will recover from disorders affecting language, then we will seek information regarding recovery from different language impairments and from the different diseases of the brain that affect language. We would hope to arrive eventually at the point where we can offer an educated prognosis to a patient. We might not achieve an understanding of what language is and how it is processed, or of the structures and events in the brain which underlie storage and use of language, for that would not be our principal concern. Of course, it may turn out that to answer questions about prognosis, we need to know about the way language is structured and the way it is processed in the brain; or it may turn out that a by-product of our study of recovery from language impairment is some insight into these other issues. But it is also possible that we will not need to concern ourselves with the question of how language is processed and stored in the brain to answer the medical question of prognosis of a language disorder. A decision to pursue the medical question of prognosis may well be the most important decision we make, one which determines what we eventually understand about language–brain relationships. This example – which is not hypothetical, as will be apparent in later chapters – stresses the importance of asking good questions. It also indicates that there are many good questions, and that our choices among them will be determined by our general purpose in approaching the field. Most scientists have found that it is, in fact, quite difficult to generate good questions, and it might be worthwhile for the reader to set this book aside for a time at this point and make a list of questions he or she considers to be important in the area of language–brain relationships.

The perspective of much work in modern neurolinguistics is very broad, and can be thought of as "biological" in the fullest sense of the word. Neurolinguistics is concerned with how the brain represents and utilizes language, how this process develops throughout human life, how it is affected by disease, and whether and how it can be compared to analogous processes in non-human species.

Linguistic aphasiology is a recent, natural outgrowth of neurolinguistics. The study of language–brain relationships has traditionally utilized the technique of establishing "clinical–pathological correlations" as the database for theory construction. We shall consider this form of analysis in Chapter 2, and shall encounter many examples of such analyses in the text proper. For our present purpose, we need only note that this form of analysis characterizes the functional abilities of a patient as a deficit in normal functioning (the "clinical" side of the correlation) and describes the neural lesion (the "pathological" side). The part of the brain which has been damaged is then concluded to be normally responsible for the exercise of the function which is impaired. This form of analysis has led to more and more detailed analyses of linguistic and psycholinguistic deficits following brain injury. In recent years, the study of these deficits has become somewhat separated from the original concerns regarding the development of neurolinguistic theories, and has been more related to theories of normal language processing – a move from "neurolinguistics" to "linguistic aphasiology". Despite this drift, the fields are necessarily closely tied, and have many questions in common. The following are some of the basic concerns of many investigators in these areas.

1. *Reductionism*

A basic question in the philosophy of science in general is how various theories and sciences relate to each other. As applied to psychology, the question has special significance, because there are a number of researchers who have maintained that psychological and linguistic terms could be replaced by neurological and physiological terms, if only we knew enough about the latter. In fact, an important movement in American psychology, Behaviorism, adopted the philosophy that psychologists should restrict themselves to descriptions of observable behavior, and that references to internal mental states, such as what an organism knows or what its motivations are, are inappropriate in the science of psychology. Many behaviorists seemed to think that all such terms would ultimately be eliminated from theories of psychology by descriptions of neurological processes. In opposition to this belief, scientific study of language is now based upon the assumption that it is reasonable to speak of the internal mental life of humans (and of other species). The very first issue facing neurolinguistics is the philosophical one of whether this assumption is justifiable, or whether "neurolinguistics" will necessarily ultimately be reduced to purely neural science.

There is a second aspect to the question of whether psychological and linguistic terms are autonomous or simply a form of shorthand for descriptions of neurological events. This approach is based on the doctrine of the unity of science. Even if we do not believe that all terms referring to the mental life of humans will ultimately be understood in neurological terms, and do not accept the methodological restrictions of the behaviorists, we must still be sensitive to the claim that linguistics and the other psychological sciences must somehow be related to physical entities. If not, we are adopting a position such as dualism, which holds that there are various forms of biological "entities", some of which obey physical laws and some of which, such as mental and emotional entities, do not. It is a very general tenet of science that one should not postulate more distinctions than are absolutely necessary, and the idea that mental life is somehow radically different from physical life, and not related to physical structures and events at all, certainly postulates a radical distinction between various parts of biology, which would be best avoided if possible. Thus, the unity of science requires that we somehow relate linguistic and psychological terms to physiological terms.

The third reason for wanting to relate neurological and linguistic and psychological terms is that we have evidence that the brain is critically involved in language. A dualist would be in a difficult position to explain the effects of disease of the brain upon language and the many correlations between events in the brain and aspects of language which shall be presented in this book. He could, of course, claim that all these correlations are purely accidental, but most of us would find this claim unconvincing.

Thus, there are methodological, philosophical, and empirical reasons for believing that the brain must be related to language in some way. But what way? Is the strongest view, that the science of linguistics and the psychology of language are some day to be totally eliminated in favor of a rich science of neurology, tenable?

We do not in fact know how this question will ultimately be answered. What we can say is that the strongest view, total reduction of linguistics and psychology to neural science, is not the only one that is compatible with empirical observations of language–brain correlations, or with the requirements of philosophy of science. Fodor (1975) has outlined two general ways in which psychological terms can be related to neurological terms. In the first, which he terms "type reductionism", the terms and laws of psychology are related to elements and laws of the brain in a principled way. In this case, a psychological law is true, or a psychological state exists, because it corresponds to some lawful event or events in the nervous system. Obviously, this approach postulates a complete reduction of psychology to neurology; in this system, psychological terms are merely shorthand expressions for neural states. However, there is an alternative to this view, which Fodor suggests – his "token physicalism". In token physicalism, every psychological state in fact is correlated with a neural state or structure, but the neural states and structures are not related to each other in any lawful way, except by virtue of whatever organization is imposed by the laws of linguistic and psychological science.

Two examples will make this position clear, both borrowed from Fodor (1975). Suppose we wish to relate economic theory to exchanges of items of value, such as currency or commodities. Clearly, there is a very large, possibly an infinite, number of methods of exchanging items of value: exchange of money, securities, land, items of trade, cattle, and so on. The laws of economics apply to exchanges in general, and are not reducible to descriptions of actual exchange. Laws such as "the law of diminishing returns" apply no matter what the medium of exchange. Thus, it can be true both that all laws of economics are in fact instantiated in some form of monetary exchange, and that they are not reducible to the laws governing actual monetary exchanges. The reason that they are not reducible is that the actual exchanges themselves consist of a large variety of activities, and no set of physical laws pertains to the purely financial aspects of all the actual instances of exchange. Only economic theory provides a lawful description of the financial aspects of exchange, and this theory cannot be replaced by a more detailed account of the exchanges themselves.

A second example is more directly pertinent. Most readers of this book will be somewhat familiar with the operations of modern computers. In these machines, various calculations are performed by the "hardware" of the central processing units of general-purpose computers. These calculations are transacted in particular computer languages via programs called "software". It is, in fact, the case that every software operation is accomplished by some part of a computer's hardware. On the other hand, it is also the case that the operations of the hardware are not organized in such a way that they can only accomplish certain software operations. Software obeys mathematical laws devised by humans. The hardware is *temporarily* organized by the particular calculation demanded by a particular program. The same hardware can be used with very different patterns of organization in any two programs or any two programming languages. Thus, although the software is instantiated in the hardware, it cannot be described by the laws of the hardware.

This situation might be analogous to the way language and other psychological entities are related to the brain. It might be that the brain provides a "hardware" for the operation of various "computational softwares", and that the software temporarily organizes the neural "hardware" in particular ways which are specific to each set of software operations. If this were the case, all linguistic and other psychological structures and operations would be related to neurological events, but the laws and regularities regulating the operation of neurological terms with respect to linguistic and psychological events would be given by linguistics and psychology, not by physics and neurophysiology. The physical laws which govern the operation of the hardware would not totally constrain linguistic and psychological events, or determine linguistic or psychological laws. Under these conditions, it might be possible to replace linguistic and psychological terms by neural terms, but it would be uninformative to do so. There would be laws of linguistics and psychology which superimpose additional organizational structures upon the physical laws that apply to the physiological operation of the brain.

We can look at this question in one other way, which may help us to understand better the issues involved. The term "natural kind" refers to motivated divisions within a science. For instance, natural kinds in neurology include the concepts of "neurons", "convolutions", "synapses", "neurotransmitters", and others; in linguistics, items such as "noun phrase", "sentence", "referent", and "phoneme", as well as larger divisions of grammar such as "syntax", are all natural kinds. A slight but important rephrasing of the question of reductionism is to ask whether the natural kinds of linguistics and psycholinguistics are related to the natural kinds of neurology. There have been many suggestions of this sort, from the notion that all of language is the function of one hemisphere of the brain, to more specific and detailed hypotheses regarding correlates between aspects of language and language processing and areas and activity of the brain. If every natural kind of linguistics and psycholinguistics were related in a one-to-one fashion to a natural kind in neurology, it would be reasonable to say that linguistics is reducible to neurology. If this is not the case, then the relationship is along the lines of token physicalism described above. The first step in investigating whether this is the case is to see to what extent elements of language are correlated with particular parts and functions of the brain.

In our present state of knowledge, it is impossible to say which of these two types of relationship between language and the brain is true. The study of language–brain relationships can be partly seen as an effort to distinguish these two possibilities, by providing a detailed theory of linguistic and neural structures and of their relationship. The point for the moment is simply that it is quite possible that the sciences which constitute the psychology of language may not be completely eliminable from a perfect science in favor of descriptions of neurological structures.

2. *Phylogenetic considerations*

What is it that enables man to master a language system for the representation of concepts and the communication of ideas, which is so useful in our adaptation to the world, and what is it that animals are missing that prevents them from developing the same system or similar systems? Putting the question this way assumes that animals have no system for the representation and communication of thoughts which is comparable to human language. Though this is a point which is the subject of debate, it seems to be the case that, although animals are capable of very intelligent behavior, they do not possess representational and communicative systems comparable to language. If we accept this assessment of non-human language abilities, and if we further accept the evidence that language is related to the functioning of the brain, we may conclude that the absence of language in other species is related to something about their brains.

It is, however, not obvious what humans have in the way of neural endowment that allows for language, and why animals do not have systems such as language. It is true that, in some respects at least, the human brain is larger than brains found in the majority of species, and that particular areas of the human brain are especially large and anatomically advanced. But some species have equally large brains which also have advanced structures, but do not appear to have similar systems. What makes the question especially difficult is the fact that many animals are capable of behaviors which require very complex calculations and plans. For instance, even so mundane an activity as a frog's snapping at one of two flies in its strike range, and not at the space in between them, requires extremely complicated mathematical considerations to describe. These descriptions of the frog's behavior can be seen as theories of the calculations accomplished by the frog's nervous system in this activity (Didday 1976). If frogs are capable of behavior which is the result of complex mathematical computations carried out by their nervous system, why do they not carry out the complex mathematical operations which are the basis for language or a similar system? Put slightly differently, considering how useful it is to have a system

9

of representation and communication of thoughts such as language, why has it not evolved in species which apparently are capable of complex operations in other areas?

One possibility is that, though other species are capable of complex cognitive tasks, language processing is still more complex. The alternative is that language, though not more complex, is special in some way, and different from other cognitive capacities. In either case, the ability to use a system like a human language must require special elements in the nervous system, or a special organization of elements of the nervous system, which are not present in animals. Note that these special features need not totally determine language functions, only support them, and thus this argument does not resolve the question of reductionism. Finding out what these elements are requires a detailed study of comparative neuroanatomy, as well as a detailed study of what functions are performed by various species, including the linguistic functions of humans. In other words, to answer the question we must have an understanding of just how language function actually differs from intellectual and complex behavioral functions of other animals, and how the parts of the nervous system responsible for language in humans and for these other behaviors in animals differ.

We may also make some progress in this area by analyzing other intellectual and psychological abilities of humans. Aside from our abilities with language, we have remarkable talents in a variety of other intellectual spheres, such as mathematics, logic, music, perception, and planning and co-ordination of action. Each of these areas differs in one way or another from language, either in terms of the organization of the intellectual or perceptual/motor system in question or in terms of the relationship between each system and items in the external world. If we compare language and music, for instance, we find that music obeys a set of internal laws, and can be used to evoke certain emotional states and memories; language also obeys a set of internal laws, and can be used to evoke emotional and intellectual states. The two systems differ significantly, though both are, for all practical purposes, unique to humans. Studying the similarities and differences in the way these systems relate to the human brain can give us information about the particular basis for language within the human brain.

3. *Developmental aspects*

Another general area of neurolinguistics is developmental (or "onto-genetic"). We are not born speaking language, and we are not born with a mature nervous system. In what way do the development of the nervous system and the development of our language abilities relate to each other?

10

One's first thought may very well be that the development of the brain has very little to do with the development of language, since brains presumably develop in similar ways in all language groups, but children learn the language that they are exposed to. If the child of English-speaking parents is taken to Japan, that child will learn Japanese, although his brain develops with no apparent difference from the ways it would develop if he were taken to France, where he would learn French, or if he remained in an English-speaking environment and learned English. Thus, to a very great extent, the development of language abilities seems to be determined by aspects of the environment, and has little to do with the developing brain.

But this view is quite superficial. Studies of the stages of language development show that children go through similar stages in the acquisition of languages, no matter what the particular structures of the language. Normal children go through a stage of babbling, followed by one in which they develop the particular set of sounds of the language they are learning, and they do the latter in predictable ways which can be stated for all languages. They then go through various other stages in the acquisition of vocabulary, syntax, intonation, and other structural elements of language. Moreover, as contemporary linguists have stressed, they acquire the language of the environment on the basis of incomplete and disorganized data, and they achieve a representation of that language that goes far beyond recall of the samples they have heard. It is this knowledge which enables them to understand and produce utterances they have never heard before. Thus, they show an ability to abstract an underlying system of knowledge of their language from the particular samples of language to which they are exposed, and to apply this knowledge in new and varied ways. All these observations point to an important contribution of internal biological factors to the acquisition of language.

Modern linguists have suggested that the acquisition of language is therefore determined by internal, innate, biologically determined abilities in conjunction with exposure to the language of the environment. One possibility is that the child has an innate system for recognizing, categorizing, and integrating linguistic information to which he is exposed, and that this system includes a framework of initial knowledge regarding the possible forms of language. Exposure to a particular language specifies particular aspects of the developing system, and constrains it within this innate framework (Chomsky 1981). The universal properties of languages are "known" by the child, because of his biological endowment, and specific features of the language he hears add to this innate knowledge to achieve a complete linguistic system.

This view suggests that the neurological correlates of language and

11

language development are of two different sorts. The first category of correlates would include those neurological structures which are related to universal aspects of language – related, that is, to those aspects of language structure which are innate, and which develop in the child due to intrinsic neural maturation. The second are those neural structures which are the result of exposure to a particular language. For instance, it might be the case that the knowledge that languages make use of systems of sounds, and that the systems of sounds are themselves structured in particular ways (such as that they consist of consonants and vowels, or openings and closings of the vocal tract), is innate universal knowledge, whereas the particular sounds of a language or a dialect are acquired on the basis of exposure. Since the universal aspects of language are, by definition, present in all languages, it is possible that they reflect universally present aspects of the human nervous system. The features of individual languages are also, clearly, related to the nervous system, but they vary from language to language, dialect to dialect, and even person to person. One consequence, therefore, of taking language development into account in neurolinguistics is that we must consider the possibility that different types of neurological structures may be related to these different aspects of language.

One way to consider this issue is for neurolinguistics to face the important and difficult question of characterizing the stages whereby both language and the brain develop. Although modern linguists have used the term "innate" to refer to the knowledge of language that humans have by virtue of their biological endowment, it is clear that this knowledge develops over time. By studying the sequence of maturational events in the nervous system, and of the language abilities of the child, we can hope to correlate neural structures and language functions, thus providing another important approach to the understanding of the relationship between language and the mature adult brain. This is not sufficient, however. We must also distinguish universal and language-specific aspects of development, and correlate each with neural structures. Since universal features of language are embedded in language-specific development, this task requires careful cross-linguistic experimentation with normal children and observation of children with abnormal language development to separate these features.

4. *Language pathology*

The final set of questions that are central to neurolinguistics are also those which constitute the subject matter of linguistic aphasiology: the study of acquired disorders of language. Aphasias – disorders of language that are caused by diseases of the brain – have been investigated scientifically for over a century. This study is a topic in its own right, and constitutes the central body of fact and theory upon which neurolinguistics is presently based.

One basic question which occurs frequently in the study of language pathology is whether language breakdown is related in natural ways to the structure of normal language. Do individual patients and groups of patients have disorders of language which are confined to particular types of language structures or processes? For instance, do certain patients or groups of patients only have trouble speaking and no difficulty understanding speech, or do they have a disorder affecting only syntactic structures and not the sound pattern of their language?

Our first reaction to questions like these must be skepticism that such patterns will be found. After all, injuries to the brain such as stroke, trauma, and tumor do not leave neat areas of destruction ("lesions") in particular locations in the brain. Stroke follows patterns of vessels, trauma depends on its cause, and tumors grow locally and spread via the blood-stream. None of these diseases causes lesions which we would expect to be related to particular aspects of language. Furthermore, even if lesions were relatively "neat", specific breakdown patterns would only arise following brain injury if particular aspects of language processing were the responsibility of individual areas of the brain, and this might well not be the case. At the very least, it would be hard to recognize such patterns, since language itself is organized in complex interactive ways, and a disorder of one aspect of linguistic structure might be due to a patient's inability to deal with a quite different aspect of language (we shall review an analysis of this sort in Chapter 15). It is therefore interesting and important that, despite these considerations, many specific patterns of language breakdown have been described. These isolated deficits bear on theories of normal language structures and processing. To the extent to which they are related to types and locations of neurological pathology, these isolated disturbances are the basis for inferences from pathological language to the relationship between normal language and the brain.

Another question which has often been raised regarding language disorders is whether they parallel language development in reverse. This question is related to another aspect of linguistic aphasiology: the regularity of language breakdown (as opposed to the specificity of isolated deficits). Some aspects of language and language processing are retained after others have been disturbed by injury. When the retained and disturbed processes and structures are within the same domain, rather than in different areas – as, for instance, when a patient cannot read long words but can read short ones – these patterns may be related to the complexity of processing of the different structures. In some cases, elements which are retained after brain injury are also those which develop first in childhood, and those which are lost are those which are last to develop. In these cases, the comparison of aphasic abilities and developmental sequences can provide powerful evidence for the relative complexity of one structure or process compared with another within a single area of language function. This is not always true, however; and the study of the areas in which it is and is not true is an important method of determining the relative complexity and inter-dependence of linguistic forms.

The question of orderly breakdown of language within a given domain is related to a third neurolinguistic question: whether the brain can support language in many different ways or whether it can do so only in one or in a limited number of forms. If language breakdown is always orderly within each sub-domain of language, no matter what the neural insult causing aphasia, we can conclude that, no matter how the brain is injured and how it reorganizes after injury, those neural elements and organizational features which support language do so in highly restricted ways. Of course, it is another matter to discover what neural elements and organizational features are responsible for language; but the existence of regular patterns of breakdown – if they exist – would indicate that the ways in which neural tissue supports language are restricted, even when neural tissue is incomplete, damaged, and partially self-repaired.

Finally, the study of linguistic aphasiology is of interest as a branch of abnormal human cognitive psychology. Whatever the relationship of specific domains of breakdown to components of normal language, and regardless of the possible ordered nature of language impairment within a domain, linguistic aphasiology deals with a field of abnormal psychology which is worth describing in and of itself, and which may be worth understanding in detail for the practical purpose of guiding rehabilitation efforts.

We have touched upon four general areas in which questions have been raised about the relationship between language and the brain. There are many other questions that can be asked about these matters, but these four are central to the fields of neurolinguistics and linguistic aphasiology, and provide a good place to start. Before turning to the ways in which these questions may be studied, it is worth noting two important points regarding all these areas of inquiry.

First, we can summarize many of the questions by saying that the goal of neurolinguistics is to characterize the relationship between elements and operations in the theory of language and language processing and elements and functions in the theory of neural tissue. If we could establish that particular structures and events in the nervous system corresponded to particular structures and processes in language and the psychology of language, and could do so over the time course of language development and in cases of disease, we would be in a position to answer almost all of the questions that have just been raised. Accordingly, it is fair to characterize the principal goal of neurolinguistics as a study of the relationship between two theories: that of language structure and processing, and that of neural tissue and its functioning. Linguistic aphasiology is partly a domain of its own, and partly a source of data on which neurolinguistic theories are constructed.

Second, it will be obvious to readers of this volume that we are a long way from answering any of the questions posed, and from achieving the ultimate goal of having a neurolinguistic theory. In part, this is the case because the sciences of linguistics and neurology are incomplete and in the midst of rapid changes. Any conclusions that we may draw about their relationship cannot be more secure than the theories of linguistics and neurology upon which they are based. However, it is presently the case that our knowledge of both linguistics and neuroscience far outstrips our knowledge of how the two are related. We shall conclude this section by considering why this is so.

In part, the reason for this discrepancy is methodological. Linguists have studied language by asking for the intuitions about language that normal adult speakers have, and by conducting psychological experiments of various sorts; neuroscientists have learned a great deal about the structure and function of the nervous system by direct manipulation and recording from the brains of animals, and from neural tissue *in vitro*. The techniques that have allowed for the advancement of these two sciences are not immediately applicable to the study of their relationship. We cannot study human brains as we do animals'; and we are only beginning the experimental study of language in abnormal populations. The absence of good "animal models" of language and the late introduction of psychological experimentation and linguistic analyses into studies of aphasia have been limitations on the investigation of language–brain relationships.

The second reason for the discrepancy between the science of language–brain relations and the sciences of linguistics and neurology is conceptual. As we shall see, until very recently the level of detail at which language was related to the brain was one which ignored the details of both linguistic and neural science. Recent work has begun to investigate language–brain relationships in light of more detailed and empirically richer theories of both language and the brain, and some of the early results of these approaches are now with us. It is this expansion of knowledge which has led to the recognition of these new fields of inquiry. It is a reasonable expectation that this more detailed level of analysis will continue to enrich our understanding of linguistic aphasiology and neurolinguistics.

To conclude, we have reviewed several basic questions in neurolinguistics and linguistic aphasiology, which we shall try to keep in mind as we explore the results of the past 125 years of research in this field. These questions do not exhaust those which can be asked, and we will come across others as we take up particular studies. We have also indicated that linguistics, psycholinguistics, and neuroscience are all more advanced in many ways than neurolinguistics and linguistic aphasiology. This, in turn, points to the fact that there are many important questions in our area of inquiry which have yet to be asked and answered.

SUGGESTIONS FOR FURTHER READING

Fodor, J. A. (1968). *Psychological Explanation.* Random House, New York.
Goldstein, K. (1948). *Language and Language Disorders.* Grune and Stratton, New York.
Lightfoot, D. (1982). *The Language Lottery.* MIT Press, Cambridge, Mass.
Marshall, J. C. (1980). On the biology of language acquisition. In D. Caplan (ed.), *Biological Studies of Mental Processes.* MIT Press, Cambridge, Mass.
Terrace, H. S. (1979). *Nim: The Story of a Chimpanzee Who Learned Sign Language.* Knopf, New York.

2

Approaches to neurolinguistics and linguistic aphasiology

As we take up the subject matter of neurolinguistics and linguistic aphasiology in the chapters to follow, we will encounter various ways of gathering evidence and of reasoning about data to draw conclusions about language breakdown and the relationship between language and brain. Before entering into the subject matter itself, it is worthwhile to consider an overview of these methods and forms of argumentation. In this chapter, we shall outline four approaches to reasoning about language–brain relationships, illustrating each with sketches of arguments which have been made by investigators at various times. (We shall consider the actual arguments in greater detail later, in the appropriate chapters.) We then shall review several techniques of study which are used in neurolinguistic research. Finally, we shall consider several issues which arise in the analysis of language disturbances which are central to the work of linguistic aphasiology. With this background, we shall be better equipped to turn to actual studies of language–brain relationships and language breakdown in the body of this volume.

Four forms of argument in neurolinguistics

1. Arguments from linguistic and psycholinguistic structures to neural structures

One form of argument relating language and the brain looks at features of language structure and the psychology of language use, and argues that these features suggest that the brain is structured and operates in particular ways. Two examples from the classical clinical literature on neurolinguistics will illustrate this type of argument.

Before he turned over his creative genius to psychoanalysis, Sigmund Freud wrote a short monograph on aphasia (1891). In the volume, he suggested that individual words, which he considered to be the basic units of language structure, were complex mental structures. In his view, each word was made up of a number of "associations", as illustrated in Figure 2-1.

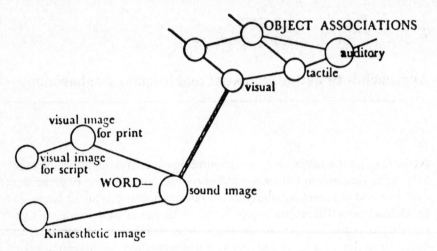

Figure 2-1. Freud's model of word structure
(*Source:* Freud 1891: 77)

Partly on the basis of this concept of the structure of words (and partly because he disagreed with other types of neurolinguistic models), Freud postulated that the area of the brain concerned with language was a single large region, whose borders abutted on areas of the brain primarily responsible for visual, tactile, auditory, and motor function. He represented this area in Figure 2-2. The inference is from the nature of the psychological make-up of words to the nature of the neural mechanisms involved in language. Freud concluded that, because word meaning involved multiple modality-specific associations, the language area of the brain must be a relatively undifferentiated region. Freud himself recognized that this was an inference, and that it needed to be confirmed by more direct observations.

Another example from the classical literature of this sort of argument is to be found in the work of Carl Wernicke (1874). Observations of aphasic syndromes led Wernicke to the conclusion that "sensory images" for words had to be mentally evoked during normal speech production. Among the reasons he gave for his belief in this hypothesis was the fact that, in his view, speech was acquired by imitation of the language that a child was exposed to. The nature of language acquisition, according to Wernicke, led to a psychological process whereby speech was tied to sensory images – a complex auditory-to-motor reflex. This had to take place over a neural pathway, and Wernicke concluded that there must be transmission of auditory images from sensory association areas to motor speech-planning areas during the act of speaking. Wernicke went on to suggest what this pathway was. Wernicke had other reasons for his belief in the arousal of

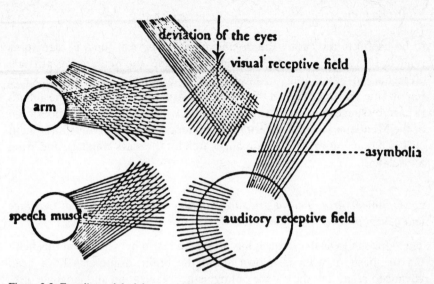

Figure 2-2. Freud's model of the neural basis for words
(*Source:* Freud 1891: 81)

auditory images of words during the act of speaking, besides the argument from language development (see the next section). Part of his rationale for this theory, however, was based on this argument from this feature of the psychology of language to the neural basis for language.

In modern times, arguments of this type have continued to be made. Contemporary linguists have suggested, for instance, that the capacity for language is a separate component of human intelligence and unique to the human species. As we saw in Chapter 1, this view has suggested the hypothesis that there must be particular features of the brain, largely yet to be discovered, which are responsible for language, and which are not found in other species. For reasons that will become apparent in later chapters, it is difficult to make specific suggestions regarding neural organization on the basis of current theories of language structure and processing (though a few such suggestions have been made). However, even the very general conclusion that it is reasonable to direct our search for neural mechanisms underlying language towards possible domain- and species-specific neural structures for this function is partly a consequence of taking seriously the argument from analysis of language structure and function to analysis of neural structure and function.

This logical approach obviously has its limits. Arguments of this sort will never be able to identify the actual physical structures that are related to language. But these sorts of arguments have been and are likely to continue to be useful in indicating the *organization* of physical (neural) structures related to language, and they can *help* guide the search for physical elements. In other areas of biology, such arguments have proven quite important. The discovery of the molecular structure of DNA was hastened, in part, by suggestions as to what to look for, which came from consideration of the Mendelian laws of inheritance of phenotypes. This type of argument clearly has an important place in our search for the ways language and brain are related.

2. *Arguments from neural structure and function to the nature of language and neural processing of language*

The opposite logical approach has also been taken by workers in this field. On the basis of what is known about the brain, arguments have been advanced regarding the nature of linguistic organization and language use, which is then conceptually linked to particular features of brain structure and function. Wernicke's paper of 1874, in which we have just encountered the first type of argument, also contains logical considerations of this second type. Again the argument concerns the question of the existence of a "flow of information" (these are not the terms Wernicke used) from auditory representations of words to motor programs for speech during the act of speaking. Wernicke bolstered his claim that such a process took place by referring to what he considered to be the basic form of neurophysiological activity underlying all movement – reflex activity. Wernicke accepted the views of Meynert, the great German neuroanatomist and physiologist, concerning reflex activity. Essentially, all movement was considered to be built upon reflex activity, by modification of elementary reflexes through higher controls. The elementary reflexes were the result of relatively uninfluenced transmission of sensory stimuli to motor nerves in the spinal cord and brain-stem. It was one of Meynert's most important discoveries that, just as the spinal cord and brain-stem had sensory and motor areas, the brain too – in particular the cerebral hemispheres – had regions towards its posterior area which were devoted to reception of sensory stimuli, and other, more anterior areas which were related to motor function. The resulting view of neurological function was that sensory-to-motor flow of impulses occurred in the cerebral hemispheres, and that complex psychological activity could be seen as a highly complex sort of reflex. Wernicke used this argument to strengthen his hypothesis that speech production required arousal of the auditory images of words because this hypothesis made language use similar to other psychological functions, such as planning and executing actions. The hypothesis was thus consistent with an accepted view of neurophysiology – a point in its favor, according to Wernicke.

Another example of this type of reasoning is found in Jackson's views of the hierarchical organization of the nervous system. Jackson developed the concept that the nervous system consisted of progressively higher levels of activity, with the function of the highest levels being largely the chronic inhibition and appropriately timed release of the activity of lower levels. This conceptual framework carried over into his approach to the description of language function and its breakdown. Jackson differed from most researchers of his day in not focussing upon the degree to which particular language tasks – speaking, reading, etc. – were disturbed after brain lesions. Rather, he concentrated on developing a descriptive framework for language disorders which was hierarchical in a certain sense. He tried to describe patients' abilities to use language in meaningful, appropriate, flexible, and innovative ways. He emphasized the extent to which patients' utterances could be considered "propositions". A proposition is a sequence of words which conveys a relationship between the objects referred to by the words. According to Jackson (1878), propositions are frequently used for the transmission of new and situationally appropriate messages. It is not clear from reading Jackson's several papers on the subject of language disorders whether he arrived at this view of how to describe abnormal language because of his belief in the hierarchical nature of neural organization; but it is quite clear that, having arrived at this way of approaching language disorders (and normal language function), Jackson linked it to his views of the functional organization of the nervous system. We shall see in Chapter 7 that this approach has been an influential one, with many classical and contemporary workers adopting it in one or another form.

Let us outline one more neurolinguistic analysis which falls into this category of logical argument. The form of the argument is quite similar to that used by Wernicke, though its substance is quite different and more detailed. The Russian neuropsychologist A. R. Luria (1947) approached the general problem of the neuropsychology of language by considering the role played by particular areas of the brain in sensory and motor functions, and by analyzing the psychology of language use in terms which were similar to those used for sensory–motor function. For instance, he concluded, on the basis of studies of brain-injured patients' abilities, that the area of the frontal lobes anterior to the motor cortex was responsible for the temporal aspects of the planning and execution of motor sequences. He analyzed the disorders of language seen after lesions in this area as being due to the loss of the "dynamic, predicative aspect of words", a function he considered similar to the sequential, temporal planning of movement. In this case, what we see is an analysis of an abnormal language performance as missing a component of the normal psychology of language; and the nature of that component is suggested by – or, at least, as in Jackson's case, consistent with – an analysis of the motor functions of the brain region in which a lesion produces the language disorder. Luria thus reached a conclusion about an aspect of language structure – that some words have a "dynamic predicative function" – and about where this function is represented in the brain, partly on the basis of an analysis of the role that brain regions have in other motor activity. Though more complex, the argument has the same structure as Wernicke's use of Meynert's psychophysiological theories to support his hypothesis regarding the role of auditory images in speech. The form of Luria's argument is also similar to that of Jackson's, insofar as an analysis of the function of the nervous system in other areas leads to a hypothesis about what language is like and how the brain processes it.

3. *Arguments from parallel structures*

A third logical approach to the way language and brain are related is, in a sense, the combination of the previous two. Indeed, it is sometimes difficult (and unnecessary) to draw a strict line between this and one or the other of the former types of reasoning. The third approach begins by joint analyses of some aspect of language and/or function, and emphasizes parallels between the two, thereby concluding that the two are related.

We shall consider just one example of this sort of argument, a well-known argument of N. Geschwind's regarding the relationship between naming objects and the inferior parietal lobule of the human brain.

Geschwind (1965) points out that there is an area of the human brain, the inferior parietal lobule, which has particular properties. Its microscopic anatomical features indicate that it is an advanced area of human cortex. It achieves certain maturational stages, such as completion of myelinization (the laying down of an "insulating" sheath around a nerve) late in life, as compared with most other areas of cortex, another indication of its neurologically advanced status. It is considerably larger in humans than in non-human primates, more so than many other areas of the brain. Finally, it has connections with the advanced "association" areas surrounding the cortical receptive areas for vision, tactile sensation, and audition. This last feature is quite unusual in the animal world, as these association areas of cortex do not emit fibers converging upon a single cortical area in any non-human species. In non-human brains, fibers from these association areas travel principally to the limbic lobe, a more elementary area of the brain.

Geschwind points out that, at the same time, non-human species have great difficulty being trained to associate two stimuli if neither is what he calls a "limbic" stimulus. Limbic stimuli are those which satisfy basic biological needs like thirst or hunger. Only humans can easily learn to associate "cortical" stimuli, such as sounds and visual images. Geschwind observes that the task of naming objects requires these purely "cortical" associations. Geschwind analyzes names as auditory representations which are associated with multiple sensory properties of the objects they refer to. Geschwind further indicates that, in his view, naming objects is the most basic function of language. The conclusion is clear: the uniquely human ability to name objects, which is at the heart of our linguistic ability, is the result of the existence and pattern of connections of this species-unique area of the brain, the inferior parietal lobule.

The logic of the argument is that there is a parallel between the structure of language and that of the brain, which indicates how the two are related. Names are associations of auditory and other sensory stimuli. The cortical areas responsible for sensory processing all connect to the inferior parietal lobe in humans, but do not do so in other species. Only man can use names. Therefore it is the inferior parietal lobe which supports naming. The difference between this argument and the preceding two types is that, in this case, Geschwind presents explicit, detailed analyses of *both* language *and* neural structures in order to draw his conclusions, while in the earlier cases, the line of argument was derived more from one domain of analysis and applied to the other. It should be clear, however, that one form of argument shades over into the next, and that all three are really variants on a similar pattern.

4. *Analysis of the results of disease of the brain*

By far the most common and important method of relating language to the brain is the analysis of the effects of naturally occurring diseases of the brain on language. Not only was the analysis of such cases the first method utilized for the systematic scientific study of language–brain relationships; because of our increasing ability to define the localization and the nature of diseases affecting the brain and to describe the resulting disorders of language, this has remained a central method of studying this topic. The difficulties in utilizing this technique as a method of learning about language–brain relationships center on our ability correctly to interpret a disorder of language in a diseased brain in relationship to a normal language system in a healthy brain.

To do this, we have to provide an analysis of abnormal language

23

performance and the abnormalities found in the brain, and clarify the relation of the two to normal processes. It is important to keep in mind that, as in the case of the first three types of arguments, conclusions drawn from the study of pathological cases are inferences regarding language–brain relationships based on data of a certain sort – in this case, on the analysis and interpretation of the effects of brain damage. Indeed, in the case of arguments derived from pathological cases, the lines of logic are usually longer and more complex than in the preceding three cases. What makes the analysis of pathological cases attractive despite these difficulties is the fact that here we have access to a system in which we know there is a missing or damaged physical component. If we can correctly analyze the damage and the resulting abnormal performance, and relate both to normal neural and linguistic function, we would be in a position to say what role the missing brain structure(s) play in normal language functioning. There are, however, many potential slips between cup and lip here, mainly due to the variety of ways brain damage might affect performance, our inability to identify what is normal and abnormal about a pathological performance, and our inability to characterize adequately the physical (neural) effects of a lesion in the brain. As we proceed through neurolinguistic work and thought, these issues will return at frequent intervals and we will consider various arguments in greater depth. At this point, we will only consider briefly some of the basic issues that arise in arguing from pathological language performances to normal neurolinguistic models.

By far the most common form of analysis and argumentation regarding pathological language, brain damage, and their relation to normal language–brain relationships is what has been called "deficit analysis" and subsequent "functional localization". Essentially, this approach sees the abnormal performance as resulting from the normal operation of the language-processing system, minus one of its components. The "missing" component is then inferred to be normally located in the region of the brain which is destroyed or damaged. The work that we shall review in the next chapter, Broca's pioneering study of aphasia, makes this sort of analysis and argument. Broca's patient, Lebourgne, was said to show normal linguistic function in all spheres other than speaking, and his autopsy was said to show a lesion whose center lay in what is now called Broca's area. Broca's conclusion was that this area of the brain was responsible for the "faculty for articulate speech".

Klein (1978) has outlined the logical requirements of this form of analysis and reasoning, which we may summarize in the following four conditions:

(1)   Pathological behavior is correctly interpreted as the failure to exercise a normal functional capacity.

24

(2)   There is an analysis of the capacity in question into sub-components (i.e. a functional decomposition), which is the best explanation of how the organism has the function in question.

(3)   The operation of the functional sub-components, minus a particular component, results in the pathological behavior, and there is no better explanation for the pathological behavior.

(4)   There is a lesion in a particular brain structure whenever the above conditions are met, and no other brain lesions cause the above conditions to be met.

It is fair to say that these are very strict requirements which have rarely been met. They may serve as a sort of logical yardstick against which the many deficit analyses and related functional localizations in the neurolinguistic literature may be measured. These requirements also indicate a variety of ways in which deficit analysis and subsequent functional localization may *not* be the correct framework for analyzing a particular aphasic symptom. We may consider the various requirements in turn.

First, it may not be the case that pathological behavior is correctly interpreted as the failure to exercise a normal function. The abnormal behavior may be something new, caused by the lesion. We shall see in Chapter 13 that certain analyses of one variety of sound errors made by aphasic patients in fact assume that the brain damage causes a new function to be superimposed upon existing language abilities. It has also been suggested that brain lesions serve to allow the expression of functions which are usually suppressed or inhibited. As we have seen, the work of Jackson was the first to stress this possibility, and his ideas have been developed by a number of investigators (Brown 1979). If this is the correct way of viewing a certain number of symptoms, the symptoms reflect functional abilities not usually exercised by the brain (or, at least, not usually responsible for overt behavior). Whether the brain damage itself produces a new function or simply releases one which was completely inhibited, these effects of brain lesions are not analyzable as failures to use the normal methods of producing a behavior or function.

Requirements (2) and (3) are, in practice, hard to meet. It is not simple to determine what the "best" functional decomposition of normal functions is, and it has proven hard to demonstrate that an abnormal performance is the result of the operation of normal sub-components of a psychological or linguistic system, minus one (or more) component(s). Such analyses seemed quite straightforward when normal language function was being decomposed into very large divisions, such as "the faculty for articulate speech", or "the ability to read". But when we try to make finer and finer divisions of the psychological and linguistic functions we are interested in, which we must do to capture the details of language structure and proces-

25

sing, we find that interactions among the postulated sub-components become very complex, and the effects of missing a sub-component or, even worse, of a partial mis-function of a sub-component are far from simple to identify. We shall see some of the complexities involved in such analyses in Chapter 14.

Finally, it is also difficult to characterize the nature of a lesion. Though radiological, electrophysiological (EEG), and even pathological data may show that a lesion is restricted to a single area of the brain, it is often the case that one or another of these methods of determining lesion extent shows abnormalities in areas where others do not; which result is the one we should take as related to the pathological functional performance? When we try to deal with groups of patients, to answer questions about how language is organized in the brains of people in general, we find that a whole host of individual factors systematically influence the extent to which a lesion in a given area will affect language. These factors include age, handedness, early injury, familial handedness, and possibly sex. Furthermore, different types of brain disease – tumor, stroke, trauma, infection, etc. – tend to produce at least slightly different symptoms even when centered in the same region. All symptoms change over time, and it is hard to measure organic changes in lesions over time completely with some imaging techniques. All these factors make it hard to collect series of patients with identical neurobiological backgrounds and identical lesions in which to determine the deficit associated with a particular lesion.

Finally, when we consider any language performance, we are forced to face the issue of variability in a person's performance. When we ask normal people to make judgements about grammaticality of sentences, or about which sound sequences constitute possible words of their language, we achieve a fair degree of reliability (though not perfectly reliable judgements). When we test normal subjects on tasks having to do with the rapid identification of words or sounds, or the detection or localization of extraneous noises in sentences, there is a moderate amount of variability from subject to subject and from testing session to testing session, which can usually be separated from the principal effects of the language stimuli by various statistical methods. When we deal with patients, the extent of variability from patient to patient, from one to another example of a language item, and from session to session, is extreme, so much so that some observers have even suggested that it is this variability itself which our analysis of the effects of brain lesions must mainly account for. This last conclusion need not be accepted for it to be obvious that the variation in capacities of brain-injured subjects is an issue that further complicates our ability to gather and use data from these "experiments of nature" to build theories of normal neurolinguistic function.

Despite the many difficulties, the use of pathological language performances following brain injury has led to the most sophisticated neurolinguistic theories currently available.

We have now considered four forms of logical inference which have been used to construct neurolinguistic models and theories. Each has its difficulties, both logical and practical. All also have limits as to the detail and complexity of the descriptions and models they can presently generate. For instance, none of these approaches can give us an indication of what neurophysiological events are occurring when a person utters a sentence, because none of them observes such events or, at present, incorporates such events into its description of the neural side of neurolinguistics. In all four approaches, the lines of inference regarding language–brain relationships are fairly long. There is little direct observation of neurological processes related to the normal use of language by a normal speaker. It would certainly be highly desirable to have more direct ways of observing the activity of the brain during normal language use, both to provide confirmation or disconfirmation of aspects of the models generated by these four kinds of logical considerations, and also to explore and suggest new theories and possibilities. We have indicated earlier that, largely for a combination of technical and ethical reasons, there are very few techniques of this sort. There are a few, however; and we shall now briefly consider five of them.

Five techniques of study in neurolinguistics

There are at present five basic approaches to gathering more direct evidence bearing on the nature of language–brain relationships.

1. *Stimulation of the brain*

In the 1870s, Fritsch and Hitzig discovered that they could produce movement in the limbs of a dog by direct application of electrical current to parts of the cortex of the dog's brain. At approximately the same time, Jackson suggested that epilepsy was the result of localized electrical discharges within the brain. From these observations, the notion developed that electrical stimulation of parts of the cortex of the brain would cause movement, and the question arose as to whether it could cause speech. No cases of talking during epileptic seizures were noted, and the question remained essentially unanswered until Penfield and Roberts (1959) stimulated the language areas of patients undergoing neurosurgery. They found that electrical stimulation did not produce speech. In most cases, it produced arrest of speech; that is, while patients were involved in counting or other repetitive automatic acts, localized current in several of the language areas inhibited their ability to carry out these activities. In a few cases, such stimulation produced vocalization or had the effect of causing mis-naming, but it never led to fluent speech. This technique has been used by several other investigators, who have reached the same conclusion. We do not fully understand why the effects of local stimulation in the language areas are almost entirely of this negative, inhibitory sort; presumably the stimuli are much more powerful than the normal electrical impulses occurring in the brain that are part of the neurophysiological basis of language function, and the inhibition of speech during external stimulation is related to this difference in strength of the stimulus.

The fact that stimulation disrupts linguistic functioning means that the way we can use this technique to learn about normal language–brain relationships is through deficit analysis and functional localization. The difference between this technique and more stable lesions lies in the precision with which we can locate the "lesion" and its briefer duration. In fact, stimulation has so far added little to our understanding of how the brain's electrical activity is related to speech, but it has been very useful for localizing areas of the brain that are involved in language. Several areas of the brain have been shown by this technique to be related to language, inasmuch as stimulating them inhibits speech. Since these areas are ones in which naturally occurring diseases do not produce permanent language disorders, our appreciation that these areas are involved in language is chiefly the result of these stimulation studies. Recent work with this technique has further enlarged our conception of the area in which words are represented, and has also provided interesting data regarding the organization of two or more languages in the brains of bilinguals and polyglots and other matters. We review work with this technique in Chapter 21.

2. *Recording neurophysiological correlates of language*

Many advances in neuroscience have come about as a result of our ability to record electrical activity from individual cells and groups of cells in a living animal at the same time as a stimulus is presented to the animal, or as the animal makes a particular movement. Our basic notions of the ways in which the nervous system transmits information are largely derived from these intra- and extra-cellular recording studies *in vivo*. In the case of language, practical and ethical considerations have limited the application of these techniques, though there are a few reported studies in which extra-cellular electrodes have been placed in the brain and the activity of small groups of cells recorded as language stimuli are presented (Bechtereva *et al.* 1979).

A more readily available technique is the measurement of "event-related potentials" (ERPs). This method involves recording of normal electrical activity of the brain; but rather than the electrodes penetrating the brain itself, the electrical activity is measured through the intact skull and scalp by the usual recording techniques of electroencephalography. If electrodes are placed appropriately, and enough repetitions of a particular stimulus are presented to a subject, a small perturbation occurs in the electroencephalographic record. This "event-related" electrical potential depends on the nature of the stimulus and also on the nature of the task that the subject must accomplish vis-à-vis the stimulus. The analysis of these potentials is complex. This is partly because the characterization of the stimulus and of the subject's psychological and physiological state must be exact, and partly because the potentials are small and hard to discern in the ongoing electroencephalographic record. Many irrelevant actions, such as eye-blinks, or clenching the jaw, can appear to be cerebral electrical events, and need to be recognized as artifacts through appropriate control monitors. It is also difficult to interpret the relationship of these potentials to cellular events within the brain, and to be certain of which structures in the brain are responsible for particular event-related (or "evoked") potentials. Despite these difficulties with the technique, a number of studies have now appeared which have established correlates between cerebral activity and particular features of language (Chapter 20). One of the important advantages of the use of ERPs to correlate brain electrical activity with language functioning is that ERPs can measure electrical events very quickly. This allows us to examine very fast, unconscious aspects of language processing, such as word recognition. As this branch of technology develops, we can expect to gain further information about the neurophysiological correlates of language structure and processing through its use.

3. *Lateralized stimulus presentation*

The previous two techniques involve direct observation or generation of cerebral electrical events which may be related to language. The application of these techniques is difficult and requires elaborate equipment, and, in the case of stimulation, can only be justified as part of neurosurgical procedures. For these reasons, their use is relatively infrequent and restricted to a few laboratories. By way of contrast, the psychological technique of presenting stimuli to one or the other side of the brain is relatively simple, and is in use in a great number of psychological laboratories. The neuroanatomical organization of the brain is such that the left side of the brain directly receives visual information coming from the right visual field (the visible area to your right as you look straight ahead), and it also receives the major share of the auditory information coming from the right ear; the opposite is true for the right side of the brain. This information is then relayed to the opposite hemisphere. Presentation of language materials to one or the other visual field, or to one or the other ear, will therefore first activate the "language-dominant" hemisphere or the "non-dominant" hemisphere. Typically, if a normal right-handed subject is asked to identify or process a linguistic stimulus, he does so more accurately and quickly when it appears in the right visual field or in the right ear.

Investigations of this sort have proven useful in determining the degree to which the left hemisphere is "dominant" for language in different groups of subjects and at different stages of development. These techniques can also be used to help determine the degree to which various components of language are processed by one or the other hemisphere. It is now clear that, in normals, the "non-dominant" hemisphere is not totally uninvolved in language, and the question of just what role it plays can be approached through these techniques. For instance, there are studies indicating that second languages are processed to a greater extent by the "non-dominant" hemisphere than are first languages, particularly at early stages of second-language development (Albert and Obler 1978), that the development of hemispheric dominance for language in childhood develops over time (Kimura 1961), and that the non-dominant hemisphere is critically involved in processing some aspects of language, such as intonation (Heilman *et al.* 1975).

One particular application of this technique is worth mentioning separately. There are a small number of patients who have had the two hemispheres of the brain "disconnected" in an effort to relieve epileptic seizures. In these patients, the major fiber tract connecting the two hemispheres – the corpus callosum – is surgically cut. Under these conditions, unlike what occurs in the normal state, presentation of a stimulus to one visual field does not lead to subsequent transmission of information about that stimulus to both hemispheres, at least not by the usual efficient channels found in the corpus callosum. Thus, the patient's response to a stimulus lateralized to one visual field is primarily a function of the opposite hemisphere. Investigation of the role of each hemisphere in speech, language comprehension, and other psycholinguistic functions has been possible through the use of unilateral stimulus presentation in these patients.

4. *Anesthetization of a single hemisphere*

In 1949, Wada showed that it was possible to anesthetize one hemisphere of the brain for short periods of time by injecting a short-acting barbiturate into the internal carotid artery which supplies blood to that hemisphere. When this procedure was accomplished, a patient would remain conscious, but would be paralyzed on the opposite side of the body, often unable to see in the opposite visual field, and, if the injection had been carried out in the "dominant" hemisphere, unable to speak for approximately five to fifteen minutes. As the anesthetic wore off, speech returned, and numerous difficulties with naming and other language functions were seen for another short period. Using this technique, it is possible to determine which hemisphere is dominant for language. Its usual use is with patients who have had brain damage, and who may undergo surgery, as a guide to which hemisphere is dominant for language and thus to how much tissue can be removed. In particular, it is useful when considering operations on diseases which have affected the brain early in life, which frequently influence the degree and direction of cerebral dominance for language. It is also useful in determining which hemisphere is dominant in individuals in whom dominance for language is not as predictable as in right-handers, such as left-handed and ambidextrous patients. The use of this technique has provided an important source of data bearing on the issue of the variation of cerebral dominance for language in different groups of patients, which complements the study of aphasia following more permanent brain lesions.

5. *Metabolic scanning*

There are a number of ways to measure the metabolic activity of parts of the human brain while a subject performs a particular task. The first of these techniques to be used was the measurement of regional cerebral blood flow. By using radioactive material which attaches to red blood cells, it is feasible to measure small variations in blood flow to particular areas of the brain during particular activities. Small increases in regional cerebral blood flow are related to transient increases in the metabolic demands of these regions. These demands reflect increased activity of neurons in these locales. Several studies have indicated that regions of the left hemisphere which are thought to be related to language because of the language abnormalities seen after they are lesioned do show such increased blood flow during language-related activity. This technique, like that of the measurement of event-related potentials, offers the promise of allowing more direct observation of physiological events related to language functioning in the normal unanesthetized subject.

31

More advanced techniques of metabolic scanning have been developed in recent years. Positron Emission Tomography (PET) scanning makes use of radioactive labels on molecules which are directly used by the brain. Glucose, oxygen, and a number of other substances such as neurotransmitters can be labeled and their utilization by parts of the brain measured. A similar technique – single proton emission computed tomography (SPECT) – involves inhaling radioactively labeled substances which are taken up by areas of the brain. The areas of the brain which use these metabolites differ as a function of a person's activities, and the uptake of different substances can be correlated with different functions. These techniques also show "metabolic lesions" in areas where more "static" radiological techniques do not show lesions. The use of these techniques can thus be helpful in the study of language–brain relationships in both normal subjects and brain-injured patients. There are limits to these techniques. The time taken for metabolites to equilibrate is relatively long, compared to ERPs: from one or two minutes to thirty minutes or more. This restricts the sorts of function that can be studied with these techniques. Not all the uptake of a metabolite in an area of the brain is necessarily due to neuronal metabolism – some may be due to the activity of the supporting cells (glial cells) and other elements. The equipment needed to use these techniques is expensive, and found in only a few centers. Overall, these techniques are in their infancy, and have great promise for application to neurolinguistic research.

It is important to recognize that these five techniques, and others which we shall come across in later chapters, are sometimes difficult to apply, often give results which can only be interpreted with the aid of statistical and other mathematical analytical tools, are in some cases only available in patients with certain types of neurological disease, and have other drawbacks. Moreover, at present it is fair to say that they are all modifications of techniques which have achieved a higher level of technological sophistication in branches of neuroscience where animal and tissue experimentation is practised, and that their use thus cannot be expected to characterize brain functions as accurately as is done in other areas of neuroscience. Last, it is worth keeping in mind that, though these more direct ways of observing brain activity related to language do exist, these techniques are no better than the linguistic and psycholinguistic questions they are directed at, and all the variables which we believe influence language–brain relationships on the basis of pathological studies must be taken into account to interpret results coming from the use of these techniques. As we proceed, we shall attempt to determine which conclusions these methods have produced which we can be confident about, and where more work is needed. We can certainly already see that one area in which work is certainly needed is the development of more refined methods of observing the normal brain while it is using language.

Three forms of argument in linguistic aphasiology

We have seen above that an important source of information about language–brain relationships comes from aphasia, and takes the form of the correlation of a deficit analysis with a neurological lesion. We have also indicated that it is sometimes hard to establish that a deficit analysis is the correct way to characterize an aphasic symptom, and that it is particularly difficult to justify specific deficit analyses. We shall not go over these matters again here, but we note that the establishment of a correct deficit analysis for a particular symptom is the most common problem faced by contemporary workers in linguistic aphasiology. There are, however, other issues that linguistic aphasiology faces. The three that we shall consider are related to the role of group studies and studies of individual cases in the development of linguistic aphasiology and the role of compensatory mechanisms in producing symptoms.

1. *Association of symptoms: anatomical and functional bases for aphasic syndromes*

In our previous discussion of deficit analysis, we considered the analysis of individual symptoms. Symptoms might be disturbances such as the inability to produce grammatical words in spontaneous conversation, the inability to name objects, the inability to plan the sound structure of words properly, and other disturbances. We might define disturbances more specifically, so that we can recognize many different reasons for the failure to name an object or to produce a sentence correctly. Establishing the exact nature of a patient's disturbance is part of the work of establishing a correct deficit analysis. However, there is another issue to be faced as well: the co-occurrence of symptoms. Most, if not all, aphasic patients have more than one disturbance. It is crucial for linguistic aphasiology to know why symptoms co-occur.

There are essentially three reasons why symptoms might occur together. The first is simple chance. In any given patient, the neuropathological lesion might affect more than one functional ability. This should be very easy to detect. Studying even a small number of patients ought to show that the symptoms that are associated in one case can occur independently in others. If so, we would conclude that the association of symptoms in the first case

33

was due to some particularity of the lesion in that patient in relationship to how language was represented in his brain.

A second possibility is that symptoms co-occur because of anatomical factors. For instance, it is well known that disturbances in sentence planning and production known as "agrammatism", characterized by the relative omission of grammatical words in sentence production, are very frequently accompanied by a disturbance in sound production known as "dysarthria", a particular form of hoarseness, slurring, and disturbance of articulation. The co-occurrence of these symptoms is extremely frequent, but not universal. It has been suggested that the reason these symptoms frequently co-occur is that the neurological areas responsible for using grammatical words in sentence planning and for production of normal articulation partially overlap, or are in close proximity, in the brain. Thus, in most cases, a lesion will affect both these functions. However, on occasion, a lesion will spare enough of one region to allow one of these functions to escape disruption.

The co-occurrence of symptoms because of the anatomical basis for language is similar to the co-occurrence of symptoms for chance reasons, insofar as both of these explanations for symptom groupings invoke an anatomical explanation. In the case of chance co-occurrence, the anatomical determinants of a set of symptoms are idiosyncratic, either because of the peculiarities of a lesion (such as, for instance, a case of multiple emboli in which many areas of the brain might be damaged) or because of some peculiarity in the organization of language functions within the brain in a particular patient (such as an early lesion leading to a cerebral reorganization of functions). In the case of anatomical reasons for symptom groupings, the claim is that the *usual* organization of the brain is such that most lesions of a particular type will affect the neurological substrate for two functions, leading to two symptoms. Operationally, the difference between the two can be seen as the ease of finding exceptions to the rule. In anatomically determined symptom groupings, exceptions are quite rare, whereas in chance co-occurrence of symptoms, counter-examples will be frequent and the co-occurrence of symptoms will be the exceptional case.

Both of these forms of explanations contrast with a psychological account of symptom co-occurrence. The psychological or functional analysis of symptom co-occurrence links two symptoms to a single functional deficit. For instance, in the case of dysarthria and agrammatism, many researchers have claimed that agrammatism is a result of the dysarthria. On this analysis, a dysarthric patient simplifies his speech so as to produce the fewest words compatible with communication. He does so because he finds pronunciation and articulation so difficult. Agrammatism is a consequence of this simplification of speech. Another example is the analysis of the co-occurrence of word deafness and phonemic paraphasias suggested by Wernicke (1874), to be discussed in Chapter 4. Wernicke argued that the loss of auditory images for words would lead to both an inability to understand words and an inability to pronounce them properly. These functional accounts are of great interest to linguistic aphasiologists. If a functional account of the co-occurrence of symptoms is correct, the symptoms in question should always co-occur, because both are a consequence of the same functional disturbance. A prerequisite to maintaining that two symptoms are both related to a single functional disturbance is that we have a model in which the functional capacity in question (which is disturbed in disease) plays a role in the two separate aspects of language processing. In other words, we cannot entertain these sorts of functional analyses of symptom co-occurrence without good models of normal language processing.

In theory, the distinction between an anatomical and a functional basis for symptom groupings is clear-cut. In practice, however, matters are much more complex. It is often possible to find explanations for exceptions to symptom groupings. There are at least two reasons why an individual patient might show an exception to a grouping of symptoms which is functionally determined. The first reason is that the patient might be exceptional with respect to the way his cognitive functions are organized. For instance, it might be the case that for most people, speaking involves accessing the auditory representations of individual words, but that a few people speak by accessing "purely motor" representations, bypassing "auditory" memories of the sounds of words. In a person like this, disturbances of the permanent memories for the sounds of words might lead to disturbances in comprehension without disturbances in spontaneous speech.

How could we know that a patient who shows poor comprehension because he no longer appreciates the sounds of words, but who does not show sound-based errors in speech, has a particular, unusual organization of the speech mechanism? How can we distinguish this possibility from the possibility that our theory that speech requires accessing of the sound pattern of words is wrong? There is no clear answer to this question. If such a patient were drawn from an "unusual" population – if the patient were left-handed, or ambidextrous, or had had early brain injury – then we might be inclined to say that his case should not be considered a clear indication that the theory is wrong. Similarly, if the patient shows other special features – if, for instance, the patient writes words fluently but cannot write non-words to dictation, suggesting that he cannot base writing on the sound system – his retained abilities might be understandable as a particular form of compensation for his disturbance. In such a case, we might say that the theory is right as a general account of the way speech is ordinarily based upon sound memories, but that, in disease, alternate routes from thought to speech are possible. These sorts of arguments require careful consideration of both neurological and psychological aspects of a case.

The second way that we might attempt to save a theory in which one functional deficit is predicted to produce two symptoms, in the face of a patient who does not show both symptoms, would be to broaden the type of associated symptoms we might accept. Consider, for instance, the theory that agrammatism is related to dysarthria because a dysarthric patient attempts to produce the fewest words needed for communication. We have indicated that there are some dysarthric patients who are not agrammatic. One way to save the theory that agrammatism results from the economy of effort caused by dysarthria is to say that all patients with dysarthria will show some reduction of spontaneous speech, though not necessarily agrammatism. Reduced initiation of speech, use of predominantly stereotypic phrases, and other symptoms might be seen with dysarthria, as well as agrammatism. Though this would save the theory that agrammatism results from dysarthria, the analysis leads to yet another question: Why do some patients with dysarthria have agrammatism and others have other forms of reduction of spontaneous speech?

What all these considerations indicate is that the use of associations of symptoms to create a theory of normal language processing, though a very powerful conceptual tool, is very hard to put into practice. In fact, there are very few examples of associations of symptoms which hold reliably across any number of patients. A great deal of theorizing about the organization of components of the language-processing system has been due to analyses of cases of associations of symptoms, and, as we consider these analyses throughout this book (for instance in Chapters 15, 16, and 17), we shall consider how well founded the arguments are.

2. *Dissociations of symptoms: arguments from single case studies*

The opposite to arguments from association are arguments from dissociation. In an argument from association, as we have just seen, the co-occurrence of two symptoms can lead to a theory of a component of language processing common to two different processes. In an argument from dissociation, what is observed is that one patient retains one functional process and is impaired in a second, while a second patient retains the second functional process and has an impairment in the first. Arguments from dissociations vary with respect to the detail of the functions which are described, in the same way as arguments from associations. For instance, dissociations between language functions and visual–spatial functions have been described in many publications. At a more detailed level, very particular language-related processes have been dissociated from others. For instance, some patients seem to be able to read whole words, recognizing them directly from their visual form, but are unable to use the individual letters of a word to arrive at the sound of a word. These patients are unable to read non-words, because non-words cannot be recognized as units the way real words can. In contrast, there are patients who only seem to be able to read via a spelling-to-sound route, and not use whole-word information to recognize words. Such patients can read both words and non-words, as long as their spelling–sound correlates are regular. When faced with irregular words, such as *women*, *colonel*, or *yacht*, these patients mispronounce the words, producing a regularized sound pattern (see Chapter 14). Dissociations of this sort indicate that the language system is separate from a cognitive system responsible for visual–spatial function, and that particular components of the language-processing system are separate.

Unlike arguments from associations, arguments from dissociations do not depend upon large series of cases. In the extreme, a single case will do (Shallice 1979). If one patient, drawn from a "normal population", who showed no obvious unusual features of language processing before a neurological injury, manifests a dissociation of two abilities, then we may conclude that, for the normal population as a whole, the processing components related to these two abilities are at least partially separate. In fact, a great deal of contemporary research on language processing based on studies of aphasia utilizes the dissociation approach.

A particular form of the argument from dissociation is the demonstration of a "double dissociation". In a single dissociation, a patient is shown to have retained one ability and lost another. In a double dissociation we are dealing with two patients, one of whom has retained one ability and lost a second, and the other of whom has retained this second ability while losing the first. A single dissociation may not be due to the complete independence of two processes. It may instead be due to one process depending upon another. Suppose that reading by spelling–sound correspondences depends upon the ability to read via whole-word recognition. Then, one might see a disturbance of the ability to read via spelling–sound correspondences in isolation, or one might see a disturbance of both these abilities. What would never be seen is an isolated inability to read via whole-word recognition, because a disability in this function would also result in an inability to read via spelling–sound correspondences. If we see separate patients with isolated disturbances of the ability to read via spelling–sound correspondences and the ability to read through whole-word recognition, we may conclude that one of these abilities does not depend upon the other, and that both include independent psycholinguistic processes.

3. *Compensatory mechanisms*

The final issue we shall consider in linguistic aphasiology deals with the role of adaptive or compensatory behaviors on the part of patients. We have indicated several times that a patient's symptoms may not simply reflect an impairment in his normal language-processing routines. Even in cases where a patient's symptoms do result from a deficit in normal function – and these are likely to be the majority of cases – a patient's performance may not reflect this deficit in a direct fashion. Rather, the patient may adapt to his deficit, and compensate for it by one means or another. For instance, we have suggested that agrammatism in spoken language might be an adaptation to dysarthria and other disturbances of articulation. If this is the case, then the co-occurrence of two symptoms need not be due to a single mechanism producing two separate observable impairments in language use. Rather, the underlying functional disturbance produces one symptom, and the second symptom arises because of the patient's compensatory behavior.

How can we distinguish this possibility from the possibility that a single functional deficit results in two symptoms? Again, the answer is not entirely clear. It has been argued that adaptive/compensatory behaviors are optional, not obligatory (Kolk and Van Grunsven 1985). If this is the case, a patient ought to use them differently in different situations. A patient with dysarthria or some other articulatory disturbance may be agrammatic in one situation, but not in another. Two patients with dysarthria may show different types of reduction in speech. If we see these patterns, we are likely to conclude that the second symptom is the result of adaptive or compensatory mechanisms, not a fixed consequence of the underlying functional impairment.

In this chapter, we have sketched several ways of analyzing aphasic performances and several logical approaches to the question of language–brain relationships. We are about to go on to the classical clinical studies and theories of language–brain relationships. We shall therefore close this chapter by indicating something we have mentioned previously, and which will become clearer as we go into specific studies: the analysis of patients with language disorders due to acquired brain injury is the most widely used approach to the development of theories of neurolinguistics, despite its complex logical relationship to models of the normal relation of language and the brain. Our most interesting theories at present come from this approach.

We shall now turn to the first such studies, and to the models constructed by workers over a century ago. These early studies are of more than historical interest. The questions raised by these first workers are still very much alive; the concepts utilized by these investigators are still common intellectual currency in neurolinguistics; the clinical classification of language disorders developed by these scientists is in wide use today; and the models suggested in this early work are still widely accepted. Neurolinguistics has made progress, but it is firmly tied to its past, and current work can only be understood if we are familiar with these earlier writings.

SUGGESTIONS FOR FURTHER READING

Caramazza, A. (1986). On drawing inferences about the structure of normal cognitive systems from the analysis of patterns of impaired performance: the case for single patient studies. *Brain and Cognition* 5, 41–66.

Klein, B. von Eckardt (1978). On inferring functional localization from neurological evidence. In E. Walker (ed.), *Explorations in the Biology of Language*. Bradford Books, Montgomery, VT.

Marshall, J.C. (1982). What is a symptom-complex? In A. Arbib, D. Caplan, and J.C. Marshall (eds.), *Neural Models of Language Processes*. Academic Press, New York.

Shallice, T. (1979). Case study approach in neuropsychological research. *Journal of Clinical Neuropsychology* 1, 183–211.

Part II

Clinical aphasiology and neurolinguistics

3

The discoveries of Paul Broca: localization of the "faculty for articulate language"

The first scientific studies of patients with acquired disorders of language were presented in the last half of the nineteenth century. They began with an address by Paul Broca before the Anthropological Society of Paris in 1861. That presentation and Broca's work over the next four years established an approach to aphasia and neurolinguistics which has dominated the field until recent years. We therefore begin with this seminal body of work.

Broca's 1861 presentation took place during an ongoing debate about the phrenological theory of the localization of higher functions in the brain. The phrenologists – Gall, Sperzheim, and others – had claimed that the moral, intellectual, and spiritual faculties of man were each the result of the activity of particular portions of the brain, and that the size of the brain area responsible for a given ability determined the degree of development of that ability or faculty in an individual. The phrenologists also argued that the size of portions of the skull reflected the size of the underlying brain, and that they could predict the capacities of individuals by palpating their heads. This they did, in popular and remunerative demonstrations. The scientific community of the mid-nineteenth century had mixed feelings about the phrenological doctrine, and its fairly notorious and lucrative popularization and application, and by 1861 most of its claims had been refuted.

The claim which remained somewhat intact was that language was located in the frontal lobes of the brain, in particular in the portion just above the eye socket (the supra-orbital portion). Bouillaud, an influential French physician, had published papers in 1830 and 1848 arguing in favor of this localization. His son-in-law, Aubertin, a member of the Anthropological Society, was a proponent of phrenology in general, and of his father-in-law's claim about language in particular. When Broca's attention was drawn to the first of his famous cases at the Bicêtre hospital, he recognized a possible test case of the phrenological doctrine with respect to its best-established claim, that regarding language, and he invited Aubertin to examine the patient in question. Aubertin did so, and agreed that the patient should have a frontal lesion. In fact, Pierre Marie (1906b) later reported that Aubertin publicly said that he would reject Bouillaud's theory if Broca's patient did not have a frontal lesion. There was thus considerable interest in the case. As it happened, Broca's patient only lived three days beyond Broca's and Aubertin's examination, and Broca was able to present the results of the autopsy to the Anthropological Society immediately.

Broca's patient – Lebourgne – had been hospitalized for twenty-one years when he died at the age of fifty-seven. The initial reason for his hospitalization was that he was almost mute – his only verbal output consisted of the syllable "tan", and he became known as "Tan" in the hospital. Despite this severe handicap, Lebourgne functioned independently at Bicêtre hospital. He apparently understood what was said to him, and was able to respond appropriately and make his needs known. In fact, he was generally known as a difficult character. After about ten years, Lebourgne's condition worsened: he lost the use of his right arm. Shortly before his death, this paralysis extended to the right leg as well, leaving him bedridden. He developed an infection in the paralyzed leg, which brought him to Broca's attention. Very soon thereafter the infection led to generalized sepsis and death.

Broca examined the brain immediately after the autopsy. According to his report, the brain showed a lesion in the left frontal lobe, thus confirming Bouillaud's and Aubertin's theory. The lesion consisted of a cyst located at the foot of the inferior frontal convolution. Broca punctured the cyst, releasing a small quantity of fluid. He then pierced the brain underlying the cyst with a probe. The brain was softer than it should have been. As Broca passed the probe posteriorly, the softness extended into the region of the parietal operculum (the area above the Sylvian fissure), and Broca found that the brain became more normal in consistency as the probe moved more posteriorly. The softening extended anterior and medial to the cyst for a shorter distance than it did in the posterior direction. The lesion is illustrated in Figure 3-1.

Broca analyzed the case according to the traditional method of clinical–anatomical correlation. He divided the illness into three stages. In the first stage, lasting about ten years, the patient had a lesion at the so-called "foot" of the third frontal gyrus, and suffered from an isolated deficit in language. In the second stage, the lesion affected the adjacent motor strip, and the patient developed a paresis of the right arm and face. In the third stage, the lesion penetrated more posteriorly and widely, and the patient developed a paralysis of the right leg. According to this analysis, it was during the first stage, when the lesion occupied the foot of the third frontal convolution, that an isolated deficit in language was manifest.

Broca then suggested an analysis of the language abnormality, and of the factors in the brain which produced it.

The analysis of the language disorder consisted of dividing communicative

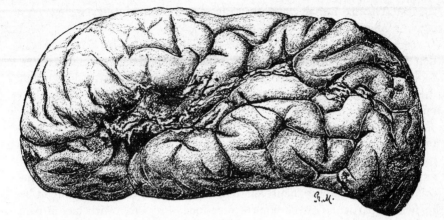

Figure 3-1. The brain of Lebourgne showing a lesion in Broca's area
(*Source:* Moutier 1908: 76)

ability along two major lines: linguistic versus non-linguistic communication; and receptive versus expressive abilities. Broca considered that Lebourgne had no deficit with non-linguistic communication or with receptive language, as evidenced by his apparent ability to understand what was said to him and to interact with others. He therefore suggested that Lebourgne had an isolated problem in what Broca termed the "faculty of articulate language". This analysis of language into faculties is one which dominated a great deal of the work of the nineteenth century, and which we shall see in almost all the theories of the "connectionist" aphasiologists.

The analysis of the neurological aspects of this syndrome was more innovative than the psychological analysis. Prior to Broca, it had been thought that the appropriate approach to localizing higher functions in the brain was to analyze lesions in terms of absolute distances from the major anatomical landmarks of the brain or skull. It had been thought that there were no divisions smaller than the major lobes of the brain which were constant from one individual brain to another, and which could be the substrates of psychological functions. Broca argued that the convolutional anatomy of the brain was relatively constant from individual to individual, and that it was appropriate to look to convolutions as possible anatomical sites of localization of the higher functions. He specifically suggested that much of the phrenological approach to localization was marred by its dependence on absolute measurements from major fissures and other landmarks of the brain and skull, which, because of the variation in the size of brains, could reflect different convolutional sites in different brains. He suggested instead that the appropriate localization of lesions was by convolutions.

From these two analyses – that the deficient function in Lebourgne was that of "articulate language", and that the corresponding lesion was in the foot of the third frontal convolution – came the now famous conclusion that the foot of the third frontal convolution was responsible for spoken language.

The 1861 paper by Broca is the first truly scientific paper on language–brain relationships. It differs from previous work in a number of ways. First, it relies on a detailed case history and excellent gross anatomical findings at autopsy. Second, it contains the insight that convolutions of the brain are relatively constant gross neuroanatomical features, and that they might be related to particular psychological functions – an idea which has proven worth investigating ever since, and which is still the basis for much neurolinguistic analysis. Third, although, as we shall see, there were many objections to and reinterpretations of Broca's paper, the central conclusion – that the expressive apparatus for speech is related to a small area of cortex just in front of the pre-central gyrus, in the pars triangularis and opercularis of the third frontal convolution – is, if not completely accurate, a very good first approximation to what we still believe to be true.

Between 1861 and 1865, Broca published several more clinical cases of aphasia (or "aphemia" as he called the syndrome), and the "language faculty" became a widespread object of study, as the prime example of the localization of a psychological function in the nervous system. In 1865, Broca published a second important paper on language disorders, the first to call the attention of the neurological community to the fact that aphasia followed lesions of the left hemisphere and not the right. We may note in passing that there is some question regarding who first suggested a "dominant" role of the left hemisphere for language. An earlier paper by Dax, cited by Broca, had been presented to a medical meeting in Montpellier, but had attracted no attention.

Broca (1865) pointed out that eight consecutive cases of aphasia he had observed had had left-hemisphere lesions, something which he concluded could not have occurred by chance. He pointed out that the conclusion that the left hemisphere is responsible for language contradicted the very general biological law that symmetrical organs (in this case, the two cerebral hemispheres) have identical functions. Broca believed that, although there were small differences in the patterns of convolutions from side to side of the brain, these differences were insignificant. The discovery that there are important lateral asymmetries in the human brain had to wait for over a hundred years (see Chapter 18). Rather, the answer lay in embryology:

observations by Gratiolet and Bertillon had shown that the formation of sulci occurs first in the left hemisphere in fetal development, and this precocity of the left hemisphere provided the basis for its "dominant" role in speech. The embryological facts also accounted for the determination of handedness; the fact that the majority of people are right-handed would be another result of the earlier maturation of the left hemisphere.

Broca then added several observations and qualifications to these claims. First, he suggested that in certain individuals the right hemisphere develops before the left, making them left-handed. It had been known that language was not always disturbed if disease in childhood or congenital malformations of the nervous system affected the left hemisphere in early life. Broca pointed out that these patients were often left-handed, implying that the right hemisphere had taken over control both of handedness and language. From these observations and inferences, Broca suggested that recovery from aphasia might be possible if the right hemisphere could take over the functions usually accomplished by the left. He concluded that the failure of most patients with aphasia to recover was due to inadequate rehabilitative efforts: he thought that adequate rehabilitation would have to consist of as much exposure to language as a child learning a first language has with his mother, something that is hardly ever provided. Finally, he pointed out that the ability of aphasic patients to understand language indicated that the right hemisphere *did* function in the broader psychology of language, which involves the establishment of relationships between expressions and meanings; the dominance of the left hemisphere was for speech alone.

As will become apparent, almost all these conclusions – that the left hemisphere is dominant for expressive language, that this is linked to handedness, that recovery from aphasia may involve the right hemisphere, that there are developmental embryological differences between the hemispheres, and that the right hemisphere has the capacity for receptive language – are still very much accepted today, with some refinements and on the basis of more evidence.

How can we evaluate Broca's contribution to the study of language–brain relationships? It is reasonable to regard him as the founder of the field. His careful attention to anatomical detail, his willingness to advance hypotheses on the basis of limited data, the framing of testable hypotheses, and the actual content of the hypotheses he put forward opened up the field to researchers. Indeed, we are still trying to solve many of the problems he left. For some fifty years after Broca, until World War I, the study of language disorders was a central part of clinical neurology, and virtually every important academic neurologist in Europe published papers on the topic. The description of the gross neuroanatomy of the language areas, and the

47

clinical classification of aphasias in use today, were the results of the concentrated activity which followed Broca.

Broca himself seems to have lost interest in the study of aphasia after 1870. By the time Wernicke published the seminal article which led to the productive "connectionist" school of aphasiology in 1874, Broca had bowed out of the field. He did travel to England in 1866 to discuss his work at a conference, which was also attended by Hughlings Jackson; the two men disagreed, and Broca is said to have carried the day. He devoted himself to anthropology, which was probably his major interest. Indeed, his work on aphasia was first discussed at the Anthropological Society which he had founded, and was a result of his interest in the relationship between brain size and the intellectual capacities of different species and human races (a controversial topic, then as now).

Like much important scientific work, Broca's has had a mixed reception. It sparked a tremendous interest in the phenomenon of aphasia and its anatomical basis, as we have noted, but it also drew great criticism and required modifications. First, the connectionists discovered other aphasic syndromes related to lesions elsewhere in the brain. Investigators then discovered that many aphasic patients who appeared to be similar to those described by Broca also had various sorts of problems in understanding speech and reading, which called Broca's analyses of his own cases into question. Finally, Pierre Marie and his student, François Moutier, criticized Broca's neuroanatomical conclusions, and debated both the clinical interpretation and the neuroanatomical basis of what, by then, had become known as "Broca's aphasia". We now can see that these debates and criticisms are testimonials to the high quality and importance of Broca's work, which provided neurolinguistics with many of its basic concepts, and also with many problems to solve and questions to answer.

SUGGESTIONS FOR FURTHER READING

Hécaen, H. and Dubois, J. (1969). *Le Naissance de la Neuropsychologie du Langage: 1825–1865*. Flammarion, Paris.

Marshall, J. (1982). Models of the mind in health and disease. In A. Ellis (ed.), *Normality and Pathology in Cognitive Functions*. Academic Press, London.

Signoret, J.-L., Castaigne, P., Lhermitte, F., Abelanet, R., and Lavorel, P. (1984). Rediscovery of Lebourgne's brain: anatomical description with CT scan. *Brain and Language* 22, 303–19.

Young, R. M. (1970). *Mind, Brain, and Adaptation in the Nineteenth Century*. Clarendon Press, Oxford.

4

Classical connectionist models

The work of Paul Broca established the study of aphasia as an important part of clinical neurology and nineteenth-century neuroscience. The localization of language capacities in parts of the brain, and the surprising fact of cerebral dominance for language, paved the way for a "scientific phrenology", the study of the relation between convolutions and other areas of the brain and "higher functions". From 1861 on, the neurological literature was filled with case reports of aphasic patients, often followed by autopsies, and, more generally, with reports of patients with a variety of psychological, intellectual, and complex perceptual problems accompanied by autopsies of the brain. The most illustrious neurologists of the day published papers on the subject of aphasia.

Among other things, it was a major point of interest to confirm or disconfirm Broca's claim that the faculty of articulate language was located in the posterior portion of the left third frontal convolution. For about a decade, controversy raged about the correctness of this claim, as cases of aphasia were discovered which had lesions elsewhere in the left hemisphere, and cases came to light of patients whose autopsied brains showed lesions in Broca's area, but who had not had disorders of language in life. As Broca pointed out, the latter cases might be explained by the right hemisphere taking over speech (though the conditions under which this was possible were not completely known), but the former indicated that Broca's analysis could not be the whole story. No unified theory relating all the observations on the aphasias was available, however, and the field became "data rich and theory poor", characterized by many interesting observations that could not be understood within any single framework.

In 1874, Carl Wernicke, then a twenty-six-year-old physician training in neuropsychiatry, published a paper which served to create a theoretical framework within which these disparate observations could be approached. He provided a classification of aphasic syndromes, and a general model of how language is represented in the brain from which new syndromes could be predicted. His paper constitutes the third great discovery of nineteenth-century aphasiologists: the discovery that there were several sub-types of aphasic syndromes, each of which resulted from lesions in different areas of the brain. One implication of this discovery is that language representation and processing by the brain is such that different areas accomplish different tasks. Normal language abilities require the integration of different areas. Wernicke's paper created the most productive school of study in this field in the nineteenth century, and one whose clinical insights are still in use.

Wernicke's paper was entitled "The symptom complex of aphasia: a psychological study on a neurological basis". In it, Wernicke described a second aphasic syndrome and predicted the existence of a third. On the basis of these cases, Wernicke set forth a model of language representation and processing in the brain, consistent with the associationist psychology and the neurophysiological theory of reflexes of his day. Wernicke described nine cases of language disorders due to acquired disease of the brain, of which the first two were the basis for his theory. These two cases were instances of an aphasic syndrome very different from what Broca had described. In both cases, the patients had a marked deficit in understanding what was said to them. The second patient, in fact, was originally thought to be deaf, because she manifested no awareness of what other people were saying to her; but it soon became apparent that she was not deaf, but simply unable to understand language. As in Broca's case, it was important for an examiner to avoid giving himself away through gesture or facial expression if he wanted to test her ability to understand language *per se*, since this patient was quite capable of understanding a great deal by observing the gestures and facial expressions of the people who spoke to her.

Wernicke's two patients also had a great deal of difficulty with spoken language, but the form of the expressive language disorder was quite different from that which Broca had described. In Broca's original case the patient was rendered virtually mute, with the exception of a single monosyllable. Other cases with anterior brain lesions had been described, and it was generally appreciated by 1874 that the characteristic speech of these patients, though not necessarily as reduced as that in Broca's first case, was always halting and effortful. Patients with anterior lesions frequently omitted many words, and often showed a great deal of difficulty in pronunciation of individual sounds. Wernicke's first two patients had quite different abnormalities in speech output. In both cases, the patients spoke fluently and maintained normal intonational patterns, but were unable to make sense. Wernicke described errors which were not in the actual production of sounds but in the selection of sounds. Instead of saying a particular word, his patients might say a word which was related either by virtue of rhyme (or some other aspect of its sound), or by virtue of some semantic relationship. At times, the words that were spoken were so different from words in

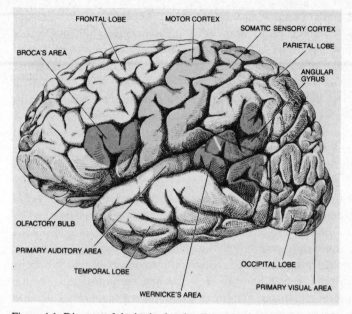

FRONTAL LOBE MOTOR CORTEX SOMATIC SENSORY CORTEX PARIETAL LOBE ANGULAR GYRUS BROCA'S AREA OLFACTORY BULB PRIMARY AUDITORY AREA TEMPORAL LOBE WERNICKE'S AREA OCCIPITAL LOBE PRIMARY VISUAL AREA

Figure 4-1. Diagram of the brain showing Wernicke's area and Broca's area. The solid line in Wernicke's area represents the junction between the temporal and parietal lobes. The lesion in Wernicke's case occupied the temporal lobe portion of Wernicke's area. (*Source:* Geschwind 1979: 111)

German that the examiners called them "neologisms" – that is, new words which did not exist in the German vocabulary, and which were not related to any words in German by normal rules of word formation. The speech of these two patients did not convey information. Wernicke and the other examiners were frequently at a loss to understand what the patients were trying to say.

One of these two patients died and her brain came to autopsy. It showed a cerebral infarct (a stroke) in the region of the first temporal gyrus on the left, occupying approximately the middle third of the gyrus and extending posteriorly towards the parietal lobe (Figure 4-1). Wernicke pointed out that this area of cortex had two important characteristics. First, it was an area directly juxtaposed to the cortical area which receives the final connections of the auditory system, the post-thalamic auditory radiations. Second, it was an area which itself was neither a primary sensory nor a primary motor area. It was one of a number of areas called "association" areas, thought to be involved in more complex elaboration and modification of sensory and motor information.

Wernicke argued that it was reasonable to consider that the association area immediately juxtaposed to the primary auditory cortex would be responsible for understanding spoken language. This was in keeping with the notion that the association cortex around each primary sensory cortex was responsible for analysis of the sensory signals which were sent to that area of primary sensory cortex. He therefore considered this area in the first temporal gyrus to be one where a lesion would cause a disturbance in understanding spoken language, and he concluded that the receptive language deficit of his first two patients was due to the lesion.

Wernicke suggested that the normal function of this area – the first temporal gyrus (which after this paper became known as "Wernicke's area") – was to be a memory store for the auditory form of words; and he reasoned that it played this role because of its close proximity to the central termination of the auditory pathway. Wernicke suggested that this region should be considered a second "center" for language, the area described by Broca being the first. Wernicke's area was hypothesized to accomplish a particular function – understanding spoken language; to contain a particular type of linguistic representation – the sound pattern of words; and to occupy a specific site in the cerebral hemisphere – the first temporal gyrus. In the connectionist literature, this triad more or less defines a "center". There are cases in which one or another of these features are absent in a postulated center, but, for the most part, the notion of a center involves the triple characterization of a brain region, a psycholinguistic function, and a linguistic representation.

Wernicke then turned to the interesting question of the origin of the expressive language deficits in these patients. A close inspection of the brain did not show a lesion of Broca's area, and Wernicke dismissed the idea that a second lesion in Broca's area was responsible for the expressive language deficit. Wernicke therefore concluded that the expressive language deficit was due to the same lesion that caused the receptive language deficit, and that it arose in the following way.

Expressive language, he argued, requires two inputs. One is an input from a thought to be expressed. The second is an input from the memory store for the auditory form of words. In other words, Wernicke envisaged a flow of information between the auditory representations of words and the representation of motor sequences that went into the articulation of these words. He suggested that, in the act of speaking, there was an excitation of the memory traces in Wernicke's area, which were forwarded in a neural code to the memory traces for articulatory movements in the anterior speech area. The anterior speech area, under the joint influence of "thought" and the auditory memories for words, activated these articulatory memories to innervate the oral musculature. He incorporated this idea into the first of

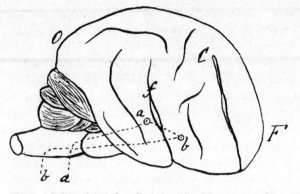

Figure 4-2. Wernicke's first diagram. Wernicke's area and Broca's area are marked as *a* and *b* respectively in the temporal and frontal lobes. Input, output, and connecting pathways are indicated in schematic form.
(*Source:* Moutier 1908: 36)

many diagrams that characterize this approach to neurolinguistics, shown in Figure 4-2.

Just as Broca's paper produced the important hypothesis that linguistic and psycholinguistic functions were localized in cerebral gyri, Wernicke's paper introduced the notion of *information flow* into our concepts of the representation and processing of language by the brain. In addition to the notion that normal language involved the co-operation of two brain areas, with information flowing from the posterior to the anterior area, Wernicke's model also involved several other features. He insisted that the components of the model and their interaction be justified not only by the facts of aphasia, but also by the facts of normal physiology and psychology. He believed that both of these requirements were met by his theory.

In the first case, he pointed to the work of his teacher Meynert, which established that sensory-to-motor flow of excitation was involved in reflex action, and he argued that language could be seen as an extremely complex modulated reflex. If it were seen in this way, then the notion of information flow from a sensory to a motor area was consistent with ideas of the control and origin of most motor movements, as understood in the physiology of Wernicke's day.

As far as consistency with normal psychology was concerned, Wernicke suggested that the usual way a child learns language was by imitating the language that he heard in the community, and that the first vocalized utterances required a transmission of linguistic information from the auditory receptive areas, through their association cortex, to the structures in the anterior portion of the brain which were involved in controlling the

53

vocal tract. Because of this ontogenetic factor, Wernicke thought that the auditory-to-motor process of information flow was a reasonable feature of any model of normal speaking.

Two other aspects of Wernicke's paper are important. The first is his prediction about other aphasic syndromes. He realized that if one type of aphasia could be caused by a lesion in Broca's area, leading to a predominantly motor syndrome, and if a second aphasic syndrome could be caused by a lesion in the first temporal gyrus leading to both a receptive deficit and an expressive disorder, his model predicted that there would be a third form of aphasia which arose from a lesion in the pathway between Wernicke's and Broca's areas. Wernicke suggested that this pathway lay in the cortex, and that it was reasonable to think of the gray matter around the Sylvian fissure as constituting a single gyrus related to language, with an auditory, sensory pole in the temporal portion and a speech, motor pole in the frontal portion.

Wernicke suggested that the aphasia that would be produced by a lesion of the intervening portions of this gray matter would be characterized by an expressive disorder similar to that seen with posterior lesions (because of the interruption of the flow of information from auditory to motor areas), but that the abilities of such patients to understand spoken language would remain intact (because the association area in which auditory representations were stored was itself intact). He suggested that, in general, there was a difference between the aphasias caused by lesions of centers, and the aphasias caused by lesions of connecting pathways.

The other point of importance in Wernicke's paper is his effort to restrict the nature and number of centers. Wernicke realized that unless one placed some restriction on what could be a center and on the number of centers, every new form of aphasia could be described by the postulation of a new center, the role of which was the normal performance of exactly the language capacity which was disturbed in a particular patient. Such multiplication of centers and connecting pathways could not lead to a testable theory of the representation and processing of language in the brain. He therefore placed the restrictions we have discussed above on the centers that he postulated: the model must be consistent with what is known about psychology and physiology. He also made one more restriction with respect to the centers: that they be "simple".

Wernicke was opposed to the localization of complex and intricate psychological functions in specific areas of the brain which had characterized the phrenological approach to cerebral localization. In its place, he adopted a much more limited notion of what could be localized, and thought that many functions resulted from connecting various brain components. He thought that the major psycholinguistic functions – understanding spoken speech, speaking, reading, and writing – could legitimately be considered to constitute psychological entities which could be represented in a center (although, as we have seen, he believed that two or more centers could participate in a single function). With respect to the posterior language area, we have noted that he proposed that a linguistic representation and psychological function were located in the first temporal gyrus. These examples are the best clues to what he meant by the notion of a "simple" psychological function. His approach became known as "connectionist", because complex functions were built up by connecting "simple" components.

Wernicke's paper was immediately successful. Despite the fact that he was a young man, without academic appointment or fame, Wernicke's contribution was immediately appreciated. By 1885, it had become the dominant way of approaching the problem of classifying aphasic disorders of language. This approach is well exemplified by a paper by Lichtheim, published in German in 1884 and in English in the influential journal *Brain* in 1885, which set forth a proposal for a complete enumeration of all aphasic syndromes based upon a connectionist model of language and the brain. Lichtheim's paper still forms the basis for the most popular clinical classi-fication of the aphasias in North America. Benson and Geschwind (1971), in a major textbook of neurology, essentially adopt Lichtheim's classification, adding three additional syndromes to the seven he proposed. Moreover, they demonstrate, in an extensive review of the literature, that the import-ant classifications of aphasia since Lichtheim's work differ from his almost exclusively in nomenclature, and not in substantive descriptions of syn-dromes or in the relationship of syndromes to areas of the brain. We shall therefore review Lichtheim's 1885 paper, focussing on his taxonomy of aphasias.

Lichtheim produced the diagram represented in Figure 4-3. He adopted Wernicke's views essentially unchanged with respect to the two major areas involved in language – Broca's area (M) and Wernicke's area (A). He thought that the first was involved in speech production, and believed that it contained the articulatory representations necessary for utterances. As for the second, he agreed with Wernicke's notion that it contained the memory traces of the auditory form of words, and that its function was primarily the perception of speech. He followed Wernicke in postulating a connection between Wernicke's area and Broca's area. In addition, he suggested that there was a "concept area", labeled B in the diagram, which he thought was

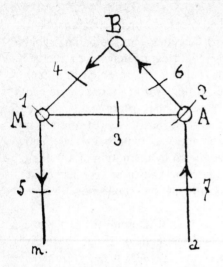

Figure 4-3. Lichtheim's first diagram. For explanation, see text.
(*Source:* Moutier 1908: 43)

diffusely represented in the brain. Whether this should be considered a "center" in the narrow sense is unclear from his writings, but it is treated very much like the other two centers in certain respects.

The types of aphasia that would be predicted from this model depend upon the nature of information flow between the various components. A lesion of M will cause the classical Broca's aphasia, in which language comprehension is spared and articulatory language is disturbed. A disorder of A will cause Wernicke's aphasia with the symptoms we have described. A disorder of the connecting pathway will cause the "conduction" aphasia predicted by Wernicke, and Lichtheim indicates that, aside from the predictions already made, the ability of such a patient to repeat would be impaired.

In addition to these classical forms of language disturbance Lichtheim argued that there were four other forms of aphasia, all due to interruption of connecting pathways. Transcortical sensory aphasia, due to a disruption of the path between B and A, would result in a difficulty in comprehension. Although the auditory form of words is intact, its connection to the concept center is disturbed, and the patient can no longer determine the meaning of language he hears. Unlike Wernicke's aphasia, repetition ought to be intact. Transcortical motor aphasia, due to a lesion between M and B, will produce the same type of output seen in Broca's aphasia, but, as in the transcortical sensory aphasia, repetition ought to be normal because the basic pathway involved in repetition is intact. Subcortical sensory aphasia, interrupting the

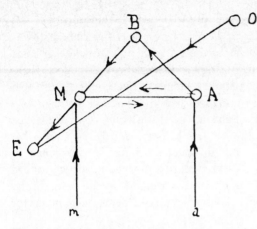

Figure 4-4. Lichtheim's second diagram. For explanation, see text.
(*Source:* Moutier 1908: 43)

pathway from the periphery to A, will lead to "pure word deafness", in which the patient does not understand spoken speech, but has none of the difficulties of the Wernicke's aphasic in speaking aloud, since the memories for the auditory form of words stored in Wernicke's area are intact and can be transmitted to the motor centers. Subcortical motor aphasia, due to a lesion between M and the oral musculature, produces a dysarthria – a disturbance of articulation.

Lichtheim's model became considerably more complicated when he added a consideration of the functions of writing and reading. In Figure 4-4, we see Lichtheim's extended diagram incorporating the center O for the memory of the visual form of words. Lichtheim also argued that clinical evidence supported the existence of a separate area for the representation of the motor sequences involved in writing. This center, E on the diagram, did not, however, operate in the same way as the motor center for speech. Joint inputs from the concept center B, and the visual storage center O, were not adequate to initiate the proper functioning of the center E. Rather, there was an additional necessary input from the center M, the storehouse for the representation of the oral motor sequences of individual words. The frequent co-occurrence of disorders of writing with Broca's aphasia testified to the link between Broca's area, M, and the writing center E.

As Wernicke had done, Lichtheim attempted to provide principled explanations for the functioning of the components of his model. An illustrative example is his analysis of the so-called "paraphasic" nature of spontaneous speech and repetition in Wernicke's aphasia. Under Lichtheim's model, it would be possible for speech to result from the triggering of oral motor commands in Broca's area, M, by concepts in the concept center B. This single pathway from B to M clearly was not the only pathway involved in triggering motor speech, as the evidence of Wernicke's aphasia and conduction aphasia showed. Basing his analysis on Wernicke's, Lichtheim therefore suggested that in spoken language one could discern two different pathological syndromes, and that each syndrome was the result of a different neuropsychological mechanism: the disturbance of Broca's area itself, M, or the pathway from the concept center, B, to Broca's area, M, would lead to slow, halting, effortful speech; whereas disturbance of Wernicke's area, A, which was only secondarily involved in speech, or the pathway from Wernicke's area, A, to Broca's area, M, would result in the varieties of fluent, paraphasic, neologistic jargon seen with posterior lesions.

Lichtheim realized that this description of different syndromes as a result of different lesions could be considered an *ad hoc* aspect of the theory, and he therefore tried to show that the same analysis was also true of written language. Given that written language depended upon the proper functioning of the center E after its reception of some form of relevant information from center M, there still remained the question of whether the *auditory* form of words was involved in writing. Lichtheim suggested that the cases of conduction aphasia might serve to settle the issue. If conduction aphasics with a lesion between A and M were totally unable to write and manifested a syndrome similar to that seen in the spoken language of Broca's aphasics, with word omissions, hesitancy, and difficulty in the actual depiction of individual graphemic characters, one would be justified in assuming that the sole pathway from the concept center B to the writing center E was $B \rightarrow A \rightarrow M \rightarrow E$. If the patients developed paraphasic writing (sometimes called "paragraphia"), then the pathways for properly activating E would be in duplicate: there would be a pathway $B \rightarrow A \rightarrow M \rightarrow E$ and a separate pathway $B \rightarrow M \rightarrow E$. A lesion of the first of these two pathways would lead to paragraphia, in exactly the same way that a lesion in the tract $A \rightarrow M$ led to paraphasia in the posterior aphasias. Finally, if conduction aphasics had no difficulty whatsoever in writing, this would suggest that the only pathway involved in writing was from the concept center B to the motor speech center M and thence to the motor writing center E. Thus, the particular set of connections Lichtheim postulated on the basis of the co-occurrence of Broca's aphasia and agraphia could be tested by other observations about patients. This rather complex hypothetical reasoning demonstrates the serious effort on the part of Lichtheim (and the other members of the connectionist school) to make the predictions of their models explicit, and to characterize in as principled a way as possible the observable differences

between performances in a given psycholinguistic function in different sub-
types of aphasia.

Lichtheim did not have the data required to settle this issue, which
remained a logical exercise in his article. He did, however, attempt to
provide a principle which would apply both to the paraphasias which
resulted from lesions in Wernicke's area and to those causing conduction
aphasia and to the form of agraphia which he predicted might arise in these
cases. This principle was that, where the activity of a center required input
from two or more other centers, the disordered output which would result
after loss of any one input would be qualitatively different from that which
followed loss of input from any other, not simply quantitatively more or less
affected. Though stated in very abstract terms, this principle could be
applied to the analysis of the disorders seen after particular brain lesions,
given that a model of centers and their interactions was adequately specified
in particular domains.

Lichtheim's paper and his model had a number of problems and, despite
its great clinical and theoretical impact, did not go uncriticized. In Chapter
6, we shall review several criticisms of the basic assumptions regarding
language and neural organization made by Lichtheim's model. At this point,
we shall simply consider three problems internal to the model.

The first of these problems is that it is not clear that Lichtheim completely
specified his model. For instance, in interpreting the lines which connect the
centers in Figures 4-3 and 4-4, it is clearly important to know which way
information may travel from center to center. Lichtheim is at best unclear,
and at worst self-contradictory about this. In the case of the pathways
involving A, B, and M, for instance, Lichtheim requires that information
move in the direction BA, to account for the activation of Wernicke's area in
speech. However, according to one model of writing Lichtheim considers,
the *lack* of a pathway BA would be critically needed to account for the
inability of Broca's aphasics to write normally. Even though the number of
centers and pathways is small in this model, enough are present to allow for a
considerable number of possibilities of information flow, and reading
Lichtheim's paper leaves one quite uncertain as to whether he finally
decided on particular directions and not on others.

The second problem we may consider at this point is the degree to which
Lichtheim was in fact committed to an anatomically based model. It is
interesting that Wernicke represented his diagram on a brain (though the
dotted lines and circles in Figure 4-2 are not intended to be serious
depictions of pathways and gyri, and though the model shows language in
the *right* hemisphere). Lichtheim's model is not drawn in this way. It is not
clear that this difference is just a matter of artistic preference. Lichtheim

certainly makes specific statements regarding the anatomical location of some of the components of the model he presented, such as Broca's and Wernicke's areas, but, equally clearly, he does not attempt to locate them all. To some extent, such as in the case of the connections between Wernicke's and Broca's area, this is simply a matter of the inadequacy of existing knowledge: Lichtheim clearly believed that the pathway AM existed *somewhere* between these two centers. But in other areas, it is not so clear that Lichtheim had any area or pathway in mind, and he may have intended to present a purely psychological model. The obvious case, of course, is the concept center, which Lichtheim admitted was diffusely located. The problem of directions of information flow is most marked regarding this center. The concept center has another peculiarity as well: it is not subject to lesions causing aphasia – that is, there is no aphasic syndrome which Lichtheim recognized as a result of a lesion of B. This is the only center or pathway in his entire system which is inviolate in this way. One's strong impression is that Lichtheim really created a mixed model, parts being purely psychological, and parts neuroanatomically based.

Finally, we may note that, despite Lichtheim's assertion that he was presenting examples of each of the seven types of aphasia his model predicted, many of the details of the cases are vague and his interpretations of the cases he presented are undetermined by the data he had at his disposal. Moreover, as we have seen, some critical observations were not available to Lichtheim, and he could not prove that some of his detailed predictions are borne out by data from aphasia.

Despite these difficulties, the model has definite strengths. These can be seen by simply inspecting the diagrams that came after his, seen in the next few figures. In comparison to Lichtheim's, these models are completely divorced from any neuroanatomical basis, and make use of connections and centers which have little or no justification, either from pathological data or from the normative psychology of language. Henry Head (1926) struck a responsive note when he labeled the theoretical positions which characterized much of this later work "chaos". Not all the work which followed in the connectionist school was as undisciplined as that represented in Figure 4-5. In the next chapter we shall consider extensions of the basic connectionist model which have conformed to the principles laid down by Wernicke regarding how these models must be constrained, and which have led to important insights into aspects of language and psychological functions related to language.

The papers of Wernicke and Lichtheim created a framework for the classification and understanding of aphasias, and, simultaneously, a model of the way language was represented in the brain. The model was not very

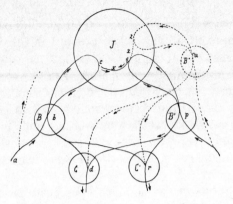

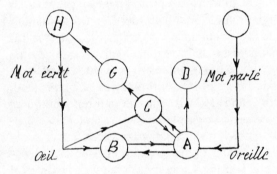

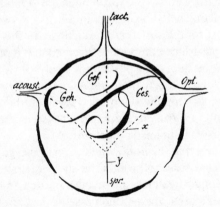

Figure 4-5. Diagrams of the functioning of the language areas according to Kussmaul, Grashey, and Moeli, developed in the late nineteenth century. Initials represent "centers". For comments, see text.
(*Source:* Moutier 1908: 41, 53).

detailed with respect to the characterization of language structures or the psychological processes which make up the various acts of language use: speaking, understanding speech, etc. In another sense, however, it was fairly complete. It included consideration of all the major tasks to which language is put, and it at least claimed to provide a complete enumeration of possible aphasic syndromes. There is no doubt that it helped to guide research, both by providing a basis upon which some workers could build, and also by providing a theory which others found worth attacking. To conclude this chapter, we shall attempt to summarize the basic features of the classical connectionist models.

Connectionist models are one type of a group which we may call "faculty" models. Faculty models are those in which the principal language functions represented in the brain are entire task-oriented processes. In Lichtheim's and Wernicke's models, we see components which are responsible for speech production, speech understanding, reading, and writing. In the classic connectionist models, the faculties which are postulated are almost exclusively the major "on-line" tasks of the psychology of language: tasks which occur quickly in real time, and in which a speaker or listener produces or recognizes sequences of acoustic or graphic elements under time constraints. These are the usual "tasks" to which language is put.

In the connectionist models, each of the psycholinguistic faculties – reading, writing, speaking, and hearing – was considered as an individual entity. Each was connected to the others, and the connectionist models do allow some provision for interaction between these components. As we have noted several times, the best examples of this interaction are the transmission of sound representations to the component involved in the production of articulate speech, and the necessary passage of signals involved in writing through the center involved in articulate speech before they reach the center for the control of the movements of writing. However, there is no provision with each component for a truly fine-grained analysis of the tasks involved in each of the major psycholinguistic functions.

It is in the connectionist models that the notion of "center" emerges most clearly. A center consists of a single psycholinguistic faculty, associated with one major type of storage for linguistic items, located in a particular area of the brain. In the case of Broca's area, the psycholinguistic function is the production of spoken language, and the linguistic representation consists of the motor programs involved in the production of spoken language. In the case of the posterior language area, the faculty is understanding spoken language, and the permanent linguistic representation is the sound pattern of words. Note that not all the "representations" are alike – the "sound pattern" for words might be a linguistic representation, but the motor programs for speech seem more "motor" than "linguistic". The connections between centers are different from the centers themselves. They do not have permanent linguistic representations, and they themselves are not involved in particular functions as a whole. Rather, they transmit information from one center to another, in order to allow the proper functioning of centers during the accomplishment of particular psycholinguistic tasks.

Connectionist theories have played a very significant role in the development of theories of language representation in the brain. In the first place, they are of tremendous clinical utility. The clinician, by assessing a patient's ability in each of the major psycholinguistic tasks – speaking, understanding spoken language, reading, writing, and repetition – is able to make reasonable hypotheses as to the location of the lesion producing the aphasia, and to move towards a hypothesis as to the pathological cause of the lesion. Especially in the era of clinical neurology in which sophisticated radiological diagnosis was not available, these hypotheses were often the best available.

Second, the notion of centers and connections being the principal method of organization of the language areas of the brain has stimulated research up to the present day. A major controversy arose between those who favored the "localizationist" view, exemplified by the connectionist approach, and others who were "holists" and believed that the brain did not process and represent language in centers devoted to particular sub-components of language performances. This controversy is not settled, and we shall see in later chapters some of the ways that this controversy has led to new discoveries in the field.

Finally, connectionist theory defined a level of observation and description of both normal and abnormal language which strongly influenced subsequent work. The features of language which enter into connectionist neurolinguistic models are the on-line tasks of language use, as we have indicated. The linguistic units which were part of the descriptions of aphasic and normal language in the work of the connectionists – words, sounds, syllables – are only roughly sketched. Similarly, the details of the processes of comprehension, speaking, and other tasks are not considered. The early connectionists stressed the assessment of the relative quantitative impairment of each of the on-line tasks as the essential observations needed for diagnosis and classification of aphasic patients. On the neurological side, connectionism emphasized localization of these functions in gyri and groups of adjacent gyri. In later chapters we shall see how these first models have been criticized, how more detailed analyses of the nature of the linguistic elements and psychological processes which are affected in aphasia have led to an empirically more detailed level of description of language disorders, and how we are slowly moving towards a more detailed analysis of the neural basis for language.

II *Clinical aphasiology and neurolinguistics*

SUGGESTIONS FOR FURTHER READING

Arbib, M., Caplan, D., and Marshall, J. C. (1982). Neurolinguistics in historical perspective. In M. Arbib, D. Caplan, and J. C. Marshall (eds.), *Neural Models of Language Processes*. Academic Press, New York.

Benson, D. F. and Geschwind, N. (1971). Aphasia and related cortical disturbances. In A. B. Baker and H. Baker (eds.), *Clinical Neurology*. Harper and Row, New York.

Head, H. (1926). *Aphasia and Kindred Disorders of Speech* (section 1). Cambridge University Press, Cambridge.

Lichtheim, L. (1885). On aphasia. *Brain* 7, 433–84.

Morton, J. (1984). Brain-based and non-brain-based models of language. In D. Caplan, A. R. Lecours, and A. Smith (eds.), *Biological Perspectives on Language*. MIT Press, Cambridge, Mass.

Wernicke, C. (1874). The aphasic symptom complex. Kohn and Weigart, Breslau. Reprinted in translation in R. S. Cohen and M. W. Warofsky (eds.), *Boston Studies in the Philosophy of Science*, vol. 4. Reidel, Boston.

5

Extensions of connectionism

The work of Wernicke, Lichtheim, and many other late nineteenth-century investigators dealt mainly with the various parts of what may be termed the "faculty for language". The identification of elementary components of this faculty, the delineation of interactions of components, and the search for the neural loci of these components and their connecting pathways, was much debated in the neurological literature of that period. Although there were many variations of these models, those we have discussed in the previous chapter are quite typical of the work in this tradition. We shall not review all this work, which would be far beyond the scope of an introductory text (we cannot devote *all* our text to the last century), but we will consider one more analysis very much in keeping with the connectionist approach, Dejerine's analysis of the syndrome of alexia-without-agraphia. The example is chosen with malice aforethought. It serves as a natural bridge to the approaches to the agnosias and apraxias undertaken within the connectionist framework, which we shall mention briefly; and, having considered its nineteenth-century description, we will be able to appreciate a twentieth-century refinement of views regarding this syndrome later in this chapter. In Chapter 14, we shall reconsider this syndrome from a psycholinguistic viewpoint.

In 1892, Jules Dejerine published the case history and neuropathological autopsy findings of a patient with a striking set of difficulties. Dejerine's patient was an engineer who had suffered a stroke which left him unable to read words, sentences, or letters. He was unable to see in the right visual half-field. He was unable to name colors. He had been a talented amateur musician, able to sight-read music, and he had lost this ability. He was, however, able to write, both spontaneously and to dictation. He was able to copy, but he had a peculiar way of copying: he copied script into script and print into print as if each were a design. Most dramatically, he was unable to read the very things he himself had written if enough time had elapsed between the writing and the attempt to read for him to have forgotten the material.

At autopsy, the brain showed the lesion diagrammed in Figure 5-1. The entire left occipital lobe, in the distribution of the posterior cerebral artery,

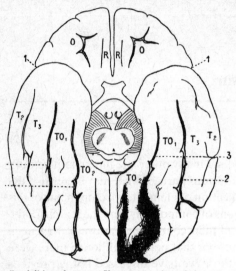

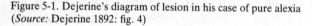

Face inférieure du cerveau. Plaque jaune ancienne de la partie postérieure des lobules lingual et fusiforme de l'hémisphère gauche.

Figure 5-1. Dejerine's diagram of lesion in his case of pure alexia
(*Source:* Dejerine 1892: fig. 4)

was infarcted, accounting for the right hemianopsia. In addition, the posterior part of the corpus callosum, the splenium, was also infarcted, as occasionally occurs in vascular lesions because of the particular areas supplied by the left posterior cerebral artery.

Dejerine suggested that the alexia could be explained in the following manner. The patient could see items in the left visual field, which were relayed normally to the right occipital lobe. However, this material could not be transferred in a visual form to the left hemisphere, because the pathway for transmission of information from the visual association cortex in one hemisphere to that in the other lies in the splenium of the corpus callosum, which was destroyed. Therefore, although the patient could see in the left half-field, he was unable to convey visual information to the language areas in the left hemisphere, and he could not establish a relationship between the visually presented orthographic representations of language and the auditory representations of language which are stored in the left hemisphere alone. Dejerine argued that reading involved the pairing of a graphemic orthographic representation with a phonological representation before the retrieval of semantic information about a word or a sentence. He postulated that there was a center for reading in the left parietal lobe, where the sound values of letters were paired with their orthographic forms. If this were the case, a disconnection between the reception of visual information and this center would produce a syndrome in which a patient could not read. Moreover, this explanation would also account for the patient's preserved ability to write. Since writing would involve accessing auditory and orthographic representations which were entirely in the undamaged portion of the left hemisphere, it would be preserved. Writing to dictation would also be possible through a route entirely involving the undamaged portions of the left hemisphere.

This analysis is an example of the natural extension of the theory of centers and connections to the callosal syndromes. In the nineteenth and early twentieth centuries, the best examples of such analyses dealt with the disconnection of motor and sensory functions of the right hemisphere from the language areas of the left hemisphere – the so-called "apraxias" and "agnosias". Alexia-without-agraphia can be seen as a special type of agnosia – an agnosia for the written form of words. In general, agnosias are conditions in which a subject can perceive a stimulus adequately but cannot appreciate its significance or meaning. Confronted with an object, he may match the object to one with a similar shape or texture, but be unable to indicate its function or match it to another member of the same category of objects. The agnosias can be seen as high-level disorders of perception, and certain forms of agnosia have been interpreted as disconnections between perceptual abilities and language functions. (For more discussion of the agnosias, see Chapter 12.)

The apraxias, by way of contrast, are high-level disorders of motor planning, some of which may also be seen as verbal-planning disconnections. The apraxias were described first in a series of papers by Liepmann (1900; Liepman and Maas 1907). Liepmann discovered that there were patients who were unable to perform skilled motor movements in response to verbal commands with the left hand, even though they were able to use the left hand perfectly normally in tasks that did not involve responses to verbal commands. He suggested that this syndrome was the result of a lesion in the anterior portion of the corpus callosum, disconnecting the motor strip on the right from the language areas on the left. This prediction was later confirmed at autopsy, leading to a "disconnection" analysis of this form of apraxia.

For a variety of reasons, connectionist theories became unpopular and were ignored for some fifty years from the 1910s to the 1960s. It has been suggested that some of the reasons may be political – connectionist models developed mainly in Germany, which lost both great wars. Other reasons were certainly scientific, as criticisms of connectionism and alternatives developed (see the following chapters). However, though connectionism was neglected, it did not die – in fact, it was revived in a major way in the 1960s.

In 1965, Geschwind published a paper in *Brain* entitled "Disconnection syndromes in animals and man". This paper presented a review and reinterpretation of a number of clinical syndromes in humans and experimental work in primates, largely based on an extension of the nineteenth-century connectionist approach to the higher functions. A good deal of the paper is devoted to an analysis of disorders of movement and sensation, but there are in addition important analyses and suggestions regarding the representation of language in the brain – the area in which the connectionist approach was originally developed. In several other papers Geschwind extended this general approach to the consideration of a variety of clinical disorders of language. The remainder of this chapter will concentrate on this reformulation of the nineteenth-century connectionist theories of language representation in the brain.

In the 1965 *Brain* paper, Geschwind first considers a number of syndromes in animals which he argues can be viewed as disconnection syndromes. The first of these, and the one which is analyzed in most detail, is the Kluver–Bucy syndrome. The syndrome can be produced in a variety of species, such as the macaque (a species of monkey), by bilateral, anterior temporal lobe resections. Several changes in behavior occur in this syndrome. The animal becomes tame and allows itself to be handled by humans, a response quite unlike its normal reaction to humans when it is caged or in the wild. It manifests a marked tendency to put all sorts of objects into its mouth, both those which are edible and those which are not. It develops an abnormality in sexual behavior and sexual preference, demonstrating increased masturbatory activity, with males mounting other males and females who are not estrous. Affected animals contravene the normal social hierarchies in activities such as grooming. A final characteristic of these animals, perhaps related to their tameness, is a lack of fear of objects, such as snakes, which these animals are usually afraid of.

Geschwind suggested that there is an explanation for this pattern of behavior which is based upon an understanding of the anatomy of the connections between visual cortex and the limbic lobe. The limbic lobe consists of a circuit, beginning with neocortex in the cingulum and the white matter buried within this gyrus, and continuing by way of the pericallosal gyrus into the more primitive cortex of the hippocampus in the medial temporal lobe. This circle is completed by a white-matter tract from the hippocampus to the mammillary bodies (the fornix), a second tract from the mammillary bodies to anterior and medial thalamic nuclei, and, finally, through projections from these thalamic nuclei, back to the cingulate gyrus

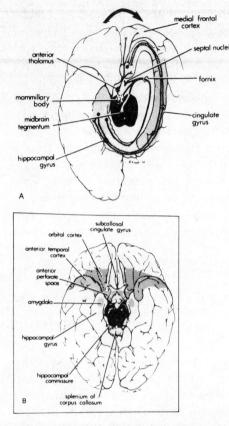

Figure 5-2. Diagram of the limbic lobe. The upper figure (A) shows the limbic lobe of the right hemisphere. In this diagram, the brain is seen from its under-surface, and the parietal and frontal lobes are rotated so that their inner surface can be visible as illustrated in the arrow. Figure (B) shows the under-surface of the brain indicating limbic structures. (*Source:* Daly 1985: 28)

(see Figure 5-2). This entire circuit, described by Papez (1937), constitutes a "lobe" or "system" in the brain, whose major functions are the regulation of endocrine secretion by the pituitary, and the control of vegetative and sustaining mechanisms such as eating, drinking, and sexual function. It is thought to be important in the areas of emotion and motivation, and it can be seen as an anatomical interface between advanced neocortex and the more automatic regulatory centers of the brain-stem and the endocrine system (MacLean 1949).

In the macaque, Geschwind argues that there are major connections from visual association cortex to the limbic lobe. Visual information from the retina passes through the thalamic relay station, the lateral geniculate, to the primary visual koniocortex in the occipital lobes (the sensory receptor cortex related to vision in area 17 of both hemispheres). From here, it passes only a short distance forward to the so-called "visual association cortex", an area of neocortex similar to the auditory association cortex in the first temporal gyrus (which is the area Wernicke considered crucial for auditory comprehension). The function of visual association cortex, areas 18 and 19, is apparently the analysis of primitive sensory data arriving in visual cortex into patterns which are of greater psychological importance to the organism. This pattern of connections from primary sensory cortex (in this case visual) to association cortex is typical of the higher primates. According to Fleisig's rule, the output from the primary sensory koniocortices is always very restricted in its dispersion, in all cases going no further than the sounding association cortex. The output from this association cortex, however, can pass very widely in brain. In the macaque, there are three principal outputs from visual association cortex:

(1)   via the splenium of the corpus callosum to the equivalent area on the opposite side;
(2)   via the white-matter tract known as the superior longitudinal fasciculus to the centers in the frontal lobes involved in eye movements;
(3)   via another major white-matter tract to the inferolateral portion of the temporal lobe.

It is this third connection which is important in the understanding of the anatomical basis of the Kluver–Bucy syndrome. The output from the inferolateral temporal lobe is by way of the anterior temporal lobe to medial temporal lobe limbic structures, particularly hippocampus. The destruction of tissue in the Kluver–Bucy syndrome involves the pathway from the inferolateral temporal lobe to the hippocampus and other medial temporal structures involved in the limbic system.

Geschwind explains the constellation of functional deficits in these animals on the basis of these anatomical connections as follows. He suggests that the functional deficit can be seen as a disconnection of visual stimuli from their biological "meaning" for the organism. The monkey is able to see and discriminate visual objects, but unable to appreciate their significance. It therefore approaches objects that it would ordinarily avoid, demonstrates no fear of these objects, is unable to make the correct selection of sexual partners, violates the social hierarchy, and is unable to learn which of the various stimuli in his environment are edible and which are not. Those aspects of visual stimuli which are relevant to the functions served by the limbic lobe are unavailable to the monkey, and his behavior reflects this deficit.

Geschwind suggests that this deficit can be seen as one of a number of disconnection syndromes in animals. This syndrome is particularly interesting because it reflects a basic anatomical feature of the primate brain. All the sensory association areas project in a fairly direct fashion to the limbic lobe in the primate. Geschwind argues that this is consistent with the abilities of primates and other infrahuman species in learning associations. In most animal-learning experiments, associations can be formed between a "limbic stimulus" such as food or water and a "non-limbic stimulus" such as a visual form or an auditory percept. What is difficult for infrahuman species is the task of forming associations between two non-limbic percepts. Thus, for instance, in so-called "preconditioning" experiments, in which animals are presented with a tone and a visual image and are then taught to perform a motor task in response to the visual image, the monkey does not generalize the performance of the motor task to the auditory tone with which the visual image was initially paired. Geschwind argues that this is the result of the paucity of direct connections between the visual and auditory association areas themselves, with the vast majority of fibers from these areas each going in separate tracts to the limbic lobe. Each "non-limbic" stimulus must therefore be paired with a "limbic" stimulus for association to occur.

This example of a disconnection syndrome and the analysis of learning capacities in the macaque serve as an introduction to Geschwind's views regarding the anatomical basis of language capacity, and regarding the nature of a number of disorders of language seen in humans. Geschwind points out that the anatomical arrangement of fibers in the human is substantially different from that in the primate. Fleisig's rule, that the projections from primary cortical sensory areas are limited to the surrounding association areas, still holds; but the efferent fibers from the association areas project to a structure not found in non-human species. This important structure is the inferior parietal lobule, consisting of two gyri, the supramarginal and angular gyrus. In the human, the majority of fibers from visual association cortex, auditory association cortex, and somesthetic association cortex project to this structure, which is found at the junction of these three association cortices. This structure is histologically advanced, representing an example of phylogenetically late, complex association cortex. This structure is absent in all species studied other than man (see Figure 5-3).

Geschwind suggests that the function of this structure is to act as a center for the association of non-limbic stimuli, thus allowing man to be "freed from the limbic system" and permitting him to establish direct associations between stimuli in the auditory, somesthetic, and visual modalities, without each of them being reinforced by a limbic event. The occurrence of major memory disorders following disruption of the limbic system in man shows

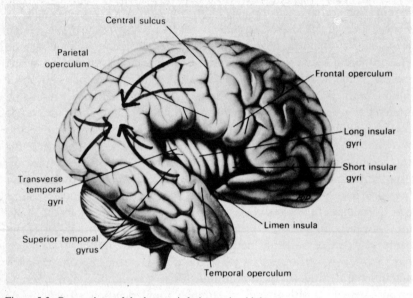

Figure 5-3. Connections of the human inferior parietal lobe
(Modified from Carpenter and Sutin 1983: 31)

that the limbic system is critically involved in human memory, but its role is
not so pervasive as to preclude the laying down of cross-modal non-limbic
associations, as is the case in infrahuman species.

Geschwind argues that this anatomical arrangement and its functional
importance are critical in the development of human language. According to
his theory, it is this arrangement and this functional capacity which allow
the development of naming. Geschwind suggests that the most basic act in
language is the assignment of names to objects. He analyzes naming as
consisting of the psychological association of a sound – the name – and other
physical properties of the named object. He suggests, therefore, that the
anatomical basis of naming is to be found in the existence of an area of
convergence of fibers from the association areas for the separate modalities
in the inferior parietal lobule. The absence of this anatomical arrangement
in non-humans precludes the development of naming, and hence of other
aspects of language.

If we compare this theory to those that we discussed in Chapter 4, it is
clear that there are many similarities. We noted in Chapter 4 that the
connectionists argued for the existence of centers, each of which was
involved with a particular language function, contained a particular form of
linguistic representation in long-term storage, and was located in a particular area of the brain. Geschwind's analysis of naming corresponds to a large

extent to the notion of a center that emerged in the nineteenth-century literature. A particular psycholinguistic function, naming, is associated with a particular set of linguistic representations, the sound pattern of words and the representations of sensory properties of objects, and is located in a particular area of the brain, the inferior parietal lobe.

There are several differences between this analysis and the notion of center to be found in the earlier literature. One is that there is more than one set of representations assigned to the center: in this case, a linguistic representation (the sounds of words) and a non-linguistic representation (the coded sensory properties of objects) are both involved in the processing going on in this area. In fact, it is not clear whether this area itself houses either of these representations, or is simply involved in their juxtaposition, while they themselves are stored in other areas of the brain. If the representations are not actually stored in the inferior parietal lobe, this area actually acts more like a pathway in Lichtheim's or Wernicke's models than like a center. A second difference lies in the type of psycholinguistic functioning attributed to the inferior parietal lobe. First, this functioning is not one of the usual on-line psycholinguistic tasks of speaking, understanding spoken speech, writing, and reading. It is rather an additional function, that of assigning names to objects, or, conversely, assigning semantic properties reflecting the physical characteristics of objects to names. If we assume that activating the words for objects during speech involves the same psychological processes as naming an object one sees, we can include this function within the "task" of speaking. This process, and this anatomical region, would thus be a necessary component in speech. In this way, they would seem to function similarly to how Wernicke's area was thought to function in speech production (recall that Wernicke's area obligatorily supplies the sound pattern of words in speech, on the classic view).

A third, and very important, feature which distinguishes Geschwind's model from those of the nineteenth-century connectionists is his commitment to an anatomical basis for the functional components and processes he postulates. There are no disembodied psychological elements such as "concept centers" in his work. Geschwind goes to great lengths to be explicit about which anatomical pathways and regions he has in mind. As we can see from his analysis of the species-specific aspects of naming, he also utilizes comparative neuroanatomical data to help ascertain the correct neuroanatomical analysis in the human. In Chapter 18, we shall see that this attention to the precise delineation of the neuroanatomical extent and nature of the language areas was to lead Geschwind to the discovery of important asymmetries in the size of comparable areas in the two hemispheres of the brain.

We have not considered Geschwind's analysis of aphasic symptoms, only his analysis of a normal function – naming – and its neuroanatomical basis. In terms of the forms of argument we discussed in Chapter 2, this analysis is an "argument from parallel structures". Geschwind (1965) also presents important analyses of many aphasic symptoms and syndromes, and of the agnosias and apraxias. Many of Geschwind's and other modern "connectionist" analyses of aphasic disorders are fairly close to those of the nineteenth-century connectionists, though, in all cases, such analyses add linguistic and psychological details to the description of a language disorder. We shall not review this work here, partly because many of these descriptions will appear in our discussions in Part III. We will simply note that, in a major textbook account of the aphasias, Benson and Geschwind (1971) use Lichtheim's taxonomy as the basis for a clinically oriented classification of aphasia. In addition to the seven types of aphasia described by Lichtheim, they add three: anomic aphasia, in which the patient has a particularly marked difficulty in naming visually presented pictures and objects; isolation of the speech area, in which the patient can repeat but neither speak nor understand (due to a combination of the lesions which produce Lichtheim's transcortical sensory and transcortical motor aphasia); and global aphasia, in which all modalities of language use are severely affected. In all these syndromes, modern connectionism provides exact anatomical analyses to a greater extent than the first connectionist work we discussed in the previous chapter. In part this is due to a better understanding of human and non-human neuroanatomy, as illustrated in Geschwind 1965; in part it results from improvement in neuro-imaging techniques which allow lesions to be detected in life (see Chapter 19).

One final feature of modern connectionist approaches deserves particular comment, for it constitutes an important addition to the traditional analyses. Much modern work explores the possibility that the brain makes use of duplicate or multiple mechanisms for accomplishing a task, some of which may be more efficient than others. Brain damage may reveal the operation of some of the less efficient mechanisms, which ordinarily are superseded by the preferred ones.

A good example of an analysis of this sort in modern connectionism is Geschwind's analysis of the syndrome of alexia-without-agraphia, and of the agnosias. Geschwind (1965) notes that these patients are unable to form "visual–auditory associations" of certain types, as we saw earlier in this chapter, but emphasizes that they retain their abilities to form other such associations. For example, the patient described by Dejerine suffered from pure word blindness and was unable to read words. He was also unable to read letters. In other cases in the literature, patients have been able to read letters, at least to a greater extent than they could read words. Dejerine's patient was able to read numbers and do calculations, as is true of most patients with this syndrome. Geschwind has pointed out that it is characteristic of these patients to be unable to *name* colors, although they can *match* identical colors. Dejerine's patient, and most of the patients in the literature, have been able to name pictures and objects when they were presented visually. For instance, Dejerine's patient was able to name pictures of complex industrial tools. On the assumption that all visual information passes through the splenium of the corpus callosum to the language areas, it is hard to see how some of these functions are retained, because all visual information is initially presented to the right hemisphere in these patients.

There are three possible ways to account for these patterns. First, it could be the case that some visual representations are transmitted from the right to the left hemisphere through more anterior portions of the corpus callosum and some are not. Second, some visual representations could be transformed into other forms of representation, such as somesthetic or "image"-type representations, which can cross in the more anterior callosum, and other types of visual representations may not be convertible. Third, some visual representations may be associated with linguistic forms in the right hemisphere, and others not.

Geschwind (1965) opts for the second of these analyses. Geschwind's analysis of the retained ability to name objects claims that the patients retain this ability because visually presented objects arouse complex associations in other modalities in the right hemisphere. Thus, presented with a picture of a piece of fruit, for example, a patient would be able to associate tactile, gustatory, olfactory, and other sensory qualities with the visual stimulus. This association of sensory qualities constitutes the mental representation of the object in Geschwind's theory, as we have seen. The representations of qualities in other modalities can be transmitted to the left hemisphere via more anterior portions of the corpus callosum.

Geschwind claims that, to a first approximation, it is only those visual stimuli which are linguistic symbols which cannot pass from the right to the left hemisphere when the splenium of the callosum is damaged. They, presumably, do not arouse associations in other modalities in the right hemisphere directly, but require the activation of the auditory representations of words in the left hemisphere to intervene in the process of activating these associations.

This will account for object naming – but what about naming numbers? Geschwind considers the ability to name numbers to be different from reading words and letters, because numbers are overlearned. This allows for their being associated with other representations in the right hemisphere which pass to the left hemisphere. Geschwind suggests that the fact that we learn to count on our fingers suggests that these representations are somesthetic. This type of analysis can apply to certain linguistic items as well. It has been noticed, for instance, that when these patients can read a little, they have a greater ability to read words which are concrete and highly picturable, and which are rich in associations to other modalities. They have the most trouble with the grammatical words of Indo-European languages (prepositions, articles, determiners, and so on) which do not have these qualities. There are also reports that words which customarily appear on public buildings can be read when presented on cards. Geschwind argues that these words are associated in a very direct way with the cognitive representations of the items on which they appear in ordinary life, and that these cognitive representations can be passed from the right to the left hemisphere.

We have indicated that some patients with alexia-without-agraphia can read individual letters. This does not fall under the explanations above, since letters have no associations in other modalities. The preserved ability to read letters in some patients thus requires some other explanation. An interesting finding has been that what can be read depends upon the form of orthography in which it is represented. Thus, in languages such as Japanese which have both a syllabic script (Kana), in which written symbols stand for individual syllables, and also an ideographic script (Kanji), in which written symbols stand for entire words, patients with this syndrome retain the ability to read the ideographic form of writing, but lose the ability to read the syllabic form (Sasanuma and Fujimura 1971). This pattern suggests that the particular written linguistic symbols which cannot cross the callosum in this syndrome are those which correlate written symbols with individual sounds: symbols which are related to the sound of a word as a whole can be transferred from right to left. Patients who can read letters (name them and indicate their sound values) may be treating them as entire units. When they are embedded within words, they lose this property and can no longer be read.

The analyses of the different "exceptions" to the inability to name visually presented stimuli in alexia-without-agraphia are thus not identical. For object and number naming, the preservation of function is said to reflect right-hemisphere associations. For letter naming and reading Kanji, the deficit in alexia-without-agraphia is seen as one which disturbs the transmission of particular types of written linguistic representations from the right visual-association cortex to the left-hemisphere language areas across the splenium of the corpus callosum. These representations are those which establish relationships between parts of the orthographic representation – graphemes or letters – and parts of the phonological representation – phonemes. When other relationships between the visual stimulus and its phonological representation exist, which relate the entirety of the visual stimulus to the entirety of the phonological representation, other pathways can transmit these representations.

We have introduced this lengthy analysis in relationship to the idea that alternate visual structures and pathways may affect an aphasic performance. Whether Geschwind's analysis of alexia-without-agraphia and associated retained abilities is correct or not (and we shall reconsider the question in Chapter 14), the analysis is a good example of how modern connectionists make use of the concept of alternate pathways. The normal pathway for reading words, letters, and numbers, and for naming colors and objects, is entirely left-hemisphere-based, according to this theory. When this pathway is not available, alternate routes may mediate these functions. These routes are not normally geared to these functions, and carry them out inefficiently or not at all. Thus colors – non-linguistic items without non-visual associates – cannot be named at all. Words can be read under special circumstances, depending upon the nature of the orthography and how the orthography is treated. Numbers and other abstract non-linguistic symbols may be recoded into other representational forms and these transmitted to left-hemisphere language areas, as may occur with visually presented objects. The study of these patterns may reveal the particular role of parts of the brain in registering and transmitting particular forms of linguistic and non-linguistic representations.

Geschwind points out that such analyses do not necessarily provide the same groupings of linguistic items that linguistic theory does. The brain, in other words, may have multiple mechanisms for analyzing linguistic stimuli, some of which correspond to (or make use of) natural groupings within a normative theory of language structure and processing, and others which are duplicate or back-up systems, and which do not correspond to the grouping of linguistic entities described in contemporary linguistic theory. The discovery of these alternate mechanisms is one of the great advantages of studying pathological material, for the normal human processing mechanisms are so efficient that these alternate groupings and psychological processes do not emerge. In addition, of course, this detailed study of brain-injured patients allows us to determine what areas and pathways of the brain are involved in processing these alternative groupings of representations.

Thus, modern connectionism has gone considerably beyond nineteenth-century analyses. It presents more detailed hypotheses about particular aspects of language processing, emphasizes the contribution that studies of pathological populations can make to the discovery of alternate mechanisms for language representation and processing, and is more rigorous in its commitment to specific neuroanatomical bases for the processes it postulates. Modern connectionism has enormously influenced neurolinguistic theory, especially in establishing the framework for investigating the anatomical basis of language and language breakdown with new radiological techniques (see Part IV). We shall take up the influence of modern connectionism upon the classification of the aphasias again in Part III (Chapter 11), and we shall return to many "connectionist" analyses when we consider psycholinguistic analyses in Part III. We shall have a better perspective on connectionism, however, after we consider objections and alternatives to this approach. We now turn to these other approaches. We shall try to put both connectionism and other clinical theories into perspective in Chapter 10.

SUGGESTIONS FOR FURTHER READING

Benson, D. F. (1979). *Aphasia, Alexia, Agraphia*. Churchill Livingstone, New York, ch. 11.
Geschwind, N. (1965). Disconnection syndromes in animals and man. *Brain* 88, 237–94; 585–644.
  (1969). Problems in the anatomical understanding of the aphasias. In A. Benton (ed.), *Contributions to Clinical Neuropsychology*. Aldine, Chicago.
Mesulam, M. (ed.) (1985). *Principles of Behavioral Neurology*. F. A. Davis, Philadelphia.
Morton, J. (1984). Brain-based and non-brain-based models of language. In D. Caplan, A. R. Lecours, and A. Smith (eds.), *Biological Perspectives on Language*. MIT Press, Cambridge, Mass.

6

Objections to connectionism

The classical connectionist theories described in Chapter 4 were not without their critics. Indeed, it is an indication of their importance that they were subject to so many attacks; unimportant theories are ignored. In many ways, the debate about connectionist models dominated neurolinguistic theory for over a century. Some reconstructions of the history of neurolinguistics and aphasiological research essentially divide theories of language–brain relationships into two groups – the "localization" camp, of which the connectionists are the prime examples, and the "holist" camp, which includes virtually all other investigators. This dichotomy is over-simplified. First, there are many aspects of the connectionist models, such as their commitment to certain linguistic and psycholinguistic levels of description, which were taken over by at least some of their critics. Second, as we have seen in instances such as the "concept center" postulated by Lichtheim, not all aspects of the connectionist models were thought to be localized. Moreover, as has been stressed by Geschwind (1964), though the critics disagreed with the connectionists about the psychological nature of language and its processing, they were largely in agreement about the nature, classification, and pathological determinants of language breakdown. Moreover, it is an error to group together all those who disagreed with the connectionists, since there are a variety of positions which these theorists maintained.

However, despite its being misleading in these ways, the view that the history of aphasiology and neurolinguistic theory was marked by two major viewpoints, largely differing on the issue of the extent to which the functioning of a language faculty could be seen as the result of several localized centers for particular language functions connected to each other, is a reasonable *general* description of what was probably the major focus of theoretical attention in the first 100 years of work in this field. It is because of the centrality of this issue in the history of the field that we shall devote several chapters in Part II to the alternatives and objections to connectionist thought. In this chapter we shall consider the work of two investigators – Sigmund Freud (1891) and Henry Head (1926) – whose contributions can largely be seen as criticisms of the connectionist school. Our review of their reservations regarding the theories we have been considering up to now will also serve to introduce some of the issues to be taken up in Chapters 7, 8, and 9.

We can divide objections to connectionism into three main groups. The first consists of the claim that the basic observations made by the connectionists were incorrect, or that there were additional observations about aphasic performances which cast the particular theories of language–brain relationships advanced by connectionists into doubt. The second group of objections is directed towards the logic of the connectionists' inferences from aphasic symptoms to neurolinguistic theory. These objections focus on the theory without disputing the actual observations about aphasia made by the connectionists. The third set of objections consists of the view that neurolinguistic theory should be based upon a different set of observations about the behavior of aphasic patients from that which the connectionists made. In this chapter we shall be mainly concerned with the first two types of objection; the last type will be covered in Chapters 7 and 8.

The work of Sigmund Freud (1891) raised questions of the first two types regarding the connectionist approach. We shall first consider the issues he raised concerning the adequacy of the connectionist descriptions.

Freud did not dispute the level of empirical description in the work of Wernicke (1874) and Lichtheim (1885); that is, he was willing to accept the view that a reasonable way of describing aphasic symptoms and syndromes, and language functions, was in terms of the entire tasks of language use which we have seen characterized these theories. He pointed out, however, that the value of a theory such as Lichtheim's lay in its ability to predict all possible combinations of symptoms. If there were a syndrome in which the grouping of symptoms could not be adequately explained on the basis of the connections and information flow postulated by the model, this would be a serious flaw in the model. Freud discussed two such constellations of symptoms. He concluded that there were serious deficits in these models in general.

The first symptom group was the combination of an alexia, affecting both silent reading and reading aloud, with a Broca's aphasia. Lichtheim (1885) had indicated that this set of symptoms often co-occurred, and Freud stressed that the co-occurrence of these symptoms was too frequent to be due to chance. He pointed out that the centers and connections postulated in Lichtheim's model (and in several other connectionist models) could not account for the combination of a motor aphasia of the Broca's type and an alexia. Lichtheim (1885) had anticipated this criticism and had suggested that, in cases in which there was both an alexia and a Broca's aphasia, there may have been a second small lesion either in the visual language center or in one of the pathways between the visual language center and the auditory language center. Lichtheim suggested that this lesion was minor and resolved over a period of time, and predicted that, over time, these cases would show resolution of the alexia. Freud pointed out that there were well-documented cases of prolonged reading difficulties accompanying a Broca's aphasia, in one case for years after a stroke. Moreover, post mortem examination in this case failed to reveal a second lesion. Freud concluded that this combination of deficits constituted a true aphasic syndrome which cast serious doubt on the connectionist models, because it was difficult to imagine any model along connectionist lines which would account for this combination of deficits.

A second criticism which Freud leveled against the connectionists was in relation to a case described by Grashey (1885), which falls under the heading of "anomic" aphasia. Grashey's patient was able to speak fluently. He made a few paraphasic errors in spontaneous speech. He seemed to understand what was said to him. His major difficulty was in naming objects and pictures of objects. Freud pointed out that, since the patient was able to understand individual words, it must be the case that, following Lichtheim's model (Figure 4-3), the connections from the representation of the auditory form of words in Wernicke's area to the concept center were intact. The fact that the patient had trouble naming objects suggested that the pathway in the reverse direction was disrupted. Allowing for a disturbance of information flow in only one direction along a pathway opened the connectionist model to a whole range of interpretations which it had previously been unwilling to incorporate. What would the anatomical basis be for such a one-way disturbance of information flow? Were the pathways carrying information from one center to another different from those carrying information in the reverse direction? No one had suggested this possibility in the literature.

Aside from these questions, there were other problems. Under certain circumstances, the patient *could* name objects. This happened when he was given more time to view the object, or when he was given various semantic clues, such as the class of object to which the presented stimulus belonged. Grashey had claimed that the deficit in this patient was not one in a particular pathway, but rather reflected the conditions under which the pathways could work. Freud suggested that the difficulty lay with the patient's ability to achieve rapid integration of visually presented material. The ability of the patient to synthesize visual information quickly into perceptual units which could be related to a semantic representation was defective. Grashey had tested this hypothesis, and discovered an interesting feature of the patient's naming difficulties: the improvement which was seen when the patient was given more time to view a drawing disappeared when the patient was forced to look at a drawing through a small hole in a piece of paper, such that he could only see a bit of the drawing at a time. When the drawing was presented bit by bit in this way, the patient was never able to say what the object was, no matter how much time he was given. Grashey and Freud agreed that this was due to the failure of perceptual integrative mechanisms in the visual modality.

Freud pointed out that this case – and, similarly, all cases of anomic aphasia – fell outside of the connectionist framework. In this case, all the centers and the connections between them were intact, but the conditions under which a pathway could operate – in this case, some aspect of the integration of visual material by the concept center – were impaired. What this meant was that the deficit was functional, not anatomical in any sense recognized by connectionism. These functional factors must apply to the normal operation of the language system. Freud quotes with approval the work of Bastian (1887), a British neurologist who incorporated several such functional factors into connectionist models, as well as the work of Jackson (see Chapter 7).

Freud thus questioned the completeness of the connectionist models; and he pointed out that Lichtheim himself had argued that these models were much less important if they were incomplete. He also argued that there was no natural way to complete the models without introducing what he termed "functional" factors; that is, specifications of the manner in which a center or pathway operated.

This first set of objections to connectionist theory deals with the need for additional psychological, or psycholinguistic, descriptions in these models. Freud's next objection dealt with the neurological basis for the functions the connectionists postulated. Freud argued that the conclusion that elementary functions, in the connectionist sense, are localized in centers, while complex functions are built up by connecting centers, does not follow from the facts of aphasia and, in fact, is an erroneous view.

Freud argued that it was incorrect to assume that an "elementary" psychological function was related to a cerebral localization, while a "complex" psychological function was the result of the interaction of different brain regions. Freud chose as an example the nature of individual words. Freud suggested that each word consisted of a sound pattern and a set of associations – the latter largely related to the sensory qualities of the objects in the real world to which the word referred. Freud pointed out that the connectionists would consider the sound pattern of the word and each of the modality-based associations to be elementary psychological entities, whereas the entirety of the word would be a complex unit made up by connections between these elements. However, Freud argued, though this might be true on a psychological level, its psychological truth did not imply that the neurological basis for this arrangement was one in which each elementary part of the totality of a word was represented in a region of the brain and the whole word composed of the connections of these regions. Indeed, Freud argued that this was unlikely to be the way words were represented. He pointed out that any neuron which was involved in the *joining up* of the sound and the associative properties of a word must somehow represent both the word's sound properties and its associations within itself. Thus, though one could postulate that the sound properties of words were in one place and the associations of words in another, every neuron involved in connecting the representation of an associated property of a word with the word's sound must have both representations. These neurons might be localized, just as those only representing the sound or the associations; in this case, the complex function would be localized. Alternatively, each neuron representing a word's sound could be linked to neurons representing its association. In this case, all these neurons would accomplish complex functions.

Freud suggested that it would be reasonable to assume that each word was represented in a sort of "net" of neurons. The auditory, visual, somesthetic, and motor speech aspects of a word were all represented across the entire perisylvian area. Freud suggested that there might be gradients within this net, with auditory information being more densely represented near the auditory area, visual information being more densely represented near the visual cortex, etc. In this way, the association cortex near the primary koniocortices would come to be specialized with respect to linguistic representations, without there being a strict difference between a "center" and a "connecting pathway". Freud also argued that the types of language breakdown that occurred after disturbance of "centers" and "connections" in connectionist models did not differ from each other, and he thus suggested that the evidence from language pathology should be interpreted as showing that centers and connections did not exist. The lack of a difference between the types of symptom which occurred after lesions of what connectionists saw as "centers" and "connections" was consistent with Freud's neurolinguistic theory.

Freud's work was not widely read, and his arguments were largely ignored. However, a volume which did exert a great influence over the approaches to neurolinguistic models and the description of aphasia was Henry Head's *Aphasia and Kindred Disorders of Speech*, published in 1926. Head was not merely critical of the connectionists; he was blatantly contemptuous of much of their work, referring to the proliferation of centers and connections and the development of theory in this field as "chaos". In what is certainly the most widely read section of his two-volume book on aphasia, the historical survey of aphasiology, he sums up the group of "diagram makers" as follows:

Most of the observers mentioned in this chapter failed to contribute anything of permanent value to the solution of the problems of aphasia . . . because they were dominated by a philosophical fallacy of their day. They imagined that all vital processes could be explained by some simple formula. With the help of a few carefully selected assumptions, they deduced the mechanism of speech and embodied it in a schematic form. From diagrams, based on a priori principles, they deduced in turn the defects of function which must follow destruction of each "centre" or internuncial path. They never doubted the solidity of their postulates, based as they were on the rule of human reason. They failed to appreciate that the logical formulae of the intellect do not correspond absolutely to physical events and that the universe does not exist as an exercise for the human mind. (Head 1926: 65)

Interestingly enough, Head's own work is rarely cited today, and despite his enormous influence in discrediting the connectionist approach, it is uncertain how much he himself left of permanent value in this field. In positive terms, he did much to reintroduce the work of Jackson into conceptual and empirical approaches to aphasia and language–brain relationships, but whether his own thinking went much beyond that of Jackson's, or whether he merely rephrased it, is not very clear. His criticisms, however, are well worth reviewing.

Head was a great observer of detail, and, if there is a way to summarize his discomfort with the connectionists, and with other workers, it might well be to say that he took them to task for ignoring the details of aphasia. He called for "a ruthless destruction of false gods", by which he was referring to "theoretical assumptions, both positive and negative", and "a return to systematic empirical observation of the crude manifestations of disease" (Head 1926: 66). It is impossible to do justice to the richness of his descriptions of aphasic patients in a few lines, and that is not our aim here. Rather, we shall focus on features of aphasic performance which he reported, and which he felt could not be accommodated within connectionist models. It is important to consider these features of aphasia in relation to other theories we shall encounter, and to ask whether they are better integrated into any other type of model. Of the many features Head describes, we shall review two, which are arguably those he was most concerned with.

The first observation is that aphasic performances cross descriptive boundaries. We have seen how the connectionists established diagnostic categories on the basis of the relative impairments seen in the tasks of language use; and we have already seen that Freud argued that more detailed descriptions of the qualitative nature of the psychological processes underlying language disturbances indicated that functional factors were needed to explain aphasic symptoms. Head also denied that language impairments could be described in terms of the totality of language tasks. In discussing Henschen's (1920) localizations, for instance, he remarks that

the fullest and most detailed reports cannot be summarized in tabular form. The patient may have been able to carry out simple orders, but not those which were more complex; he could read with understanding, provided the word did not contain a command to act; or he could write his name but not his address. Can such a case be tabulated as one of "word-deafness," "alexia," or "agraphia"? (Head 1926: 83)

Nor is he optimistic about a linguistic analysis of the patterns of perform-ance; on the contrary, he maintains that "Defects of language cannot be adequately expressed in terms of parts of speech . . . no variety of aphasia can be dissected into grammatical elements" (121).

The second set of observations only compound the problem of description, classification, and explanation of aphasic symptoms and syndromes. Aphasic symptoms are transient, indeed ephemeral.

It is a common observation in the best observed cases that on a certain day tasks could be executed with ease, which were otherwise quite impossible. Familiar surroundings, friendly people, sympathetic handling and the mode of examination have a profound effect on the results obtained, a fact which has been widely neglected. (83)

Aside from this day-to-day variation within a single patient, there is wide variation in the abilities of different patients with similar lesions, and a universal tendency for aphasic symptoms to change over time, usually in the direction of becoming less severe, in vascular cases. How then are we to describe a patient or a syndrome, and to relate the functional disability to a lesion in brain? Chaos indeed.

It is fair to say that neither Head nor any other theorist has answers to these issues. Head proposed a Jacksonian framework for viewing aphasic symptoms, but it is far from clear that that framework, which we shall consider in the next chapter, adequately deals with these types of observa-tions. Head used these observations as evidence against the notion of centers responsible for language tasks, which were individually subject to disease, and we may accept the force of this argument while, at the same time, appreciating that it applies to many other neurolinguistic models.

As with Freud, Head did not only dispute the analysis of symptoms; he also attacked the concept of a center and that of the localization of functions on a physiological basis. Freud's argument was indirect, as we have seen. Head's is more direct, being based on observations regarding the effect of stimulation of cortical structures in animals by electrical currents in experimental procedures.

Head pointed out that experimental electrical stimulation of very small areas of motor cortex yielded patterns of motor activity which were hard to reconcile with the notion of a strictly localized function. Stimulation of motor cortex produces very discrete movements – usually flexion or extension of one joint. This might be considered a paradigmatic example of localization of a simple function. However, Leyton and Sherrington (1917) had shown that, in apes, the effect of stimulation of a point in the motor cortex is not constant, but varies with prior stimulation. Rapidly repeated stimulation of a given point in the motor cortex usually increases the amplitude of a particular movement at a joint; but if a point is stimulated at greater temporal intervals, both the character of the response (flexion as opposed to extension) and the location of the response (one joint instead of another) may change on occasion. Similarly, if tissue is removed from the motor cortex, a deficit in movement occurs and recovers over a period of time. If the cortex in the region of the ablation is stimulated after recovery has occurred, the previous movement does not occur in all circumstances. Nor does removal of a greater amount of tissue in the region of the previous excision necessarily cause the deficit to reappear. This suggests that the area in question is not organized so that adjacent areas take over a particular motor movement. Finally, Head mentions experiments which show that excision or stimulation of "sensory" regions, in particular the post-central gyrus, can greatly influence the effects of stimulation in the pre-central "motor" gyrus. These phenomena of reversal, facilitation, and deviation of response to electrical stimulation provide evidence of "functional instability" in the cortex not in keeping with a simple notion of localization of elementary functions.

Despite these observations, which indicate that the neurophysiological basis for functional localization is complex, Head was willing to accept the view that the concept of functional localization is applicable to some actions and perceptions. At the very least, he accepted the notion of the topographic representation of parts of the body, to the extent of agreeing that areas such as face, hand, and arm stood in a constant relationship to each other. On the other hand, *functions*, as opposed to topographical relationships between parts of the body, were not localized in his view:

The only form of anatomical localisation which can be unhesitatingly accepted is the relative topographical representation of the various parts of the body. We can confidently assume as the result of physiological experiment and clinical observation that, for instance, the face, hand, elbow and shoulder stand in a definite relation to one another, although the results of stimulating any one point on the surface of the brain may vary from time to time.

We can discover to a limited degree focal centres for certain simple simultaneous muscular actions in some definite part of the body. But, when we attempt to deal with a succession of synergic movements and alternating changes in the limbs or segments, this is impossible; we are face to face with an interrelation of diverse functions. The complete act in its perfect form demands the mobilisation in due sequence of a series of complex procedures; here the time relation, on which von Monakow lays so much stress, is of fundamental importance. A want of chronological exactitude will throw the whole movement into disorder; its "kinetic melody" has been destroyed.

Here there can be no question of a focal localisation of function, even though many of the necessary paths of innervation emerge here and there from definable insular centres. But, on the other hand, all actions which contain a cortical component can be interrupted by a lesion of the surface of the brain, although they cannot be "localised" within its boundaries. (88)

Head thus denies the validity of any parallel between topographic localization of parts of the body and localization of motor functions. Functional localization in the complex psychological domain of the "higher functions" is akin to motor function, and is also not localized:

Thus, all these primitive functions, motion, sensation and vision, can not only be affected independently from different parts of the surface of the brain, but the situation of the functional disturbance is associated topographically with the position of the lesion within any one of these areas.

Disorders of speech, or defects of similar high-grade functions, due to local destruction of the brain, differ from those of motion, somatic sensation or vision in that there is no such relation to parts of the body or its projection in space. Moreover, the lesion to be effective must be situated in one definite hemisphere . . . On this high level the problem of "cerebral localisation" acquires a somewhat different aspect and is greatly increased in complexity. We no longer have the comparatively simple task of associating some focus of destruction in the brain with loss of function in a definite part of the body or visual field, but are compelled to ask ourselves the much more difficult question: What form does it assume in accordance with the site of the lesion? We must first distinguish categorically the various defects in the use of language and then attempt as far as possible to determine their relation to the locality of the lesion in the left hemisphere. (438)

Head thus emphasized the differences between *topographic projections*, which, if not strictly localized, at least bear a constant neuroanatomical relation to each other, *motor and sensory functions*, which are made up of components and which are thus not localized, and *higher functions*, which are similar to motor or sensory functions in that they are not localized but differ inasmuch as they do not even project topographically onto space. Head recognized that it is a very great challenge to describe correctly the functional components of motor and sensory capacities or those of higher intellectual processes, as opposed to determining the neural locations of topographic projections. Like Freud, Head explicitly denies that the division of language functions into faculties devoted to speech production, comprehension, and so on, each task coupled with a single linguistic level of representation, was adequate. He thus rejected both the psychological and neurological claims of the connectionists.

It is inaccurate to view the work of Freud and Head as entirely critical. The observations each made were also directed towards the development of other theories, in both the area of characterization of abnormal function and performance deficits and in that of defining neurological mechanisms. Many of their positive suggestions are closely related to the theories of workers whose contributions we shall come across in the next two chapters. The present chapter utilizes parts of their work to indicate some of the forms of disagreement with the connectionist approach we have presented in Chapters 4 and 5. Having established that the connectionist theories are not the whole answer, and certainly not the only possible model of language–brain relationships, we now turn to a number of other approaches and conceptual frameworks for neurolinguistic theory.

SUGGESTIONS FOR FURTHER READING

Geschwind, N. (1964). The paradoxical position of Kurt Goldstein in the history of aphasia. *Cortex* 1, 214–24.

Marshall, J. C. (1974). Freud's psychology of language. In R. Wollheim (ed.), *Freud: A Collection of Critical Essays*. Anchor Books, Garden City.

7

Hierarchical models

In the previous chapter, we have seen several reasons to be less than completely sure that the way language is represented in the brain is through a number of centers, each responsible for a particular psycholinguistic function in a particular area of the brain, connected through tracts of white matter. But if this is not the correct general framework for viewing neurolinguistics, what is? In this and the next two chapters, we shall consider three other approaches to models of language–brain relationships, each of which answers this question somewhat differently. In this chapter, we shall consider models which view both language and brain in hierarchical terms, considering behavior to be the result of the functioning of successive levels of the nervous system, rather than the build-up of complex behaviors from simple components. In Chapter 8, we shall consider the view which sees linguistic (and other) behavior to be the result of the operation of the nervous system, and the psyche, as integrated wholes. In Chapter 9, we shall examine models in which none of the components carry out the entirety of a psychological function. In each case, after presenting work which is typical of the particular approach, we shall try to indicate strengths and weaknesses of the approach, and the ways it differs from others.

John Hughlings Jackson was one of the founders of the field of clinical neurology, and, along with William Gowers, the pre-eminent English neurologist of his day. Among his many interests was the analysis of language disorders and their anatomical basis. His approach to describing symptoms, and to the neurological basis for normal language and aphasic symptomatology, stands in marked contrast to the connectionist and faculty localization models we have considered up to this point. Indeed, Jackson's writings on aphasia and language–brain relationships give almost no hint of his having been influenced by the work of the connectionist school, though we know that he was familiar with their theories: he and Broca debated various questions about aphasia in 1866, and Lichtheim's paper was published in *Brain*, of which Jackson was founding editor. However, his work is so much a product of his own genius that it in fact borrowed little from that of other workers of his era.

Jackson viewed both behavior and neural activity as consisting of the superimposition of increasingly complex functions upon basic capacities. Basic functions were relatively automatic, involuntary, stimulus-bound, and accomplished by more primitive structures within the nervous system. Respiration, cardiac rhythm, endocrine gland function, sleep, and other sustaining functions constitute examples of these basic functions. These functions are present in species with primitive nervous systems, are seen in the human neonate, and are frequently preserved in the presence of advanced disease of the nervous system, especially when such disease is slowly degenerative in nature. Jackson argued that these functions were carried out by lower levels of the neuraxis, and subsequent findings have largely confirmed this basic hypothesis. More complex functions, such as assuming certain postures, gait, response to painful stimuli, and others, are the result of intermediate levels of the nervous system. These show some degree of independence from stimuli and some variation in character while, at the same time, exhibiting a considerable degree of stereotyped execution, at least once a movement is initiated. At a higher level are functions which are voluntary, not tightly bound to any stimulus, and which exhibit considerable latitude in their character. Normal use of language is largely of this type. These functions depend for their performance upon the highest, most evolutionarily advanced areas of the brain, the cerebral hemispheres.

This very simplified sketch of Jackson's views regarding the organization of the nervous system and its relationship to the organization of behavior already indicates several ways in which his views differ from the models of the connectionists. The functions which Jackson identifies are each entire behaviors, and the nature of these behaviors and the relationship between them is quite different from the facilities of Broca, Wernicke, and Lichtheim. Jackson focusses on the superimposition of functions: we modulate gait to produce running or climbing or, in the extreme, dancing; we inhibit basic drives because of social constraints; we modify responses to threatening elements of our environment on the basis of our knowledge of the way a danger might unfold. In each case of this type, a more primitive response is partially inhibited and partially modified by the operation of the more complex response. In neurological terms, more primitive parts of the nervous system are subject to inhibition, release, and modification by higher levels. This is quite different from the models we have reviewed thus far. Though it is true that the activity of Broca's area is modified by input from Wernicke's area, for instance, the nature of this modification is not seen as a higher-order modification of the intrinsic "lower-level" activity of Broca's area. The connectionist models do not incorporate this form of hierarchical organization; as a corollary, they lack the close ties to evolutionary phenomena – both across phyla and over the course of human development and degeneration – of the Jacksonian framework.

A second feature of this conceptual framework which serves to distinguish it from that of the connectionists is the view it suggests of the nature of symptoms. The differences between these two approaches have been stressed by many theorists, and although they are not expressly stated by Jackson, they are inherent in his work. In both approaches, pathological performance results from the operation of brain tissue affected by disease. Where the theoretical viewpoints differ is with respect to how the remaining brain functions. In connectionist theories, the performances found after brain injury are basically seen as partial performances: the organism, or a part of the organism such as a human language faculty, operates as if it had a missing component. The Broca's aphasic, in the approach we have reviewed in Chapters 3–5, operates as a person with intact language capacities other than the ability to speak. In the hierarchical framework suggested by the work of Jackson, the neurologically damaged organism acts as an integrated unit. His performance reflects the operation of lower levels of performance which are more stereotyped, automatic, and stimulus-bound. Jackson sought to capture this difference in symptom types through the terms "negative" and "positive" symptoms. The former referred to the functions which the patient could not carry out, and reflected the damaged areas of the brain. The second referred to the residual abilities of the patient, and reflected the operation of the remaining brain. The difference, however, consists of more than just identifying these two types of effects, since what a patient can do is a reflection of the remaining brain in both Jacksonian and connectionist approaches. What is at issue is how the intact brain (re)organizes itself in the face of injury, and, specifically, the extent to which it achieves integrated performances which are "lower-level" in Jackson's sense, as opposed to partial performances which reflect the absence of a functional component. It should be obvious that these are not mutually exclusive possibilities (though various writers have sometimes suggested they are), and that it might be possible to find examples of both sorts of reaction to injury in aphasic performances, depending upon which aspect of aphasic performance is examined.

Jackson reported aspects of aphasic performance which were of a very different nature than those which the connectionists had described and used for the construction of their theories. We have indicated many times that the connectionists described the relative impairment in the on-line tasks of language use in their patients, and that their concept of the elements of language which were "stored" in various areas of the brain was largely restricted to individual words, with their sounds, written forms, and "associations". Jackson's descriptions of aphasic patients focussed on quite different aspects of language and language use, and the resulting views of language–brain relationships are closely tied to the way he approached the characterization of aphasic performances.

Jackson denied the primary importance of the individual word in linguistic structure or in language use. He emphasized that words were not the principal units of either; rather, the critical feature of language was its ability to form what he called "propositions". A proposition expresses a relationship between objects and events in the world through the juxtaposition of words. His insight, which is strikingly modern in light of the focus of many current linguistic concerns, is captured in the following passage:

> It is not enough to say that speech consists of words. It consists of words *referring to one another in a particular manner*; and without a proper inter-relation of its parts a verbal utterance would be a mere succession of names embodying no proposition. A proposition, e.g. Gold is yellow, consists of two names, each of which, by conventional contrivances of position, etc. (called grammatical structure in well-developed languages), *modifies the meaning of the other*. All the names in a random succession of words may, it is true, one after the other, excite perceptions in us, but not perceptions in any relation to one another deserving the name of thought. The several perceptions so revived do not make a unit. We are told nothing by a mere sequence of names, although our organisation is stirred up by each of them. Now, a proposition is not – that is to say, in its effect on us is not – a mere sequence.
>
> When we apprehend a proposition, *a relation between two things is given to us* – is for the moment, indeed, forced upon us by the conventional tricks which put the two names in the respective relations of subject and predicate. We receive in a two-fold manner, not the words only, but the order of words also. (Jackson, 1874; pp. 130–1)

In addition to the feature of propositions that they express relationships in this way, their use shows characteristics of the highest levels of function. Propositions are frequently used in innovative yet appropriate ways, and are not bound to particular stimuli. Jackson indicates that such creative use of propositions is an inherent feature of a proposition itself, and that word sequences which express relations, but which are used in stereotyped, "automatic" ways, are not "true" propositions.

There are, therefore, two aspects to the proposition, which Jackson considered to be the central language structure. Both may be subject to breakdown. The *structure* of the proposition itself may be disturbed, or the flexibility of its conditions of *use* may be impaired. In both cases, the disturbance can be seen as a change in the normal function of language towards a more restricted, stereotyped, automatic usage – terms of analysis which can be directly connected to the framework within which Jackson wished to view the relationship between neurological and linguistic function. Moreover, this form of analysis can apply separately to either comprehension or speaking. Jackson illustrated his approach in greatest detail in an analysis of a group of patients who were impaired to varying extents in their ability to construct and produce propositional language.

In a series of papers entitled "On affections of speech from disease of the brain", Jackson (1878) described a syndrome which one might wish to call a variant of Broca's aphasia, though he did not identify it in these terms. Typically, a patient with this syndrome is able to understand spoken language to a considerable extent. His spontaneous speech, however, is extremely sparse, often being restricted to one or two words. Jackson's analysis pertains to the selection and use of these words.

The actual words that remain available to such patients are determined by the nature of their usual use. "Automatic" words, such as obscenities, are frequently retained. They can be uttered when a patient is upset, but they are also used in inappropriate situations without any indication that the patient is upset or angry. Some patients produce "stereotyped" utterances – one or two words which are used constantly. Sometimes these repeated utterances are not actual words but improperly formed phonological sequences. Jackson suggested that these words might have been in the patient's mind at the time of the lesion causing aphasia, and that the non-words which appear may be derived from these linguistic forms. Neither automatic nor stereotyped utterances have the flexibility of form which is characteristic of propositional speech.

The second aspect of Jackson's analysis bears on the use of these linguistic items. He observed that the patients are capable of utilizing their small linguistic repertoire only in limited situations. Thus, they can utilize the utterances at their disposal in emotional situations. They are also capable of responding to requests to say the words that they can utter. Occasionally, they are capable of uttering these words in response to questions. In situations of great emotional stress, the patient is capable of more propositional speech than at less intense moments. Thus, for instance, one patient, whose trade was carpentry, managed to utter the word *Master's* in response to a question from his son regarding the location of his tools. Jackson stresses the significance of locating these tools for the livelihood of the family, and the strong motivation the patient must have had to provide this information. These patients are, however, incapable of using these words to state relationships in ways freed from the immediate demands of a situation; that is, they cannot use them to perform a "propositional" function. Jackson viewed the production of these automatic and stereotyped utterances as an entire integrated function of a lower level of the nervous system.

A particularly revealing set of utterances which these patients occasionally retain are the words *yes* and *no*. Jackson argued that these are, in fact, propositional utterances. They denote assertion or denial of a proposition, and therefore themselves imply assent or dissent to a relational utterance. The fact that they are the most elementary and universal propositions is what determines their occasional retention in the speech of these patients.

Jackson considered these patients to be "speechless but not wordless". The fact that they understand what is said to them is an indication that each word is in duplicate, represented both on an expressive and a receptive level. Jackson hypothesized that both the receptive aspect of words and the more automatic aspect of language were functions of the non-dominant hemisphere. The dominant hemisphere is particularly involved in the expressive use of propositional language.

This view of language does not deny the existence of aphasic syndromes, such as those described by the connectionists. However, it maintains that the delineation of patterns of receptive and expressive language disorders must be accompanied by detailed analyses of the conditions under which expression or reception is impaired, as well as by a qualitative assessment of the vocabulary and linguistic structures which are available to a patient both in expression and reception. This analysis is more important in Jackson's work than the enumeration of the tasks in which a patient is and is not impaired. Jackson attempts to substitute a subtle and often subjective analysis of patients' motives in a given situation, and a detailed account of the particular linguistic inventory available to him, for a list of psycholinguistic tasks in which a deficit can be found.

The strengths of the Jacksonian framework include his emphasis on the integrative aspect of psychological and neural function, the concept of higher-order modulation of more primitive behavior patterns, and the close ties of his approach to language with evolutionary theory and ontogenetic sequences of development. These are features of neurolinguistic theory which are hard to incorporate into the connectionist approach. On the other hand, as formulated by Jackson, the theory has little anatomical basis; outside of the hypotheses regarding the function of the non-dominant hemisphere, there is scant reference to particular neural structures. Jackson's theory lacks even the degree of commitment to the neural basis of components of a language faculty found in the connectionists' work. The theory is unrelated to the observations regarding aphasic syndromes found in the connectionist framework, and Jackson gives no hints as to how these particular patterns of language breakdown are to be explained.

Despite these limitations, Jackson's work influenced Freud, Bastian, and a number of other workers. Overall, though, it was fated to be relatively neglected until re-emphasized by Head in 1926. Thereafter, the hierarchical view, coupled to a "holist", "gestalt" psychology, strongly influenced neurolinguistic work. We shall see its influence upon Goldstein (1948) in the next chapter. In the remainder of this chapter, we shall concentrate on two approaches closely linked conceptually to Jackson's, though widely different in their data-base: Roman Jakobson's analysis of development and breakdown of the phonemic inventory, a linguistic study; and Jason Brown's theory of "microgenesis", a strongly neuroanatomically-based model.

Jakobson's (1941) book on aphasia and child language is widely cited as the first truly linguistic study of the aphasias. In this volume, Jakobson sought to relate one aspect of the pattern of language dissolution in aphasia to language development and to universal features of language structure. It is appropriate to consider this work at this point, because the view that the effect of brain injury upon language is the reverse of the sequence of acquisition of structures in language development is easily integrated into a hierarchical theory which holds that language structure and use are the result of progressively more complex modifications of an initially simple function.

Jakobson's hypotheses were based on case reports and studies in the literature, not on his own collection of data. The observations he cites deal with the pattern of loss and retention of phonemes in aphasic language, and compare that pattern to the sequence in which phonemes are acquired in language development. Roughly, phonemes are defined as the minimal sound units which are capable of indicating a difference in meaning in a language (see Chapter 13 for more detailed discussion). The sounds represented by the letters *p* and *t* are separate phonemes, since they create different meanings in otherwise identical situations, such as in the two words *map* and *mat*. On the other hand, the difference in sound in the *p* in *pat* and in *tap* (which can be appreciated by saying the words aloud with one's hand before one's lips: in *pat*, considerably more air will be felt on the hand after the *p* than will be felt after the *p* in *tap* – a feature called "aspiration") is not a phonemic difference, since the presence or absence of aspiration of the sound *p* is completely dependent upon the location of the sound in a word and never creates a difference in meaning in English. A number of other features of phonemes have been proposed, and the definition of the term "phonemes" is debated.

Jakobson's concern in his volume on aphasia is not with the precise definition of the phoneme. For his purposes, the important feature of phonemes is their reliance upon contrasts: the greater the number of contrasts utilized by the system of phonemes of a particular language, the richer the sound pattern of that language. Jakobson points out that across the world's languages there is a definite order to the appearance of particular contrasts within the inventory of phonemes in a given language. All languages have phonemes which contrast with respect to the degree to which the vocal tract is open during the production of sounds. That is, the basic phonemic contrast is between consonants and vowels, which show relative closure and relative openness of the vocal tract respectively. Each of these two basic groups of sounds is most often represented by their most extreme member. In the case of consonants, the basic consonants are *p* and *b*, which create a momentarily total closure of the extreme end of the vocal tract, the lips. The basic vowel is the maximally open vowel *a* (pronounced as in the word *father*). When the consonantal system develops in any language, it almost always develops via contrasts of "place of articulation" (that is, the place where the constriction of the vocal tract occurs), leading to a series of labial, dental (or alveolar), palatal, velar, and glottal consonants. The second dimension of contrast for consonants is nasality, a feature which depends upon the opening or closure of the nasal cavity during the production of a consonant. A third dimension along which contrasts arise in the consonant system is the degree of vocal-tract closure, which varies from absolute closure (in stop consonants such as *p*) to various partial closures (as in *s* and *sh*). Finally, additional contrasts reflecting the position of the sides and body of the tongue (as in *r* and *l*) are available. In the vocalic series, height of the body of the tongue, rounding of the lips, the position of the body of the tongue towards the front or back of the oral cavity, the presence or absence of nasality, and other special features, are available for the creation of phonemic inventories.

Jakobson's survey of languages indicated that utilization of these contrasts (and others) as the basis for phonemic inventories follows a definite pattern. To a first approximation, certain contrasts invariably appear only when others exist in a particular language. No language, for instance, will have a high back unrounded vowel (Russian *i̵*) unless it also has a high front unrounded vowel (long *i*), and a high back rounded vowel (long *u*). The unrounded position of the lips is only used to create a high back vowel if the feature of lip rounding is already used to create a high back vowel and the feature of unrounding used to define a high front vowel. When these "laws" are broken, phonemic inventories show their instability in a number of ways, such as manifesting a proclivity towards rapid change in the direction of elimination of the unusual utilization of a particular contrast. Jakobson suggests that the order of appearance of contrasts in the phonemic inventories of the world's languages reflects a tendency towards utilization of maximal contrasts before minor ones. For instance, a consonant series consisting of consonants caused by total occlusion of the vocal tract is a prerequisite for the appearance of consonants characterized by partial occlusion of the vocal tract. The former contrasts more with the openness of the vocal tract found in the vowel series than does the latter. Jakobson thus constructed a hierarchy of phonemic contrasts which reflected a basic principle – the tendency towards utilization of maximum contrasts first – and which is a major determinant of the nature of the phonemic inventories of the individual languages of the world.

Jakobson then indicated that the same hierarchy that applies to the determination of the phonemic inventories of languages also is relevant to language acquisition and breakdown. The literature he cited supported the observation that those phonemes which are most common in the world's languages are those which are first acquired, and those which are rare are late acquisitions. Children also show an obligatory sequence of mastery of the phonemes of a language, never acquiring one of the more complex phonemes until the more basic ones are attained. The aphasic shows the same sensitivity to this hierarchy of phonemic contrasts, only in reverse. Patients lose the ability to produce more complex phonemes before simpler ones and, when their language returns, show the same sequence of regaining phonemes as children do in their initial mastery of the phonemic inventory.

Jakobson restricted his hypothesis regarding the inverse relationship between aphasic disorders of language and the stages of language acquisition to the phonemic inventory, and recent work has shown that it does not apply, at least in a straightforward manner, to other aspects of language (Caramazza and Zurif 1978). In the domain of phonemic inventories, however, the analysis seems to be valid, and has been taken to reflect the organization and development of these linguistic units in the brain. The nature of the ontogenetic sequence of phoneme acquisition is in keeping with Jackson's view that more complex functions reflect modulation of earlier psychological structures. In aphasia, simple structures are retained. The neurological bases for these structures are still unknown. Although Jakobson's analysis gives specific content to the notion of the hierarchical organization of linguistic units in this domain, it does not advance our knowledge of the anatomical basis for these hierarchical features of language.

A model which conforms to this general approach but which does draw heavily from neuroanatomical analyses, and which makes specific suggestions regarding the neuroanatomy of aspects of language processing, is Jason Brown's (1980; 1982) "microgenetic" theory of language–brain relationships. Because it is partly based on the evolution of neurological structures and the development of language, Brown's theory has an affinity with Jackson's basic conceptual approach, though, as we shall see, the exact

97

features of the language-processing sequence which Brown specifies form a "hierarchy" of a rather different sort from the types exemplified in the work of either Jackson or Jakobson.

Brown views language as a system which consists of a number of levels of symbols. The tasks of language use, such as speaking and comprehension, involve realizing these levels in sequential order. Brown theorizes that the realization of these levels of language structure is accomplished in particular areas of the brain. These include both cortical and subcortical structures. The subcortical structures involved are symmetrically located near the midline of the brain. Brown views the early stages of language production as involving these more primitive areas, and later stages of language production as accomplished by more advanced cortical structures. The neural structures involved in these processes constitute a sequence, both phylogenetically and ontogenetically. The production or comprehension of an utterance is accomplished by neuroanatomical structures which are activated in a sequence determined by their appearance in evolution and in individual development. In addition, the language structures are activated in a sequence from more primitive to more complex. Brown calls this process "microgenetic", to indicate that the ontogenetically and phylogenetically determined sequence of neural activation occurs extremely rapidly – in "micro"-time.

Brown (1980) suggests that there are two major sequences in speech production, an "anterior" and "posterior" sequence, illustrated in Figures 7-1 and 7-2. In the anterior pathway, Brown identifies four levels of representation: the "motor envelope", the differentiation of the speech act from associated behavior, the differentiation of global syntactic units, and the phonological realization of the utterance. He suggests that the motor envelope is determined bilaterally in the limbic cortex; differentiation of the speech act is determined in the limbic cortex or the generalized neocortex of the dominant hemisphere; the differentiation of the syntactic units is carried out in the dominant generalized or focal neocortex; and phonological realization is added in the focal neocortex.

Brown provides support for his theory through the method of clinical–pathological correlations. He claims that akinetic mutism, transcortical motor aphasia, agrammatism, and Broca's aphasia correspond to disturbances of these four levels of language function, and result from lesions in the cerebral areas indicated above.

Akinetic mutism involves almost total absence of language. The patient makes little or no attempt to speak. This symptom occurs in the context of a global inertia. The patient with this symptom is not paralyzed, but shows little spontaneous motor activity. Brown reports that the patients do not cry

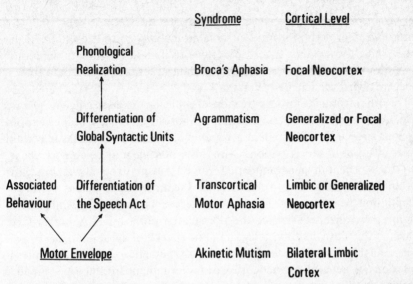

	Syndrome	Cortical Level
Phonological Realization	Broca's Aphasia	Focal Neocortex
Differentiation of Global Syntactic Units	Agrammatism	Generalized or Focal Neocortex
Differentiation of the Speech Act	Transcortical Motor Aphasia	Limbic or Generalized Neocortex
Motor Envelope	Akinetic Mutism	Bilateral Limbic Cortex

Figure 7-1. Brown's hierarchical model of the anterior speech production system, showing the stages of normal processing, the syndromes resulting from impairments at each level, and the associated neural substrate.
(*Source:* Brown 1980: 292)

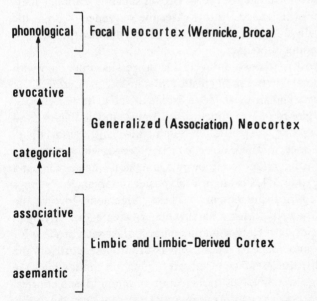

Figure 7-2. Brown's hierarchical model of the posterior speech production system, showing the stages of processing and associated neural substrate
(*Source:* Brown 1980: 295)

99

out in response to pain or attempt to communicate by gesture. The syndrome clearly goes beyond an isolated inability to utilize the linguistic code, and Brown claims that it represents an inability to initiate the motor system in any activity. It results from bilateral lesions deep in the frontal lobe, involving the cingulate cortex.

The other frontal disorders are more specifically linked to language *per se*. Transcortical motor aphasia consists of mutism or greatly reduced spontaneous speech, but the patient is capable of linguistic responses in certain situations. For instance, patients with this syndrome may be able to repeat. They may repeat in an agrammatic form, or they may repeat well but show agrammatic writing. Brown characterizes the functional deficit as a disorder of initiating the speech act. The responsible lesion is in the deep white matter and/or generalized cortex of the dominant frontal lobe. A higher-level deficit is the slow, halting, telegrammatic speech of agrammatism. Brown considers this a disturbance of generation of syntactic units, and attributes it to lesions of generalized neocortex of the dominant frontal lobe. Finally, Brown identifies a group of phonemic articulatory disorders which occur with lesions of Broca's area itself. Brown suggests that each of these disorders is a direct reflection of the patient's residual language capacity, resulting from the activity of intact areas of the brain.

Turning to the posterior language areas, Brown suggests a similar hierarchical organization of language. In this case, the sequence of linguistic structures involves individual lexical items (words) and the incorporation of lexical items into ongoing discourse.

At the first and most fundamental level, this process is concerned with establishing a relationship between linguistic and non-linguistic stimuli. At this stage both cognitive and affective factors are involved in the selection of lexical items. This operation is a function of limbic and limbic-derived cortex, and lesions in this level produce "asemantic" and "associative" verbal paraphasias in speech. These errors consist of words which have very remote connections with a target word, or no connection whatsoever. At a later stage of specification of lexical items, the posterior language system is responsible for "categorical judgements". These judgements involve the selection of particular words within a narrow linguistic category. Errors at this level consist of closely related semantic paraphasias, such as *table* for *chair*. They result from damage to generalized association neocortex in the posterior area. Finally, the last stage of speech production contingent upon the posterior language area involves the selection of phonological entities. This depends upon the focal neocortex of Wernicke's area. Damage to this area will produce disorders in the phonological nature of words, manifest in phonemic paraphasias.

Brown suggests that lesions of the deeper levels of the posterior system produce disorders that are both aphasias and general behavioral disturbances, such as Wernicke's or Korsakoff's encephalopathy. Korsakoff's encephalopathy is a severe amnestic syndrome which results from bilateral limbic lesions. One manifestation of this syndrome is confabulation, the substitution of invented memories for actual ones, which Brown suggests bears an important relationship to asemantic jargon. He argues that asemantic jargon can be seen as a sub-type of confabulation. These symptoms are not purely linguistic, just as those resulting from bilateral anterior limbic lesions are not purely linguistic. The classical posterior aphasic symptomatology, due to lesions in Wernicke's area and surrounding cortex, can be seen as a combination of phonemic and semantic errors, and reflects purely linguistic structures. Thus both the anterior and posterior language systems begin with bilateral limbic structures mediating the connection between language and non-linguistic functions, and terminate with neocortex producing formal aspects of the linguistic code. In perception and comprehension, the sequence is reversed.

Brown's model incorporates the concept that the neural levels involved in language reflect the ontogenesis of the nervous system. The evidence for this is also derived from pathological material. Young children characteristically develop mutism after left frontal lesions, and this symptom can progress to agrammatism. In older children nearing puberty, the same lesion can produce a phonemic and articulatory impairment in the context of an agrammatic aphasia. In the adult, comparatively deeper lesions are necessary to produce mutism, and superficial lesions only produce agrammatism and articulatory disturbances. The progression in symptomatology can be summarized by saying that at the earliest ontogenetic stages a focal cortical lesion produces a syndrome which corresponds to a deeper lesion in the adult. Brown suggests that, as the neuraxis develops, the neural basis for the sequence of steps in speech production matures. Deeper, more primitive neural structures accomplish the more basic earlier stages of language processing, and more advanced areas of cortex superimpose additional linguistic features upon this basic structure. Thus, in his view, there are important links between the ontogenetic development of the brain, the ontogenetic sequence of mastery of language structures, the normal sequence of processing language in on-line psycholinguistic tasks, and the syndromes of language breakdown.

Brown's model may be considered one of the "process" models we shall discuss in Chapter 9, but for the present we shall emphasize its conceptual affinity with the type of hierarchical model Jackson envisaged. It makes specific anatomical statements regarding the levels of the nervous system responsible for increasingly differentiated aspects of language processing. Though the operations carried out by each of these levels is not an entire function, as in Jackson's framework, there is a clear sense in Brown's theories that the earlier operations in the production of an utterance are more primitive and less specifically linguistic than the later operations. This is close to Jackson's notion that high levels of the nervous system superimpose more complex functions upon simpler ones.

Brown claims that his theory is incompatible with connectionist models, but it is not clear that this is so. Indeed, if we restrict our attention to the focal areas of cortex involved in language and to the analyses of the functions they carry out, it would seem that the two models are very similar, if not identical. If so, Brown's model can be viewed as an extension, rather than a refutation, of the connectionist theories. It is hard to compare the analysis of the functions carried out by a particular brain structure from model to model, and from author to author. In large part, this is due to each author's individual use of terms referring to linguistic structures and psycholinguistic operations. These terms are often not fully defined, but rather used in intuitive ways. This is a problem which we find in Brown's model. He uses terms, such as "categorical judgements", which are difficult to compare with the description of language functions in other theories. This makes it hard to say to what extent Brown agrees with other models, and it also makes it hard to test his model.

Brown's model may also not be as "hierarchical" as he claims. When one considers it in more detail, the sequence of linguistic structures and psycholinguistic processes Brown describes is not obviously one which moves from less to more complex levels. The "motor envelope" of a speech act, for instance, if taken to refer to the intonation contour of an utterance, is a complex and richly defined structure. It is not clear that it is less complex than syntactic or phonological structures (which are also hard to compare with respect to relative complexity). There is an interaction of these two problems. Since Brown is not specific about the features of language structure he has in mind when he uses terms such as "the motor envelope for an utterance", it is impossible to compare the complexity of different structures. This makes it difficult to assess the claim that the model is "hierarchical", in the "microgenetic" sense, as well as the claim that it differs from, rather than simply extends, the classical connectionist theories. The model is also hard to interpret anatomically. Brown seems to be saying that a function like initiation of speech (or of movement in general) is at first carried out by focal neocortex, and becomes the responsibility of deeper cortex bilaterally as the child matures. This is a counter-intuitive claim, which needs considerable supporting evidence for us to accept.

These problems should not obscure the new claims of this particular theory, or detract from the importance of hierarchical models in general. The fact that we need additional precision of the neurological analysis in work such as that of Jackson and Jakobson, or of the linguistic analysis in that of Brown, is testimony to the degree to which these models address important questions in terms which suggest answers, even if they do not provide them in completely convincing form. These models incorporate psychological factors, such as the automaticity of an utterance and the motivational state of a patient, and neural elements, such as limbic structures, which the connectionist models did not take into account, and which are obviously important to the totality of linguistic functioning.

In summary, the models we have reviewed here all make use of the notion of hierarchical organization in language and in the nervous system. Hierarchies are claimed to be present in the organization of linguistic systems (Jakobson), the stages of processing language in speaking and comprehension (Brown), and the structure of the central nervous system (Jackson, Brown). Language disorders affect these hierarchical organizational features. The origin of hierarchical structure may be in the evolution and developmental history of the nervous system.

The models we have reviewed here relate language and the brain on the basis of analyses of language disorders, but consider rather different aspects of these disorders than did the models we considered earlier. An important issue, not yet decided, is whether the two types of models are incompatible, or whether they are valid in different domains of language–brain relationships. We have suggested that answering this question requires that the terms of analysis used in both types of theories be made more precise, in order for the issue to be sharpened to the point that evidence can be brought to bear one way or the other.

The hierarchical models reviewed here are one of the group of theories which has been called "holist", a term which reflects the reluctance of the workers who adopt these models to accept the concept of cortical centers for components of a language faculty found in the connectionist approach. The term also has a positive connotation: it suggests the hypothesis that unitary or integrated psychological and/or neural processes underlie both normal and abnormal language function. We shall now turn to theories which incorporate this view. In Chapter 8 we discuss models which claim that all aphasic disturbances can be considered to result from a single disturbance of psychological function; and in Chapter 9 we examine theories which emphasize the integration of many functional components in every psycholinguistic task.

II *Clinical aphasiology and neurolinguistics*

SUGGESTIONS FOR FURTHER READING

Brown, J. (1982). Hierarchy and evolution in neurolinguistics. In M. A. Arbib, D. Caplan, and J. C. Marshall (eds.), *Neural Models of Language Processes*. Academic Press, New York.

Goldstein, K. (1948). *Language and Language Disorders*. Grune and Stratton, New York.

Jackson, J. H. (1874). On the nature of the duality of the brain. Reprinted in J. Taylor (ed.), *Selected Writings of John Hughlings Jackson*. Basic Books, New York, 1958.

(1878). On affections of speech from disease of the brain. *Brain* 1, 304–30; 2, 203–22; 3, 323–56.

Jakobson, R. (1941). *Kindersprache, Aphasie und Allgemeine Lautgesetze*, Universitets Arsskrift, Uppsala. Translated as *Child Language, Aphasia and Phonological Universals*. Mouton, The Hague, 1968.

8

Global models

In this chapter we shall review the work of two men, Pierre Marie (1906*a*; *b*) and Kurt Goldstein (1948), who developed models of aphasia in which a disturbance of a single functional capacity was the predominant cause of all of the signs and types of aphasia. Both investigators accepted the existence of several aphasic syndromes; neither claimed that a sole factor was adequate to describe all the various manifestations of aphasia. Despite this, their major contributions lie in the emphasis each gave to a single factor in describing and accounting for behavior, and in their attempts to explain the apparent variety of aphasic symptoms as the effect of a disturbance of the single factor they identified in difficult circumstances. In Marie's case, this attempt took the form of an anatomical analysis, while Goldstein's account was mainly psychological.

In his first writings, which were widely publicized and highly controversial, Marie (1906*a*) argued that the classification of aphasics into different clinical sub-types was an error. He argued that there was only one true aphasia, in which comprehension of language was disturbed as part of a deficit in general intelligence. This aphasia was Wernicke's aphasia, and it occurred after a lesion in the posterior areas of the brain, particularly the temporo-parietal junction of the dominant hemisphere.

Marie acknowledged that not all aphasic patients manifest an obvious disorder of speech comprehension. He claimed that the disorder of comprehension in aphasia could be relatively mild and might only be manifested through complex tests. He suggested that an adequate test was to ask patients to carry out three-part commands. He suggested that an appropriate set of commands for testing mild aphasics would be: "Of the three pieces of paper that I have put before you, take the largest and crumple it into a ball, put the smallest in your pocket, and take the middle one and fasten it to the window." He reported that in his own personal examination of over 100 consecutive aphasics, many with the syndrome associated with anterior lesions, not one had been able to carry out such complex commands properly. He considered that the ability to carry out three-step commands required "general intelligence", which was disturbed in "true" aphasia.

Marie (1908) later was to define this intellectual capacity more precisely as one which involved both language and "ideas learned in a didactic fashion" ("certaines idées apprises de façon didactique").

Marie argued that the difference in spontaneous speech which distinguished anterior and posterior aphasics was due not to the involvement of a cortical center for the planning of speech, but to a disturbance of the motor apparatus itself. Marie argued that, though not all anterior aphasics had a complete paralysis of the facial muscles or those of swallowing, these muscles were always affected to some extent. Minor degrees of impairment of the musculature of the vocal tract would be expected to cause problems only in the most complex movements made by this musculature; namely, those involved in speech. It would therefore be possible to have an anterior aphasia due to a disturbance of motor mechanisms when the disorder affected only language production, because of the relative complexity of the movements involved in producing language.

Marie argued that the portion of anterior lesions which caused disorders of language was subcortical, not cortical at all. He suggested that in cases of "true" aphasia with a speech output such as that seen in Broca's aphasia there was always a posterior lesion, which caused the comprehension disturbance he could demonstrate. The effortful, sparse output was due to an anterior extension of the lesion into the deep white matter of the left hemisphere near the central nuclei, particularly the lenticular nucleus (see Figure 8-1). Descending motor fibers in this area were injured by this extension of the lesion, causing the speech disorder typical of anterior lesions. Marie called this disorder an "anarthria". He named the area where a lesion caused anarthria the "lenticular zone" or "quadrilateral space".

In a dramatic presentation of evidence in favor of his views, Marie re-examined the brains of two of the patients originally described by Broca in the first description of the syndrome of Broca's aphasia. Marie's neuropathological findings differed from those of Broca. In the case of Lebourgne, Broca's first and most famous patient, the lesion included the anterior portion of the left cerebral hemisphere but also extended as far back as the supramarginal gyrus in the parietal lobe. It also extended deeply into the white matter of the hemisphere. It therefore confirmed Marie's argument that cases of Broca's aphasia had posterior lesions, and dramatically discredited the original basis upon which this syndrome was thought to arise from anterior lesions alone. (We should note, eighty years later, that this demonstration is less convincing than it seemed to be in 1906. In Chapter 3, we saw that Broca did appreciate the posterior extent of the lesion in this case, and based his theory on the correlation of the severity of different parts of the lesion with stages in the patient's deficits.) In Broca's second case,

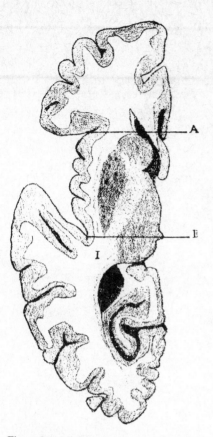

Figure 8-1. Marie's diagram of the quadrilateral space. This space involves the white matter between lines A and B on the diagram. Marie claimed that lesions in this area produced motor speech disturbances.
(*Source:* Moutier 1908: 133)

Marie claimed that the brain showed no focal lesion at all, only the diffuse atrophy seen in senile degeneration.

Marie's views were of importance largely because of the relationship of the syndromes he described to the vascular anatomy of the brain. Marie's principal neuranatomical contribution to the study of the aphasias is the description of the vascular supply to the white matter of the language zones, and the description of how vascular lesions produced the varieties of aphasia seen in the clinic. Marie (1906*a*) argued that there was considerable variation in the vascular territory supplied by the middle cerebral artery and its branches. The middle cerebral artery ordinarily divides into two main trunks, its superior and inferior divisions. The superior division supplies the frontal and parietal perisylvian areas (the frontal and parietal opercula), and

107

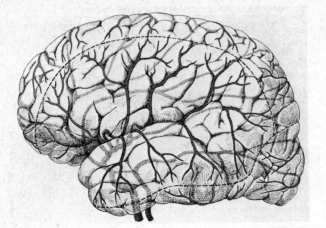

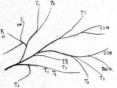

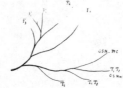

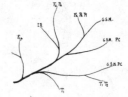

I. — Trajet rétrograde de l'artère pour le pied de F₃.

II. — Tronc commun pour Fa et F₃ (branches multiples).

III. — Artère de F₃, première collatérale. Hém. Dr.

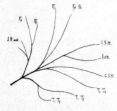

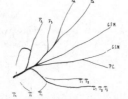

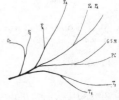

IV. — Division précoce de la sylvienne (éventail). Hém. G. (même cerveau que III).

V. — Trifurcation. Tronc commun au pôle temporal et à F₃.

VI. — Eventail : disposition moins accusée que sur la fig. IV.

Figure 8-2. The vascular anatomy of the perisylvian space. The upper diagram shows the cortex supplied by the middle cerebral artery within the dashed line. Arteries lying beneath the surface of the brain are illustrated in shaded form. The lower diagram represents variations in the branching of middle cerebral artery commonly seen in humans.
(*Sources:* Geschwind 1979: 112; Moutier 1908: 133)

the inferior division supplies the supramarginal and angular gyri as well as the superior temporal area. (This vascular arrangement is shown in Figure 8-2.) It would therefore ordinarily be the case that Wernicke's aphasia, the "true" aphasia according to Marie, would result from an occlusion affecting the inferior division of the middle cerebral artery. In some cases, the blood supply of the deep white matter of the hemisphere comes from structures supplied by branches of the posterior or inferior division of the middle cerebral artery. This white matter includes motor fibers which arise in the motor strip (pre-central gyrus) and the basal ganglia (including the lenticular nucleus). In such cases, occlusion of the inferior division of the middle cerebral artery would lead to infarction both of Wernicke's area and the more anterior deep white matter of Marie's "quadrilateral", leading to the syndrome of a Broca's aphasia.

Thus, Marie argued that the fundamental observations regarding aphasic patients that supported the connectionist models were incorrect. If the patients were examined appropriately, he argued that they would all manifest a deficit in comprehension of speech, which he considered to be a part of a general difficulty with intellectual function. The differences in spoken language were due to the involvement of motor fibers and deep gray-matter nuclei in the quadrilateral space. Because of individual differences in the areas supplied by the middle cerebral artery, some aphasias were "complicated" by anarthria; these were what had been called "Broca's aphasia". He coined a slogan which is well known in clinical aphasiology: "There is only one aphasia: Broca's aphasia is Wernicke's aphasia plus anarthria."

The most detailed presentation of evidence in favor of Marie's views was not the work of Marie at all, but of his student, François Moutier (1908), whose medical thesis constitutes one of the most extensive reviews of an aphasic syndrome that has ever been published. The bibliography alone takes up sixty-seven printed pages, and lists virtually every publication on aphasia up to 1908. Moutier reports on 387 cases from the literature as well as forty-four of his own, of which twenty-four were studied both clinically and with autopsies. The autopsy work alone was an enormous undertaking, as each autopsy included serial microscopic examination of the brain. This technique of post mortem examination had been perfected by the Dejerines (1901). It consisted of "fixing" the entire brain in a solution designed to harden it and then cutting microscopically thin sections for staining and examination. In some cases, up to 2,000 slices were cut through a hemisphere. The technique produced much greater detail regarding the extent of a lesion than any previous method of examination.

Moutier's cases were all presented to support Marie's theory. Of the autopsied cases, seven were said to show a Broca's aphasia without a lesion in the third frontal convolution; twelve were analyzed as having lesions in Broca's area without Broca's aphasia; and five were presented as cases of Broca's aphasia with a lesion in the lenticular nucleus or quadrilateral space. The thesis constituted strong support for Marie's position.

(An interesting note regarding the academic politics of neurolinguistics is that Moutier's thesis spelled the end of his career as a neurologist and aphasiologist. Apparently threatened by his student's abilities and accomplishments, Marie, whose personality, at least in the early stages of his career, seems to be have been marked by strong traits of ambition and competitiveness, blocked Moutier's further advance in academic circles. Moutier took up gastroenterology, substituting the study of "the folds of the intestine" for that of those of the brain, and became the leading academic gastroenterologist in France, pioneering the use of the gastroscope. This story is told by Lecours and Joanette (1984).)

Marie's criticism of connectionism and his unitary theory of aphasia were presented with such panache that they could not fail to attract attention. Marie (1906*a*) entitled his first major paper on the subject "The left third frontal convolution plays no special role in the faculty of language", a broadside attack on the most deeply held "truth" of aphasiology and neurolinguistics – a "truth" which, in France, was almost a symbol of French contributions to neuropsychology. He followed this article with another (Marie 1906*b*) in which he implied that Broca's theory was accepted more because of the academic political milieu in which it was presented than because of any intrinsic scientific merit. Bouillaud's importance in French neurology was seen as the critical factor in establishing the importance of Broca's studies, which by and large agreed with Bouillaud's hypothesis about language and the frontal lobes.

These challenges could not go unanswered, and a sharp controversy arose between Marie and Jules Dejerine, whose work on alexia-without-agraphia we have reviewed in Chapter 5. The controversy came to its climax in three "discussions" on aphasia sponsored in the summer of 1908 by the French neurology society (Klippel 1908). The discussions were wide-ranging, and covered questions of clinical description, pathological anatomy, and pathophysiology. The two protagonists and their students and collaborators disagreed on almost every important point.

The first meeting dealt with clinical matters, especially the clinical syndrome of Broca's aphasia. Both protagonists restated their views. Dejerine maintained that Broca's aphasics had only a mild degree of verbal deafness, and that their verbal blindness was found not in relation to words and short phrases but in relation to longer structures, and thus could be seen as a problem in association, not a true alexia. Marie argued that Broca's aphasics differed from Wernicke's aphasics only in degree, and not in kind, with respect to their receptive language impairments. On the output side, Dejerine drew a distinction between dysarthria and motor aphasia: in the former, patients mispronounced all words but retained their usual inventory of words, while in the latter they pronounced words well but utilized a reduced stock of words. The former was the result of paralytic, spastic, and ataxic disturbances of the organs of speech, while the latter resulted from a psychological impairment affecting the representation of words. For Marie, these distinctions were not clear-cut; many patients had both a reduction in the number of words they used and an element of mispronunciation. Marie maintained that only patients with disturbances of "internal language" were aphasic, and that such disturbances were similar in all forms of aphasia. The discussion ranged over cases and interpretations presented in the publications of both discussants, and several disciples (notably André Thomas) added important clarifications and hypotheses. Neither protagonist convinced the other, and the second meeting began with many clinical issues unsettled.

The second meeting dealt with questions regarding the anatomical basis of language and the pathological determinants of the aphasias. It is most memorable for the extraordinary discussion of the neuroanatomy of the anterior speech zone and of Marie's quadrilateral space presented by Augusta Klumpke Dejerine, Jules Dejerine's wife and collaborator. Mme Dejerine presented a series of microscopic sections of the normal brain which clearly showed that Broca's area – the pars opercularis and triangularis of the third frontal convolution – did not lie anterior to Marie's quadrilateral space, as Marie had maintained, but rather just lateral to it. Moreover, she demonstrated that the white-matter fibers that entered and exited from Broca's area passed through the antero-superolateral portion of the quadrilateral space. She argued, on this basis, that subcortical lesions which caused anarthria were those that affected just this portion of the quadrilateral space, and that the resulting dysarthria was related to the function of Broca's area in exactly the same way as the hemiplegia occasioned by a lesion in the descending motor tract of the internal capsule was related to the function of the cells of origin of the motor tract in the precentral gyrus. This argument accounted for the existence of subcortical dysarthria without denying the importance of Broca's area in the production of speech. Marie attempted to redefine the area he had described previously, but was unable to identify clearly a subcortical zone which was free of fibers to and from Broca's area, in which lesions caused anarthria. The remainder of the second session was taken up with additional case reports, including what must have been an interesting confrontation regarding Lelong's brain (Broca's second case). The brain was produced and examined. Dejerine saw a lesion in the third frontal convolution, while

Moutier, Marie's representative, saw "only a few scratches". Neither Marie nor Dejerine was willing to have the brain cut then and there, and the question remained unsettled.

There is little doubt that Marie's claim that all true language disorders are explicable as abnormalities in general intelligence and are of the same sort, and that they are coupled to varying degrees with motor disturbances affecting only speech production, is incorrect. Marie failed to characterize adequately the nature of the general intellectual functions he thought were disordered in language, and subsequent work has shown that the comprehension disorders in various aphasias differ qualitatively, not just quantitatively (see Chapters 12–16). Moreover, recent work describes many aphasic comprehension and production abnormalities as the result of disorders of a purely linguistic system, not as a by-product of a disorder of intelligence or motor functions. Marie's early paper had considerable impact, despite these problems, and despite the fact that his later work seems to reflect a change in stance. His work served to introduce the question of the extent to which intellectual and sensory–motor disorders are allied to, if not responsible for, aphasic symptoms. This subject has been debated and investigated continuously since his work, and answers are not yet clearly forthcoming. Head (1926) referred to Marie as an "iconoclast", who cast serious doubt on the connectionist taxonomies and descriptions of aphasia. It is probably true that, after Marie, there was increased emphasis on descriptions of aphasic syndromes in greater detail. The existence of a comprehension deficit in Broca's aphasia, for instance, had been noticed but largely ignored in the construction of neurolinguistic theories prior to Marie. This and other similar facts could no longer be so comfortably brushed aside after 1906.

Marie's failure convincingly to attribute all aphasic symptoms to a disorder of general intelligence did not settle the issue of whether some unitary explanation of the aphasias was possible. Another important attempt to approach aphasic disorders by considering the variety of aphasic symptoms as the result of a single psychological dysfunction which affected a variety of behaviors was Goldstein's (1948) emphasis on the centrality of patients' inability to assume what he called the "abstract attitude" in explaining aphasic disorders. As with Marie, Goldstein's contribution to aphasiology goes beyond this thesis, and, unlike Marie, he never claimed that a single disorder accounted for all the manifestations of aphasia. We are focussing on this one aspect of Goldstein's work because it is perhaps his most important theoretical contribution, one which enriched the approach to aphasia and to the factors which should be taken into account in an adequate neurolinguistic theory.

Goldstein's principal volume on aphasia, *Language and Language Disturbances*, published in 1948, reflects a great deal of his thought and work. Goldstein was aware of contemporary developments in linguistics, psychology, and neuropsychology, which he tried to integrate into his descriptions and explanations of aphasia. For instance, he dealt with Jakobson's theory of phonemic organization and the breakdown of phonemic inventories, which we have reviewed in Chapter 7. Goldstein basically accepted Jakobson's analysis, and the resulting hierarchical approach to neurolinguistic modeling. He discussed the concept of "inner speech", a self-regulatory use of language which emerges at a particular stage of development, and which was studied by Vygotsky (1939). He postulated that a disturbance of inner speech was the basis for a form of aphasia which he termed "central" aphasia and which closely corresponds to the "conduction" aphasia of the connectionist models. But of all the psychological theories which influenced Goldstein, perhaps the most important influence was gestalt psychology.

Put in highly simplified terms, gestalt psychology emphasized two features of psychological functioning: the contribution the organism made itself to the activities of perception, cognition, memory, and motor planning; and the integrated nature of the organism's psychological states. Gestalt psychologists concentrated on aspects of psychological function such as the subjective reversal of the three-dimensional orientation of line drawings such as the Necker cube and the occurrence of perceptual illusions (Figure 8-3). These features of perception cannot be a result of changes in the visual stimulus, which remains constant, and therefore must reflect the activity of the perceptual mechanisms in an individual.

Goldstein's principal application of gestalt concepts was in the area of the integration of psychological states achieved by a subject. He referred to this approach as the "organismic view" of psychology and psychopathology, and he believed that integration of sensory experience, cognitive and emotional states, motivational drives, and final motor actions characterized the patient with a lesion in the nervous system as well as the normal individual:

According to the general trend of organismic behavior, the aphasic patient tries to achieve a condition which allows him to react as well as possible to the tasks arising from the environment. If he is successful in this endeavor, at least to such a degree that he can fulfill those performances which are "essential" to his nature, he will be in a new order, will avoid catastrophic occurrences, and be able to use his remaining capacities. From this point of view, it follows that *every individual speech-performance is understandable only from the aspect of its relation to the function of the total organism in its endeavor to realize itself as much as possible in the given situation.* (Goldstein 1948: 21; italics Goldstein's)

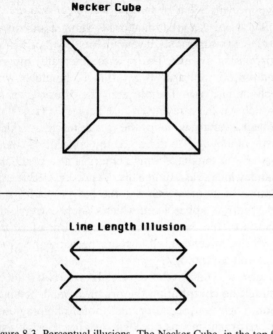

Figure 8-3. Perceptual illusions. The Necker Cube, in the top figure, can be seen as pointing either towards or away from the viewer. In the bottom figure, the three lines are in fact of equal length, but the middle line appears longer than the others because of the direction of the arrows at either end.

Goldstein identified four basic ways in which neurological disease could produce functional impairments. The first consisted of disorders due to damage to an area of the brain, which produced what Goldstein called "direct symptoms", the equivalent, in his view, of Jackson's "negative symptoms". Goldstein identified six effects of lesions upon the brain, three of which are (presumably) physiological and three psychological. The physiological effects are a rise in the threshold for neuronal excitation, abnormal lability of the threshold for neuronal excitation, and an abnormal duration and/or spread of neuronal excitation. The psychological disturbances include increased sensitivity of behavior to external stimuli, difficulty in maintaining sharp "figure–ground" boundaries, and, most important, impairment in adoption of the "abstract attitude". Since Goldstein considered the ability to assume this "abstract attitude" is crucial in maintaining normal behavior, and because its disturbance after lesions of the brain is so important a determinant of aphasic symptoms, we shall consider this feature in more detail after reviewing the other mechanisms of functional impairment Goldstein identified.

The second mechanism Goldstein identified is the separation of an undamaged area from a damaged one. Pathological behavior results from the activity of the isolated undamaged area freed from the constraints usually imposed by the damaged one. Goldstein did not actually provide neurological evidence showing that symptoms result from disinhibition in this fashion, but assumed this was so. These symptoms are one part of Jackson's "positive effects" of a lesion, and examples include increased tendon reflexes (in the motor system), and logorrhea (in the language system).

The third pathogenetic mechanism is the influence a damaged area of brain can have upon undamaged neural tissue. This mechanism was termed "diaschisis" in the work of von Monakow (1914), who developed this concept most fully. Goldstein terms the resulting symptoms "indirect", and cites as an example the improvement which is sometimes seen in functional abilities after removal of frontal-lobe scars. He notes that identifying such effects may have important therapeutic implications: in cases where damaged tissue is inhibiting the function of other areas of the brain, removal of the damaged tissue, or its disconnection from the remaining areas of the brain, might be of therapeutic value. Obviously, this would not be true of the "negative symptoms" due to the second type of mechanism discussed above, and correctly distinguishing these two pathogenetic conditions is important.

Finally, Goldstein describes a pathological mechanism which is in keeping with his gestalt approach: the avoidance of "catastrophe" by the integrated patient. "Catastrophes" are performance failures marked by disorder, disharmony, and anxiety, which the patient seeks to avoid. To do this, the patient avoids a variety of tasks which he cannot perform correctly, and adopts "protective mechanisms" which permit him to function in a circumscribed world in which he will not be threatened by "catastrophic" failures. Thus, he shows excessive orderliness, avoidance of new situations, and a requirement for highly structured situations before he will undertake a task. The integration achieved by the patient's psychology is shown in his lack of awareness of his restricted world and reduced number of undertakings. Goldstein suggests that the desire to avoid catastrophic situations accounts for some of the variability in performance which patients manifest, and which had been emphasized by Head. A difference in the ability of a patient to write on two occasions, for instance, may be due to the fact that the paper offered him was lined on one occasion and unlined on a second. In the first case, the lines offer enough structure to enable him to initiate the act of writing, while in the second instance he may not be able to decide where to begin, and thus may not try to write at all.

115

The particular integrative capacity of a neurologically and psychologically normal person which is most critical for the performance of the highest types of intellectual function, and whose loss is most responsible for the production of language (and other) disturbances, is the ability to assume what Goldstein called the "abstract attitude". Goldstein describes the abstract attitude in terms which cannot be adequately paraphrased:

We can distinguish normally two different kinds of attitudes which we call the concrete and the abstract. In the concrete attitude we are given over passively and bound to the immediate experience of unique objects or situations. Our thinking and acting are determined by the immediate claims made by the particular aspect of the object or situation. For instance, we act concretely when we enter a room in darkness and push the button for light. If, however, we desist from pushing the button, reflecting that by pushing the button we might awaken someone asleep in the room, then we are acting abstractly. We transcend the immediately given specific aspect of sense impressions; we detach ourselves from the latter and consider the situation from a conceptual point of view and react accordingly. Our actions are determined not so much by the objects before us as by the way we think about them; the individual thing becomes a mere accidental example or representative of a "category". Therefore, we also call this attitude the categorical or conceptual attitude. The abstract attitude is basic for the following potentialities:
1. Assuming a mental set voluntarily, taking initiative, even beginning a performance on demand.
2. Shifting voluntarily from one aspect of a situation to another, making a choice.
3. Keeping in mind simultaneously various aspects of a situation; reacting to two stimuli which do not belong intrinsically together.
4. Grasping the essentials of a given whole, breaking up a given whole into parts, isolating them voluntarily, and combining them to wholes.
5. Abstracting common properties, planning ahead ideationally, assuming an attitude toward the "merely possible", and thinking or performing symbolically.
6. Detaching the ego from the outer world. (Goldstein 1948: 6)

Given this framework for viewing the possible consequences of a brain lesion, Goldstein attempts to describe how the various symptoms and syndromes of aphasia occur. He does this largely by applying the concept of an impairment in abstract attitude to a function involving language or to a distinction in groups of language elements. Time after time, he ascribes the loss or quantitative or qualitative impairment of language performance to the inability of a patient to adopt the abstract attitude vis-à-vis a linguistic structure or its use. This concept is applied to a large number of phenomena, including (but not restricted to) the following: the pattern of dissolution of the phonemic inventory described by Jakobson (voiced vowels and consonants require more "voluntary attention" than voiceless segments, and thus require the abstract attitude and can be lost first (Goldstein 1948: 42)); naming disorders (61); the intellectual disorders which accompany aphasia (115); and selective impairment in using one class of vocabulary elements – the "little words", or "grammatical words". This last case is worth noting, not because it differs significantly from Goldstein's other analyses, but because the issue of differential availability of the two vocabulary classes discussed by Goldstein will recur in modern work on agrammatism (Chapter 15), and a contrast of the two analyses is revealing in a number of ways.

Goldstein's work is best known for its reliance upon this gestalt framework – in particular, for his insistence upon assessing the "abstract attitude" as part of clinical psychological diagnosis. Goldstein's conception of this functional capacity was a complex and rich one, and he sought to ascribe a host of aphasic symptoms to its loss. However, Goldstein fails to be clear about how a breakdown of the ability to assume the abstract attitude can explain all the specific deficits he described in his patients. It seems almost contradictory that the loss of the abstract attitude can produce both anomia, affecting "content words", and agrammatism, affecting "function words". Further details of how this happens are necessary. One can find clear indications in Goldstein's work that he believed that, while breakdown of psychological and neurological function followed general principles and resulted from breakdown of this "global" intellectual capacity, it could occur in particular domains, each of which would require a separate description and explanation. As has been stressed by Geschwind (1964), this admission on Goldstein's part is clearly seen in his approach to localization of functions. Though he disputed the mechanisms of symptom creation, Goldstein agreed to a large extent with the correlation of symptoms and lesion sites which had been established in the earlier clinical literature.

Goldstein identified his approach as a continuation of the work of Jackson, Marie, and Head. His concepts of "de-differentiation" of neuropsychological function, of the achievement of integrated performances by a lesioned organism, and of the ubiquity of the effects of loss of a single capacity (the abstract attitude) have much in common with their work. Perhaps it is most appropriate to view Goldstein's approach as an attempt to identify how these general features of neuropsychological function affect normal and pathological behavior in specific areas of function, such as the retention of certain aspects of the phonemic inventory or of a certain portion of the vocabulary of a language.

In the work of both Marie and Goldstein, we find a concern for general psychological factors in the generation of aphasic symptoms. These factors are indisputably important in the causation of some of the abnormal performances seen in aphasia. However, it does not seem likely that disturbances of such a general nature can account for the specific nature of language breakdown, the co-occurrence of certain symptoms, or other aspects of aphasia. Moreover, the neural basis for these factors is unclear. Marie attributed "general intelligence" (defined in a particular way) to the dominant parietal–temporal area; Goldstein seemed to ascribe the ability to assume the "abstract attitude" to the integrated activity of a great deal of the brain, probably including the non-dominant as well as the dominant hemisphere. Whether such general functions exist at all is the subject of debate (Fodor 1982), and the neural basis for such functions is far from certain.

We shall now turn to models which incorporate some of the linguistic and psychological features of Goldstein's descriptions of aphasia, but which do not accept the view that these features are due to breakdown in general principles of psychological or neurological brain function. The process models we are about to review are a form of a return to earlier connectionist models, though they differ from the earlier models in several ways. They are the last of the "clinical" models we still consider. After reviewing these theories, we shall review all these clinical models briefly, and then turn to linguistic and psycholinguistic approaches.

SUGGESTIONS FOR FURTHER READING

Arbib, M., Caplan, D., and Marshall, J. C. (1982). Neurolinguistics in historical perspective. In M. A. Arbib, D. Caplan, and J. C. Marshall (eds.), *Neural Models of Language Processes*. Academic Press, New York.
Geschwind, N. (1964). The paradoxical position of Kurt Goldstein in the history of aphasia. *Cortex* 1, 214–24.

9

Process models

The models that we shall consider in this chapter have their roots in work that has already been discussed. They are closely related to connectionist models, and they take one step further the type of model of language–brain relationships that is found in the connectionist literature. The models to be considered in this chapter may be called "process models", because the fundamental insight which motivates the development of these models is the view that the usual functions of language – speech, comprehension, reading, writing – are processes which can be further sub-divided into constitutent parts. We have seen that this view was incorporated into the models of nineteenth-century connectionist aphasiologists (Chapter 4) and their twen-tieth-century successors (Chapter 5). Both Wernicke and Lichtheim, for instance, argued that, in the process of speaking, the auditory represen-tations of words were accessed in the temporal association areas and conveyed to the motor area for speech in the left frontal lobe. In other words, Wernicke and Lichtheim appreciated that there were different inputs into the final stages of motor planning of speech. The view that overt behavior is the result of the interaction and integration of various com-ponent processes was thus incorporated into connectionist models in a limited way. The limitations of the "processing" analyses in connectionist literature can be seen in the small number of operations mentioned in the models we discussed in Chapters 4 and 5, and in the fact that certain tasks, such as word recognition (carried out in Wernicke's area), have no internal components.

The models that we shall consider here extend the processing account of language use to all tasks. They consider all the activities which involve language to be the result of several identifiable processing components. This way of approaching the psychology of language involves a number of changes in the way aphasic symptoms are described, and in the nature of the psychological processes which are to be related to the brain. As in the other "psychological" models which we have been discussing in this section, process models are concerned with the qualitative nature of language breakdown. In Chapters 4 and 5 we saw that, although connectionist theories do make mention of the qualitative nature of language impairments seen in different aphasic syndromes, the basic theory of language representation in the brain depends not so much upon these qualitative differences between different types of impairment as upon a more or less quantitative comparison of relative impairments in different language tasks. In the process models, this emphasis upon the relative impairment of one or another of the usual functions of language is completely absent, and in its place there is a concern for the particular way in which language function is disturbed in various tasks.

A second feature of many of the process models, particularly that of A. R. Luria, which we shall be considering in greatest detail, is the expectation that when language is impaired, it will usually be impaired in a number of functions. This results from the view that the sub-components of language functioning are each involved in a variety of different tasks. The interactive nature of the "language system" will become clearer as we discuss the particular models involved.

The view of what psychological functions are to be related to the brain which emerges from the process models is one in which entire linguistic functions are not considered the "simple entities" which Wernicke thought they were. Rather, it is the functional sub-components of these entire language-related functions which are conceived of as elementary aspects of the psychology of language. It is these sub-components which are related to brain structures. As with the analysis of aphasic symptoms, this is not a totally new development. We have seen that even the earliest connectionist models postulated what can be thought of as sub-components of language function, such as the storage of the sound pattern of words, and related these components to the brain. But in the process models, this is the *only* type of psychological entity which is related to the brain. Psychological functions, such as "the faculty for articulate speech" or "the faculty for language comprehension", are seen as large complex functions, which are accomplished by the interaction of different brain regions, each of which is devoted to accomplishing some small sub-component of these larger, complex, psycholinguistic functions. We should finally note that the way the process models relate sub-components to the brain is through localization; each sub-component is carried out by a particular area of the brain.

We have already encountered one example of a process model in Brown's "microgenetic" theory of speech production in Chapter 7. Brown localizes sub-components of the process of speech production in various areas of the brain: the anterior speech zones are responsible for the stages of the "motor envelope", "the differentiation of the speech act", "the differentiation of global syntactic units", and "the phonological realization of the utterance";

the posterior language zone is responsible for the relationship between linguistic and non-linguistic stimuli, the selection of individual words, categorical judgement, and "selection of phonological entities". There is no unitary "faculty for articulate speech". Rather, this faculty is seen as a complex function built up by the operation of these two sequences of psychological and linguistic operations.

Perhaps the first, most comprehensive, and most influential neurolinguistic process model is that of the Russian neuropsychologist A. R Luria (1947; 1973). Luria's model is characterized by four features.

(1)   Like Lichtheim's (1885) model, Luria's model encompasses the entirety of the uses of language. It includes models of speech production, comprehension, reading, writing, repetition, naming, and the influence of language upon self-regulation and thinking.

(2)   It is entirely modular. None of the language functions just enumerated are considered to be entire psychological entities. Each is composed of sub-components. A particularly important feature of Luria's model is that the sub-components are frequently shared between different language tasks. Thus, for instance, the component which achieves phonemic analysis is involved in a large number of tasks. Disturbance of a sub-component thus leads to impairment in more than one task.

(3)   Sub-components of psycholinguistic processes are each located in a separate area of the brain. The accomplishment of an entire neuropsychological function is consequently the result of the co-ordinated activity of a large number of brain centers. Luria sees himself as proposing a model which incorporates the best features of both connectionism and "holist" approaches to neuropsychology. There are localized functional sub-components of language and other psychological abilities, but the entirety of a behavior is the result of a complicated interaction between brain regions.

(4)   In many cases the psycholinguistic function which is accomplished by a small area of the brain is related to a non-linguistic function which that area also accomplishes. This is most clearly seen in the case of the tertiary association areas in the parietal and frontal lobes, but it is also true of the functions of the secondary association areas adjacent to primary receptive and motor cortex. Luria envisages a connection between the particular psycholinguistic functions of an area of the brain and its non-linguistic functions; indeed, he sees them as essentially the same function applied to different psychological domains.

We now turn to an examination of Luria's model in some detail. We shall outline Luria's description of the processes of speech production, naming, and repetition. In each of these cases, we shall enumerate the psychological processes that he considers to be the relevant sub-units of these psycholinguistic functions, and the areas of the brain which he considers to be responsible for each of those psycholinguistic functions. Luria's model of speech production is depicted in Figure 9-1, along with the areas of the brain involved in each component part of this process.

121

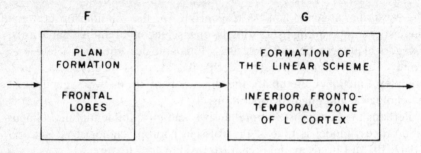

Figure 9-1. Luria's model of speech production
(*Source:* Arbib and Caplan 1979: 453)

Luria's description of the processes involved in speech production is relatively brief. The frontal lobes are essential for the creation of active intentions and the forming of plans in general. The first stage in speech production is the forming of plans for speech. Frontal lesions do not disturb the intrinsic aspects of language themselves, such as the phonemic, lexical, or logical–grammatical structures of language, but they do impair the ability of the patient to initiate speech and the regulatory role that speech plays in other human behavior (see below). The general "adynamia" of the frontal syndrome includes lack of spontaneity of speech; this is the most conspicuous language-related symptom seen with lesions of the medial frontal lobes. Luria (1973) reports that, in these patients, spontaneous speech is virtually absent, and responses to questions are passive, monotonous, and sometimes echolalic. The patient can easily respond to questions such as *Were you drinking tea?* with *Yes, I was drinking tea* because of the relative similarity between the question and the answer, but has far more difficulty with questions such as *Where have you been today?*, which requires a different knowledge base and linguistic structure for the question and the answer. In many cases these patients enter into conversations which are taking place between the examiner and other patients in the room. Luria goes so far as to say that sometimes the best way to interview these patients is to ask other patients in their vicinity the questions to which one wishes the patient to respond. This curious phenomenon is due to the role the frontal lobes play in attention: they are responsible for the selective focussing of attention upon appropriate stimuli, and with lesions in this area patients not only are unable to achieve states of arousal and attention which enable them to engage in normal conversation, but they also cannot inhibit their focussing of attention upon irrelevant stimuli.

When such lesions are more circumscribed, and involve the lower parts of the left frontal lobe just anterior to Broca's area, rather than being more medial, bilateral, and larger, they produce a particular syndrome which

Luria terms "frontal dynamic aphasia". The symptomatology of this syndrome is similar to that of the "transcortical motor aphasia" which was described by Lichtheim. Luria says that "the central feature of the disturbances in these cases is that, while the ability to utter words and even to repeat sentences remains intact, the patient is completely deprived of spontaneous speech and seldom uses it for purposes of communication" (Luria 1947: 199). Luria relates these symptoms, not to the disconnection of a hypothetical concept center from Broca's area, but rather to the role that the pre-frontal lobes play in the initiation of movement. The effect upon spontaneous speech is said to be the consequence of a lesion of the inferior dominant pre-frontal area upon the patient's ability to initiate speech. The stronger stimuli of repetition or naming can overcome this aspontaneity.

The general syndrome of adynamia and the language-specific syndrome of frontal dynamic aphasia are ones which do not affect the linguistic form of an utterance itself. The phonological, syntactic, and logical–grammatical structures of an utterance are intact when an utterance is finally produced. Similarly, the area of superior frontal cortex of the dominant hemisphere which lies between the motor strip and the pre-motor areas just described plays no direct role with respect to elements of language itself. The general function of this area of cortex is what Luria calls the "smooth execution of complex serial movements" (Luria 1947: 172). This ability to link component aspects of a motor act together into a smooth and effective whole action is disturbed when lesions occur in this area. Perseverative behavior, motor impersistence, and failure to inhibit repeated primitive reflexes, such as the glabellar (blink) response, are all consequences of lesions in this area. With respect to language, lesions in the superior part of this area produce halting speech in which "the patient no longer utters a whole meaningful complex in a single breath ... the unit becomes the individual word or syllable" (Luria 1947: 176). Patients simplify "expansive sentences" in order to keep in mind what has been said and to complete sentences grammatically. Speech comprehension is also affected, because the patient only retains isolated aspects of complex sentences. All of this is due to the inability to link the structural elements of sentences together. This inability to integrate parts of utterances is not a true linguistic impairment, according to Luria. Disorders following lesions in the superior areas of the motor association frontal cortex do not result in aberrations of the linguistic structures of sentences themselves.

Lesions in the inferior portions of the motor association cortex, which includes the classical Broca's area, do produce syndromes that affect language structures *per se*. Again, the basic disturbance is the failure to link elements in sequence, with consequent disorganization of the temporal organization of speech and comprehension. But with lesions in this area, there is actual disintegration of sentences and words. With respect to the latter, "with disruption of the dynamic schemata of words, the unit of innervation becomes the individual articulatory act, so that whereas the individual articulation may be easily carried out, there is a general decrease in the plasticity of speech and the switching from one articulation to another becomes difficult. As a result the normal articulation of words becomes impossible" (Luria 1947: 187). "Positional characteristics" which depend on the preceding and succeeding sounds are lost. Occasionally this affects writing as well, with marked perseveration of the initial letter or letters of words.

The way in which the temporal organization of *sentences* is affected with lesions in this area is through a disturbance of "inner speech". This results in disintegration of the "dynamic unity of propositions" (Luria 1947: 188). Following Vygotsky (1939), Luria believes that the transition from thought to external speech is mediated by "inner speech", in which the "rudiments of the dynamic scheme of a sentence" (Luria 1947: 188) are represented. The patient who can pronounce individual words only retains their "static nominative, designative function . . . the dynamic predicative function of the word is completely destroyed" (189). Object naming is therefore possible, but spontaneous and conversational speech is grossly impaired. Usually the impairment consists of uttering only the "kernel" of the thought, usually a few nominal phrases, which Luria considers to be the "serial naming of objects" (189) and which he calls "telegraphic style".

Luria's analysis of the naming of objects can be schematized as in Figure 9-2, in which each box corresponds to a brain region and to functions suggested by clinical data. In object naming, no acoustic model is given the subject. Instead he is obliged to look at an object and report his recognition of the object by an appropriate spoken word. Accurate performance on object-naming tasks clearly requires adequate visual perception and recognition abilities. Luria singles out the left temporal occipital zone as the anatomical site of this component (box A in Figure 9-2). Lesions here disturb both the ability to name objects and the ability to evoke visual images in response to a given word. A patient with a lesion in this area cannot draw named objects, but can copy a drawing line by line. Lesions here impair the routine transformation of an array of isolated visual features into the perceptual and cognitive unit into which the features are integrated.

The next step in naming (box B) is to access the appropriate name for the recognized object and to inhibit irrelevant alternative words. Lesions of the tertiary association area of the left parietal–occipital zone yield verbal paraphasias – the appearance of an incorrect word which resembles the

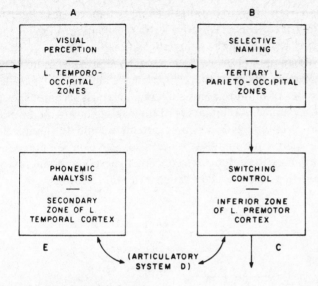

Figure 9-2. Luria's model of naming
(*Source:* Arbib and Caplan 1979: 453)

required word either in morphological form, meaning, or phonetic composition, or which is a word associated with the correct word. Isolated sensory features of the object, or partial articulatory or phonetic information associated with its name, can be the basis of a response as easily as can the entire object or word. Luria views the mis-function as one in which inhibitory constraints are removed in a competitive process. Thus, box B is involved in selection of a correct response through inhibition of incorrect responses which have become activated. Lesions here do not disturb the permanent representation of language elements. For instance, prompting with the first sound of the name triggers correct recall.

The next step in naming involves "phonemic analysis" (box E). This function is the responsibility of the left temporal region, in which lesions disturb the phonemic organization of words, yielding literal paraphasias. In literal paraphasias, words of similar phonemic organization are substituted, and often quite complex errors of sequencing of phonemes occur, in which each phoneme is properly articulated. In contrast to the verbal paraphasias induced by lesions in the occipital–parietal area, prompting with the initial sounds of the name of an object does not help the patient with a lesion in this area produce the correct word.

Luria (1973) indicates that frontal lobe mechanisms are also involved in the act of naming. Lesions of the inferior zone of the left pre-motor cortex (box C) – the area in which lesions cause the "frontal dynamic aphasia" which we have just reviewed – impair shifting from the name of one object to that of another, and lead to perseverative errors in naming. Finally, the articulatory system is involved in the final enunciation of a name.

The treatment of naming in Luria is highly typical of his view of how the brain functions. Naming involves the concerted sequential and parallel activation of a number of brain regions, each one of which accomplishes a particular task. Several of the components of the naming task – the frontal cortex involved in attention and switching attention, and the temporal cortex involved in phonemic analysis – are also active in spontaneous speech. This exemplifies the important concept that sub-components of psycholinguistic functions are shared between different functions.

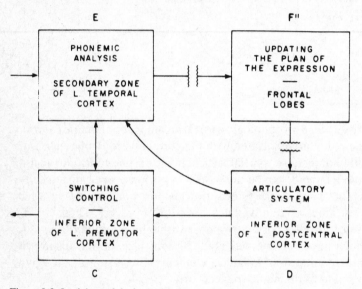

Figure 9-3. Luria's model of repetition
(*Source:* Arbib and Caplan 1979: 454)

Figure 9-3 summarizes Luria's views of the brain regions involved in repetition of sentences. The ability to discriminate the acoustic features of phonemes and to differentiate the sounds of words is a function of the left temporal region (box E in Figure 9-2). Lesions in this area yield acoustic agnosia, the inability to distinguish between sounds of speech. With large lesions in this area, all speech sounds are unintelligible, but with small lesions there is an inability to distinguish phonemes which differ by one distinctive feature, such as *b–v* or *p–b*, and a retention of the ability to discriminate phonemes which differ by more than a single feature, such as *d–p* or *b–t*. With a lesion in this area, the patient finds understanding individual words almost impossible. However, his understanding of the general meaning of a whole sentence may be preserved if he can use context to help him guess intelligently. He can also use the general intonation contour of an utterance to form some impression of the meaning of a sentence.

Luria insists that repetition is a complex function requiring several components. The programming of the response requires the participation of the frontal lobes. The frontal patient, given a logically incorrect phrase, will arrive at a likely interpretation and repeat this meaning instead of the utterance which has been presented. With a lesion of the posterior post-central cortical area, the timing of the act of speaking is impaired because of the lack of normal proprioceptive feedback. This is the basis of the syndrome of "afferent motor aphasia". Repetition is therefore somewhat dysarthric, but the dysarthria is different from that produced by more anterior lesions. If a lesion affects the lower portion of the left post-central region corresponding to lips, face, and tongue (box D), the patient may be unable to determine the position of the tongue and lips sufficiently rapidly to articulate the sounds of speech properly. Small disturbances in this area yield confusion of "articulemes" which are similar in articulation though different in acoustic properties. Secondary effects can be found in disturbances of writing involving the substitutions of letters corresponding to similar "articulemes", an effect which Luria ascribed to the interaction between speech production mechanisms and the systems for control of writing.

As we have seen previously, the motor association cortex is responsible for the "kinetic melody" of speech and other motor actions. Lesions here yield neither paralysis nor paresis, but skilled movements are no longer performed smoothly, and each component requires its own isolated "trigger". Lesions affecting the inferior zones of the left motor association cortex (box C) produce inertia and perseveration in patients' speech as part of the syndrome of "efferent motor aphasia". The articulation and pronunciation of isolated speech sounds give no serious difficulty, but the smooth pronunciation of polysyllabic words in sentences becomes impossible. There can also be corresponding defects in writing to dictation.

Finally, turning to the system underlying comprehension of spoken speech, we see in Figure 9-4 that the first step in understanding speech is the phonemic analysis which we have already seen is carried by the secondary association cortex of the left temporal lobe. Lesions in the posterior zones of the temporal region or the temporal–occipital region of the left hemisphere affect phonemic analysis, making the comprehension of words impossible.

127

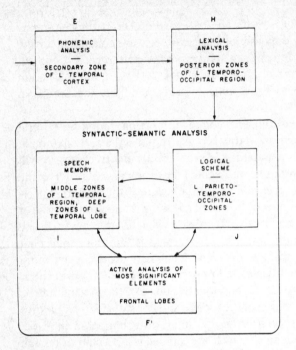

Figure 9-4. Luria's model of auditory comprehension
(*Source:* Arbib and Caplan 1979: 454)

Luria believes that this is the basis for the classical Wernicke's aphasia, thus following Wernicke's original analysis.

If this area is intact, the posterior zones of the left temporal–occipital region perform a lexical analysis (box H in Figure 9-4). Lesions here leave phonemic analysis unimpaired but grossly disturb accessing of meaning. Luria very tentatively suggests that this may be due to the impairment of concerted working of the auditory and visual analyzers. The suggestion seems to be that phonological representations, rather than evoking linguistic semantic representations directly, serve to evoke a modality-specific representation (perhaps akin to a visual image), and that this latter representation is the basis for accessing appropriate semantic and syntactic representations.

Luria identifies three sub-systems involved in "syntactic–semantic" analysis: "speech memory", "logical scheme", and "active analysis of most significant elements". Disturbance of the first of these three, caused by lesions of the middle and deep zones of the left temporal lobe (adjacent to box E) yields "acoustical–amnestic aphasia". The patient cannot retain a short sequence of sounds, syllables, or words in memory. This constitutes an impairment of the storage of information, as distinct from retrieval of information, which was said to be impaired by lesions in the tertiary parietal–occipital region. The patient confuses the order of words and forgets words, recalling only the first and last of a set of words or a sentence. Luria considers the problem to be not so much an instability of "audio-verbal traces" as a pathologically increased inhibition of these traces. In fact, if the elements are presented with sufficient time between them to eliminate "mutual inhibition", then the series can be retained.

Lesions at the parietal–occipital–temporal junction of the dominant left hemisphere (box J in Figure 9-4) yield disorders of perception of spatial relations, constructional activity, complex arithmetical functions, and the understanding of "logical–grammatical relationships". A sentence with little reliance on subtle syntax, such as *Father and mother went to the cinema, but grandmother and the children stayed home*, can be understood, whereas understanding of sentences like *A lady came from a factory to the school where Nina worked* is impaired. Understanding the meaning of this sentence requires not only the retention of individual elements, but the simultaneous synthesis of these elements into a logical scheme. Luria argues that data from patients with lesions in the parietal–temporal–occipital regions give neurological evidence for a system specifically devoted to this type of synthesis. Box J plays a role in the utilization of the grammatical codes – case relationships, prepositions, word order, etc. – which are decisive in determining how the words of the sentence combine to give its overall meaning.

Finally, the frontal lobes are required to form and maintain a program of action. Patients with frontal syndromes show deficits in the "active analysis of most significant elements of a sentence" (box F1). The process of decoding the meaning of a complex sentence, or of understanding the meaning of a narrative, is replaced by a series of guesses. The guesses are based on minimal analysis of the text and considerable reliance on pre-conceptions derived from the patient's prior knowledge of the world.

In Figure 9-5, these four systems are incorporated into a single represen-tation of a neurally based language-processing device. Figure 9-6 represents the location of these components in the brain. It should be noted that Luria specifies the localization of each of the component processes in Figure 9-6, but not that of the connections between components of this model.

Inspection of Figure 9-5 illustrates the features of Luria's approach which distinguish it from the models of the connectionists. Every psycholinguistic task is performed by several components acting in parallel and in sequence, and many components are involved in several tasks. There is no mention of entire faculties or entire functions. Component interaction in this model is

129

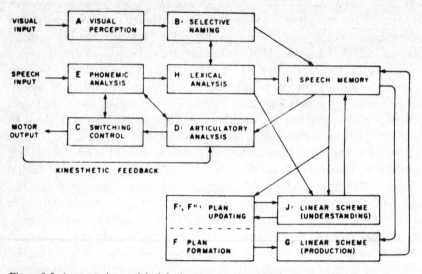

Figure 9-5. A composite model of the language-processing system according to Luria (*Source:* Arbib and Caplan 1979: 454)

far more complex than in the models we have considered so far. We shall see in later chapters that modern psycholinguists have suggested a more complex psychological model of language processing to account for normal and abnormal psycholinguistic performance.

Luria's model of language processing is embedded in a more general model of neuropsychological function. To appreciate his work, it is important to consider two other aspects of his theories: the relation of linguistic function to sensory–motor function, and the role that language plays in thinking and self-regulatory behavior.

Luria (1947) sees sensory–motor functions of areas of the brain as being closely linked to the linguistic and other intellectual functions which these areas perform. For instance, his analysis of the role of the frontal lobes begins with a description of their role in initiating plans for motor activity, and in organizing the temporal aspects of motor activity. Patients with lesions of the medial frontal lobe lapse into a state of akinetic mutism in which they do not initiate spontaneous activity. They often repeat the same activity for hours, and show other forms of perseverative behavior. This is the state described by Brown, which we reviewed in Chapter 7. With lesions of the lateral surface of the pre-frontal lobes, the smooth execution of movement is disturbed so that activity becomes a sequence of isolated gestures rather than an integrated whole. The language disorders that occur with lesions in these areas are strikingly parallel. With lesions of the medial aspect of the frontal lobes, the patient is unable to initiate conversation, and often shows perseveration in speech. The structure of speech itself is not, however, affected, once it is initiated. With lateral lesions, especially those in what is taken to be the classical speech area, including Broca's area, the syndrome of efferent motor aphasia occurs, in which the ability to produce temporally integrated sequences of words to form propositions, and to chain the phonemic constituents of individual words together, is impaired. The parallels between the motor and linguistic disturbances are not accidental, in Luria's opinion. The basic functions of these areas of the brain are the same,

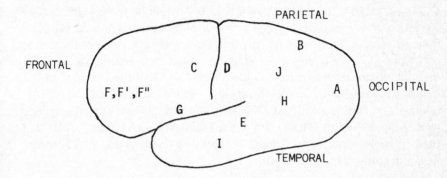

Figure 9-6. The neural correlates of the components of Luria's language-processing system

whether the domain in which these functions apply is linguistic or general motor activity. We can see that this analysis is closely related to Wernicke's and Geschwind's arguments that the auditory association cortex in Wernicke's area and the motor association cortex in Broca's area are involved in speech comprehension and speech production because of their proximity to primary sensory and motor cortex. Luria supplies a more detailed account of the relationship between language-devoted cortex and sensory–motor cortex than that specified in classical and contemporary connectionist neurolinguistic theory.

Though Luria viewed the psychology of language as an outgrowth of mechanisms regulating sensory–motor function, and extended this analysis to the level of the neural basis for language, he also conceived of language as a particular intellectual capacity which played a special role in human psychology. This role was in part to facilitate abstract thinking, categorization, drawing inferences, and other intellectual functions. Another role that language played in human psychology, according to Luria, was to regulate behavior. Luria held views which were similar to those of Jackson and Goldstein, inasmuch as he believed that human behavior consisted of primitive actions which were regulated by higher functional abilities. In

131

Luria's case, the basis for primitive behavior was the existence of conditioned reflex mechanisms such as those studied by Pavlov (1949). Pavlov's demonstration of conditioned reflexes provided an experimental basis for the study of elementary learned behavior in response to stimuli. Luria argued that when behavior was not based simply on instinctual drives, it was regulated by increasingly abstract intellectual capacities, and that language was a critical factor in the exercise of these higher faculties.

Luria (1947) criticized the classical connectionists for their over-simplification of the nature of language processing, and he rejected the work of Goldstein and of other gestalt psychologists because he thought they relied too much on general aspects of psychological functioning in their explanations of aphasic symptoms. His own approach sought to meet these two criticisms. He developed a more elaborate processing account of language than the connectionists, and he incorporated some of the concerns of the gestalt workers into his model through his discussion of the regulatory role of language. Luria provided the first reasonably detailed model of language processing related to aphasia and to the brain. We shall see in Part III that these models became much more complex as linguists and psychologists began to study aphasia in depth.

SUGGESTION FOR FURTHER READING

Arbib, M. A. and Caplan, D. (1979). Neurolinguistics must be computational. *Behavioral and Brain Sciences* 2, 449–83.

10

Overview of clinical aphasiology and neurolinguistics

In the previous seven chapters, we have considered some of the leading theories of language–brain relationships which characterize the first century of work in this field. There are several features of these theories which we shall consider before going on to more modern linguistic and psycholinguistic approaches.

The first point about this work is that it is mainly clinically based. The investigators who developed the theories we have outlined are clinicians, for the most part neurologists. With few exceptions, experimental psychologists and theoretically oriented linguists have not figured in our review. Even when the work of non-clinicians is represented in this survey, it is mainly derived from clinical observations. For instance, Jakobson's data-base for his theories of the dissolution of the sound system was clinical observation. Careful examination of the papers of Broca, Wernicke, Lichtheim, Jackson, Head, Marie, Luria, and other investigators we have cited will reveal that the vast majority of the observations upon which theories are based are clinical.

Clinical observations certainly have an important role to play, but they also have their limitations. In clinical reports, as a rule, the conditions of observation and the nature of the observations are not well defined or controlled. It is rare for the authors we have reviewed to report quantitative data regarding patients' performances, or to describe the exact conditions of testing, the exact nature of the stimuli presented to a patient, or the exact way of scoring a patient's responses. The lack of detail and precision in case reports can create important problems for theory construction. We have seen how Wernicke (1874) based his theory upon two separate cases, one of which was studied clinically and the other of which came to autopsy. Wernicke assumed that the lesion in the first case would have been in the same area as it was in the second, but this is not necessarily true. In fact, the exact area where lesions cause Wernicke's aphasia has been defined very differently by different investigators (see Bogen and Bogen 1976 for a review).

A second feature of the clinically derived theories we have been considering is the extent to which they are based on single case studies. Broca's first case exerted an enormous influence over the way neurolinguistic theory has developed, as we saw in Chapter 3. Wernicke's two cases, the case reports in Lichtheim's article, Dejerine's case of pure alexia, and many other isolated cases have been the principal observational basis for neurolinguistic theories. We have discussed the role that single case studies can play in neurolinguistic theory and linguistic aphasiology in Chapter 2. In that discussion, we concluded that single cases could provide evidence regarding *dissociations* of functional components of language processing; if one ability was retained and another disturbed in a single case, the processes underlying the two functions could be considered separate. However, we also concluded that single case studies could not establish that two deficits were functionally related; only a series of cases could establish that symptoms co-occur and thus suggest that there may be a functional basis for their co-occurrence. Despite these methodological and logical considerations, many of the clinically based theories of language–brain relationships and accounts of language breakdown use single cases to establish co-occurrences of symptoms. The best example is probably Wernicke's conclusion that the co-occurrence of a fluent speech disorder and an auditory comprehension disturbance was functionally caused; Wernicke reached this conclusion on the basis of studying a single case. We shall discuss this aspect of the psycholinguistic and neurolinguistic theories we have been considering again in Chapter 17.

The clinically derived theories we have just reviewed have proven quite durable, considering these limitations of their data-bases. This is partly because many hypotheses concerning co-occurrence of symptoms, the location of neural lesions which produce particular symptoms, and other features of the theories, have been confirmed in general terms by subsequent work. However, when one looks more closely at the details of both aphasic symptoms and syndromes and at lesion data, some of the details of the analyses become less secure or frankly untenable. We shall consider what can be reliably retained from these clinical theories in later chapters, as we come across more detailed studies of aphasic disturbances and anatomical determinants of aphasia.

For many years, the principal issue in neurolinguistic theories was thought to be the difference between "localizationist" and "holist" approaches to language–brain relationships. Localizationists, roughly speaking, were said to believe that the way the brain processed language was through the operation of centers and connections. Connectionism is archetypical localizationism. In contrast, holists held that the entire brain or, at least, large portions of the brain were responsible for the individual tasks of language functioning. The investigators we have considered in Chapters 6–8 are grouped as holists; Luria's approach deliberately incorporates some features of both points of view. Though this division has been frequently emphasized, and though there is considerable truth to the view that workers in these two camps held quite different views of how the brain supported language, the differences between the two groups have been over-emphasized in my opinion. We shall end Part II by making some of the real differences between these groups of thinkers explicit, and also by indicating the areas in which the groups had much in common.

One of the major differences between the localizationists and the holists lies in what aspects of function each group attempted to model. We have seen that workers such as Jackson, Goldstein, Brown, and Luria were concerned with the motivational states of patients, their ability to initiate actions and switch attention appropriately from stimulus to stimulus, their ability to inhibit primitive reflex actions, and other aspects of what may be called motivation and control of behavior. These workers all fall more or less into the non-localizationist camp; they all find the connectionist models too restrictive and "static", to use a term of Brown's. Classical localizationists such as the connectionists were not concerned with building psychological or neurological models which considered these aspects of performance. They concentrated on modeling the primary acts of language use – speaking, comprehension, reading, writing, naming, repetition – in the normal person, assuming that attention, motivation, and other aspects of control of cognition were functioning normally. Accordingly, one of the major differences between connectionists (and localizationists in general) and workers who are classed as holists is the range of psychological phenomena they wished to model. It is not surprising that those workers whose models encompassed a greater number and kind of psychological functions arrived at models in which each performance required a larger area of brain than is specified in models which excluded this wider range of functions.

The difference between holists and localizationists just outlined is not just a matter of what different researchers found enjoyable to study. Many of the "holist" researchers whose work we have reviewed do not consider that the study of language-processing systems can be pursued without paying attention to features of human psychology such as control of attention and motivational state. Goldstein's emphasis on the importance of being able to assume the abstract attitude, Jackson's view that the highest functions of the nervous system were mainly to inhibit more primitive responses, and his concern with the motivational state of a patient, Brown's focus upon how language production begins with the global motor envelope of an action – all these features of these models indicate the role that these abilities play in language use. This is perhaps clearest in Luria's work, where psychological capacities such as switching attention are part of language tasks such as repetition, as well as being important in tasks which are non-linguistic. There is thus a tension between the two schools: the holists implicitly or explicitly deny that one can isolate the psycholinguistic functions that the localizationists wish to isolate; the localizationists implicitly or explicitly argue that this isolation is possible, and that it is the only way to make progress in the field. Note that this difference deals with *psychological* phenomena. Though the terms "localizationist" and "holist" denote views about neural mechanisms, this fundamental disagreement is about what models of the psychology of language must include. The neural mechanisms follow the psychological analyses, in this respect.

It is worth returning at this point to a point mentioned in the Introduction to this volume: it is probably impossible at present to settle many of the disagreements in this field. The present disagreement is one which is not finally settled. Nonetheless, there is an effective, *de facto*, decision as to what approach to the psychology of language – though not to the neural basis for language – is correct. Most psychologists and linguists currently working on aphasia believe that, by appropriately controlling conditions of testing, it is possible to study the language-processing system of aphasic patients in rigorous and demanding ways, and that concern for the patient's ability to control his attention, his motivation, and similar factors can be met by proper experimental and observational techniques. The complexity of the language code and the mechanisms responsible for its processing seem to require that one approach the problem by dividing it into manageable sub-parts. The assumption is that there will be some important relationship between the operation or disturbance of a sub-component of the language-processing system in a laboratory setting and how it functions in a real-world context. This assumption underlies experimental approaches to normal psychology as well as to pathological psychology such as aphasia. We shall reconsider this issue in Chapter 17, after reviewing modern studies in linguistic aphasiology.

An attempt to reconcile the holist and localizationist approaches is found in Geschwind's (1964) paper on the role that Goldstein played in aphasiology. Geschwind points out that, though Goldstein disagreed with the classical connectionists about what caused aphasic syndromes, he agreed with them about the location of lesions that caused particular constellations of symptoms (the classical syndromes). This is partly true: Goldstein did agree that lesions in the areas identified by the connectionists caused aphasic syndromes, and by and large agreed about which symptoms occurred with which lesions. But the fact that he accounted for the symptoms differently is critical. Goldstein was not a localizationist, not because he disagreed that focal lesions could cause specific symptoms or syndromes, but because he disagreed that this state of affairs meant that individual psycholinguistic functions, linguistic representations, or language-related tasks were localized in specific areas of the brain. As we have seen, he tried to relate most aphasic phenomena to disturbances of very general and abstract intellectual capacities. He did not think these were localized. We noted in Chapter 8 that Goldstein had trouble accounting for the specific nature of aphasic disturbances. This difficulty stemmed from his refusal to recognize the same psycholinguistic components as localizationists. As we noted in Chapter 2, there is a difference between localization of symptoms and localization of functions. Geschwind correctly pointed out that Goldstein accepted the one; he did not, however, agree with the second.

Many localizationists were somewhat like Goldstein in this respect: they accepted the localization of symptoms, but did not concern themselves with the localization of functions. In fact, many did not even attempt to construct analyses of the origin of symptoms. Many of these investigators were clinical neurologists who tried to use the occurrence of symptoms to establish the location and nature of neurological disease. Volumes such as Neilson's (1936), in which symptoms are related to lesion sites, served important clinical roles in an era before neuroradiology had advanced to its present state. We see here an example of the point we mentioned in Chapter 1: the questions that are asked about language–brain relationships determine the information we obtain. In many cases, the questions that were posed were about aphasia–brain relationships, not the relationship between normal language and the brain. The analyses went no further than a description of aphasic symptoms and their associated lesions, falling short of an account of how the symptoms arose. Localization of symptoms does not, however, immediately imply localization of function, as we saw in Chapter 2. Most holists and localizationists by and large agreed about the nature and localization of symptoms. They disagreed as to what this implied about the nature and localization of language functions.

It is important to recognize that all localizationists and all holists were not alike. Localizationists – even excluding those who were only interested in localization of symptoms and considering only those who developed theories of localization of functions – differed among themselves. Functions as different as moral faculties and individual talents were localized by some researchers, as well as aspects of basic cognitive function such as we have seen in connectionist theories. Not all localizationists were connectionists. Henschen (1920), for example, possibly the greatest exponent of localization of function, would be hard to classify as a connectionist aphasiologist.

Holists, too, were not all of a kind. We saw in Chapters 6–8 that many different types of neurolinguistic theories are grouped under this term.

The localizationists and holists are similar in several respects. One is that many localizationists, such as the connectionists, conceived of some performances as the results of the integrated activity of different brain regions. The reliance of Broca's area upon Wernicke's area in speech production exemplifies this sort of interaction. As we noted in Chapter 9, this approach ultimately led to the more complex process model of Luria, and we will see further elaboration of components of a language-processing system in Part III. Thus, the localizationist approach can ultimately lead to a model of linguistic performance in which many areas of the brain act together to produce an output. In this respect, it can resemble holist approaches. The differences seem to lie in the fact that the *classical* connectionist theorists referred to these interactions sparingly, perhaps because they kept their models of performance very simple.

There is another important similarity between connectionism and the other approaches we have studied. It is the level of detail of the descriptions of language breakdown which these theories provide. We have seen a few examples of work in which detailed accounts of language structures or psycholinguistic processes are presented. Jakobson's description of the dissolution of the phonemic system is one such example; Brown's microgenetic theory is another. In Jakobson's case, his analysis of the structure of the phonemic system was strongly supported, at the time of his monograph, by developmental and cross-linguistic studies, though it has since been modified. In Brown's case, the model of sentence production he proposed has no clear connection with any models proposed by psychologists working on normal language production. Nonetheless, it does represent a more detailed process account than that found in classical connectionist theories, for example. However, even considering work on aphasia which includes the level of detail found in Jakobson, Brown, Luria, or Goldstein, we come away from these studies with the impression that much of the detail of linguistic structure and processing is not described or modeled in the theories we have reviewed. The adequacy of the level of empirical description of all these theories is an important consideration. In this respect, all the theories we have reviewed are similar, in that they fall short of the level of description of linguistic and psycholinguistic structures and processes that one sees in models of normal language.

As can be seen, the theories we have reviewed in this section have serious limitations. These occur in the areas of how data has been collected, the detail of data reported, the adequacy of deficit analyses, the reliability of co-occurrence of symptoms, and (though we have not emphasized this aspect) the variation in anatomical lesions producing aphasic symptoms. These deficiencies seem sufficiently great to warrant serious skepticism regarding virtually all of the theories we have reviewed.

Despite this, these theories have had considerable appeal. Since Geschwind's revival of connectionist theories, these models have dominated aphasiology and neurolinguistics in the USA. They are useful for the clinical neurologist, who can establish a diagnosis of a type of aphasia on the basis of a very few observations he can make at the bedside. They simplify a very complex domain in intuitively acceptable ways. They "make neuroanatomical sense", inasmuch as receptive and expressive functions are related to sensory and motor areas of the brain. It has proven very hard to disprove the basic connectionist model, and many researchers with alternate models, such as those whose work we discussed in Chapters 7–9, have not tried to disprove connectionism, but have simply stated their own theories.

We should not, however, come away from these theories with the view that they are accepted only because they simplify the problem, and that they can be disregarded. They are the fundamental analyses upon which accounts of aphasia and the neural basis for language are presently constructed, even by theorists whose work goes far beyond that reviewed in Part II. They delineate the field of inquiry. The notion that the fundamental data-base for aphasiological descriptions and for neurolinguistic theory is the pattern of performance of patients in the usual tasks of language use is a critical step towards creating a field of inquiry. The notion of isolated components of a language-processing system which interact to produce observable performances is another fundamental hypothesis that carries over from classical to contemporary work. The idea, advanced by some of the workers whose contributions we have discussed in Chapters 6–9, that the psycholinguistic processes devoted to the usual tasks of language use are influenced significantly by other factors, such as deployment of attention, motivation, or ability to initiate and switch movement, is one which cannot be ignored if we are to arrive someday at a complete theory of how the brain accomplishes linguistic functions. Finally, the neurological analysis that individual components of a language-processing system may be located in specific regions of the brain is the basis not only for neurolinguistics but also for much of neuropsychology in general.

We might put these clinically derived accounts of aphasia and language–brain relationships in better perspective if we compare them to accounts of disturbances of motor and sensory functions. In the latter areas, the late nineteenth and early twentieth centuries saw enormous advances in the identification of clinical syndromes in neurology. It was during this period that the basic manifestations of diseases such as multiple sclerosis, stroke, epilepsy, and degenerative disease of the nervous system were described, and when the relationship between clinical symptoms and location of lesions in the neuraxis was first established. This "golden age" of clinically derived neuroscience lasted for about 75–100 years, and the major advances in the clinical description of disease and in the inferences from clinical observations to how the nervous system mediated sensory–motor activity were made by the time of World War II. The enormous advances in our understanding of the normal nervous system and diseases of the nervous system that have occurred from about that time (many were also made prior to World War II) have been the results not of clinical observations alone, but of laboratory study as well. These studies can be, but need not be, inspired by clinical observations. These studies have often confirmed clinically derived analyses. In many other cases, they have revealed aspects of neural function which clinical studies could not uncover, and in some cases they have forced significant revision of clinically derived theories of disease and neural function. To cite one example of the latter, the discovery that myasthenia gravis is an immunological disease affecting post-synaptic cholinergic receptors, not a disorder of muscle itself or of release of packets of acetylcholine pre-synaptically, is a result of laboratory studies. It would have been impossible to establish the nature of this disease, and many others, without recourse to the laboratory.

Linguistic aphasiology and neurolinguistic theory have had a similar history. We have just reviewed approximately 100 years of clinically derived analyses and theories. What is perhaps most remarkable about this work is how much has been achieved with such simple observational techniques. Nonetheless, though clinical observation undoubtedly will continue to provide new insights into these areas, and will certainly inspire investigation indefinitely, its contributions are limited by what can be observed clinically and the reliability of clinical observations, just as is the case in other branches of neuroscience. In Part III, we will consider more formal approaches to language disorders, many of which involve application of concepts and techniques from psychology and linguistics to the characterization of aphasic symptoms and syndromes. In Part IV, we will see how advances in technology have added to our knowledge of the neurological basis for aphasia and for language. The work we have just reviewed provides an essential basis for these more detailed studies.

Part III

Linguistic aphasiology

11

Linguistic descriptions and aphasic syndromes

To this point in this book we have been principally concerned with neurolinguistics – theories of how language is represented and processed in the brain. We now turn to our second topic – linguistic aphasiology. The work we shall consider in Part III deals primarily with the details of the linguistic structures that aphasic patients lose and retain, and with abnormalities in the processing of these structures. The focus of this work is different from that in neurolinguistic studies. Rather than devote their attention principally to how normal and abnormal language is related to the brain, many psychologists and linguists have recently become interested in how aphasic language is related to normal language. In some instances, what we know about normal language structure and processing has helped these investigators understand the nature of aphasic disturbances. In other cases, the direction of theory construction has been reversed, and what has been discovered about aphasic language processing has led to new theories of the processing of normal language. The neural basis for language is a secondary issue, though there are implications of this work for neurolinguistic theory which we shall consider in Part IV.

Linguistic aphasiology developed in a major way well after neurolinguistics had been established. This shift in orientation and focus resulted from the slow growth of knowledge regarding the linguistic and psycholinguistic details of aphasic disorders. There has always been a concern in aphasiology for linguistic and psycholinguistic analyses, as we have seen in the work we reviewed in Part II. Linguistic and psychological analyses were also highly developed in work by many investigators which we have not covered, such as Broadbent (1879), Bastian (1887), Moutier (1908), Pick (1913), Salomon (1914), Alajouanine *et al.* (1939), and others. After World War II an international scientific community developed, complete with international societies, journals, academic structures, and related institutions, one of whose interests was linguistic aphasiology. Observations regarding the language abnormalities seen in aphasia became more numerous and more detailed. These observations, along with some of the earlier linguistic and psycholinguistic studies, form much of the data-base upon which contemporary linguistic aphasiology was developed. In the 1970s there was yet another change. New approaches to the psychology of language emerged, as the influence of Chomsky's theories of language (Chomsky 1957; 1965; Fodor *et al.* 1974) and of models of language processing developed in psychology (Morton 1969; 1970; Garrett 1976; Forster 1976) began to be felt. Linguistic and psychological models of language and language processing became more detailed, and these new theories made their mark on linguistic aphasiology, as researchers began to relate aphasic symptoms to these models.

In Part III, we shall be primarily concerned with work carried out since 1970. In Chapters 12–16, we shall consider work on the linguistic and psycholinguistic nature of language breakdown mainly as it relates to the themes and theories developed in this newer literature. In this chapter, we shall trace some of the recent background to modern linguistic aphasiology. Unfortunately, as elsewhere throughout this volume, we shall be omitting a great deal of material; the interested reader can find references to some of this material at the end of each chapter. Our purpose in Part III is to illustrate the approach and some of the results of this new literature, and to enable the reader to read and evaluate publications in this field.

We shall make the transition from neurolinguistics to linguistic aphasiology by examining the notion of an aphasic syndrome and the way aphasic patients are classified in different theories. Consideration of the basis for classification of aphasic patients will also lead us to an appreciation of some of the differences between the slightly older and slightly newer psycholinguistic approaches to aphasia. Though we cannot fully do justice to the "older" psycholinguistic approach to aphasia simply through a consideration of the taxonomy of aphasia, we will at least be able to get some sense of its accomplishments, as well as of the differences between it and the newer approaches, by considering how each deals with the issue of classification. The issue of patient classification is not a central theme in the five chapters which follow. We focus upon it here because we have dealt with it previously in our discussion of connectionist neurolinguistics, and because accrual of detailed linguistic information about patients was and still is often undertaken in relationship to the clinical syndromes. We shall see that the accrual of this information leads to important questions about these very syndromes, and raises the issue of how to relate linguistic descriptions of aphasic symptoms to theories of normal language.

We saw in Chapter 4 how connectionist neurolinguistic theory led to a specific classification of aphasic patients. Lichtheim (1885) described seven aphasic syndromes. These corresponded to disturbances of centers and pathways in his model, seen in Figure 11-1. These syndromes were: (1)

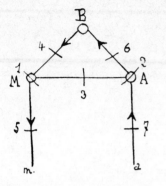

Figure 11-1. Lichtheim's model of the language-processing system
(*Source:* Moutier 1908: 43)

Broca's aphasia, due to a lesion in the center for motor speech planning (M); (2) Wernicke's aphasia, due to a lesion in the center for auditory images of words (A); (3) conduction aphasia, due to a lesion in the pathway A–M; (4) transcortical motor aphasia, due to a lesion in the pathway B–M; (5) dysarthria, due to a lesion in the pathway M–m; (6) transcortical sensory aphasia, due to a lesion in the pathway A–B; and (7) pure word deafness, due to a lesion in the pathway a–A. In Lichtheim's article, the nature of information flow between these centers and along the postulated pathways determined what deficits were found with particular lesions. Each of these syndromes was characterized by the relative preservation of one language function over another. Thus, for instance, in pure word deafness, auditory comprehension and repetition were significantly disturbed, because auditory input into the center for the sound pattern of words was disturbed. On the other hand, spontaneous speech, reading, and writing were intact, because the centers and pathways involved in these functions were not affected. Broca's aphasia, as we have seen, involved a disturbance in spontaneous speech and repetition but not in auditory comprehension. A lesion in Wernicke's area affected not only auditory comprehension and repetition, but spontaneous speech as well, because word sounds were evoked in speech planning. As we noted in Chapter 5, this approach to the classification of aphasia has had very considerable influence. Once it was revived by Geschwind (1965), it became the conceptual basis for the most widespread approach to patient classification. A modern version of this connectionist taxonomy is found in Benson and Geschwind (1971). Benson and Geschwind divide the aphasias into ten types, illustrated in Table 11-1. They indicate that, with only minor adjustments, these ten types of aphasia map onto the basic classes of aphasia recognized by a wide variety of authors throughout the history of aphasiology (Table 11-2).

Table 11-1. *Clinical varieties of aphasia*

Aphasia with repetition disturbance
Broca's aphasia
Wernicke's aphasia
Conduction aphasia
Aphasia without repetition disturbance
Isolation of speech area
Transcortical motor aphasia
Transcortical sensory aphasia
Anomic aphasia
Disturbance primarily affecting reading and writing
Alexia with agraphia
Total aphasia
Global aphasia
Syndromes with disturbance of a single language modality
Alexia without agraphia
Aphemia
Pure word deafness
Non-aphasic mis-naming

Source: Benson and Geschwind 1971: 5.

It is striking how little the connectionist approach to the classification of aphasic patients has changed in over a century of clinical observation and theory construction. As can be seen, the seven types of aphasia we have just outlined are all present in this taxonomy. In addition, Benson and Geschwind recognize three more aphasic syndromes (excluding alexias): isolation of the speech area, global aphasia, and anomia. Isolation of the speech area occurs with a lesion separating the language system from concepts; this lesion is a combination of the lesions producing transcortical sensory and transcortical motor aphasia in the Lichtheim taxonomy. Global aphasia consists of such a severe disturbance in all language functions that the patient achieves virtually no comprehension, and can at most produce stereotypic and automatic language output. The lesion responsible affects the entire perisylvian area and severely damages all the centers and connections postulated in Figure 11-1. Anomia is an isolated disturbance of confrontation naming and accessing content words in speech, which does not easily fit into the neurolinguistic model displayed in Figure 11-1.

As we have seen in Chapters 4 and 5, the proponents of this approach to taxonomy recognized that different types of aphasia produced qualitatively different language disturbances, as well as different degrees of impairment of various language functions. A good example of these qualitative features of language impairment is the difference between the spontaneous speech of a Broca's aphasic and a Wernicke's aphasic. We noted in Chapter 4 that

Table 11-2. *Aphasic syndromes arranged by symptom cluster or pathologic localization or both*

Wernicke Lichtheim (56) (1885)	Head (27) (1926)	Kleist (29) (1934)	Nielson (140) (1936)	Goldstein (26) (1948)	Brain (57) (1961)	Gloning (62) (1963)	Bay (48) (1964)	Wepman (173) (1964)	Luria (33) (1966)	BVAH
Cortical motor	Verbal	Word muteness	Broca's	Central motor	Broca's	Motor	Cortical dysarthria	Syntactic	Efferent motor	Broca's
Cortical sensory	Syntactic	Word deafness	Wernicke's	Wernicke's sensory	Central	Sensory	Sensory	Jargon pragmatic	Sensory	Wernicke's
Conduction		Repetition		Central	Central	Conduction	Sensory		Afferent motor	Conduction
				Isolation of speech area						Isolation of speech area
Transcortical motor			Transcortical motor	Transcortical motor			Echolalia		Dynamic	Transcortical motor
Transcortical sensory			Transcortical sensory	Transcortical sensory					Acoustic–amnestic	Transcortical sensory
	Nominal	Amnestic	Amnesic	Amnesic	Nominal	Amnestic	Pure	Semantic	Semantic	Anomic
Subcortical motor	Semantic	Anarthric	Subcortical motor	Peripheral motor	Pure word dumbness					Aphemia
Subcortical sensory		Word sound deafness		Peripheral sensory	Pure word deafness	Pure word deafness				Pure word deafness

Source: Benson and Geschwind 1971: 7.

Wernicke observed that the abnormalities in speech found in these two syndromes were different. Broca's patients could either barely speak or not speak at all. Wernicke's first patient had speech which was fluent and filled with phonemic paraphasias and jargon. These differences became part of the data-base upon which the diagnosis of Broca's or Wernicke's aphasia was made, as well as the "relatively good comprehension" found in Broca's aphasia.

In subsequent studies, these qualitative features of the classical syndromes were described in more detail. To pursue the syndromes of Broca's and Wernicke's aphasia, a range of abnormalities in these two syndromes became apparent. Broca's aphasia was not necessarily characterized only by mutism. A variety of reductions in speech output came to be considered as other possible manifestations of Broca's aphasia. Patients with anarthria (Marie 1906a), "phonetic disintegration" (Alajouanine *et al.* 1939), stereotypic utterances and retention of profane utterances (Jackson 1878), "agrammatism" (Tissot *et al.* 1973), and other disturbances were all classed as Broca's aphasics. The speech abnormalities in Wernicke's aphasia included phonemic paraphasias, semantic paraphasias, unrecognizable segments termed "neologisms", severely disordered and unrecognizable speech called "jargon", difficulties in producing nouns known as "anomia", and others. The early appreciation that different patients could have disturbances of speech which were qualitatively different gave rise to the recognition of a fairly large number of abnormalities of speech which could be seen in each type of aphasia. The same process occurred in all language functions in all the classical aphasic syndromes.

These observations of the qualitative nature of language disturbances formed the basis for descriptions of the *linguistic abnormalities* in aphasia. To a certain extent, these linguistic observations played a role in the system of classification. Thus, it was possible to recognize a Wernicke's aphasic not only because of his impaired comprehension, repetition, and spontaneous speech, but also because of the *nature* of his abnormal speech, which had the features we have just described. Details of the nature of phonemic paraphasias, disturbances in the processing of semantic aspects of individual words, in the formation, comprehension, and repetition of sentences, and other linguistic and psycholinguistic features of aphasia were related to the classical aphasic syndromes. Excellent reviews of these investigations can be found in Goodglass and Geschwind (1976), Lesser (1978), Benson (1979), and Lecours *et al.* (1983). As an illustration of the type of descriptions found in these and other volumes, we may consider the description of psycholinguistic research on word-finding disturbances provided by Goodglass and Geschwind (1976: 404-5):

The vocabulary of the Broca's aphasic, even though reduced by his word-finding difficulty, appears to be relatively well supplied with concrete or picturable nouns and verbs. These are sparser in the output of the anomic speech of the amnesic or Wernicke aphasic. Wepman, Bock, Jones, and Van Pelt (1956), after examining the word frequency distribution of anomic patients, felt that this disorder was not related to part of speech at all. Rather, they found an overuse of high-frequency words of all form classes in the speech of these patients. However, close examination of their data indicates that the effect of this word frequency shift is much greater for nouns than other words. Goodglass, Hyde, and Blumstein (1969) found that Broca's and fluent (Wernicke and anomic) aphasics did indeed differ in the proportion of picturable to nonpicturable nouns used but only in the highest frequency range. Fluent aphasics use many more nonpicturable words that occur idiomatically, but without much informational value, in their free-flowing speech. Broca's aphasics have an equal overuse of frequent nouns, but these include more words of specific concrete reference.

There is even stronger evidence that word-finding is a function of the semantic category of the words involved. Goldstein (1948) had noted that numbers were sometimes exempted from the difficulty experienced in naming nouns. Goodglass, Klein, Carey and Jones (1966) examined the order of difficulty of object names, body parts, actions, colors, numbers, and letters, in a test in which the patient was asked either to name a visual stimulus or to choose the correct visual stimulus in response to the spoken name. Objects were most often the hardest category to name. In auditory comprehension this relationship was however reversed, eliminating the possibility of a simple explanation in terms of word frequency. The greatest discrepancies among semantic categories were observed in anomic patients, who had much less difficulty naming numbers and letters than they did naming objects or body parts. Patients with the Broca's speech pattern had little variability in naming. The authors conjectured that the disparity in phonological information between letters and numbers places a greater information encoding load on the speaker for numbers, but a greater load for decoding on the listener for letters.

These linguistic descriptions add considerably to the observational adequacy of descriptions of aphasia, and thus significantly deepen our understanding of language breakdown. However, the addition of linguistic detail to the description of aphasic syndromes also presents a number of problems. These problems are related to the classification of patients into the traditional clinical categories, and to what linguistic features of aphasic performances can be understood in terms of linguistic theory and models of language processing. One problem is that, within each syndrome, what was once considered a single symptom now consists of a variety of possible symptoms, so that different patients classed as having the same syndrome may, in fact, have different disturbances of language. Schwartz (1984) calls this the problem of the "polytypicality" of clinical syndromes. A second problem is that many linguistic disturbances occur in more than one syndrome, and a patient who shows mainly these disturbances cannot be unequivocally classified as belonging to one or another group of patients. A third problem is that some studies have not confirmed expected differences in the linguistic nature of a symptom found in more than one syndrome.

The polytypical nature of the classic aphasic syndromes creates a number of problems. From the point of view of classifying aphasic patients, it is no longer clear just what it means for a patient to be classified as belonging to a particular syndrome. All we can say about a patient who has "Broca's aphasia" is that he has one or more of a number of abnormalities in speech, and possibly other functions such as reading aloud, repetition, and writing. This is not enough to be able to say exactly what linguistic and psycholinguistic problems the patient shows in detail. Furthermore, since different patients with "Broca's aphasia" have different linguistic and psycholinguistic disturbances, correlating brain lesions with "Broca's aphasia" does not give us information about the neural basis for a single language function. For instance, it may be the case that all the Broca's aphasics with a particular type of dysarthria have lesions in a particular area of the brain, but this correlation might not emerge from a study which looked for the neural correlates of Broca's aphasia in general. The fact that there are many different forms of speech disturbances grouped together under the heading of "Broca's aphasia" also makes it impossible for a psycholinguist to look for the consequences of having the deficit underlying Broca's aphasia in other aspects of language processing. This is because the wide range of symptoms found in Broca's aphasia do not seem to be all due to the same underlying deficit. It would be interesting to know whether a deficit in producing certain vocabulary items was always correlated with a disturbance in understanding sentences when sentence understanding depended upon the interpretation of those items (see Chapter 16 for discussion of this idea), but we cannot select patients on the basis of their having Broca's aphasia to investigate such a possibility, since different patients with Broca's aphasia have different disturbances.

The second problem faced by the clinical classification is that of symptoms which occur in several syndromes. This can be illustrated by the symptoms of anomia and phonemic paraphasias. These disturbances in the production of the content word vocabulary will be reviewed in Chapters 12 and 13. They are extremely common in aphasia, and occur in normal speech as well. Many patients are not easily classified into one or another aphasic group, because these are the predominant symptoms that they have, and these symptoms occur in many aphasic groups. In fact, the application of the Benson and Geschwind taxonomy to actual cases frequently leads to many patients being considered as "mixed aphasics" or as being unclassifiable.

This is obviously a problem for any system which seeks to classify patients. In addition, the existence of these unclassifiable cases also leads to problems in using the classical groups of patients to look for the neural basis for language functions. If these patients are excluded from neurolinguistic correlations, and these correlations are based only upon cases which can be clearly classified into one or another classical syndrome, we will arrive at wrong localizations about the neural basis of symptoms like anomia, since many patients with these symptoms are not included in the correlations. On the other hand, if we force all patients to be classified into one or another of the classical syndromes, even those with only these ubiquitous symptoms, we further dilute the already weak homogeneity of the classical syndromes.

One possible solution to this problem is to deepen the linguistic and psychological analysis of symptoms such as anomia and phonemic paraphasias. A considerable amount of work has been directed towards the question of whether symptoms which are found in many syndromes differ in subtle ways in different traditional groups of aphasic patients. Goodglass and Geschwind's review of work on anomia, quoted above, attempts to state such differences. But this, too, causes problems for the classical approach to taxonomy. If the anomia associated with Broca's aphasia does differ from that associated with Wernicke's aphasia, is anomia itself a single disturbance? Is it, or its variants, associated with each of the possible speech output disturbances that can be seen in Broca's aphasia? Which, if any, of the associations of symptoms are functionally caused (see Chapter 2)?

The third problem mentioned above has arisen when these studies have not shown expected differences between groups. For instance, Blumstein (1973a; 1973b) found that, contrary to expectations, Broca's, conduction, and Wernicke's aphasics did not differ with respect to many linguistic features of phonemic paraphasias (though subsequent work has disputed this finding – see Chapter 13). If patients do not differ as expected, the functional basis of different clinical syndromes which led to these expectations and from which the classical taxonomy is derived is called into question.

In short, there are many problems for the traditional clinical taxonomy which are raised by the introduction of qualitative linguistic and psycholinguistic descriptions of aphasic symptoms. It seems clear that a taxonomy based on these descriptions will be more detailed and complex than the classical one. It is not clear, at present, that it will retain the basic categories of aphasics specified in the clinical approach. We shall return to the way linguistic and psycholinguistic studies bear on the matter of patient classification at the end of this chapter. Before doing so, however, we shall consider an approach to patient classification which has been developed recently, and which has been widely taken to provide support for the clinical classification of patients. We shall see that it does not provide such support.

This approach is based upon statistical analysis of group performances. This approach seeks to define patient groups by clustering patients "objectively" by the use of powerful clustering methods. The statistical approaches are based upon patients' performances on "aphasia batteries". For the most part, these batteries test the language functions that are observed clinically, but they add linguistic detail. Moreover, they are standardized, so that different practitioners use the batteries in similar fashions. One of the best-known batteries of this type is the Boston Diagnostic Examination for Aphasia (Goodglass and Kaplan 1972; 1982). The BDAE divides each basic language function into a number of sub-functions. For instance, the "Auditory Comprehension" sub-test of the BDAE includes tests of word discrimination, body part identification, commands, and complex ideational materials. Word discrimination, in turn, requires selection of the correct item from among a group of nouns, actions, letters, colors, geometric forms, and numbers. Similar sub-divisions of spontaneous speech, repetition, reading, writing, and several non-linguistic abilities are found on this test. The BDAE and other tests of this nature, such as the Western Aphasia Battery (Kertesz 1979) and the Aachen Aphasia Test, thus include a number of linguistic observations on each aphasic patient. Tests of this sort have been given to large groups of unselected aphasic patients in order to determine how patients perform, and to group together patients who have similar patterns of performance.

The results of the use of these batteries are very hard to interpret. There are many technical problems regarding statistical analysis of the data these batteries provide, and these problems are not always taken into account in some of the analyses. For instance, the Western Aphasia Battery does not provide data regarding spontaneous speech which meet the mathematical requirements of the clustering procedure used to group patients (the data do not fall along the "interval scale" needed for parametric analyses). Setting this problem aside, several published studies using these batteries do not show consistent groupings of symptoms or subjects. The most widely cited analysis is that of Goodglass and Kaplan (1972), but these authors do not report a classification of patients on the BDAE at all. Instead, they report a "factor analysis" of the grouping of patients' scores. They claim that this factor analysis groups together symptoms in a way that would be predicted by the classical aphasic syndromes. However, different analyses of different patient populations, which the authors tested at separate times, do not produce the same factors. Kertesz (1979) is the investigator who makes the strongest case for the overlap of patient clusters derived from the use of his battery and traditional syndromes; but even in Kertesz' work there are problems with his conclusion. One of the traditional syndromes (conduction aphasia) must be sub-divided; there are different groupings for patients tested six weeks and six months after stroke; there are different groupings for stroke cases and tumor cases; and there are several problems with how the statistical analysis was done, as noted above. Overall, these batteries do not solve the problem of how aphasic patients are to be classified, or of which linguistic symptoms co-occur reliably in aphasia. In any case, even if these approaches did not suffer from these problems and did lead to reliable results, we would not know whether symptoms were grouped together for anatomical or for functional reasons (see Chapter 2). At best, statistical approaches could provide data regarding symptom and patient clustering which could then lead to theories of aphasic breakdown. At present, the data seem to indicate that most symptoms occur independently of most other symptoms, and do not support any special status for the constellations of symptoms identified in the classical syndromes.

In the past fifteen years or so, many classes of aphasic patients which differ from both the clinically and statistically defined groupings have been identified by psychologists and linguists. These classes – exemplified by groups such as agrammatic aphasics (Kean 1985) and deep and surface dyslexics (Coltheart *et al*. 1980; Patterson *et al*. 1986) – have several features in common. First, the symptoms which characterize patients within a class do not pertain to all psycholinguistic performances. Rather, unlike clinically and statistically defined groupings, which are defined over performances on all tasks, the symptoms which are definitional or criterial for membership in a class in this new approach are usually all related to a single task or function, such as spontaneous speech, reading, or writing. Second, the abnormalities which are considered criterial for class membership tend to be a more restricted set than those in the earlier approaches. For instance, agrammatism is separated from dysarthria, apraxia of speech, and many of the other aphasic symptoms that occur in Broca's aphasia. These changes have the effect of making these syndromes more (though not completely) homogeneous. Third, patients are considered to belong to a group if they show a symptom (or a given set of symptoms), whatever their other symptoms. For instance, different types of dyslexia may occur with or without an agraphia or other aphasic symptoms, without altering the assignment of patients to groups. This is not the case in the clinically defined patient groupings, which are entirely based upon symptom complexes, or in statistical approaches such as those described by Kertesz (1979), in which the totality of a patient's scores forces him into only one taxonomic group. In the psycholinguistic approach, a patient may belong to several groupings (e.g. Beauvois and Dérouesné 1981).

These differences result from a fundamental difference in the approach to the description and taxonomy of aphasic patients in these approaches. The psycholinguistic approach to patient description attempts to be explanatory,

153

in the sense that the descriptive terms used to characterize aphasic perform-ances are drawn from linguistic theory and psycholinguistic processing models, and symptoms and sets of symptoms are related to single impair-ments in the normal processing of language. To date, the results of this approach have mainly provided evidence regarding the nature of normal language processing and the relationship of aphasic symptoms to normal processing, as we shall see in Chapters 12–17. However, this approach can also be the basis for a taxonomy of patients. Badecker and Caramazza (1985: 113–14) set out clear criteria whereby this approach can be used for this purpose:

The strong sense of the notion syndrome corresponds to groupings of individuals according to categories delineated by the set of normal processing components. Under such a conception, the essence of a syndrome is that it is defined in terms of deficits to a specific set of processing components . . . an individual who presents with syndrome X could simultaneously exhibit additional aphasic symptoms (defined in terms of deficits to another set of processing components). These syndromes will be defined over abnormalities in autonomous components of the language processing system. Inasmuch as a syndrome is a projection of the modular system underlying linguistic performance, it may be considered a natural kind of deficit and accorded the status of a real psychological entity.

Every syndrome will be due to a deficit in an autonomous component of the language-processing device, and every autonomous component of the language-processing system will be capable of producing a syndrome.

Many of the measures of language function in the older psycholinguistic studies are not easy to relate to particular language-processing mechanisms. This is best illustrated by an example. Goodglass (1976) reviews the syndrome of agrammatism, and points out that patients cannot be clearly classed as agrammatic on the basis of their omission of function words and inflections, since this feature of aphasic speech is present in other groups of patients as well as those which meet the clinical criteria for agrammatism. Goodglass thus seeks other functional descriptors which can identify "agrammatic" patients. He rejects the criterion of simplification of syntac-tic structure for the same reasons, and advocates the criterion of phrase length. Patients with short phrases are classified as Broca's aphasics with agrammatism; those with long phrase length are not. In his work, only one patient (with "paragrammatism") is misclassified when classification is based on phrase length. Phrase length is thus pragmatically useful to distinguish agrammatics from other patients.

There are several points to be made about this analysis. The first is that the descriptive basis for these decisions consists of observations which are as detailed as any available in the literature on agrammatism, paragramma-tism, and the other aphasic conditions Goodglass is concerned with; this approach to patient classification cannot be faulted because of its lack of a detailed empirical basis. Second, the possibility that a patient may be called agrammatic if he shows a certain pattern of omission of vocabulary elements, regardless of his other symptoms, is not considered. The effort is to identify a sub-set of patients within the clinical category of Broca's aphasia as those with "agrammatism". This effort leads to the third feature of this analysis: *any* functional feature of aphasic language which emerges from the statistical analysis as heavily "weighted" in the separation of agrammatics and other aphasics is as acceptable as another to identify this set of patients. Goodglass settles on phrase length, but he would have accepted the original criterion of omission of function words and inflections, or that of structural simplification, had either or both been as useful in distinguishing the patient groups he had in mind. This approach to taxonomy creates several problems which do not arise in the psycholinguistic approach.

First, the omission of function words and inflections is an interesting symptom in aphasia, but no longer plays a role in classifying patients. Like anomia, and the presence of phonemic paraphasias, omission of these elements is found in too many classical syndromes. All the problems mentioned above, related to the inability of the classical approach to classify patients with these ubiquitous symptoms, thus arise. A second problem arises because there is a major difference between phrase length and the two parameters Goodglass dismisses. Function words, inflections, and syntactic structure are features of language specified in linguistic theory, and we can relate a disturbance affecting these items to both linguistic theory and models of speech production (see Chapter 15). Phrase length has no status in either linguistic theory or models of language processing. Formally, it is a feature of utterances which plays no role in the pairing of sound and meaning; that is, it is not specified by linguistic theory. Clearly, it must be determined by some operations involved in utterance production, but there is no reason to think that it represents the operation of a single part of this intricate system, or some combination of parts of this system which are functionally related. Phrase length is simply something one can measure that is defined over linguistic elements. In this sense, it is an arbitrary measurement, of no more significance than measuring how often a patient produces words that rhyme with each other in an utterance. Unless phrase length can be related to some part of a model of language processing, which has yet to be done, knowing that a patient has short or long phrase length tells us nothing about which parts of the sentence production system are working properly and which are not.

The new psycholinguistic approach to classification solves some of these problems and raises others. The problem of principled symptoms, such as the abnormalities in function words Goodglass discusses, not being relevant to taxonomy cannot arise in this approach. If the omission of function words and inflections represents a disturbance of an autonomous component of the language-processing system, it automatically constitutes a syndrome. The problem of syndromes based upon performance measures which are not related to isolated components of language processing – such as the grouping together of patients with short phrase length and the other functionally unassociated symptoms of Broca's aphasia – also cannot occur. As Badecker and Caramazza point out, the syndromes which result from this approach will be psychologically real.

There are two main problems with the application of the new psycholinguistic approach, one related to theoretical concerns, the other to practical matters. The first is that our knowledge of the nature of the normal processing system, and of how aphasic performances reflect disturbances of this system, is limited. This leads to considerable uncertainty regarding what symptoms are "principled" and what groupings of symptoms are due to impairments of a single autonomous processing component. The second problem is that this approach generates an enormous number of syndromes, and it is not clear that it will ever be feasible to find significant numbers of patients with a given syndrome. The usefulness of this approach is thus not clear. In fact, though Badecker and Caramazza set out these useful criteria for syndromes, their article is not designed to encourage the would-be taxonomist of aphasia. For these authors, the first of these problems is sufficient to make the use of patient groupings in neurolinguistics (and neuropsychology more generally) difficult, if not impossible at present. Despite these difficulties, however, the linguistic and psycholinguistic studies of aphasia that we shall review in the following chapters do provide a new conceptual basis upon which to approach the question of classification of patients in aphasia. We shall pursue this question in detail by considering the specific issue of agrammatism in Chapter 15.

Thus we see that studies in linguistic aphasiology increase our knowledge of aphasia, but also complicate some accepted approaches to description and classification of patients. The fact that patients within a single classical syndrome differ with respect to how a particular symptom, such as dysfluent speech, is manifest raises the question of whether the classical syndromes are homogeneous. Patients with symptoms that are seen in many syndromes are hard to classify. Some unexpected similarities between patients with different syndromes have been discovered in some psycholinguistic studies. Though our appreciation of the details of language breakdown has been deepened by psycholinguistic and linguistic analyses, the all-encompassing and satisfying modern connectionist theory of aphasic syndromes, and the related theory of language representation in the brain that was widely accepted after 1965, have become less secure and less convincing because of these same studies.

All of these considerations provide the impetus for more detailed linguistic and psycholinguistic studies of aphasia. Perhaps the most compelling reason to pursue these studies is the fact that the kinds of linguistic and psycholinguistic factors that were reported in the paper we cited by Goodglass and Geschwind – word frequency, picturability, semantic category, and so on – have been shown to be important determinants of patients' performances. If these factors, and others such as the detailed sound structure of a word, the syntactic structure of a sentence, or other features of word meaning, are important determinants of whether aphasic patients succeed or fail in a particular task, it is worthwhile to investigate these linguistic and psycholinguistic aspects of aphasia from the strictly linguistic and psychological points of view. As more of the linguistic and psycholinguistic details of aphasic performances come to light, the models of normal language functioning to which aphasic deficits can be related also become more detailed. Much of the work we shall cover in the remainder of Part III is concerned with these descriptions of aphasic impairments and their relationship to theories of normal language functioning. A taxonomy of patients can be built upon these psycholinguistic analyses, though this is a secondary issue for most contemporary linguistic aphasiologists.

The fact that more detailed descriptions of aphasia create challenges and problems for traditional ways of classifying aphasic patients means that they also raise questions about theories relating the components of language functioning to the brain which are based upon traditional clinical work. The greater empirical adequacy and theoretical development of modern linguistic and psycholinguistic descriptions of aphasia has led researchers to develop new theories of how language is represented and processed in the brain, and has encouraged researchers to look for neural correlates of particular psycholinguistic functions in new ways. We shall review some of these studies in Part IV.

We now turn to five areas where linguistic and psycholinguistic studies of aphasia have developed significantly in the past fifteen years. In each case, we shall present this work in a standard format. First, we shall consider something of what is known about the linguistic structures and their processing which are relevant to the subject under discussion. This will provide the basic account of normal function which we will use to understand aphasic deficits. Then we shall turn to studies of aphasic patients and relate these studies to our normal models. In some cases, the normal models will be largely confirmed by what we discover about aphasics; in other cases, we shall suggest revisions in the normal models because of the performances of aphasic patients. In Chapter 17, we shall look back over the material we have covered and consider some of the central features of the models we have reviewed, emphasizing the implications of these models for normal language functions and considering a number of possible new directions this work may take in the future.

SUGGESTIONS FOR FURTHER READING

Goodglass, H. and Geschwind, N. (1976). Language disorders (aphasia). In E. C. Carterette and M. Friedman (eds.), *Handbook of Perception*, vol. 7. Academic Press, New York.
Marshall, J. C. (1986). The description and interpretation of aphasic language disorder. *Neuropsychologia* 24, 5–24.
Schwartz, M. (1984). What the classical aphasia categories can't do for us, and why. *Brain and Language* 21, 3–8.

12

Disturbances of lexical semantic representation

The term "lexical semantics" refers to the meaning of individual words. It can be argued that the whole edifice of language is built upon the individual word. It is the individual word which, in a sense, makes primary contact with the real world. A simple word like "cat" somehow designates an object in the world – namely, the species of cats; a word like "pull" designates an action; a word like "large" designates an attribute. It is true, as we shall see in later chapters, that language does far more than simply designate items, actions, and attributes. For instance, it establishes the actors and recipients of an action, and it indicates which attributes are assigned to which items. However, it accomplishes these semantic tasks, and many others, only if what many people have taken to be the basic feature of language – having words for individual items, actions, and attributes in the real world – is accomplished. Researchers and theoreticians as different in their outlooks as the philosopher Hilary Putnam and the neurologist Norman Geschwind, whose views on the subject we reviewed in Chapter 5, all place the ability of the individual word to refer to items, and to carry meaning, at the center of the language system. And indeed, when one stands back and considers it, the ability to utter a simple sound and thereby designate an item or a class of items in the real world is an astonishing ability, available in the extensive form that we know of only to man. What exactly does this ability consist of? How does it break down after brain damage?

Many modern philosophers begin their consideration of the first of these questions by making a distinction between the *reference* of a word and the *meaning* of the word. Frege (1892) expressed this distinction by saying that the referent of a word is the actual item that the word designates, while the meaning of a word is the means whereby this designation occurs. Frege's most famous example actually deals with phrases, not words. Frege noted that the sentence:

(1)   The evening star is the morning star

though true, does not have the same status as the equally true sentence:

(2)   The evening star is the evening star

Sentence (2) expresses a tautology; it is true by virtue of the meaning of the words in that sentence. Sentence (1), on the other hand, is a scientific truth. Both the morning star and the evening star designate the planet Venus, and it is a matter of astronomical fact that the morning star is the evening star. In other words, both *the morning star* and *the evening star* refer to the same item – Venus – but they do so in different ways. *The morning star* means the star which is seen in the morning; *the evening star* means the star which is seen in the evening. Meaning, therefore, is not exactly the same as reference; meaning reflects the way the reference of the phrase is achieved.

The idea that phrases like *the morning star* and *the evening star* differ in their meaning and that their meanings allow these different phrases to refer to the same object – Venus – in different ways makes good intuitive sense when we are dealing with phrases. But what about individual words? What does the idea that the meaning of a word is the means by which it makes reference to something in the real world amount to? When we are dealing with phrases, the meaning of each word in the phrase combines with that of all the others to create a meaning for the entire phrase which relates to some item in the world – *the morning star* relates to a star which rises in the morning. But this doesn't solve the problem of what the meanings of each word in the phrase are. Perhaps the meaning of each word in the phrase is itself determined by the reference of that word: *morning* refers to a part of the day; *star* refers to a certain type of celestial body. This line of thinking would lead to the conclusion that the meanings of individual words are determined by the referents of each word, and the meanings of phrases are determined by the combination of the meanings of the words in each phrase.

This view of the relationship between meaning and reference is not unreasonable, but it seems to do some injustice to what we might have in mind when we consider a word's meaning. From a certain perspective, what a word means seems to be more than just what it refers to. Some idea of the difference between meaning and reference for individual words emerges from a fascinating line of hypothetical reasoning developed by Putnam (1973). Putnam accepted that the example of *the morning star* and *the evening star* indicates that two phrases can refer to the same item and have different meanings, and he posed the converse of this question: is it possible for two phrases – or words – to have the same meaning and refer to different items? At first glance, this would seem impossible. If two phrases or words mean the same thing, surely they must refer to the same item. Putnam, however, argued that this is not necessarily true. He presents the following somewhat complex but interesting scenario. Suppose there is a planet, called Twin-earth, which is exactly like Earth in every respect except that everything that is made out of aluminum on Earth is made out of another element, molybdenum, on Twin-earth. Aluminum pots and pans on Earth would have their Twin-earth counterparts in the form of molybdenum pots and pans. Now suppose also that the inhabitants of Twin-earth speak English, exactly as we do, with one exception: they use the word *molybdenum* for everything that we call aluminum and the word *aluminum* for everything we call molybdenum. This means that the people on Twin-earth use the word *aluminum* to refer to their pots and pans and other utensils. Suppose, finally, that except for some detail of their chemical structure, aluminum and molybdenum are identical: all the physical properties of aluminum are exactly the same as those of molybdenum. Now, Putnam says, the word *aluminum* on Twin-earth has exactly the same *meaning* for the average speaker of English on Twin-earth as the word *aluminum* on Earth has for the typical speaker of English on real Earth. However, despite the fact that these words mean the same thing, they actually refer to different substances.

Putnam's hypothetical case of the word *aluminum* on Earth and Twin-earth led him to the view that the meaning of a word is the knowledge about the word's referents that people *share*. *Aluminum* means the same thing on Earth and Twin-earth because people in these two worlds use the term to refer to a substance which they believe to be the same. People in the two worlds are ignorant of the fact that the referents of *aluminum* on Earth and *aluminum* on Twin-earth do not have the same chemical structure. It is the shared system of belief about the substance designated by the word *aluminum* which may be said to be the meaning of the word. Putnam (1970) makes a sharp distinction between these beliefs, which can be widely held by many speakers of a language, and both true knowledge and the ability actually to put true knowledge about a word to a test. For instance, he says that most English speakers know what the word *gold* means, but very few can tell us what its chemical structure is, and even people who do know the chemical structure of gold are not always able to tell real gold from "fool's gold". For the purposes of the average English speaker, it is not necessary to actually know what distinguishes true gold and fool's gold, or know how to apply these criteria. It is enough to know that there is a body of experts who can tell the difference in order to use the word *gold* correctly. To understand the meaning of the word *gold*, then, all that is necessary is that the average speaker of English knows that gold designates a metal with certain properties (malleability, a certain color, possession of monetary value, use in jewelry fabrication, etc.). It is not necessary for the average speaker to know the chemical structure of gold, or how to distinguish gold from superficially similar metals.

What is this shared knowledge which constitutes the meaning of a word?

Putnam suggests that this knowledge consists in part of a "prototype" – a representation of a typical item designated by a word. For instance, gold is typically gold in color, although there is "pink gold" and "white gold", and the prototype of the referent for the word *gold* is gold in color. Similarly, Putnam says, the prototypical lemon has a certain size and shape and is yellow, although lemons may vary in size and shape and, to some degree, in color. The prototype obviously is largely derived from the referent of the word, and this is why there is a link between meaning and reference. But the prototype is not entirely derived from all the referents of a word, since a word *refers* to atypical as well as prototypical items. This is one reason why meaning and reference differ. Moreover, there is more to the shared knowledge which constitutes a word's meaning than just a prototype based upon the physical properties of the referents of the word. For instance, we share the knowledge that gold is a precious metal, the knowledge that it is frequently used in making jewelry, and other facts about gold which are not simply facts about its physical properties. Even the fact that we know that there are experts who know what gold is and can tell true gold apart from fool's gold is shared knowledge about gold which may be part of the meaning of the word *gold*. According to this view, the study of *meaning* is basically a part of psychology and sociology. We will learn what a word means by learning what people believe about the entities it refers to. The study of *reference* is partly a psychological matter and partly a matter for other sciences. What items people refer to when they use a word is a psychological question, but the exact description of many of the properties of those items is a concern of the various physical and biological sciences.

Putnam's view of meaning contrasts with the classical theory, which was first developed by Aristotle (Smith and Medin 1981). In the classical theory, each word stood for a concept which was clearly defined; that is, there is a set of necessary and sufficient conditions for a concept to fall into a set designated by a word. The classical theory has been pronounced a failure, because these necessary and sufficient conditions cannot be stated for many concepts. Putnam's approach substitutes a much less precise idea of meaning for this rigorous classical concept.

Another matter to consider when thinking about meaning and reference is that not all words are the same, and not all refer in the same way or mean something in the same way. A word such as *nine* refers to an entity in a particular, formal, arithmetical system. Numbers, letters, geometric shapes, kinship terms, colors, and a few other types of words exemplify what we may call "well-defined" categories. The shared beliefs about the items in the real world designated by the words in these categories can be expressed quite rigorously. The same cannot be said for most other categories, despite the claims of the classical theory. There is some degree of variation in how well defined a category is. Biological categories are often less well defined than physical categories such as colors and shapes because scientists know less about the basis for classification in the biological than in the physical sciences. Man-made categories such as furniture, vehicles, or tools are perhaps the least well defined. Is a kitchen sink a piece of furniture? A bathroom sink? A set of drapes?

There are other types of words as well, which are quite different with respect to their reference and meaning. Some words, such as *unicorn*, do not have real referents at all. These words may have a referent in what is called a "universe of discourse" – the imaginary or fictitious setting of a story – but not in the real world. The relationship between the referent of such a word in this fictitious universe of discourse and the meaning of the word is particularly intriguing, since the referent itself has no *real* physical properties, only properties which are themselves *derived* from shared beliefs. Abstract words like *faith* or *unconstitutional* also do not seem to refer to real items in the same way as concrete words do, even if there are entities in the real world which are designated or described by these words. Function words – *the*, *or*, etc. – also do not refer to entities in the real world, but nonetheless have meaning: consider the difference between *the* and *a*, or *and* and *or*.

Going back to the idea that meaning is a set of shared beliefs about the items referred to by a word, we are tempted to conclude that the very idea of meaning itself varies for these different kinds of categories. In well-defined categories, the shared set of beliefs is very narrow, and may be identical in most English speakers. In less well-defined categories, there may be a core set of beliefs which is shared among all speakers of a language, but there is a great deal about the meaning of a word which is not shared among speakers of a language, and which may even fluctuate in an individual speaker's mind. Meaning is related to reference in quite different ways in the cases of the words without real referents, abstract words, and function words just considered. The very idea of the meaning of a word may be quite different for these different classes of words.

Psychologists as well as philosophers have become interested in the nature of word meaning. Their approach to investigation of meaning has been experimental, rather than strictly contemplative. We shall consider several experimental results in three areas: the role of prototypes in meaning; the question of whether the relationship between related words is captured in a hierarchically organized network of words or concepts; and the question of whether there are different ways of representing the knowledge a person has regarding a word – a more visual, "imagistic" form, and a more linguistic, "propositional" form.

We noted above that Putnam argued that the way a speaker represented a meaning of a word involved a "prototype" of the concept designated by that word, and that this prototype contained information about the physical properties of the concept (as well as other properties). A series of experiments reported by Rosch (1975) provided evidence for the idea that the semantic meanings of words involve a representation of prototypical members of the category referred to by a word. The experiments used a technique commonly employed by psychologists, known as "priming". In this technique, the subject is shown a picture or a word and is asked to make a response to this stimulus, such as naming the picture or reading the word aloud. The subject's reaction time is measured. On another trial, the subject is shown a so-called "priming stimulus", which may be a picture or a word related to the target item. The target item then reappears, following the priming stimulus. The subject is again required to name the picture or read the word, and his response latency is measured. When there are certain relationships between the priming stimulus and the target, the subject's response to the target is faster. For instance, if the word *apple* appears as the priming stimulus, and a picture of an apple appears as the target, subjects take less time to name the picture of the apple than when the picture appears in isolation. The priming technique can be used to establish that two stimuli are related, and that presentation of the first facilitates processing of the second.

Rosch's priming experiments were set up along the following lines. The priming stimulus was a word referring to a category which contained concrete objects. Ten such words were used: *furniture*, *fruit*, *vehicle*, *weapon*, *vegetable*, *tool*, *bird*, *sport*, *toy*, and *clothing*. The experimenter said one of these words and, two seconds later, the subject saw either a pair of words or a pair of pictures on a screen and was asked to say whether the two pictures or words were members of the same category. In one third of the trials, the words or pictures were identical; in another third of the trials the two words or pictures represented different items from the same category; and in the last third of the cases, the words or pictures came from different categories. Subjects were to answer "yes" in the first two conditions and "no" in the third. In all three conditions, Rosch systematically varied the degree to which the words and pictures were prototypical members of the category, assigning the examples of each category a value of high, medium, or low on a scale of typicality for that category, based on previous judgements of college students regarding the typicality of each stimulus item.

The result which Rosch emphasizes is that, for the situation in which the pair of stimuli were physically identical, there was a priming effect which varied with the degree of prototypicality of the presented items. For instance, when the priming stimulus was the word *fruit* and the words were *apple – apple*, subjects showed a greater saving in their reaction time than when the words were *nut – nut*. Rosch concluded that this result showed that the meaning of the word *fruit* included a representation of the prototypical members of the category fruit and that, having once heard the word *fruit*, a subject recognizes and processes prototypical members of that category more easily than atypical members of that category.

There are other possible interpretations of this result, some of which are dealt with by Rosch in her article. For instance, she argues that the effects cannot be due to subjects not thinking that the atypical members of the category were members of the category at all, because both the priming effects and the interaction of priming and prototypicality effects disappeared when items outside the primed category appeared on a certain number of trials. Rosch also showed that subjects were not simply matching the physically identical items on the basis of their physical identities. When she changed the task instructions so as to require that subjects answer "yes" only when the pair of words or pictures used as the targets were physically identical, and to say "no" when they came from the same category, the priming effects also disappeared.

Another part of Rosch's experimental work deals with the time course of these priming effects. Rosch found effects of priming and prototypicality for both word pairs and picture pairs, and explored the differences between word pairs and picture pairs in two ways. First, she demonstrated that changing the experimental session (so-called "non-blocked" presentation) did not produce different results from the original experiment in which all of the targets were either word pairs or picture pairs (so-called "blocked" presentation). Second, she varied the interval between the presentation of the priming stimulus and the presentation of the target pairs. In the original experiment, there had been a two-second interval between these two stimuli. Rosch progressively lowered the interval to one second, 500 msec., 400 msec., 300 msec., 200 msec., and 100 msec. She found that there was an effect of priming for pictures with as little as a 200-msec. interval between the priming stimulus and the target pair, but it required at least a 300-msec. interval before such effects were found with a target word pair. In addition, when the target pairs were presented in non-blocked conditions, the interval between the priming stimulus and the target that was necessary to produce an effect of priming was slightly longer. These observations led Rosch to the conclusion that, though the representation of a meaning of a term such as *fruit* was in a form that could facilitate the recognition that either the word *apple* or a picture of an apple were members of the category fruit, the processing of pictures was easier than that of words. She tentatively

165

suggested that images are closer to the representation of a category than are words (Rosch 1975: 222).

Rosch also investigated another feature of word meaning and its organization: the notion of hierarchical organization of categories. Words refer to categories which are progressively more general. A terrier is a type of dog, which in turn is a type of mammal, which in turn is a type of animal, etc. A screwdriver is a tool, which is a man-made object, which is a non-living item. Is there evidence that this hierarchical, progressively inclusive organization of categories plays a role in cognitive processes? The answer is "yes", but with some reservations.

Rosch and her colleagues (1976) report a series of observations which indicate that a hierarchical organization of concepts is an important principle for the organization of concepts, and that a level of representation which they term the "basic object level" plays an important role in human psychology. The first experiment required subjects to list properties of objects. Subjects were given one and a half minutes to write down as many features of the objects designated by a word as they could think of. The words came from three different levels of categorization: superordinate (fruit); basic level (apple); and subordinate (Macintosh apple). They found that the number of attributes listed six or more times by 200 subjects increased significantly for the basic and subordinate levels as compared to the superordinate level, except in the categories of trees, fish, and birds. These three categories are all biological classes, and Rosch and her colleagues concluded that, for biological classes, the superordinate term functions as a basic-level term. With this adjustment, the number of attributes listed frequently by subjects seems to be as great at the basic level as at the subordinate level, and higher than at the superordinate level. Rosch's second experiment required subjects to write down the muscle movements involved in the use of a named object. Again, the number of motor movements described in common increased significantly for basic-level categories compared to superordinate categories, and did not differ between basic- and subordinate-level categories. Once again, biological categories behaved as if the apparent superordinate was the basic level of description. The third and fourth experiments dealt with perceptual features of objects. In her third experiment, different pictures of objects described at the three basic levels were taken from books, magazines, and snapshots. Pictures were taken of four different members of each category, reproduced so as to be roughly identical in overall size, and superimposed. The amount of overlap of the shapes of the objects was then measured, and found to be greatest for basic- and subordinate-level categories, compared to superordinate-level categories. Finally, the fourth experiment required subjects to recognize and name a shape created by the superimposed pictures created in experiment three. Naming was significantly better for the silhouettes of overlapped basic-level categories than superordinate categories. Rosch *et al.* concluded that the basic level of object identity is one which is psychologically preferred in motor and perceptual tasks.

The remainder of the paper by Rosch and her colleagues goes on to document other features of basic objects. Basic-level objects are shown to be most easily detected under noise, to be most effective in priming tasks, and easiest to verify when subjects are asked to indicate whether or not they have seen an object of a particular type. The authors also argue that basic-level objects are acquired first in cognitive development, as measured by sorting tasks. Finally, they argue that the words for basic-level categories are those which first enter a child's vocabulary.

The importance of basic categories in perception has also been suggested by the work of several other authors. Brownell (1978) has shown that subjects can name basic-level items more quickly than either superordinate- or subordinate-level categories. Jolicoeur *et al.* (1984) have replicated this finding and extended it to the condition where items are shown for very short periods of time. These authors have suggested that when a person sees an object, his first conceptual representation is formed at the basic category level. He may go on to infer that the item can also be classified under a superordinate category, or he may continue his perceptual analysis of the object to determine the subordinate category into which the object falls. The hypothesis is that, when a person sees a particular type of apple, he first thinks of it as an apple, and then can infer that apples are fruits, or can look at the object more closely and decide what type of apple it is. This theory of object recognition has been accepted by many psychologists. Fodor (1982), for instance, develops a general theory of perceptual and cognitive processes, according to which basic perceptual processes produce a so-called "shallow" semantic conceptual output. In his theory, the output of visual perceptual processes are basic-level categories. Collins and Quillian (1969) provide experimental data showing that certain aspects of reasoning – determining whether statements such as *all canaries are birds* or *all canaries are animals* are true – requires a search through a hierarchically organized set of semantic representations.

Not all the results in the experimental psychological literature fit into the theory that semantic representations involve prototypes or are hierarchically organized. One of the most striking findings in Rosch's own work (Rosch 1975) is that the effect of prototypicality on priming only arose for physically identical stimuli. It is relatively easy to understand why this effect should only occur when subjects are asked to classify items as members of a category, and not when subjects are asked to say whether two items are physically identical, for the latter task does not require any conceptual or semantic knowledge whatsoever. However, it is very hard to see why, if categories such as "fruit" are semantically organized in terms of prototypical members, there should not be an increased effect in a priming task for two different members when both are prototypical compared to when both are atypical members of the category. Rosch has a long but inconclusive discussion of this result. Armstrong and her colleagues (Armstrong *et al.* 1983) have shown that subjects will treat well-defined categories, such as odd numbers, as if they were organized in terms of prototypes, despite knowing that no odd number is a "better example" of the concept of an odd number than another. The authors suggest that these results indicate that subjects impose prototypical structure upon a category in certain tasks, but may not represent the category in terms of prototypical members in their permanent semantic system. Similarly, though the theory that the logical hierarchical organization of concepts plays a role in certain aspects of inferencing and verification of the truth of statements also receives considerable experimental support, the extent to which concepts are organized and accessed in a hierarchical fashion does seem to be less than total. For instance, categories like "mammal", which stand between categories like "dog" and "animal" in a scientific hierarchy, do not behave as if they were intermediate categories in many tasks involving the verification of sentences: it takes *longer* to determine that dogs are mammals than to determine that dogs are animals. The results we have reviewed provide good reasons to believe that the prototypicality of an item within its category, and the level of representation of an item within a hierarchically organized system of categories, are semantic features which are involved in accessing a concept in some – perhaps many – circumstances, but the exact circumstances in which these features play a role in psychological processes are not completely known.

The third and last aspect of meaning that we shall consider relates to the separation of linguistic and non-linguistic semantic representations. In our discussion of Rosch's first paper, we saw that this investigator claimed that the representations evoked by a priming word must be abstract, because they produce priming effects for both words and pictures. She noted, however, that the priming effects occurred faster for pictures than for words, and therefore concluded that these abstract representations might be more similar to visual images than to linguistic forms.

A similar conclusion can be reached on the basis of another set of observations made by Potter and Faulconer (1975). They discovered that subjects could verify that a stimulus belonged to a particular superordinate category faster when the stimulus was a picture than when it was a word. For instance, when subjects were given the category "fruit", and then either saw a picture of an apple or heard the word *apple* and were asked to say whether the picture or word was a fruit, subjects responded faster to the picture. These results suggest that the meaning of the word *fruit* can be more easily compared to a picture of a particular fruit than to a word denoting a particular fruit. The authors conclude that this meaning may be some sort of image or, at least, a non-linguistic representation.

There are, however, several considerations and findings which are not so easy to reconcile with the view that meanings are images. For one thing, what image does a superordinate category such as "fruit" actually evoke? Since the image must be general enough to apply to any particular fruit, it cannot be an image of a particular fruit. However, we know, from the results of the second paper of Rosch's that we discussed above, that the *overlap* of pictures of instances of a superordinate category such as "fruit" is minimal, and that it is hard for subjects to recognize such composite shapes. It therefore seems unlikely that an image evoked by a word such as *fruit* could be a composite image of all fruits. Might it then be a *set* of images each corresponding to individual fruits? This is not a plausible account of meaning, when we consider the space such representations would take up, the mechanisms required to search through such a set, etc. Moreover, the whole notion of meaning as an image is hard to apply to words which do not refer to concrete objects, attributes, and actions. We may ask to what extent the results we have cited are task-specific, and depend, for instance, on what a subject must determine about an item. Suppose, for instance, that subjects had been asked to make judgements about the relative cost of pieces of fruit or particular tools; would reaction times for pictures still be faster than reaction times for words? Finally, though the concepts evoked by words like *apple* must be used to match items in the real world with the word *apple* (as required in the Potter and Faulconer task), they must also be used in other psychological tasks such as reasoning, where images may be cumbersome or impossible to use. Though a great deal of evidence indicates that human beings can and do generate some kind of mental image as part of the meanings of words which refer to classes of concrete items, the exact conditions under which such an image is generated, and the relationship of images to more abstract linguistic and conceptual representations of word meaning, are still not entirely clarified.

The philosophical and psychological literature thus provides several concepts and questions about semantic representations and the processing of these representations. We have reviewed three which are currently under investigation and which are quite basic: the prototypicality of an item in its category; the level of an item in a hierarchy of categories; and the nature of the code (imagistic vs. propositional) which represents an item. Philosophical considerations and psychological experimentation provide support for a role for these features in the representation and accessing of the meanings of words, though there are many unanswered questions about just what role these different features of meaning play in different aspects of human cognitive processes. We now turn to investigation of disorders of lexical semantics. We shall see that studies of brain-injured patients utilize many of the notions of semantic representations and processing which we have considered in normal subjects.

How would a disturbance of lexical semantics manifest itself? Two obvious areas where patients would be expected to have difficulty are in naming objects (and pictures of objects) and in matching a spoken word to one object out of a set of objects. In other words, patients who have disturbances of lexical semantics can be expected to have some sort of anomia and some form of single-word comprehension problem. However, not all patients with anomia and single-word comprehension problems necessarily have disturbances in semantic representations. Problems in the production and perception of the sounds of words have to be ruled out before it can be concluded that a patient with anomia and single-word comprehension problems has a disturbance of lexical semantic representations. In addition, we may ask many questions about disturbances of lexical semantics. We may draw a distinction between a disturbance of the permanent lexical semantic representation for a word and a disturbance in *accessing* that representation from a picture of an object, or from a spoken or written presentation of a word. We may ask whether there can be partial disturbances of permanent semantic representations and partial disturbances of accessing these representations. Finally, we may consider whether patients retain the ability to access an image-like semantic representation but not an abstract linguistic meaning for a word or a picture, and vice versa.

Warrington and her colleagues (Warrington 1975; Warrington and Shallice 1984) have described patients who have relatively pure disturbances of lexical semantic knowledge. Three patients are reported by Warrington (1975). All three were individuals who, around the age of sixty, began to experience problems with their memory. Neurological and radiological examinations revealed cerebral atrophy in all cases; in one case the atrophy was thought to be related to arteriosclerosis. Two of the patients had normal IQ scores, and one had a slightly lower than average IQ. None was dysphasic in conversation, though all had some difficulty finding words and one had "slightly impaired syntax". Reading skills were quite good (though not normal), indicating that these patients could pronounce words without phonemic errors. Finally, basic visual perceptual functions were intact in these patients: they could indicate slight variations in the shapes of objects, recognize letters presented against a confusing background, match pictures of faces taken from different views, and match pictures of objects taken in standard and unconventional views. Warrington concluded, on the basis of these performances, that these patients were not impaired in the production or discrimination of the sounds of words, or in basic visual perceptual processes. However, these patients showed major difficulties in understanding the meanings of words, and seemed not to know about many of the properties of objects depicted in pictures. Warrington explored this deficit in several ways.

First, Warrington tested object and word recognition. Performance on the Peabody Picture Vocabulary Test, in which a subject must match a spoken word to one of four pictures, was quite poor, varying from fifty-two to seventy correct out of 100 trials. The subjects also had great difficulty naming or describing pictures of objects. Nor could they give definitions of the words for these objects when the words were presented auditorily. Two of these patients did somewhat worse with naming pictures than with defining words, and the other was considerably worse with words than with pictures. All these tasks involved the same set of pictures and words, so Warrington could compare patients' knowledge of an item presented in these different modalities.

Second, Warrington explored the knowledge these patients had of items depicted in pictures. Their deficit – known as "associative agnosia" – was tested in two ways. First, subjects were given a forced-choice object recognition test. Three colored drawings were presented to the subject, and the subject was required to indicate which item or items had a particular property. The pictures were either of animals or of inanimate objects. Warrington tested knowledge of superordinate information (animal/not animal; insect/not insect) and subordinate information (dangerous animal, foreign animal, largest animal, animal with particular color; metal object, heaviest object, kitchen object, and object used primarily by a man). Patients were impaired relative to normals on almost all of these tasks, but showed the greatest difficulty in picking the correct picture on the basis of subordinate information. In a second test, the patients were given photographs of forty animals and forty objects and then were asked "yes"/"no" questions about these pictures. Superordinate information was tested by asking the questions "is it an animal?" and "is it a bird?" Subordinate information was tested by asking whether an animal was foreign, or bigger than a cat, and whether an object was used indoors, made of metal, or heavier than a telephone directory. Finally, the subjects were given a forced-choice task of recognition of the object name by being asked, for instance, "is this a picture of a swan or a duck?" Again, patients did worse on this test than normal controls, and showed particular difficulty with questions dealing with subordinate attributes of objects presented in the pictures. Performance on the task of choosing the name was no better than chance. These results reflect a major problem these patients have in understanding the "meaning" of pictures.

Warrington documented a similar problem in understanding the "meaning" of words. First, she repeated the set of questions she used with pictures after she had spoken the word to a patient. Again, performance was far below that of normal subjects, and was worse for subordinate-level attributes of animals and objects than for their superordinate categories. Second, the patients were given seventy words to define, divided into high and low concrete categories and high- and low-frequency categories. High-frequency words were well defined, and low-frequency words produced many errors. Interestingly one patient did better in giving definitions for abstract low-frequency words, such as *supplication*, *hint*, and *vocation*, than for concrete low-frequency words; the two other patients, though impaired, were better at concrete words than abstract words. Third, patients were tested on their ability to recognize real words and nonsense words, and sensible sentences and absurd sentences (such as *the woman was wearing a meringue on her head*). Though the patients were able to read the test material aloud easily, their performances were noticeably impaired. Finally, one patient, EM, was tested on a forced-choice recognition task in which she heard a spoken word and was asked to choose the correct item from a set of superordinate categories or a set of subordinate features. For instance, given the word *lion* she would be given a choice of "animal", "plant", or "inanimate object" as a choice of superordinate categories, or "two legs", "four legs", or "six legs", as a test of knowledge of subordinate features. Half the words that she was given were words which she claimed to have "forgotten" and half the words were ones for which she could give some indication of their meaning. For the known words, she did well on choosing the superordinate, but there was a significant number of errors in choosing subordinate features. She made many more errors in choosing both superordinate categories and subordinate features for the words she claimed not to know, and, again, the difficulty was worse with subordinate features than with superordinate categories.

All these tests show that these three patients had significant difficulty with what we have considered the "meaning" of words. They had lost information about items (or, at least, could not indicate their knowledge) – information that one would reasonably consider to be part of the shared knowledge which constitutes the meaning of a word. Warrington suggested that this disturbance reflected an abnormality in a particular long-term memory system known as "semantic memory" (Tulving 1972). "Semantic memory" refers to a "common pool of knowledge not unique to the individual" (Warrington 1975: 636), in contrast to "episodic memory", which is long-term memory regarding an individual's unique experiences. Warrington pointed out that, though the patients she reported in this paper did have some minor disturbances in long-term memory tests, they were quite different from the classical amnesic patients that she and other investigators had studied. She therefore took these cases as providing support for the separation of "semantic" and "episodic" memory. "Semantic memory" includes knowledge which must be very similar to that which philosophers have in mind when they speak of the meaning of a word, even if the two concepts have been developed quite independently by different investigators in different disciplines.

Warrington also reached several conclusions about the nature of semantic memory on the basis of the observations we have reviewed. The first is that items in semantic memory are organized hierarchically, as was suggested by the experiments on normal subjects we discussed above. The retention of information about superordinate categorization compared to information about subordinate features of words and pictures supports the hierarchical organization of items in semantic memory. Warrington also proposed a model of how information in semantic memory is accessed. According to this mode, this information is accessed "from the top down", so to speak. For instance, given the word *mallard* or a picture of a mallard, the first semantic information a normal subject accesses is that the word or picture designates a living entity, then that it designates an animal, then a bird, then a duck, and finally a species of duck. If this is the case, the theory that we normally access the "basic level" first when we recognize an object (see above) must be incorrect.

The second major conclusion about semantic memory that Warrington draws is that there may be "structurally and presumably functionally partially distinct modality-specific meaning systems. That is, a particular concept, say 'canary', would be represented in two semantic memory hierarchies, the one primarily visual and the other primarily verbal" (Warrington 1975: 656). The evidence for this is the relative preservation of the "meanings" of pictures in case EM, and of words in case AB. Warrington argues that these patterns cannot be due to a simple disconnection of the semantic memory system from words in EM's case and from pictures in AB's case, because of the (relative) preservation of superordinate category information, the internal consistency of the words and pictures for which

173

meanings could be accessed in different trials, and the importance of semantic variables such as concreteness in determining whether meaning could be accessed. All of these features suggested to Warrington that the patients have disturbances in the long-term representations of meanings, and not in the process whereby meanings are accessed (see below). As we have seen, the postulation of separate systems for more abstract linguistic representations and for visually based images has also been suggested by work on normal subjects.

Warrington's 1975 paper thus provided important documentation of the existence of patients who have a major disturbance which is largely restricted to the level of word meaning. These patients also cannot extract semantic features from pictures. The pattern of abnormalities suggested that there may be a distinction between "visual semantics" and "verbal semantics", and that both of these systems are organized hierarchically and accessed from the top of a conceptual hierarchy. We shall review one more paper by Warrington before taking a critical look at these and her related theories.

An important set of observations came from what at first seems to be an unusual source, a case of alexia, which was reported by Warrington and Shallice (1979). The patient, AR, had an abscess in the left parietal lobe which was successfully treated. Beginning four months after his treatment, he was tested for a period of approximately four years. During this time, he showed considerable difficulty in naming objects (anomia) and in reading, but intact speech, writing, and comprehension of spoken words. His anomia was not due to an inability to recognize the meaning of pictures, as in the cases we have just reviewed. He had no difficulty describing the functions of objects, or in the tests examining knowledge of pictures and spoken words which the patients we have just reviewed failed. He was said to have the syndrome of "optic aphasia", which we shall consider later in this chapter. Warrington and Shallice argue that this disturbance is separate from AR's reading problems, which, they argue, partially arise at the stage of comprehending written words.

First, Warrington and Shallice argue that AR could not recognize words by sounding them out. The evidence for this is that he had great difficulty naming individual letters, in pointing to the odd letter in a series of three mixed upper- and lower-case letters, in arranging wooden letters in correct alphabetical order, in categorizing letters as belonging to the beginning, middle, or end of the alphabet, and in reading three-letter nonsense words. Because of all of these impairments, Warrington and Shallice conclude that AR could not sound out words. This is an important conclusion, because it implies that AR could not gain access to the meaning of a word by sounding it out first and then using the auditory form of the word to achieve understanding (see Chapter 13). Rather, Warrington and Shallice argue, any understanding AR achieves of a written word must be through accessing semantic representations directly via the written form of the word.

AR was extremely bad at reading aloud; on a series of tests he only read 42.5 per cent of words correctly, and omitted 36.8 per cent of words. Syntactic class, imageability, concreteness, and word length did not affect his ability to read words aloud. His performance on a single set of words on two separate occasions was very inconsistent. Warrington and Shallice argue that these features of AR's performance are quite different from those of the patients studied by Warrington (1975). Those patients showed important effects of semantic features such as imageability and concreteness, and were highly consistent in their performances. Warrington and Shallice argue that this pattern of performance in AR's reading reflects an "access" disturbance, rather than a loss of the permanent representations. We shall return below to the question of exactly which representations are affected by this access disturbance.

Warrington and Shallice characterized in considerable detail the written-word comprehension problems of AR. He did poorly on a written form of the Peabody Picture Vocabulary Test (59/100), and considerably better (89/100) when given the same words in auditory form. He was unable to mime the action of written words (verbs) that he was unable to read aloud. Despite this, Warrington and Shallice observed that AR's deficit was not total. He was able to respond correctly to some of the stimuli on each of these tasks. Accordingly, they went on to characterize his residual knowledge of written words.

AR was first given a test of categorization of written words. He was asked to read 125 words. He could neither read nor indicate the meaning of eighty-seven. He was then tested on his ability to understand the words he could not read aloud. Of the eighty-seven, he correctly chose the superordinate category for sixty-eight when given a forced-choice categorization task. For instance, despite being unable to read or give the meaning for *crocus*, he could correctly answer the question "is it an animal or a plant?" This ability to categorize words that he could not read did not decrease when words were presented in a tachistoscope for as little as 100 msec. It also extended to words other than concrete nouns. For instance, he could categorize names as either surnames or forenames, as boys' names or girls' names, and as names of authors or politicians, and he could categorize words as referring to measurements or academic subjects. All these performances were well above chance for words that AR could not read. Unlike the patients of Warrington we described above, AR was as good on forced-choice tasks testing his knowledge of subordinate features of words as he was on forced-choice tasks testing his knowledge of the superordinate categories to which words belonged. These observations show that AR could access some semantic information about many words that he could neither read, nor give definitions for, nor match to pictures.

Warrington and Shallice concluded their testing of AR's residual semantic knowledge by investigating the effects of "priming" upon his ability to read words and name pictures. These "priming" experiments were not conducted in the rigorous fashion that we have seen done with normals, with careful attention to the interval between the priming stimulus and the target stimulus and measurement of reaction times. Rather, the priming stimulus was simply a word or phrase that was semantically related to the target, and the target was either a picture or a written word. The increase in the number of times pictures were named and words were read correctly was the measured (dependent) variable. AR benefitted more from these verbal prompts in reading words aloud than in naming pictures. In a second experiment, the target stimuli were eighty written words, and the priming stimuli were either words which were semantically related or pictures of the items designated by the target word. Again, AR benefitted more from the word primes than from the picture primes.

Warrington and Shallice point to the "substantial preservation of AR's capacity for semantic categorization of words that he failed to comprehend" (1979: 57) as the most important finding in this case. They argue that the fact that AR could often partially understand a written word he could not read aloud indicates that "his letter and word recognition deficit falls within the domain of semantic processing systems" (58). In other words, AR cannot read these words aloud for some reason, but understands them partially. Warrington and Shallice then pose two questions of theoretical significance: (1) is the deficit in AR an impairment of permanently stored semantic representations or one of access to these representations? and (2), is the semantic memory system involved specific either to the visual modality or to particular materials?

As we noted above, Warrington and Shallice argue that AR has a disturbance in *accessing* the semantic memory system from print. They suggest four criteria according to which a disturbance affecting semantic representations may be characterized as one of loss of permanent representations or as a deficit in accessing those representations. The first is that a disturbance affecting low-frequency words is due to a loss of permanent representations, while an impairment which does not seem to be frequency-sensitive is one of access. Second, consistent failure on specific items is associated with a disturbance of permanent representations; inconsistent performance on individual items over different trials is associated with an access disturbance. Third, the preservation of superordinate information is associated with a loss of permanent representations, and the failure to show selective presentation of superordinate information with access disturbances. Finally, priming effects should not occur in association with the loss of permanent representations. For these reasons, Warrington and Shallice argue that AR has a deficit in accessing semantic representations from print; hence the name of the abnormality: "semantic access dyslexia". (Warrington and McCarthy (1983) add a fifth criterion dealing with the existence of a "refractory period" during which a representation cannot be reactivated, but we shall only deal with the original four in this chapter. The reader is encouraged to consult these authors' paper for a more complete exposition of their views.)

Second, the authors argue that the case of AR also supports the subdivision of semantic systems into visual and verbal systems that had been suggested by Warrington (1975). They argue that if there were only one semantic system, verbal prompts should have shown equal priming in object naming and word reading and, in addition, picture and word priming should have been equally effective in facilitating reading. Since this was not the case, the authors conclude that there are "independent semantic systems subserving object recognition and word comprehension" (Warrington and Shallice 1979: 59). They also argue that AR's superior performance in auditory-word comprehension compared to written-word comprehension "is *prima facie* evidence for a meaning system, or at least access to its semantic representation, partially specific to the written word" (61).

Warrington and Shallice, therefore, develop two extremely important ideas regarding disturbances affecting semantic representations in their 1979 paper. The first is that these disturbances may be due to loss of permanent semantic representations or due to an inability to access these representations. They lay down four criteria which they say will distinguish abnormalities due to loss from abnormalities due to access impairments. Second, Warrington and Shallice argue that semantic representations are modality-specific. We have already seen that Warrington (1975) concluded that there were "visual" and "verbal" semantic memory systems, and that this conclusion is consistent with the work on normal subjects we discussed earlier. However, Warrington and Shallice go much further than a distinction between "visual" and "verbal" semantics in their 1979 paper. They also suggest that, within verbal semantics, there may be two separate systems – one for the written word and one for the spoken word.

A model of the process of reading and understanding a word, and of hearing and understanding a word, may help us to understand their model more easily. Actually, we are trying to choose between three models, illustrated by the "box-and-arrow" diagrams in Figures 12-1–12-3. It is obvious that these models have forms which are very similar to the box-and-arrow models made by the early connectionist aphasiologists (Wernicke and Lichtheim, reviewed in Chapter 4) and more recent aphasiologists such as Luria (Chapter 9). We will consider some of the features of these models in Chapter 17. For the moment, we may consider these box-and-arrow models in the following way. The boxes contain representations, such as sound patterns of words or meanings of words. The arrows indicate which representations feed into which others. We shall use a popular term for these modern box-and-arrow diagrams: we shall call them "information-processing models". Readers familiar with the flow charts used in some aspects of computer programming will recognize similarities between these diagrams and flow charts.

In all the models captured in the diagrams of Figures 12-1–12-3, there is an intermediate level of representation between the auditory or visual analysis of a word and semantic representations. This level of representation is called a lexical representation, and it represents the form of a word. Figure 12-1 embodies the idea that there is a single lexical representation of a word, which we access when we read a word or when we hear it. Figures 12-2 and 12-3 embody the claim that the lexical representation of word form is

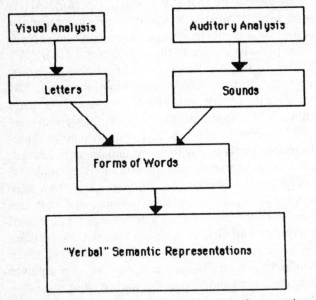

Figure 12-1. A model of the word recognition system incorporating one lexicon and one verbal semantic system

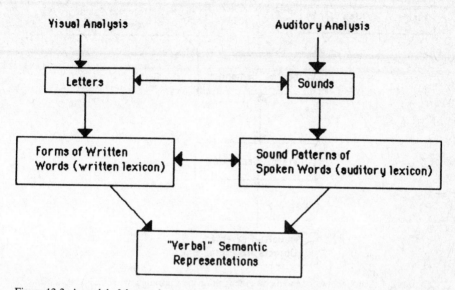

Figure 12-2. A model of the word recognition system incorporating two lexicons and one verbal semantic system

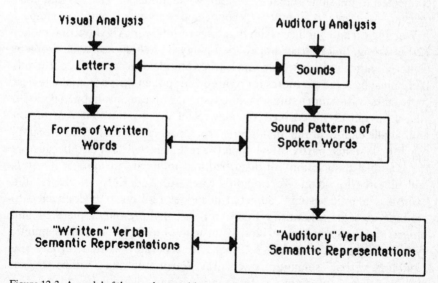

Figure 12-3. A model of the word recognition system incorporating two lexicons and two verbal semantic systems – one "written" and one "auditory"

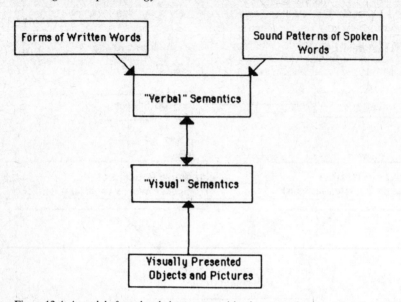

Figure 12-4. A model of word and picture recognition incorporating two semantic systems – one "verbal" and one "visual"

different for written and spoken words. Model 12-2 differs from model 12-3 in that model 12-2 claims that each lexicon – written and auditory – is connected to the same semantic system, while model 12-3 claims that each lexicon – written and auditory – is connected to its own semantic system.

Warrington and Shallice claim that their results with AR show that model 12-1 is wrong. Since, according to their analysis, AR has a specific problem comprehending written words which arises after lexical access has occurred, there must be separate routes for written and spoken words from the lexical representation system to the semantic system. This can only happen if model 12-2 or model 12-3 is correct. We may recall at this point that Warrington and Shallice also argue that there are separate "verbal" and "visual" semantic systems, partly based upon the results in AR, but also because of the "double dissociation" of disturbed and retained "meaning" of words and pictures found in Warrington's cases AB and EM. Therefore, the "verbal semantic system" depicted in model 12-2 must be connected to another "visual semantic system" for visually presented pictures and objects, as shown in Figure 12-4. If, instead of a single "verbal" semantic system, as shown in model 12-2, there are separate "written verbal" and "auditory verbal" semantic systems, as Warrington and Shallice suggest may be the case, the number of semantic systems is very large indeed.

Warrington and Shallice's approach to modeling the way people recognize a spoken or written word, or a picture or an object, and access its meaning thus involves postulating many different semantic and lexical systems. The cases they have studied show "multiple dissociations", as Shallice (1986) points out. Their view, expressed in the papers we have reviewed and in many other publications, is that these multiple dissociations of functional abilities reflect impairments to one or more of the many storage systems and access routes to these stores that constitute the psychological system responsible for representing and accessing the meanings of words and objects in normal human beings.

It is undeniable that cases such as those we have reviewed, and other published cases, show many patterns of relatively retained and impaired functional abilities in the area of storing semantic representations and/or accessing those representations from written and auditory modalities. What is unclear is whether these dissociations are as striking as Warrington and Shallice find them to be, or that they necessarily imply that there are multiple semantic stores and access routes to each. Let us consider more critically the cases we have reviewed, to see how strong the evidence is for these dissociations. We shall consider three aspects of their theory: the question of multiple semantic systems; the criteria for distinguishing an "access" from a "storage" disorder; and the issue of what information is retained when a patient only retains partial knowledge of an item.

First, let us consider the empirical facts regarding the extent of the dissociations between "verbal semantics" and "visual semantics" in Warrington's cases. On close examination, the evidence that AB and EM behave differently in answering questions about words and pictures is not strong. As Riddoch and Humphreys (in press) point out, both these patients are better overall on the picture than on the word version of this task (112/120 for pictures and 109/120 for words for AB, and 132/160 for pictures and 104/160 for words for EM). Though Warrington is correct that only EM shows a statistically significant improvement with pictures compared to words, these data fail to show a double dissociation (see Chapter 2) between impairments of knowledge regarding pictures and words. In fact, as Riddoch and Humphreys point out, both these patients are impaired on both the picture and the word versions of these tests, compared to normals.

Another interesting feature of the performance of both these patients is related to the particular questions that they got right. Both patients did better on words than on pictures in response to the question "is it English?" Riddoch and Humphreys point out that this is one of the few questions for which an answer may *not* be provided on the basis of "information represented in the picture . . . without access to semantic information", and this may explain why neither patient did better with pictures than with words for this question. Another consideration is that *word*-to-*word* associations between some of the stimulus words and the word "English" may have led to some of the correct answers when the word stimuli were presented, but would not help the patient when the picture stimuli were presented.

All these aspects of the patients' performance suggest that the interpretation placed on these data by Warrington, and subsequently by Warrington and Shallice, needs to be closely examined. Perhaps the data are yet compatible with the existence of a single "semantic" system. If so, we have to say that when we recognize a word or an object, the process of recognition involves several intermediate stages, and that the "information" or "representations" accessed in these intermediate stages may be adequate to respond correctly in many tasks that seem to require "semantic" information. For instance, we have just seen that Riddoch and Humphreys consider that some correct responses to questions about pictures may be given on the basis of non-semantic information in a picture, and we have suggested that word-to-word associations may allow for some correct responses to questions about words. We shall return below to the question of what "non-semantic information contained in a picture" might be, and to the relationship between such information and what Warrington and Shallice call "visual semantics". Our present points are that: (1) the data showing a double dissociation between answering questions about pictures and words are weak; (2) what appears to be a relative preservation of knowledge about words or pictures may really be a preserved ability to answer certain questions (or carry out certain tasks or gestures) on the basis of information obtained in the process of getting to a semantic representation from a word or a picture; and (3) this "intermediate" information may not be what we want to call "semantic" information.

AR's case is also not a simple one to interpret. It is certainly true that AR could answer certain questions about words which he could not read aloud. Since he could answer some questions about these words, it seems reasonable to assume that he must have recognized them even if he could not read them aloud – otherwise, how could he answer any questions about them at all? One possibility is that he sounded out these words and accessed the word from its sound. However, as Warrington and Shallice point out, AR's ability to sound out written words was very poor, and he could not have used this route very efficiently, if at all. Moreover, AR often could give more specific information about a word he heard than one he read. This is hard to explain if he sounded out written words and used the sound of a written word to access semantics, since he would be using the sound of the word (either the presented stimulus or the "computed" sound pattern of the word) to access semantics for both written and spoken words – why should he then be more accurate with auditorily presented than written words? As we noted above, Warrington and Shallice conclude that AR accesses a lexical representation for written words, but intermittently fails to access the semantic representation associated with that written lexical representation.

This, however, cannot be the only problem AR has in the reading process. In addition to his problems sounding out words, AR was very bad at reading words by a non-sounding-out, direct, route. He read only 42.5 per cent of words aloud correctly, and omitted 36.8 per cent of words he was asked to read, showing that his "direct" reading was very impaired as well. He did not seem to achieve lexical access well from written words by *any* means, since his lexical decision performance (that is, his ability to say whether a stimulus was a word or not) for written words was poor. These impairments in the reading process may be related to AR's ability to extract meaning from printed words. AR may have to spend so much mental effort in the task of accessing the lexicon from print that he may not have enough computational "time" or "space" available to evoke all the semantic knowledge he has. In other words, AR's impairment in accessing semantics from print may be secondary to an inability to devote "resources" to that stage of processing. If this analysis is correct, AR's performance is consistent with the existence of a single semantic system, which he cannot access easily from print because he is so bad at reading itself.

If we review AR's abilities and difficulties in extracting meaning from written words with this idea in mind, we note that AR cannot give a verbal definition for a written word, and cannot match written words with one of *four* pictures (the Peabody Picture Vocabulary Test), but that he can select one of *two* items about a word as being relevant to the word in forced-choice recognition, and that he shows facilitation in word reading with prompting. Giving a definition of a word requires conscious retrieval of the relevant information about a word that distinguishes it from other related words. This is a much harder task than simply recognizing whether one of two words is semantically related to a given word. Matching a word to one of four pictures is harder than matching it to one of two. In general, the tasks with which AR has difficulty are those tasks which require considerable processing, and active, conscious retrieval and production of information; while the tasks testing his knowledge of the meaning of written words that he succeeds at are relatively easy, and can be accomplished without conscious retrieval and production of this information. If the task of reading itself is difficult, it is possible that the more difficult semantic tasks will suffer before the easier ones.

AR's difficulty may thus be one of accessing the lexicon from the written form of words, and not one affecting a specific route to lexical semantics from a written lexicon or a specific lexical semantic store associated with the written representations of words. It is possible to access some semantic information directly from the general form of a word, without even being able to recognize all the letters in a word or the word itself (Seymour and MacGregor 1984); AR may be accessing semantics without achieving normal lexical access by a mechanism such as the one these authors postulate. Though Warrington and Shallice may be correct that AR is showing an impairment of a route from a written lexical representation to semantic representations when he shows partial knowledge of words that he cannot read aloud, there are other possible accounts of his retained ability to understand some semantic features of a word that he has difficulty reading.

If Warrington and Shallice are right, we may wonder how many semantic systems there are. One can quickly see that, following their line of reasoning, there could be as many semantic systems as there are sense modalities (vision, hearing, touch, etc.), modes of linguistic representation (speech, writing, sign, braille), and the many different forms of some of these modes (different forms of orthographies, for instance). If all these semantic systems, or even a few of them, are available, we will want to know whether the information in each is the same or partially different, how information in one system is accessed by another, and the answers to many other similar questions. On the other hand, if there is only one semantic system, we will want to know what role different types of representations (imagistic and propositional, for instance) play in that single system, how each is activated, how each activates the other, and what the intermediate representations which are activated along the different routes to this single semantic system are.

Warrington and Shallice are not the only researchers who argue that there are visual and verbal semantic systems. One line of evidence comes from the study of a fairly rare but revealing disturbance known as "optic aphasia" (Beauvois 1982; Lhermitte and Beauvois 1973). In this syndrome, the patient JF could not name pictures of objects or objects themselves when he was able to see them, but he was immediately able to name the same objects when he was allowed to hold them and manipulate them with his hands. At first glance, it would seem that JF must have had something wrong with his visual perceptual processes, but detailed testing of his perceptual abilities showed that they were intact. The second possibility that comes to mind is a "disconnection" between the output of visual perception and language, along the lines of the disconnections postulated by Geschwind. The question that Beauvois and her colleagues raised is: what stage of processing is disconnected from what part of language? Several additional observations help to answer this question.

First, JF could immediately draw from memory objects that he had just seen, even though he could not name them. This not only indicates that his low-level perceptual abilities were intact but also suggests that JF could recognize pictures as representations of objects. Second, although he frequently mis-named objects and pictures, JF could correctly mime their use. Third, many of his mis-namings were close semantic associates, such as *shoes* for *boots*. All of these observations suggest that JF understood the pictures that he saw, in some sense, but simply could not name them. This in turn suggests that there is some sort of semantic representation that the patient could access from pictures, but which was disconnected from words.

A second patient who had a more restricted form of this syndrome was studied in greater detail by Beauvois and Saillant (1985). This patient, MP, could not name colors, much as JF could not name objects. Like the first case, MP performed normally on tests of color discrimination, indicating that she was not color-blind and had no low-level deficit in color perception. In addition to not being able to name colors, MP could not select the correctly colored objects among several differently colored objects, could not color drawings of objects correctly, and failed other tests involving knowledge of colors. On the other hand, when the tests of knowledge of colors were entirely verbal or entirely visual, MP performed well. For instance, MP could answer questions such as "what category does the word 'blush' belong to: brown, red or yellow?" She could also answer questions such as "what is another name for 'Parisian ham', which is a color name?" Parisian ham is also known as "white ham", although it is in fact pink. MP could correctly answer these sorts of questions. She therefore could answer questions about colors when these questions were presented verbally.

MP failed every test that required an interaction between visual and verbal processing, but did well on "purely visual" or "purely verbal" tests. Beauvois and Saillant tested this finding in a number of ways. For instance, they found that MP could perform a variant of the test of selecting the correctly colored picture among five, when she was given explicit instructions not to think about the problem verbally and her mouth was taped shut. This presumably reduced her use of a verbal code, and therefore helped her by encouraging her to treat the task purely visually. Finally, Beauvois and Saillant constructed tests which were superficially similar to the tests that MP had done well on, but which were different in subtle ways. For instance, compared to the test in which MP was asked to give another name for Parisian ham, MP was asked to say what color a gherkin was. Whereas the first of these tasks is a purely verbal task, the second task very likely involves visual imagery. MP could not do the second task. In fact, Beauvois and Saillant showed that they could manipulate the way MP performed a task.

For instance, they gave MP the purely verbal task of saying that snow is white under two separate conditions. In the first condition, instructions biassed MP towards using verbal strategies: for instance, MP would be asked a question such as "what do people say when they are asked what color snow is?" In the other set of instructions, MP was encouraged to use visual imagery. For instance, she was told, "It is winter. Imagine a beautiful snowy landscape. There are mountains and you can see skiers going down the slopes. Now tell me what color snow is." MP's performance dropped from 19/20 to 13/20 from the first to the second of these two tasks. In other words, merely using a visual strategy to answer a verbal question made it hard for MP to accomplish the task of giving the color of an object. These results were interpreted as showing that there are two semantic stores, one visual and one verbal. In optic aphasia, the patient cannot connect the two normally, according to Beauvois and Saillant.

Again, these results, though extremely interesting, have been subject to other interpretations. Riddoch and Humphreys (forthcoming) point out that the results in these cases can be compatible with the existence of a single semantic system, just as Warrington and Shallice's results can, so long as we postulate the existence of intermediate levels of representation along the pathway from visual input to semantic representations. A diagram of Riddoch and Humphreys' model is presented in Figure 12-5. As the reader can see, Figure 12-5 is an elaboration of model 12-2, with the addition of a stage of "structural descriptions" which input from the visual modality passes through before reaching the "semantic system". Riddoch and Humphreys suggest that the information in a "structural description" is sufficient to allow a person to judge whether a picture is of a real object or not, to allow a person to indicate the use of an object through gestures, and to answer questions about the physical properties of an object. However, this information is not enough to allow a person to answer questions about the functions of an object (except insofar as an object's functions reflect its physical properties). For instance, the structural description of a steering wheel of a car would allow a person to show a number of possible actions associated with wheels, but would not allow him to indicate the actual use of a steering wheel. Riddoch and Humphreys claim that there may be a disturbance in the pathway between "structural descriptions" and "semantics" in the case of optic aphasia.

Riddoch and Humphreys base their alternate analysis on results in a case of their own, JB. Like other optic aphasics, JB could not name objects, but could show how they were used through gestures. Humphreys and his colleagues (Humphreys *et al.* forthcoming) tested JB on a wide variety of tests of object recognition. First, they showed that JB could do a so-called

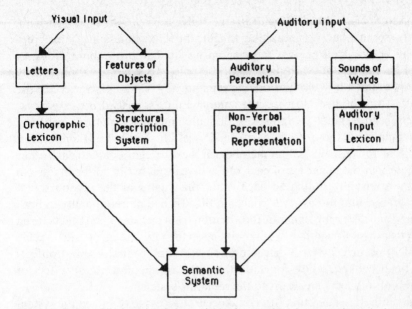

Figure 12-5. A model of word and picture (object) recognition incorporating a single semantic system and a stage of structural descriptions for object and picture recognition

"object decision" task. This is the equivalent of a lexical decision task, using pictures instead of words. The false items in this task are pictures in which parts of an object are replaced with parts of other objects. JB did as well as normal control subjects on even the most difficult version of this test, demonstrating that his knowledge of the way objects looked was excellent. JB also was able to give excellent definitions of auditorily presented words. This pattern of results is the same as in the other optic aphasic cases.

However, Humphreys and his colleagues discovered several additional features of JB's performances which they claim put his deficit in a different light. JB was significantly worse at matching words to pictures when the foils were *both* semantically *and* visually similar to the target than he was when the distractor pictures were *either* semantically *or* visually similar to the target. The authors conclude that JB did not have a disturbance of semantic representations, because purely semantic similarity did not disturb his functioning, or of structural descriptions of objects, since purely visual distractors did not impair his performance. They concluded that his deficit lay in accessing semantics from structural descriptions of objects. Second, they investigated his ability to answer questions, using Warrington's method of forced-choice responses to questions about line drawings or the names for these drawings. JB did perform better with the words than with the pictures, but there was a close relationship between how he performed in both tasks.

Whenever he made an error with an auditorily presented word, he also made some error in a question regarding the line drawing of the same object, and overall he was well below chance in answering questions about drawings when he had trouble with their names. Finally, JB's naming ability partly depended upon how similar-looking semantically related items were to the target. Thus, he had most trouble naming animals, birds, fruit, crustacea, insects, and vegetables, and less difficulty naming furniture, vehicles, implements, clothes, body parts, and possibly buildings. Independent ratings of how visually similar members of these categories are to each other indicate that the members of each of the categories in the "difficult" group are more visually similar to each other than items in the second set of categories. Humphreys *et al.* conclude that JB had more difficulty in both naming and accessing semantic information from pictures when the pictured object was visually similar to other objects in the same category, and that his problem occurred after a "structural description" of the pictured objects had been evoked. They conclude that "the results indicate an effect of structural similarity on access to the semantic system".

The authors argued that this could occur if access to the semantic system occurred "in cascade", rather than strictly linearly. A "cascade" means of accessing semantic representations would work roughly as follows. A picture would temporarily activate all similar-looking items at the "structural description" stage of processing, and each of these structural descriptions would activate a semantic representation, as shown in Figure 12-6. However, the correct item receives a maximal activation, and structurally similar items are less activated. The way that such a system ultimately recognizes the correct item is through the use of inhibitory connections. Each "node" in this sort of system activates the corresponding node at the next processing stage and inhibits all other nodes at its own processing stage. The degree of inhibition is proportional to the degree of a node's activation. Since the correct node receives the most activation, it will eventually inhibit all other nodes at its stage of processing. Ultimately, the activation and inhibitory activity in the system will converge upon the correct item; this might happen very quickly if the process of activation and inhibition is very fast.

The fact that JB showed difficulty with structurally similar items within a given semantic category can be explained in this system in the following way. Given a picture of, say, an apple, all similar-looking items will be activated at the level of structural descriptions. Each of these will activate a semantic representation. The correct structural description will inhibit all the others, and the correct semantic representation will inhibit all the others. However, at one point, quite a few semantic representations will be activated that are similar to the semantic representation of an apple. Those that refer to objects which are also structurally similar to apples will be particularly highly activated, though never as highly activated as the semantic description for "apple" itself. If JB has trouble selecting among relatively highly activated nodes, he will have trouble knowing whether the correct semantic representation to choose is that which corresponds to an apple or another highly activated semantic representation. If this is the problem JB has, he will have difficulty matching objects to words, and in doing other tasks that require extracting "meaning" from pictures (or from objects themselves).

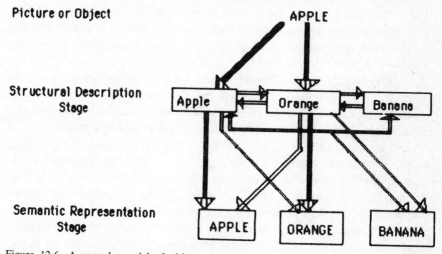

Figure 12-6. A cascade model of object recognition. Solid arrows represent activation. Outlined arrows represent inhibition. For details, see text.

However, this difficulty would reflect a disturbance internal to a single semantic system, not a disconnection of a "verbal" and a "visual" system, each of which contained "semantic" information.

We should not leave this "cascade" model without indicating that it too has its problems. For instance, how many similar structural descriptions are activated by an object? Is the structural description of the moon activated when we see an orange? Both are round, and the moon can be orange in color. We shall return to some more general issues regarding this type of model in Chapter 17. There are also questions that can be raised about case JB. Warrington (personal communication) has suggested that JB may have more than one deficit. We shall not pursue all these issues here; the basic point is that cascade models can account for some of the data regarding optic aphasia, and JB illustrates how this may happen.

We should return to our main theme at this point. We have discussed Warrington's cases with deficits in "semantic memory" (AB and EM), Warrington and Shallice's case AR, with "semantic access dyslexia", and the cases of "optic aphasia" (JF, MP, and JB) to see what they show about the number of "semantic systems" that exist. We have seen that many investigators conclude that these cases support the existence of at least separate "verbal" and "visual" semantic systems, and possibly even more semantic systems (such as "written" and "auditory" verbal semantic systems). However, questions arise about how strong the evidence is for the dissociations which lead to the postulation of separate semantic systems; and the patterns of performance in these cases can be explained by postulating deficits other than those suggested by the original authors in a system with a single set of semantic representations. If there is a single set of semantic representations, though, there must also be stages in processing visually presented objects which compute "structural descriptions" of objects. The relationship of both these concepts to the concepts of "mental images" and "prototypes" that have emerged in the literature on normal subjects is not completely spelled out, and remains an area for further clarification and theory construction.

Warrington and Shallice's second point deals with the criteria for distinguishing an "access" disorder from a "storage" disorder. We listed four of their criteria whereby the two can be distinguished. Storage disorders are expected not to allow priming (or cueing or prompting) to be effective; to show consistent patterns of success and failure on specific words or pictures across trials; to affect low-frequency items more than high-frequency items; and to affect knowledge of subordinate features of an item more than knowledge of the superordinate category of an item. Let us consider each of these criteria.

The first seems quite clear. If an item shows semantic priming effects, its semantic representation must be available in some way. In fact, in addition to Warrington's use of cueing and prompting, recent studies have used more precise priming techniques to investigate the semantic disturbances in different groups of aphasic patients, with some surprising results. Milberg and Blumstein (1981) found that Wernicke's aphasics, who could not do spoken-word–picture matching, nonetheless showed semantic priming effects in a lexical decision task. Interestingly, Milberg and Blumstein found that Broca's aphasics, who did far better at the initial word–picture matching task, did not show these priming effects. Milberg and Blumstein suggested that these results demonstrate that their Wernicke's aphasics still retained some semantic knowledge of a word, even if they cannot match the word to a picture, but could not use their residual semantic knowledge in conscious processes. According to Milberg and Blumstein, this semantic knowledge can only be activated unconsciously. (The authors refer to this as "automatic" activation of this knowledge, but more research would be needed to show that this activation is indeed automatic (Posner and Snyder 1975).) The Broca's aphasics tested by Milberg and Blumstein, on the other hand, were able to access this knowledge consciously, but several of the unconscious processes that use this knowledge – such as those that mediate priming effects – were not functioning normally. The use of various tasks, like priming, to investigate the residual knowledge a patient has of a word or picture's meaning and to determine the ability of a patient to use that knowledge in conscious and unconscious, automatic and non-automatic, and other types of tasks appears to be a new, potentially powerful approach to the study of disorders of semantic representations.

Warrington and Shallice's second and third criteria – word-frequency effects, and consistency of success and failure on individual items – seem less convincing means of distinguishing storage and access disorders. They seem to depend upon a fairly simplistic view of the actual physical basis for storage and access of an item, according to which storage is either present or not present but access can be variable, and storage is organized in terms of word-frequency but access channels are not affected by frequency. However, this need not be the case. Suppose that a particular item is "stored" through the pattern of activity in a set of neurons, and is "accessed" by the activity in a set of connections to these neurons (for models making similar claims, see Chapter 22). There is no reason why the electrical activity in the set of neurons might not be drastically changed for a period of time – a focal seizure might accomplish this, for instance. For that period, the "storage" of the items would be "lost", but this would be temporary. Similarly, the activity in the connections to that set of neurons could be temporarily or permanently disturbed, resulting in an "access" disturbance which was either intermittent or constant. In a similar vein, we may observe that the reason that high-frequency items are less easily affected is precisely because the neural nets and pathways associated with them are so frequently used. But, if use can make a neural net more resilient to damage, surely it can also make a connection to a neural net equally resilient to damage; at least, nothing we now know about neurophysiology makes this impossible, and most neurophysiological theories assume that the activity in connections and nets is equally affected by their use for a particular psychological purpose, such as understanding a word (see Chapter 22). Both these criteria, therefore, are questionable.

Finally, Warrington and Shallice suggest that retention of superordinate information reflects a storage disorder. In addition to being a criterion for distinguishing storage from access disorders, this feature of the retained information in these cases leads to the last major hypothesis of Warrington and Shallice that we shall consider: the hierarchical organization of semantic information, and its "top to bottom" access. We therefore need to consider this criterion especially closely.

One way to begin is by asking what partial semantic information is retained in patients with all varieties of semantic disorders. The patients of Warrington's and Shallice's sometimes show preservation of superordinate information (the patients in Warrington's 1975 paper do), but sometimes do not (AR, and other patients reported by Warrington). If we look further afield, many different types of partial preservation of semantic information seem to occur in aphasia and following brain damage. Goodglass and Baker (1976) document patients with various patterns of retained ability to recognize superordinate categories, "contrast co-ordinate" items (*apple* in relationship to *orange*), similarly shaped objects, functionally related objects, and items related in other ways. It is not clear what disturbances all the patients tested by Goodglass and Baker or other investigators had, but there does seem to be a large number of patterns of retained partial semantic information that can arise. In addition, there seem to be different ways the retained information can be organized (Zurif *et al.* 1974; Grossman 1981; Caramazza and Berndt 1978; see Lesser 1978 for review). All these results suggest that the retention of superordinate information is one of a number of patterns of retention and loss of semantic information that can occur after brain damage.

The other studies dealing with semantic disturbances we have just cited have involved groups of patients. Often these studies were directed towards the questions of whether two clinically defined groups of patients showed different patterns of semantic breakdown, or whether a particular pattern was found in a particular clinical group. We do not know what was wrong with the patients in these studies in as much detail as we do in Warrington and Shallice's cases. Warrington and Shallice therefore add considerably to our approach to these disturbances by advancing the claim that retention of superordinate information reflects a particular type of disturbance of the semantic system – one of storage. In the other studies, some patients may have had "access" disturbances, and others "storage" impairments; others almost certainly had problems with lexical access or visual analysis that might impair semantic access (see the discussion of AR above). If so, it is not surprising that many forms of partial retention of semantic knowledge might be seen in these cases, since the patients in these groups have many different deficits.

How can we test this claim? The claim rests on an analysis of the co-occurrence of symptoms: preserved superordinate information is said to co-occur with consistency of responses, frequency effects, and the absence of priming. As noted in Chapter 2, mere co-occurrence of deficits (or, in this case, co-occurrence features of abnormal performances) does not prove they are functionally related; only theoretical explanation can do that. In this case, we have rejected the features of consistency and word-frequency effects as relevant to the storage/access distinction. This leaves us with the relationship of retention of superordinate information to priming. According to Warrington and Shallice, a disturbance of storage of semantic representations should *not* allow priming to happen, and *should* allow superordinate information to be preserved. Therefore, if priming *is* possible, storage would *not* be affected, and superordinate information would *not* be preferentially preserved. This association needs to be documented in a large number of cases before we can accept that better retention of superordinate information reflects a disturbance of storage of semantic representations.

Finally, we should again note that Warrington and Shallice's claim that semantic information is accessed "from the top down" when a person is shown a picture of an object directly contradicts the claim that *basic*-level categories are accessed first in object perception (see our previous discussed results in normals). Warrington and Shallice tested subordinate information by probing for knowledge of an item's features (cats have four legs), while many studies of normal subjects test subordinate information by asking about category inclusion (a mallard is a duck), so perhaps the difference between the brain-injured and normal populations can be reconciled (as was pointed out to me by M. Rosenblum, 1985). However, at present, this aspect of Warrington and Shallice's theory must also be treated with caution.

Overall, we have many questions about the details of Warrington and Shallice's formulation. As elsewhere in this book, these reservations should not blind us to the importance of these papers. The theories enunciated by these researchers set up a quite detailed framework for describing disturbances of lexical semantic representations. By contrasting access and storage disorders, and making specific claims about what information is preserved in storage disorders and about the number of semantic systems, Warrington and Shallice have allowed researchers to approach a large number of questions within a theoretical structure. This has already stimulated new observations and new theories of these disturbances.

Finally, let us consider one last feature of Warrington and Shallice's work regarding semantic impairments – the investigation of what they call "category-specific" impairments. Warrington and Shallice (1984) documented several patients who have particular difficulties in comprehending both words and pictures of living things, but much less difficulty comprehending words and pictures of common inanimate objects. Two of their patients, JBR and SBY, could identify less than 10 per cent of pictures and words presented to them when they represented living things, but could identify between 75 and 90 per cent of pictures of inanimate objects, and between 52 and 79 per cent of words of inanimate objects. On a second set of stimuli, the results were much the same. JBR had considerable difficulty with foods, identifying only 20 and 30 per cent of visually presented food items and their names presented auditorily, compared with 87 and 77 per cent of inanimate objects presented visually and auditorily. These effects were not simply due to increased frequency of the words for inanimate objects, because frequency was balanced across the stimulus sets. Nor were the effects simply due to the familiarity of the pictures of items in each of these categories, since, in a separate experiment, the authors factored out the degree of familiarity of pictures using an analysis of co-variance. Two other patients, KB and ING, had such difficulties with expressive language that their verbal responses could not be taken as reliable indications of what they knew. Therefore, these two patients and JBR were tested on a matching-to-sample task, in which they were presented with five colored pictures of animals, foods, or inanimate objects and asked to match a spoken word to one of the five items. For both these patients, performance on the inanimate objects was significantly better than the two other categories.

Warrington and Shallice analyzed these cases as patients who have lost permanent semantic representations for items within the categories of living things and foods. The facts that the patients frequently produced superordinate information but not subordinate information, and that their responses were consistent, follow these researchers' criteria for disturbances of permanent semantic presentations. The authors indicate that the differences between inanimate objects and animals and living things may represent the differences between the salient features of these different categories. Inanimate objects are mainly distinguished by their functions. Even similarly shaped objects, such as chalk, crayons, and pencils, have subtly different functions. On the other hand, foods and living items by and large have similar functions (within each category), and distinctions among items within each of these categories depend more on each item's physical characteristics than its function. Warrington and Shallice suggest that these different salient features of items within these different categories may be the determining factor in setting these categories apart. Not all performances are completely explained along these lines, however. JBR, for instance, did poorly on tests of his knowledge of musical instruments, which are inanimate objects, and quite well on body parts. A "fine-grain categorical organization of semantic systems" (Warrington and Shallice 1984: 849), allowing for information within a particular category to be lost, is also consistent with these results. This possibility receives support from a case of Hart *et al.*'s (1985), who had a loss of knowledge about fruits and vegetables but not about other foods. Since all foods serve similar functions and are mainly distinguished by their physical properties, this case provides evidence for such a fine-grained, category-based organization of semantic knowledge.

Warrington and her colleagues were not the first researchers to notice category-specific semantic impairments, although their studies are the first to find these deficits in what we considered to be "less well-defined" categories (see the discussion at the beginning of this chapter). A more commonly described selective impairment with the meanings of abstract words compared with concrete words has been described by several investigators, such as Goldstein (1948), whose work we reviewed in Chapter 7. By way of contrast, Warrington (1981) reported a patient who had greater difficulty in understanding concrete written words than abstract written words, as demonstrated on a specially designed test matching pictures to both types of words. There are other instances of category-specific comprehension and production disorders. For instance, Goodglass *et al.* (1966) reported that a large proportion of 135 patients they tested in comprehension and naming of body parts, common objects, actions, colors, letters, and numbers showed particular difficulties in either the comprehension or the production of one or another category. Most of the patients had difficulties with body parts, colors, letters, and numbers, which are more "well-defined" categories in the sense that we discussed in the first part of this chapter. The existence of category-specific difficulties in comprehending or producing words within all these categories suggests that the organization of semantic systems involves grouping together items by category, or, perhaps, in relationship to whether an item is in a more or less well-defined category, or in a category whose members are distinguished by their physical properties or by their functions. Exactly how this organization is accomplished, and, if there is more than one semantic system, which is so organized, remain questions to be explored.

Interestingly, the semantic feature which philosophers and psychologists consider to be so central to meaning, and with which we began our discussion of semantics – prototypicality – has received little attention in aphasia. However, there is some work on the subject, and it does show some effects of prototypicality.

Brownell (1978) found that, though normal subjects were more likely to name typical objects with the basic-level name (thus replicating Rosch's results), they were more likely to name atypical members of a category with a subordinate-level name. Thus, for instance, given a picture of a dress shirt, they were likely to name the picture with the word "shirt", but given a picture of an undershirt, they were more likely to say "undershirt". An undershirt is not a typical member of the category shirt, while a dress shirt is. Brownell (manuscript) also found a similar effect in five Broca's aphasics and five Wernicke's aphasics. These subjects, like normals, were more likely to produce the basic-level term for a typical member of a category, and a subordinate term for an atypical member of a category. These patients also made more errors naming atypical items than typical items. An interesting feature of the responses was that the patients sometimes named an atypical item with a basic-level name, and then elaborated on their response. For instance, given a picture of a racing car, one subject said *car, one that goes fast*; and another said *car, racing car*. These responses indicate that these patients had in fact identified the picture as a racing car, but were unable to retrieve the words *racing car* without considerable effort or, in some cases, were unable to retrieve it at all. It thus seems that the degree of typicality of an item may influence a patient's ability to retrieve its name. In many cases, this does not seem to be due to the patient having difficulty understanding the concept of a subordinate-level item, but simply reflects an inability to produce the name. In other cases, an impairment of this sort may reflect difficulty at the level of concepts, as Brownell has also found that there is a slight effect of prototypicality upon a patient's ability to say whether a picture falls within a particular category when given the name of the category auditorily. Typicality, therefore, is yet another feature which enters into semantic systems, and interacts with the level of an item in a semantic hierarchy, though, again, its exact role is still largely unexplored.

Summary

We have covered a considerable amount of material in this chapter. We have seen how the simple notion that a word gains its meaning by being associated with the sensory properties of objects is far too simple a characterization of word meaning. When we stop to think about the subject, what words mean is a complicated and elusive concept. What a word refers to is one part of this concept, but its meaning is more than that. As Frege (1892) said, "meaning is the method whereby words and phrases refer to items in the real world". It is easy to see how different phrases, such as *the morning star* and *the evening star*, refer to the same object in different ways, but it is not so easy to see what is meant by the term "the way in which a word refers" when we are talking about *words* and not *phrases*. One theory is that word meaning is based upon the mental evocation of a set of prototypical items belonging to a category. We have considered the development of this view in Putnam's philosophy of word meaning, and reviewed some of the experimental psychological literature supporting the claim that words do evoke mental representations of prototypical members of their categories.

However, in our discussion of the psychological experiments dealing with prototypicality, we rapidly came across many other issues. The first is that concepts seem to be organized hierarchically, as well as in terms of prototypicality, with subordinate, basic, and superordinate levels of representation. Moreover, there seems to be a preference for the basic level of representation, both in perceptual tasks and in language tasks. At the end of this chapter, we mentioned studies that suggest that there is an interaction between prototypicality and this conceptual hierarchy, with atypical members of a category being most easily accessed at the subordinate level, and typical members of the category being most usually accessed at the basic level. A second major consideration that emerged from Rosch's experiments is that there seems to be a difference between processing pictures of objects and processing words for objects. Exploring this difference led us to a consideration of the literature on normal subjects dealing with "visual semantics" and "verbal semantics". Many results suggest that humans can process concepts in either a visually based, imagistic mode, or a more abstract, verbally and linguistically based mode. Whether these different types of representations are simply different modes of processing of a single underlying semantic representation, or whether there are two or more sets of semantic representations which are interconnected, remains the subject of debate and investigation.

Turning to abnormalities in the semantic system, we found first that patients could be identified whose sole or major problem seems to be in word meaning. These patients show major deficits in providing definitions, in matching words and pictures, in naming objects, in providing words from definitions, and in a variety of other tasks that require word meaning; but they do not have difficulties in repetition, reading aloud, categorizing different views of an object as the same, or in other aspects of long-term or short-term memory. These patients' problems, therefore, seem to be largely limited to the system of representations related to word (and object) meanings. Investigations of these patients by Warrington and her colleagues have led the authors to conclude that the data from brain-damaged subjects largely support the views of organization of meaning that we discussed in the experimental psychological literature. Warrington found that superordinate category information was more likely to be preserved than subordinate feature information, and that patients could have greater difficulty with visually presented pictures than with auditorily spoken words, thus confirming the basic notion of hierarchical semantic organization, and the distinction between "visual semantics" and "verbal semantics", which had arisen in the literature on normals. In addition, Warrington and Shallice argued that evidence from brain-injured subjects suggested that the semantic system was much more finely divided than was apparent in experiments on normals. They presented evidence that certain patients had difficulty in comprehending the concepts associated with concrete items, but not abstract items, and others had the reverse difficulty; some patients had more difficulty in accessing meaning of written words than with auditorily presented words; other patients had difficulty in accessing the meanings of specific sets of concepts, such as living things and foods, but no such difficulty in comprehending the meanings of inanimate objects. Warrington and Shallice argued that breakdowns in the semantic system show multiple dissociations of impaired and preserved abilities along highly specific category and modality lines. The conclusion they draw is that the semantic system is organized along these category and modality lines, even to the point, perhaps, of there being a separate semantic system for written words as opposed to spoken words. Finally, Warrington and Shallice have suggested that, in pathological cases, it is important to distinguish between disturbances of the permanent representations found in these multiple semantic systems, and disturbances of accessing these representations, and they have attempted to provide criteria to distinguish access disorders from storage disorders.

We have subjected the data and analyses of Warrington and Shallice to considerable scrutiny, and raised many questions about their models and their analyses of deficits. Though this process may have weakened our acceptance of their particular theories, it has led to an even richer approach to modeling the nature of semantic representations and the processes whereby they are activated or accessed. We have seen that it may be proper to separate out information about the physical properties of an object from information about its functions; that we may activate many concepts in parallel and inhibit all but the appropriate concept, rather than simply accessing a single concept, after an item is presented visually; that there may be various patterns to a patient's partial preservation of knowledge about an item; that some semantic information may be available for unconscious processes, such as priming, and unavailable for conscious processes, such as matching words and pictures, and vice versa; and other features of disorders of semantic representations. The theory of disorders of semantics which Warrington and Shallice present is extremely valuable as a framework for thinking about all these findings, even if aspects of their theory may be suspect.

Much of the work that we have reviewed is very preliminary. Though recent observations on features of semantic disturbances, such as the category specificity of impairments in comprehension, are far more detailed than the clinical observations found in the older literature, there are clearly many unanswered questions about semantic disorders in aphasia, which are likely to be studied in the future. Some of these questions are psychological. What is the exact relationship between a priming stimulus and a target word that produces facilitation in the face of particular impairments in accessing meaning? Is there some way to distinguish between the theory that there are two separate semantic systems – one imagistic and one linguistic – and the theory that there is one semantic system and a stage of processing at which structural descriptions of objects are computed? Some of the questions are neurological. What areas of the brain are involved in the specific impairments in storage or accessing semantic representations? What diseases are particularly prone to produce particular types of impairments? Some of these questions are aphasiological. Are there correlations, or causal connections between other aphasic symptoms and particular types of impairments in accessing or storing semantic representations?

We may end this chapter by returning to two early themes – one raised at the beginning of this chapter and one which we have considered at other points in this volume. The first is the question of what words mean. We saw that one view of meaning is that meaning is the shared knowledge people have about an item designated by a word. The psychological and aphasiological investigations we have reviewed in this chapter show us that shared knowledge involves many types of representations, consists of many different sorts of information, and needs to be accessed from a number of different types of stimuli presented in different sense modalities. How much of the structures and representations we have discussed would be considered to be part of the shared knowledge of an item or the prototype of an item, and, therefore, would be considered to be part of a word's "meaning" by a philosopher like Putnam, is a question we cannot answer. But, at this point in our understanding of semantics and its disorders, it is certainly premature to imagine that any hard-and-fast lines we may draw between concepts such as "meaning" and concepts such as "structural descriptions" or "visual" and "verbal" semantics will ultimately prove to be correct, however helpful the statement of clear and testable hypotheses may be. An ongoing process of theoretical clarification, consisting in part of distinguishing these related concepts, based upon empirical data from normal and pathological cases, will, we hope, eventually lead to a clear and empirically well-established theory of lexical semantic representations and concepts, and their disorders.

The second issue emerges from the first. Our review of the nature of meaning and disturbances of meaning has begun to give us some insight into the complexities of the questions surrounding the meanings of words, how words are related to objects and items in the world, how these meanings are accessed, and other related issues. We may compare our present approach to a theory of word meaning with the vastly simpler theory of "names" developed by Geschwind, which we reviewed in Chapter 5. However appealing that theory may be in its simplicity, and however neatly that theory meshes with a certain level of neuroanatomical fact, we must conclude that the theory does not deal with a great many aspects of meaning, reference, and lexical semantic representations which need to be considered if the question of what words mean and how their meanings are disturbed in aphasia is to be answered in any sort of detailed way. Indeed, our present knowledge, though more adequate, is itself very incomplete and tentative, with many questions left open. In this chapter, we have reviewed some of the major current issues regarding the nature and organization of semantic representations, the processes whereby they are accessed, and the way these representations and access mechanisms break down. It is to be expected that future work will add to and change many of the theories and conclusions presented here. The basic questions of what semantic representations are, how they are organized and accessed, and what the consequences of disease are in this system, will remain. In all likelihood, the major theories which have been presented here as possible answers to these questions will continue to define some of the issues in the field, and to be debated and revised on the basis of new data and reanalyses of old data, for some time to come.

SUGGESTIONS FOR FURTHER READING

Beauvois, M.-F. (1982). Optic aphasia: a process of interaction between vision and language. *Philosophical Transactions of the Royal Society of London* B298, 35–47.

Goodglass, H., Klein, B., Carey, P., and Jones, K. (1966). Specific semantic word categories in aphasia. *Cortex* 2, 74–89.

Hart, J., Berndt, R., and Caramazza, A. (1985). Category-specific naming deficits following cerebral infarction. *Nature* 316, 439–40.

Rosch, E. (1975). Cognitive representations of semantic categories. *Journal of Experimental Psychology (General)* 104, 192–233.

Warrington, E. K. (1975). The selective impairment of semantic memory. *Quarterly Journal of Experimental Psychology* 27, 635–57.

Warrington, E. K. and Shallice, T. (1979). Semantic access dyslexia. *Brain* 102, 43–63.

(1984). Category specific semantic impairments. *Brain* 107, 829–54.

13

Disturbances of the sound system

When we speak of the form of words, we usually have in mind some representation of their sound. Our first topic in this chapter will therefore be a brief description of the nature and organization of the sounds of words. The second topic we shall address is the psycholinguistic question of how these sounds are produced. We shall review studies dealing with the stages involved in the planning and production of sounds of words. We shall then turn to studies of aphasic patients' abilities to produce the sounds of words correctly, and relate their difficulties in this function to the structure of the sound system and to the stages of production of the sounds of words.

The sounds that make up words are organized in quite specific ways. Some features of the organization of the sounds of words are universal to all human languages. Others reflect particular properties of individual languages. The way linguists approach the investigation of the structure of the sound system is to look for words that are minimally different in their sound patterns and then to build a theory of the sounds of a language on the basis of these differences. For instance, the words *bat* and *pat* differ in their first sound. The words *blackboard* and *black board* differ in their stress contours. The word *pulley* can be spoken so that the first syllable is /pull/ and the second syllable is /ey/, or so that the first syllable is /pul/ and the second syllable is /ley/. These three contrasts exemplify three different levels of organization of the sound system. The difference between *bat* and *pat* represents a difference at the level of sound segments, known as phonemes. The difference between *blackboard* and *black board* represents a difference at the level of stress contours. The differences in the two pronunciations of *pulley* represent differences in the way phonemes are grouped into syllables within a word. Each of these elements is related to the others. Groups of phonemes make up syllables, and different syllables receive different degrees of stress to make up the stress contour of a word. Each of these parts of the sound system – phonemes, syllables, and stress contours – has its own internal structure and its own set of universal and language-specific rules. We shall consider each of these levels briefly.

The phonemes of a particular language are identified by contrasting words which are minimally different with respect to their sequences of sounds. A particular sound is a phoneme in a language if that sound can be contrasted with another in a single position in a word and both of the resulting forms are words of the language. For instance, the contrast between *pat* and *bat* leads to the conclusion that *p* and *b* are each phonemes of English. The application of this procedure leads to the identification of a small number of phonemes. Not all the different sounds which occur in a language are phonemes, if we define phonemes this way. For instance, if you place your hand in front of your mouth while saying the word *pat* and the word *tap*, you will notice that there is a burst of air that occurs after the /p/ in *pat* that does not occur after the /p/ in *tap*. This burst of air, known as "aspiration", distinguishes these two /p/ sounds. However, there is no word of English in which one can substitute an aspirated /p/ for unaspirated /p/ and produce a new word. Aspirated /p/ always occurs in certain positions in a word (the beginning of syllables) and unaspirated /p/ occurs in other positions (the end of syllables). Whether or not the sound /p/ is aspirated therefore depends entirely upon the phonological context in which the sound is found; that is, aspiration of /p/ is completely predictable from context in English. Accordingly, these two realizations of the sound /p/ are not different phonemes of English. They are termed different "allophones" of the same phoneme, /p/.

This example illustrates an important feature of phonemes; namely, that they are linguistically defined. Although each phoneme must be a sound that can actually be produced by the human vocal tract, and distinguished from other phonemes by the human auditory system, phonemes are not themselves defined physically, but linguistically. A working definition is that a phoneme is a segment of sound which determines the identity of some word in a language, in the sense that substituting that segment for another changes a word into another word. As we have seen, this linguistic definition entails that many changes in sounds do not create new phonemes. Some, for instance aspirated and unaspirated /p/, create allophones; other non-phonemic changes in speech sounds reflect particular accents, or result from the speed at which a person talks, or from other factors.

Phonemes that are identified in this way can be described in terms of the positions, movements, and flow of air through the vocal tract that occur when the phoneme is being produced, and also in terms of the acoustic properties of the sounds which are produced by this flow of air. One of the important discoveries about the production of individual speech sounds is that the way a sound is actually produced depends upon what sounds surround it. We have already noted the difference in aspiration of the sound /p/ in word-initial and word-final position. This is one example of how the context of a sound determines its exact nature. But there are more subtle examples. The pronunciation of a single consonant at the beginning of a syllable is influenced by the particular vowel in that syllable. The /b/ in *beet* is different acoustically from the /b/ in *bit*, *boot*, *but*, *bat*, etc. The same is true for vowels. There are subtle acoustic differences in the sound /i/ in the words *lit*, *bit*, *fit*, etc. This spreading of an articulatory gesture over several segments is known as "co-articulation". The limits of co-articulation are obviously important for understanding how speech sounds are produced and perceived. How many segments affect the final articulatory pattern is not yet known. Similarly, how much of the speech signal has to be present before a phoneme or a syllable can be identified is not known. Some studies (Stevens and Blumstein 1978) suggest that there is enough information in the first 20 msec. of speech signal for a listener to identify an entire syllable.

The existence of co-articulatory effects confirms our view that a phoneme is a *linguistic* entity. We said that the phoneme was the minimal sound unit which distinguishes two words in a language, and that a phoneme can be considered a representation of a single sound segment. These acoustic and articulatory results show that the idea of a "segment" does not correspond to the way sounds are actually executed. Rather, sequences of what we consider to be phonemic "segments" jointly exert an influence over a portion of the actual speech signal. These segments do not stand in a one-to-one relationship with the units of speech production. Said another way, phonemes are abstract representations of the sound segments relevant to the words of a language, which are mapped in complex ways onto articulatory gestures and acoustic waveforms.

The conclusion that phonemes are not actually articulatory or acoustic entities – in the sense that they do not map in a strictly linear way onto sequential portions of the speech signal – is a very important concept. Even though, when we talk about the form of a word, we are referring to its sound, this observation shows that we cannot represent its sound in a way which is both linguistically significant – as a sequence of phonemes – and in a way which corresponds to a simple linear division of the physical sounds we hear and produce. All linguistic representations, even those which represent sounds, are abstract. All of them must be mapped in one way or another onto output devices, and recognized by input systems.

Having recognized that phonemes are abstract representations of the sound segments of a language which are relevant to the distinction between words in a language, we may further ask whether there is any way to characterize different phonemes. In the past sixty years or so, a system of describing different phonemes in terms of positions of the vocal tract and the manner of production of sound through this tract has been developed by linguists. We have already seen one example of this system in our discussion of aspirated and unaspirated /p/. The difference between syllable-initial /p/ and syllable-final /p/ can be described in terms of the amount of air that escapes from the lips following these two instances of the same phoneme, a feature known as aspiration. Similarly, the difference between /p/ and /b/ is one of voicing. If you put your hand over your Adam's apple and say the word *bat*, you will feel a vibration immediately upon beginning to speak. This vibration only occurs once you begin to say the sound /a/ in the word *pat*. This is because the vocal cords vibrate during the production of the sound /b/, but not /p/. In other words, /b/ is a "voiced" phoneme, and /p/ is "unvoiced". It is now thought that all of the phonemes which occur in all the world's languages can be described by different groupings of a relatively small set of these features pertaining to positions and manners of articulation of the vocal tract. These include whether or not the flow of air is totally obstructed during the pronunciation of a segment (as it is in the so-called "stop" consonants /p/,/t/,/k/,/b/,/d/, and /g/), whether the air flow is partially constricted, as it is in other consonants, or whether the air flow is minimally constricted, as it is in vowels. The point in the vocal tract at which a constriction occurs – at the lips, behind the teeth, at the level of the palate, or further back at the level of the velum – also gives rise to another set of distinctive features. For vowels, and for some systems of consonants, features such as whether the lips are rounded or not, and where the body of the tongue is in relationship to the floor and roof of the mouth, constitute other distinctive features (see Chomsky and Halle 1968).

Ideas about distinctive features have evolved considerably as more and more languages have been studied, and as knowledge about the entire organization of the sound system has advanced. There have been many changes made in the sets of distinctive features proposed for specific languages and across different languages of the world. Study of languages whose sound system is quite different from European languages, such as African languages with clicks operating as phonemes, has raised serious questions regarding the set of distinctive features which had originally been proposed.

Despite these changes and challenges, there seem to be aspects of the distinctive feature system which are found in all the world's languages. Many investigators have suggested that each distinctive feature should be seen as reflecting one pole of a binary opposition: voiced vs. unvoiced (referring to activity of the vocal cords); high vs. low (referring to the position of the body of the tongue); rounded vs. unrounded (referring to the position of the lips), etc. In a strictly binary theory, aspects of sound production such as the point of maximal closure (point of articulation) of a consonant cannot be expressed as one of four different positions – lips, teeth, palate, velum – as we did above, but rather requires a combination of distinctive features, each expressed in binary oppositional terms.

Distinctive features, though based upon the positions of the articulatory muscles and the vocal tract, are also not actual descriptions of the action of the articulators (or features of the acoustic waveform). They too are abstract entities. In fact, most of the discussions in the phonological literature dealing with distinctive features do *not* deal with the way distinctive features actually map onto positions and manners of articulation or onto acoustic form (even though there is a considerable body of work dealing with these topics in the acoustic-phonetic literature). They deal with the optimal set of distinctive features for the description of a particular language, taking into account the entire sound pattern of the language, and the language-universal features of sound systems. Many refinements and modifications of the sets of distinctive features postulated for particular languages have come about because of considerations regarding how one way of formulating the set of distinctive features for a language would better capture regularities in the sound system of that language, explain the interaction of phonemes and syllables, or account for the interaction of the sound system with the way words are formed in the language. Though the distinctive features which are thought to make up phonemes are expressed as features related to the physical production of language sounds in terms of the vocal tract, they too, like phonemes, are basically abstract linguistic entities, which find their primary justification in terms of linguistic – not articulatory or acoustic – facts about the phonology of languages.

Syllables are an important and somewhat different level of phonological structure. We saw above, in the contrasts between *bat* and *pat* and *blackboard* and *black board*, that changing one phoneme for another or changing one stress contour for another can change the meaning of a word. Such changes are not possible at the level of syllables. Any syllabic change that leads to a change in a word's identity also involves a phonemic change, as in the difference between *receive* and *deceive*. If one changes the syllabification of a word by including a phoneme in one syllable and omitting it in another (as in /pat-tern/ vs. /pa-tern/), the word's meaning has not changed. For this reason, the level of the syllable is different from the level of the phoneme and the level of word stress contour.

Despite this feature of syllables, the level of syllable structure plays an important role in the sound system. First, it is at the level of the syllable and its structure that important constraints on the sequences of phonemes which can be found in any language can be stated. Second, the nature of syllables in a word is one of the major factors determining the stress contour of a word. Syllables themselves have structure, and this structure is a major factor determining what sound sequences there can be in a language. Syllables are divided into two major parts, the second of which is again divided in two. The basic components of a syllable are the "onset" and the "rime", and the rime is divided into a "nucleus" and a "coda". These structures are organized as in Figure 13-1. The onset consists of the consonant or set of

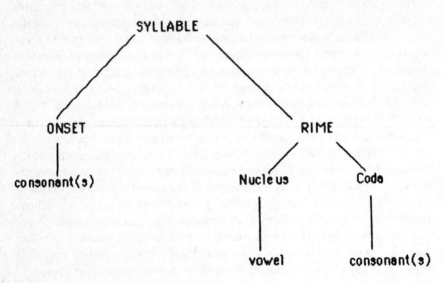

Figure 13-1. The universal structure of syllables

consonants that precede the vowel, the nucleus consists of the vowel, and the coda consists of any consonants which follow a vowel. (There can be non-vocalic nuclei in special circumstances, but we will not deal with them here.) A general constraint upon the nature of the sounds in words in all languages of the world can be stated in terms of these features of the syllables; namely, as we move from the onset to the nucleus of a syllable, the phonemes gain in sonorance, and as we move from the nucleus of a syllable to its coda, phonemes diminish in sonorance. "Sonorance" refers to the degree of unimpeded flow of air through the vocal tract. Consonants are less sonorant than vowels; and within consonants, stop consonants (e.g. /p/, /b/), consonants with near-total occlusion of the vocal tract (e.g. /f/, /s/), "liquids" (/r/ and /l/), and "glides" (/w/ and /y/) are progressively more sonorant. The sonorance hierarchy constraint thus predicts that the sequence /tr/ will occur at the onset of syllables, as in *tray*, but not syllable-finally, while the sequence /rt/ will occur syllable-finally, as in *art*, but not syllable-initially. There are exceptions to this constraint, but it applies extremely widely over the entire range of human languages that have been studied.

Second, each language has its own constraints on possible syllables. For instance, there are languages such as Italian in which all word-final syllables must be so-called "open" syllables ending in a vowel. There are languages in which no consonant clusters can occur in the coda or in the onset position. In most languages, only certain consonant sequences can occur in the onset or coda positions. The interaction of these language-specific constraints on the consonantal and vocalic make-up of syllables with universal constraints on syllable structure determines the nature of the pattern of segmental phonology – the sequences of phonemes – in a language.

Finally, syllable structure influences the last phonological structure which we shall consider: word stress contour. There are differences in the degree of emphasis of individual sounds within a word. In English, these differences are captured in the stress contour of a word. In other languages, these differences result in different sequences of rising, falling, and steady tones on portions of a word. The assignment of stress (or tone, which we shall not consider) is intimately tied to syllable structure. For one thing, stress can only fall on the nucleus of a syllable, which means that, in most cases, it is one or another vowel of a word which receives stress. In a language like English, there are different degrees of stress which vowels can receive. Vowels which receive no stress whatsoever do not retain their distinctive vocalic qualities, but are "reduced" to a common vowel, known as a "schwa", /ə/, which is almost eliminated from the sound of a word, as in the first syllable of the word *concern*. One of the major accomplishments of contemporary investigations of phonology has been to begin to understand the process whereby assignment of stress contours to words occurs in English and other languages. Until this recent work, which began with *The Sound Pattern of English* (Chomsky and Halle 1968), it was thought that a child learning English had to learn where the stress fell on each word. It now is clear that a set of rules can apply to the phonemes and syllables of each word of English to arrive at its stress contour. These rules involve the assignment of the phonemes of a word to different syllables, and the application of a complex set of rules to the resulting syllables to yield a stress pattern. These rules also interact in quite complicated ways with the process of word formation (see Chapter 15).

These three aspects of phonological structure – phonemes, syllables, stress contours – are all features of the sound patterns of words as they are actually spoken. We have referred to them as "different types of representation" in a linguistic sense, meaning that they are separate (though interrelated) aspects of a sound of a word. However, there is another sense in which these three *types* of representations all occur at the same *"level"* of representation of the sound system. We have said that phonological representations are abstract characterizations of the actual sounds of speech. However, the phonological representations we have considered thus far are still not the *most* abstract ones that linguists recognize. These (relatively abstract) representations of the way words are spoken may be different from the representations of the sounds of words that are permanently stored in the mental lexicon. For instance, the word *coròllary* can be pronounced with emphasis on the second syllable. In this case, the first vowel is a schwa. However, since *còrollary* can also be pronounced with emphasis on the first syllable, making the first sound an /ɔ/, and since it is related to the words *correlate*, *correlation*, and others in which the first vowel is pronounced as an /ɔ/, it is reasonable to say that the permanent representation of the first vowel of *corollary* is an /ɔ/, and not a schwa, /ə/. This is particulary true since the fact that the first vowel is reduced to a schwa, /ə/, when the word is pronounced with stress on the second syllable is due to the fact that there is no stress on the first vowel, since all vowels that have no stress are pronounced /ə/ in English. The conclusion is that the permanent representations of sounds of words can be different from the sounds of a word as they are actually spoken.

These differences between so-called "superficial" levels of phonological representation apply to each of the aspects of the sound system we have discussed – phonemes, syllables, and word stress contours. We have noted that stress contours do not have to be represented for each word, but can be derived by general rules of English phonology. Similarly, the nature of the syllables in a given word can be derived from the sequence of phonemes in a word on the basis of the universal constraints on syllable formation we have discussed and language-specific considerations. Therefore, neither the syllable structure nor the stress contour of a word has to be specified in its permanent mental representation in the lexicon. Finally, we noted that for some sounds, such as the /ɔ/ in *corollary*, the permanent representation can be different from the superficial representation. Many linguists have proposed that most of the distinctive features of each phoneme in a word do not need to be specified in the lexical representation of a word, but can be derived by general rules which are partly language-universal and partly language-specific. Discussing these complicated sets of rules is far beyond the scope of this chapter, and the interested reader is referred to Kiparsky (1982) for discussion of some of these rules. We simply need to appreciate that the permanent phonological representation of a word is less specified and more abstract than the superficial phonological representation of a word. Rules "fill in", change, and add to the phonological information at the lexical level to arrive at the superficial level. Additional rules then map the superficial level of phonological representations onto an "articulatory" level of representation.

We have thus begun to identify the different elements that make up the sound system of human languages. We have identified three separate types of phonological representation: phonemes, syllables, and word stress contours. Each of these different aspects of word sounds has its own internal structure, and is related to the other types of representation by a set of universal and language-specific rules. We have stressed that these representations are *linguistic* – that is, they constitute an abstract representation of the sounds of words which is related to the structure of a language. Though they are mapped onto articulatory and acoustic structure, they do not correspond to or represent the actual production of speech or the actual acoustic features of the sounds of a language in a direct, simple way. Finally, we noted that each of these aspects of the sound system is represented at an even more abstract "level", which linguists believe constitutes the permanent lexical representation of word sound. A large number of language-specific and language-universal rules and conditions on the well-formedness of phonological representations connect the underlying lexical and superficial levels.

Are all these aspects of the sound pattern of a word, and the different levels of lexical and superficial phonological representations, relevant to the process of planning and producing the sound of a word? Evidence that these types and levels of phonological representation are used in the process of word production comes from slips of the tongue made by normal speakers in normal conversations.

Fromkin (1971) analyzed approximately 600 slips of the tongue made by normal subjects. She argued that these slips of the tongue demonstrate the reality of a variety of phonological structures. The first of these is the individual phoneme. Errors such as those in (1a) and (b) below indicate anticipation of later phonemes, (1c) and (d) perseveration of a phoneme, (1e) and (f) metathesis (exchange) of a consonant, and (1g) and (h) metathesis of a vowel:

(1a)   John dropped his cup of coffee: John dropped his cuff of coffee
(1b)   also share: alsho share
(1c)   I am not allowing any proliferation of nodes: . . . proliperation of nodes
(1d)   John gave the boy: . . . gave the goy
(1e)   keep a tape: teep a kape
(1f)   the zipper is narrow: the nipper is zarrow
(1g)   ad hoc: od hac
(1h)   Wang's bibliography: Wing's babliography

209

Individual phonemes within consonant clusters are also subject to similar errors, as in (2):

(2a)   fish grotto: frish gotto
(2b)   split pea soup: plit spea soup

In each of these two examples, one phoneme from a consonant cluster has been moved. Individual phonemes can be omitted from clusters, as well as moved, and the clusters in which these errors arise can occur word-finally as well as word-initially. An important negative finding is that the segments *ch* and *j*, which can be split into a stop consonant and a so-called "fricative" consonant – *ch* being pronounced as *ts* and *j* being pronounced as *dz* – do not show splitting of these two component articulatory elements. Thus, errors such as those in (3) are present, but errors such as the hypothetical examples given in (4) do not occur in the corpus:

(3a)   pretty chili: chitty pili
(3b)   "In St. Louis," John said: "In St. Jouis," John said

(4a)   pinch hit: pint hich (where the *t* is separated out from the affricate *ch*)
(4b)   "In St. Louis," John said: "In St. Douis," John said (in which the *d* portion
        of the affricate is split off and duplicated)

Similarly, diphthongized vowels (*ey*, *uw*, *aw*, as in *hay*, *who*, *how*) are always treated as a single vowel, as would be expected from a phonological analysis of English. On the other hand, the sound of *ng*, in words like *sing*, can give rise to errors involving either the *n* or the *g* part of this complex sound. This, too, corresponds to the underlying representation of this consonant in English. All of these features indicate that phonemes are psychologically real, and are subject to unconscious errors during speech-planning processes.

Fromkin also presents several errors which show that the distinctive features which make up the phonemes are also relevant to the speech production process. For instance, the errors in (5) show changes affecting only the nasality of particular consonants, while those in (6) show only changes affecting the voicing of particular consonants:

(5a)   spell Mother: smell other
(5b)   bang the nail: mang the mail

(6a)   what does the course consist of?: what does the gourse consist of?
(6b)   big and fat: pig and vat

Fromkin also argues that the speech errors demonstrate the reality of phonological and morphological constraints. For instance, none of the errors that she observed contained illegal sequences of sounds. The error in (7), for example:

(7)   sphinx in the moonlight: minx in the spoonlight

shows a change of the initial cluster *sf* in *sphinx* to *sp* when that cluster is interchanged with an *m*. *sf* does occur word-initially in a few technical words and words borrowed from other languages, but by and large cannot appear in English in syllable-initial position. Therefore, when the first sounds of these words are exchanged, phonological rules further change the *sf* into *sp*. The operation of phonological rules which are conditioned by morphology is illustrated by the examples in (8):

(8a)   tab stops: tap stobz
(8b)   plant the seeds: plan the seets

In (8a), the *b* of *tab* is interchanged with the *p* of *stops*. In English, when a word ending in a voiceless stop consonant such as *p* is pluralized, the plural marker takes the form of unvoiced *s*, but when a word ending in a voiced stop such as *b* is pluralized, the plural takes the form of the voiced *z*. As can be seen in (8a), although the stops interchange, the correct phonological plural marker appears on the newly created word, demonstrating the automatic application of this phonological rule. Similarly, the plural marker in (8b) is corrected for the new consonant that it follows after *d* has been changed to *t* in *seeds*.

Finally, Fromkin indicates that errors tend to preserve the number of syllables in a word and even the stress contour of the original sequence.

Fromkin argues that these data suggest a model of how utterances are produced. We will only concentrate on the planning of the sounds of utterances in this model at present. Because intonation contours are preserved across phrases, she claims that one stage of utterance planning (her Stage 3) is devoted to the establishment of an intonation contour and the placement of primary stress. At the next stage, the actual sounds of words are accessed from their semantic representations. Errors at this point involve selecting similar-sounding words, and mis-ordering and changing the phonological segments of words as the sounds of words are copied over from the permanent lexicon into the developing structure of the sentence. Subsequent to this, the morphophonological constraints of the language operate to yield the phonological form of the utterance; and, finally, articulatory processes are activated. This study of speech errors therefore not only shows that many of the types of representations, and some of the levels of representation, needed to describe regularities in linguistic form are relevant to the planning of speech, but also gives some clue as to the stages of the planning of utterances.

One of the operations specified by Fromkin – one that obviously must go on when one plans an utterance – is finding the particular phonological form of the word after we have identified its meaning. How is this connection made? Answers to this question have also come from the study of speech errors. Fay and Cutler (1977) studied a particular type of speech error called a "malapropism". Malapropisms have three characteristics: the error is a real word; the error and the target are unrelated in meaning; and the error and the target are closely related in pronunciation. Simple anticipations, perseverations, omissions, and metatheses of segments, such as the errors illustrated in (1) above, are not malapropisms. Nor are abnormalities due to the blending of two words, or semantic errors. Malapropisms are of particular interest because they presumably reflect a process of mis-selection of a word based upon the phonological similarity of the uttered word (the error) and the target word, and are not due to intrusion of sounds from neighboring words or to any semantic relationship between the error and the target.

Fay and Cutler studied 183 clear malapropisms in a corpus of over 2,000 errors that they collected. They found that in over 99 per cent of the cases, the target and the error had the same grammatical category. In addition, they had the same number of syllables in 87 per cent of cases and the same stress pattern in 98 per cent of cases. Fay and Cutler compared these features to 79 semantic errors found in their own corpus and that of Fromkin. They found that, for the semantic errors, the target and error had the same number of syllables in 75 per cent of cases and the same stress contour in 82 per cent of cases, and the same grammatical category in all cases. These percentages do not differ significantly. More detailed studies showed that malapropisms and semantic errors are similar in other phonological ways as well. When Fay and Cutler examined the first phoneme which differed in the error and the target in these two classes of errors, they found that the number of distinctive features separating this phoneme in the error and the target was more likely to be small than large for both malapropisms and semantic errors. The striking finding, therefore, is not only that malapropisms are very similar to their targets in terms of their sound pattern – which would be expected, since these are errors which consist of similar-sounding words – but also that semantic errors are equally similar to their target in terms of basic aspects of the sound system.

Fay and Cutler suggest that these findings have implications for the way the mental lexicon is organized. They point out that it would be advantageous to have a lexicon organized according to the sound pattern of words for comprehension. For instance, if words with identical first syllables were listed together, all of these words could be activated when the first syllable of a word is heard, and subsequent recognition of the word would only have to discriminate among this relatively restricted set of words of the language. On the other hand, for word production, a semantically organized lexicon would be advantageous, since one has to access the words in the lexicon on the basis of their meanings when one speaks. Of course, it is possible that there are two lexicons – one for production and one for comprehension – which are connected. Fay and Cutler, however, argue that their data suggest that there is only one lexicon, and that it is organized phonologically. They suggest that the fact that semantic errors share the same phonological similarities with their targets as do malapropisms indicates that a phonologically organized lexicon is used in production as well as in comprehension. Malapropisms would arise when the words "nearest" a target are inadvertently activated instead of the target word.

Garrett (1984) has suggested another possibility. He proposes that the meanings of words are accessed in a conceptual or semantic system, and that there is a "linking address" from the semantic to the phonological form of a word. This linking address actually contains phonological information: a specification of the first syllable of the word, the number of syllables in the word, and the stress pattern of a word. If there is an abnormality in the system such that the linking address no longer "points" directly to the correct phonological form of the word, a person can still base his output on the phonological information contained in the linking address itself. This would lead to the production of another word with the same number of syllables, the same stress contour, and often the same initial syllable.

If Garrett is correct, there is a representation of the word consisting of its first syllable, the number of syllables in the word, and the stressed syllable in a multisyllable word, which is activated when a speaker converts the semantic representation of a word to its final pronunciation. This has an important implication. This representation, linking the lexical semantic and lexical phonological representations of a word, is one which is used in the psychological process of speech production but which is not required to describe phonological linguistic structures. Thus, the mechanisms involved in planning speech may *add* to the number of ways phonological information is organized, by utilizing combinations of phonological features above and beyond those specified at various levels of linguistic structure *per se*.

All these features of the sound pattern of words and of the representations of word sounds involved in word sound production constitute the framework within which we can approach the characterization and understanding of disturbances in the production of word sounds.

Disturbances in the production of sounds have traditionally been divided into those affecting the actual mechanism of articulation and those affecting the processes of planning the sounds in a word. These two major types of disturbances of the sound system overlap to some degree with the traditional division between non-fluent and fluent aphasia. One goal of research into disturbances of word sounds has been to see exactly how different the patterns of disturbance of word sounds are in these different types of aphasia. This goal is heavily influenced by researchers' interest in the clinically defined patient groups we have discussed in Part II and Chapter 11. Other researchers have investigated single cases or groups of cases from a more psycholinguistic perspective, trying to understand these errors in relationship to the normal system of sound production without much concern for the issue of patient classification.

There are three basic approaches to the investigation of disorders of sound production currently in use. The first is a linguistic approach, which consists of tape-recording aphasic patients' speech, transcribing the recording in phonetic notation, and analyzing the transcription for phonological abnormalities. The second approach is to analyze these tape-recordings, using one of a variety of instruments which display features of the acoustic signal. A third approach is to make measurements of the motion of the vocal tract during speech production. We will not cover the third area here, and shall begin our discussion with the second, acoustic, approach.

Blumstein and her colleagues (1977*b*; 1980) have made many observations of acoustic features in the speech of patients with disturbances in sound production. These researchers used computers and a spectrograph to analyze the waveforms produced at each point in each sound. A typical spectrograph of the sound /ba/ is illustrated in Figure 13-2. Blumstein and her colleagues (1980) studied the characteristics of voiced and voiceless stop consonants (*b*, *d*, *g*, *p*, *t*, *k*) in recordings from a variety of patients with speech disturbances. They found different patterns of abnormality in different types of patient.

The principal acoustic feature that distinguishes voiced from voiceless consonants in English is known as "voice onset time" (or VOT). The difference between /b/ and /p/ lies in the timing of the onset of voicing. The VOT is determined by the time between release of the consonant and the onset of periodic voicing. In a voiced stop consonant, such as /b/, periodic voicing begins 40 msec. earlier than in the production of an unvoiced stop consonant such as /p/. There is a range of VOT associated with voiced consonants and another range of VOT associated with unvoiced consonants. There is also an intermediate range, during which voicing never begins in normal subjects. This relationship between VOT and voiced and unvoiced stop consonants is illustrated in Figure 13-3.

Blumstein and her colleagues found that patients with Broca's aphasia

TYPE B/65 SONAGRAM ● KAY ELEMETRICS CO. PINE BROOK, N. J.

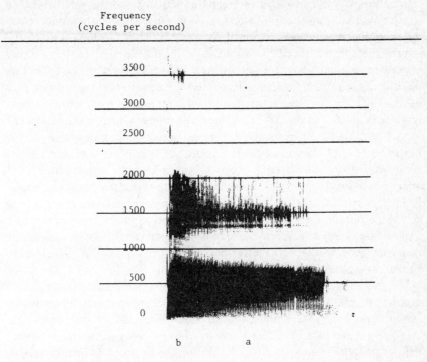

Frequency
(cycles per second)

3500

3000

2500

2000

1500

1000

500

0

b   a

Figure 13-2. A spectrogram of the sound /ba/. The opaque areas are the formant frequencies which determine the sounds in this syllable.

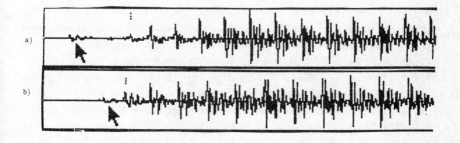

a)

b)

Figure 13-3. Oscillographic record indicating onset of periodic voicing relative to consonantal onset. ⌐ indicates consonantal onset. ⦂ represents onset of periodic voicing. The "voice onset time" is greater for the unvoiced consonant (pa – line a) than the voiced consonant (ba – line b).

215

III Linguistic aphasiology

were different from those with Wernicke's aphasia with respect to their production of VOT in syllables beginning with voiced and unvoiced stop consonants. The Broca's aphasics did not respect the basic constraints on the production of voiced and unvoiced consonants. They frequently produced intermediate forms, in which voicing began during the period where voicing never begins in normals. The Wernicke's aphasics did not do this. Though they would frequently mispronounce the target syllable, they never produced VOTs in the "no man's land" between voiced and unvoiced consonants. In addition, the Broca's aphasics produced a narrow range of VOT for /ba/ stimuli, tending towards the production of phonemes whose voicing began more in the unvoiced range. Again, the Wernicke's aphasics did not show this feature. The Broca's aphasics also produced a sound with a VOT appropriate for /pa/ when asked to produce the sound /ba/, and vice versa. Blumstein concluded that the Broca's aphasics were at times incapable of actually programming the articulators accurately, and at times mis-selected a phoneme, while the Wernicke's aphasics were capable of programming the articulatory muscles correctly but suffered from an inability to select the appropriate phoneme correctly on a given trial.

In a later series of studies, Schiff *et al.* (1985) studied different types of non-fluent aphasic patients. They found that one group of patients (with so-called "aphemia") were consistent in their abnormalities with respect to VOT. Aphemic patients consistently produced early voicing, regardless of which target they had to produce. Erratic productions of VOT characterized the remaining Broca's aphasics, who were said to have so-called "apraxia of speech". These patients sometimes produced phonemes correctly, sometimes produced the wrong phonemes with a "legal" VOT, and sometimes produced "illegal" VOTs (i.e. VOTs between those for voiced and unvoiced stops). It thus appears that there is more than one type of speech disturbance in Broca's aphasia. "Apraxia of speech" consists of difficulty both in actually programming the articulators, resulting in "illegal" VOTs, and in selecting phonemic values, leading to incorrect VOTs. The problem in programming the articulators in apraxia of speech is variably present. This contrasts with another motor speech disorder associated with Broca's aphasia, "aphemia", in which there is a consistent abnormality in the production of particular sounds.

Many other investigators have also analyzed speech through spectrographic records and similar devices. The first such investigation was undertaken by Alajouanine, Ombredane, and Durand in 1939. Using considerably less sophisticated recording devices than are available today, they nonetheless obtained important information about the physical properties of sounds in a class of aphasic patients whom they described as having a syndrome of "phonetic disintegration". The four patients studied were probably similar to the Broca's aphasics with apraxia of speech studied by Blumstein and her colleagues, since inconsistency in the production of the acoustic values of phonemes was frequently found.

An important feature of the abnormalities reported by Alajouanine and his colleagues is that the speech patterns were dependent upon the context in which a sound was found. For instance, consonantal simplification occurred in syllable-final position much more often than it occurred in syllable-initial position, indicating that the tendency towards reduction of sequences of consonants to a single consonant is somehow influenced by the position in the syllable in which a sequence of consonants occurs. Similarly, the substitution of voiceless for voiced stops occurred much more frequently word-finally than word-initially.

Alajouanine and his colleagues considered that different aspects of the errors they described could be explained in terms of specific types of motor impairments, each due to different types of damage affecting a patient's ability to control movements of the vocal tract. They postulated three types of impairments: (1) paresis – weakening of muscular strength; (2) spasticity – abnormality in the tone of muscles and in their reflex reactions; and (3) apraxia – an inability to co-ordinate movements. Alajouanine and his colleagues often did not specify which particular aspects of the errors they described were due to each of these three motor impairments, thus leaving many questions unanswered about the pathophysiological basis of these abnormalities. Though many parts of this theory are still not stated in detail, one aspect of this theory has been recently developed by MacNeilage (1982).

MacNeilage based his account of one aspect of the output disorders in apraxia of speech upon observations made by Trost and Cantor (1974). Trost and Cantor observed that voiced stop consonants in word-final position were changed to voiceless consonants more frequently than vice versa, and more frequently than occurred in word-initial position. In fact, in their corpus of errors, there were no changes from unvoiced to voiced stop consonants in word-final position. MacNeilage gives a physiological explanation for this phenomenon. He points out that it is harder to produce a voiced stop than a voiceless stop. In the production of any voiced phoneme, the vocal cords have to be held apart at a very specific distance, so that the passage of air through them from the lungs to the superior part of the vocal tract achieves a particular pressure effect (known as the Bernoulli effect) which makes the vocal cords vibrate rapidly, producing the sound we recognize as voicing. The nervous system must both keep the vocal cords exactly the right distance apart and also create exactly the correct difference in air pressure from below to above the vocal cords. This is particularly hard to do when there is a complete closure of the vocal tract above the glottis, as occurs with a stop consonant. It is also harder to do at the ends of words than the beginnings of words, because the pressure of the air in the lungs – the subglottal pressure – is lower at the end than at the beginning of a word. The consequence is that unvoiced stop consonants are much easier to produce than voiced stop consonants at the ends of words, and patients with apraxia of speech substitute unvoiced for voiced stop consonants in these circumstances. The fact that they are much less likely to make this particular substitution in other phonological contexts indicates that they have a "motor" or "execution" disturbance, not one of "planning" the phonemes in a word. There is no obvious reason why it should be hard to *plan* a voiced stop consonant word-finally, but there is a reason why these segments are hard to actually *produce* in this position.

This physiological explanation of the pattern of substitution of voiced for unvoiced stop consonants reinforces the oscillographic evidence of Blumstein's that one group of aphasic patients has difficulty with executing the movements of the vocal tract required in the production of phonemes. Some of these patients – those with aphemia – seem to have fairly consistent difficulties in this respect, while others have intermittent difficulties. Other patients do not have problems with actual execution of sounds, but nonetheless make many, sometimes quite complex, errors in the sounds of words. As we noted above, Blumstein concluded that Broca's aphasics without "aphemia" made both execution and planning errors, and that Wernicke's aphasics made mostly planning errors. A particularly complex example of a planning error is the utterance /aplaʒɛ̃ dɛ plɔtis/ for the phrase *agent de police*, the French term for policeman. Each of the phonemes in this utterance was perfectly formed. The patient's problem was not one of execution of the individual sounds of a word, but in the selection, sequencing, and organization of those sounds.

We have now identified two large classes of disturbance of sound production: those involving a disturbance of the actual production of sound segments, and those involving an abnormality in the planning of the phonemic content of a word. We have discussed the first class in some detail, and have seen that more than one type of problem produces this form of output disturbance. We have also seen that it is not simple to tell at what level an error arises. Though overtly dysarthric productions obviously must partially reflect an "execution" disorder, execution factors, such as those cited by MacNeilage, may be responsible for errors which are not obvious mis-articulations and which at first appear to be phonological. Despite the fact that there is some lingering doubt about the class into which some apparently "phonemic" errors actually fall, many investigators have accepted that errors which are not obviously dysarthric can be taken as representative disorders of planning word sounds, and have studied the nature of these errors.

The first study that we shall consider in this regard is one by Blumstein (1973*a*; 1973*b*). Blumstein studied particular types of errors in the spontaneous speech of five Broca's, six conduction, and six Wernicke's aphasics. Those errors which consisted of substitution of one word for another (*teeth* for *teethe*), those which were obviously dysarthric in nature, and those which were not obviously related to the presumed target word (/tufbei/ for *birthday*) were excluded from the analysis. Thus, she concentrated on what seems to be a corpus of phonemic errors, for which the target was known and largely uncontaminated by dysarthric or lexical effects. The first aspect of her analysis was simply to investigate whether these three classes of patients each demonstrated a full repertoire of English consonantal phonemes. Her results indicate that each did. Second, she asked whether the frequency of each phoneme was similar in each group and in normal subjects. Here again, groups did not differ: phonemes which were frequent in normal speech were also frequent in the speech of the three groups of aphasics, and those which were infrequent in normals were infrequent in all three aphasic groups. Rank-order correlations of phonemes by frequency indicated a high degree of correlation among the three groups, and between each of the three groups and normal speakers.

Blumstein then investigated the errors that these patients made. She assigned every phonemic error to one of several categories. The first category consisted of omissions, additions, and substitutions affecting a single consonant in a word. The second group of errors involved more than one phoneme in a word. These were the so-called "blends", in which phonemes later or earlier in a word substituted for the target phoneme. Blends were classified as either "regressive" or "progressive", depending on whether the affected phoneme occurred before or after the interfering phoneme. Blumstein also classified the blends into those which occurred within a single word and those which occurred between two words. For each type of error Blumstein investigated the frequency of the error in each aphasic group. She found that the groups did not differ in the frequency of error types.

These analyses indicate that these three groups of aphasic patients do not differ with respect to the total phonemic inventory at patients' disposal, the frequency with which each phoneme occurs in the inventory, and the types of error that occur with respect to phonemes. Blumstein therefore concluded that, whatever the differences between the aphasic syndromes, they each affect phonological aspects of the linguistic code in the same way. She suggested that brain damage respects the organizational principles of language, whatever the nature of the damage.

A different conclusion was reached by Nespoulous and his colleagues (Nespoulous *et al.* 1984) on the basis of a study of four Broca's and four conduction aphasics. Nespoulous studied the patients' ability to repeat single words, so that the target word was known on each trial. Under these conditions, the patients made numerous non-dysarthric errors in the production of word sounds. Considering only the cases in which a single phoneme of a word was changed to another phoneme, Nespoulous and his colleagues found that the relationship between the substituting and the substituted phoneme was different in the Broca's aphasics and the conduction aphasics. In the Broca's aphasics, there was a great deal of similarity between the substituting and the substituted phonemes. In most cases, the two phonemes differed by only a single distinctive feature, such as voicing or place of articulation. In the conduction aphasic cases, this was not the case: the substituting phoneme was as likely to have two or three distinctive features which differed from those of the substituted phoneme as one distinctive feature. Furthermore, there were preferred errors in the Broca's aphasics. Voiced stop consonants were more often changed to unvoiced stop consonants than vice versa, and when changes occurred at the point of articulation of a phoneme, there was a tendency for the point of articulation to become the alveolar ridge behind the teeth. These preferred directions of substitution seem to reflect articulatory factors. There were no such preferred directions of substitution of distinctive features in the errors produced by the conduction aphasics. The difference between the Nespoulous and Blumstein results probably reflects the features of phonemic paraphasias each investigator considered. Though Blumstein's study looked at more types of errors, Nespoulous considered a single error type in greater detail. The differences between patient groups only arose when the errors were examined in this more detailed fashion.

Despite the differences between their results, Nespoulous' study is consistent with, and extends, the first conclusion reached by Blumstein: that a sub-group of Broca's aphasics have difficulty in the actual execution of word sounds. Nespoulous did not study the "dysarthric" components of these patients' problems but rather their "phonological" problems. Errors that were mis-articulated (as judged by observers' perceptions) were eliminated from consideration. In the remaining, properly articulated, errors, substitutions of phonemes were heavily influenced by articulatory factors in the Broca's aphasics but not in the conduction aphasics. Coupled with the fact that it is the Broca's aphasic group that showed disturbances in the actual execution of the articulatory gestures involved in phoneme production in Blumstein's work, this finding suggests that many of the errors made by patients in this group are due to disturbances at a fairly late stage of the production of the sounds of words, at which the actual articulation of the word is already specified. In some cases, this articulation is mis-specified at the articulatory level, leading to abnormal positions and manners of articulation of the vocal tract, and in some cases one phoneme is specified rather than another. In these later cases, the ease of production of a particular phoneme in a particular context seems to play an important role in whether an error is produced and what the error will be, as MacNeilage has indicated. In yet other cases, when substitutions of phonemes occur in relatively "easy" articulatory contexts, the articulatory similarity between phonemes is a major factor in determining what phonemes substitute for a particular phoneme in a target word.

None of these constraints on the production of phonemic paraphasias was found in the more fluent conduction aphasics. This does not, however, mean that their errors are totally unconstrained. Conduction aphasics hardly ever produced sequences of sounds which are not permitted by universal syllable-formation rules or the specific rules of syllable structure of their language. For instance, their phonemic paraphasias rarely violated the sonorance hierarchy. A second feature of all these neologisms is that they almost always arise on content words, not function words. This "constraint" must reflect the way the disorder producing phonemic paraphasias affects the planning of sounds in sentences. It suggests that most phonemic paraphasias arise at a stage of sentence planning at which the sound of content words – but not of function words – is being planned.

Given the many processes involved in selecting and planning the sounds of words, we should not be surprised to find several types of errors arising at these more "central" planning stages. Several studies support this conclusion. Butterworth (1979) studied what he termed "neologisms" – word-like units that are not true words in English – in the speech of a patient who made numerous phonemic paraphasias. He found that these neologisms could be divided into two groups – those that occurred after a pause of 450 msec. or longer, and those that occurred immediately following the preceding word in the utterance. Neologisms in the second group bore a significant resemblance to words of the language which could occur in that position in the sentence (the so-called "target" word). In many instances, these "quickly occurring" neologisms actually consisted of sequences of neologisms all related to the target. In these cases, Butterworth argued that the patient knew the phonological form of the word that he was attempting to utter, but that he mis-selected or mis-ordered phonemes in the word. In the neologisms that occurred after a longer pause, there was no such relationship to a discernible target. Butterworth discovered an interesting feature of these "delayed" neologisms: there was no tendency for these neologisms to begin with any particular sound of English. He therefore concluded that these neologisms were produced by the patient when he could not find the phonological form of a word at all, and resulted from a mechanism that randomly generated phonemes in sequences.

We should stress that this "phoneme generator" was, however, not *completely* random. The phonemes in the neologisms it produced obeyed the general constraints on phonemes in syllables in English. The randomness applied only to the selection of the first consonant of this type of neologism. This random phoneme generator is an example of a particular mechanism which results in the production of abnormal phonological patterns because of an abnormality at the stage of sound planning. This particular abnormality is not actually one of mis-selection or mis-ordering of phonemes of a given word, since, if Butterworth is right, the patient does not actually access the sound pattern of a word when he produces these neologisms. It is the first type of neologism – those that are related to a target – which results from mis-selection and mis-ordering of the phonemes of a particular word. We have thus identified two broad types of "phonemic" errors. There are probably many more.

In Chapter 11, we discussed some recent work which relates detailed descriptions of the linguistic abnormalities found in aphasics to the traditional aphasic syndromes considered in Part II. We noted that a considerable amount of work indicates that patients who fall into different syndromes have similar symptoms, and that this finding poses an important challenge to the notion of the clinical syndromes. We further noted that more detailed linguistic investigations might reveal differences between apparently similar symptoms when symptoms are considered in yet greater detail. So far, the work we have reviewed in this chapter seems to illustrate this process. All patients make phonemic paraphasias, and there are many similarities in the phonemic paraphasias made by different groups of patients, as Blumstein showed; but it seems that the phonemic paraphasias made by non-fluent patients are different from those made by fluent patients. The former arise in processes closely related to the actual execution of speech sounds or are constrained by those processes, while the latter are due to the inability to plan the sounds of words correctly, and are not constrained by articulatory factors. It would thus seem that the distinction between "non-fluent" and "fluent" aphasia is well founded, at least insofar as it serves to distinguish two different basic mechanisms for the production of phonemic paraphasias, even if there are many further distinctions to be made within each of these types of errors which may not be neatly associated with further sub-grouping of patients on clinical grounds.

However, a larger study of Nespoulous puts the view that these different types of phonemic paraphasias are related to different classical clinical syndromes in a slightly different light. Nespoulous and his colleagues (Nespoulous *et al.* 1985*b*) repeated their analysis of the distinctive features involved in single consonantal substitutions in a larger group of twenty-four aphasic patients, including the original eight. They performed a mathematical clustering analysis to group together patients who made similar types of errors. They discovered that the division of patients into those who made substitutions which were closely linked to the target phoneme and those who made substitutions which varied considerably from the target phoneme was not so clear-cut. While the eight patients previously studied fell into distinct groups, six of the remaining sixteen patients showed mixed patterns. This means that some patients who make phonemic paraphasias have disturbances affecting more than one aspect of sound production. If these patients can be clearly classified into Broca's, conduction, Wernicke's and other types of aphasias, this implies that there are several disturbances underlying the production of phonemic paraphasias in each of these syndromes. If these patients cannot be clearly classed into one or another syndrome, this means that the syndromes themselves only identify a number of aphasic patients. Moreover, as we have seen, there is more than one problem that gives rise to each of these two broad classes of phonemic paraphasias.

To this point in our discussion of phonemic paraphasias, we have produced evidence that aphasic patients make errors at various levels of the sound system. We have broadly classified these levels as those of "execution" and those of "planning". This distinction is the first step in an effort to relate disturbances in the production of word sounds to stages in a processing model of phonological representations. By the term "processing model", we have in mind a model which expresses the sequence in which particular types of representations are activated in the accomplishment of a psycholinguistic task. Saying that phonemic errors can arise at either the planning or the execution stage of sound production specifies two stages in a processing model for the phonological aspects of a language. For the remainder of this chapter, we shall discuss the way that phonemic paraphasias have been related to processing models of phonology, and the implications of phonemic paraphasias for the nature of processing models of phonological representation.

We have been assuming in our discussion that phonemic paraphasias arise on what we may call the "output" side: that is, at a stage of processing which is related to the planning or execution of aspects of the sounds of words. It is, however, possible that many of these disturbances arise on the "input" side; that is, in relationship to processes involved in the recognition of the sounds of words or the recognition of words on the basis of their sounds. One way to rule out this latter possibility is to test patients for their ability to distinguish the sounds of words, or to identify words upon auditory presentation. Perhaps surprisingly, very few patients whose phonemic paraphasias have been studied in any detail have been thoroughly tested for their ability to discriminate, identify, and otherwise process word sounds. Testing of many patients whose sound errors have been described in the work above was limited to the use of standardized diagnostic aphasia tests, which provide only limited observations regarding these functions. Patients whose auditory receptive abilities have been explored in more extensive tests have mainly been patients who showed disturbances in auditory single-word comprehension. Some of these patients with "word deafness", who have disturbances in discrimination of phonemes under various conditions (Saffran *et al.* 1976), also make at least some phonemic paraphasias. How many of the phonemic paraphasias that have been investigated in the studies we have reviewed are due to these perceptual and "input-side" impairments is not known, but we can assume some are.

Another set of disturbances in word sounds that may be due to impairments on the input side are phonemic paraphasias which occur in reading words. In Chapter 14, we shall consider the nature of reading disorders. We shall see that the process of recognizing a printed word involves multiple stages, which can be impaired in isolation or in combination. If a patient makes a phonemic error in reading a word aloud, it may be that one of the stages is defective. Some errors in reading are "visual" errors, which many investigators define as those in which 50 per cent or more of the letters of the target word are shared with the erroneous version produced. Researchers attribute these errors to disturbances in the perception of letters, letter sequences, or words. In those studies in which phonemic paraphasias have been studied in reading and repetition tasks (such as the study by Nespoulous *et al.* 1986), there are differences between the errors subjects make on these tasks, which seem to reflect the differences in these tasks. For instance, Nespoulous found that there were fewer phonemic errors in reading than in repetition, which may be due to the presence of the written word during the planning of speech. Certainly, phonemic errors in reading may partially reflect input-side impairments.

The study of reading disorders also shows that there are many stages of processing that lie between perception and production, and illustrates how phonemic errors can arise because of disturbances of these intervening stages. For instance, patients who have a syndrome known as "surface dyslexia" have been said to be unable to recognize written words on a purely visual basis. They have trouble reading aloud words which are irregularly spelled. Rather than recognizing words visually, these patients apparently sound out the words on the basis of correspondences between letters and sounds. In a language like English, there are many graphemes which are ambiguous. For instance, the grapheme "c" can be pronounced as either /k/ or /s/. These patients tend to sound out words using the most common phoneme associated with any grapheme. This naturally leads to the production of phonemic errors. This mechanism for the production of phonemic errors is hard to classify as one belonging to input- or output-side processing. Rather, it seems to represent an abnormality in the processing of different representations of a word sound at some central stage of processing. We may recall our earlier observations that all phonological representations are in fact abstract representations of properties of sound. A tendency to convert graphemes into their most common phonemic values represents a particular limitation on the rules related to abstract representations of a word's sound – one set pertaining to the way a word is spelled, and the other pertaining to the way it is pronounced.

Despite the fact that these observations suggest that some phonemic paraphasias occur because of abnormalities on the input side, or in central aspects of the processing of phonological representations, many phonological speech errors are certainly due to output-side disturbances. The acoustic abnormalities found in the sounds produced by different Broca's aphasics strongly suggest an output-side focus for these errors, because the errors can be naturally accounted for by disturbances arising in the actual mechanism of speech sound production. Consider, for instance, the production of intermediate values of VOT by Blumstein's Broca's aphasics. For this to be due to a perceptual or central disturbance would require that a subject misperceive a voiced or voiceless stop consonant as a sound somewhere between the two, or somehow develop a representation of an intermediate sound during the processing of such a stimulus. This seems extremely unlikely. Normal subjects, in fact, tend to do the opposite. They think they hear voiced or unvoiced stop consonants even when presented with intermediate values of VOT. It is, of course, conceivable that, after brain injury, the perceptual process is so radically changed that it now perceives real phonemes as non-phonemic sounds; but this is extremely unlikely. Similarly, the idea that these non-phonemic sounds might somehow arise at a central stage of sound processing is extremely implausible. It is not even clear how they would be *represented* at a central stage of processing, since they are not actual phonemes but rather acoustic structures intermediate

225

between actual phonemes. The representation would have actually to specify acoustic values, and there is good reason to think that central representations do not include information about these peripheral aspects of sound structure.

A second argument which suggests that many of the phonemic paraphasias we have discussed are due to disturbances of output-side processes is that they are similar across a variety of tasks. Caplan *et al.* (1986*a*) showed that one conduction aphasic, RL, made errors which have phonological similarities in the tasks of repetition, reading single words, and naming objects. All of RL's errors were phonological in nature, not dysarthric, and they increased significantly when he was required to produce words of three syllables or more. Since these errors occurred in naming pictures of objects, they could not be solely due to disturbances of sound or letter perception. If a deficit at a single stage of processing phonological representations were responsible for all the errors in these three tasks, that stage would have to lie after a point at which these three tasks become similar; that is, somewhere on the "output" side of processing. Let us therefore consider several accounts of where these errors may arise on the "output" side.

Garrett (1982; 1984) has suggested that one point in the processing of phonological representations at which deficits can give rise to phonemic paraphasias is at the stage at which the "linking address" between word meaning and word sound is utilized. One observation that led Garrett to this analysis is that many conduction aphasics are able to produce the first syllable of a word even when they cannot produce the entire word (Goodglass *et al.* 1976). Garrett argued that this is part of the linking address between word meaning and word sound, which the patient has retained. Another observation upon which this theory is based is that conduction aphasic patients often make "successive approximations" to a target word in spontaneous speech. An extensive study of these successive approximations was undertaken by Joanette *et al.* (1980). They found that many successive attempts to produce a word became progressively more similar to a target, suggesting that the patient must have known something about the phonological form of the target all along. One possibility is that he retains the phonological information in the linking address.

Caplan *et al.* (1986*a*) point out that disturbances of this sort can only account for errors made in naming pictures and other tasks which involve deriving phonological forms from semantic representations, and cannot apply to any task in which there is a route from a phonological representation on the input side directly to a phonological representation which is involved in speech planning. The reason for this is that the linking address links word meaning with word sound, and need not be involved in repetition or reading. If repeating a word or reading a word aloud *necessarily* involves understanding the word and then accessing its pronunciation from its meaning, a "linking address impairment" could account for disturbances in all these tasks. However, there is no reason to believe that when we repeat or read aloud we necessarily access the meaning of a word. If repetition and reading aloud can proceed simply by perceiving the form of a word and accessing its sound directly from its form, then the common stage of processing at which a disturbance could produce phonemic paraphasias in all these tasks must involve the processing of the phonological representation of a word on the output side. Accordingly, the case RL described by Caplan *et al.* (1986*a*) cannot only have a disturbance in the use of a linking address, since the same types of errors are found in repeating and reading words as are found in naming pictures. Caplan and his colleagues suggest that the case they describe provides evidence for a stage of phonological processing involving the lexical phonological representation of a word. On their analysis, their patient had difficulty in computing a superficial phonological representation from a lexical phonological representation. Since both lexical and superficial phonological representations are involved in all of the tasks with which their patient had difficulty, this analysis provides a unified account of their patient's disturbance.

If both these analyses (Garrett's and Caplan *et al.*'s) are correct, then there are at least two different types of disturbance of sound planning which can give rise to phonemic paraphasias – a disturbance in accessing lexical phonological representations when a subject has the linking address from lexical semantics to lexical phonology, and a disturbance in accessing superficial phonological representations when a subject has accessed lexical phonological representations. There are probably other types of difficulty that patients have in the planning of sound which can also lead to phonemic paraphasias. For instance, we mentioned the possibility that some patients generate at least part of the phonological representation of neologism that they produce in a random fashion, as suggested by Butterworth. It is not clear what stage of normal word processing failed in Butterworth's patient, but the response to the impairment is different from the response that other patients make. Other disturbances in the sound system have also been described which suggest still other types of impairments and adaptive mechanisms. For instance, the fact that phonemic paraphasias occurring in sentences affect mainly content words shows that they may arise at the stage of inserting the sounds of content words into sentences – Fromkin's fourth stage of utterance planning – as noted above. This has been suggested by Buckingham (1980) and Shattuck-Hufnagel (1986).

Let us finally turn to the last phonological (as opposed to articulatory) stage of speech production. Some features of phonemic paraphasias have suggested several properties of this stage of sound production. For instance, longer words tend to be more subject to phonemic paraphasias than shorter words. We already know, from co-articulation effects, and from the fact that intonation contours are defined across entire sets of words, that more than one sound segment must be planned at once. However, there is very little information about how many phonemes are considered together at an output stage that is responsible for the planning of the superficial phonemes of a word, as opposed to an output stage which is involved in co-articulation or one that is involved in intonation contours. The fact that phonemic errors occur more frequently with words of three or more syllables indicates that one mechanism which plans phonemic representations finds it increasingly difficult to accomplish its function when a word has three syllables or more. This may be because this processing mechanism usually handles three syllables at a time, and has trouble with items that contain more than this number of syllables. Since this happens in all tasks in some patients, it must be an output stage. Since it happens in non-words as well as words, this must be an output stage relevant to both words and non-words. The only possibility is that this stage is a late stage of planning, responsible for certain aspects of the phonemic content of a word (and non-words). This stage is often called the "response buffer" (Morton and Patterson 1980). Its role may be no more than to "read off" phonemes from a superficial phonological representation onto an "articulatory" representation, or it may do more processing of superficial phonological representations than just that. The evidence from aphasia gives an indication of how many syllables this buffer can process easily.

One other observation bears on the operation of this stage of sound planning, which lies between the computation of the superficial phonological representation of a word and the representation relevant to its motor execution. Patients who have disturbances at this level of sound planning have more difficulty in producing non-words than real words, though the three-syllable limit applies to both words and non-words. The case RL described by Caplan and his colleagues showed this feature, as did another case recently described by Bub *et al.* (1986). Many other cases in the earlier literature also show this feature (Dubois *et al.* 1964). This feature of these patients' performances suggests that this stage of sound planning is more difficult for non-words than for words. One reason for this difference between words and non-words may be that words occur more frequently than non-words, and the additional experience with actually occurring words makes them easier to plan phonologically. This possibility is rendered somewhat less plausible by the observation that even quite infrequently occurring words are better pronounced than equally long and complex non-words. Another possibility is that the fact that an item is a word is carried over to the stage of processing which we have been discussing, which relates the representation of the sound of a word or a non-word to the motor mechanism responsible for its production. If this is the case, it has important implications for a model of speech planning. It means that the *processing history* of a representation can be relevant to later stages in its processing: the fact that a phonological representation has been accessed through the lexicon makes it different from a phonological representation which has been accessed through perceptual analysis, but which does not have a lexical status. It is quite possible that many aspects of the word-processing system are sensitive to the history of processing of a representation, but, on general methodological grounds, researchers have tried to describe as much of word processing as they can without recourse to this kind of "feedforward", because it vastly complicates the models that they consider. It may, nonetheless, be a feature of word processing which has to be included in processing models (see Chapter 17 for further discussion of this issue).

Let us review the disturbances of word sound production that we have discussed in relationship to a model of the production of the sounds of words. The model we shall consider is presented in Figure 13-4. We have described disturbances at each of the stages of processing shown in Figure 13-4 and we have sometimes been able to suggest aspects of the processing mechanisms operative at each stage on the basis of errors patients make.

Starting at the most peripheral level, we have identified several types of disturbance affecting the execution of the speech output. MacNeilage's analysis of the substitution of unvoiced for voiced stop consonants in syllable-final position indicates that some errors arise at this execution stage. Factors intrinsic to this stage influence errors that arise at previous stages in some patients, such as in the Broca's aphasics studied by Nespoulous, whose substitutions were constrained by articulation-related factors. It is hard to determine the exact locus of some errors within the set of relatively late output stages of processing. For instance, some of the VOT errors documen-ted by Blumstein may have arisen at the stage we have called the "neural commands to speech musculature", or at that labeled "articulatory code", as easily as at the execution stages or at the stages of conversion of one representation into another labeled (g), (h), or (i) in Figure 13-4. Presum-ably, each of these stages can yield errors; it is not clear at present what distinguishes many of the errors which arise at each stage from others arising at other late stages of processing.

Determination of the stage at which the other major class of error arises depends largely upon the tasks in which errors occur. Phonological, non-dysarthric errors that occur in words in all output tasks must arise after a lexical phonological representation has been accessed. If non-words are also affected (in reading and repetition), the only possible single locus of error in Figure 13-4 would be the "response buffer", since non-words do not evoke stored lexical phonological representations according to this model. This

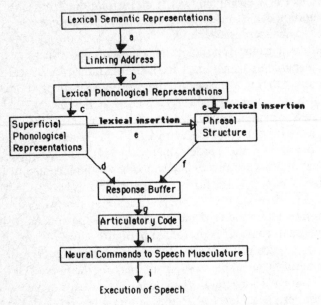

Figure 13-4. A model of the sub-components of the sound production process for words. The step at which words are inserted into phrase markers ("lexical insertion") may involve either underlying lexical or superficial phonological representations, and is indicated with outlined arrows.

leads to problems in cases like RL (Caplan *et al.* 1986*a*), who was more impaired in repeating non-words than words, unless having lexical status confers an advantage on an item's processing in the response buffer. Two solutions to this problem have implications for how the normal system operates. The first confers this advantage on an item because of its frequency of production; the second confers this advantage because the item carries with it an indication of its antecedent processing. We shall discuss the second of these possibilities in greater detail in Chapter 17. These issues aside, disturbances which can be attributed to the operation of the response buffer are associated with strong length effects, and suggest that the upper bound of the number of segments which can be easily processed at this stage is about three syllables.

Other phonemic errors may arise at earlier stages of processing. Garrett has suggested that some phonological errors arise at the level of a postulated "linking address", which connects lexical semantic and lexical phonological representations. Buckingham attributes some phonemic errors to the stage at which lexical or superficial phonological representations of individual words are inserted into developing phrasal structures. Caplan *et al.* (1986*a*) argue that some errors arise during the conversion of lexical to superficial phonological representations. Each of these stages involves many operations which take place over many different types of elements. It is to be expected that future work will identify many specific error patterns, which may help to characterize the elements and operations of each of these processing stages further.

We shall end this chapter by pointing to a few of the questions about the planning and production of word sounds, and about disorders in these processes, which remain unanswered. Despite the considerable progress which has been made in this area in the past decade or so, there are many of these unanswered questions. Some are linguistic. Other than the fact that there are constraints on phonemic paraphasias that lead to preservation of the basic sound structure in a language and that phonemic paraphasias arise mainly on content words, we know very little about the detailed structural properties of phonemic errors. In fact, studies such as Nespoulous *et al.* 1984 and Butterworth 1979 show a large degree of randomness in these errors. However, the investigation of these errors in relationship to the detailed and complex structure of phonological representations described in modern linguistic theory is now beginning (Béland and Nespoulous 1985), and is likely to lead to greater appreciation of structural factors constraining these errors. Such studies can also be expected to clarify further the details of the processing stages involved in word sound production. This is the other major area of uncertainty. Though studies of normal errors provide a framework for describing the processing stages at which phonemic paraphasias and dysarthric errors arise, the models we have now are clearly under-specified in major ways. Worse yet, they may be based upon the over-simplified assumption that processing stages are not sensitive to the processing history of their input representations. We have seen this issue come up in relationship to the treatment of words and non-words at a late processing stage in this chapter, and we have noted a similar concern in our discussion of the "cascade" model of object recognition in Chapter 12. The issue will arise again in our discussion of reading in Chapter 14, and will be discussed in more general terms in Chapter 17. Other processing and structural issues also arise. We have not mentioned disorders of intonation contours nor attempted to identify stages of processing related to the processes of word formation and inflection. We shall discuss some of these issues in Chapter 15, but deal with the *phonological* aspects of these processes only in a cursory way. Overall, there is much that remains to be investigated and understood in the domain of word sound production and its disorders. The interested reader will find suggestions for further reading at the end of this chapter, and will no doubt be able to find new studies of these classical aphasiological symptoms appearing in the literature for many years to come.

SUGGESTIONS FOR FURTHER READING

Blumstein, E. B., Cooper, W. E., Goodglass, H., Statlander, S., and Gottlieb, J. (1980). Production deficits in aphasia: a voice-onset time analysis. *Brain and Language* 9, 153–70.

Blumstein, S. (1973). Some phonological investigations of aphasic speech. In H. Goodglass and S. Blumstein (eds.), *Psycholinguistics and Aphasia*. Johns Hopkins University Press, Baltimore.

Caplan, D., Vanier, M., and Baker, C. (1986). A case of reproduction conduction aphasia I: word production. *Cognitive Neuropsychology* 3, 99–128.

Fromkin, V. (1971). The non-anomalous nature of anomalous utterances. *Language* 47, 27–52.

Garrett, M. F. (1982). Production of speech: observations from normal and pathological language use. In A. Ellis (ed.), *Normality and Pathology in Cognitive Functions*. Academic Press, London.

Joanette, Y., Keller, E., and Lecours, A. R. (1980). Sequence of phonemic approximations in aphasia. *Brain and Language* 11, 30–44.

Nespoulous, J. L., Joanette, Y., Béland, R., Caplan, D., and Lecours, A. R. (1984). Phonological disturbances in aphasia: is there a "markedness" effect in aphasic phonemic errors? In F. C. Rose (ed.), *Progress in Aphasiology: Advances in Neurology*, vol. 42. Raven Press, New York.

Trost, J. G. and Cantor, G. J. (1974). Apraxia of speech in patients with Broca's aphasia: a study of phoneme production accuracy and error patterns. *Brain and Language* 1, 63–79.

14

Acquired dyslexia

Reading and writing have often been considered "secondary" forms of language representation. Though all normal humans exposed to spoken language learn to speak and comprehend auditory language, many people do not learn to write or read, and many languages have never developed a written form. Normal children learn to use spoken language before they learn to use written language. For all these reasons, spoken language is undoubtedly the basic form of language, and written language a secondary means of expression. Nonetheless, written language is obviously an extremely valuable form of linguistic representation, since it allows humans to keep a permanent record of specific linguistic messages. Only very recent technological developments allow us to achieve this with spoken language. In this chapter, we shall consider aspects of the process of normal reading and its disturbances. As elsewhere, we shall begin by a consideration of the representations involved in reading – "orthographies" – and then proceed to consider the way these representations are processed and how the system breaks down. In this area especially, studies of brain-injured cases have contributed greatly to our understanding of how normal reading occurs.

Writing systems for language vary considerably in how they represent a language. They can be as different as Chinese characters and English letters. An important feature *common* to all orthographic systems, however, is that they all represent words of a language. There are no known orthographic systems in which the only units of representation depict phrases or sentences and not words, though there are frequently aspects of an orthographic system which indicate the beginnings and ends of sentences and some aspects of their internal structure (as the punctuation marks , . ; : do in English). Words are thus the basic units of representation in orthography. However, orthographies represent words in a variety of quite different ways.

Some orthographies represent words in quite direct phonological fashion. Italian and Serbo-Croatian, for instance, are languages in which each sound of a word is represented by a letter or a sequence of letters, so that a person who knows the sound value of each letter or sequence of letters in the orthographies for these languages is able to read correctly any word of the language, or any newly coined word which enters these languages, upon seeing its written form. The term for a letter or combination of letters which represents a particular sound is a "grapheme". Languages like Italian and Serbo-Croatian have very simple "grapheme–phoneme conversion" rules. There is a single phoneme for every grapheme and there is a single grapheme for every phoneme in these languages. We say that graphemes and phonemes stand in a one-to-one relationship to one another when going from print to sound and vice versa.

French, on the other hand, is a slightly more complicated language with respect to how words are represented orthographically. French has a one-to-one system for conversion of graphemes to phonemes, but a set of one-to-many correspondences between phonemes and graphemes. That is, any given grapheme in French only receives one pronunciation, but a given sound of French – particularly the vowel sounds – can be written in many ways. For instance, the forms *o*, *au*, *eau*, *aux*, *eaux*, and many others all represent the sound /o/ in French. A person who knew the sound value for each grapheme of French, and what the graphemes of French were, could read any word of French or any new word which entered the French language correctly, just like someone knowledgeable in Italian. However, such a person would not necessarily know how to spell a given word of French, since any one of a number of graphemes might represent some of the phonemes in a French word.

English is yet more complicated. In English the correspondences between graphemes and phonemes are many-to-many in both directions. A single sound of English, such as the sound of "long i", can be written in a variety of fashions: *i* + consonant + *e* (as in *pike*), *ay*, *ey*, *ie*, etc., just as it is true of the sounds of French. In English, however, graphemes are also ambiguous. The sequence of letters *ea* sounds like /ɛ/ in *bread* and *head*, like /i/ in *heat* or *beat*, and as the sound /ɚ/ in a word like *search*. A person who knew the set of correspondences between graphemes and phonemes in English would not automatically be able to read an English word correctly. For instance, given the word *read*, even a native English speaker does not know whether it is to be pronounced like *reed* (as in the present tense) or *red* (as in the past tense), because the grapheme *ea* is in fact ambiguous in this word.

These examples also demonstrate another way in which the orthography of English is more complicated than that of Italian or French: the sound associated with a particular grapheme depends to some extent upon the graphemes which occur near the grapheme in question within a word. For instance, the sound of *ea* in the word *search* depends upon the grapheme *ea* being followed by the letter *r*; the particular sound that *ea* represents in the word *search* only occurs for the grapheme *ea* in this particular "context". It is not the case that every time the grapheme *ea* is followed by *r* it is pronounced as it is in the word *search*; in the word *ear*, for instance, *ea* is pronounced as it is in the word *beat*. However, the only time that *ea is* pronounced as it is in the word *search* is when it is followed by the grapheme *r*. In other words, the system of grapheme–phoneme correspondences in English is many-to-many and context-dependent. English is a relatively hard language to learn to read and write compared to Italian, Serbo-Croatian, or French.

Despite these differences, Italian, Serbo-Croatian, French, and English all have one important characteristic in common. Each of these languages has an *alphabetic* script. However complex the relationship between graphemes and phonemes, the orthographies in these languages are such that the smallest unit of representation is an individual phoneme, and almost all the phonemes of a word are somehow represented in the orthography. Other orthographies do not have these properties. Hebrew and Arabic orthographies, for instance, are *consonantal scripts*, which do not represent the vowels of a language. In these languages, skilled readers determine what the vowels of a word must be. They do this partly through recognition of the word itself, and partly because many or all of the vowels are determined by rules of word formation and syntactic agreement and therefore can be deduced from the context in which a word appears. Another type of orthography is a *syllabary*. In languages such as the Indian language Kannada, the elementary orthographic units represent syllables, not phonemes. There are approximately sixty syllables in the language Kannada, and there are about sixty elementary orthographic signs, each representing a different syllable.

Consonantal and syllabic orthographies obviously contrast with the alphabetic, phonemically based orthographies of English, French, Italian, and most European languages. However, all of these orthographies also have one important feature in common: they all represent some aspects of the sounds of words. In other words, to a greater or lesser extent, and by the application of a set of rules of greater or lesser complexity, it is possible for many or all words in languages with these types of scripts to be "sounded out" by a person who knows the sounds associated with individual elements in the orthography of the language. In other words, these orthographies allow words to be recognized *after* all or part of its sound has been recognized from its orthographic form. Following the terminology we used in Chapters 12 and 13, we can say that languages with these types of orthography allow for phonology to be accessed from orthography without lexical access having been achieved; a reader can recognize at least part of a word's sound from the way it is written without recognizing the entire word itself. One could conceivably use the sounds so recognized to help recognize the entire word.

These types of orthographies all stand in contrast to writing systems such as Chinese and one form of written Japanese (Kanji), which are "ideographic". In an ideographic script, words are not represented phonologically. Rather, they are represented through a set of symbols, each of which corresponds to a particular word (or a portion of a word in a compound or morphologically complex form). In a script like Kanji, a skilled reader must memorize the visual forms of about 2,000 characters, and can rarely deduce the sound of a character from more elemental units. (To be accurate, ideographic orthographies usually have a few "phonological radicals" that indicate a few phonological features of each symbol.) Ideographic orthographies, therefore, offer almost no possibility of achieving "prelexical phonology" by means of a limited set of grapheme-to-sound relationships.

Orthographies, therefore, represent the words of languages in a wide variety of ways, and different orthographies potentially lend themselves to different ways of reading individual words. To a greater or lesser extent, alphabetic, consonantal, and syllabic scripts are compatible with a "phonologically mediated" reading process, in which some or all of the sounds of a word are computed on the basis of the orthographic elements of the language, and the word itself is then accessed from its sound. This phonologically mediated process is one route for reading. Ideographic languages are much less open to this type of reading. Although some phonological information can be gathered from the diacritic features in ideographs, many ideographs must simply be mapped directly onto a lexical entry. The same is true for highly irregular words in languages with alphabetic scripts (such as the English words *women* and *colonel*). We shall call this route a "whole-word recognition route" or a "direct route" for reading. The two routes are depicted in Figure 14-1. Though both a phonologically mediated and a direct, whole-word recognition route are possible ways to read single words in languages with alphabetic scripts, the fact that both routes are possible does not prove that both routes are actually used. A great deal of psychological research into reading is directed towards the question of whether both routes are used, and the subsequent question of how both routes operate. We shall briefly review some of this literature here.

Let us start with the phonologically mediated route, since the consideration with which we began this chapter – the fact that, in some sense, written language is a secondary form of expression compared to spoken language –

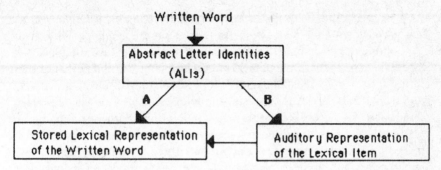

Figure 14-1. A two-route model of the reading process. Route A represents the "direct" route and route B represents the "phonologically mediated" route.

has suggested to many investigators that the process of reading involves accessing the sounds of words from a printed stimulus and then accessing the word from its sounds. Many early connectionist neurolinguistic theoreticians such as Wernicke, Lichtheim, and Dejerine, whose work we reviewed in Chapters 4 and 5, advocated this point of view. Dejerine (1892), for instance, believed that reading consisted primarily of converting each letter (or perhaps grapheme) into a phoneme, and recognizing a word on the basis of the phonemes which were derived in this way. Geschwind (1962) and many contemporary neurologists subscribe to the idea that most reading is phonologically mediated in alphabetic languages.

Though this idea has considerable intuitive appeal because of the "secondary" nature of written language, it also faces some enormous *a priori* problems. Chief among these problems is the existence of exception words, which simply cannot be read in their entirety through a phonologically mediated route at all. A second major problem that this view faces is the many-to-many and context-sensitive nature of orthographies in languages like English. How can a reader be certain that a word like *bread* is to be pronounced *bred* and not *breed*, since *ea* can be pronounced either as /ɛ/ or /i/? Similarly, how can a reader know which pronunciation to give to a word like *read*? Finally, what are the orthographic and phonological units which are relevant to phonologically mediated reading? In a word like *search*, do readers appreciate that *ear* can impart a particular sound to the grapheme *ea*? If they can, what are the largest units that are used in phonologically mediated reading? Is phonologically mediated reading based upon syllables, morphemes, or other units larger than the individual grapheme?

Though these questions pose problems for advocates of a phonologically mediated basis for most reading, it is perhaps possible to outline an answer to them. One way of looking at phonological mediation in reading is to see it as a mechanism that helps to access a word. Even in highly irregular words, such as *yacht*, *women*, and *colonel*, some graphemes are mapped onto their usual phonemes. It is possible that reading proceeds by accessing a set of words which have these phonemes, after which context (and perhaps other features of the knowledge a person has of his language) selects the correct word from this group. Alternatively, phonological mediation might proceed on the basis of progressively larger orthographic units, with the phonological value of each unit contributing in some way to recognizing the word (Marcel 1980). We shall have more to say about both these ideas later. For now, we simply note that both these accounts are much weaker versions of a phonologically mediated theory of reading than one which says that a specific word is accessed directly through a computation of its specific sounds on the basis of its orthography. However, it is simply a fact that purely phonologically mediated reading will not correctly identify all the words of a language with an orthography like that of English, and a somewhat weakened version of a phonologically mediated reading mechanism will be the only one that can be maintained, if it can be maintained at all.

If the phonologically mediated theory is right, we would expect there to be some difference between reading those words which *can* be directly accessed in their entirety through a pre-lexical phonological mediation process and reading those words which are only indirectly accessible through this process (perhaps via one of the mechanisms we have just outlined). To test this prediction, we need to know which words can be correctly identified through pre-lexical phonological mediation and which require some additional processes. And to do that, we need to know what the rules used by the postulated pre-lexical phonological mediation mechanism are. In short, the question of whether phonological mediation is the basis for normal reading cannot be settled until we know what the units of analysis of a written word are which map onto the sounds of a word.

Three principal theories have been proposed regarding the units involved in "spelling–sound correspondences". The first is a theory advocated by Coltheart (1978; 1980; 1985). This theory holds that the spelling units that are relevant to phonologically mediated reading are graphemes and that the phonological unit related to each grapheme is the most common phonological value for that grapheme. Thus, when a grapheme, such as *ea*, is ambiguous, the most common phonological value for that grapheme is produced by the phonologically mediated route. A second theory, advocated by Hansen and Rodgers (1968), holds that syllables are the letter groups relevant for phonologically mediated reading. A third theory, developed by Marcel (1980), holds that any orthographic unit may yield a phonological value. There are many difficulties in putting both the second and third models into operation, mostly centering around how a reader can identify orthographic units such as syllables and intermediate units. Though the idea that orthographic units as large as a syllable, or intermediate between syllables and graphemes, such as the sequence of letters *ear* in the word *search*, might be relevant to reading by a phonologically mediated route, we shall not discuss these aspects of phonologically mediated reading here. We postpone discussion of them primarily because, if there is a phonologically mediated route, it almost certainly makes use of basic, regular grapheme-to-phoneme correspondences as well as any other larger orthographic-to-phonological correspondences. We therefore now turn to a discussion of the evidence that grapheme–phoneme correspondences play a role in the normal reading process.

There are several lines of evidence that are pertinent to this question, but we shall concentrate on only one: the effects of orthographic regularity upon reading. Grapheme–phoneme correspondences (GPCs) convert graphemes into phonemes. If, as Coltheart (1978; 1980) has suggested, GPCs convert each grapheme into the most frequent phoneme the grapheme stands for, then the GPC system will correctly identify words with regular spelling, but will yield incorrect pronunciations for exception words, and for any word in which a grapheme is converted to an infrequent phoneme (such as the *ea* in *search*). If the only basis for phonologically mediated reading is the use of regular GPCs, and if phonological mediation sometimes is the basis for reading, then words which are spelled regularly should be easier to read than exception words, or words in which graphemes are mapped onto less frequent phonemes. Even if there are other spelling–sound cor-respondences used in phonologically mediated reading, regular words should still be easiest to read, all other things being equal.

Several experiments seem to show that this in fact is true. Baron and Strawson (1976) and Coltheart *et al.* (1979) found a so-called "regularity effect" in reading word lists, demonstrating that subjects read lists of regular words faster than lists of irregular words. Several investigators have ques-tioned the importance of the Baron and Strawson results because they were obtained with lists rather than single words; and others have suggested that the regularity effect might reflect the time it takes to pronounce a word rather than the word-recognition stage of reading. However, these potential interpretive problems were answered by Gough and Cosky (1977), who found a regularity effect in reading single words aloud but discovered that this effect disappeared if subjects were instructed to wait a variable amount of time (until a signal appeared) to report the word they read. Gough and Cosky argued that delaying the motor response emphasized the importance of the time it took to prepare for articulation or to articulate a word, because enough time passed between the presentation of the word and the signal to respond for any word to have been recognized. Any increase in reaction time (RT) in the "delayed report" condition must therefore reflect difficulty a person has in saying a certain type of word, not in recognizing that type of word. Since delaying the response had the effect of abolishing the RT advantage for regular words, Gough and Cosky concluded that regular words were read faster in the normal situation without a delay because they were recognized faster, not because it was easier to pronounce them.

Coltheart (1978) nonetheless argues that any reading-aloud task, with or without a delay between the presentation of a word and speech, involves more than simply accessing the lexicon: it involves speaking as well. Therefore he argued that reading aloud is not a good task with which to measure lexical access, and therefore not a good task with which to assess the role of GPCs and phonological mediation in the basic aspect of reading – accessing the lexicon from print. He claims that the lexical decision task, in which a subject must say whether a letter string is a word or not, is a much better task, since it is very close to being a task which requires accessing the lexicon and nothing more. Coltheart (1978) therefore reviewed the literature dealing with regularity effects in lexical decision tasks.

In these tasks, there is an effect of regularity, but Coltheart (1978) points out that it only affects subjects' appreciation that non-words are not words, and does not affect the speed with which a subject recognizes real words. Rubenstein *et al.* (1971) first reported that so-called "pseudo-homophones" such as *burd* or *blud*, which are orthographically non-words but are pronounced like real words (*bird*, *blood*), take longer to reject as non-words in a lexical decision task than non-words that are not pseudo-homophones. These results have been confirmed by several authors, and are quite reliable. They suggest that non-words are recognized in part by a GPC-based system, and that the fact that these non-words sound like words temporarily interferes with a subject's ability to appreciate that they are not real words of the language. In addition, several dyslexic patients who cannot use GPCs do not show this pseudo-homophone effect in non-word recognition in lexical decision tasks, as we shall see below. Coltheart takes all these results as strong evidence that phonological information based upon regular GPCs is involved in recognizing non-words in a lexical decision task.

But what of real words? Here the results are quite different. Coltheart (1978) reviewed the literature on regularity effects for real words in lexical decision tasks, and found that there are no such effects. Coltheart's conclusion is that phonologically mediated reading based upon regular GPCs is not an important method by which subjects recognize a real printed word. Since the results with pseudo-homophones show that normal readers can and do use GPCs to read non-words, the conclusion Coltheart draws is that phonologically mediated reading is so slow that normal reading is based upon the direct, whole-word recognition route simply because it is faster. The pseudo-homophone effect for non-words arises because a subject keeps searching his lexicon when he is presented with a non-word in a lexical decision task, and does so for a long enough period of time for the GPC system to yield a phonological representation of the presented stimulus. Since this is, in fact, a phonological word, a subject must check this phonological word against the printed stimulus to appreciate that the actual stimulus is incorrectly spelled. This means that pseudo-homophones take more time to reject than "normal" non-words.

More recently, regularity effects have been re-explored in both reading aloud and lexical decision tasks by Seidenberg and his colleagues (Seidenberg *et al.* 1984). They presented several types of words to normal subjects in these tasks. We shall return to the entire set of stimuli shortly, but for now we need only consider that some of the words were regular in spelling and some were exception words. Words in each of these groups were matched for frequency and length. Seidenberg and his colleagues found an effect of regularity upon reading aloud latencies, as other authors had reported, but they found that this effect was almost entirely confined to words of low frequency. Moreover, they too found no significant effects of regularity upon lexical decision reaction times. Seidenberg and his colleagues conclude that there is a pool of high-frequency words which are recognized directly by the whole-word recognition route, and whose subsequent pronunciation makes use of the lexical entry so accessed. For infrequent words, pronunciation may use this route, but is also based upon synthesizing the pronunciation of the phonemes in a word, which are yielded by the operation of GPCs.

Seidenberg and his colleagues caution against accepting the conclusion that GPCs play no role in normal-word recognition on the basis of the results obtained in lexical decision tasks. They point out that a lexical decision task requires a *decision* as to whether a stimulus is a word or a non-word, and therefore that it can be performed in various ways, depending upon the nature of the stimuli used in a particular experiment. For instance, a lexical decision task in which the non-words were all pictures could be performed without recognizing any of the words, simply because subjects would realize that anything that is not a picture must be a word. Conversely, if most of the real words in a lexical decision task were exception words or irregular words, the use of a GPC strategy for recognizing words might be minimized. Therefore, there is likely to be a great deal of task-specificity in the results of a lexical decision task because part of the task requires setting some criterion for deciding what is and is not a word. Part of setting or applying this criterion could involve the use of strategies which determine to what extent word recognition is to be accomplished through a direct, whole-word route and to what extent it might be accomplished by a phonologically mediated route. Seidenberg and his colleagues point to results by Bauer and Stanovich (1980), which we shall discuss below, as demonstrating the effects of stimulus list composition upon the regularity effect in lexical decision tasks.

To appreciate Bauer and Stanovich's results, we need to consider one more model of the reading process. In this model, sequences of letters are assigned pronunciations on the basis of "analogies" with real words. Consider, for example, the sequence of letters *ave*. In most words, this sequence is pronounced with a long *a* (*pave*, *rave*, *shave*, etc.). However, there is one very frequent word in the language, *have*, in which *ave* is pronounced with a short *a*. According to the model of reading which incorporates the concept of "lexical analogies", the fact that there are words in the language such as *have* affects one's reading of a word such as *gave*. *Gave*, though regular, has "inconsistent" orthographic neighbors. An orthographic neighbor is a word that ends with the same sequence of letters, and the existence of *have* makes the set of "neighbors" of *gave* not totally regular. Glushko (1979) found that both lexical decision and reading latencies for "regular inconsistent" words were longer than for completely regular words with no inconsistencies in their sets of orthographic neighbors. Bauer and Stanovich (1980) also found an effect of regularity in lexical decision tasks using Coltheart's own set of materials (Coltheart *et al.* 1979), when the "regular inconsistent" words were removed from the original set, leaving regular consistent words. These results suggested to the authors that something other than lexical access via the direct whole-word route was taking place during the process of reading real words in these experiments, but that this additional process did not consist entirely of the use of GPCs or any other sort of phonological mediation. A word like *gave* is completely regular if considered in isolation. Glushko's results suggest that, despite this intrinsic regularity, a word like *gave* is recognized by a system which is sensitive to the existence of similarly spelled words with irregular pronunciations. This process is one which makes use of knowledge of similar *lexical entries*, not spelling–sound correspondences.

Let us review the line of reasoning we are pursuing. We started by hypothesizing that regular GPCs are basic aspects of a pre-lexical, phonologically mediated reading process. We concluded that, since GPCs can yield the correct sound of regular words, if pre-lexical phonological mediation plays a role in normal reading, regular words should show some benefit from this route. We found that this was true for reading aloud. Since Gough and

Cosky's experiment provided evidence that orthographic regularity was not helpful in *pronouncing* a word, it therefore seems as if orthographic regularity must help *recognize* a written word, and, therefore, that pre-lexical phonological mediation, based on regular GPCs, is used in recognizing written words. However, Coltheart objected to the use of *any* reading-aloud task as a way to assess lexical access from print, because it does involve speaking as well as accessing the lexicon. He advocated the use of the lexical decision task to assess lexical access, and found no regularity effects for words in that task. But this, unfortunately, is not the end of the story, either. Seidenberg and his colleagues pointed out that lexical decision tasks involve setting criteria, and allow for adopting strategies upon which to base the *decision* regarding the lexical status of a stimulus. These strategies may depend upon the nature of the stimuli used in each experiment, and may favor the employment of a direct whole word or a pre-lexical, phonologically mediated reading route for real words. The results obtained by Glushko and by Bauer and Stanovich do show an effect of orthographic regularity in lexical decision experiments, when regular words are not only regularly spelled themselves but also have no "orthographic neighbors" which are irregular in their spelling–sound relationships. These results have three implications. First, lexical decision tasks are very sensitive to subtle changes in stimulus list composition. Second, orthographic regularity effects can be demonstrated in lexical decision tasks, if stimuli are carefully selected. Third, orthographic regularity effects disappear in lexical decision tasks if "regular inconsistent" words are included among the orthographically "regular" words, suggesting that activation of "lexical analogies" occurs during word recognition, even for orthographically regular words. Let us continue to explore the role of lexical analogies in written-word recognition before returning to the primary theme of phonological mediation in this process.

Later experimentation has shown that the effects of inconsistent ortho-graphic neighbors are also very sensitive to task-specific situations. We noted above that Seidenberg *et al.* (1984) used a number of different types of words as stimuli in their reading and lexical decision experiments. Among these sets of words were regular inconsistent words. They found no effects of regular inconsistent words upon reaction times in either reading or lexical decision tasks. They attribute this major difference between their results and those of Glushko to the fact that, in Glushko's experiments, the analogous exception words (e.g. *have*) were present in the same list and quite close to the regular inconsistent words (e.g. *gave*). They suggest that the effects of these exception words may only arise when one word is presented very soon after another. If this is the case, the longer latencies for regular inconsistent words found in the earlier experiments would reflect a particular task situation which is not usually found in normal reading conditions. What Glushko's results would show, on this view, is that lexical analogies *can* play a role in recognizing printed words, but that they do so only under special circumstances.

Having raised the question of the role of lexical analogies in reading, we may also consider several issues which arise when we ask how the processes using a lexical analogy actually work. One possibility has been developed by McClelland and Rumelhart (1981). They postulate a mechanism which is very similar to the spreading activation/inhibition process we have discussed in relation to the cascade model of object recognition proposed by Humphreys and his colleagues (Chapter 12). In this "interactive activation" model, a word like *mint* activates a word like *pint* because of the similarities in their spelling. In Chapter 12, we indicated that one major question regarding these models is how far activation spreads. This question arises in relationship to word recognition as well as object recognition. Glushko suggested that the endings of these words are at the basis of spreading activation, but it is not clear exactly how to define the ending of a word. Moreover, it is not *a priori* clear why the beginnings of words, or, for that matter, any segment of a word, might not be the basis upon which other orthographic elements are activated. Furthermore, once the phonological value of a word or a portion of a word is accessed, words with similar phonological values may also be activated. Thus, *gave* might not only activate *have* through orthographic similarity, but also *salve*, through a secondary, phonologically based activation process. As Seidenberg and his colleagues point out, though this is possible, it has the intuitively unappealing consequence that an enormous number of words in a language would be activated prior to the recognition of a simple, orthographically regular, four-letter word such as *gave*.

Let us return to the question we started with – the role of a pre-lexical, phonologically mediated reading mechanism in normal reading. We must conclude three things. First, there is good evidence that pre-lexical (or non-lexical) phonological mediation can occur in normal readers. The evidence for this is the strong, often replicated, "pseudo-homophone effect" in lexical decision tasks, which is most easily explained by saying that pseudo-homophones are converted into phonological form, and that this phonological form, having the sound of a word, interferes with the subjects' rejecting the item as a non-word. Second, we do find evidence for the use of a pre-lexical, phonologically mediated route in normal reading. Regular words are read aloud faster than irregular words, and this does not appear to be due to any advantage they have at the pronunciation stage, since their advantage disappears if pronunciation is delayed. Regular words can also be faster to recognize in lexical decision experiments, if the stimuli in these experiments are very carefully set up. To get an effect of orthographic regularity in a lexical decision task, "regular inconsistent" words cannot be used as part of the set of regular words, and the set of real-word stimuli must not contain too many irregular and exception words (which induces a subject to use the whole-word reading route).

This leads to the third conclusion: the role of pre-lexical phonological mediation in reading is almost certainly very limited, at best. There is still considerable disagreement as to whether the fragile effects of orthographic regularity of words in lexical decision tasks should be taken as evidence that pre-lexical phonological mediation is used in recognizing written words. For one thing, the effects are very fragile: Seidenberg and his colleagues did not find such effects, even when "regular inconsistent" words were eliminated from the set of regular words, perhaps because of the existence of a larger number of exception words in their stimulus lists than was true of Glushko's or of Bauer and Stanovich's experiments. Since there are many irregular and exception words in most real texts, perhaps the Glushko and the Bauer and Stanovich experiments are not representative of normal reading. Another point about the regularity effect in lexical decision tasks is that it seems to require that we exclude "regular inconsistent" words from the set of regular words. This seems to show that "lexical analogies" are activated by regular words (at least under certain task conditions). Though it is possible both that GPCs operate to yield phonological representations pre-lexically for regular words, and that the written form of a regular word activates "orthographic neighbors", most theorists have assumed that one or the other of these operations takes place, but not both. If only one takes place, the regularity effect in lexical decision tasks seems to favor the "lexical analogy" mechanism, since the effect disappears when "regular inconsistent" words are included among the regular words. The lexical decision results are not definitive at this point, and more experimentation, varying list composition, is needed to determine their implications. In reading-aloud tasks, the advantage of orthographically regular words is also small. Reaction times are usually not more than 25 msec. faster for regular than irregular words in reading-aloud tasks, suggesting to many researchers that the times at which a pre-lexical, phonologically mediated, GPC-based route and a direct, whole-word recognition route arrive at a lexical entry overlap, even for regular words (Henderson 1982: ch. 6). Regularity effects seem to arise only with infrequent words (Seidenberg *et al.* 1984). At most, pre-lexical phonological mediation based on GPCs seems to be used for infrequent words, and, even there, all irregular words and some, perhaps many, regular words

245

are recognized by the direct, whole-word route. We must conclude that the model of reading with which we started – that reading requires the conversion of orthographic elements to their sounds – is wrong. Spelling unit–sound unit conversion is possible, but its role in normal reading is at best very limited.

Two more points about phonologically mediated reading need to be made. First, we have only discussed a GPC-based mechanism, which converts each grapheme to its most frequent phoneme. Perhaps a more complex mechanism, based upon larger units as well as graphemes, is used in a pre-lexical, phonologically mediated route. This may be true; our discussion to this point does not deal with this possibility. The problem in evaluating this possibility is that we need to have very specific suggestions about what the spelling–sound conversion rules are to test this idea. We have seen just how sensitive critical effects are to slight variations in experimental stimuli. There are many possible "larger" spelling–sound correspondences which could be used in a pre-lexical, phonologically mediated route. We need to consider specific suggestions, one by one. So far, the proponents of this type of system have not been precise enough to generate critical experimental tests of specific hypotheses. (Note that the use of "lexical analogies" is quite different from what we are considering here since these do not yield a pronunciation on the basis of converting groups of letters or graphemes directly to sounds. Though the large orthographic units which could be converted to sounds in the system we are considering are letter groups, and though orthographic neighbors are activated by a stimulus word because they share letter groups with the stimulus word, the activation of lexical analogies is not the same as the conversion of letter groups to sounds.)

Second, we should be precise about the nature of the lexical representation accessed by any of these routes. Our discussion shows that the route (B) shown in Figure 14-1 is not the basis for much of normal reading; it does *not* show that the representation labeled "stored lexical representation of the written word" in that figure is an *orthographic* representation. In Chapter 13, we distinguished between "lexical" and "superficial" phonological representations. We pointed out that linguists consider the lexical phonological representation to be a very abstract representation of sound. Though it maps onto superficial phonological representations, this lexical phonological representation is very removed from the fully sounded-out form of the word. Several authors have suggested that this abstract representation is accessed from print, as well as being relevant to pronunciation and auditory word recognition. Most of the researchers who maintain this view argue that graphemes sometimes correspond better to phonemic segments specified in the lexical phonological representation than to those in the superficial phonological representation (Chomsky and Halle 1968; Henderson 1982). This might suggest a role for a lexical phonological representation in some phonologically mediated reading mechanism. However, we do not have to take this last step. We can think of the permanent representation of the form of a word as being a very abstract form, which can be recognized by a direct whole-word route when the word is presented in written form. In other words, the fact that reading mainly involves a direct whole-word recognition route does not imply that the representation which is recognized is in orthographic form. It only means that a phonological representation is not "assembled" from orthographic elements in a written word (to use a term employed by Patterson (1985)) and lexical access achieved from this assembled phonological representation. The exact form of the permanent lexical representation which is accessed is a separate question from how it is accessed (see Caplan *et al*. 1986*a* for further discussion of this issue).

We finally should note that our discussion of normal reading has been very brief and selective. We have only considered the regularity effect as a source of evidence for phonologically mediated reading. The interested reader is referred to Coltheart (1978) for a much more extensive discussion of this question, which deals with other types of evidence as well as the regularity effect. We have not discussed how words with affixes and compound words are recognized (are they broken down into their components, for instance?). We have not even discussed any of the theories of how lexical access actually occurs, except to mention the "interactive activation" model of McClelland and Rumelhart. Fortunately, we do not have to resolve all the questions that come up regarding normal reading mechanisms to begin the linguistic and psycholinguistic characterization of acquired disturbances of reading. In fact, studies of acquired dyslexia have been helpful in clarifying some of the questions we have just raised regarding the nature of the reading process. We therefore now turn to studies of acquired dyslexia.

We have already briefly discussed acquired dyslexia in Chapter 5, where we noted that Dejerine developed an analysis which distinguished alexia-without-agraphia from alexia-with-agraphia. Alexia-without-agraphia was thought to be due to a disconnection of early visual processing from the language zone, due to destruction of the left occipital (visual) cortex and the connections between the right occipital cortex and the language areas in the left hemisphere. Alexia-with-agraphia was thought to be due to a disruption of the set of grapheme–phoneme correspondences, which Dejerine believed were permanently stored in the left angular gyrus. Other authors (Kleist 1934; Geschwind 1962; 1965; Benson 1979) also adopt this approach to the characterization of dyslexia. Some other authors recognized other types of dyslexia, such as "aphasic alexia" – an alexia which occurs in association with an aphasic disturbance affecting spoken and auditory language (Benson 1979). Other authors (Hinshelwood 1899) have distinguished different types of alexia in patients who have impairments in letter recognition, patients who have intact letter recognition but who cannot read words, and patients who can read words in isolation but have difficulties in reading sentences. These approaches provide clinical data regarding the occurrence of alexia and its co-occurrence with other symptoms, and begin the study of the acquired dyslexias in relationship to aspects of the language code and the normal processing of written language. However, these studies do not deal with the breakdown of single-word reading in detail. The psycholinguistic approach to acquired dyslexia began in a major way quite recently, with a paper by Marshall and Newcombe (1973) which gave rise to a large series of papers and books dealing with how the reading process breaks down.

Marshall and Newcombe described two quite different types of dyslexic performance in six different patients. One case, JC, made errors which consisted of the production of items which were phonologically and visually similar to the presented written stimulus word. For instance, when required to read a word like *island*, he said /izland/. The other patient, GR, made very few errors of this type, but produced a very striking type of error, which Marshall and Newcombe called a "semantic paralexia". This error consisted of producing a word which was semantically or associatively related to the target word, such as *play* for *act*, *shut* for *close*, and even *Eisenhower* for *Krushchev*. Marshall and Newcombe considered that the first type of error arose at a relatively "superficial" level of linguistic structure, the level of the orthographic or phonological code, and termed the first pattern "surface dyslexia". They considered that the second type of error arose at a relatively "deep" level of linguistic structure – semantic structure – and termed the pattern "deep dyslexia". Subsequent research has shown that both surface and deep dyslexia are complex syndromes.

A number of reports dealing with patients with deep dyslexia have been gathered together in a volume entitled *Deep Dyslexia* (Coltheart *et al.* 1980). In an introductory chapter to this book, Coltheart reviews the characteristics of the reading performances of patients who make semantic paralexias when reading single words aloud. These patients also make derivational paralexias, substituting morphologically related words for each other (*wisdom* for *wise*, *true* for *truth*). They also make "visual" errors, producing responses whose spelling is similar to that of the target word (e.g. *shock* for *stock*). They show a part-of-speech effect, being better able to read nouns than adjectives and verbs. Abstract words are much more difficult than concrete words (e.g. *honest* versus *yellow*). They also show an extreme degree of difficulty in reading aloud two particular sets of stimuli: function words (e.g. *the*, *which*, *because*, *if*) and non-words (e.g. *bote*, *kald*).

The investigators who described the first cases of deep dyslexia attempted to account for all of these symptoms by postulating a single functional lesion in one or another part of the reading process. New data, which we shall review below, has required that most of these original formulations be changed. It is, however, worthwhile to view these earlier models, because the more recent models are extensions and modifications of them.

The first models of reading that these theorists postulated were ones that included both a "semantic" and a "phonologically mediated" route from print to meaning. This relatively simple model is illustrated in Figure 14-2.

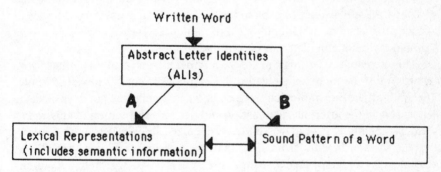

Figure 14-2. The model of the reading process which was first related to deep dyslexia, simplified to show its essential components

We note that this model assumes that there is only one lexical entry for a word, and that this entry includes semantic as well as other information. We have already seen that this is unlikely (see Chapters 12 and 13, as well as the previous discussion in this chapter), but we will accept this model as a place to start thinking about these syndromes. The semantic route in this "two-route model" immediately accesses the meaning of a word from its printed form, and the phonologically mediated route accesses a representation of the sound of the word from its spelling which then leads to appreciation of word meaning. In this model, the disturbance in deep dyslexia was thought to consist of an inability to use the phonologically mediated route. The symptoms of deep dyslexia are accounted for by this hypothesis as follows.

First, since non-words do not have semantic representations and therefore cannot be accessed by the semantic route, they will not be read correctly. The production of semantic paralexias and derivational errors was thought to be due to the fact that the semantic system is inherently "unstable". When it is accessed by the semantic route, a number of related forms are all activated. In normal reading, the choice of the correct form then depends upon additional information about that form supplied by the phonologically mediated route. Since the phonologically mediated route is inoperative in this syndrome, any one of a number of semantically or morphologically related forms can be produced. The increased difficulty with adjectives and verbs was also thought to be due to the internal organization and nature of activation of lexical entries in the cognitive system, as was the fact that abstract words often produced no responses at all. The lack of response to function-word stimuli was also attributed to the fact that function words have no intrinsic semantic meaning, or an abstract type of intrinsic meaning, and therefore could not be read through the semantic route efficiently. Several accounts (Coltheart 1980; Morton and Patterson 1980) also try to explain the occurrence of visual errors as a result of a disturbance of the phonological route in this syndrome, using a model similar to the one depicted in Figure 14-2.

This explanation clearly makes a number of assumptions. First, non-words must be read entirely through a phonologically mediated route. Second, all the morphological and semantic paralexias seen in deep dyslexia must reflect the internal organization and nature of activation of entries in a lexical–cognitive system when that system is accessed through a direct reading route. It is far from clear that these assumptions are correct. For instance, as we noted above, several researchers have suggested that reading non-words is partly accomplished by recognizing "analogies" between non-words and existing words, not through a process solely involving the conversion of each spelling unit into a unit of sound and combining these sounds together. If the process of reading non-words involves a mechanism such as this, then the inability to read non-words must reflect an inability to use lexical analogies normally, as well as an inability to read by a phonologi-cally mediated mechanism. This would imply that several processes are impaired, not just phonologically mediated reading. Second, the features of lexical and cognitive organization which this type of explanation postulates need to be independently evaluated. Studies of word associations and priming (which we partially reviewed in Chapter 12) do provide support for the idea that the mental lexicon contains sets of associatively related words, and that the presentation of a word activates its associates. However, it is not clear that this feature of lexical organization is different for nouns, verbs, and adjectives, or for abstract or concrete words, or radically different for function words by comparison with the major vocabulary classes. Nor is it clear that reading via the "semantic" route automatically leads to activation of a large set of associatively and semantically related lexical items, any one of which would be produced in an oral-reading task were it not for the presence of a check on word pronunciation due to the phonologically mediated route. In languages with ideographic scripts, for instance, normal readers should constantly be making semantic paralexias if this were the case, since there is little phonologically mediated reading in an ideographic language. Clearly, skilled readers of Chinese and Japanese Kanji do not show this pattern of single-word reading.

In short, the initial attempts to explain the deficits in deep dyslexia raised many more questions than they answered. As has been the case in many areas of linguistic aphasiology, these questions led to other theories, and to more detailed descriptions of patients' impairments. In the present case, the major questions which were raised by attempts to model the reading process, and to account for the syndrome of deep dyslexia, pertained to the details of both the "semantic" reading route and the phonologically mediated route. Data bearing on both of these questions have come from additional studies of reading disorders. Three patterns of dyslexia have received particular attention, because of their implication for the nature of the different reading routes. These three conditions are the "syndromes" of surface dyslexia, which we mentioned above, a syndrome known as "phonological alexia" described by Beauvois and Dérouesné (1979), and a type of alexia described by Schwartz and her colleagues (Schwartz *et al.* 1979).

As we noted above, patients with surface dyslexia make errors which are closely related to the form of the target word. Some of these errors have been considered to be "visual" in origin. The exact definition of a "visual" error is somewhat arbitrary, but most researchers consider an error to be visual in origin if the response word contains 50 per cent or more of the letters found in the target word and these letters appear in the same sequence as in the target word. It is assumed that such errors arise because of visual mis-analyses of letters in the target word. Another possibility, which has not been explored in detail, is that such errors are a form of phonemic paraphasia, due to disturbances in the planning of the phonemic content of a correctly identified target word during output processing, as was described in Chapter 13. These types of error appear in many forms of dyslexia, and do not bear in any specific way upon the nature of the conversion of print to sound, since they may arise during the process of letter identification or the final selection and planning of phonemes in a spoken word.

However, a second feature of the errors of surface dyslexics is important for the development of a theory of how surface dyslexia arises, and has implications for the normal reading process. This type of error is known as a "regularization error". In this error, a grapheme which is ambiguous, such as *ea* in English, is mispronounced in a particular word. A regularization error occurs when the target word contains the less common sound of the grapheme and the response contains the more common sound. For instance, in English, the letter *i* is usually pronounced as a short *i* (as in *hit*), but in certain words, such as *pint*, this rule is broken. A regularization error would consist of pronouncing the word *pint* with a short *i* sound, to rhyme with *hint*. Regularization errors can occur whether an error is a "visual error" or not; that is, they can occur whether or not half of the letters in the response match the letters in the target.

Regularization effects are extremely common in surface dyslexia, in the reading of ambiguous words, completely irregular words, and non-words. With real words, these effects cause errors; with non-words they lead to patients most frequently reading the non-words in a completely regularized form, and rarely, if ever, attributing a phonemic value to a grapheme which is other than its most common phonemic value. Patients misread words like *women*, *colonel*, and *yacht*, producing non-words which are formed by the application of the most regular and common grapheme–phoneme correspondences of the language.

In addition to making regularization errors, patients with surface dyslexia often show two interesting behaviors when confronted with pseudo-homophones. First, they sometimes do not realize that these are not real words. They read them in a phonologically regular fashion and believe them to be the word they have pronounced. This indicates that they are achieving lexical access *after* converting the written stimulus to its spoken form, and that the process of lexical access does not take into account the entire spelling pattern of the presented written word, but only the sound structure created by blending together the phonemic values of each of the graphemes of the presented stimulus. Second, some surface dyslexics incorrectly class pseudo-homophones as real words in lexical decision tasks. This performance also indicates that they are not sensitive to the spelling pattern of a non-word in its entirety, but only pay attention to the sound of the non-word, which they achieve by conversion of graphemes to phonemes. The regularization errors made by surface dyslexics and their treatment of pseudo-homophones have led some theorists to conclude that the impairment in surface dyslexia consists of an inability to access the lexicon through a whole-word recognition route (Coltheart 1978; 1985). The performance of surface dyslexics is taken to reflect the functioning of the phonologically mediated route in isolation. The pattern of oral reading errors seen in these patients has suggested that this route makes use of the most frequent grapheme–phoneme correspondences in the language (Coltheart 1978; 1985).

A question which the data from surface dyslexia can help resolve is what the units of analysis and conversion are in the phonologically mediated route. We have made reference numerous times to the fact that, in a language such as English, a single grapheme can stand for many phonological values. It is also the case that, in a language such as English, the graphemic context in which a grapheme occurs helps to decide which phonological value a grapheme has. For instance, we noted above that the grapheme *i* is usually pronounced as a short *i*, as in *hid*, and that the regularization of a word like *pint* would produce a misrepresentation with a short *i*. However, in one particular context, *i* is more likely to be pronouned as a long *i* than a short *i*, namely when it is followed by the letters *ld* (as in *wild*, *mild*, *child*, etc.). How surface dyslexics pronounce words like these becomes an interesting and important question. If surface dyslexics are always likely to produce regularizations, the pattern of response to these words would indicate to what extent graphemic context is taken into account in the phonologically mediated reading route. If words like *wild* are pronounced with a short *i*, then phonemic context is not part of the information on which the phonologically mediated route operates. If the *i* in *wild* is pronounced correctly but the *i* in *pint* is not, then phonemic context is taken into account in the phonologically mediated route, but *word-specific* information is not. At present, this empirical question is unresolved. Leading researchers disagree as to the actual data from surface dyslexia in this respect. Marcel (1980) argues that surface dyslexics make errors which reflect their use of phonemic context, while Coltheart *et al.* (1983) maintain that regularization errors that involve graphemic context rarely occur in this syndrome.

The issue of what the units of analysis are in the phonologically mediated reading route is a particularly good example of an area of inquiry in which the study of brain-injured subjects and that of normals complement each other. Coltheart (1978; 1980) was a major proponent of the view that the phonologically mediated route relies exclusively upon the most frequent grapheme–phoneme correspondences in the language, but he has since slightly revised his position. He now (Coltheart 1985) accepts that graphemes may occasionally be converted into less than the most frequently associated phonemes, on the basis of evidence that normal readers assign phonemes to graphemes in part on the basis of what sort of word they are reading. He notes that Campbell and Besner (1981) showed that normals pronounced word-initial *th* differently in non-words that appeared in the position of function words and in non-words that appeared in the position of content words in printed sentences. Since word-initial *th* is pronounced differently in function words and content words (being voiced in function words like *the* and unvoiced in content words like *thin*), this finding suggests that syntactic class determines which phonemic value a particular phoneme can take, even if the value is not the one with the greatest overall frequency for that grapheme. Similarly, Coltheart (1985) accepts the finding of Kay and Lesser (1985) that normals pronounce the grapheme *ea* differently in non-words in which *ea* is followed by the letters *n*, *k*, and *d*. Since the likelihood of *ea* being pronounced as *ee* is directly influenced by which of these letters follows it, this finding also indicates that graphemic context does affect the phonemic value assigned to a grapheme. Since all these effects occurred with non-words, Coltheart accepts that they reveal something of the nature of the phonologically mediated route. However, Coltheart (1985) still points out that these effects are limited. For instance, in Kay and Lesser's study the most common phonemic value of *ea* in all these types of words was *ee*, suggesting that the use of context is very limited. Since surface dyslexics overwhelmingly make regularization errors which do not involve the use of orthographic context, and occasionally produce the phonemic value which is not the most frequent overall value of a grapheme but is correct in that context in reading non-words, the data from both normals and surface dyslexics point to the major role of regular GPCs in the phonologically mediated reading route, and to the occasional use of context to determine the phonemic value of a grapheme by this route.

A second feature of the performance of surface dyslexics is also interesting with respect to the operation of the phonologically mediated route. Many surface dyslexics show a "lexicalization" effect as well as a regularization effect. That is, when they read non-words, they not only make regularization errors, they also tend to produce existing words of the language, which are phonologically close to the regularized target. How do these lexicalizations arise? One possibility is that they arise because of the nature of the phonologically mediated reading route, which may make more use of the process of analogy than a simple theory would postulate. Alternatively, the phonologically mediated route may produce a phonological output which is itself a non-word, and this form may activate phonologically similar words in the mental lexicon. We have seen in Chapter 13 that words are more easily produced than non-words when there are output disturbances in aphasia, and it may be that the activated words are more readily produced than the regularized form of the presented non-word.

This second possibility might reflect a disturbance *within* the phonologically mediated route. Coltheart (1985) indicates that there must be at least three steps in the conversion of print to sound in phonologically mediated reading: letters must be grouped into graphemes; graphemes must be converted to phonemes; and individual phonemes must be "blended" together to form a unified utterance. Individual cases described by different authors appear to have problems with each of these steps. A patient of

Beauvois and Dérouesné (1979) could not read non-words in which letters had to be grouped together into phonemes. The patient could read real words well, indicating that the impairment affected the phonologically mediated route alone. Moreover, the patient could read non-words in which *single letters* were mapped onto phonemes, showing that the grouping of letters into graphemes was impaired, not grapheme–phoneme conversion. A second case (Newcombe and Marshall 1985) assigned a phonological value to each letter of a word, reading a word such as *advice* as (/ædvɪki/. Coltheart (1985) analyzed this performance as a failure in assigning letters to graphemes and the direct conversion of letters to phonemes. Both cases thus have disturbances at the first stage of the phonologically mediated route – "graphemic parsing". A patient of Funnell's (1983) showed an impairment of the second step – grapheme–phoneme conversion. The patient could not produce the sound of any graphemes, whether made up of one or more letters, but could identify words quite well when given the sounds of the phonemes in the words individually, indicating that the final step – phoneme blending – was intact. Finally, Coltheart (1985) reports a case in which the patient produced the sounds of each of the letters (or graphemes) of very short (three-letter) non-words but could not blend them – evidence for the final "phoneme-blending" stage of the phonologically mediated route. The lexicalization effects seen in non-word reading in surface dyslexia may arise because of the greater ease of "blending" the sounds of words than of non-words at this last stage of the phonologically mediated route.

Surface dyslexia thus seems to be a disturbance of the use of the whole-word reading route, and the performance of surface dyslexics is relevant to the nature of the phonologically mediated route. We began this discussion by entertaining the possibility that deep dyslexia represented a disturbance of the phonologically mediated route and that the characteristics of deep dyslexic patients reflected the operation of a "semantic" reading route. However, as we noted above, further research into acquired dyslexia has shown that this is not the case. Two types of disturbances shed light upon the whole-word reading route, and indicate that deep dyslexia is due to a number of different functional impairments.

The first of these forms of alexia is "phonological alexia" (Beauvois and Dérouesné 1979). The patient described by Beauvois and Derouesne was similar to the deep dyslexics previously described, inasmuch as he could not read non-words, and showed a number of other symptoms which would be expected to arise following disruption of the phonologically mediated reading route. However, unlike deep dyslexics, he did *not* make semantic paralexias. This pattern bears on the existence and the nature of the direct whole-word reading route.

First, Coltheart (1985) has argued that the very existence of cases of phonological alexia shows that there must be a direct, whole-word reading route, as well as a non-lexical reading route (the non-lexical route being phonological). Coltheart argues that we can account for the existence of this syndrome, if there are two such routes, by postulating that the phonologically mediated route is impaired and the direct route spared; but there is no way to account for the fact that non-words cannot be read and words read very well if there is only one way to read that applies to both words and non-words. This argument of course depends upon what models we have of reading. Coltheart (1985) argues that only a model of Marcel's (1980) could lead to the pattern of reading abilities seen in phonological dyslexia and is explicit enough to be testable. Marcel maintains that all written stimuli – words and non-words – are read by a process that first recognizes orthographic segments of all sizes (graphemes, morphemes, words), then segments spoken words into equivalent units and relates the two, and finally blends the phonological segments together to achieve a pronunciation. Though Coltheart argues that this model is worth considering, he believes it is shown to be wrong by data from a phonological alexic studied by Funnell (1983). What Funnell showed is that her patient, WB, could accomplish each of these operations, but could still not read non-words and could read words. Coltheart (1985) takes this as evidence that Marcel's model of reading is incorrect, and thus maintains that the only model of the reading process compatible with the existence of phonological alexia is one which incorporates both a direct lexical route, and a non-lexical, phonologically mediated route.

The second conclusion that can be reached based upon evidence from phonological dyslexia is that the operation of the whole-word reading route in isolation does not lead to the activation of associated and morphologically related items whose production must somehow be inhibited; that is, this crucial feature of the model underlying the initial explanation of deep dyslexia is wrong. Rather, the whole-word reading route must be capable of producing the correct phonological item when operating in isolation. Deep dyslexics must have some disturbance aside from their problems with phonologically mediated reading. Their other problem may arise within the lexical semantic system, and give rise to the semantic and derivational paralexias that these patients produce.

Phonological alexia allows us to investigate the way the "lexical" route operates. For instance, one feature of phonological alexia is that there is no word-class effect favoring nouns, adjectives, or verbs – or only a very minor one. The conclusion that can be drawn is that the whole-word reading route is capable of accessing nouns, adjectives, and verbs equally easily. Nor is there an abstractness effect, which leads to the same conclusion as regards words that have abstract meanings.

A feature of deep dyslexia that is also found in phonological dyslexia, however, is that there is frequently an associated disturbance of reading morphological endings and free-standing function words. In the original case described by Beauvois and Dérouesné, the patient had trouble reading both these types of vocabulary element. New cases of phonological dyslexia have been described in which bound morphemes could be read better than function words (Patterson 1982), and vice versa (Job and Sartori 1984). It thus appears that patients who cannot use the phonologically mediated reading route do not necessarily have disturbances in reading in either of these vocabulary classes. Assuming, though, that all these patients have problems with some aspect of the non-lexical route, these patterns suggest that, within the direct whole-word reading route, there can be separate disturbances affecting the reading of words in each of the major lexical categories (nouns, verbs, and adjectives, as opposed to morphological affixes and free-standing function words). The study of phonological alexia has thus begun to provide data regarding different processes that exist within the direct whole-word reading route.

Further studies have been directed towards the question of just how affixes are recognized. First, researchers have shown that, in phonological alexia, the difficulty patients have in reading affixes is due to a problem in recognition that is specific to the written word. Moody (1984) showed that four patients with phonological alexia could not recognize that written sentences in which an affix was incorrect, such as *Tomorrow, he will cooked the dinner*, were anomalous, but they had no trouble recognizing the anomaly when the sentences were spoken. This is consistent with an impairment of recognition of the affix in the written version of the sentence. Second, it has been shown that the problem with affixes does not occur in words that seem to have affixes but actually do not (so-called "pseudo-affixed words") such as *corner*. These two results suggest that words with affixes are treated differently from unaffixed words in the process of reading by the whole-word route.

Several accounts of how this happens have been presented. Job and Sartori (1984) suggest that affixes are separated from the stems of complex words, and that both the affix and the stem are recognized separately and later combined to yield the entire complex word. If this is the case, however, patients with phonological alexia who make errors on affixes must "lose" the affix somewhere during the process of recognition or of combining the affix and stem, and there is evidence that this does not happen. Moody (1984) had his phonological alexics do a lexical decision task, in which the real words were all complex words with affixes (*biggest*, *calling*) and the non-words were composed of the same stems and affixes in illegal combinations (*callest*, *bigging*). The patients did very well on this test. Coltheart (1985) takes this as evidence that phonological alexics who make errors in reading affixes aloud nonetheless are able to recognize the affixes, and to combine them with stems to yield complex forms which they can recognize as real or illegal words. Since Moody's first result shows that the problem these patients have with affixes is one that arises at the visual recognition stage, the conclusion to be drawn is that the theory that affixes are stripped from complex words, and that stems and affixes are separately recognized and subsequently blended together, is wrong. In fact, at present, the investigation of the ability of patients with phonological alexia to read and make judgements about affixed words has not led to *any* convincing theory of how affixes are read. Investigators such as Coltheart (1985) and Seidenberg (personal communication) have begun to wonder whether effects such as misreading of affixed words in phonological alexia (and increases in reading latencies for affixed words in normals) might not be due to orthographic features of these words. The data from phonological alexia certainly suggest that affixes are recognized differently during the process of reading by the whole-word route, but many questions about how this takes place remain unanswered.

The study of *surface* dyslexia has also begun to provide information regarding some of the features of the whole-word recognition route for basic, non-compositional, major-class lexical items. Bub and his colleagues (1986) have studied a surface dyslexic who had great difficulty reading irregular words. MP was able to read some irregular words correctly, however, and these were all words with relatively high frequencies of occurrence. Since irregularly spelled words can only be recognized by the whole-word route, this suggests that the whole-word reading route was operating in the recognition of high-frequency words in MP. This result confirms that the frequency of a written form partially determines whether the form can be recognized by the whole-word route, and complements the results of Seidenberg and his colleagues (1984), cited above, which show a frequency by regularity interaction. All these results suggest that the whole-word recognition route works efficiently for high-frequency words, and is somehow supplemented by information derived from the phonologically mediated route in the recognition of infrequent words.

Finally, a form of dyslexia described by Schwartz and her colleagues (1979; 1980*a*) also bears on the nature of the whole-word recognition route. Schwartz *et al.*'s. patient had Alzheimer's disease, a degenerative neurological disease affecting cognitive functioning. Among the many symptoms that this patient had was a progressive loss of information about the meanings of individual lexical items. During the relatively late stages of the patient's disease, when her reading was tested, the patient was quite poor at naming most common objects, matching spoken words to pictures or objects, and other tasks that require knowledge of the meaning of words. This was true of her performance with written as well as spoken words. Moreover, the patient was unable to read non-words, suggesting that she could not read through the process of phonological mediation. Nonetheless, the patient was able to read a large number of words aloud, quickly and correctly. Most strikingly, she was able to read aloud irregular words, even infrequent irregularly spelled words such as *yacht* and *colonel*.

This set of observations is very revealing about the nature of the direct reading route. The direct reading route must be involved in this patient's reading, not only because she did not read non-words, but also because she correctly read irregularly spelled words, which can be only read by this route. This case shows that the direct reading route does not necessarily make contact with semantic information, as the model in Figure 14-2 supposed. Reading can proceed by a whole-word recognition route in a patient in whom semantic representations are largely destroyed or disturbed. This case also provides evidence that the lexical entry accessed through the direct reading route can be mapped onto speech production stages without activating a semantic representation.

The overall model of the stages and processes involved in reading that emerges from the studies is represented in Figure 14-3. As this figure indicates, there are several routes from orthographic representations to their sounds. One is a route that involves phonological mediation. This route seems to involve grapheme–phoneme conversions, and may involve appreciation of the context in which a grapheme occurs. It may be more correct to call this an "indirect" route than a "phonologically mediated" route, since this route may also involve reference to existing words through the process of analogy. In addition to this route, there is a direct route which allows a reader to recognize a whole word on the basis of its written form. The lexical entry so accessed may activate a semantic representation, but a reader can convert this "input" lexical representation of a word directly into an "output" representation of the sound of a word without activating the word's meaning. There may also be some process whereby lexical semantic representations are accessed directly from the letters or graphemes in a word.

Many questions remain to be answered about the processes involved in these reading routes, the time course of the activation along these various routes, and the interactions of the outputs of these various routes in

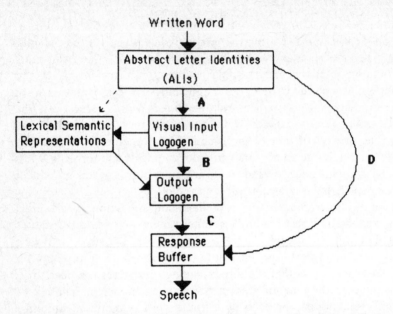

Figure 14-3. A revised two-route model of the reading process. The pathway A–B–C represents the "lexical" route, and the pathway D represents the "phonologically mediated" or "indirect" route. The dotted line indicates a possible route from letter identities to lexical semantic representations, originally postulated in relationship to deep dyslexia. For details, see text.

feedback and feedforward systems. The study of the acquired dyslexias has been extremely helpful in providing evidence for the existence of these different reading routes and has begun to provide information about the nature of each route and about their interactions. This study is just beginning; much work on this topic lies ahead.

SUGGESTIONS FOR FURTHER READING

Beauvois, M.-F. and Dérouesné, J. (1979). Phonological alexia: three dissociations. *Journal of Neurology, Neurosurgery and Psychiatry* 42, 1115–24.

Coltheart, M. (1978). Lexical access in simple reading tasks. In G. Underwood (ed.), *Strategies of Information Processing*. Academic Press, London.

Coltheart, M., Patterson, K., and Marshall, J. C. (1980). *Deep Dyslexia*. Routledge & Kegan Paul. London.

Marshall, J. C. and Newcombe, F. (1973). Patterns of paralexia: a psycholinguistic approach. *Journal of Psycholinguistic Research* 2, 175–99.

Patterson, K., Marshall, J. C. and Coltheart, M. (1985). *Surface Dyslexia*. Erlbaum, London.

Seidenberg, M. S., Waters, G. S., Barnes, M. A., and Janenhaus, M. K. (1984). When does irregular spelling or pronunciation influence word recognition? *Journal of Verbal Learning and Verbal Behavior*. 23, 383–404.

15

Disturbances of sentence production: agrammatism

In Chapters 12, 13, and 14 we have discussed a number of disturbances that affect single words: disturbances of lexical semantic representations, of the phonological output from the lexicon, and of accessing the lexicon from the written word. In Chapters 15 and 16, we shall be discussing disturbances that affect the form and meaning of *sentences*. In this chapter, we shall discuss disturbances of sentence production, and in Chapter 16 disturbances of sentence comprehension. In keeping with the philosophy that we have adopted throughout Part III of this book – that of discussing a few aphasic symptoms in detail in relationship to normal processes, rather than presenting a general survey of a large number of studies dealing with a particular topic – we shall focus here upon the symptom (or syndrome) of agrammatism, and upon a particular type of sentence comprehension disturbance in Chapter 16. As elsewhere in Part III, we begin with studies that describe the normal structures and processes involved in sentence production, and then move to disturbances in this functional domain.

We began our discussion of linguistic structures in Chapter 12 by considering the question of what individual words mean, and we continued our investigation of language by outlining some of the properties of the sound system and of the orthographic representations of words in Chapters 13 and 14. Crucial though words are to language, they are not the only elements of linguistic structure, and the meanings of individual words by no means exhaust the semantic features conveyed by language. As John Hughlings Jackson (1874) pointed out, words are generally grouped together into larger structures which convey meanings above and beyond those inherent in each lexical item. We shall refer to the semantic features conveyed by groups of words as "phrasal" and "sentential" semantic features, although these terms do a slight injustice to the actual linguistic structures which convey these additional aspects of meaning, as we shall see. Among these phrasal and sentential aspects of meaning are: thematic roles – who did what to whom in an action; attribution of modification – which qualities are associated with which items; scope of quantification – what items are included within the "domain" of quantifiers such as negative elements and numerals; and co-reference – which nouns, pronouns, reflexives, and other nominal expressions refer to the same item in the real world.

Language makes use of a number of formal devices to convey these aspects of meaning. We shall be concerned primarily with phrases and sentences, but for completeness, and because it is relevant to several distinctions we shall be making between types of vocabulary elements, we shall also consider the process of word formation, which creates derived and compound words (*constitutional, nightwatchman*, for example) which can also convey certain "phrasal" semantic features. (It is because of the existence of word formation that the terms "phrasal" and "semantic" are not entirely accurate descriptions of the linguistic structures which convey the types of semantic information arising beyond the level of the single word.)

Word formation and the construction of phrases and sentences are all based upon the ability to combine vocabulary elements to yield larger structures. Vocabulary elements never combine freely in language. Just as there are rules regulating the combination of sound segments in single words in a language, such as the syllable structure rules that we discussed in Chapter 13, so there are rules regulating the combination of lexical elements in the processes of word formation and phrase and sentence construction. As with the rules regulating combinations of sounds, rules regulating combinations of lexical elements have some features that are universal to all languages and others which are specific to each individual language. Much of the "revolution" in modern linguistics which began with the publication of *Syntactic Structures* by Chomsky in 1957 consists of an increasingly detailed and abstract characterization of the linguistic elements, rules, and constraints which govern the combination of words into these larger linguistic units. In this chapter, we shall be primarily concerned with a number of distinctions among types of lexical elements, some of the properties of word formation, and the most elementary aspects of sentence structure. In Chapter 16, we shall present a brief description of some of the more abstract aspects of sentence structure. The reason for this division of the topic has to do with the focus of investigation in the studies that we shall review which deal with aphasic patients. For the most part, analyses of the linguistic structures *produced* by aphasic patients have concentrated on patients' abilities to produce particular vocabulary elements and very elementary aspects of sentence structure, while, to a greater extent, recent studies of *comprehension* have focussed on aphasic patients' abilities to construct and interpret some of the more abstract aspects of sentence structure.

We shall begin our discussion by outlining some of the major divisions between vocabulary elements in English. Vocabulary elements in English, and many other languages, can be divided into several major categories. Informally, we may make a distinction between "content" words and "function" words. Content words consist of nouns, adjectives, verbs, many adverbs, and perhaps some prepositions; function words are exemplified by articles, pronouns, auxiliary verbs, other prepositions, possessive adjectives, and a few other items. The second major division is between items which are entire words – which includes both the class of content words and that of function words – and "affixes". Affixes, also called "morphological items", are vocabulary elements which are appended to words during the process of word formation. They are exemplified by items such as the past tense marker *-ed*, the progressive marker *-ing*, and the plural and possessive *-s*. We shall consider each of these distinctions among vocabulary types in turn.

The class of function words receives this informal name because of the particular role that function words play in syntactic structures. The "function" served by function words is to create certain aspects of syntactic structure. The function words italicized in the sentences below introduce relative clauses, verbal complements, and questions:

(1a)   The boy *that* the dog bit is feeling fine
(1b)   John knows *who* can fix this car
(1c)   *Why* did you go downtown yesterday?

Function words also introduce certain semantic notions, such as possessive (2a) and future tense (2b):

(2a)   The owner *of* that car must be very wealthy
(2b)   They *will* each lunch at the airport

Our intuitions about words such as these tell us that they are not serving the same functions as the "content" words of a sentence. Our intuitions are certainly right about this, but, as often happens when considering language structures, it is hard to capture what these intuitions are telling us in a specific way. For instance, we can express some of the syntactic and semantic structures in (1) and (2) without using function words, as in (3):

(3a)   The boy the dog bit is feeling fine
(3b)   That car-owner must be very wealthy
(3c)   They plan to eat lunch at the airport

Of course, this does not mean that the function words in the sentences (1) and (2) do not play roles in determining the syntax and sentential semantic features of these sentences, but it does mean that there are other devices in English which can play similar roles.

If we ask what roles can only be played by function words, we must embark upon a detailed examination of all the relations between particular syntactic structures and semantic features. For instance, one of the ways of expressing the semantic feature of attribution is to make use of sequences of content words, as in (3a) and (3b). In (3a), a relative clause is signaled by the juxtaposition of the words *the boy the dog bit*, which can only be analyzed as a structure in which *the dog bit* is a relative clause which is attached to *the boy*. In this particular construction, the relative pronoun, *that*, can be omitted. What is important about the construction in (1a) and (3a) is that it expresses a relative clause. The relative pronoun *that* signals the relative clause, but it itself is not a necessary feature of the relative clause. Similarly, in (3b), the word *car-owner* is a compound word, formed by a certain type of word-formation process which does not make use of function words. This is not the same syntactic structure as (2a) but, rather, an alternate way of combining words to yield a structure which captures a semantic feature very similar to that expressed in (2a).

Despite the fact that there are a variety of structures which express similar sentential semantic features, and that some syntactic structures do not require the overt presence of function words, there are particular syntactic roles associated with the *syntactic categories* to which function words belong. Let us consider examples (1a) and (3a). In most versions of contemporary syntactic theory (Bresnan 1982; Chomsky 1981), the word *that* in (1a) is a member of the syntactic category "complementizer" (COMP, for short) and this *category* is present in both (1a) and (3a) even though the actual word *that* – the "overt" complementizer – can be deleted in (1a) to yield (3a). All relative clauses have an introductory complementizer; indeed, all clauses – main clauses and subordinate clauses as well as relative clauses – have an introductory complementizer at an abstract level of representation. The hypothesis that all clauses have an introductory complementizer, which may be omitted in certain cases, such as sentence (1a), and *must* be omitted in other cases, such as main clauses, results from an effort to describe the syntactic structures of English and other languages in as simple a form as possible. Postulating the existence of abstract complementizers, which may or must be deleted in certain circumstances, greatly simplifies descriptions of other aspects of syntactic structure (Bresnan 1982; Chomsky 1981). There are many other syntactic structures which make use of function word categories. In Chomsky's theory, for instance, another category closely related to function words is the category INFL, a shorthand for the term "inflection". INFL is related to the auxiliary verb of a sentence, but is actually an abstract category which determines many aspects of sentence structure. The syntactic roles played by COMP and INFL are quite different. In other cases, the particular consequences of a function word reside in the particular function word itself, and not its category. This is the case with pronouns and reflexive elements which we shall discuss in Chapter 16. Overall, there are many syntactic structures which are created by the presence of function words and function word categories.

Some of the structures signaled by function words are also signaled by content words, especially verbs. For instance, consider the role of complementizers in indicating the presence of a subordinate clause. Some subordinate clauses are required because of the nature of the main verb of a sentence, as in (4):

(4)   John hopes that he will be elected

The verb *hopes* requires that a sentential complement be present. *Hopes* cannot be followed by a noun (as in **John hopes the presidency*), and it cannot stand by itself as an intransitive verb (as in **John hopes often*). Though the complementizer *that* signals the presence of the embedded complement sentence in (4), the verb *hopes* itself also specifies that a subordinate complement sentence is going to occur in sentence (4). The syntactic information conveyed by the actual complementizer *that* and the function word category COMP is critical in structuring the embedded clause, but there is a sense in which the verb *hopes* also expresses the fact that sentence (4) has a subordinate sentential complement. Though the syntactic information that is conveyed by function words and function word categories is different from the syntactic information conveyed in content words, the simple generalization that function words convey syntactic information and content words convey semantic information is too simplistic.

The other intuition that we have about function words is that they express a particular type of semantic information. Often this information is said to be "abstract". While it is certainly true that the information expressed by words such as *and* or *of* is abstract, this feature also does not adequately capture the difference between some function words and many content words. First, many function words seem to be reasonably concrete in meaning: prepositions such as *under*, pronouns such as *she*, and demonstrative adjectives such as *those*, all convey semantic information which is quite concrete. On the other hand, we have already noted in Chapter 12 that there are content words which are abstract in meaning (such as *honesty*) and others that have no referent at all in the real world (such as *unicorn*). A somewhat more satisfying characterization of the differences between the semantic information conveyed by content and function words might make use of the notion of "reference" which we also discussed in Chapter 12. We might wish to say that content words are "referential" – that they somehow refer to objects, actions, and attributes in the real world – while function words do not refer in this way. We might try to extend the notion of reference to say that a word like *honesty* "refers" to a situation or a certain type of behavior. Though distinguishing between the semantics of content words and function words on the basis of their ability to make reference may be slightly more accurate than trying to do so on the basis of their being "abstract" in meaning, this attempt is also not entirely satisfactory. Prepositions such as *under* do seem to refer to something in the real world, even though we may feel that what they refer to is different from what is referred to by any of the content words we have discussed; and, conversely, we have certainly had to extend the notion of "reference" in relatively undefined ways to advance the claim that abstract words refer to situations and behaviors in the real world. Therefore, the two semantic criteria that we have considered – abstractness and referentiality – do not seem to be able to capture the differences between the semantic features of these two classes of vocabulary elements in a specific way.

We therefore see that it is not a simple matter to distinguish function words and content words on the basis of either the syntactic or the semantic information that they convey. While it is certainly possible to distinguish the syntactic information conveyed by function words and function word categories from that conveyed by content words and content word categories, this is a task that requires the construction of an abstract theory of syntactic structure, and is not a simple matter. The function words and function word categories themselves specify a wide variety of syntactic structures, which makes it hard to capture what they have in common syntactically. The effort to distinguish between the lexical semantic information conveyed by function words and content words also leads to a number of difficulties and uncertainties. Since the distinction between function word and content word classes is based upon our intuition that there are syntactic and semantic differences between words in these two classes, we may at this point feel that our distinction is at best difficult to specify and justify, and at worst incorrect. Perhaps surprisingly, however, it is possible to distinguish two vocabulary classes which correspond very closely to "function words" and "content words" by referring to two other parts of language structure – namely, phonological structure and the processes involved in word formation.

A very simple phonological feature distinguishes function words from content words in English and many other languages. Function words never bear the main stress of a sentence when a sentence receives a normal intonation contour. Only content words can bear main stress. Of course, it is possible to put emphatic stress on any word of a sentence, but, aside from this circumstance, the stress rules of English apply to sentences to place main stress on content words. In fact, function words never bear stress at all, and do not seem to be relevant to the assignment of intonation contours in sentences, except insofar as they contribute to syntactic structure. This quite simple property serves to distinguish two vocabulary classes which overlap almost completely with the set of function words and content words in English. In many other languages, similar phonological properties distinguish these two sets of vocabulary items.

Second, function words tend not to enter freely into word-formation processes. English allows words to be combined to form compound words, such as *greenhouse*, *bedtable*, *housefly*, or *cutthroat*. Though there are several examples of prepositions which can enter into word-formation processes, (e.g. *runoff*, *overthrow*), most function words – determiners, auxiliary verbs, complementizers – do not combine with other words to form compound words. In English, nouns, verbs, and adjectives can combine relatively freely to form compound words. Restrictions on word compounding involving these vocabulary elements are primarily due to the fact that certain words have no relationship to one another semantically. On the other hand, the few examples of word compounding that involve function words are usually quite restricted and very semantically constrained, as in the examples we have given and others (*he-man*, *she-wolf*). Compound formation is a *productive* process when it involves the content word vocabulary; it is *unproductive* when it involves the function word vocabulary. This difference is also relatively clear-cut, and serves to distinguish these two vocabularies.

Finally, there are features of the function word vocabulary which are not directly relevant to linguistics – that is, they are not directly relevant to the formal nature of linguistic structures involved in the pairing of sounds and meanings – but which are nonetheless of considerable significance to psychological processes involving language. The two most important purely psychological or psycholinguistic characteristics of the function word class are that it consists of a fixed number of elements, and that its members are extremely frequent in spoken and written language. There are approximately 500 or so function words in English, and, of the 100 most common words in English, most are function words. The fact that the set of function words is a "closed class" of vocabulary elements may have important consequences for psychological processing. Once a person has learned the function words of English he does not need to learn any more. Since, as we have just seen, he also does not have the opportunity to use these words to form new words, any features of the representations or processing of words which are related to the fact that new words can be learned, and that words can be formed from other words, are irrelevant to the function words of English. Similarly, the fact that a word is extremely frequent has important consequences for how easy it is to recognize and produce. These two features of function words, therefore, may be important in determining how these vocabulary elements are processed, though they do not have any particular significance for the structural role that function words play in creating linguistic structures and their meanings.

To summarize our discussion of function words and content words, we have seen that our original intuitions about the differences between function words and content words, though undoubtedly important and correct in some sense, are very difficult to make explicit. On the other hand, other aspects of the linguistic roles played by function words, having to do with the sound pattern and word-formation processes of English and other languages, provide straightforward ways of distinguishing these two vocabulary classes on linguistic grounds. In addition, it is possible to distinguish these two vocabulary classes on psychological grounds, in terms of the "closed" nature of the function word vocabulary class, and the frequency of many of its members. As we have seen in Chapters 9, 11, and 13, and as we shall discuss in greater detail in relationship to sentence production in this chapter, different aphasic impairments affect the function word and the content word vocabularies.

The second distinction we drew was between both these vocabulary classes and affixes. There is no difficulty in distinguishing these two classes of vocabulary elements, because affixes are not themselves words, while both function and content words are. We may therefore concentrate on the different types of affixes, and their different roles in the processes of word formation and phrase and sentence construction.

Affixes are divided into two large categories: "derivational" and "inflectional" affixes. Derivational affixes are those which are involved in word-formation processes which are essentially independent of the form of sentences, while inflectional affixes are dependent upon sentence structure for their correct use. For instance, if we take a verb such as *destroy*, derivational processes can change this verb into the noun *destruction*, and inflectional processes will create the particular form of the verb *destroy* which is appropriate for certain syntactic environments, as in *he destroys*. Though the proper use of *destroy* as a verb or as a noun does, of course, depend on the sentence context in which it is located, there is a difference between the way a sentence context determines the presence of the noun or verb form of *destroy* and the presence of an appropriate agreement marker on the verb *destroys*. In the first case, the use of *destroy* as a verb or as a noun depends upon the entire form of a sentence. Since we can express essentially the same idea using either the verb or noun form of *destroy*, as in example (6) below, the decision to use either the verb or the noun form depends upon very general decisions as to the entire syntactic structure of a sentence:

(5)   The way the enemy destroyed the city was particularly barbaric
(6)   The destruction of the city by the enemy was particularly barbaric

In contrast, agreement between a verb and a noun is a relatively "late" and "local" aspect of syntactic structure, which is determined well after the general syntactic structure of a sentence is already fixed, and which depends solely upon the relationship between the noun in the subject position of a sentence and the verb of that sentence. A related feature of derivational processes that distinguishes them from inflectional processes is that derivational processes can change the syntactic category of a word from a verb to a noun or an adjective (*destroy–destruction–destructive*) and from each of these categories to another. Inflectional morphology cannot change syntactic category. We therefore have two criteria by which to distinguish derivational from inflectional processes: (1) derivational processes involve syntactic features related to much more general aspects of sentence form; and (2) inflectional processes do not change the syntactic categories of words, while derivational processes do.

Both these types of affixation have consequences for the sound patterns of words – that is, they have phonological as well as syntactic consequences – and an account of linguistic form must specify the way morphological processes affect the sound pattern of words. Seen from the point of view of their phonological consequences, affixes can also be divided into two groups. The first group consists of affixes which do not change the phonological form of the word to which they are attached. All inflectional affixes in English fall into this group, and some derivational affixes – such as *-ly*, *-ment*, *-ness* – and most prefixes also do. The remaining derivational affixes – *-ive*, *-tion*, and others – do affect the sounds of the words to which they are attached (*destroy–destruction–destructive*). We may term the first set of affixes "word boundary" affixes, since they are added to words beyond some boundary which marks the end of the *phonological* word. The remaining affixes may be termed "formative boundary" affixes, since they are added to words after a boundary which does not mark the end of the phonological form of a word. For the most part, in English, formative boundary affixes are derived from Latin, and are used in word-formation processing involving the Latinate portion of our vocabulary, while word boundary derivational affixes are derived from Anglo-Saxon forms and are used in word-formation processes involving the Anglo-Saxon portion of the vocabulary of English (Chomsky and Halle 1968).

Finally, in addition to there being rules that govern the selection of a particular affix (as, for instance, in subject–verb agreement in English), there are also rules of word formation that determine the way affixes can be combined with word stems and with each other to yield well-formed lexical items. These rules are based upon both the syntactic and the phonological aspects of affixation.

Derivational affixes are attached to English words before inflectional affixes. Thus, we have words such as *horrifies*, in which a noun, *horror*, has been turned into a verb *horrify*, through a derivational process, and then the inflectional marker *s* has been added to form the third person singular present tense form of the verb. On the other hand, we have no forms such as *considersation* (asterisk indicates an unacceptable form) in which the verb *consider* has undergone an agreement process to yield the third person singular present tense form, *considers*, which is then subject to further word-formation processes turning that form into a noun. As elsewhere with respect to linguistic form, we should note that this constraint is not due to the fact that a form such as *considersation* would be impossible to understand. We can easily imagine that this item would mean something that an individual person is considering, thereby incorporating both a nominal sense and the fact that we are dealing with a process going on in the present tense, being accomplished by a single individual. The word-formation rules of English, however, do not allow us to produce this word.

A second aspect of the rules of word formation which involve affixation is that formative boundary affixes precede word boundary affixes. Thus we have words such as *receptiveness*, in which the formative boundary affix *-ive* has been added to the root *receive*, and then the word boundary affix *-ness* is added, but we have no words such as *homelessity*, in which the word boundary affix *-less* has been added to the root *home* to form the adjective *homeless* and that adjective then turned into a noun through further addition of a formative boundary affix. We may contrast the illegal form *homelessity* with the legal form *homelessness*, in which a second word boundary affix is added. Formative boundary affixes may be added one after another (*capture, captive, captivate, captivation*), word boundary affixes may follow one another (*home, homeless, homelessness*), and word boundary affixes may follow formative boundary affixes (*receive, receptive, receptiveness*), but formative boundary affixes may not follow word boundary affixes. Thus we have a very strict set of rules governing word formation in English, which determines that formative boundary derivational affixes are added to roots first, followed by word boundary derivational affixes, followed by word boundary inflectional affixes. Details of this system, along with many other interactions between morphological aspects of word formation and phonological consequences of different types of morphology, can be found in many recent linguistic studies, mentioned at the end of this chapter.

We have outlined some of the general constraints upon how words are formed using affixes, and we have commented on the way function word categories and syntactic features of content words are involved in the determination of the syntactic structure of sentences. We will not attempt to discuss sentential syntactic structure in detail in this chapter. A slightly more detailed account of syntactic structures is presented in Chapter 16. We shall close this discussion of the linguistic structures relevant to the aphasic phenomena to be discussed below by describing one very elementary feature of syntactic structure. This aspect of syntactic structure is known as "word order".

We indicated above that the linear sequence of content words in a sentence can sometimes give an adequate clue as to the abstract syntactic structure of a sentence. In discussing the sentences in (7):

(7a)   The boy that the dog bit is feeling well
(7b)   The boy the dog bit is feeling well

we noted that the sequence of words at the beginning of sentence (7b) is compatible with only one syntactic structure – the relative clause which is more fully expressed in sentence (7a). This fact indicates that we can construct a considerable amount of the syntactic structure of a sentence solely by considering the linear sequence of nouns, verbs, and adjectives in a sentence. However, the actual syntactic structure of a sentence consists of more than just the strictly linear sequence of nouns, verbs, adjectives, and other words in the sentence. It includes hierarchical relationships between the categories to which these words belong, and a variety of relationships between words which are defined over these hierarchically organized structures (see Chapter 16). The strictly linear sequence of content words is one of a number of clues to this hierarchical syntactic structure.

When linguists speak of an "underlying", "canonical", or "basic" word order for a particular language, they have in mind the most common sequence of grammatical functions found in simple sentences of that language. Thus, for instance, English is said to be a "subject–verb–object" (SVO) language, because subjects precede verbs and verbs precede objects, while Japanese is said to be a "subject–object–verb" (SOV) language, because subjects precede objects and objects precede verbs in simple Japanese sentences. In German, the basic form of main clauses is SVO, while the basic form of subordinate clauses is SOV. Since the grammatical functions of subject and object are instantiated as nouns, SVO languages mostly contain sequences of the form noun–verb–noun (N–V–N), and SOV languages sequences of the form N–N–V. Psychologists and aphasiologists sometimes use the term "word order" to refer to sequences of major categories (noun, verb, adjective).

The underlying, canonical order of the subject, verb, and object in simple sentences is altered in sentences such as those in (8):

(8a)   Salami, Seymour doesn't like
(8b)   Did you bake that cake yourself?

In (8a) the object, *salami*, has been "topicalized" and placed in sentence-initial position, while in (8b) there is an inversion of the subject and the auxiliary verb to mark the interrogative form. Constructions such as the passive (in sentence (9)) and sentences in which there has been object relativization (such as (10)) also show deviations from the canonical, underlying SVO word order of English:

(9)   The cake was eaten by the boy
(10)   It was the cake that the boy ate

Many theories of syntactic structure relate these overt forms to an underlying sequence of categories in the canonical SVO form, and derive the surface order from the underlying order from a series of syntactic rules.

In very simple sentences, such as simple active forms, the order of words is quite directly indicative of the syntactic structure of the sentence. In these cases, it is not unreasonable to speak of the order of words or syntactic categories in a sentence as conveying the thematic roles of words in the sentence – although we should keep in mind that this is a potentially misleading shorthand for indicating that the subject, object, and indirect object are mapped onto thematic roles in a very straightforward way in these sentences. For instance, in a simple sentence like (11), we may informally say that the word order "noun–verb–noun" expresses the fact that *boy* is agent and *girl* is theme.

(11)   The boy pushed the girl

If sequences of nouns and verbs directly express thematic roles, what role is there for the function words or function word categories in creating syntactic structure in these canonically ordered sentences? Function words and function word categories (and inflectional agreement markers as well) may only be important in establishing the nature of deviations from canonical form, as in sentences (8)–(10). Though thematic roles are related to the grammatical functions of subject and object in sentence (11) just as in sentences (8)–(10), and function word categories such as COMP and INFL are present at an abstract level of syntactic structure, speakers of English may produce or understand simple sentences such as (11) by mapping thematic roles directly into much simpler structures, such as N–V–N sequences. In other words, though linguistically incorrect, the description of the structure of sentences like (11) as consisting solely of the sequence N–V–N may be appropriate for the processing of the sentence. Indeed, it is even possible that the syntactic structures relevant to the production and comprehension of sentences with non-canonical word orders, such as (8)–(10), may also involve little more than sequences of major class categories (N, V, A, and possibly prepositions). Though more complex sentences, such as those to be discussed in Chapter 16, do require that syntactic categories be hierarchically organized, many sentences could be processed on the basis of quite superficial syntactic analyses.

These considerations lead from the study of syntactic structures themselves to the question of how sentential syntactic structures are processed. In this chapter, we shall confine our discussion to sentence production, and consider sentence comprehension in Chapter 16. In this chapter, we shall review work that deals with the different roles that function words, content words, and affixes play in sentence production. This research establishes that the creation of the syntactic structure of a sentence is separate from the selection and structuring of the semantic values conveyed by the sentence.

As we have seen in Chapter 13, one way to study the process of planning and producing the forms of sentences is to study spontaneously occurring errors in people's speech. The logic relating observations on speech errors to a model of speech planning has been developed by Garrett (1976) as follows. If two elements of a sentence are both involved in an error, then these two elements must be simultaneously available at the stage of processing at which the error occurs. Similarly, if two types of elements are never involved in an error together, then these two types of elements must be processed at different points in sentence planning and production. The application of these principles to the study of speech errors has been undertaken by a number of researchers. We shall review the results of a large-scale study by Garrett (1976; 1982; 1984), which has been particularly revealing with respect to the stages of planning sentence form.

Garrett, studying a corpus of several thousand naturally occurring speech errors, observed that a number of different types of error had particular characteristics. Four error types which he considered to be especially revealing as to the nature of sentence production are the following:

(1)   Semantic substitutions, such as *boy* for *girl*, or *black* for *white*. These errors only occur with the content word vocabulary and certain prepositions.

(2)   Word exchanges, such as *he is planting the garden in the flowers* for *he is planting the flowers in the garden*. These exchanges affect words of similar categories (nouns exchange with nouns, adjectives with adjectives, verbs

273

with verbs), and also only affect the content word vocabulary. In addition, as would be expected by these constraints, word exchanges do not affect words within a single phrase. For instance, exchanges of the form *this is a room lovely* for *this is a lovely room* do not occur.

(3)   Sound exchanges, such as *shinking sips* for *sinking ships*. Sound exchanges also affect the content word vocabulary. Sound exchanges usually affect adjacent words. They therefore mainly occur within a single phrase, and frequently affect words in different categories within the content word vocabulary, as in the example illustrated.

(4)   "Stranding" errors, as in *he is schooling to go*, for *he is going to school*, in which the suffix *-ing* has been "stranded" in its original position, and the verb stem to which it was originally attached has been moved elsewhere in the sentence. The elements which are "stranded" – that is, which are left in their syntactic positions – are affixes; it is the content words which are moved.

Garrett has built up a model of the sentence-production process based on the observation that these are frequent errors in speech production. As noted, he makes the assumption that, for an error to occur, the vocabulary elements which are involved in the error must be processed simultaneously during a certain stage of the sentence-production process. Using this principle to analyze these data, Garrett first draws a major distinction between the sentence-planning processes which determine which content words there are in a sentence and the sentence-planning processes which determine the choice and location of the function words and inflectional morphemes in a sentence. These distinctions are based on the observation that these two types of vocabulary class are subject to different errors.

The stages of sentence planning identified in Garrett's model are illustrated in Figure 15-1. The first level is termed the "message" level. This is not a linguistic level, strictly speaking, but rather consists of the elaboration of the basic concepts which a speaker wishes to talk about. The first truly linguistic level is the "functional level". At the functional level, lexical items are found for concepts. At this stage, the speaker has accessed the *lexical semantic* representation of a word, but not its *phonological* representation. In addition, the functional level contains information about aspects of meaning which are related to *sentences*, not just words. For instance, information about *thematic roles* – what is the agent of an action, what is the recipient of an action, etc. – is specified at the functional level. Garrett refers to this as information about the "argument structure" of verbs; that is, the number and type of functional arguments – thematic roles – that are associated with each verb in the sentence. As with lexical semantic information, this sentential semantic information is not related to the *form* of the sentence at this stage of processing. These "functional argument struc-

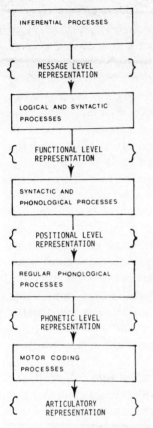

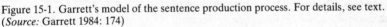

Figure 15-1. Garrett's model of the sentence production process. For details, see text.
(*Source:* Garrett 1984: 174)

tures" do not, for instance, require that a sentence take a particular syntactic form, such as the active or the passive.

It is at the "positional level" that information about the form of words and sentences is specified. At the positional level, the syntactic form of a sentence is produced, and the phonological forms of words are inserted into their appropriate positions in the syntactic structure of the sentence. An important feature of Garrett's model is that syntactic structures contain function words and inflectional morphemes at the point when the positional level of representation is created. Because the phonological forms of function words are not inserted into the positional-level representations, as is true of the phonological forms of content words, function words are not subject to certain types of error, and are subject to others (see below).

Following the creation of the positional level, the phonological form of words is specified in greater detail to yield a phonetic level of representation, which is ultimately transformed into a series of commands to the vocal apparatus.

The types of error that Garrett has documented in normal speech can be attributed to disturbances arising at these different levels as follows. Word exchanges and word substitutions arise at the functional level. Since the representations at the functional level only specify content words, these errors only apply to content words. Sound exchange errors arise during the insertion of content words into syntactic structures at the positional level. The fact that sound exchanges occur primarily between adjacent words suggests that the process of inserting the phonological form of content words into syntactic structures takes place on a phrase-by-phrase basis. Function words are not subject to sound exchanges because they are already present in the structures at the positional level. The stranding errors, in which function words and bound morphemes are stranded while the content words and stems are moved, also arise during the creation of the positional level, when content words are mis-ordered. The fact that bound morphemes remain in place while stems move is one piece of evidence suggesting that the syntactic structures accessed during the creation of the positional level of representation already contain bound morphemes and function words in their final position.

This entire model is obviously very under-specified with respect to the linguistic representations involved in the stages of sentence planning. For instance, the exact specification of the phonological form of words is not indicated (see Chapter 13). Differences between different types of morpho-logical endings are not taken into account. The whole problem of how syntactic structures are created, and of their exact form, is not specified: for instance, it is not determined whether speakers only construct major category sequences for sentences with canonical word order. Garrett is well aware of these limitations, and has frequently indicated that it is not possible to go beyond this level of specification of a model of sentence production on the basis of the errors that he has collected, though the nature of the language code clearly indicates that many more details of planning are necessary (Garrett 1984). Despite these limitations, this model has the advantage of being based upon empirical observations relevant to the speech production system – naturally occurring speech errors – and it is well enough specified to serve as a reference model for the study of the breakdown of the sentence-production process as seen in aphasia.

We shall illustrate how the identification of different types of vocabulary elements, the appreciation of the role of "word order" in sentence structure,

276

and this model of the stages of planning the form of sentences have provided conceptual tools with which to approach disturbances of sentence production by considering the symptom of expressive agrammatism. Agrammatism is a symptom that we have discussed briefly before (Chapters 8, 9, and 11), in relation to the syndrome of Broca's aphasia. The most noticeable deficit in agrammatism is the widespread omission of function words and affixes and the greater retention of content words in spontaneous speech, and often in repetition and writing. Contemporary work deals with the exact delineation of the class of items which are affected in this condition, the abnormalities of processing which give rise to these disturbances, and the ancillary symptoms which are associated with these abnormalities.

The class of words which are affected in agrammatism has been described in two quite different frameworks. The first is a psychological framework, and the second is linguistic. According to the psychological account, the words which are affected in agrammatism are those which belong to the closed class of vocabulary elements. As we have seen, this set consists of all the vocabulary elements of languages such as English and French other than nouns, verbs, adjectives, and derived adverbs. One distinguishing feature of these vocabulary elements is that their number is fixed in the language at any given point in time, while the number of nouns, verbs, and adjectives in a person's vocabulary may increase. It is the fact that certain vocabulary elements belong to this "closed class" which sets them apart and which is related to their impairment in this syndrome, according to this psychological account.

The linguistic approach to the characterization of agrammatism has been explored by several researchers. Kean (1977) first enunciated a theory of the vocabulary elements affected in agrammatism in relationship to linguistic theory. Kean proposed that the class of elements affected in this syndrome was defined in terms of aspects of their sound pattern. As we have seen, the rules for assignment of stress to words, phrases, and sentences in English assign stress to phonological words – stems and roots of nouns, adjectives, and verbs – and ignore function words and word boundary affixes. Kean suggests that agrammatics have difficulty with items which are not phonological words. One of the principal pieces of evidence which Kean takes as support for her analysis is that agrammatism affects both free-standing function words and inflectional affixes. She emphasizes the point that these different elements accomplish quite different functions syntactically and semantically, but have in common the feature that they are all "phonological clitics", elements that do not affect stress placement in English. Other linguistic descriptions, mainly proposed in reaction to Kean's theory, have also been suggested. Lapointe (1983), for instance, argues that the class of elements affected in agrammatism can be described morphologically as well as phonologically, and that the particular theory of phonological structure upon which Kean's formulation was based has been superseded by other theories and is not, therefore, an appropriate framework for characterizing agrammatism.

These different accounts of the elements affected in agrammatism are difficult to compare because the vocabulary elements identified in each of these theories largely overlap. However, there are some differences in the vocabulary elements specified by each of the theories of agrammatism we have considered, and it is possible to devise experimental tests that can choose between these theories. For instance, the psychological theory would not distinguish between formative boundary and word boundary affixes, since both are members of the "closed class" of vocabulary elements in English. However, both Kean's and Lapointe's theories would predict that formative boundary affixes should be retained in agrammatism, while word boundary affixes should be omitted. Though the rarity of either of these forms in derivationally formed words makes this hard to test by examining normal discourse, specially designed experiments, such as word or sentence repetition tests, might be useful in exploring these predictions.

Linguistic theory and psycholinguistic concerns have thus begun to be used as the basis for symptom description in agrammatism. On a less theoretical plane, linguistic analyses have also led to a greater appreciation of the detailed "profiles" of agrammatism, and this work shows that agrammatism varies from patient to patient. Many studies of this syndrome (Goodglass 1973; Luria 1973; Tissot *et al.* 1973; Miceli *et al.* 1983) have shown that patients with agrammatism can have different patterns of loss of inflectional morphology, derivational morphology, and the function word vocabulary. Moreover, these patients vary considerably in their ability to produce certain open-class vocabulary items, notably verbs (Miceli *et al.* 1984). In addition, recent observations have rediscovered the fact that agrammatism is not easily distinguishable from so-called "paragrammatism", in which substitutions of morphological elements and free-standing function word vocabulary items predominate in expressive speech (Grodzinsky 1984). Obler *et al.* (1984) report the results of a large cross-linguistic study of agrammatic patients, and note that all the patients studied showed both omission and substitution of vocabulary elements. Heeschen (1985) argues for the co-occurrence of omission and substitution of free-standing function words and morphological elements in so-called "agrammatism", and de Bleser (in press) points out that this co-occurrence had also been noted by earlier writers, whose observations had been largely ignored. These linguistic descriptions – some new, some old – indicate that the symptom of agrammatism itself includes a variety of profiles of omission of vocabulary elements, and is not easily separated from other speech production abnormalities affecting the same vocabulary elements.

Badecker and Caramazza (1985) illustrate this variation with several speech samples, all labeled agrammatic, which show many different features: omission of main verbs, incorrect nominalization of main verbs, and semantic ill-formedness, as well as different patterns of omission of inflections and function words. Several examples are shown in Table 15-1.

Table 15-1. *Examples of agrammatic speech cited in Badecker and Caramazza 1985*

(A) Short excerpts from discourse showing function word and inflectional omissions:
  (1) ah . . . Monday . . . ah, Dad and P.H. (the patient's name) and Dad . . . hospital. Two . . . ah, doctors . . ., and ah . . . thirty minutes . . . and yes . . . ah . . . hospital. And, er Wednesday . . . nine o'clock. And er Thursday, ten o'clock . . . doctors. Two doctors . . . and ah . . . teeth. Yeah, . . . fine
  (2) My uh mother died . . . uh . . . me . . . uh fi'teen. Uh, oh, I guess six month . . . my mother pass away. An' uh . . . an'en . . . uh . . . ah . . . seventeen . . . seventeen . . . go uh High School. An'uh Christmas . . . well, uh, I uh . . . Pitt'burgh

(B) Omission of main verbs:
(Patient attempts to describe the picture of a girl presenting flowers to a teacher)
  (1) The young . . . the girl . . . the little girl is . . . the flower
  (2) The girl is . . . going to flowers

(C) Nominalizations used instead of verbs:
(Same situation as in B)
  (1) The girl is flower the woman
  (2) The girl is . . . is roses. The girl is rosin'
(Picture of a man taking a photograph of a girl)
  (3) The man kodaks . . . and the girl . . . kodaks the girl

(D) Semantic ill-formedness:
(Picture of a man painting a house)
  (1) The painter washed the paint . . .
(Picture of a cat peeping out from behind an armchair)
  (2) The cat leans the sofa up . . .
(Picture of a boy giving a valentine to a girl)
  (3) The boy put the valentine into this girl

They also cite other patterns. One Italian agrammatic patient showed preservation of verbs but produced incorrect verbal inflections, while another English patient correctly inflected verbs. An English patient produced speech almost entirely restricted to nominal phrases, but produced plural nominal inflections correctly, while another patient who produced some subject–predicate sequences failed to produce properly inflected plural noun phrases.

Badecker and Caramazza (1985) indicate that this variation poses two problems. First, it can be taken to represent dissociations in symptoms, indicating that separate processing impairments underlie each of these patterns, following the logic we discussed in Chapter 2. If so, agrammatism is not a single category. Second, these patterns suggest that it is not appropriate to distinguish agrammatic patients from those with paragrammatism. The authors thus call for the abolition of the category of agrammatism.

Badecker and Caramazza may be correct that the intra-category variation seen in patients with agrammatic speech is evidence that several separate syndromes are present in what is presently termed agrammatism. If so, the "profiles" of agrammatism must each be related to separate deficits in linguistic elements and stages of language processing: difficulties with subject–verb agreement can be distinguished from those with adjective–noun agreement; different abnormalities affecting different types of affixes can be separated from each other; etc. Linguistic and psycholinguistic theories provide a large number of possibilities for specific impairments, since each type of linguistic element and each individual processing mechanism can, in principle, be separately disturbed.

On the other hand, linguistic and psycholinguistic investigations suggest that some of this observed variation may not result from impairments to separate processing components. The explanation for some variation runs as follows. There are groups of vocabulary elements which are defined by sets of features, as we have seen. For instance, though subject–verb and adjective–noun agreements differ, they are both agreement phenomena, determining the location of members of a specified class of vocabulary elements – inflectional morphemes. As we saw above, inflectional morphology in English and French is affixed to derivational morphology, and is always outside the scope of word-level phonological processes. These features define a class of vocabulary elements. Agrammatism could result from a disturbance affecting lexical items which have these features. A "higher-order" disturbance of this sort would presumably produce effects in the entire class of inflectional affixes, but these effects might not be equally apparent in all members of that class in a given task. The expression of the impairment would be affected by other symptoms a patient has, and by other linguistic features of the affected elements.

Let us consider a well-studied example of these effects. Goodglass and Berko (1960), studied the ability of twenty-one agrammatic aphasic patients to produce the suffix -*s*. In English, the suffix -*s* can mark the plural, the third person singular present tense inflection of verbs, and the possessive. These are so-called "morphological" facts about this ending. In addition, the phonological form of the suffix *-s* varies systematically regardless of the morphological use to which it is put. When *-s* follows an unvoiced stop consonant, it is unvoiced (*he hits*; *two cups*; *Jack's tie*); when it follows a voiced consonant or a vowel, it is voiced (*he runs*; *two ties*; *John's cup*); and when it follows voiced affricates, such as *ch*, it is produced in a syllabic form, with the sound of a reduced vowel as part of the suffix (*he watches*; *two churches*; *Mitch's glasses*). Goodglass and Berko found that the possessive and third person singular forms of *-s* were more frequently omitted than the plural, and that the third person singular inflectional ending was omitted about as frequently as the possessive. They replicated this finding in another group of twenty-eight aphasic patients, whom they grouped into fluent and non-fluent sub-groups on the basis of an "objective" measure of speech, phrase length, previously investigated by Goodglass *et al.* (1964). Both sub-groups of patients had more difficulty with the possessive and third person singular inflection than the plural. This result confirmed the earlier results, and also indicated that the pattern of difficulty with these affixes did not differ in different types of aphasia. Goodglass (1973) suggested that there is a universal hierarchy of difficulty of grammatical inflections, which determines the order in which aphasic patients experience difficulty with these forms. In this connection, Kean (1977) has pointed out that stranding errors affect inflectional affixes (the possessive and third person singular forms) more often than derivational affixes (the plural form) in normal speech errors, which also indicates that there are important processing differences between these two types of affix. These factors make certain items more "omission-prone". In the present case, all these forms of the suffix *-s* are word boundary affixes, and all are subject to omission in agrammatism. The fact that they are not all omitted equally frequently is due to other aspects of their processing.

Goodglass and Berko's study also shows that the agrammatic patients had less trouble producing the syllabic form of the suffix (e.g. *churches*) than in producing the non-syllabic forms (e.g. *bats*, *cubs*) regardless of the morphological role the suffix played. Kean (1977) points out that this aspect of the differential susceptibility of these word boundary affixes to omission can also be explained linguistically in terms of the sonorance hierarchy we discussed in Chapter 13. The syllabic form of *-s*, /əz/, is more sonorant than either of its non-syllabic forms, /s/ and /z/. We have seen how important the sonorance hierarchy is in determining syllable structure; Kean suggests that it also affects agrammatic patients' tendency to omit a word boundary affix.

Though it is straying from our main theme of how variation in agrammatics' production of a linguistically defined class of vocabulary elements can be explained, we should take the opportunity created by reviewing Goodglass and Berko's findings to mention what these authors say about their own work. These interpretations bear on the nature of agrammatism, and also reflect the differences between the "slightly older" and "slightly newer" psycholinguistic approaches to aphasia we mentioned in Chapter 11.

Goodglass (1973) suggests that it is possible to integrate data from a number of experiments to define a class of words which are less "salient" and therefore more difficult for an agrammatic patient. Salience is the "psychological resultant of stress, of the informational significance, of the phonological prominence, and of the affective value of a word" (Goodglass 1973: 204). Function words have low information and affective value, and are consequently more vulnerable to omission than other vocabulary elements. Phonologically prominent suffixes, such as /əz/ as compared with /s/, are better produced. In other work, Goodglass showed that function words following phonologically stressed words were better produced by agrammatic patients. Stress itself, even when it applies to a syntactically complex item like a negative auxiliary, makes it significantly easier for an agrammatic to produce a word. These elements combine into a single factor – salience – which determines performance. The factor of salience does not apply to all agrammatic patients, some of whom seem to have a problem at a more conceptual level of language involving relationships between words, statements, and concepts; but Goodglass postulates that it is the factor which influences the performance of those agrammatic patients who do not have this "conceptual" form of the syndrome.

In introducing the concept of salience, Goodglass is making a strong claim about the nature of the psychological factors which determine aphasic, and presumably normal, language performance. He is claiming that, in addition to properties of words such as their "informational" and "affective" value, or their carrying main or emphatic stress, there is a property of words in sentences, salience, which combines all these separately identifiable factors into one more general feature. In some ways, this higher-order feature is reminiscent of the very general, "global", psychological factors we encountered in Chapter 8; but it is different from Marie's notion of intelligence or Goldstein's concept of the "abstract attitude" in important ways. One way in which it differs is that it simply does not deal with the wide range of abilities or mental states of a patient that these other concepts do. Salience is a descriptive term applied by Goodglass to linguistic material. Though it is a concept which could be applicable to other domains of function, Goodglass quite carefully defines it in terms of properties of words and restricts its use to language. Second, Goodglass's concept of salience, though it seems to be a factor which could be applied to the description of linguistic materials in a fashion which might be relevant to any aphasia, is in fact a function which Goodglass claims has special significance for agrammatic performance. Thus, it is not a global factor like those described in Chapter 8.

As a term which is supposed to be relevant to linguistic structure or psycholinguistic processing, "salience" is similar to the other construction Goodglass uses to describe agrammatism – phrase length (see Chapter 11). Like phrase length, "salience" is not a purely linguistic term. Some of the elements contributing to Goodglass's notion of salience, such as whether an item is the first word in a sentence, are not features of linguistic structure *per se*. Like phrase length, they are defined over linguistic structures, but are not formally specified in theories of the sound–meaning pairing. The combination of features Goodglass identifies as making up "salience" cannot, therefore, be a linguistic concept. Nor is it easy to specify the exact role the concept of salience might play in a psycholinguistic processing model. The "slightly older" psycholinguistic approach to aphasia does not see this as a reason not to use this concept; the "slightly newer" approach, though respectful of the notion – based as it is on a serious analysis of carefully collected details of patients' performance – does.

What is at issue here is whether it is possible to describe aphasic symptoms and syndromes in terms derived from linguistic and psycholinguistic processing models. Goodglass, Geschwind, and others have argued that aphasiology and neurolinguistics must not be slavishly derivative from linguistics and psycholinguistics, and that analyses of aphasic performances may suggest new ways of viewing the organization of language. Perhaps a concept like salience is one example of an analysis of various aspects of language structure which cuts across both linguistic and non-linguistic structures and processing in a revealing way. On the other hand, we must be cautious in accepting this conclusion. Linguistic structures, and the principles behind them, as well as certain aspects of their processing, are very well worked out at present, and there is good justification for many structural features of natural language and aspects of their processing. At the very least, it is reasonable to try as far as possible to characterize aphasic symptoms in terms derived from these theories, while recognizing that brain damage may confer important roles upon combinations of linguistic and non-linguistic factors in ways that need to be explored as well. These combined factors may also be important in normal language processing in some circumstances. The development of our understanding of the role of strictly linguistic and processing factors, and that of "combined" factors like salience, in the genesis of an aphasic symptom like agrammatism is part of the effort to separate the effects of disturbances of "core" psycholinguistic processing from disturbances of related, more integrative, functions which interact with core psycholinguistic processes. In this sense, it is a continuation of the work begun by researchers like Luria (Chapter 9), who sought to incorporate both the "core" processes explored by connectionist neurolinguists and the more general factors identified by many holist theorists into an explicit, integrated model of language functioning. Present studies are more detailed, and the separation of "core" and "general" factors more difficult, especially since the "general" factors, like salience, are only related to language functions. It is possible that here, as elsewhere, different approaches might be more compatible than they at first seem to be.

Returning to our main theme – variation in the expression of agrammatism – we have seen that some patterns of relative impairment of affixes within the class of affixes affected in agrammatism can be explained on psycholinguistic and linguistic grounds. Let us turn to the specific problems Badecker and Caramazza (1985) cite as reasons to abandon the category "agrammatism". Recall that they argue that there is too much intra-category variation in patients with agrammatism for agrammatism to be a single deficit. However, as we have just discussed, one would *expect* some variation due to the interaction of agrammatism and aspects of language structure and processing. The particular variation cited by Badecker and Caramazza can largely be accounted for on linguistic grounds.

One of the major variable features they cite is a number of disturbances of main verbs. However, we may exclude any problems with main verbs from agrammatism, for the following reasons. As we have seen, there are several possible characterizations of the affected elements within one or another version of linguistic theory and psycholinguistic processing models. These formulations all identify sets of affected language elements, and also *exclude* certain language elements from these sets. These theories thus identify the *agrammatic* features in utterances with complex sources of aphasic pathology. Verbs are excluded from these sets of vocabulary elements. Therefore, abnormalities affecting verb roots, such as their absence or replacement by nominal stems, are not part of the agrammatic features of speech, but have some other source. It is, of course, possible that other formal characterizations would group the elements designated in these theories together with verbs, but to date no such characterization has been stated. Tests directly investigating the mechanisms responsible for verb omission have also suggested that this symptom is a form of anomia for verbs, and has nothing to do with the other symptoms in agrammatism

(Miceli *et al.* 1984). Variation in this aspect of the speech of agrammatic patients, though interesting, does not affect our ability to define agrammatism.

Other aspects of the variation noted by Badecker and Caramazza can also be accounted for. The presence of inflection on Italian main verbs has been related to the fact that Italian verb roots are not lexical items, and require inflections to become real words. Kean (1977) has proposed that agrammatics are con-strained to produce real words. The severity of the patient's deficits also determines some of this variation. The patient who produces largely correct verbal inflections in English is obviously only mildly agrammatic, compared with the patient who omits plural agreements. This latter could not omit verbal agreements because no verbs were produced. It would obviously be an exaggeration to claim that the range of patterns which are seen in agrammatism is known or understood; but the situation is not as bad as Badecker and Caramazza make out. Several principled distinctions – the separation of main verbs from the items affected in agrammatism, the sonorance hierarchy, the status of an affix with respect to derivational or inflectional morphology, the lexical status of a root or stem, and others – go quite a long way towards accounting for part of the variation found in agrammatism.

The variation we have been discussing is of three types: (1) inter-language variation due to different structural features of different languages; (2) variation due to different degrees of complexity of different affixes or function words within a language; (3) variation according to how severe a case of agrammatism a patient represents. Clearly, not all the different profiles of agrammatism can be accounted for by these three factors. Patients of about equal overall severity, speaking the same language, differ considerably with respect to the particular function words and affixes which they tend to omit. Some of these profiles of impairment appear to reflect relatively isolated disturbances with particular types of function words or morphological forms. As we noted above, even if some restricted patterns of agrammatism result from an impairment in a "higher-order" processing component which shows up in a sub-set of the items within the domain of that process, Badecker and Caramazza may be right that other patterns of agrammatic speech may reflect restricted disturbances of particular affixes, function words, or their related processing components.

However, even these apparently restricted patterns of agrammatic output may reflect a more widespread disturbance in the function word/inflectional vocabularies than is immediately apparent. Nespoulous and his colleagues (Nespoulous *et al.* 1985*a*) studied a patient with one of these restricted forms of agrammatism. The patient, MM, had particular trouble with certain pronouns in French (the "weak" forms of pronouns – *le, la, lui* – but not the "strong" forms – *il, elle, moi, toi*), and with auxiliary verbs, but less trouble producing other function words. This problem only occurred when these words were presented in sentences, or when the patient had to produce sentences. Thus, MM had no trouble reading or repeating these words in isolation nor in recognizing them as words in a lexical decision task; but he tended to omit them often in speech, repetition, and reading, when dealing with sentences.

The proof that MM's problem is related to processing these words in sentences is that he sometimes realized that a sequence of words was a sentence, and only then began to have trouble with these words. For instance, he was asked to read words written vertically, one to a page. He did so perfectly, turning the pages over and reading each word, until he quite suddenly realized that the sequence of words formed a sentence. From that point on, he had difficulty with the items in these affected groups of words. Realizing that MM had trouble with these words in sentences, Nespoulous hit upon the idea of presenting a written sentence to MM and highlighting these difficult words with a rose-colored magic marker. MM then read these highlighted words and the content words in the sentences correctly, but began to omit *other* function words. When both the original and the second set of affected function words were highlighted in subsequent trials, MM began to omit yet other function words. MM never omitted content words (nouns, verbs, or adjectives) in any of these experiments. His impairment seems, therefore, to be limited to function words, but the extent of the impairment was not limited to the particular sub-set of function words he omitted in spontaneous speech. More detailed testing showed that other function words were affected, under particular task conditions.

There are many intriguing aspects of MM's case which raise questions for which there are no answers at present. The kind of processing impairment that would give rise to this pattern of performance is far from clear. In terms of the question of whether some patients have a restricted form of agrammatism related to a sub-set of the function word/inflectional vocabulary, MM's case certainly shows that a deficit may be more extensive than it first appears to be. We must still ask why the most affected items are the particular ones MM had trouble with. Perhaps there are two impairments at work in this case – one related to function words as a whole, and one making for particular difficulty with a sub-set of function words. The point, for now, is simply that this case shows that a "higher-order" impairment affecting function words and inflectional affixes might be manifest in subtle ways.

The other question raised by detailed studies of agrammatic patients' speech is how far agrammatism is unique. Agrammatism is classically contrasted with another syndrome that also affects function words and affixes – paragrammatism. Paragrammatism is usually associated with fluent speech, and is one of the many manifestations of Wernicke's aphasia in the classical taxonomy. In paragrammatism, patients tend to select incorrect function words and affixes, not omit them. However, as noted above, several researchers have recently suggested that paragrammatism and agrammatism may be closely related, or even be one and the same syndrome.

A paper which made this point dramatically was Grodzinsky's (1984) report of several Hebrew-speaking agrammatics. As we noted briefly in Chapter 14, the vowels in Hebrew words are determined by inflectional and derivational morphological considerations. For example, the word for a single male child is *yeled*, for a single female child *yalda*, and in the plural the corresponding forms are *yiladim* and *yiladot*. The three consonants *y–l–d* form a root, into which the markers for gender and number are interpolated. These markers consist of vowels (and a terminal consonant), and the particular vowel patterns are used in many words in the language: the various forms of the word for "dog", whose triconsonantal root is /k–l–v/, are *kelev*, *kalva*, *kilavim*, and *kilavot*. As Grodzinsky (1984) pointed out, a patient who omitted the inflectional and derivational morphemes carried in this "vowel tier" would not be able to say anything, because the triconsonantal roots are unpronounceable. In fact, what Grodzinsky found his patients did was to omit free-standing function words, but substitute vowels from within the appropriate set of morphological items. Thus, they appeared to be agrammatic in certain respects and paragrammatic in other respects.

Grodzinsky suggested that omission of elements simply reflects a preference for phonologically null elements of these morphological sets, whenever null elements exist, constrained by the requirement that lexical items be produced. Thus, the basic psychopathological disturbance in agrammatism is substitution or mis-selection, and the syndrome is the same as paragrammatism in terms of the basic abnormality. This formulation, however, also provides the basis for *distinguishing* agrammatism from paragrammatism, since the preference for the phonologically null element of a set is not present in paragrammatism. The difference between the two is not with respect to the deficit itself, but affects a constraint on what is produced. Both agrammatism and paragrammatism affect the same set of items: their formal linguistic locus in a theory of language structure is identical. The basic psychopathological disturbance is the same: mis-selection of items in a morphologically determined paradigm. The disturbance is subject to constraints: word status must be respected in the output; the selection involves a hierarchy of the legitimate items in a paradigm. The difference is that one phonological constraint on the output is present in agrammatism and absent in paragrammatism: the preference for phonologically null items of the paradigm.

Assuming that this formulation is correct, we may ask whether we should consider agrammatism and paragrammatism to be separate syndromes, or as various forms of a single, large syndrome. The answer would seem to depend on how we answer two questions: can we account for the extra constraint in agrammatism in some way, and, are we interested in a classification relevant to aphasia or to normal processes? For instance, this phonological constraint may only occur in patients with motor speech disturbances, and may be related to these disturbances. If, however, the presence of this constraint is not derivable from other features of language structure or processing, or from other aspects of the aphasia of patients, it is a qualitatively different constraint on a psychopathogenetic process. It constitutes a new mechanism, and hence generates a new syndrome from the point of view of aphasiology. Whether this would have a special effect on other aspects of language processing is another matter. If we are interested in aphasic syndromes for their utility in exploring the nature of the normal system, we may be able to overlook this difference for certain purposes.

This leads us directly to our next concern. A question which has been raised since the early twentieth century (Pick 1913) is whether the omission of function words is related to other abnormalities in sentence structure. Classical and modern investigations show that it is. Goodglass *et al.* (1972) documented the syntactic constructions produced by one agrammatic patient and found virtually no syntactically well-formed utterances. Based on these results, Caplan (1985) suggested that agrammatic patients do not construct phrasal nodes (NP, VP) in their utterances, but encode semantic values only through linear sequences of major category nodes (N, V, A). This characterization is now known to be too restrictive, but all agrammatic patients studied so far show some impoverishment of syntactic structure in spontaneous speech. For instance, all fail to produce embedded verbs with normal frequency (Nespoulous *et al.* 1985a; Obler *et al.* forthcoming).

These observations suggest that these patients have an impairment in the construction of normal syntactic structures. As discussed above, based upon patterns of occurrence of normal speech errors, Garrett (1982) has suggested that syntactic structure is constructed at the same stage of sentence planning at which function words and inflections are accessed. Though the details of this process remain to be clarified, this suggestion implies that a single impairment may underlie both the omission of vocabulary elements and the simplification of syntactic structure in agrammatism. This deficit would involve the construction of aspects of Garrett's "positional" level of sentence representation (Kean 1982; Caplan 1985).

Other researchers have suggested a more "profound" disturbance in this syndrome. Saffran *et al.* (1980*b*) presented data regarding the order of nouns around verbs in sentences produced by five agrammatic patients describing simple pictures of actions. The authors noted a strong effect of animacy upon the position of the nouns around the verbs. When an animate noun acted upon an inanimate noun (as in a picture of a boy hitting a ball), the resulting sentence almost always had the animate noun before the verb, while when an animate noun acted upon another animate noun (as in a picture of a boy pushing a girl), the animate noun agent preceded the verb in only about two thirds of sentences. A similar set of results occurred when the experiment was replicated using a sentence anagram rather than a verbal production task. The authors suggested that thematic roles are not even mapped onto "word order", and that animacy determines the position of nouns around verbs. They concluded that agrammatic patients have either lost the basic linguistic notions of thematic roles (agency, theme) or else cannot use even the basic "word order" of the language to express this sentential semantic feature. They argue that this more profound deficit cannot be related to problems with the function word/inflection vocabulary, and therefore that agrammatic patients have more than one impairment affecting sentence planning and production.

There were, however, some data in Saffran *et al.*'s study which did not entirely correspond to the notion that animacy alone determined word order. When two inanimate nouns appeared in a picture (as in a picture of a boat pulling a truck), the noun depicted as instrument (in this case, *the boat*) was produced before the verb virtually all the time. Furthermore, when an inanimate noun was acting upon an animate noun (as in a picture of a ball hitting a boy), the inanimate noun preceded the animate noun about half the time, with the animate noun preceding the inanimate noun the other half of the time. If animacy alone determines word order of nouns around verbs, one should find that the inanimate/inanimate pairs were treated like the animate/animate pairs (either noun appearing first), while the inanimate/animate pairs should have shown consistent reversals. The authors mention these problems, and conclude that a more general factor might account for these orderings. They invoke Goodglass's concept of "salience" or another notion, "potency", but do not define these terms, except to say that knowledge of the thematic role played by a noun does *not* enter into potency or salience. They specifically claim that such knowledge is not available to agrammatic patients, who, they say, lack the linguistic concept of thematic relations.

Caplan (1983) reanalyzed these data, and pointed out that there is a quite simple set of rules which does account for the pattern of results, but which assumes that the patients know that language encodes thematic relations. The rules are the following:

(1)   The patient is producing sentences in the active voice.
(2)   The patient tends to put animate nouns before the verb.
(3)   The patient tends to put nouns bearing the thematic role of agent or instrument before the verb.

Principle (2) assumes that the patient knows which words are animate, and principle (3) assumes that he can assign thematic roles to items in a picture, assign these thematic roles to words, and order words on the basis of their thematic roles.

Assuming these principles are additive in their effects, they account for the data in a straightforward way. In the animate–agent/inanimate–theme cases, principles (2) and (3) both dictate that the animate agent will go first. In the animate–agent/animate–theme cases, principles (2) and (3) will both lead to the animate agent going first, but principle (2) will also lead to the animate theme going first (because of its animacy). The animate agent goes first two thirds of the time; the animate theme goes first one third of the time. This two-to-one ratio exactly reflects the additive effects of each of these factors upon "word order". In the inanimate–instrument/animate–theme cases, principle (2) dictates that the animate theme goes first, and principle (3) dictates that the inanimate–instrument goes first, leading to the 50/50 split in responses. Finally, in the inanimate–instrument/inanimate–theme cases, only principle (3) applies, putting the inanimate instrument first. This is how the patients behave.

Thus, we must reject the claim Saffran *et al.* make that agrammatic patients do not appreciate thematic relations. If the analysis just presented is correct, agrammatic patients do appreciate that language encodes thematic roles, and can map these semantic functions onto individual words in particular positions in a sentence. It does not appear that the agrammatic has lost all of this system. What seems to be the case is that the agrammatic has added a set of principles dealing with intrinsic animacy of nouns to the set dealing with the thematic role of nouns in establishing the mapping between "word order" and thematic relations conveyed by a sentence. The data and this analysis establish that agrammatics can use "word order" in the sense of the order of major categories (N–V–N) to encode thematic roles. Coupled with the observation that agrammatics simplify syntactic structure, this fact indicates that the prediction that Garrett's "functional level" is intact and his "positional level" is affected in agrammatism is confirmed.

The linguistic and psycholinguistic approach to agrammatism also led to hypotheses regarding abnormalities patients might have in language functions other than speech production. Zurif *et al.* (1972) postulated that, if agrammatics' disturbances with the function word vocabulary were a result of a disturbance of a central aspect of processing related to these vocabulary items, agrammatic patients might have difficulties on tasks that require the use of the function word vocabulary, whether or not these tasks involved spontaneous speech. They discovered that agrammatic aphasics did, in fact, perform abnormally on a task of judging the degree of relatedness of words in sentences. Given sets of three words from a particular sentence and asked to say which two words were most closely related, normal subjects indicated that words that were syntactically grouped together in the sentence were most closely related. Agrammatics, in contrast, grouped together the major lexical items on a semantic basis, and totally omitted the function words from these relatedness judgements. This result suggested that agrammatics may have a "central" disturbance in the processing of the function word vocabulary. The most obvious manifestation of this disturbance was in sentence production, but it could be demonstrated in other tasks as well.

This hypothesis was directly tested by a series of experiments dealing with sentence comprehension in agrammatism. Caramazza and Zurif (1976) showed that agrammatic patients were unable to interpret certain sentences whose meaning required syntactic analysis. Somewhat similar results were obtained by Heilman and Scholes (1976) and Schwartz *et al.* (1980*b*). All of these results indicated that the disturbance in an agrammatic patient may not be limited to expression, but may also affect the ability to construct syntactic structure, no matter what tasks he is required to perform (Berndt and Caramazza 1980). To the extent that constructing syntactic structure relies on the use of the function word/inflectional vocabulary, all these problems may be related to one "central" disturbance. However, some agrammatic patients without syntactic comprehension disturbances have been described. The relationship between expressive agrammatism and disturbances of comprehension of syntactic form thus does not appear to be universal. We shall consider this question in more detail in Chapter 16.

Why do agrammatic patients have these difficulties in producing function words and certain affixes and, at times, in comprehending certain syntactic structures? One study of agrammatic aphasics' language-processing abilities attempted to answer this question by investigating how agrammatic patients access these vocabulary items. Bradley *et al.* (1980) reported that the recognition of the function words was abnormal in agrammatic aphasics. Bradley and her co-workers gave agrammatic patients and normal controls a number of lexical decision tasks, testing recognition of function words and content words. Normal subjects' reaction times are inversely correlated with a word's frequency, with faster reaction times for more frequent words. Bradley and her colleagues discovered that this inverse linear relationship between frequency and RT was only true for the "open-class", content word vocabulary. The "closed-class", function word vocabulary did not show any effect of frequency upon RT in the experiments conducted with normal subjects. Agrammatic aphasic patients, however, continued to show the normal relationship between RT and word frequency for open-class words but also showed this same inverse relationship between RT and frequency for closed-class words. In a second set of experiments, Bradley *et al.* investigated the way in which the presence of a sub-string of letters which actually constitutes a word interferes with a person's ability to reject a longer string of letters which is not a word. Bradley *et al.* found that if a non-word string began with an actual word, there was an interference effect upon the rejection of the non-word. This "non-word interference effect" was only observed when an open-class word occurred at the beginning of a non-word letter string. Words occurring later in the letter string did not produce any interference effects, and closed-class words did not produce interference effects. Agrammatic aphasic patients, on the other hand, did show interference effects for both open-class and closed-class words when they occurred at the beginning of a non-word letter string.

Bradley and her colleagues concluded that the basic process of recognizing closed-class words was abnormal in agrammatic patients. They argued that closed-class words are recognized by a specialized recognition routine, which is not frequency-sensitive and does not operate in a "left-to-right" manner. Open-class words are recognized by a routine which *is* frequency-sensitive and *does* operate in a left-to-right manner. The authors concluded that agrammatics are forced to use this "open-class" routine for the recognition of closed-class items. They further suggested that this reliance upon an inappropriate (and, for these words, inefficient) recognition routine characterizes not only the perceptual recognition abilities of agrammatic patients, but also the way they access closed-class items in general. They suggested that this disturbance in lexical access underlies the inability of the agrammatics to use these elements in spontaneous speech, and leads to the disturbances in syntactic expression which we have reviewed, as well as to other disturbances found in agrammatism, such as difficulties in syntactic comprehension.

This work has not gone unchallenged. Gordon and Caramazza (1982) reanalyzed the Bradley *et al.* results, using a different set of statistical analyses. They argued that, when non-linear regression analyses were used, closed-class and open-class words behaved similarly in Bradley's experiments with respect to the relationship between word frequency and recognition RT. They also repeated Bradley's experiments, and found no differences between agrammatic patients and normal controls, other than a generally increased reaction time on the part of the agrammatic patients. They therefore concluded that a disturbance in lexical access for the closed-class vocabulary did not underlie the abnormality seen in agrammatic patients. Close study of the Gordon and Caramazza results, however, still leaves open the possibility that the relationship between word frequency and recognition RT differs between closed-class and open-class elements, since the stimuli which were recognized most quickly in all of these experiments were the ones which were most frequent, and these stimuli are mainly closed-class items. It is, therefore, possible that agrammatic patients have a disturbance in word recognition affecting their ability to access the most frequent words of the language as quickly as normally, and that, because the most frequent words in the language are primarily closed-class items, this disturbance primarily affects these elements. This account, however, is inconsistent with a *linguistic* as opposed to a psychological analysis of agrammatism (see above, p. 277).

Our survey of work on one aspect of the problems in sentence production seen in aphasia – agrammatism – has taken us over a fair amount of ground. Fundamental questions regarding the nature of this impairment have forced us to refer to quite detailed models of linguistic structure and processing to begin to fashion a coherent account of this clinically observed symptom. Our discussion has brought up some of the difficulties in analyzing symptoms such as agrammatism, and shown how some of these – certain aspects of the variation in agrammatism seen across languages or across vocabulary elements in a single language – may be explained by postulating interactions between a primary "higher-order" deficit and features of languages themselves. The interaction of a primary deficit with other aphasic symptoms is another issue we have discussed: the interaction of a primary deficit (misselection of vocabulary items within a morphological paradigm) with another aphasic disturbance (some form of motor speech disturbance) may actually give rise to agrammatism instead of paragrammatism in a particular patient. As usual, we have raised many questions which we have not been able to answer; but our discussion has indicated the level of empirical detail and theory development that now characterizes the study of sentence-planning disturbances, as well as illustrating some of the experimental techniques that researchers use to approach these questions. The interested reader will find more material on this and related topics in the "Suggestions for further reading" section which follows this chapter.

III *Linguistic aphasiology*

SUGGESTIONS FOR FURTHER READING

Badecker, B. and Caramazza, A. (1985). On considerations of method and theory governing the uses of clinical categories in neurolinguistics and cognitive psychology: the case against agrammatism. *Cognition* 20, 97–125.

Bradley, D. C., Garrett, M. F., and Zurif, E. B. (1980). Syntactic deficits in Broca's aphasia. In D. Caplan (ed.), *Biological Studies of Mental Processes*. MIT Press, Cambridge, Mass.

Caplan, D. (1983). A note on the "word order problem" in agrammatism. *Brain and Language* 20, 155–65.

Goodglass, H. (1973). Studies on the grammar of aphasics. In H. Goodglass and S. Blumstein (eds.), *Psycholinguistics and Aphasia*. Johns Hopkins University Press, Baltimore.

Goodglass, H. and Berko, J. (1960). Agrammatism and inflectional morphology in English. *Journal of Speech and Hearing Research* 3, 257–67.

Goodglass, H., Gleason, J. B. Bernholtz, N. A., and Hyde, M. R. (1972). Some linguistic structures in the speech of a Broca's aphasic. *Cortex* 8, 191–212.

Gordon, B. and Caramazza, A. (1982). Lexical decision for open- and closed-class items: failure to replicate differential frequency sensitivity. *Brain and Language* 15, 143–60.

Grodzinsky, Y. (1984). The syntactic characterization of agrammatism. *Cognition* 16, 99–120.

Kean, M. L. (1977). The linguistic interpretation of aphasic syndromes: agrammatism in Broca's aphasia, an example. *Cognition* 5, 9–46.

    (ed.) (1985). *Agrammatism*. Academic Press, New York.

16

Disturbances of sentence comprehension

As we noted in Chapter 15, sentences convey information not expressed by words in isolation. Which person or object is accomplishing an action, which is receiving an action, where actions are taking place, and similar information – known as "thematic roles" – is not part of the lexical semantic information associated with each word, but rather depends upon the relationship of words to each other within a sentence. Similarly, sentences convey the information of which adjectives and other modifiers are associated with which nouns, how pronouns are related to nouns, and other aspects of meaning. When we understand speech, we must extract this "sentential" and "phrasal" semantic information from the sentences that we hear, or we have failed to understand a significant part of the information conveyed by spoken language.

There is a fundamental difference between the way sentential semantic information is represented in sentences and the way lexical semantic information is associated with individual words. For a simple lexical item, essential semantic information must be connected in a direct fashion to the representation of the word in a mental lexicon. We have seen in Chapters 12, 13, and 14 that accessing the mental lexicon from sound or print is not a simple process, nor is accessing a semantic representation from the mental lexicon. Despite the complexity of the processes involved in identifying words and recovering the meaning of a word, the meaning of a word is "directly" associated with its form, in the sense that each word has one meaning (except homophones, homographs, and ambiguous words). Sentential semantic information is not represented in this fashion. Rather, there is a complex interaction between the syntactic structure of a sentence and the words in the sentence that determines what the sentence means. Unlike words, syntactic structures do not "mean" anything by themselves. By placing words in certain positions in syntactic structures, we add sentential semantic features to the intrinsic lexical semantic features of those words. A few simple examples will illustrate this interaction.

If we consider sentences (1) and (2) below, the words in the sentences are identical, but the thematic roles of the nouns differ because of the syntactic structures into which the words are inserted. In (1), *cat* is the subject of an active sentence, and hence the agent of the sentence; this role is played by *dog* in (2):

(1)   The cat scratched the dog
(2)   The dog scratched the cat

The subject of a sentence is not always its agent, as the passive of (1) shows:

(3)   The dog was scratched by the cat

In (3), *dog* is the subject of the sentence, but carries the thematic role of theme (the recipient of the action of the verb) because of the presence of the passive form. Nor is it always the case that the subject of a sentence with an active verb is the agent, as (4) and (5) show:

(4)   The boy received the gift
(5)   The saucer cracked

In (4), *receive* is a verb that assigns the thematic role of goal to its subject, while the intransitive form of the verb *crack* in (5) is a so-called "inchoative" verb that assigns the thematic role of theme to its subject.

Thus, verb voice (active, passive) and intrinsic aspects of the way each verb assigns thematic roles determine what thematic roles are assigned to particular grammatical positions such as the subject and object of a verb. The nouns in these positions receive these roles, as (1) and (2) illustrate. The nouns themselves contribute to the determination of the exact thematic role assigned. For instance, in (6), *boy* is agent because it is an animate noun, while in (7), *ball* is instrument because it is inanimate:

(6)   The boy broke the window
(7)   The ball broke the window

Attribution of modifiers is also determined by the syntactic structures into which modifiers are placed. In (8), *big* can only modify *girl*, while in (9) it can only modify *boy*. Again, the actual words in the sentences have not changed – only the syntactic structures into which they are inserted differ:

(8)   The boy and the big girl went downtown
(9)   The big boy and the girl went downtown

Another aspect of semantic meaning which is constrained by syntactic structure is the possibility of co-reference between pronouns, reflexives, and nouns. In (10), *He* and *John* cannot refer to the same person (i.e. cannot be "co-referential"), while in (11) *John* and *his* can refer to the same person. Again, this is a function of the syntactic structure of the sentence. The relevant aspects of the syntactic structure are different from those which determine the possible thematic roles in (1)–(7) and attributions of adjectives in (8) and (9), and we shall return to the way syntax constrains co-reference later.

(10)   He read John's book
(11)   John read his book

The sentential aspects of meaning that we mentioned above – thematic roles, the way that modifiers are attributed to nouns, the reference of pronouns – and other sentential semantic features are determined by the "constituent structure" of a sentence. For instance, in sentence (12):

(12)   The dog that chased the cat killed the mouse

there is a sequence of words – *the cat killed the mouse* – which by itself is actually a sentence, but is not understood as a sentence. The reason that the sequence *the cat killed the mouse* is not understood as a sentence is that the structure of sentence (12) does not group *the cat* together with *killed the mouse*. Rather, *the cat* is grouped together with the preceding verb (*chased the cat*), and the entire relative clause *that chased the cat* is related to the noun phrase, *the dog*, which is the "head" of the relative clause. The constituents of sentence (12) are, roughly, those indicated in (13):

(13a)   The dog that chased the cat – noun phrase
(13b)   that chased the cat   – relative clause
(13c)   chased the cat   – verb phrase
(13d)   the cat   – noun phrase
(13e)   killed the mouse   – verb phrase
(13f)   the mouse   – noun phrase

The noun phrase constituents of (12) each play particular *grammatical roles*, illustrated in (14):

(14a)   The dog that chased the cat – subject of *killed*
(14b)   the cat   – object of *chased*
(14c)   the mouse   – object of *killed*

Grammatical roles are defined in terms of the hierarchical relationships between constituents. The subject of a sentence is the noun phrase (NP) directly dominated by a sentence node (S); the object of a sentence is the NP directly dominated by the verb phrase (VP), etc. The easiest way to conceive of these structures is through a tree diagram representation of the grammatical structure of a sentence, as illustrated in Figure 16-1. Thematic roles – agent, theme, etc. – are assigned to constituents on the basis of the grammatical role of the constituent in relationship to the verb of its clause. Since *the cat* is a constituent that does not have a grammatical role in relationship to the verb *killed*, we do not take (12) as expressing the proposition that the cat killed the mouse. It is the hierarchical organization

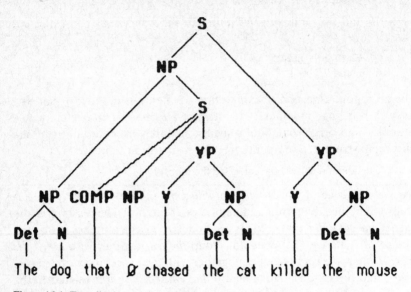

Figure 16-1. Tree diagram of the syntactic structure of sentence (12)

of sentence constituents which determines the grammatical roles of each constituent and hence the thematic role of each NP, not the strictly linear order of either words or constituents.

Syntactic structures thus consist of hierarchically organized constituents. Each constituent is made up of syntactic categories – nouns, verbs, adjectives, pronouns, conjunctions, etc. – and is itself a syntactic category of one sort or another – a noun phrase, a verb phrase, a sentence, etc. The "terminal" syntactic categories in a "tree" such as the one represented in Figure 16-1 are directly attached to lexical items. We say that each category is a "node" in a syntactic structure, and a node "dominates" another node if it is higher in the syntactic structure than the second node. Thus, in Figure 16-1, the node VP dominates the nodes V and NP. We also say that a node "directly" dominates another node if there are no intervening nodes between them. Thus, VP also directly dominates V and NP, while the node S, standing for "sentence", directly dominates one NP (*the dog that chased the cat*) and a VP (*killed the mouse*) and also dominates the nodes within these constituents, though not directly. Dominance is one relatively simple relationship between nodes that can be defined over hierarchically organized syntactic structures. We have just seen that the relationship of dominance is important in defining grammatical roles of constituents, and therefore in determining thematic roles of noun phrases. Other more complex relationships defined over syntactic trees are relevant to other

298

aspects of sentential semantic information. Before turning to other relationships between nodes and their roles in determining aspects of sentential semantic representations, however, we should note two features of syntactic structures.

The first is that there is an infinite number of syntactic structures in each of the languages of the world. For instance, in English it would be possible to form relative clauses indefinitely, as illustrated in sentence (15):

(15)   The dog chased the cat that found the mouse that bit the snake that . . .

Because there are an infinite number of syntactic structures, we cannot mentally represent our knowledge of syntactic structures in the form of a list. We must represent syntactic structures in the form of rules, which can generate an infinite number of syntactic structures. Chomsky (1957) was the first to recognize this feature of syntactic structures, and he developed a way to represent an infinite number of syntactic structures in a finite set of rules by using rules with a property known as "recursion". In Chomsky's (1957) system, one set of syntactic rules consisted of formulae which allow a category (sentence, noun phrase, verb phrase, noun, etc.) to be "rewritten" or "expanded" as another set of categories. The property of recursion occurs in a set of "rewrite" rules when one of the elements which is being rewritten also appears as one of the rewriting elements. For instance, the rules that are needed to produce the structures shown in Figure 16-1 are listed below:

(16) $S \rightarrow NP + VP$
(17) $NP \rightarrow Determiner + N$
(18) $NP \rightarrow NP + S$
(19) $VP \rightarrow V + NP$

Rules (16)–(19) indicate that a sentence can be expanded as a noun phrase plus a verb phrase, that a noun phrase can be expanded as a determiner plus a noun, that a noun phrase can be expanded as another noun phrase plus a sentence, and that a verb phrase can be expanded as a verb plus a noun phrase. These rules can be used over and over again. They are recursive because the symbol for sentence – S – is found as both a symbol that is rewritten (in rule (16)), and as a rewriting symbol (in rule (18)). Repeated application of rules (16), (18) and (19) can lead to an indefinitely long sentence, as in example (15) above.

The fact that syntactic structures cannot be represented as a list but rather require a system of rules is an important feature distinguishing syntactic and lexical representations. Though lexical items may be organized and accessed according to rules, each lexical item requires its own entry in a lexicon, since each is an independent entity which has some idiosyncratic features. A list of the basic words in a language – excluding those formed through the word-formation processes we discussed in Chapter 15 – though long, would be finite, and therefore could be stored. A list of the syntactic structures of a language would never end, and therefore could not be stored. Therefore, words can and must be stored in a list, and syntactic structures *must* be stored in the form of a set of rules. Of course, it might be the case that certain simple or frequent syntactic structures are also represented separately as individual items, in addition to their being generated by a rule system. We shall explore this possibility in our discussion of aphasic breakdown of syntactic comprehension.

The second point to be made about syntactic structures is that linguists have postulated a considerable number of syntactic categories and elements in their search for the underlying regularities in syntactic structures. The syntactic structure represented in Figure 16-1 is a simplified representation of the structure of sentence (12). Different versions of syntactic theories postulate different structures and different syntactic elements (Chomsky 1981; 1982; Bresnan 1982; Gazdar *et al.* 1985). Each of these theories represents an attempt to express the rules governing syntactic form in as economical and accurate a way as possible. A considerable effort has gone into trying to decide which of these competing theories is correct, and to make each theory account for more data, and account for "old" data in a more general fashion.

In Chomsky's work, for example, an initial theory made extensive use of so-called "transformational" rules, which supplemented the "phrase structure" rules illustrated in simplified form in (16)–(19) (Chomsky 1957). This theory has been replaced by a model in which there is only one transformational rule applicable to the structures created by phrase structure rules, and in which that rule can move any constituent to any position in a sentence (Chomsky 1981). What prevents this rule from producing an enormous number of ungrammatical sentences is the presence of a set of "constraints" and "conditions" on the resulting syntactic structures, which must be satisfied if a syntactic structure is to be well formed. These constraints themselves are then related to different "modules" or "sub-systems" of the syntactic component of a grammar, such as one dealing with the assignment of thematic roles, or one dealing with how far an item may be moved. As with phonological representations and rules, some aspects of the rules and constraints relevant to syntactic structures are thought to be language-universal, and others specific to particular languages.

With these considerations in mind, let us return to the question of the way the relationships between nodes in hierarchically organized syntactic structures determine the reference of pronouns and reflexives. We saw in

Chapter 12 that nouns such as *girl* refer to items in the world. Words such as *her* or *herself* do not refer in the same way as a word such as *girl*. Though pronouns like *her* and reflexives like *herself* do constrain the class of real-world items that they designate, because they convey information about the sex of these items, the particular item they designate is unspecified. The reference of these words is achieved through the pronoun or reflexive being related to another noun in a sentence. Thus, for instance, in (20), *herself* refers to *Mary*, and in (21), *her* cannot refer to *Mary* and may refer to *Susan*. The subscripts in (20) and (21) indicate these patterns of reference. *Co-reference* is indicated by identical subscripts, as in (20), and *disjoint* reference is indicated by different subscripts, as in (21):

(20)   Susan said that Mary$_i$ washed herself$_i$
(21)   Susan said that Mary$_j$ washed her$_i$

The examples show that the noun phrase to which a reflexive is related (its "antecedent") must be in the same clause as the reflexive, and that the antecedent of a reflexive cannot be the antecedent of a pronoun in the same grammatical position. Example (22) shows that the antecedent of a reflexive is not simply *any* noun phrase in the same clause. Of the various NPs in the same clause as *herself*, only *a friend* can be the antecedent of *herself*:

(22)   Susan said that a friend$_i$ of Mary's washed herself$_i$

Conversely, in (23), only *a friend* cannot be the antecedent of *her*:

(23)   Susan said that a friend$_j$ of Mary's washed her$_i$

What is special about *a friend* in both (22) and (23) is the particular position it has in the syntactic structure of the sentence. *A friend* is the subject of the clause in which *herself* and *her* are found. We might therefore conclude that a reflexive can only refer to the subject of its clause and a pronoun may not refer to the subject of its own clause. However, though almost correct, this is not quite true, as sentences (24) and (25) show:

(24)   Susan said that Mary's$_i$ portrait of herself$_i$ pleased Helen
(25)   Susan said that Mary's$_j$ portrait of her$_i$ pleased Helen

In (24), *herself* refers to *Mary* and in (25) *her* cannot refer to *Mary*, even though *Mary* is not the subject of the clause in question.

These sentences show that there are two constraints on which NP can function as the antecedent of a reflexive and be unable to be the antecedent of a pronoun. First, this NP must be within a particular syntactic domain. In the cases we have been considering, this domain is the S or NP within which the reflexive or pronoun occurs. Second, the NP in question must stand in a particular structural relationship to the reflexive or pronoun. In (20)–(23), the subject of the sentence stands in that relationship, and in (24) and (25), the head of the subject NP does. That relationship is defined in terms of the hierarchically organized syntactic structure in which the reflexive or pronoun is found, and its exact nature has been explored and debated in great detail by syntacticians. Chomsky (1981) gives that relationship the name "c-command" (standing for "constituent-command"), which he defines as in (26):

(26)   A node *A* c-commands a node *B* if (and only if) the branching node immediately dominating *A* also dominates *B*

This quite abstract and complex relationship is illustrated in Figure 16-2; and Figure 16-3 demonstrates why only one node in the clause with the reflexive satisfies the c-command relationship in sentences (22) and (24) and thus can be the antecedent of the reflexive in these sentences.

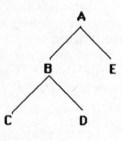

C-command relations:

C c-commands D
D c-commands C
B c-commands E
E c-commands B, C, and D

C and D do not c-command E, because they are dominated
by the branching node B which does not dominate E

Figure 16-2. Diagram illustrating the syntactic relationship of c-command

In addition to the relationships between nodes in a syntactic tree, we must also consider the nature of the category each node contains. Though there is much to say about the "higher" nodes in syntactic trees (see Jackendoff 1977, for instance), we will concentrate on one aspect of the lower, "terminal" nodes – the question of so-called "empty" terminal nodes in syntactic structures.

As we have indicated, noun phrases (NPs) are the linguistic categories which designate items in the real word. NPs must be assigned references in

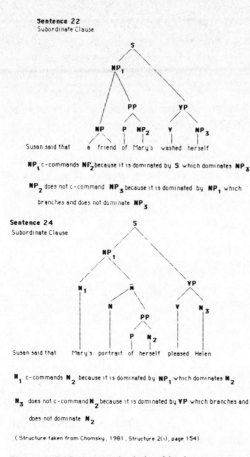

Sentence 22
Subordinate Clause

Susan said that   a   friend of Mary's   washed herself

NP₁ c-commands **NP**₂ because it is dominated by S which dominates **NP**₃

NP₂ does not c-command **NP**₃ because it is dominated by **NP**₁ which

branches and does not dominate **NP**₃

Sentence 24
Subordinate Clause

Susan said that   Mary's portrait of herself   pleased Helen

N₁ c-commands **N**₂ because it is dominated by **NP**₁ which dominates **N**₂

N₃ does not c-command **N**₂ because it is dominated by **YP** which branches and

does not dominate **N**₂

(Structure taken from Chomsky, 1981, Structure 2(1), page 154)

Figure 16-3. C-command relationships in sentences (22) and (24)

the world. Each NP must also be assigned a single thematic role (e.g. agent, theme, goal) around every verb it is associated with. In every sentence, thematic roles are assigned to the NPs in the sentence by the sentence's predicate. For example, in (27), the predicate verb *introduce* assigns three thematic roles: that of agent to the subject NP (*John*), that of theme to the direct object NP (*Bill*), and that of goal to the indirect object NP (*Mary*):

(27)   John introduced Bill to Mary

Now consider the following sentences:

(28)   Who did John introduce to Bill?
(29)   Who did John introduce Bill to?

We know that *who* is the theme of *introduce* in (28), and that it is the goal

303

in (29). This exactly parallels the role of *Bill* and *Mary* in (27). Furthermore, we can see that the grammatical roles occupied by *Bill* and *Mary* in (27) – the direct and indirect object positions – are empty in (28) and (29): an NP is "missing" after *introduce* in these positions in (28) and (29). In Chomsky's theory of syntax (Chomsky 1981; 1982), these facts are related. The interrogative pronoun *who* is said to have originated in the position of direct object in (28) and indirect object in (29), and to have been moved to its final position during the syntactic derivation of the sentence. At one level of syntactic structure, a trace (t) occupies the original position of *who*. This trace is co-indexed with *who*. The trace is an empty NP. It receives a thematic role (theme in (28), goal in (29)), and this thematic role is transmitted to its antecedent, *who*. The traces and their relationship to their antecedents are indicated in (30) and (31):

(30)   Who$_i$ did John introduce t$_i$ to Mary?
(31)   Who$_i$ did John introduce Bill to t$_i$?

Sentences with interrogatives (*who*) are not the only sentences with traces or empty NPs. Another type of trace is illustrated in (32):

(32a)   It seems to Bill that John is shaving
(32b)   John$_i$ seems to Bill [t$_i$ to be shaving]

In (32a), *shave* assigns the role of agent to *John*. In (32b), *John* has been moved to its surface position, leaving a trace, with which it is co-indexed. The trace is assigned the role of agent of *shave*. Since the trace transmits its thematic role to its antecedent, *John*, we understand that it is *John* and not *Bill* who is shaving. The trace in (32a) is known as an NP trace, because the antecedent of the trace is a lexical NP, as opposed to the *wh-* traces in (28) and (29), which are co-indexed with a *wh-* word (*who*).

Wh- traces are also found in relative clauses, and NP traces in passive sentences. The reader may have noticed that there was no lexical item dominated by the subject NP in the relative clause in Figure 16-1. In Chomsky's theory, this NP dominates a trace, and the trace is co-indexed with the complementizer, *that*, which is logically connected to the head NP of the relative clause, *the dog*. Since the trace transmits its thematic role around *chased*, *the dog* is understood to be the agent of *chased*. NP traces are postulated in passive sentences, such as (3), repeated here, whose more abstract representation would be that shown in (3a):

(3)   The dog was scratched by the cat
(3a)   The dog$_i$ was scratched t$_i$ by the cat

In Chomsky's theory, *the dog* has moved from its original position as object of *scratched*, leaving a trace. The trace is the theme of *scratched*, and this thematic role is transmitted to *the dog*.

There is one more type of empty NP, which is not a trace. In (33)–(35), there is an empty NP – called PRO by Chomsky (1981) – which occupies the position of subject of the embedded verb *shave*. In (33) and (34), PRO is co-indexed with a lexical NP in the sentence, as indicated. Which lexical NP is the antecedent of PRO depends upon the main verb of the sentence. In (35), PRO refers to anyone; that is, its reference is free:

(33)   John$_i$ promised Peter [PRO$_i$ to shave]
(34)   John persuaded Peter$_i$ [PRO$_i$ to shave]
(35)   It is hard [PRO to shave]

PRO differs from trace in several respects. As (35) demonstrates, PRO can refer to something outside the sentence it is in. Traces always have an antecedent within their sentence. In Chomsky's theory, the relationship of PRO to its antecedent is not due to movement of the antecedent from an original position in the syntactic structure of the sentence, as with trace, but to the semantic process of "logical construal", which ties PRO to certain NPs. Therefore, the antecedent of PRO can be partially determined by properties of verbs such as *promise* and *persuade*, while the antecedent of trace is always determined by where an NP has moved in a sentence.

Empty NPs are thus similar to reflexives and pronouns, in that they all share the property of receiving their reference by being related to a lexical NP. We have just noted that there are two basic types of empty NPs – PRO, which may refer outside the sentence it is in, and trace, which must refer to an NP within its sentence. Pronouns (e.g. *him*), also may refer to other nouns in the sentence they are in, or may refer to an entity outside the sentence, as in sentences (21), (23), and (25) above. The only restriction on pronouns is that there are certain NPs which they may *not* refer to. Reflexives (e.g. *himself*), must refer to a particular NP in their sentence, as sentences (20), (22), and (24) illustrate. Thus, there is a similarity between traces and reflexives, on the one hand, and PRO and pronouns, on the other. Traces and reflexives always co-refer with a sentence; PRO and pronouns may refer outside the sentence.

We thus see that syntactic structures consist of far more than simple linear strings of words or even of syntactic categories. Syntactic categories are organized hierarchically, and relationships defined over these hierarchical structures – subject, object, c-command – play crucial roles in determining aspects of sentential semantics such as thematic roles and co-reference. Different aspects of the hierarchical structure of sentences are relevant to different sentential semantic features. Syntactic structures are abstract in another way as well: many theorists have postulated the existence of syntactic elements, such as the empty categories trace and PRO in Chomsky's work, which are not physically present in the uttered sentence. Theories which postulate such elements do so in order to simplify the description of other aspects of sentential structure, such as the assignment of thematic roles (in passive sentences and questions, for instance) and co-reference (in so-called "control" sentences such as (33)–(34), for example). There is much debate as to what formulation of syntactic structure is correct in this relatively new science of linguistics; but all theories have properties of the sort we have been discussing – abstract elements and hierarchical organization of categories. All syntactic theories consist in one way or another of sets of rules specifying structures with these features.

The fact that syntactic structures must be represented as a set of rules has led researchers to conclude that the process of recognizing the syntactic structure of a sentence also involves the use of rules. According to this view, when a person recognizes a sentence, he builds up a syntactic representation such as those shown in Figures 16-1 and 16-3, using something like the reverse of rules such as (16)–(19). Words such as *the* and *dog* are recognized, and their syntactic category obtained from their lexical entry. This category, "determiner" in the case of *the*, or "noun" in the case of *dog*, triggers a so-called "pattern-action" rule. A pattern-action rule takes as its input a syntactic category, such as determiner, noun, or noun phrase, and creates a syntactic structure as its output. For instance, the "pattern" determiner can trigger the creation of the larger category noun phrase; the category noun phrase can trigger the category sentence. As can be seen, pattern-action rules can be generative phrase structure rules in reverse.

However, the existence of sentences such as (28) and (29) shows that the pattern-action rules used in assigning syntactic structure cannot be quite this simple. In the case of a sentence with an interrogative pronoun, a passive construction, or other types of constructions, the structures created by pattern-action rules must either contain empty categories or include some special indication that the assignment of thematic roles to noun phrases is different in these sentences from what it is in simple active declarative sentences.

The pattern-action rules specified in any particular "parser" (a device which yields the syntactic structure of a sentence when presented with that sentence in spoken or written form) must bear a close relationship to a particular theory of syntax, because the output of such rules must be a structure specified in that theory. Thus, there now are parsers which are related to Chomsky's theory (Marcus 1980; Berwick and Weinberg 1984) and to other theories (Bresnan 1978). We cannot review all these parsers here, but we note that they all share the property of creating a syntactic structure from the words of a language on the basis of pattern-action rules related to a particular theory of syntax. In most cases, the operation of the pattern-action rules is subject to a number of constraints, some related to the syntactic theory associated with the parser, and others derived from considerations internal to the operation of the parser itself.

A parser can be considered to be a psychological theory of how humans construct syntactic structures. Although most parsers are devices run on computers, and their internal structure is heavily influenced by computational constraints imposed by computer software, many are, in fact, designed to incorporate constraints on parsing which are derived from human psychology, or their operations are said to explain certain aspects of how humans understand sentences. They are therefore often said to be psychologically real. For instance, Marcus (1980) is concerned with the problem that a particular node – say, determiner or verb – can trigger a very large number of pattern-action rules which might overload a working memory system. Therefore, Marcus wishes to restrict the number of syntactic structures the parser actually creates. His parser imposes a severe restriction on the number of structures created: the parser only carries one structure along as it goes through a sentence. But this also means that the parser could often be wrong. For instance, sentence (36) could finish in any of the ways indicated:

(36)   John read that
      (a) story
      (b) it might rain

If the parser assigns the category "determiner" to *that*, it will be correct if the sentence finishes as (a), but wrong if it finishes as (b). Marcus deals with this problem by creating a "buffer" in the parser which allows the parser to "look ahead" before committing itself to a structure. Since the whole point of not creating two possible structures in a sentence like (36) when the word *that* comes up is to reduce the memory load of the parsing process, this solution may be self-defeating. Therefore, Marcus restricts the number of places in the buffer to three. This is an arbitrary number, which works for the sentences Marcus deals with. Though this particular feature of Marcus' parser may have no psychological validity, the idea that a parser waits to hear several words before creating a structure, and never erases a structure it creates, is an important concept which has the status of a hypothesis regarding human parsing. Not all parsers are structured this way. The so-called "HEARSAY" parser (Lesser *et al.* 1975) and the HWIM parser (Woods 1982), for instance, postulate many syntactic structures, and finally select the most "highly valued" structure at the end of a sentence.

The parsers we have considered so far are implemented on computers, and their "psychological reality" is claimed to be due to the fact that their outputs resemble certain syntactic theories (which are assumed to be real representations of what a person knows about his language) or to be due to the plausibility of the internal workings of the parser (as in Marcus' claim that the parser reduces memory load by being "deterministic"). Psychologists have preferred to approach the study of human parsing another way – by investigating how people parse and understand sentences, and building up a theory of parsing from the results of such investigations.

Let us consider one example of this sort of work, the parser developed by Frazier and Fodor (1978). We can appreciate one part of its operation by considering a particular example. Consider the following sentence:

(37)   John bought the book for Susan.

One's first interpretation of sentence (37) is that it is Susan for whom John bought the book. On reflection, it is clear that sentence (37) is ambiguous, and can also mean that what John bought was the book for Susan. Since both meanings are possible, the fact that one is preferred must be due to the parser arriving at the preferred interpretation before the alternative. This, in turn, suggests certain features of the parser.

To see what these features are, we first need to represent the differences between the two possible interpretations of these sentences. Figure 16-4 illustrates the two structures that underlie the two possible interpretations of sentence (37). Following Frazier and Fodor, we see that the relevant aspect of these structures is the structural configuration into which the node PP (prepositional phrase) is inserted in both these sentences. In Figure 16-4(a), the prepositional phrase *for Susan* is attached directly to the verb phrase, whereas in Figure 16-4(b) it is attached to an NP that is itself attached to the VP. Frazier and Fodor postulate that, when a structure (such as an NP) is identified in a sentence, it is attached to the phrase marker that has previously been constructed using the smallest number of non-terminal nodes – a principle called minimal attachment (MA). Having identified *the book* as an NP in (37), the parser, following MA, will attach it directly under the VP. When *for Susan* is recognized as a PP, the phrase marker constructed by a parser will have the form shown in Figure 16-4(c). At that point, there is only one place for the PP *for Susan* to be attached: as a "sister" to the NP *the book*. Attaching the PP *for Susan* as in Figure 16-4(b) would entail both adding an additional node and revising the previously constructed phrase marker. The parser therefore attaches the PP *for Susan* to the VP, with the result that the sentence is first interpreted to mean that it was for Susan that John bought the book.

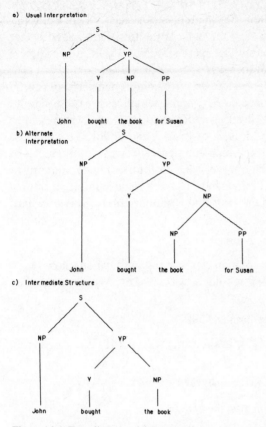

a) Usual Interpretation

b) Alternate Interpretation

c) Intermediate Structure

Figure 16-4. Tree diagram of the syntactic structure of the two readings of sentence (37), and of the intermediate structure created by the parser at the point where *John bought the book* has been assigned its structure in this sentence. See text for discussion.

In the Frazier and Fodor model, these principles are two of several which are embedded within a two-stage model of parsing that leads to more detailed predictions about preferred and possible interpretations of other sentences. Other models (in particular, augmented transition network models (Wanner 1980)) provide alternate analyses of these and other phenomena related to parsing. Nonetheless, this simplified example serves to illustrate several important features of the human parser. What this example shows is that a psychologically real parser must do more than assign the correct structure to a sentence. It must do this the way humans do it. Sentence (37) is ambiguous and has a preferred meaning. The preferred meaning cannot be given by linguistic theory, which specifies *all* the legitimate structures and meanings of a sentence. It is not given by context in

309

this case, since it exists when the sentence is presented in isolation. Therefore, it must result from how the parser operates. Frazier and Fodor model this aspect of the parser in the manner we have seen; other parsers achieve similar results in different ways.

Before going on to disturbances of sentence comprehension, we should return to a point we briefly raised earlier. Some sentences are quite simple, such as the first two example sentences in this chapter. Do we use the entire machinery of a parser such as Marcus' or Frazier and Fodor's to parse and interpret them, or do we create much simpler structures – a sequence of nouns and verbs, perhaps – which serve as the basis for our understanding of a simple sentence? Some researchers have claimed we use simple structures in these cases. Bever (1970) points out that a sentence like (38) is very hard to understand:

(38)   The horse raced past the barn fell

Most people think that (38) is not a proper sentence and, when told it really is a sentence of English, think it is somehow related to (39) (although they are not sure how):

(39)   The horse raced past the barn and fell

In fact, (38) is derived from (40), in the same way as (41) is derived from (42):

(40)   The horse that had been raced past the barn fell
(41)   The horse racing past the barn fell
(42)   The horse that was racing past the barn fell

Bever (1970) argues that we mis-analyze (38) because it contains the sequence *the horse raced past the barn*, which we think of as a sentence. He claims we think of it as a sentence because we match it to a "template" of the form N–V–Prep–N. Sequences of the form N–V–Prep–N are understood through the application of one of a number of "heuristics". In this case, the heuristic interprets the first noun in the sequence N–V–Prep–N as agent of the verb. These heuristics contrast with the pattern-action rules of parsers in that they do not create fully developed syntactic structures, and they often take as input a string of terminal categories and assign only one sentential meaning to that string. They therefore sacrifice the considerable flexibility of parser-based pattern-action rules for speed and simplicity of analysis. It is not clear whether these heuristics are really used by normal people in comprehending sentences (we do not, for instance, misinterpret the N–V–N sequence *the cat killed the mouse* in sentence (12) that we discussed extensively above), but they might be very important in aphasia.

Finally, we should note that some sentences do not require syntactic analysis at all to be understood. The sentences we have considered so far all do require syntactic analysis, but a sentence like (43) does not:

(43)   The boy ate the cake

If we understand the words *boy*, *ate*, and *cake*, and know something about the real world – that only animate items can eat, and that cakes are objects which are frequently eaten – we can infer that *boy* is agent and *cake* theme in (43) without analyzing the syntax of the sentence at all. Sentence (44) is more complex syntactically than (43), but is equally easy to understand if this "lexical–pragmatic" route to meaning is employed:

(44)   The cake was eaten by the boy

As with the use of heuristics, we do not know whether normal subjects bypass syntax in interpreting these "semantically irreversible" or other semantically constrained sentences, but aphasic patients who have trouble constructing or interpreting syntactic representations might.

We now turn to studies of aphasic patients. We shall focus on disturbances in constructing and interpreting syntactic structures, leaving aside the whole area of how patients deal with sentences such as (43) and (44) in which syntax can be avoided. As we shall see, there is a fair amount to consider regarding "syntactic" comprehension – enough to serve as an introduction to the larger topic of sentence comprehension in general.

In certain aphasic populations, comprehension of some sentential semantic functions is not determined or constrained by syntactic form in a normal manner. Studies which demonstrate this phenomenon fall into three groups: survey studies of more or less unselected aphasic populations, using test batteries designed for screening purposes; more focussed studies of small selected groups of aphasic patients, which concentrate on one or two syntactic structures and sentential semantic features; and case studies. Taken together, these three types of studies clearly establish that there are patients who fail to use syntactic structures normally in the determination of sentential semantic functions, and begin to characterize these disorders in some detail. We shall review several studies of each sort in turn.

By far the largest experience with a sentence comprehension battery which involves comprehension of syntactic structure by aphasic patients has accrued with the Token Test (De Renzi and Vignolo 1962) and its many translations and variants. The more popular abridged versions of the Token Test consist of sequential sections in which commands are given to manipulate colored geometric forms. In all but the last section, the subject is required to touch one or two tokens, which are specified with increasing precision, as in (45)–(48):

(45)   Touch a large square
(46)   Touch the large red square
(47)   Touch a large square and a small circle
(48)   Touch the large red square and the small blue circle

The final section requires that the subject delay before touching a token, touch tokens in a particular order, touch only one of the two mentioned tokens, etc. The commands in the final section involve a variety of structural forms, including *if . . . then* statements, subordinate clauses with *before* or *after*, and prepositional phrases. From a linguistic point of view, all sections but the last of the Token Test test attribution of modification (a sentential semantic function) through the presentation of adjective–noun sequences of increasing length. The final section tests a wide variety of syntactic structures, and requires their interpretation with respect to attribution of modification as well as assignment of thematic roles and the temporal ordering of actions.

The Token Test has been used in many studies of aphasic populations. It is well established that scores on the Token Test distinguish patients considered aphasic from normal subjects, from non-aphasic left-hemisphere-damaged patients, and from right-hemisphere-damaged patients. It is also known that failure on the Token Test increases with subsequent sections, and that failure on the last section, with its more complex linguistic and response demands, is more severe than on previous sections, and out of proportion to failure on previous sections. Degree of failure also correlates strongly with short-term memory limitations (Lesser 1976).

Published analyses of performance on the Token Test allow only limited characterizations of the syntactic structures assigned and interpreted by patients on this test. Clearly, many patients are unable to assign modification normally. This difficulty is increased when several modifiers have to be assigned to one or more nouns. No published data regarding the actual errors made in the first sections of the Token Test exist. Multiple studies indicate that errors occur far more frequently in the final section than in the earlier sections of the Token Test. Unfortunately, the final section is made up of heterogeneous structures, so that a raw score for performance on this section is not revealing with respect to specific structures which occasion difficulty in parsing or interpretation. Moreover, many of the test items in the final section involve the interpretation of the lexical semantics of subordinate temporal conjunctions, and errors may result from misinterpreting the meaning of these words, or from being unable to carry out the

actions in the required order when that order is opposite to the spoken order
of clauses in the test item. Neither of these sources of error would reflect a
failure to understand syntactic structures. In short, the experience with the
Token Test, though valuable in the identification of aphasic patients, does
not clearly lead to hypotheses regarding the syntactic structures which are
assigned and interpreted in aphasia. It should be noted that this was
probably not the goal of its creators.

Caplan and his colleagues (Caplan *et al.* 1985) studied a large number of
aphasic patients using a different test, requiring comprehension of a number
of syntactic structures. The authors presented the nine sentence types (49)–
(57). Subjects were required to indicate the thematic roles of NPs in the
sentences by manipulating toy animals – a technique used extensively to
study sentence comprehension in children.

(49)   Active (A): The elephant hit the monkey
(50)   Passive (P): The elephant was hit by the monkey
(51)   Cleft Subject (CS): It was the elephant that hit the monkey
(52)   Cleft Object (CO): It was the elephant that the monkey hit
(53)   Dative (D): The elephant gave the monkey to the rabbit
(54)   Dative Passive (DP): The elephant was given to the monkey by the rabbit
(55)   Conjoined (C): The elephant hit the monkey and hugged the rabbit
(56)   Subject–Object relative (SO): The elephant that the monkey hit hugged
        the rabbit
(57)   Object–Subject relative (OS): The elephant hit the monkey that hugged
        the rabbit

The authors report three studies of fifty-six, thirty-seven, and forty-nine
patients. In each study, they determined the relative difficulty of each
sentence type. The mean number of correct responses for each sentence
type in each of the three studies is shown in Table 16-1. The same sentence
types produced the highest mean correct scores in each study, except for
some variation in how difficult conjoined sentences are. Caplan *et al.* argue
that these results indicate that syntactic structure influences sentence interpretation in aphasia. Sentences with "canonical" word order were consistently easier than those with deviations from canonical word order: (A vs.
P, CS vs. CO, D vs. DP, and C and OS vs. SO). Verb argument structure
also affected performance: D sentences were more difficult than A sentences, and DP harder than P sentences. Sentences with two verbs were
harder than those with one verb, when canonical word order was controlled
(C and OS vs. A and CS; SO vs. CO).

The authors considered the presence of a non-canonical word order, a
third thematic role, or a second verb, as elementary structural features of a
sentence which partially determine the complexity of a sentence. To a
considerable extent, the relative complexity of a sentence type could be

Table 16-1. *Mean correct scores for different types of semantically reversible sentence*

Pilot study		Experiment 2		Experiment 3	
CS	3.9	A	4.4	A	4.1
A	3.9	CS	4.2	CS	4.0
P	2.8	D	3.2	P	3.2
D	2.8	P	2.9	D	2.9
CO	2.4	C	2.7	C	2.8
OS	1.9	CO	2.6	CO	2.7
DP	1.8	OS	2.3	OS	2.1
C	1.5	DP	2.0	DP	1.9
SO	1.2	SO	1.3	SO	1.4

Note: The maximal possible score for each sentence type is 5. Bracketed sentence types do not differ significantly. Sentence types not bracketed together show significant differences in mean correct scores.
Source: Caplan *et al.* 1985.

predicted from the number of these features that occur in a sentence. The length of a sentence may have influenced its complexity, but sentence length could not be the sole determinant of complexity, because sentences of equivalent length differed with respect to the number of correct interpretations (CS vs. CO; C and OS vs. SO).

Caplan *et al.* suggest that the results are due to constraints upon how syntactic comprehension can break down in aphasia, and these constraints are themselves due to certain aspects of the normal parsing/interpretive process. One is the lower and upper bounds of a string upon which some part of the parser/interpreter operates. The lower limit is suggested by the greater ease all patient groups have with cleft-subject and active sentences than with cleft-object sentences. This suggests that the parser/interpreter is sensitive to the entire N–V–N or N–N–V configuration, for if it were able to consider only the N–V part of these strings, accurate assignment of the immediately pre-verbal noun to the role of agent in cleft-object sentences should result. The upper bound may be the number of nouns needed to fill the argument positions of a verb. The evidence for this upper bound is the greater difficulty of two-verb sentences by comparison with one-verb sentences (equated for canonical form). This suggests that one part of the parser/interpreter operates on one verb and its arguments at a time. The part of a parser/interpreter that operates on these input strings may be the part that is involved in the assignment of thematic roles.

This study thus begins to describe the way syntactic structures influence patients' interpretation of sentences. The exact nature of and the reasons for a syntactic comprehension disorder in a single patient or a group of patients have been explored by more detailed investigations of small groups of patients and single cases. The characterization of disturbances of syntactic comprehension in agrammatic aphasics, which we mentioned in Chapter 15, constitutes part of this literature. Indeed, this work on agrammatic patients' comprehension provided much of the impetus for the recent investigation of syntactic comprehension disorders. We shall therefore begin our discussion of small group studies with a consideration of syntactic comprehension in agrammatic patients.

Caramazza and Zurif (1976) first investigated the question of sentence comprehension in agrammatic patients. They tested Broca's, conduction, and Wernicke's aphasics on a sentence–picture matching test, using four types of sentences illustrated in (58)–(61):

(58)   The apple the boy is eating is red
(59)   The boy the dog is patting is tall
(60)   The girl the boy is chasing is tall
(61)   The boy is eating a red apple

Each sentence was presented with the correct picture and one of four "foils": a picture in which one of the adjectives was altered (yellow for red; short for tall); one in which the verb was altered (kicking for patting); one in which both these changes were made; and one in which the agent and the theme of the verb were inverted (e.g. a girl chasing a boy in (60)).

The patients were scored on the number of errors they made in selecting the correct picture. Broca's and conduction aphasics made almost no errors when pictures with incorrect adjectives or verbs were used as foils. Their errors were confined to pictures presenting reversals of the thematic roles of the nouns in the sentences. Moreover, these patients only made errors on sentences such as (59) and (60), in which the syntax of the sentences indicated an improbable event in the real world, or in which the thematic roles are reversible. In the semantically irreversible sentences (58) and (61), these patients made no more errors than normal subjects.

Caramazza and Zurif interpreted the results as indicating that patients with Broca's aphasia cannot construct syntactic structures. They claimed that these patients relied upon the meanings of individual content words and what they knew about events in the real world to determine the meaning of the sentence. This could account for their inability to select the correct response in sentences such as (59) and (60), where the syntax of the sentence determines the thematic role of the nouns, and their retained ability to understand (58) and (61), in which a lexical–pragmatic route to meaning is adequate to determine the thematic roles in the sentences.

Caramazza and Zurif also claimed that these results showed that agrammatic patients use heuristics based upon basic word order to interpret sentences. However, as Schwartz and her colleagues pointed out (Schwartz *et al.* 1980*b*), there is no evidence that this is how the patients in Caramazza and Zurif's study interpreted sentences, since no semantically reversible sentences in canonical word order were presented. Schwartz *et al.* (1980*b*) therefore tested this important hypothesis. They presented sentences such as

(62)	The dancer applauds the actor
(63)	The actor applauds the dancer
(64)	The dancer is applauded by the actor
(65)	The actor is applauded by the dancer

in a sentence–picture matching test, in which there were two pictures to choose from – one correctly representing the meaning of the sentence, and one representing a reversal of the thematic roles of the NPs in the sentence. Five agrammatic patients interpreted the active sentences (62) and (63) correctly about 75 per cent of the time. On a case-by-case basis, two patients performed well above chance on the actives, and one patient's performance was exactly at the cut-off point for statistical reliability. In the passive sentences (64) and (65), the patients performed at chance as a group, choosing sixty-eight out of 124 correct pictures. Four of five patients performed at a chance level, and one consistently chose the incorrect picture. Schwartz *et al.* repeated the study with the same patients using stimuli designed to eliminate any subtle lexical effects. The results were similar overall, although the patients who did well on the active sentences in the first trial and those who did well in the second were not the same individuals.

Schwartz and her colleagues claim that the results indicate that these patients could not use the basic N–V–N or SVO word order of these sentences to assign thematic roles. According to these investigators, their patients did not even use this aspect of sentence structure in a heuristic way. However, Caplan (1983) pointed out that the group results for the active sentences (62) and (63) suggest that the patients did appreciate the word order of the sentence but were also influenced by the animacy of each noun. The pattern of interpretations could result from the patients' taking the first noun, or any animate noun, as the agent of the sentence. This is exactly the same way these same patients performed in sentence production, according to Caplan (1983) (see Chapter 15). Though the intrusion of an "animacy effect" complicates the responses (and requires an explanation), the results suggest these patients do appreciate basic SVO or N–V–N word order in active sentences.

The results also show that the patients are unable to interpret passive sentences correctly. However, this too could result from several impairments. One possibility is that the patients assign no structure to a sentence at all, as Schwartz *et al.* suggest. Another possibility is that they take both the subject NP and the NP in the *by* phrase as possible agents, and cannot decide between these possibilities. This would imply that they appreciate many syntactic features of sentences, including both word order and the passive construction, but cannot use this information normally.

This alternative was suggested by Grodzinsky (1986) as part of a more general analysis of agrammatic patients' difficulties with syntactic comprehension. Grodzinsky (1984) suggested that agrammatic patients make errors in producing items which are not phonologically specified at one level of syntactic structure (Chomsky's S-structure). Grodzinsky (1986) argued that agrammatics have difficulty in comprehending these same items. These items include most function words and inflectional affixes, and also all the empty categories specified in Chomsky's theory that we reviewed above.

Grodzinsky thus claims that agrammatic patients have a much less severe deficit than that postulated by Schwartz *et al.* (1980*b*). He claims that agrammatics misunderstand passive sentences because they do not co-index the trace in the passive with the subject NP (illustrated in sentence (66)), and take both the subject NP and the NP in the *by* phrase as agents, leading to an ambiguous sentence:

(66)   The dancer$_i$ was applauded t$_i$ by the actor

Grodzinsky bases his analysis on the fact that five agrammatic patients he studied had trouble both with passive sentences, such as (66), and with sentences with object relativization, such as (67) and (68), but not with sentences with subject relativization, such as (69) and (70):

(67)   The dog$_i$ that the cat chased t$_i$ followed the rat
(68)   The dog chased the cat$_i$ that the rat followed t$_i$
(69)   The dog$_i$ that t$_i$ chased the cat followed the rat
(70)   The dog chased the cat$_i$ that t$_i$ followed the rat

Grodzinsky argues that sentences (66)–(68) require co-indexation of traces to be understood, but sentences (69) and (70) can be understood by a heuristic that takes the head NP of a relative clause as agent of the verb of that clause. The fact that both passive and object relatives are misunderstood can thus be accounted for economically by postulating that agrammatics cannot co-index traces.

Caplan and Hildebrandt (1986), however, argue that this analysis is not adequately supported by Grodzinsky's data. They point out that there is no evidence that Grodzinsky's patients assigned all the syntactic structure Grodzinsky assumes they did. There is no evidence that they were sensitive

317

to the constraints on co-indexation of overt referentially dependent items (pronouns and reflexives) which we discussed above, or that they could interpret sentences with empty NPs other than trace (such as PRO). Certainly, Grodzinsky's analysis does not apply to all agrammatic patients. Another agrammatic patient described by Caplan and Futter (1986) did not construct all this structure. She treated sentences as linear sequences of the major lexical categories N and V. This patient, SP, interpreted sentences (71)–(73) all the same way:

(71)   The elephant hit the rabbit and hugged the bear
(72)   The elephant that hit the rabbit hugged the bear
(73)   The elephant hit the rabbit that hugged the bear

SP understood the first clause correctly in (71)–(73). She also correctly assigned the last NP as theme of the second verb. However, she randomly picked either the first or second NP as agent of the second verb in each of these sentence types. Caplan and Futter argue that this resulted from SP considering these sentences as sequences of the form (74):

(74) N_1–V_1–N_2–V_2–N_3

and assigning agent and theme to pre- and post-verbal nouns which had not already been given thematic roles. This would lead to the assignment of N_1 as agent of V_1, N_2 as theme of V_1, and N_3 as theme of V_2 in (71)–(73), but would leave the agent of V_2 unspecified. SP would then randomly take either N_1 or N_2 as agent of V_2. Caplan and Futter argue that this more complex heuristic would lead to correct interpretation of object–object relatives (75), but not subject–object relatives (76).

(75)   The elephant hit the rabbit that the bear hugged
(76)   The elephant that the rabbit hit hugged the bear

In (75), the first clause is correctly interpreted by this heuristic, and N_3 (*the bear*) is correctly assigned as agent of V_2 (hugged). However, in (76), the heuristic cannot apply to the initial N–N–V sequence, leading to errors. This is how SP performed on these sentences.

Caplan and Hildebrandt (1986) argue that SP's performance illustrates that some agrammatics assign less structure than Grodzinsky claims. Schwartz *et al.*'s cases fall into this category. Other agrammatic patients assign more structure than Grodzinsky claims. Two agrammatic patients studied by Miceli *et al.* (1983) had no impairment in several tests of syntactic comprehension. The patient of Nespoulous described in Chapter 15 had no trouble understanding any of these types of sentences ((66)–(76)). Thus, Caplan and Hildebrandt argue that Grodzinsky's analysis at most applies to a sub-set of agrammatic patients. In fact, the nature and the severity of the syntactic comprehension disorders found in agrammatic patients is no different from that found in the unselected aphasic population studied by Caplan *et al.* (1985). The uniformity, specificity, and ubiquity of a syntactic comprehension deficit in agrammatism is therefore called into question.

A related question is whether the syntactic comprehension deficit found in some agrammatic patients is secondary to whatever impairment is causing their expressive agrammatism, or whether it is due to some other cause. Researchers at first thought that it was secondary to the deficit underlying expressive agrammatism. Zurif *et al.* (1972), Berndt and Caramazza (1980), Bradley *et al.* (1980), Caplan (1985), and others argued that syntactic comprehension was abnormal in agrammatic patients because of their inability to use function words or a parser, and that this impairment also caused the more readily observable abnormalities in speech output. However, the results we have just reviewed make this hypothesis very unlikely. Since some agrammatics have no syntactic comprehension deficits (at least on these materials), the deficit causing expressive agrammatism does not necessarily produce a syntactic comprehension impairment. It is possible that there is a single impairment underlying both expressive agrammatism and syntactic comprehension limitation in some patients, but it will require close study of the exact expressive profile, and of the syntactic structures which are and are not interpreted, and a theory connecting these two deficits, to substantiate and prove this hypothesis.

Expressive agrammatism is one of two deficits which has been said to cause an impairment of syntactic comprehension. The other is an impairment of auditory-verbal short-term memory (STM). As we noted above, patients with STM impairments do poorly on the Token Test. It is logical to suppose that an STM deficit could cause a sentence comprehension deficit, since words are presented one at a time in sentences and some memory is needed to operate on more than one word at a time. The questions we must ask are: what memory system(s) is (are) used in sentence comprehension, and what aspects of sentence comprehension is a particular memory system used in?

In the past ten years, the concept of short-term verbal memory has undergone considerable revision. The traditional view was that a phonological "short-term store" (STS) served as an intermediary between perception and a semantic long-term store (LTS). This view has been revised, and the functions of STS have been increasingly related to language processing, especially aspects of sentence comprehension (Warrington and Shallice 1969; 1972; Shallice and Warrington 1970; Baddeley 1976). A second change has been the development of a model of "working memory" (WM) which includes a "phonological store" (PS) and an "articulatory loop"

319

(AL) (Baddeley and Hitsch 1974; Baddeley 1981). In this model, a "Central Executive" (CE) performs a wide variety of operations upon input stimuli and relays information to semantic memory. The CE can make use of the PS when its own memory capacities are exceeded; in turn, the PS uses the AL to maintain items through rehearsal. Among the functions performed by the CE is the initial assignment of meaning to sentences. Both these changes to the older notion of STM have the effect of relating a short-duration memory store, in which items are maintained in a phonological code and in which rehearsal helps maintain an item's strength, to some aspect of sentence comprehension.

Evidence supporting this view has come from neuropsychological studies of patients with STM deficits. These patients are said to have a number of impairments in sentence comprehension, which have been related to their verbal memory deficits. The conclusion drawn from this literature is that one or another aspect of verbal STM is a component of the mechanisms involved in sentence comprehension. One possibility is that this system plays a role in syntactic comprehension, and that impairments of STM (or parts of the WM system) cause syntactic comprehension disorders. We shall consider three cases – PV (Vallar and Baddeley 1984), MC (Caramazza *et al.* 1981), and TI (Saffran 1985) – to try to discover exactly what role an STM deficit plays in producing a comprehension impairment, and whether syntactic comprehension deficits are secondary to STM or WM impairments.

The very first case we shall consider, PV, would appear to show that WM deficits do *not* lead to syntactic comprehension impairments. PV showed evidence of retained ability to assign and interpret syntactic structure, performing almost perfectly on a test of syntactic comprehension devised by Parisi and Pizzamiglio, which tests comprehension of passive sentences, subject–verb agreement, adjective–noun agreement, and other syntactic features of Italian, in sentences whose length exceeded her repetition span. PV also did well on several other specially designed tests of sentence comprehension. However, she did fail on one specially designed test, in which she was required to judge whether sentences such as (77) were true:

(77)   The world divides the equator into two hemispheres, the Northern and the Southern

The authors interpret this failure as evidence that PV was not able to interpret "word order", and imply that they believe she had a syntactic comprehension disturbance.

As we noted in Chapter 15, there are many different senses of the term "word order". Vallar and Baddeley use the term with one particular meaning which we did not consider in Chapter 15. They use the term to refer to the inversion of two nouns within a sentence (which may be in canonical form), yielding a semantically false or anomalous sentence. Vallar and Baddeley's "word order" variations lead to "syntactically encoded semantic anomalies" (Saffran 1985). In some cases, these are very hard to detect. For instance, sentence (77) is misleading even for normals, who often do not see or hear the reversal of the words *world* and *equator*.

The reason for the difficulty in detecting the falsehood of (77) may be due to the existence of parallel routes to sentential meaning which occur in normal sentence processing. We have seen that one route involves the assignment and interpretation of syntactic structure. The use of this route would lead to appreciation that (77) is anomalous. However, the "lexico-pragmatic" interpretive route would lead to an interpretation of (77) according to which the sentence is taken to mean that the equator divides the world into two hemispheres; that is, a reading which is true. In normals, when there is a conflict between syntactically derived and lexico-pragmatically derived readings, the former is usually selected. Intuitions indicate that this may take some thought, and that it may require review of the verbatim form of a sentence to determine which interpretation is consistent with the sentence actually presented. Because of her STM impairment, this review may not be available to PV. If this analysis is correct, PV is able to interpret sentences syntactically, but is unable to choose a syntactic over a lexico-pragmatic reading because she cannot review the verbatim form of the sentence. Her deficit lies in a post-interpretive checking or editing function, not in syntactic comprehension itself.

A more complex case is MC (Caramazza *et al*. 1981). MC clearly has a disturbance in interpreting syntactically complex sentences, failing to choose the correct picture over lexical and syntactic foils in tests of passive and center-embedded relative clauses with auditorily presented, semantically reversible sentences. MC was also tested on the same battery with visual presentation. The authors note that his error rate declined from about 50 per cent with auditory presentation to about 25 per cent with visual presentation. Since MC had a disturbance of "auditory-verbal" STM and not "visual" STM, as determined by the memory testing the authors carried out, the increased number of errors on these sentences with auditory presentation was said to indicate that auditory-verbal STM is used when interpretation of syntax is required for auditory sentence comprehension.

However, a close examination of the actual data makes this analysis less convincing. MC's increased impairment with auditorily presented sentences did not come about because of an increased selection of *syntactic* foils, but because of an increased selection of *lexical* foils. MC evolved from an initial stage of severe word deafness, and it is entirely possible that his poorer performance with auditory presentation reflected a residual word deafness. In fact, the magnitude of the increase of selection of lexical foils from visual to auditory presentation was about the same for simple word–picture matching as for syntactically complex semantically reversible sentences. There is no evidence that MC was more impaired in *syntactic* comprehension with auditory than with visual presentation of sentences; on the contrary, there was actually a slight *decrease* in the number of syntactic foils MC selected when he went from visual to auditory presentation of these sentences. MC's syntactic comprehension deficit also cannot be related clearly to his memory impairment. With visual presentation of sentences, MC was allowed to look at the sentence while he selected the picture, but he still did poorly. This suggests that the source of his syntactic comprehension deficit was not an inability to keep a verbatim record of the presented sentence in mind for reinspection, but rather some other impairment in assignment or interpretation of syntactic structure.

Saffran (1985) reports a third illustrative patient with an STM impairment. TI failed to understand semantically reversible sentences of the sort we have been considering – passives, relative clauses, etc. However, here too there is evidence that the syntactic comprehension impairment may not be related to the memory deficit. For instance, Saffran varied sentence length, keeping basic aspects of a syntactic construction the same, and found this often did not change TI's performance. For example, TI performed as poorly on "truncated" passives, without a *by* phrase, as in (78), as on full passives:

(78)   The dog was chased

This indicates that if TI's STM impairment underlies his syntactic comprehension problems, it does not do so in any simple way. His problem cannot be directly related to keeping the verbatim record of a sentence in memory, since if this is how an STM impairment affects syntactic comprehension, shorter sentences should be easier. Another possibility is that STM abilities interact with the parser/interpreter to assign and interpret a syntactic structure. Saffran investigated this possibility by having TI judge whether strings of words were grammatical sentences or not. The non-grammatical sentences often contained a single violation of an agreement rule. Saffran varied the number of words between the elements involved in the violation, as in (79) and (80):

(79)   The *boy* in the car *are* wearing a hat
(80)   The *boy* in the car parked illegally next to the doughnut shop *are* wearing a hat

TI could recognize that these stimuli were ungrammatical (and recognize that correct sentences were correct). The number of words intervening between the critical items did not affect her ability to make these judgements. Saffran concluded that TI could assign syntactic structure but could not interpret it. Thus, she concluded that the auditory-verbal STM functions which TI was lacking are not involved in assigning syntactic structure, though they might be used in *interpreting* a parse.

Thus, different patients with auditory-verbal STM impairments have been able to interpret a variety of syntactic structures (PV) and assign syntactic structures when they have a syntactic comprehension deficit (TI). There is evidence that the syntactic comprehension deficit in patients like MC and TI is not secondary to their STM deficit. MC had the same sort of syntactic comprehension deficit with written sentences as with oral sentences, despite the fact that his visual STM was good and that the written sentence remained in view while he was responding. TI had no more trouble comprehending long sentences than short ones. These patterns suggest that the syntactic comprehension deficit in these patients was not a simple direct consequence of their verbal STM limitations. The role of auditory-verbal STM in the comprehension process may be limited to checking different interpretations against the original sentence, recovering from a "garden path" situation (as in sentence (38)), and other functions which occur after the syntactic structure of a sentence has first been assigned and interpreted.

We thus see that the study of syntactic comprehension disorders in patients with expressive agrammatism and auditory-verbal STM impairments, which originally was taken to show that these supposedly "primary" impairments cause "secondary" disturbances in assigning and comprehending syntactic form, in fact suggests that syntactic comprehension impairments are often independent primary disorders of sentence processing. It is entirely understandable why this should be the case, given the specificity and complexity of the parsing process which we discussed at the beginning of this chapter. Case studies reporting very specific primary disorders of syntactic comprehension are just beginning to appear in the literature (Caplan *et al.* 1986*b*; Hildebrandt *et al.* in press). We shall end this chapter with a description of one such case, who shows a specific disturbance in understanding sentences with traces as well as a general limitation of his parsing and interpretive abilities.

Hildebrandt and her colleagues (Hildebrandt *et al.* in press) report an extensive study of the performance of a patient, KG, on a number of tests of syntactic comprehension using an object manipulation paradigm. The stimuli were constructed to test KG's ability to co-index the referentially dependent noun phrases discussed in the first part of this chapter – overt lexically dependent items (pronouns and reflexives) and empty categories (PRO and trace). Table 16-2 presents the results of this study. In this table, sentences are classified according to the type of category that needs to be co-indexed.

As can be seen, KG has no trouble with most sentences containing overt referentially dependent items. He does make some errors on sentences containing pronouns and reflexives, but only when these sentences also contain empty categories. Moreover, even in these circumstances, KG understands the lexical semantic content of reflexives and pronouns: he

Table 16-2. *Summary of results from KG on syntactic comprehension batteries*

Number correct	
COMPARISON STRUCTURES WITHOUT A REFERENTIALLY DEPENDENT NP	
12/12	*The monkey kicked the elephant*
11/12	*The monkey gave the elephant to the goat*
11/12	*The monkey kicked the elephant and kissed the goat*
11/12	*Patrick expected a friend of Joe's to be praying*
10/12	*Patrick knew that Joe kicked Eddie*
OVERT REFERENTIAL DEPENDENCIES	
Overt pronouns (+ pronominal):	
12/12	*Patrick said that a friend of Joe's hit him*
10/12	*Patrick said that Joe hit him*
9/12	*Patrick promised Joe that he would kneel* [antecedent = Patrick]
9/12	*Patrick told Joe that Eddie had hit him*
Overt reflexives (− pronominal):	
12/12	*Patrick said that a friend of Joe's hit himself*
12/12	*Patrick told Joe that Eddie had hit himself*
10/12	*Patrick said that Joe hit himself*
SENTENCES CONTAINING PRONOMINAL VERSUS NON-PRONOMINAL EMPTY NPS:	
PRO:	
Object control:	
12/12	*Patrick persuaded Joe$_i$ [PRO$_i$ to wash]*
12/12	*Patrick persuaded a friend$_i$ of Joe's [PRO$_i$ to wash]*
10/12	*Patrick allowed Joe$_i$ [PRO$_i$ to hit himself]*
10/12	*Patrick forced Joe$_i$ [PRO$_i$ to hit him]*
Subject control:	
10/12	*Patrick$_i$ vowed to Joe [PRO$_i$ to pray]*
9/12	*Patrick$_i$ promised Joe [PRO$_i$ to pray]*
7/12	*Patrick$_i$ promised Joe [PRO$_i$ to cover him]*
4/12	*Patrick$_i$ promised Joe [PRO$_i$ to hit himself]*

Table 16-2 (*cont.*)

Number correct	
Trace:	
12/12	*The goat$_i$ was hit t$_i$ by the frog*
12/12	*The monkey$_i$ was pushed t$_i$ by the frog and the rabbit*
11/12	*[$_{NP_i}$ The monkey and the goat] were pushed t$_i$ by the rabbit*
11/12	*It was the goat [that$_i$ [the frog hit t$_i$]]*
10/12	*The goat [that$_i$ [t$_i$ hit the frog]] kissed the cow*
10/12	*The goat hit the frog [that$_i$ [t$_i$ kissed the cow]*
9/12	*Patrick$_i$ was believed by Joe [t$_i$ to be praying]*
8/12	*The goat$_i$ was given t$_i$ to the frog by the cow*
8/12	*Patrick$_i$ was persuaded t$_{ij}$ by Joe [PRO$_j$ to pray]*
7/12	*The goat hit the frog [that$_i$ [the monkey kissed t$_i$]]*
6/12	*It was the goat [that$_i$ [the frog gave t$_i$ to the cow]]*
4/12	*Patrick$_i$ seems to Joe [t$_i$ to be praying]*
4/12	*Patrick$_i$ seems to Joe [t$_i$ to have hit himself]*
4/12	*Patrick$_i$ was believed by Joe [t$_i$ to have kicked himself]*
3/12	*The goat [that$_i$ [the frog hit t$_i$]] kissed the cow*
2/12	*Patrick$_i$ seems to a friend of Joe's [t$_i$ to be praying]*

Source: Hildebrandt *et al.* in press.

always takes reflexives as reflexive in meaning and always takes pronouns as disjoint in meaning. KG makes errors on sentences containing empty categories. Here, he makes many more errors with sentences containing trace than sentences containing PRO. He makes errors with PRO when PRO is controlled by the subject of the sentence (*John$_i$ promised Bill PRO$_i$ to shave*), but not when PRO is controlled by the object of the sentence (*John persuaded Bill$_i$ PRO$_i$ to shave*). He makes errors with trace when a sentence containing trace is more "complex". Simple passives do not cause KG trouble, but dative passives, many relative clauses, so-called "NP-raising" sentences (*John$_i$ seems to Bill t$_i$ to be shaving*), and sentences with passive main verbs and sentential complements (*John$_i$ was believed by Bill t$_i$ to be shaving*) cause difficulty.

Hildebrandt and her colleagues argue that KG has a limitation of his ability to devote mental resources to the task of syntactic comprehension, and probably a particular difficulty in co-indexing traces. The overall limitation of parsing resources causes KG's mildly impaired performances with reflexives and pronouns in sentences which are otherwise difficult because they contain an empty category. It also leads him to misinterpret PRO when it must be co-indexed with an NP from which it is separated by a verb. Finally, it shows up in the fact that simple sentences with trace are correctly understood, while more complicated sentences are misinterpreted. The great difference between KG's ability to interpret superficially similar sentences with PRO and trace, however, suggests that KG has a particular difficulty with trace. For instance, KG interprets sentences like (81) correctly nine out of twelve times, but sentences like (82) correctly only four out of twelve times, a statistically significant difference:

(81)   John promised Bill PRO to shave
(82)   John seems to Bill t to be shaving

Though it is possible to account for this difference in terms of the overall complexity of parsing and interpretive operations involved in co-indexing PRO and trace in some parsers, there is no way to know whether the different treatment of these two types of empty categories in these parsers is enough to create this large difference in KG's performance. Therefore, Hildebrandt *et al.* suggest that the process of recovering and co-indexing trace may be particularly affected in KG. Since, unlike the Grodzinsky cases we discussed above, KG has been shown to have quite intact parsing and interpretive abilities for many sentence types, including the co-indexation of pronouns and reflexives, his case constitutes an example of a primary disturbance of one aspect of syntactic comprehension superimposed upon a more general, mild limitation of the resources available for this function.

We see from all the studies we have reviewed that there are many different degrees of impairment of syntactic comprehension, many specific impairments of this ability, and many heuristic compensations to impairments that occur in this functional domain. We should also keep in mind that most of the studies we have reviewed only test (or at least, mostly concentrate on) the assignment of thematic roles to NPs. When we consider that syntactic structures constrain and determine the assignment of other sentential semantic functions as well – co-reference, scope of quantification, assignment of modification – and that we have not even considered patients who do not understand semantically constrained sentences despite good single-word comprehension, we gain some appreciation of the magnitude of the task that lies ahead of us as we search for the entire set of primary and secondary disturbances of sentence comprehension.

SUGGESTIONS FOR FURTHER READING

Baddeley, A. D. (1976). *The Psychology of Memory*. Basic Books, New York.
   (1981). The concept of working memory: a view of its current state and probable future development. *Cognition* 10, 17–24.

Caplan, D., Baker, C., and Dehaut, F. (1985). Syntactic determinants of sentence comprehension in aphasia. *Cognition* 21, 117–75.

Caplan, D. and Hildebrandt, N. (1986). Language deficits and the theory of syntax: a reply to Grodzinsky. *Brain and Language* 27, 168–77.

Caplan, D., Vanier, M., and Baker, C. (1986). A case study of reproduction conduction aphasia II: sentence comprehension. *Cognitive Neuropsychology* 3, 129–46.

Grodzinsky, Y. (1986). Language deficits and the theory of syntax. *Brain and Language* 27, 135–59.

Vallar, G. and Baddeley, A. D. (1984). Phonological short-term store, phonological processing and sentence comprehension: a neuropsychological case study. *Cognitive Neuropsychology* 1, 121–41.

17

Overview of linguistic aphasiology

We have covered a great deal of material in Chapters 11–16, and we shall take this opportunity to review some of the most important features of the work we have discussed, to relate this work to the material we covered in Part II, and to discuss a number of directions that work in linguistic aphasiology may take in the future.

Perhaps the first major feature of the research that we have been discussing is that it relates to a relatively new domain of investigation – linguistic aphasiology. Though it has implications for neurolinguistics (and we shall discuss some of these implications in Chapters 19 and 23), linguistic aphasiology is not neurolinguistics. Nor is it purely psycholinguistics or theoretical linguistics. Linguistic, psycholinguistic, and cognitive psychological concepts are applied to aphasia by linguistic aphasiologists to describe the phenomena of disturbed language processing and related cognitive impairments. As we have seen, this process can be carried out with little or no reference to the neurological basis for cognition or language, or to the neuropathological determinants of functional abnormalities in these spheres. Similarly, though linguistic aphasiology does seek to describe aphasic impairments in terms of deficits in sub-components of a language-processing system and related cognitive capacities, linguistic aphasiology is also separate from normal studies. This is partly because brain-injured subjects are often quite impaired with respect to their ability to process language normally, and therefore studying aphasic patients often does not lead to a consideration of the full range of linguistic structures or psycholinguistic processes that normals are capable of. For this reason alone, linguistic aphasiology is in some ways more limited than the study of normal language and its processing. In addition, aphasic symptoms often reflect the employment of heuristic strategies to circumvent deficits in the normal processing system, and aphasics' overt performances may reflect adaptations and compensations which are seen only after brain damage. For all these reasons, linguistic aphasiology is becoming a domain of study in its own right, separate from the parent disciplines which gave rise to it and which continue to sustain it.

Nonetheless, many aspects of linguistic aphasiology have emerged from the clinical studies of aphasia which we discussed in Part II. The very domain of study of contemporary linguistic aphasiology is that emphasized by connectionist neurolinguistics. It consists primarily of modeling breakdown in the principal tasks of language use: speaking, auditory comprehension, reading, writing, and naming objects. The broader questions of how the mechanisms involved in accessing, recognizing, and converting various forms of linguistic representation into others are related to more general features of psychology, such as motivational state, level of arousal, consciousness, and others, is not a major concern of contemporary aphasiology. Recently, several researchers (Marcel 1986) have suggested that researchers should concentrate more on the interaction of the language-processing system with these more general aspects of human psychology; but, to date, the research approach adopted by most workers in this field adopts a "divide and conquer" philosophy, according to which the "language-processing" part of the general psychology of language is isolated for intensive study.

A second part of the heritage of contemporary linguistic aphasiology from classical connectionist neurolinguistic theory is the basic type of model which is postulated. We have referred to this type of model as a "diagram" or a "box and arrow" model. A more revealing name might be "serial processing stage models", because these models attempt to establish the sequence of processing stages involved in any psycholinguistic task. For the most part, the processing stages specified in these models are ones at which particular types of linguistic representation are activated. In these models, these stages are usually represented in "boxes", and the operations which convert one representation into another are represented in the "arrows". For instance, in Figure 17-1, the boxes "contain" various representations of a linguistic stimulus – surface phonemic representations, abstract letter identities, lexical–phonological representations, etc. – and the arrows represent the processes whereby one of these representations is turned into another – visual whole-word recognition (A), grapheme–phoneme conversion (D), etc. Models such as the one illustrated in Figure 17-1 constitute efforts to establish the sequence whereby these linguistic representations are activated during a language-related task. The use of this type of model is being challenged, as we shall see below.

A third feature found both in much of clinical neurolinguistics and in contemporary linguistic aphasiology is the constraint that aphasic phenomena must be related to models of normal language structure and normal language processing. Wernicke (1874) took pains to justify his model of speech comprehension on the grounds that it could account for the normal process of language acquisition (see Chapter 4). Dejerine (1892) postulated

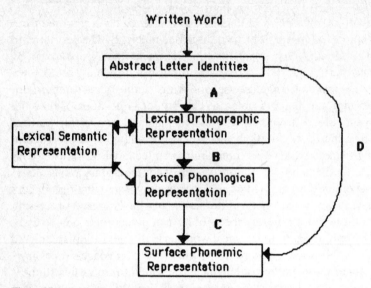

Figure 17-1. A sketch of part of a model of the reading process

that pure alexia resulted from the disconnection of visual input from the neural area responsible for converting graphemes to phonemes, secure in the belief that the function of grapheme–phoneme conversion was a necessary part of the reading process. Geschwind (1965) postulated that the inferior parietal lobe plays an important role in establishing word meaning, based upon an analysis of normal language acquisition which holds that words receive their meanings, at least initially, because of the establishment of associations between the physical properties of objects and the sound of a word. Jackson (1878) attempted to relate aphasic breakdown to a theory of the hierarchical organization of the nervous system. Goldstein (1948) tried to do the same in relationship to gestalt views regarding human psychology. Contemporary linguistic aphasiology follows this well-trodden path. What distinguishes contemporary linguistic aphasiology from earlier models is the increased linguistic and psychological detail in contemporary studies, and the relationship of contemporary studies in aphasiology to explicit models of linguistic structure and psycholinguistic processing. These differences mark all aspects of linguistic aphasiology, and can be appreciated by comparing the work we reviewed in Chapters 12–16 with the psycholinguistic formulations presented in Part II.

We touched upon this change in focus and in commitment to specific types of psycholinguistic models of language processing in Chapter 11, when we referred to what we called a "slightly older" and "slightly newer" psycholinguistic approach to describing aphasic symptoms. In Chapters 11 and 15, we illustrated these "older" and "newer" approaches by contrasting Goodglass' (1973) characterization and explanation of certain aspects of speech production in agrammatic patients with the description and explanation of the same abnormalities by linguists such as Kean (1977). We noted that Goodglass uses the phenomenon of short phrase length as a criterion for diagnosing agrammatism, and that short phrase length is a feature of speech which is not easily related to either linguistic theory or psycholinguistic processing models. Contemporary linguistic aphasiology would not use phrase length as a way to describe a patient's utterances. Rather, it would attempt to describe aphasic abnormalities in terms of disturbances of particular vocabulary classes, syntactic structures, and other features of language which are recognized in linguistic theory and psycholinguistic models.

Because of its greater attention to detail and its close connections with theories of language structure and processing, linguistic aphasiology has made a number of contributions to our understanding of normal language processing. The view that normal reading largely proceeds by direct, whole-word recognition, rather than by sounding out a word and achieving lexical access on the basis of the auditory form of a word, received important support from studies of reading disorders. We have not discussed all of the areas in which linguistic aphasiology has contributed to normal models of language and processing. The early investigations of the short-term memory syndrome led to the conclusion that stimuli are entered into both the STM and the LTM systems directly; this was a modification of the previously held view that stimuli entered STM before they entered LTM. We mentioned Saffran's discovery (1985) that a patient with an STM impairment could make judgements about the grammaticality of sentences despite being unable to understand semantically reversible sentences with any syntactic complexity such as passives. Linebarger and her colleagues (1983) were the first to report the phenomenon of retained grammaticality judgement abilities, in the face of severe disturbances in syntactic comprehension, in agrammatic patients. These findings suggest that parsing operations are partially separable from the process of interpreting the structures created by a parser in normal people. In all these areas and others, linguistic aphasiology has suggested features of normal processing mechanisms. Because brain damage does affect parts of the language system and spares others, the detailed study of aphasic patients has always been recognized to be a potentially valuable way of gaining information about normal processing mechanisms. As linguistic aphasiology has explicitly attempted to relate aphasic phenomena to detailed and otherwise justified models of normal language processing, this potential is beginning to be realized.

These changes in the content of contemporary linguistic aphasiology have brought with them a number of changes in the methods of study employed in aphasiology. Probably the most noticeable of these changes, and one whose significance has been frequently discussed, is an increasing reliance upon single case studies as evidence for the nature of normal functions. We discussed single case studies in Chapter 2, and it is appropriate to return to their use after having reviewed the material in Chapters 12–16.

Though there is increased reliance upon single case studies in linguistic aphasiology, the use of single cases goes back to the beginnings of clinical neurolinguistics. The earliest studies in aphasia, which we reviewed in Part II of this book, relied heavily upon single case studies. Broca, Wernicke, Lichtheim, Jackson, Dejerine, and many others developed both psycholinguistic and neurolinguistic theories on the basis of single cases. Modern connectionists have also done the same: Geschwind and Kaplan (1962) presented a case of a callosal patient which led to the revival of the entire connectionist model in Geschwind's 1965 paper (see Chapter 5). However, single case studies were somewhat less popular during a fairly lengthy period during which investigators tried to characterize the particular aspects of language disturbances in recognized aphasic syndromes, and to answer questions about the organic basis for language. The resurgence of interest in single case studies has gone hand in hand with increased interest in the use of data from aphasic patients to bear on normal language processing. There are good reasons for this shift in methodology, which are related to the questions the study of aphasia has undertaken to answer.

The earlier studies using single cases – those of Broca, Wernicke, Dejerine, and others – were primarily devoted to neurolinguistic models. On the basis of a single case, Broca suggested that the third frontal convolution was responsible for planning speech. On the basis of two cases, Wernicke suggested that there was a single "phonological lexicon", and that it is located in the association cortex adjacent to Heschl's gyrus. On the basis of a single case, Dejerine concluded that the language system responsible for reading was based in the angular gyrus of the left hemisphere, and that visual linguistic stimuli reaching the right occipital cortex could only be transferred to this area through the fibers of the splenium of the corpus callosum. If we think about the logical form of these analyses, we see that they are all arguments based upon associations of deficits. In each of these cases, there is a functional deficit – difficulty in speaking, the combination of a particular speech output disturbance with auditory comprehension abnormalities, and alexia – and an organic deficit – the lesion. In each case, the theorist postulates that the two are causally connected. We indicated in Chapter 2 that the first step in verifying an analysis based upon associations of deficits is to show that the deficits are reliably associated. The use of single cases to *validate* a hypothesis about the neural basis for language on the basis of the association of a lesion and a functional deficit is, therefore, questionable. A great deal of effort has thus gone into investigating the question of whether the syndromes described by Broca, Wernicke, and other investigators do in fact arise after lesions in particular brain regions, as these investigators hypothesized (see Chapter 19).

What role do single case studies play in neurolinguistics and linguistic aphasiology? Our discussion in Chapter 2, and the considerations just mentioned, do not do full justice to the arguments of Broca, Dejerine, Wernicke, and many other researchers who use associations of deficits in single cases as the basis for the development of both psycholinguistic and neurolinguistic theories. What we have left out of our considerations is the fact that the particular associations found in the cases which became important for neurolinguistic theory were *predicted* or, at least, expected on the basis of plausible theories of language processing or the neural basis for language. Broca's and Wernicke's theories made anatomical sense, because they postulated that motor planning functions and auditory comprehension took place in areas of cortex near the primary motor regions and primary auditory receptive regions of the brain. Wernicke's theory made psychological sense as well, at least to him, because the role of a "storehouse for the auditory form of words" in speech production was consistent with the idea that children learn to speak by repeating what they hear. If two deficits are found in a single patient, and this co-occurrence is exactly what a theory would predict, the co-occurrence of deficits is much more theoretically important than if two deficits co-occur but there is no way to understand why they co-occur. This is true regardless of whether the two deficits are both psychological, or one is psychological and one is organic. In either case, the relationship of the association of deficits to a plausible theory of psycholinguistic or neurolinguistic function gives the association of deficits added theoretical importance, even at the point at which it is first discovered in a single case.

Despite this consideration, which accounts for the acceptance of neurolinguistic theories based upon associated deficits in single cases as being at least worth further investigation, it is nonetheless a fact that, if the theories which predict the associations of deficits are true, the deficits in question must continue to be frequently associated in all patients, and exceptions to the associations of deficits must receive some explanation. Therefore, neurolinguistic theories based upon aphasia inevitably led to group studies, because these theories absolutely required that functional and organic deficits in fact be associated in many, if not all, aphasic patients.

333

In other words, the fact that neurolinguistic theories based upon aphasia can only be built upon the observation that a functional deficit and an organic deficit co-occur inevitably leads to a scientific approach to neurolinguistic theory based upon aphasia to the study of groups of patients with similar deficits or similar lesions.

In the case of linguistic aphasiology, the situation is similar in certain respects but different in others. The association of two or more functional impairments in a single patient has led researchers to postulate shared processing components in the normal language system. For instance, we reviewed claims that some aspect of the processing of function words and inflectional morphemes is carried out by a single processing mechanism in both speech production and speech comprehension, claims which were based upon the observation that both the speech and the syntactic comprehension of agrammatic aphasics were abnormal (see Chapters 15 and 16). These arguments from association of deficits in the functional sphere have the same criteria for acceptance as arguments from associations of deficits which cross the functional–organic boundary. In the case of the analysis of agrammatism, we noted in Chapter 16 that the association of a syntactic comprehension deficit with expressive agrammatism is not universal, and that there is no obvious way to account for the cases in whom this association is not seen. This led to the abandonment of the argument, based upon agrammatism, for a processing component related to the use of function words and inflections which is shared between speech production and speech comprehension. The process of hypothesis formation and validation is very similar in the neurolinguistic and psycholinguistic domains in this respect. Hypotheses about processing components or neurolinguistic relationships are advanced upon the basis of association of deficits, often found in a few cases. Subsequent research is, in part, devoted to seeing whether the association of deficits found in the original cases is generally found in the population. If it is, the theory receives some support. If not, the theory is abandoned or modified.

In addition to arguments based upon association of deficits, however, linguistic aphasiology can also base arguments upon *dissociations* of deficits. In particular, "double dissociation" is an important and revealing phenomenon which can bear on a psycholinguistic theory (see Chapter 2). For instance, the fact that there are some patients that have LTM impairments but excellent STM function, and others with the reverse pattern of impaired and intact memory abilities, is consistent with the view that STM and LTM systems are independent. Dissociations and double dissociations of deficits are an inadequate means of investigating the existence of processing components *common* to two or more tasks, but they are an invaluable means of investigating the possibility that *separate* processing components are involved in two or more tasks. A great deal of linguistic aphasiology can therefore proceed on the basis of individual case analyses, which demonstrate a particular pattern of retained and disturbed abilities. The accumulation of cases can lead to the documentation of a double dissociation. This accumulation of cases does not have the same status as a group study. On the contrary, the accumulation of cases for the purpose of demonstrating a double dissociation is explicitly designed to find cases who do *not* have the same functional deficits. Since single cases and series of cases are useful in this way, linguistic aphasiology need not lead to group studies, as neurolinguistics based upon data from aphasia must.

Single case studies published in recent years show highly specific, quite restricted, impairments of psycholinguistic functioning, as we have seen in many case reports in Chapters 12–16. These analyses provide direct evidence for the existence of particular components in the language-processing system. If patients with identical functional disturbances could be found, then the association of impairments in these patients could be studied to indicate the nature of shared components in the language-processing system. In large part for practical reasons, due to the great degree of specificity of impairments in individual patients, detailed psycholinguistic studies showing associations of very specific deficits in series of patients have been less forthcoming in recent years than individual case studies documenting a particular deficit in great detail.

Single case studies can also be used to *suggest* at least the existence of shared components of a language-processing system, in much the same way as early neurolinguistic theory was based upon an association of functional and organic deficits in a single case. If deficits occur in two closely related functions – such as the repetition of words and non-words – and if the disturbances in both of these similar functions are *qualitatively similar*, researchers have argued that it is reasonable to postulate that a single processing component, common to both of these functions, is disrupted. We saw in Chapter 13 how Caplan *et al.* (1986*a*), argued for the existence of a stage of lexical–phonological representations in single-word processing on the basis of qualitatively similar performances in word repetition, word reading, naming functions, and non-word repetition abilities of a single patient. As with neurolinguistic theories based upon associations of deficits in single cases, such theories rely heavily upon the plausibility of the suggested model for their appeal. For instance, in the Caplan *et al.* analysis, the model is consistent with the nature of phonological representations postulated by linguistic theory.

The fact that a great deal of linguistic aphasiology is based upon single case analyses does not imply that group studies are not used. We reviewed a study by Caplan *et al.* (1985) in Chapter 16 which investigated syntactic comprehension in unselected patients. Studies of patients with particular deficits, such as STM disturbances, were also discussed in Chapter 16. The use of single case studies by contemporary linguistic aphasiology does not constitute a sharp break with the methodology employed by researchers in the past, and does not exhaust the methods used by linguistic aphasiologists, though this tendency is more widespread today than previously. What is truly new in modern work is the degree of detail and reliability of the observations made on aphasic patients, and the relationship between relatively detailed models of psycholinguistic processing and aphasic disturbances which characterizes contemporary linguistic aphasiology.

Linguistic aphasiology is a new and relatively rapidly evolving area of science, and it draws heavily upon psycholinguistics and cognitive psychology, as well as on linguistics, for the theories of normal language processing to which aphasic phenomena can be related. Because these models are themselves changing, theories of aphasia are also changing. One particular aspect of normal modeling is clearly gaining in importance in aphasiology, and we shall consider it here. This aspect of modeling is the possibility that what are known as parallel distributed processing systems (PDP systems) are important ways of representing and processing information in a variety of psycholinguistic tasks.

We have seen one example of this type of analysis in our discussion of the "cascade" model of object recognition proposed by Humphreys and his colleagues (see Chapter 12). In that model, the physical properties of a stimulus activate structural descriptions of objects. The level of activation is highest for the structural description that has the most properties in common with the presented stimulus. Each structural description inhibits all other structural descriptions with an inhibitory force equal to its level of activation, so that, ultimately, the structural description corresponding to the presented object is the only one that remains activated. If the level of activation exceeds a certain threshold, the structural description "fires" and the object is recognized. In this PDP model, many items are activated in parallel when a stimulus is presented, and information about the stimulus is distributed over the entire set of structural descriptions which have a particular property by means of a rise in their level of activation.

One of the differences between this PDP model and the serial-processing stage models is the presence of inhibitory feedback among items in the PDP model. In the model we have just discussed, the inhibition affects items at the same stage of processing (structural descriptions). In other models (McClelland and Rumelhart 1981; Rumelhart and McClelland 1982) there is also a form of *feedback inhibition*, where a representation activated on one level reduces the activation of items on a previous level. These models also provide for *feedback reinforcement*, in which an activated item increases the activity of selected items at a previous level. For instance, in the Rumelhart and McClelland model of the reading process, a sequence of letters presented visually activates a representation of a written word at the level of the visual lexicon. This lexical entry feeds back in a positive way onto the letters in it, and in a negative inhibitory way upon all the other letters in the alphabet. This process is represented in Figure 17-2. PDP systems with so-called "interactive activation" and "feedback inhibition" have been developed for object recognition (Chapter 12), aspects of reading, aspects of the

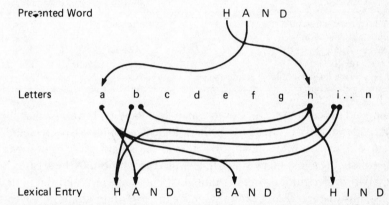

Figure 17-2. An interactive–activation model of letter and word recognition, modeled on Rumelhart and McClelland 1982. ⟶ represents activation, ⟶● represents inhibition. The effects of presenting the word *hand* are shown with respect to the letters *h* and *a*. These presented letters activate their corresponding representations in the set of all letters and in the words *hand*, *band*, and *hind*, and inhibit all other letters. Ultimately, the word *hand* is most highly activated. However, visually similar words, such as *band* and *hind*, can be strongly activated at some points in the recognition process. For further details, see text.

production of the sounds of words, and other areas of psycholinguistic functioning. Increasingly, researchers are trying to describe aphasic symptoms in terms of breakdown in PDP models, and to make inferences about models incorporating PDP systems on the basis of aphasic breakdown.

The similarities and differences between these PDP models and present serial-processing stage models are summarized in Table 17-1. As can be seen, PDP models basically involve more types of operations than simple serial-processing stage models. Each type of model specifies that a linguistic specification is accessed or recognized, and specifies that one linguistic representation is converted into another type of representation. Neither type of model allows processes to carry along the processing history of an item (see Chapter 13). Both types of models involve feedback, but the feedback is different in the two cases. In PDP models, the feedback consists of reinforcement or inhibition of elements at an earlier stage of processing, as we have seen in Rumelhart and McClelland's model of the reading process and the cascade model of object recognition discussed in Chapter 12. In the serial stage model, feedback is really more of a means of bypassing

Table 17-1. *Comparison of parallel distributed processing and sequential stage-processing models*

	Serial stage models	PDP models
Sequential representational stages	Present	Present
Within-stage inhibition	Absent	Present
Feedback inhibition	Absent	Present
Feedback reinforcement	Stage bypassing	Present
Item processing history available at late stages	No	No

a damaged processing stage. For instance, in Chapter 14, we saw that some surface dyslexics who read by a phonologically mediated route seem to access the lexicon after having recognized the sound of a printed word, rather than through direct visual whole-word recognition. In these cases, the whole-word recognition route is thought to be damaged, and the patients bypass this disturbed processing stage by the use of an alternate route, as illustrated in Figure 17-3. This process is not the same as the inhibitory or excitatory feedback used in PDP models. PDP models also differ from serial-processing stage models in that they are explicit about the actual computational mechanisms that underlie the processing of linguistic representations. They make use of only two basic mechanisms – activation and inhibition.

This list of similarities and differences between PDP models and serial-processing stage models is not the only way to look at these different approaches to modeling psycholinguistic functions. Another way is to compare these models with respect to what level of psycholinguistic modeling each focusses on. Marr and Poggio (1976) have suggested that there are three separate levels at which a cognitive process is to be modeled. The highest stage is the so-called "computational" stage. At this stage, the actual representations that are involved in a process are stated. With respect to psycholinguistics, this stage is specified by constructs of linguistic theory. The second stage is the so-called "algorithmic" level. At the algorithmic

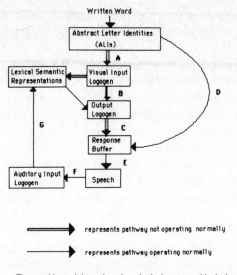

Figure 17-3. A model of lexical access in surface dyslexia, showing bypassing of the whole word recognition route

level, the representations specified at the computational stage are accessed, recognized, and converted from one form to another by processing mechanisms. All of the models that we have been considering in Part III are formulated at the algorithmic theory stage. The final level of the "Marr hierarchy" is the "neural level". At the neural level, the algorithms are actually carried out by real physical elements.

Both PDP models and serial-processing stage models are specifications of the algorithmic level of this hierarchy. Serial-processing stage models are more influenced by computational-level representations, and seek to establish the sequence in which representations specified at the computational level are accessed and converted one into another. PDP models are more detailed specifications of the algorithmic level. They advance hypotheses about particular computational mechanisms: namely, parallel and distributed processing, activation, and inhibition. The two are not incompatible. It is entirely possible for a serial-processing stage model, such as the one represented in Figure 17-1 or 17-3, to be implemented through a number of PDP systems, each of which specifies a set of activations and inhibitions of items at each of the processing stages specified in the model. Proponents of PDP models often represent their models as being no more than a specification of how the algorithms hypothesized in the stage models are to be carried out. They often add that their computational mechanisms have a certain neural plausibility, a claim that we shall return to in Chapters 22 and 23.

It is far too early in the development and investigation of PDP models to know whether this particular form of computation is neurally plausible, psychologically necessary, or psychologically justified; but it is clear that a considerable amount of work in theoretical psycholinguistics is directed towards the statement and evaluation of these models, and that one of the directions that modeling in linguistic aphasiology is taking is the incorporation of PDP models. Though not a logical break with the past, this is yet another step towards increasingly detailed psycholinguistic modeling of aphasic phenomena that distances linguistic aphasiology from clinical work.

Linguistic aphasiology is a very new science, at least in its present form. The methods of study, the reliability of data, the logic of inferences from deficits in single cases to the nature of the normal language-processing system, the question of whether patients can be grouped together when their deficits are grossly similar but differ in detail, the nature of the linguistic theories and models of psycholinguistic processing which are relevant to aphasic data – these are some of the areas in which theory and empirical study are evolving relatively rapidly. The accomplishments of this relatively new science are impressive, but there is a great deal that remains to be clarified both about the particular theories that are being advanced at present, and about the most basic aspects of data gathering and data interpretation in this field. Contemporary linguistic aphasiology represents one domain in which cognitive psychology and experimentally oriented work on brain-damaged subjects are beginning to come together. In principle, brain damage can provide valuable external evidence for models of particular psychological processes. Though any one of the particular analyses and models presented in Part III of this book may prove to be wrong, the general direction of research does appear to be well founded and headed in the right direction at present; and continued work on the problems presented here, and on other aspects of the psychology of language, can confidently be expected to increase our knowledge both of aphasia and of normal language processing.

We have indicated at several points that linguistic aphasiology has distanced itself in significant ways from neurolinguistic theory. This is unquestionably true if we consider the work in the field at present, but it is not true that linguistic aphasiology as it is presently being developed has no implications for neurolinguistic theory. At the very least, linguistic aphasiology serves to define damaged sub-components in the language-processing system in individual patients, and it is the correlation of these damaged sub-components with lesion parameters which is still the fundamental basis of our understanding of how language is processed in the brain. Several researchers have begun to look for the neural correlates of damage to processing components specified in contemporary psycholinguistic models, using psycholinguistic analyses of aphasic breakdown to identify patients of interest. Linguistic aphasiology serves as an important caution to accepting neurolinguistic theories based upon the traditional aphasic syndromes. The detailed characterizations of individual patients that we have reviewed in Chapters 12–16 illustrate that the ten or so classic syndromes cannot capture the full variety of impairments in aphasic patients. The problem of the heterogeneity and polytypicality of the aphasic syndromes which we referred to in Chapter 11 is amply illustrated in Chapters 12–16. It is not clear what correlations between neuropathological features of cerebral lesions and the classical aphasic syndromes tell us about the neural basis for sub-components of the normal language system. Thus, though a great deal of linguistic aphasiology has not yet been applied to the problem of developing neurolinguistic theories, there are important implications of this work for the development of such theories.

In summary, linguistic aphasiology has emerged in the past fifteen years or so as an independent area of scientific inquiry, with a subject matter which is partially unique and partially related to psycholinguistics, cognitive psychology, and linguistic theory. The field also has a special set of methods. These differ from those employed in cognitive psychology, because of the nature of the subject population in whom observations and experiments are undertaken. The field is concerned with many basic issues, such as the reliability of data, the validity of inferences based upon aphasic patients for normal function, and the types of models which should be used to explain patients' and normals' performances. Empirical work, theory construction, and "metatheory" (the development of a theoretical understanding of the methods and logic used in this field) have all developed very quickly in the past fifteen years in linguistic aphasiology. The subjects discussed in Part III of this book are designed to provide the reader with a glimpse of some of this activity, and to relate linguistic aphasiology to the related fields of cognitive psychology, linguistics, psycholinguistics, and neurolinguistics.

SUGGESTIONS FOR FURTHER READING

McClelland, J. L. and Rumelhart, D. E. (1981). An interactive activation model of context effects in letter perception, part 1: An account of basic findings. *Psychological Review* 88, 375–407.

Marr, D. and Poggio, T. (1976). From understanding computation to understanding neural circuitry. *Neurosciences Research Program Bulletin* 15, 470–80.

Rumelhart, D. E. and McClelland, J. L. (1982). An interactive activation model of context effects in letter perception, part 2: The contextual enhancement effect and some tests and extensions of the model. *Psychological Review* 89, 60–94.

Part IV

Contemporary neurolinguistics

18

Cerebral dominance and specialization for language

In Part II, we discussed a number of clinically derived theories of how language is represented and processed in the brain. In Part III, we presented recent studies of the linguistic and psycholinguistic aspects of aphasic disturbances. In the final part of this book, we shall consider a number of recent studies of the neural basis for language. Chapters 20 and 21 review studies based upon new techniques – recording electrical activity in the brain, and stimulating cortical and subcortical areas during neurosurgical operations. In Chapter 23, we shall consider theoretical approaches to modeling neural activity which can be related to language and language breakdown. In this chapter and the next, we shall take up two old themes – lateralization, and localization of language functions – in the light of recent studies.

One of the major neurobiological discoveries of the nineteenth century was that language functions were primarily carried out in one hemisphere of the brain. This feature, known as lateralization of language functions, was first brought to widespread scientific attention by Broca in 1865 (see Chapter 3). Broca recognized that the fact that eight consecutive aphasic patients had lesions in the left hemisphere was unlikely to have occurred by chance, and he therefore hypothesized that the left hemisphere was dominant for language. Broca also recognized that the left hemisphere was responsible for right-handedness, and he postulated that left-hemisphere dominance for language and for manual preference were linked. The connection between the two, according to Broca, was due to the fact that the convolutions in the left hemisphere developed earlier than in the right, a finding which he attributed to Gratiolet. Because Broca thought that left-hemispheric dominance for language and for manual preference were related in this way, he also hypothesized that cerebral dominance for language would be reversed in left-handed individuals.

Broca's 1865 paper therefore stated a number of hypotheses which have remained foci of research regarding the role of each cerebral hemisphere in language. The first hypothesis is that language is primarily the responsibility of one cerebral hemisphere – the left – in the right-handed population.

Second, Broca hypothesized that there were anatomical features of the left hemisphere which were responsible for both right-handedness and the role of the left hemisphere in language. Third, Broca thought that left-handed individuals would be right-hemisphere dominant for language. In addition, Broca hypothesized that early injury to the left hemisphere would shift cerebral dominance from the left to the right hemisphere. Finally, Broca advanced a hypothesis regarding the particular language function which was localized in the left hemisphere: he believed that it was "the faculty for articulate speech". We shall review the results of 120 years of research into these and related hypotheses in this chapter.

Broca (1865) was right with respect to his major hypothesis. In a very large number of adult human beings, one hemisphere – the left – is responsible for a great many, if not all, language functions. The most important evidence supporting this neurobiological discovery are large series of neuropsychological examinations of brain-injured subjects. Such examinations were carried out after both World Wars and more recent wars, as well as in civilian life. The war-related studies took place in most of the European combatant countries, and therefore involve patients who speak a variety of Indo-European languages. The war-related studies generally consist of series of younger patients with head injuries, while the civilian studies largely consist of considerably older patients with strokes and/or brain tumors. Because of the wide range of ages and etiologies which are represented in all of these studies, and the "replications" of these studies by different investigators in different languages, we can be quite sure that the results do not reflect the effect of just one type of brain injury upon patients of a particular age who speak a particular language.

All of these studies show left-hemisphere dominance for language in the right-handed population. Luria (1947) studied sixty-four absolute right-handed patients with left-hemisphere lesions in the language area. Sixty-one had severe forms of aphasia, and three had slight forms of aphasia in the "initial period" following brain injury; forty-eight had severe aphasia, and fourteen had a slight form of aphasia in the "residual period" following brain injury. In another series reporting on brain-injured subjects from World War II, Russell and Espir (1961) stress the difference in the incidence of aphasia following left-hemisphere and right-hemisphere injury in right- and left-handed populations. As compared with the 213/348 instances of aphasia following left-sided wounds in right-handed patients, only 10/276 right-sided injuries caused aphasia in right-handed patients. The difference between the incidence of aphasia following left- and right-hemisphere lesions in the right-handed population is highly significant.

Similar figures apply to stroke and tumor cases. The incidence of aphasia following strokes in the left perisylvian region in right-handed individuals is generally put at above 95 per cent (Lecours *et al.* 1983). Perhaps because it is so well established on the basis of clinical observations that left-sided strokes cause aphasia in right-handed individuals, studies directly comparing the incidence of aphasia following stroke in right- and left-hemisphere injuries in right-handers are hard to come by in the published literature. Hécaen and Albert (1978) cite an incidence of crossed aphasia in right-handed individuals of between 0.4 and 2 per cent according to four different estimations (Hécaen *et al.* 1971: 0.4 per cent; Benson and Geschwind 1971: 1 per cent; Gloning *et al.* 1963: 1 per cent; Zangwill 1967: 2 per cent). In a study limited to stroke patients, Kimura (1983) reports aphasia following left-hemisphere stroke in 95/216 right-handed subjects, and in 3/169 patients following right-hemisphere stroke. These differences in the incidence of aphasia following stroke in the two hemispheres in the right-handed population are also statistically significant.

Similar figures are reported following induced transient anesthetization of a single hemisphere. Wada (1949) first described a procedure whereby a short-acting barbiturate is injected into one carotid artery, thereby temporarily inactivating one hemisphere. Milner and her collaborators (Milner *et al.* 1964; 1966; Milner 1974) have shown that transient aphasic language disturbances occur with injection of barbiturate into the left carotid artery in over 98 per cent of right-handers. Similarly, Penfield and Roberts (1959) demonstrated that stimulation of the left perisylvian cortex during neurosurgical procedures produced speech arrest or aphasic errors in approximately 95 per cent of right-handed cases (see Chapter 21) but in almost no cases when the comparable structures in the right hemisphere were stimulated. Finally, when linguistic stimuli are presented simultaneously to both hemispheres – either auditorily, in the so-called "dichotic listening" task, or visually, through the use of tachistoscopic presentation – a so-called right-ear or right visual field "advantage" for linguistic stimuli occurs in the vast majority of right-handed individuals (Bryden 1982). Though the exact mechanisms responsible for the right-sided advantage are not entirely clear, and may be partly related to the control of attention or to memory factors, the fact that stimuli which occur on the right side are initially transmitted to the left hemisphere has universally been taken as one of the factors which account for the right-sided advantage for linguistic material, thus providing additional support for the role of the left hemisphere in processing language.

Recognition of the existence of cerebral dominance – the fact that one hemisphere is primarily responsible for language – constituted a major discovery regarding the neurological basis for language. A second major finding was that hemispheric specialization and hemispheric dominance for language is not the same in all adult humans. The results that we have discussed above all pertain to right-handed individuals. Broca (1865) hypothesized that left-handed individuals without early brain damage would be the mirror image of right-handed individuals with respect to cerebral dominance, having language represented in the right hemisphere. Studies of left-handed individuals have proven that this hypothesis is wrong, but hemispheric specialization and dominance for language are different in the non-right-handed and the right-handed population.

Goodglass and Quadfasel (1954) studied 123 left-handed patients. Fifty-three of 65 patients with unilateral left-hemisphere lesions had aphasia, and 50/58 with unilateral right-hemisphere lesions had aphasia. Similar figures are found in a report by Hécaen *et al.* (1981) and Bryden *et al.* (1983). In their study, 66/87 (75.9 per cent) of left-handed patients with left-sided lesions became aphasic, and 17/53 (32.1 per cent) of left-handed patients with right-sided lesions became aphasic. As the reader will notice, in both these series, if we add the percentage of aphasic cases following left-hemisphere lesions to that following right-hemisphere lesions in left-handers, we arrive at a figure greater than 100 per cent. There is only one way to explain this: in some left-handed individuals, language must be represented in both hemispheres of the brain, and a lesion in either hemisphere must cause an aphasia. These data from stroke and tumor cases therefore indicate that language is organized differently in the cerebral hemispheres of left-handers and right-handers. In the left-hander, speech and language functions are carried out in both hemispheres far more frequently than in the right-handed population.

There is some conflicting evidence regarding which hemisphere is responsible for language when language functions are carried out by one hemisphere in a left-handed individual. Penfield and Roberts (1959) found that the incidence of speech arrest and aphasic errors following electrical stimulation of the perisylvian cortex in either hemisphere was about the same in left-handers and in right-handers. They concluded that the left hemisphere is as likely to be dominant for language in left-handers as in right-handers. However, Penfield and Roberts' conclusion may reflect the use of the electrical stimulation technique, which only interferes with the functions of a very small area of cortex during a very brief time period (see Chapter 21). Studies of patients with larger and more permanent lesions tend to agree with the Goodglass and Quadfasel data that lesions to the right hemisphere frequently produce aphasia in left-handed individuals. Russell and Espir (1961) found that aphasia followed left-hemisphere damage in 10/28 and right-hemisphere damage in 4/30 left-handed patients. Luria (1947) found similar percentages. Using the Wada carotid amytal injection technique, Milner (1974) found that 69 per cent of seventy-four left-handed patients (none of whom had had a left-hemisphere lesion in childhood) showed unilateral left-cerebral dominance for language. In this population, 13 per cent of the patients showed bilateral language representation, and 18 per cent were right-hemisphere dominant for language.

All these results indicate that cerebral dominance for language is not the same in different sub-groups of the adult human population. Right-handers overwhelmingly develop aphasia following left-hemisphere lesions and not right-hemisphere lesions; left-handers tend to show aphasia after left-hemisphere lesions, but a significant number of left-handers develop aphasia after right-hemisphere lesions or after lesions to either hemisphere. Manual preference, therefore, is one way of beginning to identify sub-groups of adults which differ with respect to the lateralization of language functioning. However, since a significant number of left-handed individuals are left-hemisphere dominant for language, and since there are rare cases of crossed dextral aphasia, handedness alone is not an adequate guide to establishing which hemisphere is dominant for language.

The picture is yet more complicated. Not only do some left-handers have right-hemisphere dominance or bilateral hemisphere participation in language, but different groups of right-handers and left-handers seem to have different patterns of hemisphere dominance for language. Again, the most important clue as to the different sub-groups of right-handers and left-handers is related to handedness – not the individual's handedness, but the presence of left-handers in his family.

There are two sorts of evidence for increased right-hemisphere participation in language in right-handers with left-handed family members. The first observation is that the aphasias that occur after left-hemisphere lesions in these patients are less severe than the aphasias that occur after left-hemisphere damage in "pure" right-handers. The second observation is that aphasia following left-hemisphere damage in these patients is not as long-lasting as aphasia following left-hemisphere damage in right-handers without left-handed family members (Luria 1947). There is no evidence that indicates that right-handed individuals with left-handed family members are more likely to have right-hemisphere dominance for language than right-handers without familial sinistrality (Bryden *et al.* 1983, table 3). For instance, the incidence of crossed aphasia – aphasia following right-hemisphere lesions in a right-hander – is no higher in right-handed patients with left-handed family members than in right-handed patients from purely right-handed families. These observations are consistent with the idea that the right hemisphere of right-handed individuals with left-handed family members is capable of taking over some language functions after left-hemisphere damage (thus accounting for the mild nature and the short duration of aphasia following left-hemisphere damage in this population) but is not necessary for language functioning (since lesions in the right hemisphere do not cause aphasia). The capacity of the right hemisphere to take over language in this population is greater than that in the right-handed population without left-handed family members, but does not actually lead to a shift in cerebral dominance for language. This situation therefore differs from that in both the "pure" right-handed and the left-handed population.

In the left-handed population, the picture is somewhat different but has some similarities. It appears that left-handers from left-handed families are more likely to have right-hemisphere dominance for language, or bilateral language representation, than left-handers from right-handed families (Bryden *et al*. 1983, table 3). Left-handers are all more likely to have right-hemisphere dominance or bilateral representation for language than right-handers, whether or not they come from left-handed families. However, the left-hander from a right-handed family seems to be more likely to resemble a right-handed individual than a left-hander from a left-handed family.

Another factor affecting hemispheric involvement in and dominance for language is the degree of right- or left-handedness in an individual. Extensive studies on manual preference (Hécaen and Ajuriaguerra 1963; Subirana 1964; Luria 1947) have investigated the nature of manual preference in great detail. Though many so-called "right-handers" are strongly right-handed, there are a considerable number of people who are clearly right-handed but who use the left hand for one or more activities on a regular basis. These patients, who are "relatively right-handed", do not seem to have the same degree of left-hemisphere dominance for languages as "pure" right-handers. Luria (1947) found that only 2/64 pure right-handed patients with aphasia following left-hemisphere brain injuries recovered, but 29/56 "relatively right-handed" patients recovered from their aphasia following left-hemisphere damage. Subirana (1964) found similar differences between the duration of aphasia following left-hemisphere injuries in "pure" and "relative" right-handers. The degree of right-handedness may interact with the presence of left-handers in a person's family to determine the likelihood of left-hemisphere, right-hemisphere, or bilateral representation of language (Subirana 1969). It has so far proven impossible to acquire comparable statistics regarding aphasia following left- and right-hemisphere damage in left-handers as a function of the degree of their left-handedness, due to the relative rarity of absolute left-handed individuals.

A fourth factor which may influence the pattern of cerebral localization for language is an individual's sex. Several studies (McGlone 1977; Bryden *et al.* 1983) suggest that language may be more bilaterally represented in the brains of right-handed women than men. McGlone (1978) found a significant depression of verbal IQ scores after left-hemisphere lesions in men, but not in women. Bryden *et al.* (1983) estimate that only about 80 per cent of right-handed women are left-hemisphere dominant for language, on the basis of a number of statistical assumptions and mathematical extrapolations from data reported by Hécaen *et al.* (1981). However, these results are extremely tenuous. In an extensive review of the subject of sex differences in cerebral dominance, covering both language and non-verbal function, McGlone (1980) argued that there are "enough data . . . to take seriously the notion of sexual variation in brain asymmetry" (227). However, there are many studies reported by McGlone in which different degrees of cerebral dominance for language functions in men and women are reported but the differences are not large enough to be statistically reliable. There are also several studies (Kimura 1983) which do not show different patterns of cerebral dominance for language in men and women. Whether there are truly differences in the degree of cerebral dominance for language in right-handed men and women remains an open question. The differences between men and women are small, if they exist at all, and they seem to be overshadowed by the differences between left- and right-handers. Among left-handers, women are fairly similar to men, according to the analysis of Bryden *et al.* (1983).

It thus appears that the degree of left-hemisphere dominance for language varies in different sub-groups of the adult human population. Handedness and the presence of left-handers in a person's family are a basis upon which to classify an individual into a group which is likely to have left-hemisphere dominance, or right-hemisphere dominance, or to have both hemispheres active in language functions. However, classifying an individual on the basis of these factors (and perhaps by sex) is only a rough guide to the actual pattern of hemispheric involvement in language functions in that individual. There are occasional right-handers who have crossed dextral aphasia, and many left-handers, even with left-handed family members, are left-hemisphere dominant for language. This implies that the pattern of hemispheric involvement in language functions is partially independent of manual preference, although the two are statistically related. The fact that they are frequently separable in left-handers (and occasionally separated in right-handers) indicates that, contrary to Broca's original hypothesis, the neural mechanisms which produce hemispheric dominance for language must be at least partially different from the neural mechanisms which produce manual preference.

The question of differential lateralization of language and language-processing components as a function of handedness, sex, and other factors, is part of a larger set of questions regarding the biological basis for language. A narrow approach to neurolinguistics would only be interested in the neurological aspects of this problem, such as what aspects of the language-processing system are located in which hemisphere. The larger *neurobiological* question is what determines differential lateralization. What we have seen so far is that there are statistically significant trends towards different degrees of lateralization of language function in adult humans as a function of handedness, degree of handedness, consistency of familial handedness, and possibly sex. One striking feature of these factors is that they are all totally determined by intrinsic organic factors. Handedness can be changed through practice, but it is an individual's original handedness, not the manual preference derived through practice, which affects the probability of left- or right-hemisphere participation in language. As far as is known, original handedness is largely determined through genetic mechanisms. Similarly, an individual's sex is determined by his or her genetic endowment, which codes for the development of organs that secrete male and female sex hormones. So far, we have not indicated that there are any environmental factors which affect the lateralization of language. This, however, is not entirely the case. It is well known, as Broca hypothesized, that early damage to the left hemisphere results in a shift of language functions to the right hemisphere.

Lenneberg (1967) reviewed the experience at the Boston Children's Hospital with children who had had early brain damage to the left hemisphere. Regardless of handedness, he found that left-hemisphere injuries that occurred before the child learned to speak were not associated with permanent aphasia. Similarly, evidence from Wada testing (Milner *et al.* 1964; Milner 1974) indicates that neonatal damage to the left hemisphere is associated with right-hemisphere-based language functions. Lenneberg concluded that the right hemisphere could take over functions that were normally accomplished by the left hemisphere when the left hemisphere was damaged, provided the damage occurred prior to approximately age two or three. If the damage occurred between this age and puberty, aphasia occurred but was transient, and recovery was usually excellent. Lenneberg suggested that there was a "critical period" during which language was acquired by the left hemisphere – approximately between age two and puberty – before which the right hemisphere could assume language functions, and following which the right hemisphere could not easily take over language functions. These dates regarding the "critical period" have been the subject of considerable discussion. Based on data in Basser's (1962) study of childhood aphasia and Kimura's (1963) studies of dichotic listening,

Krashen (1973) argued that the critical period seems to end much earlier than Lenneberg suggested – at approximately five years of age. Whatever the upper bound on the age beyond which changes in lateralization can no longer occur, the fact that early damage to the left hemisphere does often shift language into the right hemisphere indicates that environmental factors can affect cerebral dominance. However, the environmental factors involved are organic: they consist of physical damage to the left hemisphere of the brain.

Another type of environmental factor that might affect hemispheric specialization would be psychological. Factors such as what language a person learns, whether he learns more than one language, and whether he learns to use written language through reading and writing, are ones which do not affect the brain directly through an obvious organic process. Whether these inorganic, psychological, environmental factors affect the degree or nature of lateralization for language is unclear. To date, there are very few studies of this question. The studies that do exist seem to indicate that psychological factors do not affect lateralization of language-processing components. Thus, the incidence of aphasia following left-hemisphere damage is as high in bilinguals as in monolinguals with similar handedness profiles (Paradis 1977). There are a considerable number of studies that suggest that the second language of a bilingual (or later languages in polyglots) may be more right-hemisphere-based than the first language, especially during the early stages of language learning (Albert and Obler 1978; Obler 1984), but there is no strong evidence that the first language of bilingual individuals and polyglots is lateralized differently by comparison with monolinguals. Similarly, there is no strong evidence that languages with different syntactic structures or phonological structures are differentially lateralized.

There is some discrepancy in the results of studies regarding literacy. Cameron *et al.* (1977) found that the incidence of aphasia differed in literate and illiterate right-handers with left-hemisphere lesions: 78 per cent of the literate subjects, 64 per cent of the semi-literate subjects, and only 36 per cent of the illiterate subjects developed aphasia following left-hemisphere lesions. The authors concluded that cerebral dominance for language differed as a function of having acquired the ability to read. However, Damasio *et al.* (1976) found that 114/208 literate subjects and 21/38 illiterate subjects developed aphasia following unilateral cerebral lesions. Only one of the twenty-one illiterate subjects who developed an aphasia had a right-hemisphere lesion, an incidence of aphasia following right-hemisphere damage which did not differ from that which is observed in literate subjects. A number of dichotic listening tests have also been performed on literate and illiterate groups. Tsavaras *et al*. (1981) showed a right-ear advantage for linguistic stimuli in a group of sixty-one illiterates which was actually greater than that in fifty-one literate subjects. Tsavaras *et al*. also indicated that this right-ear superiority was not due to a different strategy of deployment of subjects' attention, since it continued to be present when the subjects only had to report a stimulus presented to a single ear. In a recent, as yet unpublished study, Lecours and Mehler (1985) report results which by and large indicate that aphasic impairments are as likely to follow left-hemisphere lesions in illiterates as in literate individuals.

The conclusion to be drawn from these studies is that environmental factors which do not directly affect the brain – the nature of the representations in a language, whether or not an individual has mastered the written form of a language, and whether or not a person has learned a second or subsequent language – do not to any important extent influence the lateralization of language-processing components for a person's first language. As far as we know, the extent and nature of lateralization for language are entirely determined by organic factors and, in the absence of early cerebral disease, entirely determined by factors which are ultimately genetic in nature. We know very little about the genetic structures that determine language lateralization, but recent studies have begun to reveal neuroanatomical features which seem to be related to this phenomenon. We shall return to the neural basis of hemispheric specialization and cerebral dominance after considering one more psychological issue regarding cerebral specialization for language.

So far, we have been considering the linguistic aspect of the question of cerebral dominance in a very superficial fashion, speaking of "speech" and "language" functions as undifferentiated functions which are primarily exercised by one or another hemisphere. However, some of what we have said about the nature of aphasia in subjects other than "pure" right-handers should make us realize that the linguistic and psycholinguistic aspects of hemispheric specialization and cerebral dominance cannot be ignored. We noted that aphasias were not as severe or as long-lasting in right-handed individuals with familial sinistrality as in "pure" right-handed patients following left-hemisphere injuries (Luria 1947). It is very hard to know just what this observation implies about the cerebral organization of language in these right-handers with familial sinistrality. One possibility is that undamaged areas of the left hemisphere happen to be responsible for more aspects of language processing in these patients than in "pure" right-handers. However, another possibility, which has been widely accepted, is that some aspects of language processing are carried out in the right hemisphere of these patients. Since these patients do become aphasic after left-hemisphere lesions, albeit mildly so, some aspects of language processing must also be carried out in the left hemisphere. An obvious question is: what aspects of language processing are damaged in these patients, and what aspects retained? If we could answer this question, we could begin to develop a theory of how components of the language-processing system are distributed between the two hemispheres in these patients. Exactly the same considerations arise when we consider the aphasias that occur following unilateral brain damage in left-handers. Though the studies cited above indicate that aphasia follows either left- or right-sided lesions in left-handed individuals, it is also clear that the aphasias that follow unilateral lesions in left-handers are milder and shorter-lasting than those which occur in right-handers. Close analysis of the patterns of deficit and of the retained linguistic capacities in these patients would reveal which language-processing components can be disrupted following unilateral lesions. Coupled with information about where the remaining language functions are carried out, this would reveal the distribution of language-processing components between the hemispheres in the left-handed population.

Unfortunately, aside from the observation that aphasias are less severe and shorter-lasting in left-handers and in right-handers with left-handed family members than in "pure" right-handers without familial sinistrality, there are no systematic surveys of the exact nature of language disturbances found after unilateral brain injury in these different populations. Some authors have noted peculiarities of the aphasias that occur in the not strictly right-handed population. Lecours *et al.* (1983) claim that "unexpected symptom constellations (that is, unclassifiable clinical forms) and intriguing dissociations . . . are more frequently observed in non-right-handers than in right-handers" (277). They cite a case of their own, that of a twenty-five-year-old ambidextrous female, who had extremely reduced oral language and great difficulty with comprehension of spoken language, but was able to write and to understand written language quite well following an extensive left-hemisphere stroke. They suggest that "this patient's residual behaviors may constitute evidence of right-hemisphere participation in the control of certain aspects of her linguistic functioning" (276). Further detailed cases of this sort are available in many monographs, but so far no one has systematically reviewed the available cases to see just what aspects of language functioning are preserved and disturbed following unilateral brain injury in these cases. The symptomatology in crossed dextral aphasia also seems to be unusual. Hécaen and Albert (1978) indicate that patients with crossed dextral aphasia cannot be easily classified into one of the traditional clinical aphasic syndromes. Given the problems in discerning the language-processing deficits in a patient on a basis of his falling into one of the traditional syndromes (see Chapter 11), it is not clear how much further ahead we would be in knowing what aspects of the language-processing system can be located in one or another hemisphere simply on the basis of a patient's clinical classification. However, the fact that non-right-handers and right-handers with right-hemisphere dominance for language have unusual aphasic symptoms from the point of view of classical aphasiology does suggest that, in these patients, components of the language-processing system which are usually all located together in the left hemisphere of a right-handed individual can be partitioned separately across the hemispheres.

Some indication of the inadequacy of present data regarding the differential lateralization of different language functions can be seen if we review the studies on sex differences in lateralization for language. McGlone (1980) cited studies by Lansdale (1961) which suggest that proverb interpretation and word associations are impaired following temporal-lobe resections on the left in men to a greater extent than in women, but also indicating that many other tests – multiple-choice vocabulary tests, verbal reasoning, spelling, clerical speed, and others – do not show sex-by-laterality interactions. Though this pattern is not very specific, it suggested to McGlone that the relevant factor is whether overt speech production is required: in studies in which overt speech is required, men showed greater deficits following left-hemisphere damage than did women, but on tests requiring language or verbal functions which do not require overt speech production, this is not the case. The implication is that it is the capacity for speech which is more likely to be left-hemisphere-based in men than in women. On the other hand, in the same article, McGlone (1980) cites her own results (McGlone 1977) to demonstrate that it is the verbal IQ score which may be somewhat lower in men than in women following left-hemisphere damage (when patients with aphasia are removed from the patient population under consideration). Thus, it is not clear whether differential lateralization involves the speech production mechanism, intellectual functions which involve language and verbal capacities, or both (if it is even present). More detailed studies are needed if we are to use data from differential lateralization of language functions in the two sexes as the basis for a theory of which language functions can be individually lateralized in individual subjects.

These results – especially those coming from crossed dextral aphasics and aphasia in non-right-handers – do indicate that different components of a language-processing system can be separated from the bulk of components of this system and lateralized in one or another hemisphere. The extent of such possible separations is not known on the basis of present studies, because present studies have not attempted to analyze the language deficits in these cases in detailed psycholinguistic terms. In fact, we are not even sure that what is separately lateralized are individual components of the language-processing system. It is possible that verbal reasoning abilities, aspects of "verbal memory" systems, and other capacities which make use of the language system but which are not part of the processing system related to the recovery and assignment of the literal meaning of words and sentences, are the psychological functions which are separately lateralized, at least in some cases. However, given the fact that there are mild aphasias following unilateral brain damage in many non-right-handed patients, it is a reasonable hypothesis that components of the "core" language-processing system can be separately lateralized in at least the non-right-handed population. This hypothesis assumes that mild aphasias arise because of the disturbance of a limited number of components of the language-processing system, which seems to be a reasonable assumption.

One population in which we can advance specific hypotheses regarding hemispheric specialization for language is the strongly right-handed population without familial sinistrality. Because we know that there are an enormous number of different patterns of aphasia in these right-handed individuals – from mild aphasic deficits that seem to involve a very small part of the language system to devastating language and communication deficits – our initial hypothesis regarding what can be lateralized on the left must be that virtually any aspect of the language system can be carried out by the left hemisphere in a right-hander. Not only can all parts of the psychological processes that are responsible for the processing of individual words and sentences be subject to disruption following left-hemisphere damage, but psychological functions which rely upon the language system – verbal memory systems, verbal reasoning systems, etc. – can also be disrupted following left-hemisphere lesions in right-handers. Since a severe enough disturbance of the system responsible for the recovery of words and sentences would necessarily affect the ability of a person to make use of language in memory or reasoning tasks, it is possible that disturbances of verbal memory or verbal reasoning, or impairments in "verbal intelligence" as measured on standard intelligence tests, which arise following left-hemisphere damage, are frequently secondary to an aphasia. However, there are reports in the literature (Kimura 1983; McGlone 1977) which indicate that there are patients with left-hemisphere lesions with decreased verbal intelligence, as measured on standard IQ tests, who do not have aphasia. Therefore, it seems that the left hemisphere can be the structure responsible for these language-related/language-dependent intellectual processes, as well as the neural structure responsible for the more narrow, psycholinguistic aspects of language processing in right-handers.

Recently, several studies of language deficits following right-hemisphere damage in right-handed adults have been published. These studies are of special importance, because any permanent deficits found after right-hemisphere disease in right-handed individuals indicate what aspects of language processing can be carried out by the right hemisphere in right-handers. To date there are three types of disturbances which have been documented following right-hemisphere damage in right-handed individuals.

The first disturbance is a particular type of abnormality of speech, which affects the intonation contour of utterances. Studies by Ross and Mesulam (1979) have documented abnormal intonation contours in right-hemisphere patients. On the receptive side, Heilman and his colleagues (Heilman *et al.* 1975; Tucker *et al.* 1977) have shown that patients with right-hemisphere damage have great difficulty recognizing the emotional tone of voice of an utterance. It therefore appears that a particular form of disturbance of intonational contour does occur with right-hemisphere damage in right-handed patients, and can be a long-lasting and possibly permanent deficit. The deficit does not seem to be one that is "narrowly" linguistic. It does not affect patients' abilities to understand the role that sentential stress plays in establishing new and old information, or in determining what is known as the "illocutionary force" of an utterance – whether or not the utterance is a question, a statement, etc. It is a disturbance which affects patients' abilities to express emotional states, such as surprise, happiness, anger, etc., and to recognize these states through the voice patterns of others. Whether there are other disturbances related to intonational contours that occur in right-hemisphere patients is, at present, not known.

The second disturbance is related to a certain type of logical inferencing. Gardner and his colleagues (Gardner *et al.* 1983), have found that right-hemisphere-damaged patients have difficulty in understanding jokes. They are unable to pick the ending of a story which is humorous; instead, they often pick an ending which does not make sense but which is not particularly funny. What they seem to fail to do is to realize that a joke is a story that has a particular logical structure that leads the listener to expect a particular statement, and then a "punch-line" that provides a conclusion which the reader has not been conditioned to expect but which is anomalous or absurd in particular ways. A number of other studies have also found disturbances at the level of "discourse" – that level of structure which is related to drawing inferences and reasoning about groups of sentences. It has frequently been noticed that right-hemisphere patients seem to "miss the point" of a story, or are able to give the general gist of a conversation or something that they read but not supply any of the details, or seem unable to understand the relationship between the details and the general point of a story (Locke *et al.* 1973). Joanette *et al.* (1984) have found that the narratives of right-hemisphere-damaged patients have many abnormal features when analyzed according to the criteria for coherent and cohesive discourse developed by Kintsch and his colleagues. This area – the ability to extract the logic and to structure the main ideas and supporting details of discourse – seems to be a functional sphere which is permanently damaged in many right-handed patients with right-hemisphere lesions.

A third group of studies that investigate deficits following right-hemisphere lesions in right-handed adults shows a very wide variety of disturbances of language, but shows that each of these disturbances occurs only to a very mild degree. Perhaps the largest such study is by Joanette and his colleagues (Joanette *et al.* 1983). These investigators studied forty-two right-handed individuals with unilateral right-sided strokes, using a standard French aphasia battery, somewhat similar to the Boston Diagnostic Aphasia Battery (Goodglass and Kaplan 1972). The authors found that thirty-three patients had statistically discernible language deficits. These language abnormalities were similar in nature to classic aphasic symptoms. They consisted of phonemic paraphasias, disturbances similar to agrammatism and paragrammatism, repetition and reading disturbances, etc. However, these disturbances were unlike the vast majority of aphasic disturbances in that they were excessively mild. This study, therefore, clearly established that many right-handed patients with right-hemisphere lesions do have language disturbances of a sort seen in aphasia, but ones which are very minor in degree.

What can be concluded about the role of the right hemisphere in psycholinguistic processes, and those intellectual processes which use the language code, on the basis of these observations in right-hemisphere-damaged right-handed patients? There are two features of the deficits seen in these patients which are suggestive. The first is that the severe disturbances seen after these lesions all affect aspects of language use which are not part of what we may consider to be "core" language functioning. By "core" language functioning, we mean those aspects of psycholinguistic processes which are involved in the production and recognition of the form and literal meaning of words and sentences. As we noted in Chapters 10 and 17, traditional clinical aphasiology as well as contemporary linguistic aphasiology sets aside these areas of psychological functioning related to language as the area of psychological function relevant to aphasiology and neurolinguistics. Emotional aspects of prosody and inferencing are not part of these "core" psycholinguistic processes. One conclusion that the data suggest is that several of these non-core psycholinguistic processes are usually carried out in the right hemisphere, even in right-handed individuals.

The second observation is that, when core psycholinguistic processes are affected after right-hemisphere damage in the right-handed subjects, they are only mildly disturbed. How might this happen? One possibility is that the right hemisphere serves as an area in which certain psycholinguistic computations can take place; on a computer analogy, we might think of it as some additional part of a work-space. If this is correct, the right hemisphere work-space may be utilized when computations become particularly complex, or when the left hemisphere is using some of its work-space for other computations. If this is the case, we might expect a fair degree of variability in performance among patients, and from item to item in a single patient, after right-hemisphere damage, since the right-hemisphere work-space would be used as needed. This account still maintains a quite strong notion of hemisphere specialization and dominance for language: the left hemisphere is the permanent repository of linguistic representations, and the preferred site for the computations that arise in core psycholinguistic processes related to those representations. There are other possibilities as well. One is that the right hemisphere is involved in focussing attention on a microsecond-by-microsecond basis, and that disturbances in the unconscious deployment of attentional processes affect a person's ability to handle language normally, leading to more errors than occur in normals. More work is needed by way of description of the exact nature of the abnormalities found in right-hemisphere-damaged right-handers to choose between these, and other, theories of the role of the right hemisphere in core psycholinguistic processes. Currently available data is compatible with a strong view of hemispheric specialization and left-hemisphere dominance for core psycholinguistic processing in right-handed adults.

We must make a clear distinction between those language processes (whether related to core psycholinguistic functions or the more general language-related psychological functions we have been considering at various points in this chapter) which *are* carried out routinely in the right hemisphere of right-handers, and those language functions which *can* be carried out in the right hemisphere of right-handers. One of the most exciting developments in the last fifteen years in neurolinguistics has been the intensive study of patients who have had surgery cutting the corpus callosum, the major white-matter fiber tract connecting the two cerebral hemispheres. This surgery is done on rare occasions for the relief of epileptic conditions which are not responsive to medication. Many discoveries regarding the role of the right hemisphere in a large number of psychological spheres, including the possible maintenance of a separate consciousness, have been made. In fact, the only Nobel Prize ever given in neuropsychology was awarded to Roger Sperry for his pioneering work in animals and man regarding the effects of this operation. The study of patients who have undergone this operation has been a major source of data regarding what the right hemisphere can do when it is isolated from the left.

Gazzaniga (1983) has reviewed the studies demonstrating right-hemisphere language following section of the corpus callosum. He emphasized that only about 10 per cent (five patients out of approximately fifty who have undergone this operation) have right-hemisphere language. In these five patients, the degree and type of right-hemisphere language functions vary considerably. Two cases (PS and VP) developed the capacity to generate speech from the right hemisphere. These patients can name objects presented in the left visual half-field, but cannot compare objects across the visual fields, indicating that naming is originating in the right hemisphere. The remaining three patients with right-hemisphere language cannot use the right hemisphere to initiate speech. However, they are all capable of matching pictures to words, and can extract considerable semantic information from both pictures and words presented to the right hemisphere. They can recognize synonyms and functional associates, as well as determine superordinate and subordinate class membership. They can match action pictures to verbs as easily as pictures of objects to nouns, although three of them cannot carry out commands presented to the right hemisphere. PS and VP, the patients who developed speech in the right hemisphere, also showed the ability to understand syntactic constructions as tested with passive sentences or parts of the Token Test.

The exact extent of language capacity in the right hemisphere of these patients is not yet known, and is a subject of considerable controversy. Zaidel (1978a; 1978b) has argued that the two split-brain patients with right-hemisphere language that he has studied were unable to perform rhyming or phoneme discrimination tasks, and he therefore suggested that the right hemisphere was incapable of representing or accessing segmental phonology. Gazzaniga (1983) has subsequently reported other split-brain patients who can do these tasks. Zaidel (1978a) also suggested that visual language was better understood than auditory language by the right hemisphere, a claim equally disputed by Gazzaniga. Despite these differences, investigators who have studied the split-brain cases do agree that the right hemisphere is capable of processing at least some aspects of language following surgical section of the corpus callosum.

A very considerable literature has been directed towards investigation of the right hemisphere's contribution to language processing in normal subjects. This literature makes use of tachistoscopic visual presentation and dichotic listening techniques, which allow for simultaneous presentation of visual or auditory stimuli in both visual half-fields or to both ears. As we indicated above, there is usually a right-sided advantage for linguistic material in both tachistoscopic and dichotic listening tasks, and this advantage has been taken as evidence that the left hemisphere customarily processes linguistic stimuli. However, the extent of this advantage varies, and differences in the extent to which there is right-sided advantage for language material have been considered to reflect the participation of the right hemisphere in language functions. An evaluation of these claims is far beyond the scope of this volume. What makes these claims so difficult to evaluate is that factors other than the language-processing functions of the two hemispheres are also a determinant of the right- or left-sided advantage in these tasks. These factors include how the subject employs his attention, whether the task involves verbal memory as well as other language processing, whether the subject makes a verbal or a manual response, and whether a manual response is made by the right hand or the left hand. The interested reader is referred to Bryden (1982) for a review of many of these issues. A few studies have used these techniques in brain-damaged subjects. For instance, Saffran and her colleagues (Saffran *et al.* 1980*a*) investigated the hypothesis advanced by Coltheart (1980) that the semantic paralexias made by deep dyslexics reflected a right-hemisphere-based reading mechanism, using tachistoscopic half-field presentation of written words to deep dyslexic subjects. However, to date, the use of these interesting but technically difficult experimental techniques to investigate the hemisphere which is responsible for residual language following a unilateral injury has been quite limited.

In all, both the split-brain studies and the half-field tachistoscopic and dichotic listening studies do support the view that the right hemisphere is capable of some language functioning even in some strongly right-handed individuals. As indicated above, we must be careful to distinguish between what the right hemisphere can do and what it actually does. An argument that it does not exercise many language functions, whether or not it is capable of exercising these functions, has been made by Kinsbourne (1978). Kinsbourne bases his argument on the fact that there are many severely aphasic patients with unilateral left-hemisphere injuries, in both right- and left-handed individuals. If the right hemisphere can do all the things that some of the studies of split-brain patients suggest it can, how can these aphasic patients suffer such severe disturbances? One possibility suggested by Kinsbourne, is that the left hemisphere is the preferred site for language processing, even when it is damaged and language processing is inefficient. According to this view, the left hemisphere is somehow activated upon the presentation of linguistic stimuli or in accomplishing a task which requires language output, and it inhibits the functioning of the right hemisphere. This inhibitory process occurs even when the left hemisphere is inefficient and damaged, and when the organism as a whole might be better off if the right hemisphere were free to exercise its language abilities.

To this point, we have been making the assumption that the linguistic capacities of the left hemisphere are exactly that – linguistic capacities. We have tried to narrow them down to what we have called core psycholinguistic functions or processes. We should briefly note that some researchers claim that the specialization of the left hemisphere is not for language at all, but for some other psychological ability. The two leading candidates for what the left hemisphere might be specialized for, if it is not specialized for language, are: (1) that it is specialized for some aspects of the planning of motor sequences (Kimura 1976); and (2) that it is specialized for a certain type of thinking or cognitive processing known as "analytic" processing, as opposed to "holistic" or "gestalt" processing (Bradshaw and Nettleton 1981). Both of these ideas are problematic, however. It is likely that some aspects of speech make use of motor planning capacities which are also used in other tasks; but many aspects of the core psycholinguistic processes we have discussed in Part III are computations which take place upon abstract linguistic elements and do not involve sequences of motor acts at all. We may think of them as "analytic" processes, but it is far from clear what calling them "analytic" tells us, because this term has not been defined. These views are reminiscent of the attempts to derive language processes from motor (and sensory) functions, or from global psychological capacities, which we reviewed in Chapters 8 and 9. As we have seen in Part III, far more detailed "domain-specific" representations and processes (Fodor 1982) need to be, and have been, developed to account for language functions.

Leaving psychological issues aside for the moment, let us return to studies of the organic basis for hemispheric dominance. Recent observations have led to a greater understanding of these factors. Studies have shown that the cerebral hemispheres are not symmetrical, but rather that there are import-ant, grossly discernible differences in the size of areas of the brain from side to side. Many of these differences are situated in areas serving language, and may underlie differential hemispheric participation in language.

The first modern study demonstrating these asymmetries was reported by Geschwind and Levitsky (1968). These investigators sectioned the brain in a non-standard manner, passing the section in the plane of the sylvian fissure posteriorly to the occipital lobes. This cut showed the superior temporal gyrus clearly, and revealed the "planum temporale", a structure extending from Heschl's gyrus to the intersection of the temporal lobe with the sylvian sulcus, and continuing posteriorly along that sulcus until its end. This structure is illustrated in Figure 18-1. When the brain is cut this way, it is clear that the planum temporale differs from side to side. In 100 adult brains, Geschwind and Levitsky found that the left side sloped backwards more sharply in fifty-seven, the right side more sharply in eighteen, and twenty-five were identical. A sharper anterior slope was found on the left in 40 per cent of cases and on the right in 24 per cent of cases. The planum temporale

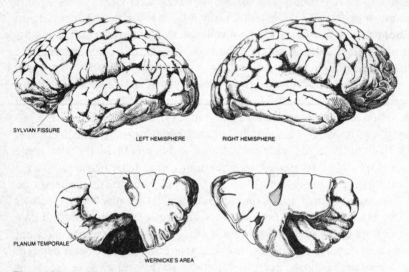

SYLVIAN FISSURE

LEFT HEMISPHERE   RIGHT HEMISPHERE

PLANUM TEMPORALE

WERNICKE'S AREA

Figure 18-1. An illustration of the planum temporale demonstrating its asymmetry in the two hemispheres
(*Source:* Geschwind 1979: 115)

was larger on the left in 65 per cent of cases and larger on the right in 11 per cent. The average length of the planum temporale was 3.6 ± 1.0 cm. on the left and 2.7 ± 1.2 cm. on the right. This work has since been extended by other investigators. It is now clear that there are other differences between hemispheres, as well as those related to these measurements of the planum temporale.

An important discovery is that these asymmetries affect well-defined areas of the brain. One way to define a brain area is through the examination of the cells in it. This feature of the brain is known as "cytoarchitectonic structure", and has been used by many researchers to define brain areas. It is now clear that the cytoarchitectonic areas differ in size from side to side. This proves that the asymmetries are not due simply to the nature of the folding of areas of the brain, but reflect true differences in size of microscopically defined brain areas. Galaburda and his colleagues (1978) have reported that one such area (TpT) in the temporo-parietal association cortex can be up to seven times larger on the left than on the right.

Asymmetries are demonstrable through radiological study as well as in post mortem examinations. In an angiographic study, LeMay and Culebras (1972) have shown that the sylvian fissure is usually longer and more horizontal on the left than on the right in adults and fetal brains. Right-handed subjects show a higher right sylvian point in 65 per cent of cases and left-handed subjects show a higher right sylvian point in 20 per cent of cases. The reverse asymmetry is found in 8 per cent of right-handers and 10 per cent of left-handers, with an equal height of the sylvian point in about 25 per cent of right-handers and 70 per cent of left-handers. Geschwind (1984) has interpreted this finding as indicating that the inferior parietal lobe is larger on the left than on the right. He argues that the larger inferior parietal lobe pushes the sylvian fissure down and straightens it out on the left.

Many other asymmetries have been noted in computed tomography (CT) studies. There is a wider left occipital lobe and a wider right frontal lobe in these studies. The occipital horn of the lateral ventricle (the fluid-filled cavity in the brain) has been shown to be longer on the left than on the right in a majority of cases, with the reverse asymmetry found in only 10 per cent of normal subjects. The asymmetry of frontal and occipital lobes causes asymmetries in skull x-rays corresponding to the underlying growth of the brain. Larger lobes produce indentations of the skull known as " ptalias" which parallel the brain asymmetries (as the phrenologists claimed – see Chapter 3).

These asymmetries differ as a function of handedness. Thus, the hemispheric asymmetries seen in CT scans indicate that there is a wider right frontal lobe in 70 per cent of right-handed individuals, but only in 40 per cent of left-handed individuals; similarly the left frontal lobe is wider in approximately 10 per cent of right-handers and 20 per cent of left-handers. (The remaining cases are equal in width.) Similarly, the occipital lobe is wider on the left in 64 per cent of right-handers but only in 10 per cent of left-handers, with a reversed asymmetry in 16 per cent of right-handers and 15 per cent of left-handers. These asymmetries indicate differences in the size of these areas in right- and left-handers.

These asymmetries are found in the skulls of the earliest hominids on record. LeMay and her colleagues (LeMay and Geschwind 1978) have observed asymmetries in the impressions of sylvian fissures in the skulls of Neanderthal man and Peking man. The Neanderthal skull shows a shortened, upwardly curving sylvian fissure on the right compared to the left. Other early hominid brains show asymmetries of occipital lobes, manifested by a right occipital ptalia or left occipital ptalia.

The great apes also have some asymmetries similar to those found in humans. The right sylvian fissure is angled up more sharply than the left in the orangutan and in the gorilla. The brains of monkeys have not yet shown structural asymmetries. It seems as if the migration of the sylvian fissure downwards and backwards, occasioned by the over-growth of the inferior parietal lobe, is more commonly seen on the left than on the right in a variety of species of great apes, though not in all. Geschwind (1984) has suggested that these asymmetries reflect functional asymmetries in systems unrelated to language, particularly attentional systems, whose investigation is just beginning.

Functional and anatomical asymmetries extend very far back along the phylogenetic scale. They have been found in turning behavior in rats, where they are correlated with dopamine content and size of the caudate nucleus, and are related to other locomotor preferences in other species. The demonstration of such asymmetries indicates that lateral asymmetries in the brain which are correlated with functional differences are not a unique feature of language. One of the contributions of work on language in the brain to neurobiology has been to open the door for the investigation both of lateralized functions and of anatomical and physiological asymmetries underlying lateralization and dominant function in many species, and in domains other than language (Geschwind and Galaburda 1985).

The anatomical asymmetries are obvious candidates for the neural basis for hemispheric specialization and dominance, and Geschwind and Galaburda (1985) have explicitly argued that these asymmetries are responsible for the partitioning of language functions between the hemispheres, and for the primary responsibility of the left hemisphere for language. The accruing weight of evidence certainly supports the claim that the asymmetries are related to hemispheric specialization for language; but we should note that there are problems with this hypothesis. For instance, in the Geschwind and Levitsky (1968) study, there are too many cases in which the right planum temporale is larger, if we consider that the language-dominant hemisphere is the hemisphere with the larger planum temporale. It is, of course, possible that particular cytoarchitectonically defined regions within this region, or in other regions of the brain, are larger on the left in these cases, but only a thorough search will be able to substantiate such detailed claims regarding the relative size of very specific areas in the two hemispheres in relationship to cerebral dominance. Some investigators (Ratcliff *et al.* 1980) have attempted to correlate anatomical asymmetries seen on angiography with cerebral dominance as defined by dichotic listening and other tests. These approaches may also yield direct evidence in support of the hypothesis that the anatomical asymmetries are the basis for hemispheric dominance for language functions.

We have covered a fair amount of material in this chapter, and we shall take this opportunity to review the highlights of what we have presented. Since Broca's 1865 paper, it has been appreciated that language is very frequently primarily the responsibility of the left hemisphere. This neurobiological fact – termed "cerebral dominance for language" – is overwhelmingly true in a sub-set of the human population. Detailed studies of large populations have shown that strongly right-handed individuals from right-handed families have over a 98 per cent chance of being left-hemisphere dominant for language. In this population, we have seen that the right hemisphere does play a role in language-related functions but we have claimed that available evidence suggests that core psycholinguistic processes – those that are responsible for the recovery of the form and literal meaning of words and sentences – are the sole responsibility of the left hemisphere in this population. In left-handed individuals and right-handed individuals with left-handed family members, as well as individuals who are not strongly right-handed, the situation is far more complex. Both hemispheres seem to be involved in core psycholinguistic processing in some of these individuals, and some of these individuals are right-hemisphere dominant for language. Some individuals have claimed that there are differences between men and women with respect to hemispheric involvement in language, but the evidence for these differences is extremely weak; certainly it is nowhere near as strong as the evidence for differential involvement in language of the two hemispheres as a function of handedness.

All of these factors are ultimately genetic. Though early organic injury to the left hemisphere can shift language to the right hemisphere, there is no evidence that psychological variables such as how many languages a person knows, or whether he knows how to read or write, affect hemispheric specialization or dominance for language. Though there are many uncertainties about how sub-components of the language-processing system are divided between the two hemispheres in non-right-handers, what language capacity the right hemisphere is capable of in right-handers, and whether factors such as genetic or hormonal sex influence hemispheric specialization for language functions, one reasonably certain conclusion appears to be that hemispheric specialization and dominance for language are overwhelmingly under genetic control, and are not influenced to any important extent by exposure to particular language phenomena.

The anatomical basis for hemispheric specialization and dominance for language is just beginning to be explored. One of the exciting neurological discoveries of the 1970s was the finding that the language areas of the brain are not the same size in the left and the right hemisphere. They are larger on the left in many individuals. The investigation of the extent of asymmetries in the nervous system is just beginning, and the full significance of these anatomical asymmetries is far from known. Though there are many detailed questions which remain unanswered about the relationship of the neuroanatomical asymmetries to hemispheric specialization and dominance for language, the hypothesis that the two are related, and that language is more likely to be carried out in the hemisphere with the larger "language area", has received some initial support and is being actively investigated.

In all, our understanding of the contribution of each hemisphere to language processing has increased enormously since the first systematic investigations of this problem in large populations following World War II; and the recent discovery of the neuroanatomical asymmetries in language areas have opened up a whole new area of investigation regarding this aspect of the neural basis for language. Many questions about the detailed nature and neural basis of hemispheric specialization and dominance for language remain to be explored. Future work will no doubt increase and change our present understanding of this neurobiological phenomenon.

SUGGESTIONS FOR FURTHER READING

Galaburda, A. M., LeMay, M., Kemper, T. L., and Geschwind, N. (1978). Right–left asymmetries in the brain. *Science* 199, 852–6.

Gazzaniga, M. S. (1983). Right hemisphere language following brain bisection: a 20-year perspective. *American Psychologist* 38, 525–49.

Geschwind, N. and Galaburda, A. (1985). Cerebral lateralization: biological mechanism, associations, and pathology I–III: a hypothesis and a program for research. *Archives of Neurology* 42, 428–59, 521–52, 634–54.

Joanette, Y., Lecours, A. R., Lepage, Y., and Lamoureux, M. (1983). Language in right-handers with right hemisphere lesions: a preliminary study including anatomical, genetic and social factors. *Brain and Language* 20, 217–48.

Luria, A. R. (1947). *Traumatic Aphasia*. English translation, Mouton, The Hague, 1970.

McGlone, J. (1980). Sex differences in human brain asymmetry: a critical survey. *Behavioral and Brain Sciences* 3, 215–63.

Zaidel, E. (1978). Auditory language comprehension in the right hemisphere following cerebral commissurotomy and hemispherectomy: a comparison with child language and aphasia. In A. Caramazza and E. B. Zurif (eds.), *Language Acquisition and Language Breakdown: Parallels and Divergences*. Johns Hopkins University Press, Baltimore.

19

Cerebral localization for language revisited

Like the concept of cerebral dominance and specialization for language, the concept of localization of the language system and its components has undergone considerable development since it was first enunciated by Broca in 1861 with respect to motor speech functions. We have traced some of the development of this concept in Part II of this book. The first major innovation to Broca's formulation that we mentioned was that of Wernicke (1874), whose hypothesis that the function of auditory comprehension and the permanent representation of the sound patterns of words for language were located in the association cortex of the first temporal gyrus became the cornerstone of the connectionist theories of language processing in the brain. We traced the development of these connectionist models through the work of Lichtheim (1885) and other nineteenth-century neurologists, and into the twentieth century with the work of Geschwind (1965). In Chapter 9 we reviewed Luria's (1973) theories, which go yet further with respect to the localization of sub-components of a language-processing system. We also reviewed a number of objections to the connectionist theories in Chapters 6, 7, and 8 of Part II.

Recent developments in neuroradiology have greatly increased our ability to study the exact location of lesions which cause particular types of aphasia, and therefore have allowed investigators to test the correlations between symptom complexes and lesion sites predicted by the classical connectionist theory. They also permit us to document new sites in the brain in which lesions can produce aphasias. This new work has led to new theories of localization of language functions. In addition, recent psycholinguistic analyses of deficits in patients following localized lesions have also suggested new theories of language localization. We shall review this recent body of work in this chapter.

We shall divide the topic that we shall cover in this chapter into two areas. The first may be called "gross" localization. The question we shall pursue in this section is whether there are regions of the left, dominant hemisphere *other* than the association cortex in the perisylvian area which are involved in language function. The second topic is what might be called "narrow" localization. Narrow localization refers to the question of the internal organization of the perisylvian association cortex with respect to language functions – the so-called "functional neuroanatomy" of this region for language. In both these areas we shall be concerned only with right-handed subjects, who can be thought to have left-hemisphere dominance for language. We saw in Chapter 18 that a reasonable hypothesis is that the left hemisphere is the neural substrate for core psycholinguistic functions in this population. We shall, therefore, be concerned with how these core processes are related to areas of the dominant hemisphere. We shall consider these two topics in turn.

Gross localization

In the last ten years or so, the use of the computerized axial tomographic (CT) scan has greatly increased our ability to visualize small lesions in patients at the time at which they experience symptoms. The use of this technique has documented the existence of left-hemisphere lesions which lie outside the perisylvian cortex in patients who have aphasias. In addition to CT scan studies, recent reports of clinical–pathological correlations relating aphasia to a lesion in one of these sites have also appeared. Four sites have been associated with these aphasias: the thalamus, the caudate, the white matter in the region of the internal capsule, and the supplementary motor area. These areas are illustrated in Figure 19-1. We shall consider the nature of the language impairments that arise following lesions in each of these areas in turn.

Language disturbances following lesions to the thalamus have been reported by a number of authors. Mohr *et al.* (1975) report a retrospective review of patients at the Massachusetts General Hospital with aphasia following thalamic hemorrhages demonstrated at autopsy, and review the literature on the subject to that date. The authors stress the rarity of this condition: only four cases could be found by reviewing a fifteen-year experience with over 16,000 autopsies in the files of the Massachusetts General Hospital. Two cases were observed by the authors themselves. These patients showed language impairments which were different from the widely recognized aphasias which follow cortical lesions. One patient produced unintelligible jargon, with "fading vocal volume" which led quickly to silence, steady respirations, and closed eyes. When she was aroused, she was able to accomplish many language tasks – repeat long and unfamiliar words, spell dictated words, recognize words dictated in spelled form, name animals on the basis of their characteristic sounds, read headlines, and name a few items presented in visual form. Within two

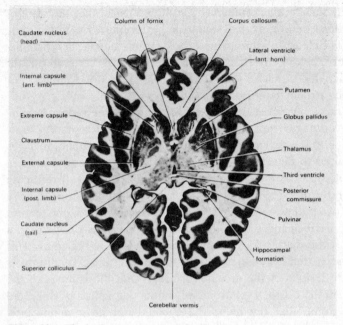

Figure 19-1. The basic neuroanatomy of subcortical gray-matter structures and related white-matter tracts
(*Source:* Carpenter and Sutin 1983: 38)

months, all of these abnormalities had completely cleared. A second patient also produced "logorrheic paraphasia and fading vocal volume leading to silence" (5), unless vigorously prompted by the examiner. This patient showed a good deal of echolalia (repetition of the examiner's questions and utterances) and was able to repeat multisyllabic familiar words and answer simple questions, but was unable to name objects, presented visually or tactilely, or give words from definitions. The patient became less and less responsive to the examiner during a testing session. In both these cases, CT scans showed hemorrhages involving the left thalamus. Mohr *et al.* report three more cases from the records of the Massachusetts General Hospital and an additional three cases from the literature.

These authors emphasize that the patients with thalamic hemorrhages whom they studied personally showed two distinct states: a state of arousal for brief periods, sustained by vigorous examiner stimulation of the patient, during which the patient could perform in what they term a "highly complex and appropriate fashion over a large range of materials . . . as to undermine serious considerations of a disorder in language or speech function" (16), and a second state, in which the patient's state of arousal was so reduced

371

as to preclude language functioning. The authors suggest that the state of arousal is a critical determinant of language performances with thalamic hemorrhages. The clearly abnormal logorrheic jargon seen in their patients may, they believe, be due to a thalamic role in "regulating cerebral surface gray-matter activity", such that thalamic dysfunction allows for unmoderated logorrheic paraphasia (16).

The authors are concerned that these disturbances may reflect impairments of the overlying cortex, and present an argument designed to show that they are due to the thalamic lesion itself. They note that hemorrhages are not well suited to determine the exact site which is responsible for a language deficit, since the hemorrhage can exert pressure on surrounding structures, thereby affecting their ability to carry out language functions. In the case of the two patients Mohr and his colleagues described, one feature of the patients' performances suggested that the aphasia was *not* due to a disturbance of white-matter tracts immediately around the thalamus. This feature was· the patient's retained ability to repeat. Since repetition is interrupted with lesions of the arcuate fasciculus and the isthmus of the temporal lobe, in the classical syndrome of conduction aphasia, Mohr and his colleagues argue that the hemorrhage could not have significantly compressed the arcuate fasciculus of the temporal isthmus. Mohr and his colleagues are tentative about this conclusion, because they had discovered other cases with subcortical lesions involving the temporal isthmus in which repetition was spared.

Because of the uncertainty regarding the role of pressure effects in generating aphasic symptoms following hemorrhagic lesions, it is important to search for cases with small, non-hemorrhagic strokes in the thalamus. If such patients show aphasia, the conclusion that the thalamus itself is responsible for aspects of language would be better supported. McFarling *et al*. (1982) reported two such cases.

One patient initially showed the extreme fluctuation in language abilities noted by Mohr and his colleagues, and also showed a tendency towards perseveration and echolalia. A few days later, spontaneous speech was extremely reduced but no syntactic errors were noted. The patient could answer 12/20 simple questions such as *Is your name Smith?* and *Is a hammer good for cutting wood?* Of interest was the fact that seven consecutive questions were missed, preceded and followed by correct responses. The authors take this as an indication of fluctuation in the patient's comprehension deficit. The patient was unable to point to objects in response to words, but was able to repeat all single words presented to him with only some dysarthric disturbances. The patient was unable to name common objects. The CT scan in this patient showed a vascular lesion in the left internal capsule and the adjacent portion of the left thalamus, possibly affecting the internal portion of the left occipital lobe. Two weeks after admission, the patient developed a new infarction in the left temporal parietal area and became more severely aphasic.

The second case, who presented with a small abnormal density in the CT scan in the left thalamus, also showed extremely reduced speech, with very short but correct responses to questions. The patient could not produce the names of objects beginning with a specified letter, but was able to answer 20/20 simple yes/no questions, point correctly to forty-two objects when given their names auditorily, and identify twenty objects presented to him. He was good at identifying parts of the body and had a good short-term verbal memory, with a digit span of seven, and no problems following commands which required sequential actions. The patient was also able to understand sentences with reasonably complex syntactic structure, such as, *He showed the boy's dog the cages*, on a sentence–picture matching test.

The authors stress the similarities between these two patients. They both had non-fluent speech with relatively preserved repetition. One had poor comprehension and the other quite good comprehension. The authors classified these as patients with "mixed transcortical aphasia" and "transcortical motor aphasia", in keeping with the classification we have discussed in Chapters 4 and 11. At the time that repetition was preserved, there was no CT evidence of a lesion in the cortex, or in the arcuate fasciculus or other white-matter tracts which the classical clinical theory postulates are involved in repetition. The authors do not, however, account for their patients' deficits in terms of classical or modern connectionist theories, since there was no cortical lesion in their cases. Rather, they argue that their cases confirm the general ideas of Jackson regarding the hierarchical organization of the nervous system, according to which lower structures are involved in automatic functions (see Chapter 7). In the present case, the basic function which the authors suggest is subserved by the thalamus, more specifically the ventral lateral nucleus of the thalamus, is an alerting function, without which intact cortical language mechanisms are not sufficiently aroused to perform their usual functions. This results in the loss of more complex functions with relative sparing of repetition, often to the point of echolalia. McFarling *et al.* therefore also come to a similar conclusion as Mohr and his colleagues: that the thalamus plays a role in language functions by activating the cortical areas responsible for language.

Additional cases of aphasia following thalamic injury are reported by Cappa and Vignolo (1979). Three of their patients showed reduced verbal output and some disturbance of auditory comprehension but good repetition, a pattern which is quite similar to the pattern in the cases we have described above. Alexander and LoVerme (1980) also noted the similarities between the aphasias following thalamic lesions and the "transcortical aphasias" in the clinical classification, emphasizing the fact that repetition is spared in these patients. In these and many other cases, the symptomatology is quite varied, but the presence of echolalia, spared repetition, and wide fluctuations in performance which parallel the patient's state of arousal are frequently found.

Researchers in the literature are of two minds about whether the disturbances found in association with lesions of the thalamus are "true aphasias" or not. As we noted above, some of the language disturbances seem to be tied to the level of arousal of a patient, and Mohr, McFarling, and others have suggested that the language problems in these patients arise because the alerting influence of the thalamus upon the surrounding cortex is lost. On the other hand, many of the patients with thalamic lesions seem to have relatively stable and restricted disturbances in language functions, such as problems with naming, non-fluent speech, and phonemic paraphasias. It is difficult to invoke a general alerting mechanism to account for all of these isolated disturbances. It may be that both theories are correct: the thalamus may play an important role in activating the left-hemisphere perisylvian cortex responsible for language, and it also may be responsible for certain aspects of language processing in at least some individuals. We shall, however, express an important reservation regarding this last conclusion after we discuss the types of aphasia which follow other subcortical lesions.

Two groups of researchers – Naeser *et al.* (1982) and Damasio *et al.* (1982) – have reported a total of twenty patients with subcortical lesions affecting the internal capsule, the putamen, and the head of the caudate nucleus (see Figure 19-2). Naeser *et al.* reported on nine patients with CT lesions in the area of the internal capsule and the putamen. Eight cases had occlusive, non-hemorrhagic strokes, and one case had a hemorrhagic stroke. The authors divide their cases into three groups, depending upon the exact location of the lesions. All patients had lesions in the region of the internal capsule and the putamen, with extensions in an anterior–superior direction, a posterior direction, or both. The authors claim that "*small* differences in subcortical extension on the CT scan (a few mm. in one direction or another) were associated with *large* differences in language behavior" (3).

Three cases had antero-superior extensions of the lesions. The authors claim that the predominant aphasia pattern in these cases was one of good semantic comprehension, poor syntactic comprehension, and grammatical but slow and dysarthric speech. They suggest that the dysarthria in these patients might be due to white-matter lesions deep to Broca's area, or in the area deep to the cortical representation of the face, lips, and tongue in the

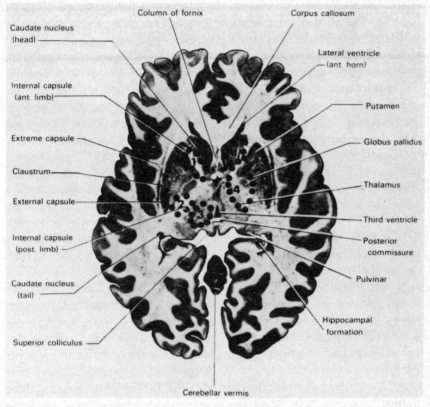

Figure 19-2. Horizontal section of the cerebral hemisphere showing location of lesions in subcortical aphasia: (1) represents anterior capsular lesions; (2) represents posterior capsular lesions; (3) shows thalamic lesions; (4) shows large capsular lesions; (5) shows pericaudate lesions. (4) and (5) are depicted in the right hemisphere for clarity. (Modified from Carpenter and Sutin 1983: 38)

pre-central gyrus, or to a combination of both these lesions. They note that the language profile of these cases does not completely resemble any of the classically clinically defined aphasic syndromes, but has features of both Broca's and Wernicke's aphasia. The pattern of preserved and disturbed abilities in fact differed in these three patients. Thus, for instance, silent reading returned to a high level of efficiency in the two patients who had the greatest difficulty in naming pictures.

The second group of three cases were tested from one month to five years after a stroke (one of these cases had a hemorrhagic stroke). The authors say that the pattern of aphasia in these cases included poor comprehension and fluent paraphasic speech shading into jargon. The language picture is similar to that found in typical cases of Wernicke's aphasia. The lesions in these cases extended posteriorly across the auditory radiations in the temporal isthmus. The authors suggested that interruption of these auditory fibers, which transmit information from the thalamus (the medial geniculate body) to the cortical receptive area for audition in Heschl's gyrus, might cause the comprehension deficits.

The third group consisted of three cases, tested two months to eleven and a half years post-stroke. Spontaneous speech was absent, or reduced to stereotyped monosyllables, in all three. Comprehension of single words was poor, as was repetition, naming, and silent reading, where these functions were even possible. The patients were unable to write. The CT scan showed lesions which extended anteriorly to the white matter beneath Broca's area and posteriorly across the temporal isthmus. In addition, the lesions in these cases also extended superiorly. The authors estimate that more than 10 per cent of the left hemisphere was damaged in these patients. The authors believed that the extremely limited speech output was likely to be due to isolation of Broca's area, and the comprehension disturbance to interruption of thalamo-cortical auditory fibers.

Naeser *et al.* discuss two possible determinants of the aphasic impairments found in their cases: lesion site and lesion size. They conclude that the lesion site is more important than lesion size. The patient with the largest lesion (case 3) did not have the most severe aphasia, and one of the most severely aphasic patients had a relatively small lesion. On the other hand, the site of the lesion was associated with different patterns of symptoms, as we have seen. The authors allow for the possibility that the size of the lesion within a particular region may affect the degree of impairment of a particular function; specifically, patients with small lesions in the white matter beneath Broca's area had less dysarthria than patients with larger lesions in this region.

Naeser *et al.* indicate that their cases differ in three ways from other patients with subcortical lesions. First, their patients had impaired repetition, while patients with thalamic hemorrhage have spared repetition or echolalia. Second, cases with purely posterior lesion extensions had good articulation but poor bucco-facial movement for non-linguistic tasks, which is an unusual dissociation of abilities. Third, their cases did not all recover well. Naeser and her colleagues suggest that the particular nature of the language deficits and their long duration reflect damage to white-matter pathways or to the putamen.

A second group of patients with non-hemorrhagic vascular lesions in this area was reported by Damasio *et al.* (1982). Six patients had aphasic symptoms following lesions in this area. Five cases showed non-fluent speech, which was not typical of Broca's aphasia because of the presence of frequent phonemic and semantic paraphasias in three cases. In addition, auditory comprehension, reading for comprehension, writing ability, and repetition varied considerably in these cases. The authors indicated that all of these cases were difficult to classify with respect to the clinical classification of aphasia. The remaining case had fluent speech, semantic and neologistic paraphasias, word-finding difficulty, severely impaired auditory and reading comprehension, and impaired repetition. Five other patients showed no "central" language disturbances, but had dysarthria and dysprosodia following lesions in this area.

The authors emphasize the frequent presence of dysarthria following lesions in this area. The aphasic symptoms that were seen in their patients were not grouped together, as in the classical aphasic syndromes, and the authors claimed that they are more reminiscent of the symptoms described in thalamic hemorrhages. They recognize that these symptoms constitute a heterogeneous group of disturbances. The lesions which they claim are responsible for these impairments involve the anterior limb of the internal capsule, the head of the caudate nucleus, and the putamen. Other structures in this region – the globus pallidus, the thalamus, and the posterior limb of the internal capsule – were not involved. The authors conclude that "there is a powerful association between aphasia and a well-circumscribed anatomic region, the anterior limb of the internal capsule and both the head of the caudate nucleus and the anterior aspect of the putamen" (Damasio *et al*. 1982: 19). According to these authors, lesions anterior to this region produce transcortical motor aphasia, and lesions posterior to this region produce motor disturbances but not aphasia. Damasio *et al*. claim that the language disturbances may be due to the interruption of descending white-matter fibers in the internal capsule, or to lesions in the caudate and the putamen. They argue that the caudate and the putamen receive important visual, auditory, and somesthetic projections, and send fibers to the pre-motor, motor, and somato-sensory cortices through a series of neuronal connections. They claim that damage to these subcortical gray-matter structures could "disrupt language decoding and encoding, disturbing aural comprehension and giving rise to paraphasias" (20). The anterior limb of the internal capsule contains many fiber tracts relevant to language: descending fibers from the motor cortex, auditory fibers destined to arrive in the caudate, fibers from the thalamus ascending to the pre-frontal lobe, and fibers connecting the various nuclei of the subcortical gray structures we have been discussing. Damage to these fiber tracts could lead to aphasic syndromes by interrupting the transmission of linguistic representations from one cortical area to another cortical area, to a subcortical area, or to the motor nuclei in the brain-stem responsible for speech.

These cases of thalamic and more anterior subcortical lesions producing aphasias clearly document that language disturbances can arise following lesions in these areas. It is very hard to say whether particular patterns of language disturbance are correlated with lesions in one or another of these subcortical structures. The largest experience is with lesions in the thalamus. In these cases, a typical language picture does seem to emerge. The disturbance involves alternation between a depressed and a hyper-attentive state of arousal, which correlates well with the level of language production. In addition, most lesions in the thalamus spare repetition. Whether this is because repetition is inherently an easier, more automatic, task which can be triggered by more "immediate" stimuli as Jackson (Chapter 7) and Luria (Chapter 9) maintained, or whether repetition is spared because it depends upon a set of purely cortical and immediately subcortical structures not affected by the lesion (the classical connectionist analysis, Chapters 4 and 5), is not known. We should also note that the involuntary echolalia often seen with these lesions may differ from the preserved repetition found in other patients, and that its exact characteristics are not known. It is not impossible that echolalia is simply one manifestation of a hyperattentive state, in which the patient focusses upon auditory linguistic stimuli. Aside from these relatively common features of the language abnormalities following thalamic hemorrhages, the remaining language symptoms in subcortical lesions are quite varied, both in cases with thalamic lesions and in cases with lesions in the internal capsule, the caudate, the putamen, and related structures.

The anatomical basis for these disturbances is said to be the affected subcortical structures. Naeser argues that lesions are likely to produce dysarthria if they extend anteriorly in the region of the internal capsule and affect the white-matter tracts originating in Broca's area, and likely to be associated with comprehension disorders if they extend posteriorly and interrupt some of the fibers conveying auditory information to Heschl's gyrus and Wernicke's area. Damasio *et al.* also attribute the disturbances seen in their patients to white-matter lesions and to the lesions in the caudate and the putamen. However, a critical question regarding these cases is whether the language deficits should be attributed to the subcortical lesion itself. The authors we have cited have been concerned to show that there are no signs of edema or small cortical lesions in the perisylvian language zone in their patients. Whenever possible, non-hemorrhagic stroke cases have been studied, since these lesions have the least likelihood of producing cerebral edema. Mohr *et al.* argue that the preserved repetition in their cases suggests that white-matter tracts quite close to the thalamus are preserved if the classical analysis of the neural basis for repetition is correct. It seems that the language deficits in these cases are not due to the effects of edema upon surrounding structures, nor to lesions in perisylvian cortex which are visible on CT scans. Nonetheless, we must be cautious in accepting that the language deficits in these patients arise because of impairment of subcortical structures and not because of physiological abnormalities in the overlying perisylvian cortex, for several reasons.

First, most of these lesions are vascular, and when there are vascular lesions in the deep structures of the left hemisphere, there are frequently abnormalities in the cerebral vessels which supply the more lateral, cortical parts of the hemisphere as well. Blood flow to the overlying cortex may not be completely normal in all these patients. More importantly, lesions in the white-matter fibers that come from a region of cortex, in the groups of neurons to which a set of neurons project, and in sets of neurons which project to a set of cortical neurons, are all known to produce abnormalities in the metabolic and physiological functioning of the original set of neurons. These abnormalities can be seen through electro-physiological recording and, more recently, through metabolic scanning, using techniques such as positron emission tomography (PET). In experimental animals, even tiny lesions in subcortical structures are frequently associated with severe reductions in blood flow and metabolism in overlying cortical areas. To date, there is not a single published case of an aphasic patient with a subcortical lesion in whom EEG and PET scans demonstrate the physiological and metabolic integrity of the overlying cortex. On the contrary, Metter *et al.* (1985) found no correlation between the degree of metabolic impairment in the caudate, measured using labeled glucose uptake by PET scanning, and the extent of comprehension impairment (measured on the Western Aphasia Battery) in ten patients with left temporo-parietal strokes. There was a correlation between metabolic impairments in the temporo-parietal lobe and comprehension deficit, however, in these patients. Even in the absence of edema, subcortical lesions may produce language deficits because they impair the functioning of overlying cortical regions, not because of damage to subcortical structures themselves.

Another set of studies that deal with language disturbances following lesions in regions other than the perisylvian cortex are those documenting aphasias following infarctions of the left supplementary motor area. Masdeu *et al.* (1978) report one such case with a typical "supplementary motor syndrome". The patient suffered from a single stroke in the supplementary motor area of the left hemisphere, resulting in the lesion seen in Figure 19-3. On initial examination the patient was able to understand, and to follow simple auditory and written commands, but was totally unable to speak. By the third day, she could whisper, uttering a few simple phrases such as *good*

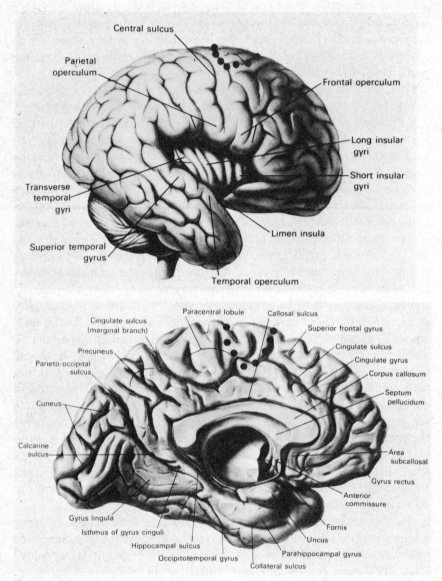

Figure 19-3. Illustration of the lateral and medial surface of the brain, showing the location of lesions affecting the supplementary motor area
(Modified from Carpenter and Sutin 1983: 31, 33)

morning, and *yes* and *no*. Two weeks after her stroke she performed well on the single-word auditory comprehension parts of the Boston Diagnostic Aphasia Examination, and could name objects, colors, and letters. She could repeat single words and phrases (though she failed on unfamiliar polysyllabic words), could read simple sentences and paragraphs slowly, and continued to show good auditory comprehension. A month after her stroke she showed a reduced amount of spontaneous speech, and rare paraphasias and circumlocutions, especially in response to "open-ended" questions. Her speech was slow and hesitant but well articulated. She was not agrammatic. She continued to have some impairment in repeating low-probability items. At six weeks, her speech was still slow, but naming, repetition, and auditory comprehension were normal. Writing remained slow and effortful and showed paraphasic errors, and she would not write more than a single word.

Masdeu and his colleagues reviewed the published cases of language disturbances following infarctions, excisions, and electrical stimulation in the left parasagittal region including the supplementary motor cortex. Interference with speech and mutism are the most frequent disturbances following lesions in this area. Inability to speak either spontaneously or in repetition distinguishes this syndrome from the classical transcortical motor aphasia seen after more lateral lesions, and the impairment in writing is said by the authors to distinguish this syndrome from the syndrome of "aphemia", in which the patient is mute but able to write. The fact that the disturbance is transient, and that language returns suddenly in a quite intact fashion, differentiates the language impairments in this syndrome from those seen in Broca's aphasia, in which persistent abnormalities in articulation, sentence formation, and other tasks are present (see Chapters 4, 5, 11, and 15).

The language disturbances found in these cases with lesions in the supplementary motor cortex have been considered to be true aphasias by researchers such as Masdeu and his colleagues because of features such as the severe writing disorder, the occurrence of literal and verbal paraphasias, and the lower scores on the more complex items of tests such as the Token Test seen in their patients. If true aphasias follow lesions in the supplementary motor area, then the language areas of the brain must include this area, and cannot be grossly localized to the association cortex of the perisylvian region. In the case of lesions in subcortical structures, we have expressed reservations about the conclusion that the aphasia following these lesions is due to the abnormalities of the subcortical areas alone, since there is some reason to believe that physiological and metabolic function in the overlying perisylvian association cortex may be abnormal when a lesion occurs in

381

subcortical structures. In the case of lesions of the supplementary motor cortex, this reservation seems less important. Though there are cortico-cortical connections between this region and the perisylvian association cortex devoted to language, there is no direct major connection between one region and the other. It is much less likely that disturbances following small infarcts in the supplementary cortex are really due to physiological abnormalities in the perisylvian association cortex than is the case with subcortical lesions. On anatomical grounds, therefore, we must accept the disturbances which arise following lesions in the supplementary motor cortex as indications of the existence of language functions in this area of the brain.

On the other hand, despite the claims of Masdeu and his colleagues and others, there is reason to doubt that the abnormalities found after supplementary motor lesions are "true aphasias", similar to those which follow lesions in the perisylvian association cortex. The mutism which is the most common language symptom arising after these lesions is not like the mutism found in Broca's aphasia, as Masdeu and his colleagues note. The striking difference between the two is, as Masdeu *et al.* say, that the mutism following supplementary motor infarction rapidly resolves, to leave the patient with perfectly normal language, while the mutism following lesions in the perisylvian association cortex very rarely suddenly resolves to leave the patient without some disturbance of spoken language production. It may be that the mutism following supplementary motor-area lesions is due to the patient's inability to initiate speech, rather than to a disturbance of a component of the speech production system (see Chapter 15). In non-human species, the supplementary motor region is important in the control of vocalization. This region may exercise a regulatory and initiation function for vocalization function in man as well. The fact that recovered speech is often whispered suggests that the role of this area in vocalization has to do with the control of sub- and supra-glottal pressures, and the absence of major disturbances of segmental phonology or intonation contours in recovered speech in these cases suggests that truly linguistic aspects of processing are not affected by this lesion.

Patients with lesions of the supplementary motor area make occasional paraphasias and other minor errors on complex linguistic items such as the latter segments of the Token Test. These mild aphasic symptoms are similar to those which follow right-hemisphere damage in strongly right-handed individuals, which we discussed in Chapter 18. We argued in Chapter 18 that these errors may arise because of the use of the right hemisphere as a computational area for language processing when language processing becomes complex, and exceeds the capacity of the perisylvian association cortex of the left hemisphere. The same considerations apply to lesions of the supplementary motor area. Indeed, the fact that the lesions in these two areas – the right hemisphere and the supplementary motor region – lead to similar mild disturbances of language reinforces the possibility that these areas are used as additional computational working space for the language system, but are not the permanent loci of linguistic representations.

The third type of abnormality that has been described following lesions to the supplementary motor area is an agraphia. This agraphia is severe, and has a linguistic character; it is not simply a disturbance of handwriting. It may be somewhat premature to attribute the agraphia to a lesion to the supplementary motor area itself; one possibility is that it arises because of some disturbance in the adjacent motor cortex. Interestingly, unpublished reports of patients with amyotropic lateral sclerosis, a disease which affects motor neurons but not association cortex to any significant extent, have documented agraphias (Funkenstein and Kuban, personal communication). However, whether or not the agraphia in patients such as the case reported by Masdeu *et al.* is due to a lesion in the supplementary motor cortex or in the motor cortex itself, it cannot be attributed to a lesion in the perisylvian association cortex, and it is clearly a disturbance in what we have been considering as core psycholinguistic processing. It thus appears that some core language processing does not take place in the perisylvian association cortex in some individuals. We should note that writing is perhaps the least established of the primary psycholinguistic tasks – auditory comprehension, speech, reading, and writing. Reading and writing do not develop in humans without special exposure and instruction, and, of the two, reading skills and habits are frequently better developed than writing. As we indicated in Chapter 14, this does not mean that either reading or writing is dependent upon the psycholinguistic processing routines used for auditory language in the skilled reader or writer. However, the fact that writing can be disturbed following lesions in non-perisylvian association cortical regions is consistent with the hypothesis that only this late and frequently poorly developed function is represented outside of the perisylvian association cortex.

Let us summarize the results of these studies. Researchers have documented a wide variety of aphasic symptoms following lesions in the thalamus, the internal capsule, the putamen, the caudate, and surrounding white-matter structures. Lesions in the thalamus seem to be frequently associated with language disturbances that are correlated with the state of the patient's arousal. These language disturbances may be due to an impairment in arousal or attentional mechanisms. Lesions in the deep white matter of the hemisphere tend to produce dysarthrias when they extend anteriorly and auditory comprehension deficits when they extend posteriorly. Both these effects are likely to be due to the interruption of white-matter tracts descending from Broca's area and ascending to Heschl's gyrus, respectively. Aside from these relatively constant features of subcortical lesions, the language disorders which arise following subcortical lesions are extremely varied, and encompass virtually the whole range of aphasic symptoms. Though direct pressure on overlying cortex does not seem to be responsible for these disturbances, we cannot as yet be confident that these language disturbances are not due to metabolic and physiological abnormalities in the overlying perisylvian association cortex secondary to the deep lesions. The second non-perisylvian region in which damage causes language disturbances is the supplementary motor area. Here too, the effects of the lesion may be primarily non-linguistic, affecting the ability to control vocalization and initiate speech, and to use this cortical area for additional language-related computations when needed. The only permanent aphasic language disturbance found in association with supplementary motor-area lesions is an agraphia.

Overall, with the exception of the representation of written language, which seems to be at least occasionally located in the supplementary motor region or the adjacent motor strip, it is possible that there is considerable gross localization of language functions in the perisylvian association cortex. All of the core psycholinguistic language processes that we have reviewed in Part III may go on in this area. The ability to initiate and regulate this activity does seem to depend upon the functioning of other areas of the brain, such as the thalamus and the supplementary motor area. The use of the representations yielded by these core processes in verbal memory, verbal reasoning, and verbal learning also seems to involve other brain regions.

Narrow localization

What of "narrow" localization of sub-components of the system devoted to core language processing? The basic, traditional, neurolinguistic model pertaining to the functional neuroanatomy of the perisylvian cortex, which we have discussed in Chapters 4, 5, and 11, maintains that narrow localization of language-processing sub-components exists. According to this model, the permanent representations for the sounds of words are stored in Wernicke's area, the association cortex of the second temporal gyrus. These auditory representations are accessed following auditory presentation of language stimuli. They, in turn, evoke the concepts associated with words in the "concept center". According to Lichtheim (1885), the concept center is diffusely represented in association cortex (Chapter 4); according to Geschwind (1965), a critical part of this process involves the inferior parietal lobe (Chapter 5). In spoken language production, concepts access the phonological representations of words in Wernicke's area, which are then transmitted to the motor-programming areas for speech in Broca's area, the association cortex of the pars triangularis and opercularis of the third frontal gyrus, and possibly that of the rolandic (frontal) operculum. Simultaneously, according to Lichtheim (1885), the concept center activates Broca's area. The proper execution of the speech act depends upon Broca's area receiving input from both these different cortical areas, each conveying different types of linguistically relevant representations. The principal evidence in favor of this model is the occurrence of specific syndromes of language disorders which can be accounted for by lesions of these centers and the connections between them. We have reviewed these syndromes in Chapters 4, 5, and 11.

The Wernicke–Lichtheim–Geschwind analysis has been subject to considerable criticism, some of which we discussed in Chapters 6, 7, 8, 11, and 17. Among the questions raised in those chapters was that of the reliability of the correlation between aphasic syndromes and lesion sites. As mentioned in Chapter 17, most of the classical connectionist views regarding the neural basis for the components of the language-processing system were based upon single cases or, at most, on a small series of cases. Close reading reveals the remarkable fact that Wernicke himself based his entire theory upon two cases, one of which was studied clinically but not pathologically, and one which was studied pathologically but not clinically! Because of the difficulty in obtaining good indications of where lesions were in the brain in a living patient before the modern neuroradiological era, researchers relied primarily upon clinical–pathological correlations, which greatly reduced the number of cases in which lesions relating to particular types of aphasia could be established. One of the first research goals of several contemporary neurologically oriented aphasiologists was, therefore, to investigate the correlates of the classical aphasic syndromes using modern radiological techniques, especially the CT scan. There are many such studies; we shall review a few of the most typical and representative.

Naeser and Hayward (1978) studied nineteen aphasic patients using CT scans to locate the lesion sites and the Boston Diagnostic Aphasia Examination (Goodglass and Kaplan 1972) to describe symptoms and classify patients. Patients were primarily right-handed men (17/19), aged between thirty-four and eighty-four, who were victims of a single left-hemisphere stroke.

Three Broca's aphasics had lesions in the pre-rolandic area, the inferior frontal lobe including Broca's area, and underlying structures including the caudate, the anterior limb of the internal capsule, the globus pallidus, the putamen, and the insula. In most patients, at least some tissue in the upper portion of the temporal lobe just beneath the sylvian fissure was also affected. The patients also had damage in the inferior parietal lobe. Four Wernicke's aphasics had lesions which involved the first temporal gyrus. One lesion was relatively anterior in this gyrus, and involved the post-central gyrus and part of the parietal operculum. A second was relatively small, and involved more of the inferior parietal lobe. The other two primarily involved the first and second temporal gyri, with some very minor extension into the parietal operculum or the inferior parietal lobule. In four conduction aphasics, the lesions were primarily posterior to the rolandic fissure. They were either subcortical lesions deep to Wernicke's area or lesions in the supramarginal gyrus and the structures beneath this gyrus. The four patients with transcortical motor aphasia had small lesions primarily anterior and superior to Broca's area. Two patients had lesions that partly included Broca's area, and none had lesions directly involving Wernicke's area. Four patients with global aphasia had extremely large lesions involving the entire perisylvian cortex.

The authors conclude that there was "good correlation between CT findings and BDAE syndromes" (551). They do, however, indicate that there were some unexpected findings in their study. For instance, two patients with small lesions in Broca's area had transcortical motor aphasia, not Broca's aphasia. In general, small lesions correlated with milder types of aphasia. The authors further suggested that variability in the degree of infarction in an area (which can be measured in part by the degree of hypo-density on the CT scan) may correlate with the severity of the corresponding aphasic deficit.

Other authors have reported much larger series of cases. Basso *et al.* (1985) studied 257 aphasic subjects who had CT scan examinations. They report on the classification of patients into "fluent" and "non-fluent" groups. They emphasize exceptions to the classical predictions. Leaving aside fifty patients in whom there were no CT scan lesions, or lesions which only occupied subcortical areas, thirty-six of the remaining 207 patients had unexpected findings. Three patients had no aphasia, despite lesions in the classical speech areas. None of these patients was non-right-handed, or had any other reason for not becoming aphasic after these lesions. One patient with an anterior lesion outside of the classical speech area had a Broca's aphasia, and one with a posterior lesion outside of the classical speech area had a Wernicke's aphasia. Ten global aphasics had lesions which spared Wernicke's area, and eight cases with Wernicke's aphasia had large lesions in the entire perisylvian cortex which the authors expected to produce global aphasia. Seven patients with anterior lesions had Wernicke's aphasia or transcortical sensory aphasia. Finally, six patients with posterior lesions which spared the lower half of the pre-central gyrus and Broca's area had non-fluent aphasia.

Basso *et al.* make several comments about these findings. First, they suggest that it might be possible to exclude the ten patients with global aphasia but sparing of Wernicke's area from the group of "exceptions". If this group is excluded, there are 9.7 per cent of the cases which show unexpected CT scan findings; if the group is included, 13.5 per cent of the patients show unexpected findings. They are impressed that the anatomical–clinical principles underlying the connectionist neurolinguistic theory "turn out to be roughly valid for 86.5 per cent to 90.3 per cent of cases" (226) and they say that these principles should be "adhered to as a basis for standard teaching" (226). They emphasize that "the present study does not lead us to reject, at least with regard to the population so far extensively investigated in this respect, the main anatomical–clinical principles of European aphasiology" (226). Still, the authors are disturbed by the presence of these exceptions and they say that "one can offer no satisfactory 'explanation' of the type of 'exceptions' that we have discussed here, to the best of our knowledge" (226). They suggest that perhaps pre-natal brain damage occurred in these patients, with consequent reorganization of the language zone.

Several studies report on CT (and sometimes pathological) correlates of particular types of aphasia. Mohr *et al.* (1978) report patients with small infarcts in Broca's area or other parts of the frontal or insular cortex, or large lesions affecting the opercular and insular regions. They found that twenty-two patients with small inferior frontal infarctions had mutism which lasted from hours to days and a variety of other language deficits, but these patients all improved within hours to weeks. In a review of 1,600 autopsies at the Massachusetts General Hospital, they found ten patients with small infarcts in Broca's area and immediately surrounding structures. In two, the neurological examination did not indicate the presence of an aphasia; in the remaining eight patients, the aphasia disappeared within two months. Four patients that the authors studied personally with small lesions in other frontal sites, including the insula, also initially had severe motor speech disturbances and other aphasic symptoms, but returned to normal within weeks to months.

On the other hand, large infarcts involving Broca's area, other frontal and parietal regions of the operculum, and the insula showed much more severe and long-lasting syndromes. The typical picture was one of severe language output disturbances, often mutism, and comprehension deficits severe enough to have the patient be considered a global aphasic. In these patients, comprehension improved but speech frequently remained abnormal, so that the patients were classified as Broca's aphasics when several months had elapsed after their strokes. Fifteen patients from the autopsy files of the Massachusetts General Hospital showed large infarctions in this region. All had language disorders which were initially considered to be severe and total. Not all patients were followed clinically, but one reported by Mohr and his colleagues showed recovery of comprehension six years after her stroke, and was then considered to be a Broca's aphasic. The authors refer to Henschen's (1920) neuropathological study in which thirty-eight cases with similar large lesions were reported. Mohr and his colleagues note that, in each of these cases, deficits lasted for months or years, and affected speaking aloud to a far greater extent than they affected comprehension.

Mohr and his colleagues argue that a number of relatively isolated disturbances of speech production can follow small lesions in Broca's area, the frontal operculum, or the insula: dysarthria, mutism, dyspraxia of speech, and bucco-facial apraxia. These symptoms may be associated with mild disturbances in comprehension, writing, and other functions. These disturbances are extremely short-lasting. The full syndrome of Broca's aphasia – which the authors stress typically includes agrammatism (see Chapter 15) – is only found with much larger lesions, involving Broca's area, the frontal and parietal opercula, the insula and adjacent white matter, and often temporal lobe structures. This is the vascular territory supplied by the upper division of the middle cerebral artery. The authors suggest that when this syndrome follows infarction it arises because of occlusion of this artery. The authors note that the initial symptoms in these cases are usually very severe, and that Broca's aphasia is a syndrome which only appears in the recovery period.

Mohr and his colleagues suggest that these findings might be the result of what they term "synergistic interaction" of the lateral perisylvian cortex and the insula. Small lesions in this area involve relatively minor language deficits which improve quickly, and they speculate that different sub-areas of this region "to some extent overlap one another in their contribution to language functions" (323). They believe that the "severity and persistence of the clinical deficit is proportional to the size and distribution of the infarct" (323). They liken this state of affairs to that of a team, which can be weakened when one or more players are sent off the field, but only ceases to be a team when a critical number of players are lost. This view of the way language is represented in this particular portion of the perisylvian cortex has been termed "mass action" by Lashley (1950). Lashley argued that many intellectual functions, particulary memory, depend upon large portions of the brain and are impaired in direct proportion to the size of brain lesions, regardless of the location of these lesions. Mohr and his colleagues do not believe that the whole brain is involved in the functions disturbed in Broca's aphasia, but only the upper bank of the perisylvian fissure and the insula. They maintain that mass action operates within sub-areas of the brain such as this region.

A CT study of another classical aphasic syndrome – conduction aphasia – was reported by Damasio and Damasio (1980). The authors studied six patients who showed fluent, meaningful speech with phonemic paraphasias, a profound repetition defect for sentences with sparing of digit repetition, and slightly to substantially impaired auditory comprehension (auditory comprehension scores varied from the twentieth to the seventieth percentile on Benton's Multilingual Aphasia Examination). The patients showed remarkable dissociations of digit spans and ability to repeat sentences. Three patients had a digit span of seven, one of six, one of five, and one of four. Despite being able to repeat digits with this degree of proficiency, these patients had a profound deficit of sentence repetition, varying from being unable to repeat a single sentence correctly to being able to repeat no more than three-word sentences.

Lesions in these cases were relatively small. In five of the six cases, the lesion involved a good deal of the insula, and in the sixth case the lesion was primarily subcortical in the region of the putamen. All lesions affected the arcuate fasciculus, the tract which Geschwind (1965) argued was critical in carrying auditory representations from Wernicke's area to Broca's area (see Chapter 5). In addition, the lesions extended into the temporal lobe, affecting the auditory complex, and frequently into the inferior parietal lobe, affecting particularly the supramarginal gyrus.

Damasio and Damasio note that the involvement of the arcuate fasciculus is in keeping with classical connectionist predictions. They single out the involvement of the temporal lobe and the insula for particular consideration. They note that the lesions in the temporal lobe do not affect much of Wernicke's area, and are not as posterior as those seen in cases of Wernicke's aphasia. Damage to the auditory complex and the arcuate fasciculus also occurs in Wernicke's and Broca's aphasia, and the authors suggest that "the specific pattern of compromise to either structure ... renders conduction aphasia distinctive, anatomically and behaviorally" (347). The authors speculate that the lesion in the cortex of the insula may not be as important as that in the adjacent white matter which contains connections from the temporal and parietal lobes to pre-motor structures. Because some conduction aphasics have lesions which spare the insula but damage other white-matter connections between the temporal–parietal area and the pre-motor region, they suggest that there are many anatomical bases for conduction aphasia: "in sum, it appears that damage to a specific set of temporal–parietal connections, be it in the parietal operculum or beneath the insula, can be associated with impaired repetition" (349).

Damasio and Damasio then make an important claim regarding the correlation of behavioral deficits with lesion sites. They note that several authors, such as Warrington and Shallice (1969), whose work we reviewed in Chapter 16, postulate that the clinical syndrome of conduction aphasia may arise because of a memory disturbance, rather than an inability to transmit auditory representations from Wernicke's area to Broca's area. Damasio and Damasio suggest that disturbances in different anatomical structures may be associated with different types of behavioral deficits. They say that "the variety of structures potentially involved makes it necessary to cast doubts on the explanations based on a single disruptive factor (for example, amnesic deficit)". They identify a number of functional components involved in repetition: identification of phonemes, memory for phonemes and sequences of phonemes, access to an intact motor system, and others. They say that these steps depend upon the left auditory cortex and its connections to frontal and parietal cortex, and possibly to the basal ganglia. The authors claim that the number of lesions responsible for conduction aphasia makes it unlikely that all the forms of conduction aphasia are due to a single factor, and conclude that different anatomical structures are responsible for the different psycholinguistic processes involved in repetition. As opposed to Mohr *et al.*'s conclusion that a large area of cortex is organized so that particular psycholinguistic functions are shared and overlap in many small regions of the area, producing some degree of "neural plasticity" or "functional reserve" within the area, Damasio and Damasio argue that specific psycholinguistic functions are carried out in quite small regions and tracts without any such duplication. While Mohr *et al.* propose a theory of language representation in the brain which involves a mechanism like Lashley's mass action, Damasio and Damasio favor the view that there is an exquisitely narrow localization of particular sub-components of the language-processing system within very small areas of the perisylvian language-devoted cortex.

The neurological correlates of the transcortical aphasias have also been studied using CT scans. Kertesz *et al.* (1982) identified fifteen patients who had a single infarction and whose clinical picture was one of "transcortical sensory" aphasia. On the Western Aphasia Battery (Kertesz and Poole 1974), these patients had repetition scores of eight or better, comprehension scores of less than seven, and fluent speech, thus confirming their membership in this group of patients (see Chapters 4 and 11). Nine patients had CT scans, thirteen had radio-isotope scans, and one had an arteriogram. (Some patients had several tests.) The authors report on the areas of the brain which were affected in all of the CT scan examinations and all of the isotope examinations. The primary visual areas were spared. Most of the lesions were near the junction of the temporal and occipital lobes, and three extended into the parietal lobe. Twelve of the cases had lesions between the territory of the posterior and middle cerebral arteries. The authors comment that these lesions were deeper and more posterior than those producing the "Gerstmann syndrome", and posterior to those seen in cases of alexia-with-agraphia. Correlations between initial severity and degree of recovery and lesion size were poor. Thus, the authors conclude that "the location of the lesion is a more important factor in the development of the syndrome than the lesion size" (Kertesz *et al*. 1982: 477).

The authors indicate that the location of lesions in their patients in the parietal–occipital region is a new finding. They interpret this finding as showing that this posterior association area plays an important role in semantic processing. They argue that the impaired comprehension in these patients reflects a disconnection of auditory input and "a semantic processor" (478). The authors stress that their study dealt with patients at an acute stage of their illness and that the symptoms frequently resolved to an anomia after a period of months. On the other hand, some Wernicke's aphasics they had seen improved over time to become "transcortical sensory" aphasics. In these cases, the lesions were considerably larger than those in the patients in this study.

We have now reviewed five studies of the CT correlates of the classical syndromes which have been taken to provide support for the classical localization of these syndromes. Naeser and Hayward found that patients with Broca's aphasia, Wernicke's aphasia, conduction aphasia, transcortical motor aphasia, and global aphasia (as defined on the BDAE) had lesions in the predicted areas. Basso *et al*. (1986) find that non-fluent patients generally have anterior and fluent aphasics posterior lesions; Damasio and Damasio (1980) claim their results support the classical localization of conduction aphasia; and Kertesz *et al*. (1982) argue similarly regarding transcortical sensory aphasia. These results have been taken as direct support for the classical connectionist neurolinguistic theory. Mohr *et al*. (1978) argue that for a lesion to produce a permanent Broca's aphasia it must be relatively large, but acknowledge that it must include Broca's area. Their results are consistent with a modification of classical connectionist neurolinguistic accounts, which claims that a lesion in Broca's area is necessary rather than sufficient to cause Broca's aphasia. The neurolinguistic claim that Broca's area is involved in speech production would still be intact, if this modification were true.

391

Most of the authors of the papers we have reviewed argue that their results are quite consistent with the predictions made by classical and contemporary neurolinguistic theories. Damasio and Damasio say that their study "supports, in good measure, Wernicke's original prediction and Geschwind's now classical anatomical account of the syndrome [of conduction aphasia]" (1980: 349), and Basso *et al.* emphasize that, despite the exceptions to the classical localizations that they have documented, the neuroanatomical principles underlying the connectionist theory deserve to be kept as the standard teaching on the subject. In a general way, these studies do confirm what was predicted on the basis of clinical studies and neurolinguistic theories. However, a closer look at these studies suggests that a number of reservations regarding the classical doctrine are in order.

The study by Naeser and Hayward does show that most patients with the classical aphasic syndromes have lesions in more or less the expected locations. However, even in this small group there are counter-examples to connectionist predictions, such as the few patients with transcortical motor aphasia who have lesions in Broca's area. In the large study by Basso *et al.* (1986), there are many exceptions. Moreover, we must remember that Basso *et al.* say that there are many aphasic syndromes which are *expected* after a lesion in a particular area. For instance, both Broca's aphasia and global aphasia are expected following anterior lesions; Wernicke's aphasia, conduction aphasia, anomia, and certain forms of reading disorders are "expected" after lesions in the posterior language area. If so many syndromes are compatible with particular lesion sites, it is not surprising that there are a relatively small number of exceptions to the predictions made by the classical theory. While the connectionist theory certainly generates these expectations, it generates much more detailed expectations. Wernicke's aphasia should follow lesions in Wernicke's area; conduction aphasia should follow lesions in the arcuate fasciculus; anomia should follow lesions in the inferior parietal lobe. The large studies by Basso and her colleagues, and others such as those undertaken by Kertesz (1979), do not bear on whether these specific correlates are found.

If we look at the correlation of lesion site with aphasic syndrome in the studies of selected aphasic groups we have reviewed, we find these specific predictions are not borne out. Mohr *et al.*'s (1978) results showed that a permanent Broca's aphasia requires a large lesion, which leads to the change in connectionist neurolinguistic models mentioned above. Kertesz and his colleagues showed that auditory comprehension is disturbed, not by a lesion disconnecting Wernicke's area from the inferior parietal lobe, but rather by a lesion at the junction of the parietal and occipital lobes. If the traditional "concept center" is thought to be located in the inferior parietal lobe, as

Geschwind (1965) suggests (see Chapter 5), we would expect that the lesion producing transcortical sensory aphasia should disconnect the temporal and parietal lobes, not the parietal and the occipital lobes. Damasio and Damasio's cases show an unexpected site for conduction aphasia, and the authors indicate that this site is different from the sites in conduction aphasia recorded in other studies. The Damasios' findings suggest that the contemporary connectionist theory is not complete.

There are also problems in the Damasio study related to interpreting the disturbance that the patients had. Two of the patients had difficulty comprehending, and it is not clear what relation the comprehension problem had to the repetition problem. The most puzzling question is why these patients were unable to repeat sentences despite such good digit spans, reasonable auditory comprehension, and fluent spontaneous speech. If a patient can speak fluently, he can map concepts onto speech; if he can understand sentences, he can map sentences onto concepts. These retained abilities should, by themselves, allow for repetition, as the patient should be able to understand a sentence and then generate a form of the sentence from the concept he has extracted from the auditorily presented sentence. In addition, if the patient can repeat seven digits, it is not clear why he cannot repeat more than three-word sentences. Most normal subjects can repeat more words in sentences than in lists, precisely because they use the additional structure in sentences to group words together in meaningful ways and thereby increase their repetition span. The Damasios' patients should have been able to do this. Looked at from a psycholinguistic point of view, the linguistic abnormalities in these patients raise a large number of intriguing questions. It is very hard to conclude that the anatomical basis for repetition has been clarified by a study in which the repetition performance is so unusual.

These problems with the Damasio and Damasio study reflect a general problem which arises with all of these studies. We have noted in Chapter 11 that the classical aphasic syndromes are not homogeneous, and we have explored the specific nature of disturbances in individual psycholinguistic functions in some detail in Part III of this book. We noted in Chapter 11 that the fact that the classical syndromes are not homogeneous, and that different patients classified in a single syndrome can be quite different with respect to their deficits, makes it impossible to correlate disturbances in isolated psycholinguistic functions with lesions on the basis of the correlation of the classical syndromes with lesions. We see this problem emerging in several ways in the studies we have reported. In the Damasio and Damasio (1980) study, patients were not homogeneous with respect to functions like auditory comprehension, and the deficit causing their impaired repetition is unclear. In the Kertesz study (1979), some of the patients had fluent jargon speech output, and others only a few phonemic paraphasias. In the studies by Naeser and Hayward (1978) and by Basso and her colleagues (1986), in which a larger number of patients were classified into few relatively large syndromes, we can expect that there would be a great deal of intra-category variability with respect to the symptoms found in individual patients.

These investigators, who use instruments like the BDAE to classify patients into the classical syndromes, tend to assume that, if the deficits were more narrowly characterized, there would be a good deal of correlation between specific deficits and specific lesion sites; but this is an assumption, not a proven fact. In addition, these investigators find slight but theoretically significant discrepancies between actual lesion sites in some syndromes and those predicted by connectionist theories. We should not lose sight of the fact that the interpretation of some of these discrepant findings – such as the attribution of a semantic processor to the area betwen the parietal and occipital lobe by Kertesz and his colleagues – are really quite significant changes in the modern theory (as developed by Geschwind at least), even if they only involve "moving" a function a very short distance in the brain. As we saw in Chapter 5, Geschwind (1965) had very important reasons for claiming that one aspect of the semantic system is located in the inferior parietal lobe. These reasons do not apply to the parieto-occipital junction, even if it is very close to the area Geschwind discussed.

If the classical syndromes are unreliable guides to specific deficits, perhaps we could make more progress by looking at individual *symptoms* rather than the symptom complexes of the classical syndromes. As we have seen in Part III, symptoms may be either primary or secondary (for instance, see the discussion of syntactic comprehension disorders in Chapter 16). If we are to examine individual symptoms as reflections of deficits in a single psycholinguistic processing component of the language-processing system, it would be well to pick a symptom which cannot be secondary to other disturbances. There are several disturbances which seem to meet this requirement, and one of them has been studied in relationship to different types of aphasia and, to some extent, in relationship to lesions associated with aphasia in a number of patients. This symptom is the ability to discriminate and identify phonemes. Because this is such a specialized ability, and because it is a function which occurs prior to most other processes involved in auditory comprehension, a disturbance in phoneme discrimination and identification is likely to be a primary disturbance (assuming that hearing deficits are excluded). Several authors have recently reported a variety of interesting studies regarding disturbances in phoneme discrimination and their neuropathological basis.

Blumstein *et al.* (1977*a*) studied phoneme discrimination in twenty-five patients: six Broca's, six "mixed anteriors", six Wernicke's, and seven unclassified posterior aphasics. The Broca's and the mixed anterior aphasics all had anterior lesions, and the Wernicke's and the unclassified posterior aphasics had posterior lesions. The Broca's and mixed anterior patients had non-fluent speech, but the former had good comprehension and the latter bad comprehension on the Boston Diagnostic Aphasia Exam. The unclassified posterior aphasics had a variety of fluent aphasias (anomic aphasia, conduction aphasia, transcortical sensory aphasia). The authors tested these patients on several tasks. The subjects had to discriminate words which differed in a single phoneme, such as *pear/bear*. The phonemes differed either in voicing, as in the example given, or in place of articulation, such as *pin/tin*, or in both voicing and place of articulation (*pen/den*). Some of the words were monosyllabic and some were bisyllabic. In addition, the subjects had to discriminate words that had a change in one syllable, such as *describe/prescribe*. On a third task, the subject had to discriminate words in which the sequence of phonemes was inverted (*tax/task*). For each of these stimuli, some of the discriminations required discriminating two real words, and others required discriminating two nonsense words.

The authors report their results for each of the four groups of aphasic patients. Averaging across the two groups with anterior lesions and the two groups with posterior lesions, there are no differences in performance for any of these anatomically defined groups on any of these tasks, except for the fact that discrimination of phonemes differing in place of articulation was more difficult than discrimination of phonemes differing in voicing for the Wernicke's and residual posterior aphasics, but not for either of the other two groups. However, this was because the Broca's aphasia group performed extremely well on the entire task, and the differences between the two types of phoneme differences were not large enough to be significant (a ceiling effect), and the mixed anterior aphasics performed so poorly on all of the tasks that there were no differences between any of the two types of phoneme discrimination tasks (a floor effect). In all tasks in which floor and ceiling effects did not occur, the groups with anterior and posterior lesions *did* produce quantitatively similar behavior. For instance, discrimination of phonemes differing by two distinctive features was easier than discrimination of phonemes differing by a single distinctive feature in all groups.

Another study by Basso and her colleagues (Basso *et al.* 1977) shows a similar result. These researchers used synthetic stimuli to test their patients, focussing on the ability of the patients to discriminate phonemes that differed in voicing. As noted in Chapter 13, the differences between voiced and unvoiced consonants at the acoustic level consist in large part of the differences in the onset of periodic voicing. Voiced stop consonants have voicing that begins earlier than unvoiced stop consonants. Basso and her colleagues presented synthetic syllables in which either a voiced or unvoiced stop consonant was followed by the sound /a/, and subjects were asked to identify each stimulus as either *ta* or *da*. They studied 137 subjects, sixty-two of whom had left-hemisphere lesions, of which fifty were aphasic. There were ten globally aphasic patients (group 1), eleven patients with non-fluent aphasia with good comprehension (group 2), eighteen patients with fluent aphasia with poor comprehension (group 3), and eleven patients with fluent speech and good comprehension (group 4). There were no significant differences between the groups with respect to age, years of schooling, time elapsed since the aphasia began, or the etiology for the aphasia. Patients' performance on this test were estimated through analysis of the boundary zone between the voiced and unvoiced consonants. Patients were divided into four groups on the basis of how well they did on this test.

The non-aphasic patients had no detectable impairments. The authors were "unable to detect any significant association between fluency/non-fluency and presence/absence of a phoneme identification deficit" (93). The authors do not report the lesion sites in their patients, but it is known from Basso's own study, reviewed above (Basso *et al.* 1985), that there is considerable overlap between non-fluency and anterior lesions and fluency and posterior lesions. On the basis of this study, we may infer with some confidence that the incidence of phonemic identification deficits in patients with anterior lesions and posterior lesions does not differ.

A third study, of a yet more technical nature, was undertaken by Blumstein and her colleagues (Blumstein *et al.* 1977*b*). In this study, the ability to discriminate synthetic stop consonants was investigated, as well as the ability to identify these synthetic stimuli. Stimuli similar to those in the study by Basso and her colleagues were used. In the discrimination task, two stimuli which varied by 20 msec. with respect to the onset of voicing (VOT) or which were identical were presented, and the subjects had to say whether they heard two different stimuli or two identical stimuli. Normals are able to discriminate stimuli whose VOTs fall on either side of the middle zone which differentiates voiced from unvoiced consonants, but are unable to discriminate two synthetic consonants differing by 20 msec. of VOT when both fall on the "voiced" or the "unvoiced" side of this acoustic boundary.

Patients consisted of eight cases with anterior brain damage – six Broca's and two mixed anteriors – and eight with posterior brain damage – four Wernicke's, two conduction, and two anomics. The authors report their results in terms of how patients did both on this discrimination task and on a task of identifying phonemes similar to that used by Basso and her colleagues. Eight patients did well on both tasks – three Broca's, one mixed anterior, one Wernicke's, one conduction, and two anomics. A second group of patients were capable of performing the discrimination task, but were unable to identify the test stimuli reliably. This group consisted of three Wernicke's aphasics and one Broca's aphasic. Presumably, their disturbance is one of phoneme identification, and is possibly specific to linguistic stimuli. The third group, who were unable to do either the labeling or the discrimination task, consisted of one mixed anterior patient, one Broca's aphasic, and one conduction aphasic. This group had a more basic perceptual deficit, which is tied to the psycholinguistic task of phoneme identification. If we take these three groups as representing normal performance, intact low-level auditory processing but impaired linguistically relevant labeling, and impairments in both these functions, we see that there is no correlation between lesion site and the type of disturbance that these patients have.

A similar set of findings were found by Caplan and his colleagues (Caplan *et al.* 1985) with respect to the study of syntactic comprehension which we reviewed in Chapter 16. Caplan studied three groups of fifty-eight, thirty-seven, and forty-nine aphasic patients on a test requiring comprehension of sentences with a variety of syntactic structures. The authors performed clustering analyses to identify sub-groups of patients. These sub-groups primarily reflect overall severity of patients' impairments, with a lesser contribution of how patients differ on particular sentence types. The best-performing sub-groups were excellent on the test, and the worst patients were unable to perform the test at all, with many different levels of performance between the best- and worst-performing groups. Caplan (1987) also performed discriminant function analyses to see whether aphasic patients could be separated from normal controls. He discovered that most of the aphasic patients did not do as well as normals, but that a few patients in each of the three studies were indistinguishable from normals. Caplan *et al.* (1985) then attempted to correlate the sub-groups they found with lesion sites. They found that patients with strictly frontal, parietal, or temporal lesions within the dominant perisylvian cortex were equally likely to belong to any of the sub-groups of patients identified by the clustering procedure. In addition, patients identified through the discriminant function analyses as performing normally also could have lesions restricted to any one of these three lobes. This means that a lesion in any one of these lobes can be associated with no demonstrable deficit in syntactic comprehension, any degree of deficit, or a total impairment of this function.

The fact that some lesions confined to a single lobe give rise to severe or total impairment of syntactic comprehension implies that, for some individuals, the functions needed for syntactic comprehension are carried out in a single lobe; that is, that they are narrowly localized. (A failure of syntactic comprehension can be secondary (see Chapter 16) but, in the Caplan *et al.* study, it cannot be secondary to a failure to understand single words, at least.) The fact that these severe impairments arise following lesions in single lobes rules out the possibility that the perisylvian cortex is "equipotential" for these language functions (Lashley 1950). Equipotentiality refers to the idea that any area of cortex can carry out a function. If this were true of the perisylvian cortex with respect to the functions involved in syntactic comprehension, severe deficits in this ability should not arise with damage restricted to one part of this cortex. The fact that the lobe associated with these severe impairments varies across the population indicates that this narrow localization is not the same for all adults. In addition, the fact that any lobe can be lesioned without affecting syntactic comprehension at all rules out any theory based upon "mass action" (Lashley 1950) as the neural basis for language. As we have seen, "mass action" claims that the amount, not the location, of the damage determines a deficit. In these cases, some damage causes no impairment at all, which contradicts this principle.

All these results suggest that different areas within the perisylvian cortex are capable of supporting particular aspects of language functions in different individuals. The notion of localization of function applies, but in a rather different sense from that which theorists have so far considered. A particular function may be narrowly localized in an individual in a particular area of perisylvian dominant cortex, localized equally narrowly in another area in another individual, and carried out in a much larger area of perisylvian cortex in a third. The only constraint seems to be that core language processes are accomplished in this area of neocortex.

Let us review our discussion of the narrow localization of sub-components of the language-processing system within portions of the dominant perisylvian association cortex. All the traditional theories we have reviewed which postulate narrow localization of components of the language-processing system share two features. First, they all claim that, ignoring the issue of lateralization, the localization of components of the language system is the same in all normal adults. Second, they all derive the specific functions of the sub-areas of language-related cortex from the relationship of these sub-areas to motor and sensory areas of the brain. For instance, Geschwind (1965) relates the language functions of the inferior parietal lobe to its connections, as discussed in Chapter 5, not to its intrinsic elements and organization – indicating that pre-frontal cortex, which does not have similar connections, has no language functions, despite its equally advanced structural character. Similarly, Luria (1947) explicitly derives the particular role of areas of cortex in language from the role of adjacent cortex in motor and sensory function (Chapter 9). These theories are said to receive support from studies correlating lesions seen in modern radiological images (especially CT scans) with the classical aphasic syndromes.

We have seen that this evidence is not easy to interpret. First, there are exceptions to the general correlation of classical syndromes with lesion sites found on CT. Second, lesion sites are sometimes subtly different from those predicted by theory, and these differences are hard to interpret. Third, the classical syndromes are polytypic, and do not reflect disturbances of isolated psycholinguistic functions. For all these reasons, though the classical clinical syndromes tend to follow lesions in particular areas of the brain, it is not completely clear what this fact tells us about the localization of sub-components of the language-processing system. The fact that some functions which can reasonably be taken to be independent stages of language processing, such as phoneme discrimination and identification, can be disturbed or spared with lesions in either the anterior or posterior portions of the language zone, adds to our uncertainty about what CT scan correlates of the classical aphasic syndromes are telling us about narrow localization.

One possibility which has been suggested by many researchers is that those aspects of the language-processing system that interact with sensory and motor systems may be narrowly and invariantly localized near motor and sensory areas of cortex, while those processes which make use of abstract representations are not localized at all. Though this is an appealing formulation, the evidence which we have reviewed indicates that the matter is more complicated. On the one hand, functions such as categorical perception are certainly as closely tied to perceptual functions as any operation related to language processing can be. Nonetheless, the data from Blumstein's study suggest that categorical perception can be impaired with anterior lesions as frequently as with posterior lesions. In this respect, categorical perception is no different from phoneme discrimination, phoneme identification, or multiple aspects of parsing and sentence interpretation, which all seem to be affected and spared with roughly equal frequency with either anterior or posterior lesions. It therefore does not appear that early sensory-related functions are always carried out by association cortex which is close to the primary receptive areas of the brain. Neither, on the other hand, does it seem to be the case that abstract aspects of language processing are *not* localized. Results such as those of Caplan *et al.* (1985) indicate that abstract functions such as syntactic comprehension can be severely disturbed through focal lesions. As we noted, this is only consistent with some form of localization of the functions necessary to accomplish syntactic comprehension; but that localization seems to vary considerably in the adult human population.

Is the fact that there is some localization of the traditional aphasic syndromes a reflection of non-variant localization of at least certain language-processing sub-components? Most researchers have found that anomias and some types of phonemic paraphasias tend to arise after lesions of the posterior regions of the brain. Conversely, omission of function words in agrammatism tends to follow lesions which are more anterior. Does this reflect a uniform localization of processing related to content words in the posterior part of the perisylvian association cortex, and of processing related to function words in the anterior part of this cortex? The answer is far from clear. As we noted in Chapter 11, anomia does occur in conjunction with Broca's aphasia, following primarily anterior lesions. Though agrammatism does tend to occur more frequently with lesions that involve portions of the frontal lobe, it can be seen after a wide variety of lesions in the perisylvian cortex including the insula, and with lesions which spare the frontal lobe entirely (Vanier and Caplan, in press). Moreover, paragrammatism, a syndrome very similar to agrammatism insofar as it affects the function word vocabulary, is somewhat more likely to follow posterior than anterior lesions. It is, therefore, not at all clear that processing of these two vocabulary classes takes place in different areas of the brain in any systematic way.

Overall, we can say that narrow localization does exist, but it is not clear that particular sub-components of the language-processing system are located in the same areas of the brain in all adult humans. On the contrary, there is reason to believe that there is considerable variation with respect to the exact narrow localization of individual processing components. Several obvious dimensions of language structure and processing which could be related to particular brain locations – the relationship between a process and sensory functions; the content word/function word vocabulary class distinction – do not appear to map onto brain locations in completely systematic ways. The extent of individual variation of the language-processing system within the perisylvian association cortex remains a matter for further investigation. The genetic, organic, environmental, and phenomenological determinants of any regularities in the localization of sub-components of the language-processing system also remain to be determined. Despite these unanswered questions, important advances have been made. Perhaps chief among these is the recognition of the need for far more detailed functional analyses of patients' deficits to be used in lesion–deficit correlational studies. A second advance is the recognition that a function need not be diffusely represented in the brain if it is not localized in the same brain region in all members of the species. Some variation in the location of language-processing components could be present, subject to genetic and environmental influences.

These considerations lead to a very different view of the significance of narrow localization of the sub-components of the language-processing system than that which emerges from the existing theories in this domain. We said above that the uniform localization of the sub-components of the language-processing system postulated by traditional theories went hand in hand with the view that the location of a language-processing sub-component was largely dictated by how the area in which it was located connected to sensory and motor cortex. This view is most appealing if we believe that language processing is closely related to sensory or motor functions. However, a large number of components of a language processor are devoted to operations affecting abstract representations of the language code. There is no reason to believe that these "central" stages of language processing have any similarity to processes related to non-linguistic sensory and motor functions, or are in any way derived from these functions. Thus, there is no *a priori* reason to think that most areas of cortex devoted to language processing derive their specific language functions from their connections to sensory and motor association cortex, or from their adjacency to such cortex. For the central aspects of language processing, what matters is not how a brain region is related to the sensory or motor areas of the brain, but what types of computations can go on in that region. The studies we have reviewed in this chapter are consistent with the view that the association cortex in the perisylvian region is uniquely suited to accomplish core psycholinguistic computations. Whether there is a greater degree of uniform localization of individual processing components within this cortex is unclear, as is the question of whether genetic factors (such as sex (Kimura 1983) or those related to handedness) or environmental factors determine systematic narrow localization of processing components in this cortex in a sub-set of the population. As elsewhere in neurolinguistics, new formulations of theory and new observational capacities in linguistic aphasiology, as well as in neuro-imaging, combine here to open up new research areas touching on the old question of localization of language functions.

SUGGESTIONS FOR FURTHER READING

Basso, A., Lecours, A. R., Moraschini, S., and Vanier, M. (1985). Anatomoclinical correlations of the aphasias as defined through computerized tomography: exceptions. *Brain and Language* 26, 201–29.

Caplan, D. (in press). The biological basis for language. In F. Newmeyer (ed.), *Linguistics: The Cambridge Survey*. Cambridge University Press, Cambridge.

Damasio, H. and Damasio, A. R. (1980). The anatomical basis of conduction aphasia. *Brain* 103, 337–50.

Kertesz, A., Sheppard, A., and MacKenzie, R. (1982). Localization in transcortical sensory aphasia. *Archives of Neurology* 39, 475–8.

Mohr, J. P., Pessin, M. S., Finkelstein, S., Funkenstein, H. H., Duncan, G. W., and Davis, K. R. (1978). Broca's aphasia: pathologic and clinical. *Neurology* 28, 311–24.

Vanier, M. and Caplan, D. (in press). CT scan correlates of agrammatism. In L. Obler, L. Menn, and H. Goodglass (eds.), *A Cross-Language Study of Agrammatism*. Benjamin Press, New York.

20

Cerebral evoked potentials and language

Technological advances have not only greatly increased our ability to document the sites of lesions associated with aphasias through CT scans and other modern radiological techniques, but have also enabled us to record electrical activity in the brain that is correlated with language functions. Electrical activity in the brain can be measured through the use of electrodes placed on the scalp. Electroencephalographic (EEG) recordings have a major role in the assessment of neurological functioning in many patients. Abnormalities in the EEG can be used to help diagnose the location of neurological disease and its nature in cases such as epilepsy. Many changes in the physiological activity of the brain, such as those associated with sleep, are associated with changes in the EEG. However, because it reflects the activity of millions of neurons, all of which generate electrical charges, the EEG itself does not change in relation to specific cognitive functions in any way that can be reliably measured. For instance, the EEG changes dramatically when a person resting quietly with his eyes closed opens his eyes. In these conditions, the "alpha-rhythm" in the posterior portions of the brain disappears, and the EEG becomes "de-synchronized". Though this change reflects the fact that the subject is attentive to visual stimuli and more aroused with his eyes open than with his eyes closed, the particular visual stimuli or the particular content of a person's thoughts do not induce further detectable changes in the general EEG record.

We do know, however, from physiological studies in animals that patterns of electrical activity in individual neurons are altered in specific ways by the presence of particular stimuli. For instance, the number of "spikes" – discharges in a nerve fiber – increases when that nerve is stimulated. Physiologists have recorded electrical activity from individual cells and groups of cells within the brain when an animal is exposed to a particular stimulus or trained to perform a particular act. Many such studies have shown that small groups of cells respond quite selectively and specifically to particular types of stimuli. Some of the best-known work on this subject is that by Hubel and Wiesel (1962), who showed that cells in the occipital (visual) cortex of cats and monkeys respond to very particular types of visual patterns. Some cells in this area respond to concentric circles with dark centres and bright surrounding areas; other cells respond to concentric circles with the opposite pattern. Still other cells respond to lines which are presented at certain orientations, and other groups of cells respond to more complex geometric forms. A good deal of work has refined the analysis of just what aspects of the visual stimulus are important in triggering different firing rates in different cells in different areas of this cortex. Mountcastle (1978) has demonstrated that cells in the motor cortex, the post-central gyrus, and in other areas of the parietal and pre-frontal lobes, as well as groups of cells in subcortical gray-matter nuclei, all fire in fairly regular patterns just before and during the execution of a motor act in a trained monkey. Kandel (1985*b*) has pioneered the investigation of single-cell responses to simple learning situations in certain types of molluscs known as aplysia. All of this work indicates that selected groups of cells develop specific patterns of electrical activity in response to particular stimuli, in preparation for motor activity, and when an organism "learns" something new.

Though it is not possible to investigate the responses of single cells and groups of cells in the human brain through these direct methods (except in very selected populations who require certain neurosurgical diagnostic or therapeutic procedures), it is possible to study the electrical activity of individual groups of neurons within the brain through specialized techniques which allow specific event-related electrical activity to be separated from the background EEG. These techniques are all based upon the idea that if a stimulus is repeated enough times, and each repetition produces the same response in a part of the brain, it might be possible to find that response by averaging together all the electrical activity of the brain for a short period of time, beginning with the onset of the stimulus and ending after the electrical response is finished. In these conditions, the general electrical activity of the brain should form a sort of background "noise" against which the particular activity associated with the stimulus begins to stand out. The electrical activity associated with a stimulus or an internally generated action is known as an "event-related potential" (ERP), because it is an electrical potential associated with a particular event, either an external stimulus or an internal state of the organism. The development of computer-based recording and averaging techniques has allowed the use of ERPs to develop considerably in research and clinical neurology.

Before considering several studies which report ERPs related to language functions, several features of the use of ERPs in language studies should be borne in mind. First, not all electrical potentials which occur after a stimulus or in preparation for a motor action are necessarily cerebral in origin. For instance, there are very large electrical potentials associated with contraction of the facial muscles in preparation for speaking. In order to know that an electrical potential which occurs prior to a speech act is coming from the brain, and not from the articulatory muscles, electrodes measuring electrical activity in these muscles must be used in addition to electrodes measuring electrical activity in the brain. This is because an electrode placed on the scalp will measure activity coming from these muscles as well as activity coming from the brain. Similarly, the eyes are electrically charged, and movements of the eyes generate large electrical potentials which are picked up by electrodes placed over the anterior portion of the scalp. Monitoring horizontal and vertical eye movements is also an important control measurement in determining that an electrical potential measured in electrodes over the anterior portions of the scalp is truly coming from the brain.

Second, we must bear in mind that, while the presence of a true cerebral potential in relationship to a language stimulus does indicate that some electrical activity is occurring in the brain when that stimulus is presented, the absence of an electrical potential in relationship to a stimulus does not mean that there is no electrical activity in the brain that occurs when the linguistic stimulus is presented. Many electrical currents generated in the brain simply do not reach the surface. Others are too small and inconstant to be recorded by surface electrodes, even using averaging techniques.

Third, the exact location in the brain at which a response occurs cannot always be accurately discovered by examining the ERP. For instance, the visual ERP that occurs in the left hemisphere is actually largest over the right side of the scalp, because the visual cortex is located medially in the occipital lobe, and electrical activity is generated in such a way that it is more easily conducted to the opposite side of the head. Interpretation of the location of a generator of an ERP must be made in conjunction with information about the functional anatomy of portions of the brain which might be generating the ERP.

Last, ERPs are quite complicated electrical events. Typically there are "early", "middle", and "late" parts to an ERP. The early parts, which occur within approximately 20 msec. of a sensory stimulus, reflect the early transmission of information into the subcortical portions of the nervous system. The middle component, from approximately 20 to 75 msec. after a stimulus, reflects the arrival of the stimulus in the primary cortical processing areas. The late components, from approximately 75–100 msec. to 400–700 msec. after a stimulus, reflect the processing of these stimuli. The late components are in many ways the most interesting, from the point of view of language studies. The late components (and the early and middle components as well) are not simple. Typically, they consist of a series of negative and positive electrical waves which vary in their exact form, size, and temporal duration. It is far from clear just what parts of this complex waveform are related to different psychological processes. For instance, some researchers have taken a particular wave, such as a positive wave which occurs approximately 300 msec. after a stimulus, as an entity which correlates well with certain psychological processes. Other investigators have taken the difference in amplitude between a negative and positive wave as being of psychological significance. Still other researchers have developed complex mathematical analyses – principal components analyses – to identify factors which contribute to the entire waveform, and have taken these factors as relevant to psychology. Some researchers have taken the energy in part or all of the ERP as the significant feature of the ERP, while yet others have looked at the degree of coherence or synchronization of the waveform as a reflection of the degree to which a portion of the brain is active during the processing of the stimulus. These different ways of evaluating ERPs do not always lead to the same results in a particular task.

Despite all these reservations, the use of event-related potentials is an exciting development in neuropsychology and neurolinguistics. Event-related potentials have the capacity to measure millisecond-by-millisecond electrical events in the brain. We know from the studies reported in Part III and many other psycholinguistic studies that processes such as the recognition of a written or spoken word, understanding certain aspects of syntactic structure, and other psycholinguistic processes, take place extremely rapidly, probably within a few hundred msec. of the presentation of a linguistic stimulus. It is not easy to find physiological correlates of these psycholinguistic processes, but event-related potentials at least have the temporal resolving power that makes them potentially capable of being correlated with these processes. Moreover, the information we have from neuropsychological and neurophysiological studies in animals gives us strong reasons to believe that electrical events are at least some of the information-processing physiological processes used by the brain. Investigation of the electrical potentials that arise in relation to linguistic processing is therefore a promising new field of neurolinguistic inquiry.

We shall review studies in three different areas that make use of these techniques: speech production, auditory discrimination, and comprehension. Though we shall find that many of the published results are preliminary and need to be accepted with caution, the potential these studies have for many new discoveries regarding the neurophysiological correlates of language processing will also be apparent throughout our review.

Cerebral potentials preceding speech

There are two types of cerebral potentials related to speech which have been measured. The first is the so-called "readiness" potential. To measure the readiness potential, a subject is either asked to repeat a particular word or phrase, or to speak freely with pauses of three or more seconds between various portions of his utterance. The EEG is recorded continually, and a portion of the EEG preceding the onset of speech is analyzed, averaging across many utterances to discover any speech-related potentials. In the second paradigm, which measures the so-called contingent negative variation (CNV) or "expectancy" waveform, the subject is given two separate stimuli, usually visual. The temporal interval between the first stimulus (S_1) and the second stimulus (S_2) is fixed, and the subject is required to say a particular word or phrase when the second stimulus arises. In these conditions, an "expectancy" potential appears following S_1. This potential is negative in polarity and "contingent" upon S_1 signaling that a response must be made at S_2, from which it gets its name. The location and shape of both the readiness and expectancy potentials can be measured.

The first researchers to describe readiness potentials preceding speech were Ertl and Schafer (1969). A well-known early study was also reported by McAdam and Whitaker (1971). McAdam and Whitaker found late negative potentials emanating from what they thought was Broca's area, which occurred approximately 150 msec. before a subject uttered a single polysyllabic word. These potentials were larger over the left hemisphere than over the right. As a control, the authors reported potentials related to non-speech activities using the vocal tract, such as coughing. They found that non-speech activity produced negative waves in a symmetrical way over both hemispheres. The authors interpreted their findings as showing that Broca's area on the left was involved in the planning of speech.

This interpretation was criticized by many investigators, who argued that the readiness potentials described in these studies were not cerebral at all. Grozinger and his colleagues (1970; 1977) provide many arguments against the McAdam and Whitaker interpretation of their findings. First, they argued that the use of a voice microphone to indicate the onset of speech cannot measure the activity in the articulatory muscles accurately. Compared with electromyographic recordings of muscle activity in the muscles of the lips (the orbicularis oris muscle), a recording made through a microphone can begin up to 150 msec. after muscle activity has already started. Grozinger and his colleagues found that there were asymmetrical potentials over the two hemispheres as early as two to three seconds before the onset of speech, not just a few hundred msec. before speech began. They also found that in some cases these very early potentials correlated well with potentials of cerebral origin that are related to respiratory function. The relationship of cerebral potentials related to respiration (the so-called "R-wave") to the onset of speech is highly variable, and the authors argued that only detailed studies of individual subjects can separate potentials related to motor speech planning from cerebral potentials related to respiration. The problem is even more complicated because certain aspects of the control of respiration may, in fact, be integrated with the motor control of the supra-glottal vocal tract needed for speech (see Chapter 13 for additional discussion). How much of the hemispheric asymmetry reported by McAdam and Whitaker was due to potentials related to respiration and how much due to potentials relating to speech planning is not clear.

Other sources of electrical potentials were not completely controlled in these early studies. Grozinger and his colleagues mention that galvanic skin responses can contaminate scalp-recorded potentials, and that potentials coming from the tongue (glossokinetic potentials) may also interfere with the recognition of purely cerebral electrical events. Finally, the authors mention that electrical activity arising in the muscles of articulation may be mistaken for electrical activity coming from the brain itself. This last point is emphasized by Szirtes and Vaughan (1977). These investigators reported potentials over Broca's and Wernicke's areas, the inferior portion of the pre-central gyrus, the inferior frontal lobe anterior to Broca's area, and several additional scalp sites. In addition, they recorded electrical activity in many articulatory muscles, including those of the lips, tongue, and jaw. Their first finding was that, in individual subjects, the form of the evoked potential measured over a particular area, such as Broca's area, depended upon which sound the subject produced. Their second finding was that there was a very wide distribution of speech-related electrical activity over the head and face region, with the largest potentials in the area of the nose. Of greatest importance is the fact that electrical activity recorded from the cheek was similar in shape to that recorded in the inferior frontal electrode. Some of the potentials recorded in both these locations probably originated in the tongue and in the jaw. These potentials were frequently asymmetrical, and the asymmetry in the cheek electrode paralleled the asymmetry found over the brain regions in relation to speech. The gradient of asymmetrical electrical activity had its maximum potentials in the area around the nose, and the smallest potentials were recorded over the upper lateral portion of the scalp.

The authors indicate that their results "lend strong support to the suggestion that scalp-recorded speech-related potentials either represent activity of solely extra-cranial origin or are heavily contaminated by such activity" (Szirtes and Vaughan 1977: 120). The authors question how much any of these potentials is related to the "net cortical neural activity associated with differences in the verbal engrams as opposed to programming commands associated with movements of the bulbar musculature" (122). The authors see no way to study cerebral potentials preceding speech through the scalp without heavy contamination from electrical activity of non-cerebral origin, and advocate direct cortical recordings from these areas as the best approach to solving this technological problem.

The second approach to measuring cerebral potentials related to speech is to measure "expectancy" potentials. In the paradigm discussed above, a slow negative wave develops after the presentation of a warning stimulus (S_1). This is known as a Contingent Negative Variation (CNV). Low and Fox (1977) used this technique to study cerebral potentials related to speech in volunteer subjects and epileptic patients. They used a technique in which S_1 was a flash of light and S_2 was a tone. S_2 followed S_1 by 1.5 seconds. The subject was instructed to say either a particular word (*Hi*) or his own name, upon hearing the tone. On control trials, the subject saw just a flash, heard just a tone, or saw a flash and heard a tone and was required to press a button. Twenty-two normal volunteers from eighteen to thirty years of age, eleven right-handed and eleven left-handed, took part in this experiment. The averaged negative shift (CNV) which occurred between S_1 and S_2 was measured over the left and right temporal lobe in each of these subjects. The average CNV was significantly larger over the left hemisphere than over the right in the right-handed subjects and vice versa in the left-handed subjects. The authors also noted that there was considerable variation between individuals in the relative size of CNVs in the two hemispheres. Larger CNVs occurred in the hemisphere dominant for language as measured by Wada testing in 12/15 epileptic patients. (The three mismatches were all cases in which the larger CNV occurred in the right hemisphere of a right-handed subject in whom Wada testing ultimately showed left-hemisphere dominance for language.) The authors conclude that there is a "speech CNV" which shows an asymmetry related to hemispheric dominance in a particular population. The authors were concerned about possible contamination of their results by potentials arising in horizontal ocular movements, but concluded that there was little chance that potentials coming from the tongue were sources of artifact in their results. The authors discussed the occasional mismatches between cerebral dominance as measured by Wada testing and the size of the CNVs in the two hemispheres. Since there are CNVs in *both* hemispheres, they concluded that their observations "support the idea that both left and right hemispheres contribute to the language system in a dynamic way" (Low and Fox 1977: 111), and they are cautious about the functional significance of the asymmetries in the CNV that they recorded, saying that this remains an "open question". Nonetheless, they argue that they have discovered potentials specifically related to speech which are largest over the hemisphere which is dominant for language.

These results and interpretations have been questioned by Curry and his colleagues (Curry *et al.* 1978). Curry and his colleagues studied four right-handed and two left-handed subjects between the ages of twenty-one and thirty, and determined hemispheric dominance for language using Kimura's Dichotic Listening Test (Kimura 1967). Five of the subjects were consistently left-hemisphere dominant for language, and one right-handed subject was mildly right-hemisphere dominant for language. Subjects were presented with a CNV paradigm in which S_1 was the word to be spoken, presented for 1.5 seconds on a screen, followed by a flash of light (S_2). In one condition the subjects then had to say the word aloud, and in a second condition they had to press a button using their preferred hand. In control conditions, S_1 consisted of a tone, followed by a flash, (S_2), at which the subject had to press a button. CNVs were recorded at sites in the inferior frontal and inferior temporal lobes. The results showed significant asymmetrical CNVs at both inferior frontal and inferior temporal sites, with a larger CNV occurring in the left hemisphere. However, these CNVs occurred both in the condition when the subject had to say the presented word and in the condition when he had to press a button after having seen a written word. There were CNVs of quite different size which were not symmetrical which occurred in the control paradigm involving a light, a tone, and a button press, but no linguistic processing. The authors concluded that hemispheric differences in CNVs are not related to preparation for speech, and suggested that asymmetrical CNVs may be obtained in any paradigm which uses a word as the S_1 stimulus.

Overall, the studies on electrical stimulation in the brain preceding speech are suggestive, and show a variety of directions which further research could take. Readiness potentials preceding speech are obtainable through the scalp, and probably partly reflect cerebral activity, but this cerebral activity is very hard to distinguish from electrical impulses which arise in the muscles of the vocal tract and other electrically charged structures in the head. Like the cerebral potentials, these non-cerebral potentials seem to be asymmetrical preceding speech. Expectancy potentials using the CNV paradigm can also be recorded preceding speech, but it is not clear to what extent these potentials are specifically related to speech or are potentials which arise in relationship to any linguistic process. Moreover, the possibility that there are cerebral potentials which differ considerably with respect to their form, and possibly their location, as a function of the particular linguistic structure of an utterance is suggested by the work of Szirtes and Vaughan. The use of evoked potentials to study the electrical activity related to speech planning is an area which will require a considerable number of very detailed controlled studies to clarify the role of particular potentials in particular speech processes.

Cerebral potentials related to phonological processing and auditory comprehension

A large number of studies using ERPs have focussed on the electrical potentials which correlate with the recognition of sounds and meanings of individual words. These studies have been concerned with both the intra-hemispheric locus of these ERPs and with asymmetries between the hemispheres in these ERPs. We shall review several studies related to the recognition of the sounds of words first, and then studies related to word meanings.

Molfese and his colleagues (Molfese 1977; 1978; 1980a; 1980b; Molfese *et al.* 1975) have reported one of the most extensive sequences of experiments dealing with the ERPs related to sound discrimination and identification. Molfese (1977) reported on the evoked potentials related to non-meaningful speech stimuli (/ba/, /da/), piano chords, noise bursts with a frequency of 250 to 4000 Hz, and two words (*boy* and *dog*). Five male and five female subjects between the ages of eighteen and twenty-nine, nine right-handed and one left-handed, were studied. Electrodes were placed over the temporal lobes for recording.

Molfese and his colleagues first attempted to characterize the form of potentials which were evoked by these different types of stimuli. The largest potentials occurred between 90 and 160 msec. following the presentation of the stimulus. Molfese and his colleagues chose the largest negative (N) and positive (P) potentials for analysis. The latencies of these peaks – that is, the time of appearance of these peaks after the presentation of a stimulus – did not differ significantly amongst the stimulus types. The difference between the largest N and P value was measured, and an index of the laterality of the auditory-evoked potential (AEP) was obtained by comparing the N–P amplitude difference for the two hemispheres. There was a consistent (8/10) tendency for the NP amplitude difference to be greater in the left hemisphere than in the right hemisphere in the ten subjects, but the differences between the two hemispheres were extremely small. There was no significant difference between the NP amplitude difference for words and for syllables; but both were different from the NP amplitude differences for

411

mechanical noises, which were greater over the right hemisphere than over the left.

To investigate the meaning of these differences in greater detail, Molfese and his colleagues used more specific stimuli to evaluate the determinants of the responses, and also used more sophisticated analyses of the data to support their conclusions. Molfese and his colleagues presented subjects with stop consonants which varied in VOT (voice onset time). As discussed in Chapters 13 and 19, synthetic stimuli of this sort with VOTs of less than 20 msec. are perceived as voiced consonants (/b/) and stimuli with VOTs greater than 40 msec. are perceived as unvoiced consonants (/p/). Molfese presented stimuli with VOTs of 0, 20, 40, and 60 msec., and recorded the evoked potentials from the mid-temporal regions of each hemisphere in response to sixteen repetitions of each type of stimulus. The averaged waveforms were then analyzed using a Principal Component Analysis (PCA). Such analyses make use of the entire waveform, not just the amplitude differences between the greatest negative and positive peaks, as was done in Molfese's first study. Therefore, they probably more accurately reflect the entirety of the cerebral processes which are responsible for the waveform, especially since the amplitude difference between the largest negative and positive peaks may be an arbitrary measurement.

The results showed that several of the factors in the PCA differed across the hemispheres. For instance, the first and fourth factors of the PCA were significantly different in the right hemisphere but not over the left hemisphere for the boundary between voiced and unvoiced stop consonants (20–40 msec. VOTs). In another study, Molfese (1980*a*) studied similar stimuli which were not linguistic, but differed with respect to the onset of one tone relative to others. These "tone onset times" (TOTs) were structurally similar to the VOTs used in the first experiment. In this study, Molfese reported that the eighth factor in a PCA also showed a significant change in the right hemisphere when the TOT moved from 20 to 40 msec. On the basis of these studies, Molfese concluded that there is a right-hemisphere-based mechanism responsible for the discrimination of voice onset times which is not purely linguistic, but which is also responsible for TOT perception and probably for other aspects of auditory processing of non-linguistic stimuli.

It is very difficult to assess these results. The factors contributing to a PCA decrease in importance from the first factor on. Therefore, an effect that shows up in the eighth factor of a PCA contributes very little to the total ERP. Moreover, the eighth factor in the PCA related to the TOT experiment had maximum values at a latency of 355 msec., which is significantly sooner than the maximum values for the first factor in the VOT experiment (430 msec.) and considerably later than the maximum value for the fourth factor in the VOT experiment (135 msec.), as Picton and Stuss (1984) point out. These potentials might have originated from non-cerebral generators, since no control electrodes over the muscles of the face or the eyes were used. Finally, Molfese himself (Molfese 1977) notes that, in studies of infants and children, there is a significant difference between the pattern of results which is obtained when the peak NP amplitude differences are considered to be the important way to measure the ERP and the pattern obtained when a PCA is used. As we mentioned in the introduction to this chapter, just which feature of the evoked potential is the correct one to use for psychological purposes is not always apparent.

Other studies searching for ERPs related to the perception of sounds have been reported by Wood and his colleagues (1971). These investigators required subjects to discriminate between the sounds /ba/ and /da/ in one condition and between the sound /ba/ played with two fundamental frequencies in another condition. These two tasks use extremely similar acoustic stimuli, but one is a task which is relevant to linguistic discriminations and the other one requires only acoustic discrimination. Potentials were recorded from the temporal region as well as from the central region of the scalp. There were no differences over the right hemisphere between the two tasks, but there were significant differences over the left-hemisphere electrodes in the two tasks. These consisted of a larger early negative peak during the discrimination of stop consonants than during the discrimination of fundamental frequency charges. Though these experiments were very carefully undertaken, they have not proven to be replicable. Grabow and his colleagues (1980) could not find significant differences between these tasks using electrodes over either hemisphere, but they noted that the responses over the left temporal lobe were smaller than those over the right. Grabow suggested that these smaller waveforms over the left hemisphere reflected the fact that the left hemisphere was occupied with other types of linguistic activity during both of the tasks. Here again we see part of the difficulty involved in interpreting the meaning of a finding in an event-related potential. Grabow suggests that a *smaller* ERP reflects the increased activity of the left hemisphere in a discrimination task, while one of the measures used by Molfese (1977) is the maximum NP amplitude difference, which assumes that *larger* potentials occur in the hemisphere which is processing the stimulus.

ERPs related to aspects of meaning

A number of investigators have reported ERPs that correlate with semantic or syntactic aspects of an auditorily presented stimulus. For instance, Brown

413

and his colleagues (Brown *et al*. 1973) found that there were different ERPs evoked by a word in different contexts, such as *sit by the fire* vs. *ready, aim, fire*. These investigators calculated the differences between the waveforms evoked by the word *fire* in these different contexts, and found that these differences were greatest over the anterior portion of the left hemisphere. In another experiment, Brown and his colleagues (Brown *et al*. 1976) told subjects to think about one meaning of a word, and presented a sentence containing a homophone. For instance, subjects would be instructed to think about the verb *led* by thinking of a sentence such as *The horse was led*, or the noun *lead* by being given a sentence such as *The metal was lead*. Then they heard the sentence *It was* /lɛd/. Again, the correlation between the waveforms obtained when the subject was thinking about these two meanings of the word were compared, and were found to be maximally dissimilar in the left anterior region. In other work (Brown and Lehmann 1979; Brown *et al*. 1980), Brown and his colleagues showed that there were differences between the noun and the verb senses of a homophone such as *rose–rows*. They presented phrases such as *a pretty rose* and *the boatman rows*, and recorded the maximum and minimum peaks in the evoked potentials themselves, and in portions of the evoked potentials isolated by a PCA. The maximum positive peaks associated with the verb meanings were more posterior than those of the nouns at the beginning of the potential (under 175 msec.), and the largest negative waves were more anterior for verbs than nouns in the first 330 msec. of the recording.

Picton and Stuss (1984) summarized these results, and expressed several reservations about some of the analyses undertaken by Brown and his colleagues. With respect to the first experiment, Picton and Stuss point out that the use of correlational analyses is very susceptible to very slight changes in latencies, and that a so-called "coherence analysis", in which waveforms of similar shape which differ with respect to their latency are considered similar, might be more appropriate than a simple correlational analysis when comparing two waveforms in this kind of experiment. Moreover, they point out that the PCA of some of the Brown data found components with peak latencies that were significantly affected by meaning of the items presented, but did not appear maximally over the left anterior portion of the scalp. With respect to the second set of results, Picton and Stuss are concerned that the differences in location of the maximum positive and negative potentials of verb and noun readings treat the location of the ERP independently of its waveform over time, and that such differences therefore are very difficult to interpret. Nonetheless, these critical reviewers do call these results "impressive", and it seems likely that semantic aspects of linguistic stimuli do produce discernible ERPs.

Another series of experiments deals with aspects of *sentence* meaning in relationship to ERPs. Friedman and his colleagues (Friedman *et al.* 1975*a*; 1975*b*) showed that one of the late positive waves – the positive wave occurring at approximately 300 msec. after a stimulus is presented, known as the "P300" – can be measured following the presentation of each word in a sentence, when the words of the sentence are presented visually one at a time. The P300 is known to be sensitive to the information carried in the stimulus. Friedman and his colleagues suggested that the P300 occurs when information is acquired by the subject, and that the size of the P300 might vary with the informativeness of each word. They therefore studied sentences in which there were redundant and non-redundant words, and they found that all words, whether redundant or not, evoked a P300. They therefore abandoned their initial hypothesis, but, based on the observation that the P300 was largest for the last word in the sentence, suggested that the P300 enhancement seen at the end of the sentence might reflect what they called "syntactic closure", by which they meant the point-in-processing at which a sentence is complete and a certain amount of syntactic analysis is finished. Moreover, though the size of the P300 did not vary with the information contained in each word, the latency of the P300 did. This wave occurs at about 300 msec. overall, but occurred at a slightly longer latency when the word it was related to was informative than when the word was redundant. The authors looked for hemispheric asymmetries in the size and latency of the P300 in this task, but did not find any.

Another set of late waves in the potential related to sentences is the so-called "N400", a negative wave which occurs after the positive P300. Kutas and Hillyard (1980) reported that an N400 appears if a semantically inappropriate word occurs towards the end of a sentence, using a paradigm in which the words in the sentences were presented individually in visual form. Sentences such as *I take coffee with cream and dog* produced these large waves, while sentences such as *I take coffee with cream and sugar* produced a positive wave rather than a negative wave at a latency of about 400 msec.

Since the late components of an evoked potential, such as the P300 and N400, are waves which arise in experiments measuring ERPs in relation to many cognitive processes, it is possible to relate these waves to cognitive processes which occur in domains other than language. The P300 is often taken as a reflection of expectancies. For instance, the P300 occurs when a subject expects to hear a tone or see a flash in a particular temporal rhythm, and no stimulus occurs at the expected time. In other words, the P300 can actually be evoked by the absence of a stimulus, rather than its occurrence; the "event" in the "event-related" P300 can be a non-event physically, in these cases. The P300 is therefore an "endogenous" potential (Picton and Stuss 1984) or a task-enhanceable potential (Desmedt and Robertson 1977). Desmedt and Robertson suggest that the P300 corresponds to the completion of a perceptual task and the clearance of an item from an information channel to make way for other activities. The P300 results obtained by Friedman are consistent with the theory that this wave marks the end of certain processes related to the recognition and comprehension of linguistic elements, and using it as an on-line measure of psycholinguistic processing might be extremely interesting.

In this chapter we have presented a number of studies dealing with electrical activity in the brain which precedes speech or follows linguistic stimuli. Technological advances allow us to identify very small electrical events which occur within milliseconds after an auditory or visual stimulus is presented. Because these electrical events are generated by neuronal pools which constitute a minute fraction of the total neuronal population of the brain, these event-related potentials are extremely difficult to find. It is easy to mistake non-cerebral potentials for cerebral events. Once true cerebral potentials are found, they are very difficult to analyze. It is not clear what portions of these potentials are psychologically important, and the use of sophisticated mathematical analyses of these potentials has, if anything, made even more complex the problem of identifying the psychologically real features of these ERPs. Despite these problems and challenges, the use of event-related potentials to measure physiological processes in the brain which correlate with language processing is an exciting development. Only the ERP can demonstrate neural activity which happens fast enough to be relevant to the psycholinguistic processes which we have discussed in Part III of this book. Use of ERPs in relationship to language holds out the promise of investigating psycholinguistic aspects of language processing with a technique that does not require subjects' attention. This technique also allows us to explore the physiological basis of language in normal subjects. Thus its use complements and extends the many studies of the anatomical features of the brain related to language which we have reviewed in this book; and future experience with ERPs may lead to a data-base upon which to begin the construction of theories of the physiological events responsible for language.

SUGGESTION FOR FURTHER READING

Picton, T. W. and Stuss, D. (1984). Event-related potentials in the study of speech and language: a critical review. In D. Caplan, A. R. Lecours, and A. Smith (eds.), *Biological Perspectives on Language*. MIT Press, Cambridge, Mass.

21

Electrical stimulation of the language areas

In 1959, Wilder Penfield and Lamar Roberts published a book dealing with their experience in electrically stimulating small portions of the brain during neurosurgical procedures designed to relieve epilepsy. Penfield was one of the great pioneers of neurosurgery. Among his many accomplishments and innovations was the beginning of the use of surgical excisions for the relief of certain forms of epilepsy. In some patients, a small scar, tumor, vascular malformation, infection, or other abnormality is the cause of seizures. Although many of these seizures can be controlled with medication, a few cannot, and in these remaining cases, it may be possible and worthwhile to remove the epileptogenic area of the cortex. Obviously, if the removal of this area of cortex leaves the patient with a severe functional impairment, the treatment will have been worse than the disease. Therefore, if the epileptogenic lesion is in primary motor cortex, or in some other area which is important in an essential function, this surgery is not performed. One of the areas which obviously must be avoided during such surgery is any portion of the brain which is necessary for language functioning. One of the first challenges facing Penfield in the development of this type of surgery, therefore, was to find a method to determine what portion of the brain was responsible for these basic functions, including language.

The technique that Penfield developed was to stimulate tiny portions of the brain electrically during the neurosurgical procedure. Because the brain itself has no pain receptors, it is possible to undertake neurosurgical procedures under local anesthesia when the patient is lightly sedated. With the patient conscious in this fashion, one can stimulate areas of the cortex and see what the effects are upon speech, control of motion, and elementary sensory function. Areas of the brain in which stimulation produces alterations in these functions would then be left untouched during any subsequent removal of epileptogenic tissue.

Because electrical impulses and electrical potentials are part of the information-carrying elements in the brain, it might be expected that stimulation of small areas of cortex would produce "positive symptoms"; that is, that such stimulation would produce speech or conjure up images of word meanings or word sounds, etc. This is not the effect of stimulation, as shown by Penfield and many subsequent workers. Rather, even the small voltages applied through cortical electrodes in these studies basically inhibit speech processes. Typically, a patient who is talking will cease to be able to speak while the stimulation is being applied to the language area. Even more automatic functions such as counting are interrupted during cortical stimulation far more frequently than positive symptoms are evoked. When speech *is* possible during the stimulation of part of the language zone, it is frequently abnormal, with paraphasias, and other abnormalities found in aphasia, being seen. Presumably, the stimulation being used in these procedures is far greater than that in the resting activity of the brain, and acts to depolarize many nerve cells in an area of the brain, thus rendering them non-functional for a period of time. Electrical stimulation may therefore be considered to create a very small, temporary lesion in a specified area of the brain. The relationship of the symptoms to the lesion is identical to the relationship of symptoms to lesions in larger, more permanent lesions such as strokes. We have discussed the logic of the use of lesion cases to construct neurolinguistic theories in Chapters 2 and 17.

Focal electrical stimulation offers possibilities for controlled experimentation which stroke patients and other brain-damaged cases do not permit. First, the "lesion" is restricted to a relatively small area of the brain, in many studies not more than a millimetre or two in diameter (when bipolar electrodes are used). Moreover, the exact temporal point at which the lesion begins can be recorded, and the end of the effective lesion is usually very soon after the end of the stimulation, when after-discharges are kept to a minimum. Therefore, changes in language abilities and functions can be directly correlated with the timing of the lesion. Moreover, electrical "lesions" can be applied several times in the same patient, both in the same spot and in different areas of the brain. These repetitions and different locations of stimulation are clinically important, because they tell the surgeon whether an area is consistently involved in language or only variably so, as well as which areas are involved in language functions and which are not. Whether a lesion of a particular sort is continually related to a particular deficit or only occasionally related to it, and whether the same or different deficits follow stimulation in different locations, cannot be determined in single cases with more permanent, larger lesions.

On the other hand, there are many limitations on what can be studied in the operative setting in which the stimulation occurs. For one thing, stimulation cannot last for more than five seconds or so, or it may trigger a clinical seizure. Therefore, any abnormality in function which is produced by the stimulation must be one which can be documented in a very short period of time. Although, as we have pointed out, it is possible to stimulate the same point several times in the course of one operation, there are also serious limits to how often a single point can be stimulated. Usually, a point is stimulated three times at most, though occasionally it may be stimulated up to five times. In many cases, especially in the earlier series of cases reported by Penfield and Roberts (1959), points on the cortex were stimulated only once or at most twice. Though we can say that an area of cortex in which stimulation produces a language abnormality is clearly involved in language, this limitation on the number of times a point can be restimulated makes it very difficult to know in just what aspect of language functioning a particular point is involved. We simply cannot go back to stimulate a point in all of the various tasks that are related to language.

Finally, as any reader who has come this far in this book now knows, it is not a simple matter to analyze a pathological performance as a deficit in normal psycholinguistic processing. Let us take as an example the most common symptom that occurs after cortical stimulation: speech arrest. Speech arrest can occur for many reasons. It may occur because of inter-ference with the neuronal system which is responsible for the movement of the articulatory muscles. It may arise following impairment of any one of the stages of speech production outlined in Chapter 15, from the "message level" through many levels of elaboration of the linguistic form of an utterance. Speech arrest can be due to much more general problems in the elaboration of thought or the initiation of action (see, for instance, Brown's analysis of the stages of the speech act discussed in Chapter 7). As many of the analyses presented in Part III indicate, to decide exactly what the psychological problem leading to speech arrest is requires a number of "control" observations. If the problem is with the muscles of articulation, writing should be intact. If the problem is with the construction of a particular level of linguistic representation, speech arrest should not be total, but a particular form of language disorder should arise. If the problem is with more global aspects of cognition or the initiation of any motor activity, many problems other than the inability to utter linguistically encoded messages should arise during stimulation. It is impossible to check on all of these possibilities in a single patient in relationship to the functions of a particular point in the cortex, because of the limitations on the number of times a point can be stimulated and on the duration of this stimulation. In practice, researchers such as Ojemann, whose work we shall review below, attempt to get around these difficulties by studying a series of patients, and stimulating roughly identical points in each patient. Since these points are never exactly identical, the areas involved in the stimulation vary over a slightly larger area than any one point, and we must assume that these slightly larger areas are all responsible for the same functions in different individuals. We have, however, seen several reasons to be skeptical of the idea that language functions are carried out in the same small areas of the brain in all members of the species, which makes this approach to the problem of control observations less reliable.

Despite these limitations, the use of cortical stimulation offers opportunities that no other technique provides, and it has been used by several researchers to investigate the language areas of the brain and their internal organization. In this chapter, we shall review the work of Penfield (Penfield and Roberts 1959) and Ojemann (Ojemann 1983) using this technique.

Penfield and Roberts carried out their "speech mapping" by requesting the patient to name pictures presented on cards, count, write the names of pictures on the cards, or read aloud. They report on the results when the patient is naming and counting. They note two effects on speech: "positive, or vocalization" and "negative, or inability to vocalize or use words properly" (20). They point out that "no intelligible word has been induced [by stimulation] while the patient is silent" (120). Vocalization consists of a vowel cry with the occasional "consonant component". Vocalization is produced by stimulation in the pre- and post-central gyri in the areas where the lips, jaw, and tongue are represented, and in the supplementary motor area. They note that vocalization occurs with stimulation of either the right or the left hemisphere.

Interference with speech occurs in a much larger area. Total arrest of speech occurs with stimulation of the motor areas and of a large number of points in the perisylvian region, as well as a few points in the superior frontal, superior parietal, and inferior temporal lobes. Hesitation and slurring of speech also occur in this wide area, and distortion and perseveration of words and syllables occur in a slightly more restricted area nearer to the sylvian fissure. Confusion of numbers while counting occurs following stimulation in a variety of sites, mostly in the inferior frontal lobe, in the parietal and temporal opercula, and in the second temporal gyrus. A sixth type of impairment is the inability to name despite a retained ability to speak. Stimulation in the inferior frontal lobe, the inferior parietal lobe, the first and second temporal gyri, and a few sites just above the inferior parietal lobe gives rise to this isolated difficulty with naming. Perseveration on the previously uttered word occurs with stimulation in this same area. In these cases, a patient who has just named a butterfly, for instance, will call a table a butterfly, but name the picture correctly after the electrodes are removed. Stimulation in this same area of the cortex can also produce the last type of response these investigators noticed, which they considered "the most unusual". This response is also a form of mis-naming, but is not due to

THE APHASIC TYPES OF RESPONSES

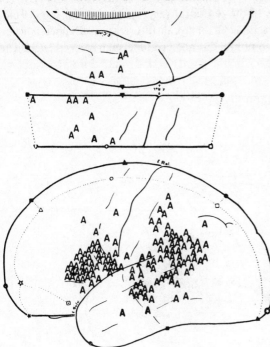

Figure 21-1. Diagram of the lateral surface of the brain, showing locations in which stimulation produced aphasic or dysphasic errors
(*Source:* Penfield and Roberts 1959: 130)

perseveration of a previously uttered word. The authors note that "the patient may use words somewhat closely related in sound, such as 'camel' for 'comb', or he may use a synonym, such as 'cutters' for 'scissors', 'hay' for 'bed', and 'moth' for 'butterfly'. Or an entirely unrelated word, such as 'rink' for 'scissors' or 'cone' for 'hammer', has been used" (124). Figure 21-1 shows the areas in the left hemisphere in which one of these abnormal responses occurred in the Penfield and Roberts study, and Figure 21-2 shows the representation of the language areas of the left hemisphere which these authors propose. The authors note that other parts of the left hemisphere have also been stimulated without affecting speech, but that too few trials in these areas have been performed to rule out the possibility that they too may be involved in speech.

Several points regarding the details of language representation in the brain are made by Penfield and Roberts in their discussion of these results. They claim that, in the areas where effects on speech occur, there is what they call an "area-localization" and not a "point-localization" (134). They point out that stimulation in the temporal region, 5 cm., 7 cm., and 9 cm. back from the tip of the temporal lobe, can interfere with speech, when stimulation at intermediate points did not produce such interference. The same is true for stimulation in the first, second, and third frontal gyri.

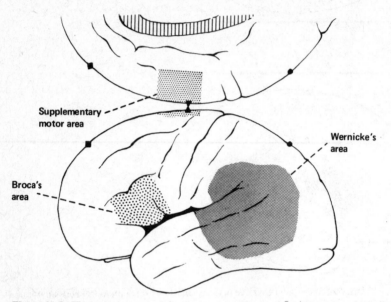

Figure 21-2. The speech areas of the brain, according to the results of cortical stimulation experiments
(*Source:* Penfield and Roberts 1959: 189)

Additionally, they point out that electrical interference in a given area is only effective 50 per cent of the time. These observations have been replicated and extended by Ojemann (1983), and form part of the basis for a general theory of how language is represented in the brain advanced by this contemporary researcher. Finally, Penfield and Roberts point out that "there is no difference between the effects of the electrical current applied to the dominant Broca's area, supplementary motor area, or parietal–temporal region as regards the various alterations of speech" (136). This was not what they had expected; they had thought that different language functions were carried out in these regions, and that the effects of cortical stimulation would be different. They suggest that the reason for this lack of difference might be that the areas are connected by transcortical and subcortical pathways and form a single system, damage to any part of which can produce the same symptoms.

Penfield and Roberts' work with cortical stimulation was mainly directed towards the location of the language cortex. They partly confirmed what was already known: that the cortex around the sylvian fissure was involved in language. They discovered that stimulation of the supplementary motor area also caused interference with speech, and they concluded that this area was integrated into the language areas of the brain. Another aspect of their work, which we have not reviewed, also confirmed the fact that speech is lateralized to the left hemisphere in the vast majority of right-handers. Penfield and Roberts' results, both from stimulation and subsequent excision of epileptogenic cortex, suggested to them that the left hemisphere was dominant for language in left-handed as well as in right-handed individuals.

Following publication of this monograph, work on stimulation of the cortex was not pursued actively for many years. Neurosurgeons did pursue the effects of stimulation of areas of the brain on language functions, but they began to concentrate on stimulation in subcortical areas, such as the thalamus. However, after an interval of almost twenty-five years, George Ojemann and his colleagues revived the use of electrical mapping of the language areas. Ojemann (1983) provided a review of his results using this technique.

Ojemann studied multiple language-related behaviors at particular sites in the cortex. Five different language functions were tested in three "protocols". The first protocol consisted of a sequence of slides. The first slide in the sequence was a picture of an object with the incomplete sentence *This is a* . . . printed above the picture. The patient's task was to read this phrase and name the object. The second slide contained an eight- to ten-word incomplete sentence that the patient had to read aloud and complete. Each completion had to have a particular syntactic feature to be well formed. The third slide had the word *Recall* printed on it, and the patient's task was to name the object presented on the first slide of the series. Stimulation occurred during the naming, reading, or recall portions of the sequence. The second protocol assessed patients' ability to imitate single movements of the facial musculature, or sequences of such movements. The patient was asked to produce the movements or sequences of movements shown on the series of slides. The final protocol measured the patient's ability to identify the phonemes *p*, *b*, *d*, *t*, *g* and *k* (the stop consonants in English) presented in the "carrier phrase" /a – ma/. Sequences like /agma/ and /atma/ were played on a tape-recorder, and the subject was required to point to the letter representing the second phoneme on a card. Stimulation in the second protocol occurred during the presentation of the slide with the single or sequential movements which the patients had to produce. On the

423

third protocol, the stimulation occurs during the presentation of the tape-recording.

Ojemann reported a number of results from the use of these protocols. First, he found that there is considerable discreteness of the effects of stimulation: stimulation of one cortical site might alter a language function such as naming on every trial, while stimulation at the same current at a site within a half-centimetre along the same gyrus may have no effect whatsoever. For instance, in one patient stimulation produced errors on nearly all naming trials at one frontal and two posterior temporal sites, but not at sites 0.5 to 1.0 cm. further along in the same gyri. Ojemann suggested that a particular function may have a "mosaic" or "macro-columnar" pattern of representation in cortex. These terms refer to the fact that sensory and motor cortex is organized in terms of small vertical columns, within which there is considerable electrical activity before impulses move to another part of the cortex. On the basis of these findings, Ojemann suggested that the association cortex may also be organized the same way.

A second discovery was that the frequency with which a particular language process is disrupted when a site is stimulated reflects the importance of that site in language processing. When Ojemann removed parts of the temporal lobe in which stimulation caused intermittent disturbances of language, he found that the resulting language deficit depended upon the total pattern of how stimulation affected that function. When there were many unresected sites at which stimulation affected the function 100 per cent of the time, no language disturbances arose. When there were only a few "100 per cent sites" very close to the margin of the resection, post-operative defects of language were "substantial". Ojemann suggested that sites at which there is 100 per cent interference with a function (that is, interference on all trials) are those which are necessary for the function, and the sites in which there is occasional interference with a function are held "in reserve" to mediate that function if necessary.

A third finding was that frequently only one language function was affected at a particular site. In a series of seven patients in whom all of the language functions mentioned above were tested at a total of fifty-two sites, changes in only a single function were observed at seventeen sites (39 per cent). The only function Ojemann tested which was never affected in isolation was oral–facial mimicry.

A particular extension of this discovery had to do with the representation of multiple languages in the brain. Sites that affected naming in one language did not affect naming in another language in bilingual or polyglot patients. Though some of Ojemann's patients were much more proficient in one language than in another, the patients in whom this observation was made were equally competent at naming the presented pictures in all the relevant languages when stimulation was not occurring. In one patient, the sites at which naming was affected were more spread out when the patient was tested in the less proficient language. Ojemann hypothesized that increasing familiarity and facility with a language may reduce the cortical area that is involved in processing that language.

Ojemann's purpose in utilizing electrocortical stimulation was not simply to map the sites at which disturbances in particular tasks occurred. Like most theoretical neurolinguists who base their work on aphasia, Ojemann was concerned with the nature of the components of the language-processing system, and with the organization of the language-processing system in the brain. He argues that his results bear on both these topics.

The most interesting and controversial claim that Ojemann makes on the basis of his data deals with the relationship between speech production and speech perception. Ojemann found that 86 per cent of the sites at which stimulation interfered with the ability to mimic sequences of oral facial movements were also sites at which phoneme identification errors arose upon stimulation. Conversely, 81 per cent of the sites showing abnormalities in phoneme identification during stimulation were sites at which sequential oral–facial mimicry was disturbed. He argues that "this relationship seems to identify a cortical area that has common properties of speech perception and generation of motor output, one with the common functions described by the motor theory of speech perception" (195). According to this theory (Liberman *et al*. 1967), the recognition of speech sounds utilizes a perceptual system specifically geared towards recognizing sounds that can be produced by the human vocal tract. A second claim Ojemann advances is that "a large portion of the brain related to language is fundamentally part of the motor system" (195). This conclusion is based on the fact that naming and reading were affected in 71 per cent of these sites, and 60 per cent of the sites with naming or reading changes were sites at which this putative sensory/motor function was impaired. Ojemann concludes that "in pre-linguistic animals [there is an] area of the cortex [that] is probably part of the system responsible for complex sequential motor function that is incorporated into the mechanisms for language in man" (196).

Ojemann also develops a very general theory of the organization of the perisylvian cortex with respect to language functions. He points out that disturbances of recall by and large occur after stimulation in sites other than the stimulation sites which led to disturbances in speech production. Speech production was considered to be impaired at sites at which naming, reading, ability to mimic a single oral–facial movement, and the output from short-term memory were all affected. These sites lay primarily in the perisylvian area. The sites at which patients could not *recall* stimuli surrounded the perisylvian cortical zone. Ojemann concludes that "language ... seems to develop with a perisylvian, lateralized, motor-sequence phoneme-decoding system surrounded by a lateralized short-term memory system" (197). Sites that interfered only with naming or reading were found at the interface of these two zones in the frontal, parietal, and posterior temporal regions. Ojemann therefore concluded that his data do not support either a "production/understanding dissociation" or a "frontal/parietal dichotomy based on linguistic function" (197). Rather, he believes that sites in the cortex which accomplish these particular language functions can lie anywhere between a core language-producing system, which itself is based on the ability to accomplish sequential oral–facial movements, and a more peripheral system which stores items in short-term memory.

Though there are sites in frontal, parietal, and temporal regions which produce only naming or reading problems, there is some pattern to the abnormalities found during stimulation in some of these tasks. For instance, reading errors that involve verb endings, prepositions, pronouns, or conjunctions – which seem similar to the errors found in agrammatism or paragrammatism (see Chapter 15) – occur at particular places within each of these three lobes. In the temporal lobe, these sites, which Ojemann calls "syntactic", are just anterior to the sites at which stimulation affects naming alone. Similarly, posterior sites at which naming changes occurred following stimulation differ in patients with verbal IQs above or below 96: 7/10 patients with verbal IQs of 96 or less showed naming impairments with stimulation in the parietal lobe, and only 1/10 patients with IQs higher than 96 had naming impairments following stimulation in these areas. Finally, naming impairments were found for more zones in men than in women. Specifically, there were more naming changes seen following anterior frontal and to some extent parietal stimulation compared with temporal stimulation in men than in women. Ojemann concluded that verbal IQ and sex determine the localization of the naming function in normal adults.

Reaction to Ojemann's theories about the organization of language in the perisylvian cortex has been mixed. Several researchers have commented on Ojemann's claim that his data support the motor theory of speech perception. Two sets of reservations have been voiced regarding this conclusion. The first is that, even though Ojemann has managed to stimulate very small areas of the brain, his stimulation may not be circumscribed enough to affect only a single site. If two sites are simultaneously stimulated, one of which is responsible for speech production and oral–facial sequencing and the other of which is responsible for phoneme identification, the two functions would be separate, though closely juxtaposed (Studdert-Kennedy

426

1983). Cooper (1983) argues that stimulation may affect "transmission lines" that link different sites. In reply, Ojemann points out that there are no measurable after-discharges following his stimulation, which makes the "transmission line interruption" objection less problematic. He concedes that the electrode may stimulate more than one functional site in the brain, and that his "macro-columnar" view of cerebral organization certainly involves sites which are much smaller than the diameter of his electrodes. However, he points out that, even if this is the case, the sites responsible for oral–facial sequencing and phoneme identification must be very close if they are always affected together by a single electrode, and that there must be a reason for their proximity.

Another set of problems with this theory has to do with the motor theory of speech perception itself. Frazier (1983) pointed out that, since children can perceive phonemes well before they can speak, the idea that there is a motor basis for speech perception may put the cart before the horse. Perhaps speech production is somehow constrained to produce sounds which can be discriminated. Studdert-Kennedy (1983) argued that, if there is a motor basis for some aspect of the processing of phonemes, it is probably most important in language acquisition, rather than in adults.

Finally, several researchers have questioned the validity of Ojemann's inferences. Ojemann argues from the association of two deficits to the conclusion that a disturbance in a single underlying function gives rise to both deficits. In the present case, the associated deficits are difficulty in all acts of speaking, mimicking sequences of oral–facial gestures, and phoneme identification. All of these disturbances would follow from an impairment in a single mechanism on the assumption that a single function is responsible for speech, mimicking sequences of oral–facial gestures, and identification of phonemes. We discussed this form of reasoning in Chapters 2 and 17, and we have seen many examples of this sort of reasoning throughout this volume. We noted in Chapters 2 and 17 that, if two deficits are both due to a single underlying disturbance, those deficits should always occur together, unless there is some reason to believe that a person in whom only one deficit is found is somehow exceptional with respect to how his psychological functions are organized. In the case of Ojemann's data, Studdert-Kennedy (1983) pointed out that the association between the deficit in sequential oral–facial mimicry, speech production, and phoneme identification is far from universal in Ojemann's data, with approximately 20 per cent of sites constituting exceptions to the association of deficits. Since the two functions dissociate, he concludes that there is no necessary connection between them. Frazier (1983) also questioned the logic of Ojemann's argument, pointing out that there is a great difference between the gestures the subject has to make in the oral–facial mimicry task and the gestures involved in speech. She suggested that a detailed linguistic analysis, comparing specific patterns of phoneme mis-identification with patterns of phoneme mis-production, would be a more convincing basis upon which to make an argument such as Ojemann's if there were a very high degree of correlation between the ability to identify particular phonemes and the ability to produce those same phonemes.

Ojemann's response to some of these objections seems to indicate a misunderstanding of the issues involved. Ojemann argues that the fact that functions can be separately impaired by stimulation at a few sites does not mean that they are not causally connected at the sites where both functions are impaired. He says that "different associations indicate different causes at these different sites for the . . . errors evoked . . . The appropriate unit for establishing causality is the site, not the patient" (1983: 225). This reply is inadequate on two grounds. First, if there are different causes for the impairment in phoneme identification at different sites, and some of these causes are not related to the motor theory for speech perception, then the motor theory for speech perception cannot be universally true. It may be that the motor theory of speech perception is true for some aspects of speech perception and not others; but this is a major change in the motor theory of speech perception, and would need considerable investigation before it could be accepted. Second, it is very difficult to establish that the same site has been located in two individuals. Although the primary and secondary sulci define gyral areas that are relatively constant across normal individuals, finer divisions of cortex are variable across subjects. Moreover, Ojemann's patients had long-standing cerebral lesions, which can induce reorganization of gyri far from the primary lesion site (Goldman-Rakic 1982; Geschwind and Galaburda 1985). It is, therefore, unlikely that Ojemann ever stimulated the same exact site in two different patients. (It is not even clear that the idea of "identical sites" has any meaning, when sites as small as those stimulated by Ojemann are being considered across individuals.) Accordingly, Ojemann's emphasis on "the site" as the "appropriate unit for establishing causality" runs into the problem that he only has data from two or three trials at any given site within an individual patient. This is not a reliable enough data-base upon which to reach the conclusion that deficits are always associated at a single site.

In addition to investigating the cortex, Ojemann was also concerned about the role of the thalamus in language. Ojemann's work on the stimulation of the thalamus is both pioneering and provocative. Ojemann performed the first of his protocols in a number of patients in whom portions of the thalamus were stimulated as part of surgery related to the treatment of

Parkinson's disease. The protocol consists of naming a picture, a distractor task (in this case, counting backwards), and a recall task. Ojemann found that two types of naming abnormalities occurred with stimulation of the thalamus. The first is an arrest of speech. This occurs during stimulation of either the right or the left thalamus, and Ojemann believes it is due to inhibition of impulses traveling in the internal capsule which directly innervate the bulbar nuclei responsible for the control of the speech musculature.

The second type of naming disorder is more complicated. It arises after stimulation in a very small portion of the medial central part of the ventral lateral thalamus (VL) on the left. The area is shown in Figure 21-3.

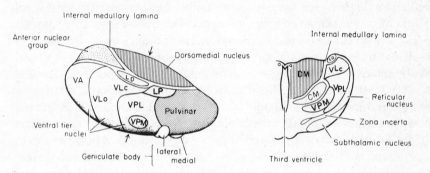

Figure 21-3. Diagram of the human thalamus. Ojemann stimulated the internal medullary lamina, the dorsal medial nucleus, and the ventral tier nuclei.
(*Source:* Carpenter and Sutin 1983: 508)

Stimulation in the posterior portion of this region produced anomic errors consisting of omissions and mis-namings. These errors are similar to the mis-namings found with stimulation of the perisylvian cortex. Errors of this sort also arise with stimulation of another thalamic structure, the pulvinar. In the anterior pulvinar, stimulation primarily produced perseveration of the first syllable of the correct name, and perseveration of an incorrect response. Ojemann concluded that this stimulation interfered with a thalamic mechanism that itself reduced perseveration. A hint as to what this mechanism may be comes from the last finding of Ojemann's. In this naming–distractor–recall task, Ojemann found that stimulation in the VL nucleus of the left thalamus during presentation of a picture – that is, the "naming" condition – actually caused the error rate to decline in the *recall* condition in 14/17 patients. Applying the current at the time of the *recall* substantially *increased* errors and shortened the response latencies for correctly recalled items. Stimulation during the distractor task had no consistent effect.

Ojemann suggests that these results indicate that the thalamus plays a "specific alerting" function: "stimulation in left ventral lateral thalamus activates this [specific alerting] mechanism, focuses attention on the verbal material in the external environment while simultaneously blocking retrieval of already internalized verbal information" (201). If this were the role of the thalamus, stimulation during the presentation of an object would lead to better encoding of that object because it would be better attended to, but stimulation during the actual time of recall would decrease the efficiency of the search in STM for the item which had just been presented. Errors and perseveration could result from the inefficiency of this search. Ojemann concluded that the anatomical substrate of this specific alerting function may be the nuclei or fibers of the thalamo-cortical activating system. These fibers and nuclei, in particular the intra-laminar nuclei, are involved in the control of attention, and activate portions of cortex electrophysiologically. Another possibility he considers is that the ventral lateral nucleus of the thalamus itself may be the locus of the specific alerting response. Since nucleus VL is a motor nucleus, Ojemann argues that this analysis also supports his view that areas of the brain that are primarily involved in motor systems in sub-human species become involved in language functions in the human. There are too many uncertainties about the reliability and the psychological cause of the effects we have reviewed, as well as their exact anatomical basis, to accept this argument. Nonetheless, the results are interesting, and invite further exploration.

We shall end this chapter with some general comments upon this technique and its present use. The majority of studies using electrical stimulation of the brain to study language–brain relationships are directed at the issues of localization of language functions. The logic of the analyses is no different from that based on studies of aphasia following cerebral lesions: it consists of deficit analysis and functional localization (see Chapter 2). "Lesions" are much smaller, much shorter-lived, and are electrical in nature, but they are nonetheless lesions for logical purposes. The deficits are explored through controlled observations, and the particular nature of the experimental setting imposes serious limitations on the exploration of the nature of a deficit. It is very hard to know exactly what function is disturbed during stimulation, when one can stimulate only a few times for a few seconds in one spot, and when one has to average performances across patients who may vary to a considerable degree in where a particular psycholinguistic function is carried out. It is far too early to make definitive statements about neurolinguistics on the basis of data from electrical stimulation; but some of the results are certainly provocative. Ojemann has presented data which clearly challenge the contemporary connectionist neurolinguistic theory, insofar as speech production and comprehension are both disturbed during electrical stimulation over a wide area of cortex. The results of thalamic stimulation are consistent with other measures of thalamic function (see Chapter 19), and suggest a possible interaction of the language-processing system and mechanisms responsible for focussing attention. Ojemann's results are extremely interesting, and are an important source of data which bear upon, extend, and challenge many present theories of language.

The use of electrical stimulation to chart the language areas has not been primarily concerned with the physiology of language. We may recall that, in his discussion of the physiological basis for localization, Head (1926) cited Sherrington's experiments showing that stimulation of a point in the motor cortex of the macaque produced a motor response which varied depending upon the recent history of stimulation of that point and surrounding points (see Chapter 6). Electrical stimulation studies allow us to explore those physiological questions by varying inter-stimulation intervals at given points in the cortex, stimulating specific points in specific sequences, and other means. Though the limitations of the experimental situation preclude as extensive a set of investigations of these more "dynamic" aspects of the neural basis for language as are afforded by animal experimentation, a step towards greater understanding of the physiological basis of language functions could be taken through the use of cortical stimulation. This is one of a number of directions that the research using this technique could take.

Electrical stimulation of the cortex is probably the technique whose use is the most restricted, since it can only be carried out during neurosurgical procedures that involve a conscious patient. The number of centers in which surgical procedures involving cortical stimulation is done is slowly increasing, and it is possible that neurosurgeons sufficiently interested in the question of language representation in the brain will allow observations regarding language to be made during precious operative time. Ojemann has indicated that infection rates are slightly higher in patients in whom cortical stimulation has been undertaken, primarily because of the increased duration of the operation. The intra-operative situation which allows for electrical mapping of the language areas is a rare and precious occasion. It has been used to provide interesting and stimulating neurolinguistic analyses, and it is to be hoped that its thoughtful use will deepen and extend these analyses, and contribute in a variety of ways to our understanding of the neural basis for language.

SUGGESTION FOR FURTHER READING

Ojemann, G. A. (1983). Brain organization for language from the perspective of electrical stimulation mapping. *Behavioral and Brain Sciences* 6; 189–230.

431

22

Towards a theoretical neurophysiology of language

We have discussed the neuroanatomical basis of language extensively in this volume, reviewing classical and modern connectionist theories, clinically derived "holist" theories of various sorts, modern studies of lateralization of language and cerebral dominance, localization of language functions in parts of the dominant hemisphere, and other related topics. Though we have considered evoked electrical correlates of language and the effects upon language of electrical stimulation of the cortex and subcortical areas, we have said practically nothing about the physiology of language – that is, the actual neural processes which are responsible for the coding of language. Nonetheless, this is a topic which is of crucial importance in neurolinguistics. Language must not only be carried out in portions of the brain; it must somehow or other actually be represented by elements and events in the brain. Caplan (1981) comments that the localization of a function would be, at most, a "convenient shorthand" for a statement of the actual physiological mechanisms which are responsible for the representation and processing of language. Marshall (1980) takes a further step, which, as we shall see in this chapter, may be correct: he argues that the physiological way a function is localized may be important in determining *what* is localized. These concerns are not new. Jackson (1878) also drew a distinction between the anatomical basis of a function (which he called "morphology") and the physiological basis of a function (which he called "anatomy"). Most of what we have covered regarding language–brain relations in this book involves Jacksonian "morphology" (our "neuroanatomy"). In this chapter, we shall take a step towards a theory of the neurophysiology of language. Though our consideration of this topic will be very abstract, it will lead to a number of conclusions that raise deep questions about the neural basis for language and how studies of aphasia are related to normal functions.

We have said in Chapters 20 and 21 that electrical and chemical events in the brain and peripheral nervous system are correlated with the transmission of sensory information and certain elementary forms of learning in lower species. Though we have every reason to assume that these events are part of the physiological activity of the brain relevant to information processing in the domain of human language, we know very little about how electrochemical activity in the brain actually represents language. The studies of evoked potentials reviewed in Chapter 21 speak to this issue, but, as we saw, such studies are in their infancy. There are very few empirical constraints on a physiological theory of language representation and processing. These lacunae have not totally prevented researchers from exploring a number of theoretical approaches to the neurophysiological basis for language. These approaches make a number of assumptions about the way in which language is represented in the brain. These assumptions are at best idealizations and abstractions from the true physiological basis for information processing, and, at worst, may be wrong in important respects. Nonetheless, making these assumptions has led to a number of interesting results in computer-based simulation studies which have been related to language. We shall review two such studies.

The basic physiological model which underlies both of these studies is the same, and is due to the work of D. O. Hebb (1949). Like many other psychologists, Hebb believed that associations between stimuli or between a stimulus and a response were among the fundamental psychological functions accomplished by humans. He developed a model of the neural events which are responsible for such associations. In Hebb's model, associations were the result of changes in neural activity. He hypothesized that each time a neuron fired, it produced a change in the neuron it was directly connected to, which made it easier for that second neuron to fire in response to the first neuron's activity at a later date: "When the axon of a cell 'A' is near the site of a cell 'B' and repeatedly and persistently takes part in firing it, some growth process or metabolic change takes place in one or both cells so that A's efficiency in firing the B cell is increased" (Hebb 1949: 62). Hebb's basic idea was that cells become correlated in their firing, and that this correlation is the neural basis for learned associations.

One possible site at which changes may occur that would facilitate the firing of a second cell in response to the activity in a first is the synapse between the two. Changes in biochemical reactions in the membrane of the post-synaptic cell in response to neural input have been documented in simple habituation and dishabituation learning in aplysia (Kandel 1979). Changes in the number of receptors in a post-synaptic cell also seem to occur, because of growth of dendritic spines. These anatomical changes may also make it easier for a post-synaptic cell to fire after receiving stimulation from a particular input neuron. Mechanisms such as these may be the physical basis for what has become known as "the Hebb synapse" – a synapse whose efficiency increases as a function of the number of times it is used. Not all physiological researchers agree that the evidence for the existence of a Hebb synapse is convincing, but this theoretical concept has received some empirical support, and has been incorporated into a number of abstract, mathematical, computer-based simulations of the nervous system. The studies we shall consider are based upon a model developed by Anderson (1972), which we shall review before going on to the actual simulations themselves.

In Anderson's model, two sets of neurons, alpha and beta, are connected. There are N neurons in each set. Every neuron in set alpha projects to every neuron in the set beta; that is, neuron 1 in set alpha projects to neurons $1, 2, 3 \ldots$ N in set beta, and so does neuron 2, neuron 3, etc. The feature of interest to us is the strengths of the connections between the neurons in these two sets, because the strength of each connection is an indication of the degree to which the firing of a neuron in set alpha is correlated with the firing of a neuron in set beta. The strength of the synapse between neuron i in set alpha and neuron j in set beta may be represented by the symbol $A(i, j)$. $A(i, j)$ simply stands for a number which indicates how often neuron i in set alpha and neuron j in set beta fire together.

In Anderson's model, the activity of all of the neurons in set A at any one moment may be considered an input stimulus, and the activity in all of the neurons in set B considered to represent the response associated with the input stimulus. We may represent the activity in the input set of neurons by the symbol $\mathbf{f}$, and the activity in the output set of neurons by the symbol $\mathbf{g}$. The symbol $\mathbf{f}$ represents activity in each of the N neurons of set alpha, and $\mathbf{g}$ represents the activity of each of the N neurons of set beta. In other words, there will be N values in each of $\mathbf{f}$ and $\mathbf{g}$. For instance, if there are eight neurons in $\mathbf{f}$ and the activity in each neuron can take on the value of any whole number, then a value for $\mathbf{f}$ might be $[0, 1, -2, 1, 0, 0, 3, -1]$. This value constitutes a set of integers, each of which represents the level of activity in each neuron in the set alpha. This set of integers is known as a "vector". For our purposes, a vector may simply be thought of as a set of numbers, each associated with the level of activity of a neuron in either an input or an output set of neurons. The activity in each of the neurons of the output set beta is also represented by the vector $\mathbf{g}$. Like $\mathbf{f}$, $\mathbf{g}$ has eight integer values if there are eight cells in the output set of neurons.

Now suppose that $\mathbf{f}$ and $\mathbf{g}$ are to be associated; that is, whenever $\mathbf{f}$ appears in the input set alpha, $\mathbf{g}$ appears as a response in the output set beta. To associate the pattern of $\mathbf{f}$ in alpha and $\mathbf{g}$ in beta, we need to correlate the activity of the neurons in alpha that makes up $\mathbf{f}$ with that of the neurons in beta that constitutes $\mathbf{g}$. We do so through the synapses between each of the cells in alpha and each of the cells in beta. We have said that the strength of the synapse between neuron i in alpha and neuron j in beta is represented by

A(i,j). We may now say that the level of activity in the i cell of set alpha in vector **f** is represented by $\mathbf{f}(i)$ and the activity in the j cell of set beta in vector **g** is represented by $\mathbf{g}(j)$. As we have seen above, the change in the strength of the synapse between these two cells is due to this correlated activity and can be represented as:

$$A(i,j) = \mathbf{f}(i)\mathbf{g}(j)$$

If we add up the changes in each one of the pairs of synapses, we associate all of the values in the vector **f** with all the values in vector **g**. The way to do this is to use a mathematical formula derived from the branch of mathematics known as set theory, which allows us to multiply one vector by another. Essentially, the way this happens is to align the values of the first vector along the top of a matrix (one per column) and the values of the second vector along the side of a matrix, and to multiply each column by each row. The resulting matrix (**A**) will have N × N entries. Such a matrix is displayed in Figure 22-1. If we recall that each neuron in the input set alpha is connected to each neuron in the output set beta, we will see that there are N × N synapses whose values need to be specified, and that this matrix specifies them all.

If the input vector **f** and the output vector **g** are associated through the strength of the synapses in **A**, then when we "present" **f** to **A**, we should see

Input Vector (F)

			Neuron						
			1	2	3	4	5	6	7	8
		Value	1	-2	2	-1	0	1	2	-3
	Neuron									
	1	2	2	-4	4	-2	0	2	4	-6
Output	2	1	1	-2	2	-1	0	1	2	-3
Vector	3	-2	-2	4	-4	2	0	-2	-4	6
(G)	4	0	0	0	0	0	0	0	0	0
	5	-1	-1	2	-2	1	0	-1	-2	3
	6	1	1	-2	2	-1	0	1	2	-3
	7	3	3	-6	6	-3	0	3	6	-9
	8	2	2	-4	4	-2	0	2	4	6

Figure 22-1. A matrix of two associated vectors, an input vector (**f**) and an output vector (**g**) each consisting of eight neurons. The association matrix (**A**) is contained within the solid lines. For details, see text.

the pattern of activity **g** emerging in neuron set beta. This is, in fact, what happens. Using set theory again, we may "present" **f** to **A** by multiplying **A** by **f**. Mathematically, we multiply **A** by $\mathbf{f}^\mathrm{T}$ (the transform of **f**). If the vectors are normalized, the result of this operation yields **g**:

$$
\begin{aligned}
\mathbf{Af} &= (\mathbf{g}, \mathbf{f})\mathbf{f}^\mathrm{T} \\
&= \mathbf{g}(\mathbf{f}, \mathbf{f}^\mathrm{T}) \\
&= \mathbf{g}
\end{aligned}
\tag{1}
$$

In non-mathematical terms, what happens when we present a particular vector, **f**, from the input set to the synapses between the input set of neurons and the output set of neurons is that the vector associated with **f** in the output set of neurons, **g**, automatically appears in beta. The input vectors and the output vectors associate perfectly. This, of course, is not surprising, since we have set up the system mathematically in such a way that this will be the case.

Now, consider what happens when there is more than one association between the input and output neuron pools. Since there is only one synapse between each neuron in the input pool and each neuron in the output pool, all the associations between input vectors and output vectors must use the same set of synapses. We have just said that the association between two vectors, **f** and **g**, is represented as a matrix, **A**, which represents the synaptic strength between each input neuron and each output neuron. If there are ten such associations, there must be ten such matrices, and these matrices all must be represented in the same set of synapses. The way this is done is to add up all the matrices, **A**. We can think about this by imagining ten tables such as the one depicted in Figure 22-1, each table containing a vector along the top and another vector along the side, and different values in each of the squares of the matrix. Adding up all of the values in each of the squares would then represent the activity in the synapses between the neurons in all the associated vectors in the input set alpha and the output set beta.

Again, our model makes mathematical assumptions which simplify various calculations for sets of several associated vectors. It assumes that the input vectors are all "orthogonal", meaning that multiplying any vector by another in the same set yields 0 and multiplying a vector by itself yields 1. If vectors are orthogonal, the presentation of any input vector to this more complicated set of synaptic strengths still yields the associated output vector in the output set of neurons.

Mathematically, if we represent the i input vector as $\mathbf{f}_i$, then we may "present" $\mathbf{f}_i$ to the set of synapses by multiplying $\mathbf{f}_i \times \mathbf{A}$, as follows:

$$\mathbf{Af}_i = \mathbf{A}_i\mathbf{f}_i + \sum_{j \neq i} \mathbf{A}_j\mathbf{f}_i \tag{2}$$
$$= \mathbf{g}_i[\mathbf{f}_i, \mathbf{f}^T_i] + \sum_{j=i} \mathbf{g}_j[\mathbf{f}_j, \mathbf{f}_i]$$
$$= \mathbf{g}_i(1) + \mathbf{g}_j(0)$$
$$= \mathbf{g}_i$$

As long as the vectors in the input set of neurons are unrelated to each other (orthogonal), the input and output still continue to be associated perfectly. (The mathematically more sophisticated reader will note that we have changed our use of symbols here. $\mathbf{A}$ refers to the combined matrix, and $\mathbf{f}_i$ and $\mathbf{g}_i$ refer to vectors here. In (1), $\mathbf{A}$ referred to the product of two vectors, and $\mathbf{f}$ and $\mathbf{g}$ to individual "neurons".)

Undoubtedly this completely accurate form of association of inputs and outputs is a considerable simplification of what goes in the real nervous system. Nonetheless, if associations do occur because of changes in synaptic strength between input and output neurons, and if associations do occur reliably despite any background "noise" that occurs in the nervous system, when an input stimulus is presented to an organism, some degree of association mediated by synaptic strength must be taking place. It is possible to complicate these models and make them more realistic by not assuming that the input vectors are orthogonal, but the essence of the model is contained in this idealized and simplified model. The model has some interesting properties, as we shall now see.

Wood (1978; 1982) used this model of a neural net to explore the effects of various "lesions" upon the abilities of systems such as the one we have just described to associate input and output vectors. Wood associated four 8-place input vectors with four 8-place output vectors. The input vectors, output vectors, and the resulting association matrix are shown in Table 22-1. Table 22-2 shows the computed output vectors which arise when the input vectors are presented to the matrix. As can be seen, the computed output vectors are exactly the same as the original output vectors in Table 22-1. Wood measures the similarity between each of these computed output vectors and the original output vectors, using a particular mathematical value (the cosine of the angle between the two vectors) as a measure of the similarity between the vectors. Table 22-3 shows the similarity of each of the computed output vectors to each of the original output vectors. In Table 22-3, the values can range from $+1$, representing perfect correspondence, to -1, representing complete difference. The values along the diagonal represent the goodness-of-fit of the original and the computed output vectors, and the values off the diagonal represent the confusibility of one

Table 22-1. *Input vectors, output vectors, and association matrix for a numerical example*

Input vectors				Output vectors			
f_1	f_2	f_3	f_4	g_1	g_2	g_3	g_4
0.354	−0.354	0.354	−0.354	1.000	−1.000	3.000	4.000
0.354	−0.354	−0.354	−0.354	0.000	2.000	0.000	0.000
0.354	0.354	0.354	0.354	−1.000	0.000	−1.000	−1.000
0.354	0.354	−0.354	0.354	0.000	−1.000	−1.000	−1.000
−0.354	−0.354	0.354	0.354	1.000	−1.000	−2.000	−1.000
−0.354	−0.354	−0.354	0.354	−1.000	−1.000	0.000	0.000
−0.354	0.354	0.354	−0.354	−1.000	−1.000	−1.000	−0.000
−0.354	0.354	−0.354	−0.354	0.000	2.000	2.000	1.000

Association matrix							
0.354	−1.768	2.475	0.354	2.475	0.354	−1.061	−3.182
−0.707	−0.707	0.707	0.707	−0.707	−0.707	0.707	0.707
−0.354	0.354	−1.061	−0.354	−0.354	0.354	0.354	1.061
0.354	1.061	−1.061	−0.354	−0.354	0.354	−0.354	0.354
0.354	1.768	−1.061	0.354	−1.061	0.354	−1.061	0.354
0.000	0.000	−0.707	−0.707	0.707	0.707	0.000	0.000
−0.354	0.354	−1.061	−0.354	0.354	1.061	−0.354	0.354
−0.354	−1.768	1.768	0.354	0.354	−1.061	0.061	−0.354

Source: Wood 1982: 491.

output vector with another. Wood (1982) points out that "the diagonal elements in the confusion matrix may be thought of as an index of the model's 'recognition' performance; that is, the degree to which the model corresponds to each input vector with the appropriate output vector ... [and] the off-diagonal values of the confusion matrix may be thought of as the model's 'discrimination' performance, the degree to which the model responds to each input vector with an output vector appropriate for some other input vector" (493). The combination of the mean diagonal and the mean off-diagonal values of the confusion matrix is a combined measure of the recognition and discrimination ability of the model. As can be seen in the example given, recognition is perfect in this model, and, for the most part, discrimination is also very good. However, because vectors g_3 and g_4 are very similar, discrimination of these two vectors is difficult.

Wood uses both the "recognition" and the "discrimination" measures, as well as a combined measure to indicate how well the system performs with some of its elements missing. Tables 22-4 and 22-5 show the computed output vectors and the confusion matrices after a "lesion" of input neuron 1 and output neuron 8, respectively, in this system. Wood emphasizes several

Table 22-2. *Computed output vectors for the numerical example*

Computed output vectors			
g_1	g_2	g_3	g_4
1.000	−1.000	3.000	4.000
0.000	2.000	0.000	0.000
−1.000	0.000	−1.000	−1.000
0.000	−1.000	−1.000	−1.000
1.000	−1.000	−2.000	−1.000
−1.000	−1.000	0.000	0.000
−1.000	−1.000	−1.000	0.000
0.000	2.000	2.000	1.000

Source: Wood 1982: 492.

Table 22-3. *Confusion matrix based on computed output vectors for the numerical example in Wood's simulation*

Original output vectors	Confusion matrix computed output vectors			
	g_1	g_2	g_3	g_4
g_1	1.000	−0.016	0.304	0.436
g_2	−0.016	1.000	0.312	0.016
g_3	0.304	0.312	1.000	0.911
g_4	0.436	0.016	0.911	1.000

Source: Wood 1982: 492.

features of the resulting simulation. First, though "recognition" is impaired, it is not impaired substantially. The mean of the diagonal elements in Table 22-4 is 0.994, and in Table 22-5, 0.936. Both are close to the perfect 1 of Table 22-3. Second, the off-diagonal elements of the confusion matrices show that the effects of a lesion upon "discrimination" depend upon how similar the specific output vectors in the system actually are. A lesion which removes a neuron whose activity is very important in the difference between two input vectors will have a very great effect upon performance, while a less critical neuron can be removed without much effect. Third, lesions of input and output vectors differ in the way they affect the entire system. If an output neuron is eliminated, the effect is usually small, since output vectors differ with respect to most of the values of their component neurons. A lesion of an input neuron has a more subtle, widespread effect upon the entire pattern of output. All the output neurons

Table 22-4. *Computer output vectors and confusion matrix for a lesion of input neuron 1*

Computed output vectors for lesion of input neuron 1			
g_1	g_2	g_3	g_4
0.875	−0.875	2.875	4.125
0.250	1.750	0.250	−0.250
−0.875	−0.125	−0.875	−1.125
−0.125	−0.875	−1.125	−0.875
−1.000	−1.000	0.000	0.000
−0.875	−1.125	−0.875	−0.125
0.125	1.875	2.125	0.875

Confusion matrix computed output vectors			
	g_1	g_2	g_3	g_4
Original output vectors				
g_1	0.987	0.047	0.225	0.475
g_2	0.125	0.997	0.374	−0.048
g_3	0.332	0.338	0.996	0.894
g_4	0.441	0.038	0.892	0.996

Source: Wood 1982: 495.

Table 22-5. *Computed output vectors and confusion matrix for a lesion of output neuron 8*

Computed output vectors for lesion of output neuron 8			
g_1	g_2	g_3	g_4
1.000	−1.000	3.000	4.000
0.000	2.000	0.000	0.000
−1.000	0.000	−1.000	−1.000
0.000	−1.000	−2.000	−1.000
−1.000	−1.000	−1.000	0.000
−1.000	−1.000	−1.000	0.000
0.000	0.000	0.000	0.000

Confusion matrix computed output vectors			
	g_1	g_2	g_3	g_4
Original output vectors				
g_1	1.000	−0.061	0.316	0.430
g_2	−0.016	0.875	0.053	−0.120
g_3	0.304	0.080	0.909	0.823
g_4	0.436	−0.101	0.949	0.977

Source: Wood 1982: 495.

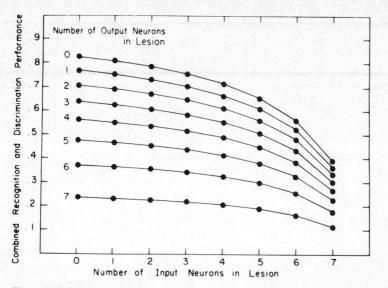

Figure 22-2. Effects of lesion size upon the model's performance in Wood's simulation study (*Source:* Wood 1982: 497)

still generate activity, but the pattern of activity across all the output neurons is slightly different from that in the original vectors.

Wood investigated the effects of lesioning an increasing number of neurons in either the input or the output set of neurons. Lesion "size" and "location" were systematically explored by eliminating all possible combinations of one through seven input neurons, one through seven output neurons, and both one through seven input and one through seven output neurons. Altogether, Wood simulated 65,024 total lesions. Moreover, to be sure that the results were not artifacts of the particular values of input and output neurons used in one simulation, Wood repeated the 65,024 lesions for each of 100 randomly selected sets of four input and four output vectors – well over half a million simulations, each involving many calculations. The fact that this can be done at all indicates some of the power and utility of simulating neural models on a computer.

Figure 22-2 shows the effects of variation of lesion size upon the performance of the entire system. Figure 22-2 shows that lesions of increasing size produced larger increases in the performance deficit. This was true for lesions of both input and output neurons. The relationship of lesion size to the system's performance is reminiscent of the concept of "mass action", proposed by Lashley (1950), which we discussed in Chapters 8 and 19. As Wood (1982) notes, however, even quite large lesions still leave the performance of the entire system well above chance.

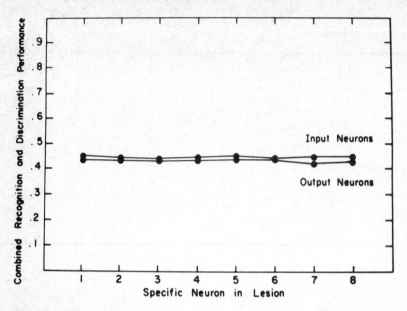

Figure 22-3. Effects of lesion location on the model's performance in Wood's simulation study (*Source:* Wood 1982: 500)

Figure 22-3 shows the effect produced by the removal of any given neuron. As can be seen, there is no significant difference between the effect of removing any one neuron and removing any other upon the performance of the model. Wood indicates that this is similar to the idea of "equipotentiality" advanced by Lashley (1950), which we have discussed in Chapter 19.

In addition to these results, which are based upon the average performance of the system in the face of lesions of various sizes in various parts of the model, Wood also explored the effects of very particular lesions upon particular associations. Here the effects depend almost entirely upon how similar the input and output vectors are to each other. Table 22-6 shows the input and output vectors for a particular system, and the effect of lesioning neuron 1 or neuron 2 upon the association performance of the system as a whole. This is a particularly interesting example. We see that input vectors f_1 and f_2 are different with respect to the values of each of their component "neurons", but that input vectors f_3 and f_4 are entirely distinguished by the activity in neurons 1 and 2. It therefore is to be expected that a lesion of neuron 1 or neuron 2 would particularly affect the association between input vector f_3 and output vector g_3 and between input vector f_4 and output vector g_4, and not affect the association of f_1 and g_1 or f_2 and g_2 to any great extent. This is just what the results show. Recognition performance of the system

Table 22-6. *Input vectors, output vectors, and confusion matrices illustrating localization of function*

	Input vectors				Output vectors			
	f_1	f_2	f_3	f_4	f_1	f_2	f_3	f_4
	−0.196	−0.229	0.114	0.912	1.000	−1.000	1.000	−1.000
	0.000	−0.459	0.912	0.114	1.000	−1.000	−1.000	−1.000
	−0.196	0.459	−0.114	−0.114	1.000	1.000	1.000	1.000
	0.392	0.229	0.228	0.228	1.000	1.000	−1.000	1.000
	0.558	−0.459	0.114	0.114	−1.000	−1.000	1.000	1.000
	0.558	0.000	−0.114	−0.114	−1.000	−1.000	−1.000	1.000
	−0.196	−0.229	−0.114	−0.114	−1.000	1.000	1.000	−1.000
	−0.196	0.459	0.228	0.228	−1.000	1.000	−1.000	−1.000

Confusion matrices

Original output vectors	Computed output vectors for lesion of input neuron 1				Computed output vectors for lesion of input neuron 2			
	g_1	g_2	g_3	g_4	g_1	g_2	g_3	g_4
g_1	0.943	−0.299	0.083	0.276	0.960	−0.319	0.209	−0.087
g_2	−0.309	0.989	−0.315	0.081	−0.259	0.933	0.163	−0.127
g_3	0.088	−0.322	0.914	0.803	0.064	0.062	0.256	0.251
g_4	0.088	0.025	0.241	0.522	−0.086	−0.154	0.809	0.956

Source: Wood 1982: 499.

decreases from 0.89 to 0.53 for input vector f_3 following a lesion in input neuron 2, and from 0.92 to 0.52 for input vector f_4 after a lesion in input neuron 1. Input vectors f_1 and f_2 are hardly affected at all.

As Wood points out, these results have very significant consequences for our understanding of the relationship between lesions, deficits, and the neurological basis for functions. Unlike the situation as regards the real brain, in this simulation of a brain we know exactly what kind of information is represented and how it is represented. The information that is represented is the "synaptic strength" of each neuron in an input set of neurons connected to each neuron of an output set of neurons. This is the *only* information represented in this simulation. This information is represented in the form of a table, each of whose elements consists of the sum of the synapses between each input and output neuron in each pair of associated vectors in the system. In this system, this information is not localized, but distributed. Each pair of input and output vectors contributes to all of the cells of the matrix, and all the cells in the matrix have contributions from each input/output pair. As noted above, if we have to characterize this simulation as representing information "locally" or "holistically", we would certainly say that the information in this simulation is holistically and diffusely represented.

And, in fact, this simulation works the way Lashley thought a brain in which information was diffusely represented would work, showing features similar to equipotentiality and mass action. The overall efficiency of association of input and output vectors varies as a function of the number of neurons which are removed from the system, and the particular neuron which is removed from the system does not on average make a difference in how efficiently the system works. On the other hand, in some special circumstances, the system appears to act in a very different way. As the examples in Figure 22-6 show, in some cases removal of a single neuron produces a very specific deficit in association of input and output vectors, and spares other input–output relationships. In fact, the particular pattern of relatively spared and relatively impaired associations illustrated in Table 22-6 shows a feature very reminiscent of a double dissociation (see Chapter 2), since the removal of neuron 1 affects the relationship between input vector f_4 and output vector g_4 and not that between input vector f_3 and output vector g_3, while the reverse situation occurs with a lesion of input neuron 2. As Wood points out, if a neuropsychologist were to see a pattern of impairments like that in Table 22-6, in which one function was impaired after a lesion in one part of the brain and spared after a lesion in another, and a second function impaired after a lesion in that second part of the brain but spared after a lesion to the first area, he would almost certainly conclude that the first function was localized in the first area of the brain and the second function localized in the second. However, if one were to infer that the "function" of associating input vector f_3 and output vector g_3 was "localized" in input neuron 2, and the "function" of associating input vector f_4 with output vector g_4 was "localized" in input neuron 1, one would be completely wrong in this simulated example. Having actually constructed the system ourselves, we know that all of the information associating all the vectors in the system is entirely distributed over all of the input and output cells in the form of the matrix of synaptic strengths, A; nothing is strictly localized in one vector.

Wood's conclusion from this exercise is that "principles of functional organization cannot be directly inferred from lesion data". He quotes Jackson's (1874) admonition that "to locate the damage which destroys speech and to locate speech are two different things" (Wood 1982: 503). Wood accepts that it is possible to characterize the deficits in performance that follow a lesion in an area of the brain but, on the basis of this simulation, denies that one can take the next step and infer the neural basis for a function from the functional deficit and the lesion. He argues that one would have to know "how the brain worked as a whole" – "the global capacities and input–output relationships of the system as a whole" (505) – in order to infer how a brain region is involved in any particular psychological function on the basis of deficit and lesion data. The most that he believes can be concluded from the fact that a deficit reliably follows a lesion is that the damaged tissue is necessary for the accomplishment of that function. The region in question may not be sufficient to accomplish that function, however. Conversely, the most that can be concluded from the fact that a lesion in a particular area of the brain reliably *spares* a function is that that region is not necessary for the production of that function; it does not follow that that region is not involved in that function, since remaining areas of the brain may be sufficient for carrying out that function, either because the function is localized in other areas or because it is distributed over the lesioned and unlesioned areas, as in the simulation.

This argument appears to be devastating to the entire methodology of inferring the nature of language representation in the brain from aphasic deficits correlated with brain lesions. Is it as devastating as it at first appears? It is important to note that Wood's argument applies to information which is diffusely represented in neuronal nets. He has shown that, under certain circumstances, application of criteria commonly used by neuropsychologists, such as the logic of double dissociation, to infer any aspect of the representation of a psychological function in the brain can be misleading when the information is diffusely represented. However, it does not seem possible that the reverse error would happen. When information is represented in a single neuron in a system such as Wood's, only a lesion in that neuron will interfere with the retrieval of that specific piece of information. The danger to the usual logic is not total. If we know *that* a function is localized, we can use the logic of double dissociation to discover *where* it is localized. Wood indicates as much when he claims that one needs to know "how the brain works as a whole" to base localization in deficit–lesion correlations.

Furthermore, we might even be able to salvage more of the traditional logic used in neuropsychology. Consider the results in Table 22-6 again. It is true that the effect of lesions in input neurons 1 and 2 is "local", inasmuch as it affects the association of vectors f_3 and g_3 and f_4 and g_4, while the information in the matrix A is distributed. But Wood's argument requires that we consider only the matrix A as the simulation of the brain. What of the input and output vectors themselves? If we think of them as part of the total neural system, we can see that input neurons 1 and 2 are particularly

445

important in pairing of $\mathbf{f}_3$–$\mathbf{g}_3$ and $\mathbf{f}_4$–$\mathbf{g}_4$. Though all of the information about synapses is represented "diffusely" throughout matrix $\mathbf{A}$, the information *distinguishing* input vectors $\mathbf{f}_3$ and $\mathbf{f}_4$ is entirely dependent upon the activity of input neurons 1 and 2.

If we look at things this way, Wood's system performs much as traditional thinking would predict. The system has different types of problems in distinguishing the output vectors associated with input vectors, depending upon how critical particular input neurons are in particular associations. When the information which distinguishes the input vectors is carried in a few neurons, removal of these neurons has major effects. The behavior of the system does in fact reveal this locality, even though on average all neurons affect the operation of the entire system in very similar ways.

Even if these considerations do partially respond to Wood's arguments, we can see the power of this simulation system. Wood has shown that a system in which information is represented in distributed fashion can act as Lashley predicted, by using over half a million simulations to document how the system behaves. It is clearly impossible to test the feasibility of a proposal such as Lashley's in an intact biological system on any comparable scale. We may have answered some of Wood's objections to the use of deficit–lesion correlations to infer that functions are localized in the brain, but we are certainly made more aware of the difficulties in showing that these arguments are valid by Wood's work. Even if our rejoinder is correct, Wood's simulation does show that inferring what is localized and what is distributed information in a neural system is an extremely difficult task. And Wood's simulation is very simple, modeling only sixteen neurons and four associations, rather than the 100 million cells in the brain!

Wood's study does not deal specifically with linguistic or psycholinguistic phenomena. Gordon (1982) uses a similar model to simulate the process of naming an object presented visually or tactilely. The simulation involves sequences of neuronal nets of the sort that we have been considering. The overall organization of the system is shown in Figure 22-4. The "visual" and "tactile" "stimuli" in this simulation consist of vectors with sixteen "neurons". Each stage of processing – visual recognition, tactile recognition, semantic recognition, and articulatory motor function – consists of two "neural nets", each also with sixteen neurons. The first of these nets is an "association net", which simply takes the input to that stage of processing and passes it on to the second net. The second net is a so-called "feedback" net. The activity in each neuron in the feedback net is "fed back" onto all the neurons in that net. When a vector is presented to a processing stage in this system, it produces a pattern of activity in the association network which in turn evokes a pattern of activity in the

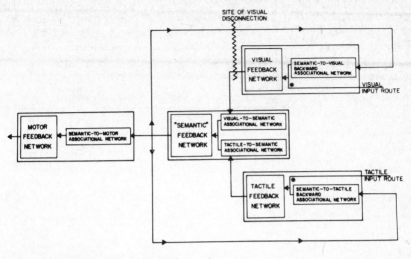

Figure 22-4. Gordon's simulation of the naming process
(*Source:* Gordon 1982: 517)

feedback network. Since the feedback network may continue to generate activity within itself forever, a "saturation limit" is imposed on individual neurons in this feedback net. When either a stable pattern of activity arises in the feedback net or this saturation limit is reached, the activity in the feedback net ceases and the level of activity in each of its neurons is passed on to the next stage of processing. The value of the neurons at that point constitutes the "output" of that processing stage. As can be seen from Figure 22-4, in addition to these "stage-internal" feedback nets, there are also "feedback *pathways*" from the semantic recognition system to both the visual and the tactile recognition stages in Gordon's model.

Gordon explores the effects of certain types of disconnections on the performance of this system. In a disconnection, the output of a particular stage of processing cannot be transmitted to the next stage. "Complete" disconnections totally disrupt this output, and "partial" disconnections interrupt from 25 to 75 per cent of the "axons" leaving each processing stage. When there is a feedback pathway from one stage to a previous stage, as between semantic recognition and visual and tactile recognition, a lesion of the output of the visual recognition stage not only interrupts transmission of information from the visual recognition to the semantic recognition stage, but also affects transmission of information in the reverse direction.

Table 22-7 shows the effects of several such lesions. Several have surprising effects. For instance, consider the effect of a complete disconnection between the visual recognition stage and the semantic recognition stage,

447

Table 22-7. *The effect of different lesions upon recognition and naming in Gordon's simulation model*

Input route and vector name	Disconnection location and type	Asymptotic recognition				Suggested analogous behavior
		Peripheral tactile	Peripheral visual	Semantic	Motor output	
1. Visual–chair	None		chair $T=4$	chair $T=6$	"chair" $T=6$	Normal
2. Visual–chair	Complete visual		chair $T=5$	0	(no name)	"Optic aphasia"
3a. Tactile–sandpaper ("poor visual" representation)	Partial tactile	sandpaper $T=8$		0	(no name)	"Tactile aphasia" – patient of Beauvois *et al.* (1978)
3b. Tactile–broom ("good visual" representation)	Partial tactile	broom $T=3$	broom $T=5$	broom $T=5$	"broom" $T=5$	
4. Visual–tree	Partial visual		tree $T=4$	house $T=5$	"house" $T=5$	Compare patient of Marin and Saffran (1975) with "pathologic verbal dominance"
5a. Visual–comb	Partial visual	(???)	comb $T=6$	(???)	(no name)	Undirectional disconnection (Mohr 1976)
5b. Tactile–comb	Partial visual	comb $T=3$	comb $T=5$	comb $T=5$	"comb" $T=5$	
5c. Visual–brush	Partial visual	brush $T=5$	brush $T=3$	brush $T=5$	"brush" $T=5$	
5d. Tactile–brush	Partial visual	brush $T=3$	(???)	brush $T=5$	"brush" $T=5$	
6. Degraded stimulus: visual–spoon	None		(???)	spoon $T=20$	"spoon" $T=20$	Semantic representation and name response available before item fully recognized
7. Degraded stimulus: visual–butter	None		butter $T=20$	(???)	"butter" $T=20$	Visual recognition and motor naming accomplished before semantic recognition achieved (cf. Heilman *et al.* 1976)
8a. Visual–pen	None		glass $T=3$	glass $T=3$	"glass" $T=3$	Misperceptions
8b. Visual–pen	Complete		pen $T=4$			

illustrated in lesion (2) in Table 22-7. Obviously a complete disconnection of visual processing and semantic processing blocks the emergence of a semantic representation after an object is presented "visually" and no name is produced. However, an unexpected finding is that it takes longer to recognize objects visually presented after this disconnection than in the absence of a lesion. Table 22-7 shows that it takes five iterations before activity in the visual recognition stage corresponds to the representation of a visual stimulus after a visual–semantic disconnection, whereas ordinarily it only takes four iterations. This is because the feedback from the semantic recognition stage normally helps stabilize activity in the earlier stage of visual recognition, when this feedback is available.

Partial disconnections produce more complex results. For instance, when a partial disconnection exists between the tactile recognition system and the semantic recognition system, it is still possible to recognize certain "objects" (vectors) when they are presented "tactilely" (that is, when they are presented to the "tactile recognition" matrices). These representations are ones which have very characteristic vectors in the *visual* recognition component. In these cases, even the somewhat inaccurate representation which arises at the "semantic" recognition stage after tactile presentation is adequate to activate and stabilize a distinctive vector in the "visual recognition" stage. This "visual" representation in turn serves to stabilize the vector at the semantic recognition and naming stages. In a similar way, partial disconnections can give rise to correct representations at a relatively peripheral stage of representation, such as the visual recognition stage, but incorrect recognitions further along, such as the semantic and the naming stages, as illustrated in example (4) of Table 22-7. Finally, partial lesions which affect both the output from a particular stage to the next and the feedback from the second stage to the first can produce a variety of effects. In example (5a), a partial visual lesion leads to the correct recognition of a stimulus at the visual stage of processing, but without a semantic or tactile representation, or a name. In example (5b), the same lesion allows for a complete representation of the same item presented "tactilely" at all stages of the processing. Almost the converse of these effects are found in examples (5c) and (5d), where a different partial visual lesion leads to complete recognition of a visually presented item at all stages of processing, but also to the failure of a tactilely presented item to arouse a visual image.

Other kinds of abnormality can also be created in this simulated system. For instance, without any disconnection at all, degrading the input by removing part of the information in an input vector can lead to unexpected results. In example (6), a visually presented stimulus whose representation has been degraded in this way produces a semantic representation and a name before there is a stable pattern of activity at the visual recognition stage; while another degradation of another stimulus, illustrated in example (7), produces a name and a visual presentation before a semantic representation has been achieved. In yet other cases, illustrated in examples (8a) and (8b), the system "mis-perceives", misunderstands, and mis-names the stimulus, but when the visual recognition stage of processing is *completely* disconnected from the remainder of the system, visual recognition of the same stimulus is correct.

Gordon's simulated model of the processes involved in naming does not attempt to be a complete account of this complicated function. According to its author, its chief value is that it postulates a very small number of processing stages, makes explicit statements about the computations which go on in each stage, and models lesions in very precise ways. A large number of deficits follow complete and partial disconnections of the processing stages. As with Wood's simulation, many of the behaviors which the model produces would ordinarily have led researchers to postulate additional stages in processing, or many connections between processing stages. Though this model is only presented as a sketch of the naming process, it clearly shows that the way information is represented is an important factor to consider in trying to understand the effects of a lesion upon the performance of an entire system.

There is no direct evidence that the way language is represented in the brain corresponds to the way vectors are represented in the set theory models that we have reviewed in this chapter. Nonetheless, these models are not completely fanciful: the idea of a synapse whose strength is a function of the activity in the pre- and post-synaptic neuron is not an unreasonable abstraction and idealization of our present ideas of how information might be represented in sets of neurons. Researchers such as Anderson (1984) have used these models to simulate a variety of psycholinguistic functions, and the researchers whose work we reviewed in this chapter have investigated some of the effects of lesioning these systems. Their results at least serve as a serious caution to anyone who draws conclusions about the way normal language is represented in the brain from the way language breaks down after brain damage. Wood's results must make us cautious about assuming that an isolated functional deficit seen after a localized lesion implies that that function is carried out exclusively in that area of the brain. Gordon's results show that it may be a mistake to postulate multiple processing stages or multiple routes between processing stages to account for certain isolated deficits, since different lesions which disconnect processing stages can produce a wide variety of behavioral effects even in very simple systems. One of the reasons that lesions behave so counter-intuitively in both Wood's and Gordon's simulations is that these models do not incorporate the usual approach to processing stages, which is to consider them as completely sequential. We have seen that this is a feature of modern psycholinguistic models of normal language processing, and that there is increasing interest in interactive–activation models in very recent aphasiological studies (Chapter 17).

The neural simulations based on Anderson's model incorporate features of both parallel and sequential processing. Each vector represents a good deal of information. Eight to sixteen elements (representing neurons) each contain information which can vary over the entire range of integers. These vectors, therefore, contain a good deal of information "in parallel". The information in each neuron is "collected up" into a vector, and transmitted through that vector to the next stage of processing. This aspect of the model is serial in nature. The combination of parallel and serial processing makes for enormous computational power. Anderson (1984) points out that one of the major advances in the design of real computers consists of increasing the number of "bits" that are used in the "words" of each computer. Without altering the basic sequential nature of computations in a computer, the extra power that occurs with the increased information associated with each word as the number of bits for each word increases has led to a situation where a micro-processor with 32-bit words could contain nearly the power of an older main-frame computer on a single micro-processing chip. The possibility that the mechanisms related to language work partially in parallel and partially in series has not yet been investigated in relationship to actual neural structures.

The studies that we have reviewed in this chapter are obviously very far removed both from real neural systems and from real psychological systems. Despite this, they can teach us much about how psychological functions *might* be represented in an actual physical system, and thereby open our minds to new ways to conceptualize the neural basis for the language. They also serve to make us cautious about certain types of inferences that we draw from the study of aphasic impairments and their associated cerebral lesions. For all these reasons, computer-implemented simulations of neural systems have a valuable role to play in adding to our understanding of how language is represented and processed in the brain.

SUGGESTIONS FOR FURTHER READING

Anderson, J. A. (1972). A simple neural network generating an interactive memory. *Mathematical Biosciences* 14, 197–220.
   (1984). Neural models and very little about language. In D. Caplan, A. R. Lecours, and A. Smith (eds.), *Biological Perspectives on Language*. MIT Press, Cambridge, Mass.
Gordon, B. (1982). Confrontation naming: computational model and disconnection simulation. In M. A. Arbib, D. Caplan, and J. C. Marshall (eds.), *Neural Models of Language Processes*. Academic Press, New York.
Rumelhart, D. E. and McClelland, J. L. (1986). PDP Models and General Issues in Cognitive Science, in Rumelhart, D. E., and McClelland, J. L. (eds.), *Parallel Distributed Processing*, Vol. 1. MIT Press, Cambridge, Mass.
Wood, C. (1982). Implications of simulated lesion experiments for the interpretation of lesions in real nervous systems. In M. A. Arbib *et al.* (eds.), *Neural Models of Language Processes*. Academic Press, New York.

23

Overview of contemporary neurolinguistics

We have learned a great deal about the neural structures involved in representing and processing language since Broca's first scientific paper on the subject in 1861. In Part IV we reviewed some of the advances in our knowledge of this subject, and began to explore some of the newer techniques for investigating the neural basis of linguistic knowledge. We may divide the neurolinguistic topics that we have discussed into three groups: the study of general areas of the brain in which language processing takes place; the development of theories of the functional neuroanatomy within a specified area of the brain; and the exploration of the cellular and the neurophysiological basis for language functions. We know progressively less about each of these three topics. This is not surprising. Neuroscience has always progressed "from the outside in", beginning by identifying the general area of the brain where a function is carried out, then developing a model of the internal workings of that area in general terms, and finally dealing with the cellular and sub-cellular events actually responsible for the function's operation. Neurolinguistics is making slow but steady progress along these lines.

In Chapters 18 and 19 we reviewed studies from the time of World War II onwards which gave us a much more detailed and clearer understanding of the general areas of the brain that are involved in language functions. These studies show that, although Broca was right that the left hemisphere is specialized and dominant for language in the vast majority of right-handed individuals, the situation is much more complicated in left-handers, and in right-handed individuals who have left-handed family members or who are not strongly right-handed. In these groups, the right hemisphere is involved in language functions to a greater or lesser extent, sometimes to the point of being dominant for language. This fact alone shows that the very first neural question – gross localization – is far more complex for language than for elementary motor and sensory functions, which do not vary in this way. It is not known just what aspects of language processing are separated from each other and located in one or another hemisphere in these populations. The partial and mild aphasias which follow unilateral injury in these populations may be limited because the uninjured hemisphere normally subserves certain language functions in an individual, or because undamaged parts of the injured hemisphere are subserving the remaining language functions.

There is one particular sub-population – strongly right-handed individuals with only right-handed family members – in which the situation seems to be relatively clear. In this population, language functions are almost always carried out by the left hemisphere. Even here, there are exceptions, which lead to crossed-dextral aphasia. The case of crossed-dextral aphasia poses all the questions we have just raised about whether all language functions or only a sub-set of them are in the right hemisphere; but in the vast majority of strongly right-handed individuals without familial sinistrality (probably over 98 per cent of cases), language functions are left-hemisphere-based. Recent studies, however, have shown that language is not normal after right-hemisphere lesions in this population. We reviewed these studies in Chapter 18, and concluded that the aspects of language functioning which are abnormal following right-sided lesions in this population are not part of what we may call "core psycholinguistic processing". By "core psycholinguistic processing", we are referring to the accessing of the form and literal meaning of words and sentences. The functions which are disturbed in patients with right-hemisphere lesions in this sub-population – inferencing, recognition and production of phonological features of speech related to emotional state – are not core functions. We also noted that, although split-brain studies showed that different aspects of core psycholinguistic functioning – such as the ability to access the literal meaning of words – *can* be carried out in the right hemisphere in a few cases, this does not mean that these functions ordinarily *are* carried out in this hemisphere. Though our conclusions in this area must be tentative, the data suggest that the left hemisphere is dominant for core psycholinguistic processing in this one sub-set of the human population.

We also were concerned with the areas of the left hemisphere which are responsible for language processing in this population. We found that lesions in subcortical areas, such as the thalamus, the caudate, the putamen, and surrounding white matter, do produce aphasic symptoms. However, lesions in this area affect the overlying cortex, and these effects may be responsible for the aphasias seen in patients with these lesions. The best case for the involvement of a subcortical structure in language can be made for portions of the thalamus; and, in this case, both the behavior of patients after strokes and hemorrhages (Chapter 19) and patients' language functioning after thalamic stimulation (Chapter 20) suggest that the language disturbances seen after thalamic lesions are due to an alerting function which interacts with the patient's ability to use the language code. The other area of the brain in which lesions produce language disturbances is the dominant supplementary cortex. Here, too, the disturbances seem to involve the initiation of speech, rather than intrinsic psycholinguistic computational processes. The only exception to this seems to be the occasional occurrence of a persistent dysgraphia after supplementary motor lesions. In all, except perhaps for the most secondary forms of linguistic expressions such as writing, core psycholinguistic processes may be accomplished only by the perisylvian association cortex. Though the conclusion that this relatively small area of the brain is the sole region involved in psycholinguistic processing really only applies to the right-handed population, there is no reason at present to believe that regions outside of the perisylvian association cortex of one or the other hemisphere are responsible for language in non-right-handers.

The second major issue that we have discussed in Part IV is the internal organization of the perisylvian association cortex with respect to language functions. This is the principal area of neurolinguistic theory construction, and has been a subject of speculation, debate, and scientific investigation since the first truly scientific paper on this subject by Broca in 1861. In this book we have traced the development of theories of the functional neuroanatomy for language in the perisylvian cortex. The dominant theory in this history is the classical and contemporary connectionist model proposed by Wernicke following Broca's work, and extended by Lichtheim, Dejerine, Geschwind, and others. There are objections to this theory, as we have seen, but no other theory has achieved the widespread acceptance that this one has. However, this theory is now under the most serious attack that it has ever faced.

Though the problems with this theory presented by Freud, Head, Goldstein, and many other researchers are serious, these objections did not lead to an alternative to this theory. Not only were opposing neurolinguistic theories phrased in very general terms (such as Jackson's or Goldstein's); the psycholinguistic approaches to aphasia advocated by critics of the connectionist models were not well grounded in a rich theoretical framework given by normal psychology and linguistics. Although researchers such as Goldstein and Luria borrowed heavily from existing theories of language structure and the psychology of language, these borrowings were not systematic, and these authors did not generate a sustained approach to linguistic aphasiology. The attack that connectionist models now face comes from the contemporary psycholinguistic approach to aphasia. The contemporary approach to linguistic aphasiology, though new, is a well-founded, sustained, scientific enterprise, and even its early results are to be taken seriously. This approach has clearly demonstrated that classical connectionist aphasiology recognizes too few primary aphasic disturbances of language, and that it groups together a variable number of primary disturbances in each of the major syndromes. Psycholinguistic studies of aphasia have also shown that many aphasic disturbances are due to disturbances in processing the abstract representations of the language code – the part of language processing which the classical connectionist models were least able to handle. Although contemporary linguistic aphasiology has not been much concerned with the neural basis for the psychological functions it describes, it has shaken researchers' faith in the adequacy of the classical connectionist model in a serious way.

Despite these concerns, classical and contemporary connectionist neurolinguistic theory has led to a number of investigations of the neuropathological determinants of the classical syndromes, using modern neuroradiological imaging techniques, especially the CT scan. We reviewed these studies in Chapter 19, and voiced a number of reservations about these studies. Some objections pertain to the interpretation of the syndrome–lesion correlates found in some of these studies. In particular, we noted that a functional analysis of patients' deficits is sometimes avoided or actually obscured by authors' satisfaction with the fact that patients fall into a classical syndrome (Damasio and Damasio 1980). We also noted that rough correlates between the lesion sites found on CT scans and those predicted by the theory, as in the localization of the lesions associated with transcortical sensory aphasia in Kertesz's work, are hard to interpret, because slight differences between what is found and what is expected are highly significant with respect to particular connectionist neurolinguistic theories. The chief reservation that was expressed in Chapter 19 about these studies, however, was that the classical aphasic syndromes have become too heterogeneous and polytypical for the correlation of these syndromes with lesion sites to be informative about aspects of a neurolinguistic theory which deals with the functional neuroanatomy of the language area at the level of detail that is now of interest.

Contemporary linguistic aphasiology has just begun to be used as a way to analyze patients' deficits for correlation with lesion parameters. Studies by Roeltgen and Heilman (1983; 1984) and Vanier and Caplan (1985; in press) correlate some of the more narrowly defined psycholinguistic syndromes – the various forms of alexia and agraphia, agrammatism – with lesion site as defined by CT scanning. In some cases – for instance, the dyslexias – connectionist neurolinguistic models made no explicit predictions about deficit–lesion correlations, and the data do not bear on specific aspects of connectionist theories. In other cases – for instance, agrammatism – there were specific predictions made by connectionist neurolinguistic models and

455

these predictions are not clearly borne out by the data. In addition, the almost universal view that localization of a function must be uniform across all adult members of the species (except for the issue of lateralization) is not borne out by lesion–deficit correlates reported by Caplan *et al.* (1985) for syntactic comprehension or for other simpler psycholinguistic functions that we reviewed in Chapter 19. These findings all point to a need to rethink the most fundamental tenets of this theory: the uniform localization of sub-components of the language-processing system within a portion of the perisylvian cortex in all adult members of the species, and the determination of this putative uniform localization by the relationship of an area of association cortex to sensory and motor cortex. In place of a theory which allocates language-related tasks – speaking, auditory comprehension, reading – to areas of the cortex because these tasks seem tied to sensory or motor functions of adjacent areas of association cortex, linguistic aphasiology indicates that we need to develop a neurolinguistic theory which establishes the basic facts about localization of sub-components of the language-processing system in relationship to neural structures, and then account for the localization of these processing components in terms of genetic and environmental influences.

Several modern neuroscientists (e.g. Kandel 1985*a*) have concluded that the localization of the "higher functions" is so well established that objections to localization are of historical interest only. We have seen that the localization of language functions is far from understood, though there is good reason to believe that there is gross localization of core psycholinguistic processing functions. Just what the actual "elemental" operations and processing stages related to language functions are is not established in many areas of psycholinguistic functioning. Where we have reasonably good ideas about particular processing stages, and can identify disturbances of these processing stages reasonably reliably, we have only very general information about the neural lesions which are related to these impairments. We have better information about the neural basis of the classical aphasic syndromes; but these syndromes are clearly not the result of a disturbance of a single processing stage, and the variation of symptoms between patients with a single syndrome makes the interpretation of these correlational data in terms of localization of processing components impossible.

We may consider the question of localization the other way around as well, beginning with neural considerations. We do not know what the appropriate units of the brain for localization are. Broca suggested that they are gyri, grossly defined parts of gyri (such as the pars triangularis and opercularis of the third frontal convolution), and groups of adjacent gyri. This concept has dominated the neural side of neurolinguistic analyses since

1861. We know, however, that gyri contain more than one cytoarchitectonically defined area, a fact which makes the localization of any function within a gyrus likely to be empirically insufficient. Moreover, we know that cytoarchitectonically defined areas differ as a function of the stains used to visualize aspects of neural structure: which way of dividing the brain is relevant to functional localization? We also know that there are ways to define brain areas other than in terms of histological structure or gross anatomical landmarks. Widespread groups of cells share neurotransmitters: for instance, Alzheimer's disease is now thought to be partly the result of a disturbance in the functions of cells which use acetylcholine as a neurotransmitter (Whitehouse *et al.* 1982). Could groups of cells which share a neurotransmitter be the appropriate units for correlation with a language-processing function? We should keep in mind that there are many different ways to "parse" the nervous system, and that the hypothesis that the relevant "parsing" is in terms of grossly definable brain areas is just one of many which needs to be considered. At present, there is no *direct* evidence that any of these types of "parsings" – cytoarchitectonically defined areas, groups of neurons related through shared neurotransmitter substances, or other "natural kinds" discovered in contemporary neuroscience – are the units which map onto specific functions in the language-processing domain. It is not even clear how to investigate some of these hypotheses. For instance, the hypothesis that cytoarchitectonically defined areas are the locales of particular linguistic processes does not seem to be approachable by any observations which can be made by presently available technology. In other cases, we can at least begin to study these questions. For instance, the investigation of the language disturbances seen in patients with Alzheimer's disease (Schwartz *et al.* 1979) may give us clues as to the role played by certain neural populations (e.g. cortical cholinergic cells) in language functions (Caplan 1981; 1982).

Influences coming from the basic neurosciences – especially neurophysiological investigations of elementary psychological functions such as planning simple motor actions, early stages of perception, and simple aspects of learning – have also influenced our concepts of the neural elements and mechanisms which may be related to language processing. The most specific suggestion coming from this area of investigation is that many computations in the nervous system make use of parallel and distributed systems for the representation of information. These systems are based upon the theory that synapses between neurons are information-bearing elements. We have seen that parallel distributed processing systems (PDP systems), coupled with interactive activation and inhibition computational mechanisms, are beginning to be used to model aspects of psycholinguistic processing (see Chapter

17). In Chapter 22, we reviewed simulations of psychological processes which make use of these PDP systems, which explicitly relate these models to problems in neuropsychology, such as inferring the nature of the representation of language in the brain from double dissociations in patients' performances, and to aspects of language disturbances, such as naming impairments. The relationship of modeling at this more "elemental" or "basic" level of psycholinguistic processing to the basic notion of localization of function is far from clear. Certainly, PDP systems, which represent and process information in a diffuse or "global", "holistic" way, can nonetheless produce very specific deficits, as the studies by Wood and Gordon that we reviewed in Chapter 22 point out. Modeling neural computations in this "bottom-up" way thus also raises questions about the fundamental concept of localization of function in neurolinguistics. Here, too, the way theory will develop is far from clear.

All these topics are aspects of the characterization of Marr's "neural level" of theory construction (see Chapter 17). We can see that there is a great deal that remains to be discovered about this level, even with respect to the most basic, gross aspects of localization of language-processing components, let alone the cellular and sub-cellular structures and physiological and biochemical mechanisms responsible for processing and representing language. A major consequence of our ignorance in these areas is that neural facts do not constrain linguistic or psycholinguistic theories as we would like them to. We cannot infer that language structure or processing has certain characteristics because of how the brain is structured. Similarly, we cannot conclude from the fact that a lesion is in a certain area of the brain, or is of a certain type, that a patient will have a particular type of language impairment, if by "language impairment" we mean a deficit in a particular language-processing component. At best, we can say that the patient is likely to have one of the classical aphasic syndromes (if the patient is right-handed and meets other criteria: Lecours 1984) – a very general characterization.

What this means is that neurolinguistic theories are not yet explanatory. As we have deepened the level of empirical detail and theoretical analysis of language structure, language processing, and language breakdown, we have distanced neurolinguistic theories from the satisfying, apparently explanatory models developed by Wernicke, Geschwind, and the other connectionists. We do not know how the particular features of neural areas make for the particular computational capacities which allow these parts of the brain to subserve language, although we do know much more about these features of the brain than we did a decade ago.

We are also living in an age of exciting technological development. It was not very long ago that our ability to image the brain in life was restricted to the use of x-rays of the skull, and highly invasive, uncomfortable, dangerous procedures such as arteriography and pneumoencephalography. Though these procedures are still in use, we now have safe, highly revealing, and quite accessible means of imaging the brain in much more detail. Chief among these tools is the CT scan. In addition, positron emission tomography (PET), single proton emission computed tomography (SPECT), and nuclear magnetic resonance imaging (MRI) are available at a few centers. Our ability to measure many dimensions of a lesion – its metabolic profile with respect to a particular nutrient or neurotransmitter, its electrical consequences – of which location is only one, is growing on almost a weekly basis. We can study deliberately created small transient "lesions" caused by cortical and subcortical stimulation during neurosurgical procedures. All of these technological developments offer exciting new possibilities for exploring the neural basis for language deficits and – through the usual logic of association of organic and functional deficits – the neural basis for language. Some of these technological developments, such as PET scanning, SPECT, and evoked potentials, can also be used in normal subjects to correlate changes in metabolic or neurophysiological activity with particular language processes. We reviewed early work using some of these techniques in Part IV of this book.

These techniques, though exciting, are not ends in themselves. Their contribution to our understanding of how the brain processes language depends upon the questions that we use these techniques to answer. If we use these techniques to determine the localization of metabolic abnormalities in lesions that correspond to the classical aphasic syndromes, we will not advance our knowledge of the neural basis for language in ways that contemporary linguistic aphasiology suggests are important. On the other hand, if we use these techniques to bear on the neural basis for functions which contemporary psychology, linguistics, cognitive science, and linguistic aphasiology suggest are basic aspects of language processing, these techniques may add enormously to our understanding of the neural basis for language. We can certainly expect – and hope! – that neurolinguistic theories will become much more complex very quickly, as this new technology begins to be used extensively.

We said at the outset of this book that much more is known about the basic neurosciences and human sciences of linguistics and psychology than is known about the hybrid science of neurolinguistics. Our review of neurolinguistic models in Parts II and IV of this book illustrates the extent to which this is true. However, the work that we have reviewed in these sections, as well as in Part III of this volume, also clearly indicates how much

459

progress has been made in many areas of this complex field. We are much better able to see how parts of this complex picture fit together than we were twenty years ago. Linguistic aphasiology can be a guide to the functions for which localization can be sought. The extent of variation of localization of a function across the population can be ascertained, and the genetic and environmental determinants of constraints on such variation established. Neural units other than grossly defined brain regions can be related to language, through the studies of patients with different pathologies. ERP, metabolic mapping, and stimulation techniques can add to our knowledge of the neural basis of language-processing components. Though there is little room for "grand theories" in contemporary neurolinguistics, the slow accumulation of data that bear on the relationship of language structure and processing to neural parameters can fill in the many gaps that presently exist in our knowledge of the levels of the Marr hierarchy. We may be on the verge of an extremely productive era of neurolinguistic research and theory construction, in which technological advances in neuro-imaging, increased ability to measure neurophysiological activity in normal subjects, and advances in our understanding of cellular aspects of the neuroanatomy of the language area, will all coalesce to lead to major new advances in our understanding of the very old question of how the uniquely human capacity for language is sustained by the human nervous system.

SUGGESTIONS FOR FURTHER READING

Caplan, D. (1981). On the cerebral localization of linguistic functions. *Brain and Language* 14, 120–37.

(1982). Reconciling the categories – representation in neurology and in linguistics. In M. A. Arbib, D. Caplan, and J. C. Marshall (eds.), *Neural Models of Language Processes*. Academic Press, New York.

References

Alajouanine, T., Ombredane, A., and Durand, M. (1939). *Le Syndrome de Désintégration Phonétique dans l'Aphasie.* Masson, Paris.

Albert, M. and Obler, L. (1978). *The Bilingual Brain: Neuropsychological and Neurolinguistic Aspects of Bilingualism.* Academic Press, New York.

Alexander, M. P. and LoVerme, S. R. (1980). Aphasia after left hemisphere intracerebral hemorrhage. *Neurology* 30, 1193–202.

Anderson, J. A. (1972). A simple neural network generating an interactive memory. *Mathematical Biosciences* 14, 197–220.

—— (1984). Neural models and very little about language. In Caplan *et al.* 1984.

Arbib, M. A. and Caplan, D. (1979). Neurolinguistics must be computational. *Behavioral and Brain Sciences* 2, 449–83.

Armstrong, S. L., Gleitman, L. R., and Gleitman, H. (1983). What some concepts might not be. *Cognition* 13, 263–308.

Baddeley, A. D. (1976). *The Psychology of Memory.* Basic Books, New York.

—— (1981). The concept of working memory: a view of its current state and probable future development. *Cognition* 10, 17–24.

Baddeley, A. D. and Hitsch, G. (1974). Working memory. In G. H. Bower (ed.), *The Psychology of Learning and Motivation: Advances in Research and Theory*, vol. 8. Academic Press, New York.

Badecker, B. and Caramazza, A. (1985). On considerations of method and theory governing the use of clinical categories in neurolinguistics and cognitive neuropsychology: the case against agrammatism. *Cognition* 20, 97–125.

Baron, J. and Strawson, C. (1976). Use of orthographic and word-specific knowledge in reading words aloud. *Journal of Experimental Psychology: Human Perception and Performance* 2, 386–93.

Basser, L. S. (1962). Hemiplegia of early onset and the faculty of speech with special reference to the effects of hemispherectomy. *Brain* 85, 427–60.

Basso, A., Casati, G., and Vignolo, L. A. (1977). Phonemic identification defect in aphasia. *Cortex* 13, 85–95.

Basso, A., Lecours, A. R., Moraschini, S., and Vanier, M. (1985). Anatomoclinical correlations of the aphasias as defined through computerized tomography: exceptions. *Brain and Language* 26, 201–29.

Bastian, C. (1887). On different kinds of aphasia with special reference to their classification and ultimate pathology. *British Medical Journal* 2, 931–6.

Bauer, D. W. and Stanovich, K. E. (1980). Lexical access and the spelling-to-sound regularity effect. *Memory and Cognition* 8, 424–32.

Beauvois, M.-F. (1982). Optic aphasia: a process of interaction between vision and language. *Philosophical Transactions of the Royal Society of London* B298, 35–47.

Beauvois, M.-F. and Dérouesné, J. (1979). Phonological alexia: three dissociations. *Journal of Neurology, Neurosurgery and Psychiatry* 42, 1115–24.

461

References

Beauvois, M.-F. and Saillant, M. F. (1985). Optic aphasia for colours and colour agnosia: a distinction between visual and visuo-verbal impairments in the processing of colours. *Cognitive Neuropsychology* 2, 1–48.

Bechtereva, N. P., Bundzen, P. V., Gogolitsin, Y. L., Malyshev, V. N., and Perepelkin, P. D. (1979). Neurophysiological codes of words in subcortical structures of the human brain. *Brain and Language* 7, 145–63.

Béland, R. and Nespoulous, J. L. (1985). Phonological models and paraphasic aphasic errors. Academy of Aphasia, Pittsburgh.

Benson, D. F. (1979). *Aphasia, Alexia, Agraphia.* Churchill Livingstone, New York.

Benson, D. F. and Geschwind, N. (1971). Aphasia and related cortical disturbances. In A. B. Baker and L. H. Baker (eds.), *Clinical Neurology.* Harper & Row, New York.

Berndt, R. S. and Caramazza, A. (1980). A redefinition of the syndrome of Broca's aphasia: implications for a neuropsychological model of language. *Applied Psycholinguistics* 1, 225–78.

Berwick, R. and Weinberg. A. (1984). *The Grammatical Basis of Linguistic Performance: Language Use and Acquisition.* MIT Press, Cambridge, Mass.

Bever, T. G. (1970). The cognitive basis for linguistic structures. In J. R. Hayes (ed.), *Cognition and the Development of Language.* Wiley, New York.

Blumstein, S. (1973*a*). *A Phonological Investigation of Aphasic Speech.* Mouton, The Hague. (1973*b*). Some phonological implications of aphasic speech. In H. Goodglass and S. Blumstein (eds.), *Psycholinguistics and Aphasia.* Johns Hopkins University Press, Baltimore.

Blumstein, S., Baker, E., and Goodglass, H. (1977*a*). Phonological factors in auditory comprehension in aphasia. *Neuropsychologia* 15, 19–30.

Blumstein, S., Cooper, W. E., Goodglass, H., Statlander, S., and Gottlieb, J. (1980). Production deficits in aphasia: a voice-onset time analysis. *Brain and Language* 9, 153–70.

Blumstein, S. Cooper, W. E., Zurif, E. B., and Caramazza, A. (1977*b*). The perception and production of voice-onset time in aphasia. *Neuropsychologia* 15, 371–83.

Blumstein, S., Katz, B., Goodglass, H., Shrier, R., and Dworetsky, B. (1985). The effects of slowed speech on auditory comprehension in aphasia. *Brain and Language* 24, 246–65.

Blumstein, S., Tartter, V. C., Michel, D., Hirsch, B., and Leiter E. (1977*c*). The role of distinctive features in the dichotic perception of vowels. *Brain and Language* 4, 508–20.

Bogen, J. E. and Bogen, G. M. (1976). Wernicke's region: where is it? *Annals of the NY Academy of Sciences* 280, 834–43.

Bradley, D. C., Garrett, M. F., and Zurif, E. B. (1980). Syntactic deficits in Broca's aphasia. In D. Caplan (ed.), *Biological Studies of Mental Processes.* MIT Press, Cambridge, Mass.

Bradshaw, J. L. and Nettleton, N. C. (1981). The nature of hemispheric specialization in man. *The Behavioral and Brain Sciences* 4, 51–91.

Bresnan, J. (1978). A realistic transformational grammar. In M. Halle, J. Bresnan, and G. A. Miller (eds.), *Linguistic Theory and Psychological Reality.* MIT Press, Cambridge, Mass. (ed.) (1982). *The Mental Representation of Grammatical Relations.* MIT Press, Cambridge, Mass.

Broadbent, W. H. (1879). A case of peculiar affection of speech, with commentary. *Brain* 1, 484–503.

Broca, P. (1861). Remarques sur le siège de la faculté de la parole articulée, suivies d'une observation d'aphémie (perte de parole). *Bulletin de la Société d'Anatomie* (Paris) 36, 330–57. (1865). Sur le siège de la faculté du langage articulé. *Bulletin d'Anthropologie* 6, 377–93.

Brown, J. (1979). Language representation in the brain. In H. Steklis and M. Raleigh (eds.), *Neurobiology of Social Communication in Primates.* Academic Press, New York. (1980). Brain structure and language production: a dynamic view. In D. Caplan (ed.), *Biological Studies of Mental Processes.* MIT Press, Cambridge, Mass.

462

(1982). Hierarchy and evolution in neurolinguistics. In M. A. Arbib, D. Caplan, and J. C. Marshall (eds.), *Neural Models of Language Processes*. Academic Press, New York.

Brown, W. S. and Lehmann, D. (1979). Linguistic meaning related differences in ERP scalp topography. In D. Lehmann and E. Callaway (eds.), *Human Evoked Potentials: Applications and Problems*. Plenum, New York.

Brown, W. S., Lehmann, D., and Marsh, J. T. (1980). Linguistic meaning related differences in evoked potential topography: English, Swiss-German and imagined. *Brain and Language* 11, 340–53.

Brown, W. S., Marsh, J. T., and Smith, J. C. (1973). Contextual meaning effects on speech-evoked potentials. *Behavioral Biology* 9, 755–61.

(1976). Evoked potential waveform differences produced by the perception of different meanings of an ambiguous phrase. *Electroencephalography and Clinical Neurophysiology* 41, 113–23.

Brownell, H. H. (1978). *Picture Perception and Semantic Memory*. Ph.D. dissertation, Johns Hopkins University, Baltimore.

(manuscript). Prototypicality and category level effects in aphasic naming.

Bryden, M. P. (1982). *Laterality: Functional Asymmetry in the Intact Brain*. Academic Press, New York.

Bryden, M. P., Hécaen, H., and DeAgostini, M. (1983). Patterns of cerebral organization. *Brain and Language* 20, 249–62.

Bub, D., Black, S., Howell, J., and Kertesz, A. (1986). Damage to input and output buffers – what's a lexicality effect doing in a place like that? In E. Keller and M. Gopnik (eds.), *Motor and Sensory Processes in Language*. Erlbaum, Hillsdale, NJ.

Bub, D., Cancelliere, A., and Kertesz, A. (1985). Whole-word and analytic translation of spelling to sound in a non-semantic reader. In Patterson *et al.* 1985.

Buckingham, H. (1980). On correlating aphasic errors with slips of the tongue. *Applied Psycholinguistics* 1, 199–220.

Butterworth, B. (1979). Hesitation and the production of verbal paraphasias and neologisms in jargon aphasia. *Brain and Language* 8, 133–61.

Cameron, R. F., Currier, R. D., and Haerar, A. F. (1977). Aphasia and literacy. *Br. J. Com. Disorders* 6, 161–3.

Campbell, R. and Besner, D. (1981). This and thap: constraints on the production of new, written words. *Quarterly Journal of Experimental Psychology* 33A, 375–96.

Caplan, D. (1981). On the cerebral localization of linguistic functions: logical and empirical issues surrounding deficit analysis and functional localization. *Brain and Language* 14, 120–37.

(1982). Reconciling the categories – representation in neurology and in linguistics. In M. A. Arbib, D. Caplan, and J. C. Marshall (eds.), *Neural Models of Language Processes*. Academic Press, New York.

(1983). A note on the "word order problem" in agrammatism. *Brain and Language* 20, 155–65.

(1985). Syntactic and semantic structures in agrammatism. In Kean 1985.

Caplan, D. (1987). Discrimination of Normal and Aphasic Patients on a test of Syntactic Comprehension, *Neuropsychologia* 25,173–84.

Caplan, D., Baker, C., and Dehaut, F. (1985). Syntactic determinants of sentence comprehension in aphasia. *Cognition* 21, 117–75.

Caplan, D. and Futter, C. (1986). Assignment of thematic roles to nouns in sentence comprehension by an agrammatic patient. *Brain and Language* 27, 117–34.

Caplan, D. and Hildebrandt, N. (1986). Language deficits and the theory of syntax: a reply to Grodzinsky. *Brain and Language* 27, 168–77.

References

Caplan, D., Lecours, A. R., and Smith, A. (eds.) (1984). *Biological Perspectives on Language.* MIT Press, Cambridge, Mass.

Caplan, D., Vanier, M., and Baker, C. (1986*a*). A case study of reproduction conduction aphasia I: word production. *Cognitive Neuropsychology* 3, 99–128.

(1986*b*). A case study of reproduction conduction aphasia II: sentence comprehension. *Cognitive Neuropsychology* 3, 129–46.

Cappa, S. F. and Vignolo, L. A. (1979). "Transcortical" features of aphasia following left thalamic hemorrhage. *Cortex* 15, 121–30.

Caramazza, A., Basili, A., Koller, J. J., and Berndt, R. S. (1981). An investigation of repetition and language processing in a case of conduction aphasia. *Brain and Language* 14, 235–71.

Caramazza, A. and Berndt, R. S. (1978). Semantic and syntactic processes in aphasia: a review. *Psychological Bulletin* 85, 898–918.

Caramazza, A. and Zurif, E. B. (1976). Dissociation of algorithmic and heuristic processes in language comprehension: evidence from aphasia. *Brain and Language* 3, 572–82.

(eds.) (1978). *Language Acquisition and Language Breakdown: Parallels and Divergences.* Johns Hopkins University Press, Baltimore.

Carpenter, M. and Sutin, J. (1983). *Human Neuroanatomy*, 8th edn. Williams & Wilkins, Baltimore.

Chomsky, N. (1957). *Syntactic Structures.* Mouton, The Hague.

(1965). *Aspects of the Theory of Syntax.* MIT Press, Cambridge, Mass.

(1981). *Lectures on Government and Binding.* Foris, Dordrecht.

(1982). *Some Concepts and Consequences of Government and Binding.* MIT Press, Cambridge, Mass.

Chomsky, N. and Halle, M. (1968). *The Sound Pattern of English.* Harper & Row, New York.

Chusid, J. (1973). *Correlative Neuroanatomy and Functional Neurology*, 15th edn. Lange, Los Altos, California.

Collins, A. M. and Quillian, M. R. (1969). Retrieval time from semantic memory. *Journal of Verbal Learning and Verbal Behavior* 8, 240–7.

Coltheart, M. (1978). Lexical access in simple reading tasks. In B. Underwood (ed.), *Strategies of Information Processing.* Academic Press, London.

(1980). Reading, phonological recoding, and deep dyslexia. In Coltheart *et al.* 1980.

(1985). Cognitive neuropsychology and the study of reading. In M. I. Posner and O. Marin (eds.), *Attention and Performance XI.* Erlbaum, Hillsdale, NJ.

Coltheart, M., Besner, D., Jonasson, J. T., and Davelaar, E. (1979). Phonological encoding in the lexical decision task. *Quarterly Journal of Experimental Psychology* 31, 489–507.

Coltheart, M., Davelaar, E., Jonasson, J. T., and Besner, D. (1977). Access to the internal lexicon. In S. Dornic (ed.), *Attention and Performance VI.* Erlbaum, Hillsdale, NJ.

Coltheart, M., Masterson, J., Byng, S., Prior, M., and Riddoch, J. (1983). Surface dyslexia. *Quarterly Journal of Experimental Psychology* 35A, 469–95.

Coltheart, M., Patterson, K. E., and Marshall, J. C. (eds.) (1980). *Deep Dyslexia.* Routledge & Kegan Paul, London.

Cooper, W. E. (1983). Brain cartography: electrical stimulation of processing sites or transmission lines? *Behavioral and Brain Sciences* 6, 212–13.

Curry, S. H., Peters, J. F., and Weinberg, H. (1978). Choice of active electrode site and recording montage as variables affecting CNV amplitude preceding speech. In D. A. Otto (ed.), *Multidisciplinary Perspectives in Event-Related Brain Potential Research.* US Environmental Protection Agency, Washington, DC.

Daly, D. D. (1985). Cerebral localization. In A. B. Baker and H. Baker (eds.), *Clinical Neurology*, ch. 8, vol. 1. Harper & Row, Philadelphia.

Damasio, A. R., Castro-Caldas, A., Grosso, J. T., and Ferro, J. M. (1976). Brain specialization for language does not depend upon literacy. *Archives of Neurology* 33, 300–1.

Damasio, A., Damasio, H., Rizzo, M., Varney, N., and Gersch, F. (1982). Aphasia with nonhemorrhagic lesions in the basal ganglia and internal capsule. *Archives of Neurology* 39, 15–20.

Damasio, H. and Damasio, A. R. (1980). The anatomical basis of conduction aphasia. *Brain* 103, 337–50.

de Bleser, R. (in press). Agrammatism and paragrammatism: a historical perspective. *Cognitive Neuropsychology*.

Dejerine, J. J. (1892). Contribution à l'étude anatomo-pathologique et clinique des différentes variétés de cécité verbale. *Mémoires Société Biologique* 4, 61–90.

—— (1901). *Anatomie des Centres Nerveux*. Rueff, Paris.

De Renzi, E. and Vignolo, L. (1962). The token test: a sensitive test to detect receptive disturbances in aphasics. *Brain* 85, 665–78.

Desmedt, J. E. and Robertson, D. (1977). Search for right hemisphere asymmetries in event-related potentials to somatosensory cueing signals. In J. E. Desmedt (ed.), *Language and Hemispheric Specialization in Man: Cerebral Event-Related Potentials*. S. Karger, Basel.

Didday, R. L. (1976). A model of visuomotor mechanisms in the frog optic tectum. *Mathematical Biosciences* 30, 169–80.

Dubois, J., Hécaen, H., Angelergues, R., Maufras du Chatelier, A., and Marcie, P. (1964). Etude neurolinguistique de l'aphasie de conduction. *Neuropsychologia* 2, 9–44.

Ertl, J. and Schafer, E. W. P. (1969). Cortical activity preceding speech. *Life Sciences* 8, 559.

Fay, D. and Cutler, A. (1977). Malapropisms and the structure of the mental lexicon. *Linguistic Inquiry* 8, 505–20.

Fodor, J. A. (1975). *The Language of Thought*. Crowell, New York.

—— (1982). *The Modularity of Mind*. MIT Press, Cambridge, Mass.

Fodor, J. A., Bever, T. G., and Garrett, M. F. (1974). *The Psychology of Language*. McGraw-Hill, New York.

Forster, K. I. (1976). Accessing the mental lexicon. In R. J. Wales and E. Walker (eds.), *New Approaches to Language Mechanisms*. North-Holland, Amsterdam.

Frazier, L. (1983). Motor theory of speech perception or acoustic theory of speech production? *Behavioral and Brain Sciences* 6, 213–14.

Frazier, L. and Fodor, J. D. (1978). The sausage machine: a new two-stage parsing model. *Cognition* 6, 291–325.

Frege, G. (1892). On sense and reference. In P. Geach and M. Black (eds.), *Translations from the Philosophical Writings of Gottlob Frege*. Basil Blackwell, Oxford, 1960.

Freud, S. (1891). *On Aphasia*. Deuticke, Leipzig. Reprinted in translation, International Universities Press, New York, 1953.

Friedman, D., Simson, R., Ritter, W., and Rapin, I. (1975a). Cortical evoked potentials elicited by real speech words and human sounds. *Electroencephalography and Clinical Neurophysiology* 38, 13–19.

—— (1975b). The late positive component (P300) and information processing in sentences. *Electroencephalography and Clinical Neurophysiology* 38, 255–62.

Fromkin, V. (1971). The non-anomalous nature of anomalous utterances. *Language* 47, 27–52.

Funnell, E. (1983). Phonological processes in reading new evidence from acquired dyslexia. *British Journal of Psychology* 74, 159–80.

Galaburda, A. M., LeMay, M., Kemper, T. L., and Geschwind, N. (1978). Right–left asymmetries in the brain. *Science* 199, 852–6.

465

References

Gardner, H., Brownell, H., Wapner, W., and Michelow, D. (1983). Missing the point: the role of the right hemisphere in the processing of complex linguistic materials. In E. Perecman (ed.), *Cognitive Processes in the Right Hemisphere*. Academic Press, New York.

Garrett, M. F. (1976). Syntactic processes in sentence production. In R. Wales and E. Walker (eds.), *New Approaches to Language Mechanisms*. North-Holland, Amsterdam.

(1982). Production of speech: observations from normal and pathological language use. In A. W. Ellis (ed.), *Normality and Pathology in Cognitive Functions*. Academic Press, London.

(1984). The organization of processing structure for language production: applications to aphasic speech. In Caplan *et al.* 1984.

Gazdar, G., Klein, E., Pullum, G., and Sag, I. (1985). *Generalized phrase structure grammar*. Harvard University Press, Cambridge, Mass.

Gazzaniga, M. S. (1983). Right hemisphere language following brain bisection: a 20-year perspective. *American Psychologist* 38, 525–49.

Geschwind, N. (1962). The anatomy of acquired disorders of reading. In J. Money (ed.), *Reading Disability*. Johns Hopkins Press, Baltimore.

(1964). The paradoxical position of Kurt Goldstein in the history of aphasia. *Cortex* 1, 214–24.

(1965). Disconnection syndromes in animals and man. *Brain* 88, 237–94, 585–644.

(1974). *Selected Papers on Language and the Brain*. D. Reidel, Dordrecht.

(1979). Specializations of the human brain. In *The Brain*. W. H. Freeman, San Francisco.

(1984). Neural mechanisms, aphasia, and theories of language. In Caplan *et al.* 1984.

Geschwind, N. and Galaburda, A. (1985). Cerebral lateralization: biological mechanism, associations, and pathology I–III: a hypothesis and a program for research. *Archives of Neurology* 42, 428–59, 521–52, 634–54.

Geschwind, N. and Kaplan, E. (1962). A human cerebral disconnection syndrome: a preliminary report. *Neurology* 12, 675–85.

Geschwind, N. and Levitsky, W. (1968). Human brain: left–right asymmetries in temporal speech region. *Science* 161, 186–7.

Gloning, I., Gloning, K., and Hoff, F. (1963). Aphasia – a clinical syndrome. In L. Halperin (ed.), *Problems of Dynamic Neurology*. Jerusalem Post Press, Jerusalem.

Glushko, R. J. (1979). The organization and activation of orthographic knowledge in reading aloud. *Journal of Experimental Psychology: Human Perception and Performance* 5, 674–91.

Goldman-Rakic, P. S. (1982). Organization of frontal association cortex in normal and experimentally brain-injured primates. In M. A. Arbib, D. Caplan, and J. C. Marshall (eds.), *Neural Models of Language Processes*. Academic Press, New York.

Goldstein, K. (1984). *Language and Language Disturbances*. Grune & Stratton, New York.

Goodglass, H. (1973). Studies on the grammar of aphasics. In H. Goodglass and S. Blumstein (eds.), *Psycholinguistics and Aphasia*. Johns Hopkins University Press, Baltimore.

(1976). Agrammatism. In H. Whitaker and H. A. Whitaker (eds.), *Studies in Neurolinguistics*, vol. 1. Academic Press, New York.

Goodglass, H. and Baker, E. (1976). Semantic field, naming, and auditory comprehension in aphasia. *Brain and Language* 3, 359–74.

Goodglass, H. and Berko, J. (1960). Agrammatism and inflectional morphology in English. *Journal of Speech and Hearing Research* 3, 257–67.

Goodglass, H. and Geschwind, N. (1976). Language disorders (aphasia). In E. C. Carterette and M. Friedman (eds.), *Handbook of Perception*, vol. 7. Academic Press, New York.

Goodglass, H., Gleason, J. B., Bernholtz, N., and Hyde, M. R. (1972). Some linguistic structures in the speech of a Broca's aphasic. *Cortex* 8, 191–212.

466

Goodglass, H., Hyde, M. R., and Blumstein, S. (1969). Frequency, picturability and availability of nouns in aphasia. *Cortex* 5, 104–19.

Goodglass, H. and Kaplan, E. (1972). *The Assessment of Aphasia and Related Disorders*. Lea & Febiger, Philadelphia.

(1982). *The Assessment of Aphasia and Related Disorders*, 2nd edn. Lea & Febiger, Philadelphia.

Goodglass, H., Kaplan, E., Weintraub, S., and Ackerman, N. (1976). The "tip of the tongue" phenomenon in aphasia. *Cortex* 12, 145–53.

Goodglass, H., Klein, B., Carey, P., and Jones, K. (1966). Specific semantic word categories in aphasia. *Cortex* 2, 74–89.

Goodglass, H. and Quadfasel, F. A. (1954). Language laterality in left-handed aphasics. *Brain* 77, 521–48.

Goodglass, H., Quadfasel, F. A., and Timberlake, W. H. (1964). Phrase length and the type and severity of aphasia. *Cortex* 1, 133–52.

Gordon, B. (1982). Confrontation naming: computational model and disconnection simulation. In M. A. Arbib, D. Caplan, and J. C. Marshall (eds.), *Neural Models of Language Processes*. Academic Press, New York.

Gordon, B. and Caramazza, A. (1982). Lexical decision for open- and closed-class words: failure to replicate differential frequency sensitivity. *Brain and Language* 15, 143–60.

Gough, P. B. and Cosky, M. J. (1977). One second of reading again. In N. J. Castellan, D. B. Pisoni, and G. R. Potts (eds.), *Cognitive Theory*, vol. 2. Erlbaum, Hillsdale, NJ.

Grabow, J. D., Aronson, A. E., Offord, K. P., Rose, D. E., and Greene, K. L. (1980). Hemispheric potentials evoked by speech sounds during discrimination tasks. *Electroencephalography and Clinical Neurophysiology* 49, 48–58.

Grashey, H. (1885). Uber aphasie und ihre beziehungen zur Wahrnehmung. *Archiv für Psychiatrie* 16.

Grodzinsky, Y. (1984). The syntactic characterization of agrammatism. *Cognition* 16, 99–120.

(1986). Language deficits and the theory of syntax. *Brain and Language* 27, 135–59.

Grossman, M. (1981). A bird is a bird is a bird: making reference within and without superordinate categories. *Brain and Language* 12, 313–31.

Grözinger, B., Kornhuber, H. H., and Kriebel, J. (1977). Human cerebral potentials preceding speech production, phonation, and movements of the mouth and tongue, with reference to respiratory and extracerebral potentials. In J. E. Desmedt (ed.), *Language and Hemispheric Specialization in Man: Cerebral Event-Related Potentials*. Karger, Basel.

Grözinger, B., Kornhuber, H., Kriebel, J., and Murata, K. (1970). Menschliche Hirnpotentiale vor dem Sprechen. *Pflingers Arch. ges. Physiol.* 332, R100–200.

Hansen, D. and Rodgers, T. (1968). An exploration of psycholinguistic units in initial reading. In K. S. Goodman (ed.), *The Psycholinguistic Nature of the Reading Process*. Wayne State University Press, Detroit.

Hart, J., Berndt, R., and Caramazza, A. (1985). Category specific naming deficit following cerebral infarction. *Nature* 316, 439–40.

Head, H. (1926). *Aphasia and Kindred Disorders of Speech*. Cambridge University Press, Cambridge.

Hebb, D. O. (1949). *The Organization of Behavior: A Neurophysiological Theory*. Wiley, New York.

Hécaen, H. and Ajuriaguerra, J. (1963). *Les Gauchiers, Prévalence Manuelle et Dominance Cérébrale*. Presses Universitaires de France, Paris.

Hécaen, H. and Albert, M. (1978). *Human Neuropsychology*. Wiley, New York.

Hécaen, H., DeAgostini, M., and Monzon-Montes, A. (1981). Cerebral organization in left-handers. *Brain and Language* 12, 261–84.

467

References

Hécaen, H. and Dubois, J. (1969). *La Naissance de la Neuropsychologie du Langage: 1825–1865*. Flammarion, Paris.

Hécaen, H., Mazars, G., Ramier, A., Goldblum, M. C., and Mérienne, L. (1971). Aphasie croisée chez un sujet droitier bilingue. *Revue Neurologique* 124, 319–23.

Heeschen, C. (1985). Agrammatism and paragrammatism: a fictitious opposition. In Kean 1985.

Heilman, K. M. and Scholes, R. J. (1976). The nature of comprehension errors in Broca's, conduction, and Wernicke's aphasics. *Cortex* 12, 258–65.

Heilman, K. M., Scholes, R., and Watson, R. T. (1975). Auditory affective agnosia: disturbed comprehension of affective speech. *Journal of Neurology, Neurosurgery and Psychiatry* 38, 69–72.

Henderson, L. (1982). *Orthography and Word Recognition in Reading*. Academic Press, London.

Henschen, S. E. (1920). *Klinische und Anatomische Beiträge zur Pathologie des Gehirns*. Nordiska Bokhandler, Stockholm.

Hildebrandt, N., Caplan, D., and Evans, K. (in press). The man$_i$ left t$_i$ without a trace: a study of aphasic comprehension of empty categories. *Cognitive Neuropsychology*.

Hinshelwood, J. (1899). *Letter-, Word-, and Mind-Blindness*. Lewis, London.

Hubel, D. H. and Wiesel, T. N. (1962). Receptive fields, binocular interaction, and functional architecture in the cat's visual cortex. *Journal of Physiology* 160, 106–54.

Humphreys, G. W., Riddoch, M. J., and Quinlan, P. T. (in press). Cascade processes in picture identification: data and implications. *Cognitive Neuropsychology*.

Jackendoff, R. (1977). *X'-Syntax: A Study of Phrase Structure*. MIT Press, Cambridge, Mass.

Jackson, J. H. (1874). On the nature of the duality of the brain. Citation from reprinted text, in J. Taylor (ed.), *Selected Writings of John Hughlings Jackson*, vol. 2. Basic Books, New York, 1958.

—— (1878). On affections of speech from disease of the brain. *Brain* 1, 304–30; 2, 203–22, 323–56.

Jakobson, R. (1941). *Kindersprache, Aphasie und Allgemeine Lautgesetze*. Universitets Arsskrift, Uppsala. Translated as *Child Language, Aphasia and Phonological Universals*. Mouton, The Hague, 1968.

Joanette, Y., Goulet, P., Ska, B., and Nespoulous, J. L. (1984). Production of narrative discourse in right brain-damaged right-handers. Manuscript presented at BABBLE (Body for the Advancement of Brain, Behavior, and Language Enterprises), Niagara Falls.

Joanette, Y., Keller, E., and Lecours, A. .R. (1980). Sequence of phonemic approximations in aphasia. *Brain and Language*. 11, 30–44.

Joanette, Y., Lecours, A. R., Lepage, Y., and Lamoureux, M. (1983). Language in right-handers with right-hemisphere lesions: a preliminary study including anatomical, genetic and social factors. *Brain and Language* 20, 217–48.

Job, R. and Sartori, G. (1984). Morphology decomposition: evidence from crossed phonological dyslexia. *Quarterly Journal of Experimental Psychology* 36A, 435–58.

Jolicoeur, P., Gluck, M. A., and Kosslyn, S. M. (1984). Pictures and names: making the connection. *Cognitive Psychology* 16, 243–75.

Kandel, E. R. (1979). Small systems of neurons. In *The Brain*. W. H. Freeman, San Francisco.

—— (1985a). Brain and behavior. In E. R. Kandel and J. H. Schwartz (eds.), *Principles of Neural Science*, 2nd edn. Elsevier, Amsterdam.

—— (1985b). Cellular mechanisms of learning and the biological basis of individuality. In E. R. Kandel and J. H. Schwartz (eds.), *Principles of Neural Science*, 2nd edn. Elsevier, Amsterdam.

Kay, J. and Lesser, R. (1985). The nature of phonological processing in oral reading: evidence from surface dyslexia. *Quarterly Journal of Experimental Psychology* 37A, 39–81.

Kean, M. L. (1977). The linguistic interpretation of aphasic syndromes: agrammatism in Broca's aphasia, an example. *Cognition* 5, 9–46.

(1982). Three perspectives for the analysis of aphasic syndromes. In M. A. Arbib, D. Caplan, and J. C. Marshall (eds.), *Neural Models of Language Processes*. Academic Press, New York.

(ed.) (1985). *Agrammatism*. Academic Press, New York.

Kertesz, A. (1979). *Aphasia and Associated Disorders: Taxonomy, Localization and Recovery*. Grune & Stratton, New York.

Kertesz, A. and Poole, E. (1974). The aphasia quotient: the taxonomic approach to measurement of aphasic disability. *Canadian Journal of Neurological Sciences* 1, 7–16.

Kertesz, A., Sheppard, A., and MacKenzie, R. (1982). Localization in transcortical sensory aphasia. *Archives of Neurology* 39, 475–8.

Kimura, D. (1961). Cerebral dominance and the perception of verbal stimuli. *Canadian Journal of Psychology* 15, 166–71.

(1963). Speech lateralization in young children as determined by an auditory test. *Journal of Comparative and Physiological Psychology* 56, 899–902.

(1967). Functional asymmetry of the brain in dichotic listening. *Cortex* 3, 163–78.

(1976). The neural basis of language qua gesture. In H. Whitaker and H. A. Whitaker (eds.), *Studies in Neurolinguistics*, vol. 2. Academic Press, New York.

(1983). Sex differences in cerebral organization for speech and praxic functions. *Canadian Journal of Psychology* 37, 19–35.

Kinsbourne, M. (1978). Evolution of language in relation to lateral action. In M. Kinsbourne (ed.), *Asymmetrical Function of the Brain*. Cambridge University Press, Cambridge.

Kiparsky, P. (1982). From cyclic phonology to lexical phonology. In H. van der Hulst and N. Smith (eds.), *The Structure of Phonological Representations*, vol 1. Foris, Dordrecht.

Klein, B. von Eckardt (1978). Inferring functional localization from neurological evidence. In E. Walker (ed.), *Explorations in the Biology of Language*. Bradford Books, Montgomery, Vermont.

Kleist, K. (1934). *Gehirnpathologie*. Barth, Leipzig.

Klippel, M. (1908). Discussion sur l'aphasie. *Revue Neurologique* 16, 611–36, 974–1024, 1025–47.

Kolk, H. H. and van Grunsven, M. (1985). Agrammatism as a variable phenomenon. *Cognitive Neuropsychology* 2, 347–84.

Krashen, S. D. (1973). Lateralization, language learning, and the critical period: some new evidence. *Language Learning* 23, 63–74.

Kutas, M. and Hillyard, S. A. (1980). Reading between the lines: event-related brain potentials during natural sentence processing. *Brain and Language* 11, 354–73.

Lansdale, H. (1961). The effect of neurosurgery on a test of proverbs. *American Psychologist* 16, 448.

Lapointe, S. (1983). Some issues in the linguistic description of agrammatism. *Cognition* 14, 1–39.

Lashley, K. S. (1950). In search of the engram. *Symposia of the Society for Experimental Biology* 4, 454–82.

Lecours, A. R. (1984). Where is the speech area, and who has seen it? In Caplan *et al.* 1984.

Lecours, A. R. and Joanette, Y. (1984). François Moutier or "from folds to folds". *Brain and Cognition* 3, 198–231.

Lecours, A. R., Lhermitte, F., and Bryans, B. (1983). *Aphasiology*. Baillière Tindall, London.

Lecours, A. R. and Mehler, J. (1985). *Illiteracy and Aphasia*. Tapuscrits du Laboratoire Théophile Alajouanine, no. 1.

References

LeMay, M. and Culebras, A. (1972). Human brain – morphologic differences in the hemi-spheres demonstrable by carotid arteriography. *New England Journal of Medicine* 287, 168–70.

LeMay, M. and Geschwind, N. (1978). Asymmetries of the human cerebral hemispheres. In Caramazza and Zurif 1978.

Lenneberg, E. H. (1967). *Biological Foundations of Language*. Wiley, New York.

Lesser, R. (1976). Verbal and non-verbal memory components in the token test. *Neuropsychologie* 14, 79–85.

(1978). *Linguistic investigations of aphasia*. Elsevier, N.Y.

Lesser, V. R., Fennel, R. D., Erman, L. D., and Reddy, D. R. (1975). Organization of the HEARSAY-II speech understanding system. *IEEE Transactions on Acoustics, Speech and Signal Processing* 23, 11–23.

Leyton, A. S. F. and Sherrington, C. S. (1917). Observations on the excitable cortex of the chimpanzee, orangutan and gorilla. *Quarterly Journal of Experimental Physiology* 11, 135–222.

Lhermitte, F. and Beauvois, M. F. (1973). A visual–speech disconnection syndrome: evidence from a case with optic aphasia, agnosic alexia, and colour agnosia. *Brain* 96, 696–714.

Liberman, A. M., Cooper, F. S., Shankweiler, D. P., and Studdert-Kennedy, M. (1967). Perception of the speech code. *Psychological Review* 74, 431–61.

Lichtheim, L. (1885). On aphasia. *Brain* 7, 433–84.

Liepmann, H. (1900). Des Krankheitsbild der Apraxie ("motorischen asymbolie"). *Monatsschr. Psychiatr. Neurol. Bd VIII*, 182–97. Monograph, Berlin.

Liepmann, H. and Maas, O. (1907). Ein Fall von linksseitiger Agraphie und Apraxie bei rechtsseitiger Lahmung. *Journal für Psychologie Neurologie* 10, 214–27.

Linebarger, M. C., Schwartz, M. F., and Saffran, E. M. (1983). Sensitivity to grammatical structure in so-called agrammatic aphasics. *Cognition* 13, 361–92.

Locke, S., Caplan, D., and Kellar, L. (1973). *A Study in Neurolinguistics*. Thomas Press, Springfield, Illinois.

Low, M. D. and Fox, M. (1977). Scalp-recorded slow potential asymmetries preceding speech in man. In J. E. Desmedt (ed.), *Language and Hemispheric Specialization in Man: Cerebral Event-Related Potentials*. Karger, Basel.

Luria, A. R. (1947). *Traumatic Aphasia*. Reprinted in translation, Mouton, The Hague, 1970.

(1973). *The Working Brain*. Basic Books, New York.

McAdam, D. W. and Whitaker, H. A. (1971). Electrocortical localization of language production: reply to Morrell and Huntington. *Science* 174, 1360–1.

McClelland, J. L. and Rumelhart, D. E. (1981). An interactive activation model of context effects in letter perception, part 1: An account of basic findings. *Psychological Review* 88, 375–407.

McFarling, D., Rothi, L. J., and Heilman, K. (1982). Transcortical aphasia from ischaemic infarcts of the thalamus: a report of two cases. *Journal of Neurology, Neurosurgery and Psychiatry* 45, 107–12.

McGlone, J. (1977). Sex differences in the cerebral organization of verbal functions in patients with unilateral brain lesions. *Brain* 100, 775–93.

(1978). Sex differences in functional brain asymmetry. *Cortex* 14, 122–8.

(1980). Sex differences in human brain asymmetry: a critical survey. *Behavioral and Brain Sciences* 3, 215–63.

MacLean, P. D. (1949). Psychosomatic disease and the "visceral brain": recent developments bearing on the Papez theory of emotion. *Psychosomatic Medicine* 11, 338–53.

MacNeilage, P. (1982). Speech production mechanisms in aphasia. In S. Griller *et al.* (eds.), *Speech Motor Control*. Pergamon, Oxford.

470

Marcel, T. (1980). Surface dyslexia and beginning reading: a revised hypothesis of the pronunciation of print and its impairments. In Coltheart *et al.* 1980.

(1986). Why we must have consciousness. Paper delivered at Fourth European Cognitive Neuropsychology Association Meeting, Bressanone, Italy.

Marcus, M. (1980). *A Theory of Syntactic Recognition for Natural Language*. MIT Press, Cambridge, Mass.

Marie, P. (1906*a*). Révision de la question de l'aphasie: la troisième circonvolution frontale gauche ne joue aucun rôle spécial dans la fonction du langage. *Semaine Medicale* (Paris) 26, 241–7.

(1906*b*). Révision de la question de l'aphasie: l'aphasie de 1861 à 1866: essai de critique historique sur le genèse de la doctrine de Broca. *Semaine Medicale* (Paris) 26, 565–71.

(1908). Discussion sur l'aphasie. In M. Klippel (ed.), *Revue Neurologique* 16, 974–1024.

Marr, D. and Poggio, T. (1976). From understanding computation to understanding neural circuitry. *Neurosciences Research Program Bulletin* 15, 470–80.

Marshall, J. C. (1974). Freud's psychology of language. In R. Wollheim (ed.), *Freud: A Collection of Critical Essays*. Anchor Books, Garden City.

(1980). On the biology of language acquisition. In D. Caplan (ed.), *Biological Studies of Mental Processes*. MIT Press, Cambridge, Mass.

Marshall, J. C. and Newcombe, F. (1973). Patterns of paralexia: a psycholinguistic approach. *Journal of Psycholinguistic Research* 2, 175–99.

Masdeu, J. C., Schoene, W. C., and Funkenstein, H. (1978). Aphasia following infarction of the left supplementary motor area: a clinicopathologic study. *Neurology* 28, 1220–3.

Metter, E. J., Sepulueda, C. A., Jackson, C. A., Mazziotta, J. C., Benson, D. F., Hanson, W. R., Riege, W. H., and Phelps, M. E. (1985). Relationship of temporal–parietal lesions and distant glucose metabolism changes in the head of the caudate nucleus in aphasic patients (abstract). *Neurology* 35, supplement 1, 120.

Miceli, G., Mazzucchi, A., Menn, L., and Goodglass, H. (1983). Contrasting cases of Italian agrammatic aphasia without comprehension disorder. *Brain and Language* 19, 65–97.

Miceli, G., Silveri, M., Villa, G., and Caramazza, A. (1984). On the basis for the agrammatic's difficulty in producing main verbs. *Cortex* 20, 207–20.

Milberg, W. and Blumstein, S. E. (1981). Lexical decision and aphasia: evidence for semantic processing. *Brain and Language* 14, 371–85.

Milner, B. (1974). Hemispheric specialization: its scope and limits. In F. O. Schmitt and F. G. Warden (eds.), *The Neurosciences: Third Study Program*. MIT Press, Cambridge, Mass.

Milner, B., Branch, C., and Rasmussen, T. (1964). Observations on cerebral dominance. In A. de Reuck and M. O'Connor (eds.), *Disorders of Language*. Churchill, London.

(1966). Evidence for bilateral speech representation in some non-right-handers. *Transactions of the American Neurological Assocation* 91, 306–8.

Mohr, J. P., Pessin, M. S., Finkelstein, S., Funkenstein, H. H., Duncan, G. W., and Davis, K. R. (1978). Broca aphasia: pathologic and clinical. *Neurology* 28, 311–24.

Mohr, J. P., Watters, W. C., and Duncan, G. W. (1975). Thalamic hemorrhage and aphasia. *Brain and Language* 2, 3–17.

Molfese, D. L. (1977). The ontogeny of cerebral asymmetry in man: auditory evoked potentials to linguistic and non-linguistic stimuli in infants and children. In J. E. Desmedt (ed.), *Language and Hemispheric Specialization in Man: Cerebral Event-Related Potentials*. Karger, Basel.

(1978). Neuroelectrical correlates of categorical speech perception in adults. *Brain and Language* 5, 25–35.

(1980*a*). Hemispheric specialization for temporal information: implications for the perception of voicing cues during speech perception. *Brain and Language* 11, 285–99.

(1980*b*). The phoneme and the engram: electrophysiological evidence for the acoustic invariant in stop consonants. *Brain and Language* 9, 372–6.

Molfese, D. L., Freeman, R. B., and Palermo, D. S. (1975). The ontogeny of brain lateralization for speech and non-speech stimuli. *Brain and Language* 2, 356–68.

Moody, S. (1984). *Agrammatic Reading in Phonological Dyslexia.* Ph.D. thesis, University of London.

Morton, J. (1969). Interaction of information in word recognition. *Psychological Review* 76, 165–78.

(1970). A functional model for memory. In D. A. Norman (ed.), *Models of Human Memory.* Academic Press, New York.

Morton, J. and Patterson, K. (1980). A new attempt at an interpretation, or, an attempt at a new interpretation. In Coltheart *et al.* 1980.

Mountcastle, V. B. (1978). An organizing principle for cerebral function: the unit module and the distributed system. In G. M. Edelman and V. B. Mountcastle (eds.), *The Mindful Brain.* MIT Press, Cambridge, Mass.

Moutier, F. (1908). *L'Aphasie de Broca.* Steinheil, Paris.

Naeser, M. A., Alexander, M. P., Helm-Estabrooks, N., Levine, H. L., Laughlin, S., and Geschwind, N. (1982). Aphasia with predominantly subcortical lesion sites: description of three capsular/putaminal aphasia syndromes. *Archives of Neurology* 39, 2–14.

Naeser, M. A. and Hayward, R. W. (1978). Lesion localization in aphasia with cranial computed tomography and the Boston diagnostic aphasia examination. *Neurology* 28, 545–51.

Neilson, J. M. (1936). *Agnosia, Apraxia, Aphasia.* Hoeber, New York.

Nespoulous, J. L., Dordain, M., Perron, C., Caplan, D., Bub, D., Mehler, J., and Lecours, A. R. (1985*a*). Agrammatism in sentence production without comprehension deficits. M S.

Nespoulous, J. L., Joanette, Y., Béland, R., Caplan, D., and Lecours, A. R. (1984). Phonological disturbances in aphasia: is there a "markedness" effect in aphasic phonemic errors? In F. C. Rose (ed.), *Progress in Aphasiology: Advances in Neurology*, vol. 42. Raven Press, New York.

Nespoulous, N., Joanette, Y., Ska, B., Caplan, D., and Lecours, A. R. (1986). Production deficits in Broca's and conduction aphasia: repetition versus reading. In E. Keller and M. Gopnik (eds.), *Motor and Sensory Processes in Language.* Erlbaum, Hillsdale, NJ.

Nespoulous, J. L., Ska, B., Joanette, Y., and Lecours, A. R. (1985*b*). The taxonomy of phonetic/phonemic disturbances in aphasia. Academy of Aphasia, Pittsburgh.

Newcombe, F. and Marshall, J. C. (1985). Reading and writing by letter-sounds. In Patterson *et al.* 1985.

Obler, L. (1984). The neuropsychology of bilingualism. In Caplan *et al.* 1984.

Obler, L., Menn, L., and Goodglass, H. (1984). Report on the cross-language study of agrammatism. Academy of Aphasia, Minneapolis.

(eds.) (in press). *A Cross-Linguistic Study of Agrammatism.* Benjamin, New York.

Ojemann, G. A. (1983). Brain organization for language from the perspective of electrical stimulation mapping. *Behavioral and Brain Sciences* 6, 189–230.

Papez, J. W. (1937). A proposed mechanism of emotion. *Archives of Neurology and Psychiatry* 38, 725–43.

Paradis, M. (1977). Bilingualism and aphasia. In H. Whitaker and H. A. Whitaker (eds.), *Studies in Neurolinguistics*, vol 3. Academic Press, New York.

Patterson, K. E. (1982). The relation between reading and phonological coding: further neuropsychological observations. In A. W. Ellis (ed.), *Normality and Pathology in Cognitive Functions.* Academic Press, London.

(1985). From orthography to phonology: an attempt at an old interpretation. In Patterson *et al.* 1985.

Patterson, K., Marshall, J. C., and Coltheart, M. (eds.) (1985). *Surface Dyslexia: Cognitive and Neuropsychological Studies of Phonological Reading*. Erlbaum, London.

Pavlov, I. P. (1949). *Complete Collected Works*. Akademia nauk SSSR. Cited in Luria 1973.

Penfield, W. and Roberts, L. (1959). *Speech and Brain Mechanisms*. Princeton University Press, Princeton.

Pick, A. (1913). *Die Agrammatischen Sprachstorungen*. Springer, Berlin.

Picton, T. W. and Stuss, D. (1984). Event-related potentials in the study of speech and language: a critical review. In Caplan *et al.* 1984.

Posner, M. I. and Snyder, C. R. (1975). Attention and cognitive control. In R. L. Solso (ed.), *Information Processing and Cognition: The Loyola Symposium*. Erlbaum, Hillsdale, NJ.

Potter, M. and Faulconer, B. A. (1975). Time to understand pictures and words. *Nature* 253, 437–8.

Putnam, H. (1970). Is semantics possible? In H. E. Kiefer and M. K. Maritz (eds.), *Language, Belief and Metaphysics*. State University of New York Press, New York; reprinted in S. P. Schwartz (ed.), *Naming, Necessity and Natural Kinds*. Cornell University Press, Ithaca, NY, 1977.

(1973). Meaning and reference. *Journal of Philosophy* 70, 699–711; reprinted in S. P. Schwartz (ed.), *Naming, Necessity and Natural Kinds*. Cornell University Press, Ithaca, NY, 1977.

Ratcliff, G., Dila, C., Taylor, L., and Milner, B. (1980). The morphological asymmetry of the hemispheres and cerebral dominance for speech: a possible relationship. *Brain and Language* 11, 87–98.

Riddoch, M. J. and Humphreys, G. W. (in press). Semantic systems or system? Neuropsychological evidence re-examined. *Cognitive Neuropsychology*.

Roeltgen, D. and Heilman, K. (1984). Lexical agraphia: further support for the two-system hypothesis of linguistic agraphia. *Brain* 107, 811–27.

Roeltgen, D., Sevush, S., and Heilman, K. (1983). Phonological agraphia: writing by the lexical–semantic route. *Neurology* 33, 755–65.

Rosch, E. (1975). Cognitive representations of semantic categories. *Journal of Experimental Psychology (General)* 104, 192–233.

Rosch, E., Mervis, C. B., Gray, W. D., Johnson, D. M., and Boyes-Braem, P. (1976). Basic objects in natural categories. *Cognitive Psychology* 8, 382–439.

Ross, E. and Mesulam, M. (1979). Dominant language functions of the right hemisphere? Prosody and emotional gesturing. *Archives of Neurology* 36, 144–8.

Rubenstein, H., Lewis, S. S. and Rubenstein, M. A. (1971). Evidence for phonemic recoding in visual word recognition. *Journal of Verbal Learning and Verbal Behavior* 10, 645–57.

Rumelhart, D. E. and McClelland, J. L. (1982). An interactive activation model of context effects in letter perception, part 2: The contextual enhancement effect and some tests and extensions of the model. *Psychological Review* 89, 60–94.

Russell, W. R. and Espir, M. L. E. (1961). *Traumatic Aphasia*. Oxford University Press, London.

Saffran, E. (1985). STM impairment and sentence comprehension. Paper presented at the Second International Cognitive Neuropsychology Meeting, Venice.

Saffran, E. M., Bogyo, L. C., Schwartz, M. F., and Marin, O. (1980). Does deep dyslexia reflect right hemisphere reading? In Coltheart *et al.* 1980.

Saffran, E., Marin, O., and Yeni-Komshian, G. (1976). An analysis of speech perception in word deafness. *Brain and Language* 3, 209–28.

Saffran, E. M., Schwartz, M. F., and Marin, O. (1980*b*). The word order problem in agrammatism II: Production. *Brain and Language* 10, 263–80.

Salomon, E. (1914). Motorische Aphasie mit Agrammatismus und Sensorischagrammatischen Storungen. *Monatschrift für Psychiatrie und Neurologie* 35, 181–208, 216–75.

473

References

Sasanuma, S. and Fujimura, O. (1971). Selective impairment of phonetic and nonphonetic transcription of words in Japanese aphasic patients: Kana vs. Kanji in visual recognition and writing. *Cortex* 7, 1–18.

Schiff, H. B., Blumstein, S., Ryalls, J., and Shinn, P. (1985). Aphemia: an acoustic phonetic analysis (abstract). *Neurology* 35, supplement 1, 122.

Schwartz, M. (1984). What the classical aphasia categories can't do for us, and why. *Brain and Language* 21, 3–8.

Schwartz, M., Marin, O., and Saffran, E. (1979). Dissociation of language function in dementia: a case study. *Brain and Language* 7, 277–306.

Schwartz, M., Saffran, E., and Marin, O. S. M. (1980). Fractionating the reading process in dementia: evidence for word-specific print-to-sound associations. In Coltheart *et al.* 1980.

  (1980*b*). The word order problem in agrammatism, I: Comprehension. *Brain and Language* 10, 249–62.

Seidenberg, M. S., Waters, G. S., Barnes, M. A., and Tanenhaus, M. K. (1984). When does irregular spelling or pronunciation influence word recognition? *Journal of Verbal Learning and Verbal Behavior* 23, 383–404.

Seymour, D. M. L. and MacGregor, C. J. (1984). Developmental dyslexia: a cognitive experimental analysis of phonological, morphological and visual impairments. *Cognitive Neuropsychology* 1, 43–82.

Shallice, T. (1979). Case study approach in neuropsychological research. *Journal of Clinical Neuropsychology* 1, 183–211.

  (1986). Impairments of semantic processing: multiple dissociations. In M. Coltheart, R. Job, and G. Sartori (eds.), *The Cognitive Neuropsychology of Language*. Erlbaum, London.

Shallice, T. and Warrington, E. K. (1970). Independent functioning of the verbal memory stores: a neuropsychological study. *Quarterly Journal of Experimental Psychology* 22, 261–73.

  (1977). Auditory–verbal short-term memory impairment and conduction aphasia. *Brain and Language* 4, 479–91.

Shattuck-Hufnagel, S. (1986). The role of word onset consonants in speech production planning: new evidence from speech error patterns. In E. Keller and M. Gopnik (eds.), *Motor and Sensory Processes in Language*. Erlbaum, Hillsdale, NJ.

Smith, E. and Medin, D. L. (1981). *Categories and Concepts*. Harvard University Press, Cambridge, Mass.

Stevens, K. and Blumstein, S. (1978). Invariant cues for place of articulation in stop consonants. *Journal of the Acoustical Society of America* 64, 1358–68.

Studdert-Kennedy, M. (1983). Mapping speech: more analysis, less synthesis, please. *Behavioral and Brain Sciences* 6, 218–19.

Subirana, A. (1964). The relationship between handedness and language function. *International Journal of Neurology* 4, 215–34.

  (1969). Handedness and cerebral dominance. In P. J. Vinken and G. W. Bruyn (eds.), *Handbook of Clinical Neurology*, vol. 4. North-Holland, Amsterdam.

Szirtes, J. and Vaughan, H. G. (1977). Characteristics of cranial and facial potentials associated with speech production. In J. E. Desmedt (ed.), *Language and Hemispheric Specialization in Man: Cerebral Event-Related Potentials*. Karger, Basel.

Tissot, R. J., Mounin, G., and Lhermitte, F. (1973). *L'Agrammatisme*. Dessart, Brussels.

Trost, J. E. and Cantor, G. J. (1974). Apraxia of speech in patients with Broca's aphasia: a study of phoneme production accuracy and error patterns. *Brain and Language* 1, 63–79.

Tsavaras, A., Kaprinis, G., and Gatzoyus, A. (1981). Literacy and hemispheric specialization for language: digit dichotic listening in illiterates. *Neuropsychologia* 19, 565–70.

Tucker, D. M., Watson, R. T., and Heilman, K. (1977). Discrimination and evocation of affectively intoned speech in patients with right parietal disease. *Neurology* 27, 947–50.

Tulving, E. (1972). Episodic and semantic memory. In E. Tulving and W. Donaldson (eds.), *Organization of Memory*. Academic Press, New York.

Vallar, G. and Baddeley, A. (1984). Phonological short-term store, phonological processing and sentence comprehension: a neuropsychological case study. *Cognitive Neuropsychology* 1, 121–41.

Vanier, M. and Caplan, D. (1985). CT scan correlates of surface dyslexia. In Patterson *et al.* 1985.

(in press). CT scan correlates of agrammatism. In Obler *et al.* in press.

von Monakow, C. (1914). *Die Lokalisation in Grosshirn und der Abbau der Funktionen durch corticale Herde*. Bergmann, Wiesbaden.

Vygotsky, L. S. (1939). Thought and speech. *Psychiatry* 2, 29–54.

Wada, J. (1949). A new method of identifying the dominant hemisphere for language: intracarotid sodium amytal injection in man. *Medical Biology* 14, 221–2.

Wanner, E. (1980). The ATN and the sausage machine: which one is baloney? *Cognition* 8, 209–25.

Warrington, E. K. (1975). The selective impairment of semantic memory. *Quarterly Journal of Experimental Psychology* 27, 635–57.

(1981). Concrete word dyslexia. *British Journal of Psychology* 72, 175–96.

Warrington, E. K. and McCarthy, R. (1983). Category specific access dysphasia. *Brain* 106, 859–78.

Warrington, E. K. and Shallice, T. (1969). The selective impairment of auditory–verbal short-term memory. *Brain* 92, 885–96.

(1972). Neuropsychological evidence of visual storage in short-term memory tasks. *Quarterly Journal of Experimental Psychology* 24, 30–40.

(1979). Semantic access dyslexia. *Brain* 102, 43–63.

(1984). Category specific semantic impairments. *Brain* 107, 829–54.

Wepman, J. M., Bock, R., Jones, L., and Van Pelt, D. (1956). Psycholinguistic study of aphasia: a revision of the concept of anomia. *Journal of Speech and Hearing Disorders* 21, 468–77.

Wernicke, C. (1874). The aphasic symptom complex: a psychological study on a neurological basis. Kohn and Weigert, Breslau. Reprinted in R. S. Cohen and M. W. Wartofsky (eds.), *Boston Studies in the Philosophy of Science*, vol. 4. Reidel, Boston, Mass.

Whitehouse, P. J., Price, D. L., Struble, R. G., Clark, A. W., Coyle, J. T., and DeLong, M. R. (1982). Alzheimer's disease and senile dementia: loss of neurons in the basal forebrain. *Science* 215, 1237–9.

Wood, C. (1978). Variations on a theme by Lashley: lesion experiments on the neural model of Anderson, Silverstein, Ritz, and Jones. *Psychological Review* 85, 582–91.

(1982). Implications of simulated lesion experiments for the interpretation of lesions in real nervous systems. In M. A. Arbib, D. Caplan, and J. C. Marshall (eds.), *Neural Models of Language Processes*. Academic Press, New York.

Wood, C., Goff, W. R., and Day, R. S. (1971). Auditory evoked potentials during speech perception. *Science* 173, 1248–51.

Woods, W. A. (1982). HWIM: a speech understanding system on a computer. In M. A. Arbib, D. Caplan, and J. C. Marshall (eds.), *Neural Models of Language Processes*. Academic Press, New York.

Zaidel, E. (1978*a*). Auditory language comprehension in the right hemisphere following cerebral commissurotomy and hemispherectomy: a comparison with child language and aphasia. In Caramazza and Zurif 1978.

(1978*b*). Lexical organization in the right hemisphere. In P. A. Buser and A. Rougel-Buser (eds.), *Cerebral Correlates of Conscious Experience*. North-Holland, Amsterdam.

References

Zangwill, O. L. (1967). The Grünthal–Storring case of amnesic syndrome. *British Journal of Psychiatry* 113, 113–28.

Zurif, E. B., Caramazza, A., and Myerson, R. (1972). Grammatical judgements of agrammatic aphasics. *Neuropsychologia* 10, 405–17.

Zurif, E. B., Caramazza, A., Myerson, R., and Galvin, J. (1974). Semantic feature representations for normal and aphasic language. *Brain and Language* 1, 167–87.

Author index

Subject index

German, 271
Gerstmann syndrome, 391
Gestalt processing, 363, *see also* Analytical
    processing; Holistic processing; Lateral
    asymmetry
Gestalt psychology, 94, 117, 132
Glial cell, 32
Global aphasia, 74, 146, 386–7, 391–2, 396
Global model, 105–18
Globus pallidus, 377, 385
Glossokinetic potential, 408
GPC, *see* Grapheme-to-phoneme
    conversion
Grammatical category, *see* Major lexical
    category; Syntactic category
Grammatical function, 271–2, *see also*
    Grammatical role
Grammatical role, 297, 304, *see also*
    Grammatical function
Grammatical word, *see* Function word
Grammaticality judgment, 26, 322, 331
Grapheme, 77, 233–5, 238, 246, 252–4, 256
Grapheme-to-phoneme conversion, 233–6,
    239–42, 245–7, 252–5, 259, 329–30, *see
    also* Assembled phonology; Non-lexical
    route; Phonologically mediated route;
    Spelling-sound correspondence
Graphemic parsing, *see* Parsing
Group performance, statistical analysis, 151
Gyrus, *see* Convolution

Habituation, 433
Handedness, *see* Ambidexterity; Cerebral
    Dominance; Crossed dextral aphasia
Head, of a construction, 297
HEARSAY parser, 307
Hebb synapse, 433–4, *see also* Synapse
Hebrew, 235, 287
Hemisphere, *see* Dominant hemisphere;
    Right hemisphere
Hemorrhagic lesion, *see* Lesion
Heschl's gyrus, 332, 363, 376, 378, 384
Hesitation, 420
Heuristic, 310–11, 315–17, 326, 328, *see
    also* Compensatory mechanism
Hierarchical model, 89–104, 113
Hierarchical organization, *see* Language;
    Lexical semantic information; Nervous
    system; Semantic category
Hierarchy of phonemic contrasts, *see*
    Phonemic contrast
High-frequency word, *see* Word
Higher function, *see* Function
Hippocampus, 68, 70
Holism, 63

Holistic approach, 79, 103, 121, 134–8, 284,
    432
Holistic processing, 363, *see also* Analytical
    processing; Gestalt processing; Lateral
    asymmetry
Holistic representation, 444, 458
Homophone, *see* Pseudo-homophone effect
HWIM parser, 307

Ideographic script, 76, 235–6, 251, *see also*
    Kanji; Orthography; Radical
Identification, *see also* Discrimination;
    Naming; Phoneme; Word recognition
    of sounds, 26, 411
    of words, 26
Illiteracy, 353
Illocutionary force, 358
Imageability, 175, *see also* Picturability
Imaging, *see* Neuroimaging techniques
Imagistic representation, 170, *see also*
    Semantic representation
Imitation, 18, *see also* Mimicry; Repetition
    of gesture, 423
Inchoative verb, *see* Verb
Indirect symptom, *see* Symptom
Inferencing, 168, 358–9, 453
Inferior parietal lobule, *see* Parietal lobe
Inflection, 154–6, 264, *see also* Affix;
    Agreement marker; Morpheme;
    Morphology
Information flow, 53
Information-processing model, 178, 423
Inhibition, 21, 28, 90, 115, 125, 135, 188,
    244, 338–9, 363, 429, 457, *see also*
    Disinhibition
    of function, 25
    mutual, 127
Inhibitory feedback, *see* Feedback
Innate language ability, 11–12
Inner speech, 113, 124
Insula, 385, 387–90
Intellectual disorder, 112, 116
Intelligence, 19
    verbal, 356–7, 426
Interactive activation, 247, 337, 450, 457,
    see also Parallel distributed processing;
    Spreading activation
Interference, with speech, *see* Speech arrest
Internal capsule, 111, 370, 372–4, 377–8,
    383, 385, 429
Intonation, 11, 30, 228, 358, 382, *see also*
    Dysprosodia; Prosody
Intra-laminar nuclei, 430
Intransitive verb, *see* Verb
I.Q., *see* Intelligence